Remedies in Public Competition Law

Remedies in Public Competition Law

Reasons and Scope for Reform

Massimo Merola

Wolters Kluwer

Published by:
Kluwer Law International B.V.
PO Box 316
2400 AH Alphen aan den Rijn
The Netherlands
E-mail: lrs-sales@wolterskluwer.com
Website: www.wolterskluwer.com/en/solutions/kluwerlawinternational

Sold and distributed by:
Wolters Kluwer Legal & Regulatory U.S.
920 Links Avenue
Landisville, PA 17538
United States of America
E-mail: customer.service@wolterskluwer.com

ISBN 978-94-035-3257-8

e-Book: ISBN 978-94-035-3267-7
web-PDF: ISBN 978-94-035-3277-6

A Clara

'Lo zelo per la tua casa mi divora' (Gio 2:13-25; Salmo 69(10))

Zelo di amare

Table of Contents

Forewords

After several decades of application of the State aid rules, a review of this adaptation to the current needs is more than timely. Professor Massimo Merola's book '*The System of Remedies in Public Competition Law*' adds in this regard a significant dimension to the discussion on '*the way forward*' as regards State aid control.

Rules are indeed only credible if they are supported by effective remedies: *ubi jus, ibi remedis*. In this regard, being the product of its author's first-rank experience, both as a leading practitioner and as a distinguished professor on this subject, this book not only highlights the shortcomings and failures of the current system of remedies but also puts forward insightful and concrete proposals for solving them.

According to the author, a combination of several remedies both at national level and before EU institutions is needed to simultaneously forfeit the competition distortions and deter further breaches. In this regard, the author does not limit himself to pure legal analyses but discusses also the inherent political dimension of the debate and in particular considers the global impact of the rules and pleads for a convergence between State aid law and foreign subsidies law.

A central idea in this book is the author's forceful plea for a clarification of the notion of '*re-establishment of the status quo ante*', *i.e.*, the situation existing before the unlawful aid was granted.

In Professor Merola's view, mere '*restorative remedies*' are indeed insufficient and may often be inadequate. The concept of '*redressive measure*' should instead be introduced. Several convincing arguments are given to show why mere repayment of the aid may be either a punitive tool or, at the opposite, not restrictive enough.

Three alternative concepts of '*recovery*' of illegal State aid are discussed, the current '*financial concept*' (the refund must equal the amount unlawfully granted), the '*economic concept*' preferred by the author (*i.e.*, the need for a repayment of the economic advantage provided immediately and directly in the beneficiary's sphere) and the '*functional concept*', (*i.e.*, removing the overall advantages caused including indirectly and together with other factors and over time) rejected by the author for being too uncertain. Whilst the author recognises that the current '*financial*' approach has the merit of simplicity, he argues that it is often not achieving the desired objective.

Overall, the application of State aid rule is found to be still often too '*formalistic*', and thus not pursuing to the full the '*modernised*' approach otherwise defended henceforth in the application of competition rules.

But the discussions go much further, the author not shying away in this regard from a discussion of possible innovative routes such as negotiated remedies or even more radical ('*behavioral*' or even '*structural*') remedies such as divestments, breaking up of companies, access remedies, *etc*. Also possible improvements to '*private enforcement*' are considered.

Similar discussions follow as to the identification of the real '*beneficiary*' of the aid or the issue of proper judicial control.

Overall, the author offers a critical approach and addresses the wider economic and political realities of State aid law.

Elegantly drafted, in an '*easy-to-follow*' style, the book culminates in a number of concrete proposals for the much-needed reform of State aid rules.

Denis Waelbroeck

This book is a slightly reworked version of the author's doctoral dissertation, which he defended on 7 November 2024 at the Faculty of Law and Criminology of the *Université libre de Bruxelles*. It thoroughly analyses the existing public and private enforcement remedies in situations of (allegedly) unlawful (and incompatible) State aid, while calling for a clarification of certain key concepts of EU State aid law and, most importantly, proposing a comprehensive and much needed reform of the current system of remedies. Effective remedies are indeed essential for achieving the objectives of EU State aid law: integration of the internal market, a level playing field for all undertakings, optimal allocation of State resources, maximised consumer welfare, to name but a few.

Whereas Part 1 of the book looks at the evolution over time of public enforcement of EU State aid law, Part 2 pays due attention to its private enforcement. Part 3 briefly explains two other systems of remedies that exist in EU law: the new Foreign Subsidies Regulation is discussed for comparative purposes in dealing with public enforcement, as it 'can serve as a model for the reform of the system of remedies in the field of State aid', while the directive on remedies in public procurement law and the damages directive in antitrust law are referred to within the framework of private enforcement, as they 'can offer some useful indications for the reform of private enforcement in State aid law'. Finally, in the very innovative Part 4, the author proposes an in-depth and ambitious reform of the current system of remedies that should meet the requirement of a coherent and complete system of restorative and, which is new, redressive remedies in EU State aid matters. The author concludes with the following, well-founded statement: 'It is submitted that the system of remedies advocated for in this book (...) meets this requirement, whereas the current system of remedies clearly does not.'

In the report that I prepared for the aforementioned defence, I wrote that Massimo's dissertation fulfilled all the requirements that an excellent doctoral dissertation must meet and makes an important contribution to legal scholarship. In his dissertation, now book, Massimo demonstrates a profound knowledge of EU State aid law, particularly its enforcement, showing a keen analytical and critical mind, and perseverance. The main research question – what is the most appropriate reaction to a violation of EU State aid rules? – is very well answered and argued, including in the form of proposals for reform. The suggested reforms of soft law and secondary EU law – amendment of the Procedural Regulation and a new law on the basis of Article 314 TFEU, including a State aid harmonisation directive – rest on solid theoretical foundations, as Massimo writes, and are well presented and argued. And as the book concludes, '[a]n effective and modernised system of remedies for breaches of the notification and standstill obligations is an essential component of the proposed solution to restore the control system's credibility, along with efficient *ex-post* monitoring and cooperation with Member States' authorities in a way that is consistent with the modernisation paradigm'. The theoretical and practical usefulness of this book for all parties concerned is beyond dispute, and it is certainly to be hoped that the proposals for urgent reform put forward in this book – some more feasible than others – will be taken to heart by the European Commission.

Massimo's book is very well written and a pleasure to read. The table of contents and the four parts are organised in a logical order. The source material is rich and the bibliography neat.

While being a full-time practitioner in and professor of EU State aid matters, Massimo took up a huge challenge in writing his dissertation and publishing this book, which is the very much welcomed result of that challenge. Given the urgency of the proposals made, this book could not have come at a better moment.

Tony Joris
17 January 2025

Acknowledgements

Drawing up a thank-you list is always difficult, especially after working as long as I have on this book. Indeed, over the course of my research, I had the opportunity to discuss various aspects of my study or writing with many colleagues of different seniorities, and I feel indebted to every single one of them. However, it would certainly be impossible to mention them all, not only because it would require too much space but also, and even more, because my memory has its obvious limits, and I would risk forgetting someone. Nonetheless, I would be remiss – and it is only natural to start here – if I did not express my deepest thanks to all the members of the *comité d'accompagnement* and the PhD jury who deemed my thesis worthy of publication, thus encouraging me to pursue this goal. This book incorporates some updates and short additions compared to my original thesis but essentially reproduces its entire structure and content.

I am profoundly grateful to all the jury's distinguished members for their attention, generosity and support. Considering their contributions individually, I am especially grateful to Prof. Marianne Dony for her warm encouragement as I took on this belated personal challenge; to Prof. Arnaud Van Waeyenberge for his guidance through the not-so-obvious technicalities of a doctoral programme; to Prof. Tony Joris for his careful reading of my thesis, for his comments, which he provided down to the slightest detail with rigour but also with great kindness, and for his generosity in agreeing to write one of the forewords to this book; to Prof. Denis Waelbroeck, who also generously agreed to write a foreword to this book, for his friendly support as president of the Jury and for his indulgent assessment of the ideas developed throughout these pages; and to Prof. Oana Stefan and Prof. Martín Martinez Navarro for their warm support and competent comments.

I would also like to express my heartfelt thanks to all former colleagues – mainly associates and trainees at BonelliErede – with whom I worked on so many State aid matters and who are now in good numbers at the European Commission or at the Court of Justice of the European Union or who have embarked on different paths: our exchanges on professional and academic issues certainly enriched me and nourished my intellectual curiosity about developments in the field. Thanks also go to those (especially one) who indirectly gave me a boost to take on new challenges, even if they caused me distress in the process. The list of people to thank would not be complete without mentioning Prof. Aurelio Pappalardo (14 September 1936-21 June 2021), who surely would have rejoiced with me - and for me - at this new achievement.

A big thank you also goes to the fantastic team at BonelliErede's English Improvement Department, with a special mention for Vincent Picciani for his expertise and unsurpassable patience; to my assistants Laura Marzilli and Federica Masucci for their help with all the book's logistical aspects and for their dedication in taking my challenge to heart; and to BonelliErede's former general manager Gabriele Zucchini for his support.

Lastly, I am moved to thank my family, namely my father (28 July 1928-3 November 2019), whose example of humility and humanity still guides me; my mother, who is still the shoulder I lean on in difficult moments; my uncle, Prof. Fabrizio Ramacci, who has set a masterful (and unreachable) intellectual example that I aspire to; my children (and grandchildren), who give me drive and purpose and who always seem to know how to lift up my soul; and, of course, Clara, to whom this book is dedicated, and who is truly half of me and so much more. The prospect of dedicating this book to her was one of the main motivations that supported me in the most difficult moments of my work.

Introduction

This book analyses remedies in public competition law with a view to promoting their reform and convergence.

Public competition law is the branch of competition law that deals with the application of competition rules to governments' conduct. In European Union ('*EU*') law, it is represented by the rules of primary, secondary and soft law that regulate control over unilateral State measures that have the effect of actually or potentially distorting competition. EU public competition law encompasses State aid rules,[1] the competition rules addressed to undertakings insofar as they can be applied to Member States in combination with the principle of sincere cooperation under Article 4(3) of the Treaty of the European Union ('TEU'), the rules applicable to State-owned or State-controlled undertakings,[2] and the rules applicable to foreign subsidies.[3] Public procurement rules are also closely related to public competition law given their purpose, though they are not normally included in that definition as they are not based on the Treaty's competition provisions but rather on internal market provisions (namely, Article 34 Treaty on the Functioning of the European Union (TFEU)). The remedies provided in relation to State measures directed at public undertakings or to State measures affecting competition between undertakings are the typical antitrust remedies or the ordinary infringement procedure. Thus, they are not the subject of analysis in this book. The focus here is instead on State aid remedies, whereas remedies in relation to foreign subsidies and remedies in public procurement law are referred to for

1. Articles 107-109 of the Treaty on the Functioning of the European Union ('*TFEU*').
2. Article 106 TFEU. Notably, Commission Directive 2006/111/EC of 16 November 2006 on the transparency of financial relations between Member States and public undertakings as well as on financial transparency within certain undertakings, OJ L 318, 17.11.2006, p. 17 ('*Transparency Directive*'), sets out transparency requirements in relation to State-owned or State-controlled undertakings and undertakings holding exclusive or special rights within the meaning of Art. 106(1) TFEU. The Transparency Directive defines 'public undertakings' as any undertaking over which the public authorities may directly or indirectly exercise a dominant influence by virtue of their ownership of it, their financial participation therein, or the rules which govern it (Art. 2(b) of the Transparency Directive).
3. Regulation (EU) 2022/2560 of the European Parliament and of the Council of 14 December 2022 on foreign subsidies distorting the internal market (OJ L 330, 23.12.2022, p. 1).

comparative reasons. Remedies in antitrust private enforcement are also briefly considered for the same reasons.

The system of remedies in State aid law is the result of an evolutionary process that spans over half a century, starting in the early 1970s but unexpectedly coming to a halt at the most auspicious moment for reform: when the European Commission ('*Commission*') announced the modernisation of State aid law.

Traditionally, State aid control in the EU is aimed at guaranteeing all undertakings in the EU a level playing field and at preventing subsidy races between Member States. Following modernisation, it is now also aimed at containing public spending, prioritising EU horizontal objectives and tackling economic crises. State aid control thus pursues not only equal opportunity but also the optimal allocation of resources, budgetary discipline and, ultimately, economic prosperity.[4] Up to this point, the progressive paradigm shift seen in the definition of the objectives of State aid control has had no impact on the system of remedies, which can be considered the missing piece (or the main missing piece) in the modernisation process.

This definition of the objectives of EU State aid policy is the result of a long evolution that has progressively shaped the Commission's enforcement in the field. Primary law, however, has remained essentially unchanged since 1957. The TFEU holds that State aid is incompatible with the internal market unless otherwise provided therein (*i.e.*, when the aid falls under one of the derogations laid down in the Treaty). All exemptions are under the control of the Commission, which has exclusive authority to scrutinise and authorise State aid - be it individually or, upon delegation by the Council, through block exemption regulations.

To be eligible for aid, an investment project (or, in exceptional cases, the ordinary running of an economic activity) must pursue a policy objective (regional development, R&D, environmental protection, energy efficiency, *etc.*) that is consistent with EU policy.

Needless to say, the rigorous enforcement and the effectiveness of the rules are key to attaining high-level objectives. The Commission is thus empowered to ascertain and declare infringements of State aid rules without having to bring the matter before the Court of Justice of the European Union (also referred to below as '*Court*' or '*CJEU*')[5] to have it declare an infringement as in ordinary infringement proceedings.

Despite this simplified (derogating) infringement procedure, neither the Treaty nor secondary law envisages any penalties for infringement. Based on Article 108(2) TFEU (as interpreted by the Court of Justice),[6] the only consequences of an infringement by Member States - besides increasingly evanescent political reprobation - are obligations to: (i) bring the infringement to an end by ceasing to grant the aid; and/or

4. On this topic, *see* M. Merola and F. Caliento, *A Few Selected Issues Regarding the Change of Scope of the Notion of State Aid*, in L'Europe au Kaléidoscope: Liber Amicorum Marianne Dony, Editions de l'Université de Bruxelles, 7 November 2019.
5. The short form 'Court' refers to the higher judicial body, the short form 'General Court' refers to the lower body, and the short forms 'Court of Justice' and 'CJEU' indicate the judicial institution as a whole (*i.e.*, the lower and higher bodies).
6. Judgment of the Court of 12 July 1973, Case 70/72, *Commission of the European Communities v. Federal Republic of Germany (Kohlegesetz)*, EU:C:1973:87.

(ii) remedy the distortion of the level playing field by recovering the amount granted. However, no effective prevention or deterrence can be achieved through these means.

On top of this, a crucial conceptual mismatch is inherent in the second consequence mentioned above, because recovering the amount granted and remedying the infringement by forfeiting the competition distortion are two different things. Recovery of the amount granted (plus interest) can fall short of or exceed, depending on the circumstances, the effects of forfeiting the competitive advantage (or, for competitors, disadvantage) caused by the aid.

Only if the Member State concerned does not comply with a Commission decision ordering recovery of the aid can it be held liable by the Court of Justice and, if the non-compliance persists, ultimately fined. In this case, the Commission may propose – and the Court may subsequently impose – suitable fines in accordance with Article 260(2) TFEU, in the form of lump sums and periodic penalty payments.

The consequences of the Treaty's incomplete sanctioning system and of the insufficient modernisation of the system of remedies go beyond the mere incongruity explained above and, in the recovery phase, can give rise to conflicting interests between the Member State granting the aid and the aid recipient. Given the increasing rigorousness in the enforcement of the recovery remedy over the last twenty years,[7] undertakings must be extra vigilant because they are directly affected by recovery orders. They cannot simply rely on assurances from Member States when making investments and location decisions.

Indeed, Member States have a vested interest in undertakings investing and setting up businesses in their country. Furthermore, governments, by their very nature, generally have short-term objectives – objectives that are more aligned with their need to gain popularity among electors than with long-term business success and profitability rates. This situation is referred to in social policy literature as 'administrative failure'.[8] By contrast, undertakings need to avoid the recovery of unlawful aid in the long term if they want to preserve their investment's profitability. This explains the increasing attention that investors, including foreign investors, are called on to pay to State aid rules and procedures.

The present recovery system does not take any account of the concrete possibility – and even likelihood – of conflicting interests. What is more, it continues to structure the enforcement procedure, even in the recovery phase, as a bilateral procedure between the Member State concerned and the Commission. This unsatisfactory situation is worsened by the lack of progress in safeguarding the rights of interested parties (and above all, aid beneficiaries) to defend themselves in administrative proceedings. In fact, beneficiaries are almost entirely excluded from the procedure despite being: (i) directly affected by recovery; and (ii) unable to rely on the possibility of cooperating with the Member State concerned for the protection of their interests.

---

7. Namely, since the adoption of the first procedural regulation (Council Regulation (EC) No 659/1999 of 22 March 1999 laying down detailed rules for the application of Art. 93 of the EC Treaty, OJ L 83, 27.3.1999, p. 1), which introduced the obligation for the Commission to order recovery of unlawful and incompatible aid (as explained later in this book).
8. Among others, *see* A.T. Peacock, *Identifying and Applying Norms for Subsidies to Industry*, in R. Gerritse, 'Producer Subsidies', Printer Publishers Ltd., London, 1990.

Furthermore, the Commission Services[9] do not seem prepared to compensate for this regulatory gap through openness to informal contact. They encourage beneficiaries to participate in pre-notification meetings (always with the presence of the Member State involved) or in state-of-play meetings, but only for notified aid.[10] Moreover, beneficiaries have no right to participate in such meetings; they can only participate if invited, and that decision is left to the competent authorities of the Member State involved. Furthermore, the Commission Services are showing increasing resistance to having informal meetings or exchanges with undertakings or their lawyers in procedures concerning unnotified aid and basically view complainants as a mere source from which to gather information. This practice is heading toward precluding undertakings (and even beneficiaries) from almost all access to the Commission Services during enforcement procedures except for when the Commission itself opens an informal channel to gather information. This is a very worrisome development for businesses and their advisors.

Against this backdrop, this book analyses the origins, stated goals and fundamental principles of the system of recovery of unlawful aid and, more broadly, the remedies available in cases of infringement of State aid rules. The aim is to highlight the need for reform and identify the main areas it should cover. The ambition is to propose a specific approach to reforming the system and to clarify its various components. Given this purpose, this book does not examine in detail the measures that the Commission may require a Member State to take – nor does it address the conditions or constraints that the Commission may impose on beneficiary undertakings – within the framework of its compatibility assessments of notified aid measures, which aim at ensuring a proper balance between a given aid measure's positive and negative effects (known as 'prospective' remedies).

The totally unforeseeable developments in State aid policy prompted by the 2008 economic and financial crisis, the COVID-19 emergency and the war in Ukraine – and more broadly by the era's geopolitical tensions, which affect international trade – also offer food for thought in relation to the reform of the system of remedies. Indeed, an examination of State aid policy from the perspective of the enforcement process and the application of remedies is a way to check the internal coherence of policy choices. A discussion of recent phenomena – such as new aid measures propelled by health and geopolitical crises and the approach the Commission has taken to ensure a coordinated response at the EU level – only further points to the need for reform. It is indeed extremely difficult to adapt the present system of remedies to new forms of State intervention, such as tax advantages granted to investors that do not qualify as undertakings to fuel fresh capital toward the real economy, or measures intended to make good the damage caused by lockdowns or to keep companies afloat if their difficulties are directly related to a crisis.

9. The expression 'Commission Services' refers to the various teams in charge of conducting State aid control procedures within the Commission's Directorate-General for Competition.
10. *See* Communication from the Commission 'Code of Best Practices for the conduct of State aid control procedures', C(2018) 4412 of 16 July 2018, paras 18 and 36.

To achieve the proposed goals, this book focuses on the essential principles, enforcement criteria, and substantive and procedural rules that constitute the backbone of the current system of remedies. Therefore, the chosen methodology combines a chronological analysis of secondary and soft law with a more original analysis by guiding principles of the relevant case law. Cases are discussed in detail only when necessary to clarify concepts, but the emphasis is on the latter with a view to providing a systematic and comprehensive analysis of the system of remedies (which is sometimes, unfortunately, missing in the case law). The book then highlights all the uncertainties and inconsistencies that a comprehensive reform should seek to address. Such a reform is long overdue in the modernisation process and would fit perfectly with the modernisation's objectives.

Remedies available to national courts are sometimes broader than those at the Commission's disposal and may theoretically fill the gap seen in public enforcement. Therefore, in assessing the need for reform, both public enforcement and private enforcement of State aid rules are considered – in Part One and Part Two of the book, respectively. The same methodology followed in Part One, based on a combination of studying the chronological evolution of the system and pointing at its essential conceptual pillars, while using references to case law mainly to illustrate the latter, is also used in Part Two to illustrate the system of private enforcement.

Therefore, both Part One and Part Two are based on a dual perspective of analysis: on the one hand, a historical perspective, which attempts to grasp the development of the system of remedies by analysing its legal sources and referring to the goals pursued by modernisation; and on the other hand, a conceptual perspective, which emphasises the fundamental principles underlying which remedies are chosen and how they are applied. The intersection of these two perspectives naturally complicates the analysis and perhaps makes it more difficult to read. However, this is a deliberate choice, because the historical perspective is functional in proving the thesis argued in this book, *i.e.*, the need for a profound (and long overdue) reform, whereas the conceptual perspective is useful for readers who wish to consult this book to study the principles underlying the system of remedies in the field of State Aid.

National laws and case law are not analysed, except for very few cases, as a broader analysis would hardly contribute to the objective of explaining the reasons and scope of the proposed reform of the EU system of remedies. Moreover, official studies on the enforcement of State aid rules at the national level already offer a broad overview of the characteristics and limits of such enforcement. Enforcement at the national level encompasses, in addition to genuine private enforcement, enforcement of State aid rules by the granting national authorities themselves, following the principle of self-protection of administrative authority (*auto-tutelle*). Although encouraged by recent case law,[11] this form of national enforcement remains exceptional and

11. Judgment of the Court of Justice (Grand Chamber) of 5 March 2019, C-349/17, *Eesti Pagar AS v. Ettevõtluse Arendamise Sihtasutus and Majandus- ja Kommunikatsiooniministeerium*, EG, EU:C:2019:172, and Judgment of the Court of 7 April 2022, Joined Cases C-102/21 and C-103/21, *KW and SG v. Autonome Provinz Bozen*, EU:C:2022:272.

can only take the form of a revocation of the act granting the aid and consequent recovery. It is therefore of little help in shaping a reform of the system of remedies.

Part three delves into other systems of remedies that exist in EU law - especially the system in the related area of foreign subsidies, the regulation of which was recently introduced in EU law - and advocates for a convergence between State aid law and foreign subsidies law when it comes to remedies. Whereas the system of remedies in the area of foreign subsidies is used for comparative purposes in dealing with public enforcement, the directive on remedies in public procurement law and the damages directive in antitrust law are briefly referred to when dealing with private enforcement.

Although the analysis of remedies against foreign subsidies introduces an international perspective,[12] this book does not ambition to fully explore the international law implications of the system of remedies in State aid., nor does it discuss whether an international law perspective should be integrated into the design of the new system of remedies, either for legal reasons (*i.e.*, coordination with other EU rules and with international rules, such as those of the WTO) or for political reasons (*i.e.*, pursuing the new 'open strategic autonomy' model) or both.

Finally, part four of this book concludes by elaborating on the objectives, scope, means, content and legal basis of the proposed reform of the system of remedies and discussing the approach that should be taken in designing a coherent and complete system of remedies.

In short, the thesis put forward in this book is that a comprehensive reform of the system of remedies is urgently needed and should encompass both public and private enforcement. The reform should be based on, among other things, the long-awaited conceptual clarification of the notion of 're-establishment of the status quo ante' (*i.e.*, the situation existing before unlawful aid was granted). Furthermore, a combination of several remedies is needed to serve the system's various objectives (*i.e.*, not only forfeiting the competition distortion but also preventing further breaches of State aid rules through means of deterrence). In this respect, although the foreign subsidies regulation (FSR) is not entirely transposable to the field of State aid, it is nonetheless a good indicator of the direction to be followed. Finally, considering the significance of the inherent challenge in reforming the system of remedies in public competition law, it is necessary to pool hard and soft law instruments in the reform process.

12. First, it would be rational to harmonise the systems of remedies for aid granted by Member States and aid granted by third countries to the extent possible, unless it is impracticable to do so in specific cases. Based on this idea, this book explores the possibility of whether the recently enacted foreign subsidies regulation can serve as a model for the reform of the system of remedies in State aid law and - *vice versa* - whether the *acquis communautaire* in State aid can be of help in the enforcement of that regulation (*i.e.*, whether a reciprocal fertilisation between the two areas is possible). Moreover, a credible and effective system of remedies in State aid law is key in order to justify the trade restrictions/controls introduced within the framework of the 'open strategic autonomy' model advocated by the EU.

Part One

Public Enforcement of State Aid Rules

Introduction to Part One

CONTENTS

This section introduces Part One by explaining how it is structured and what it covers. Part One analyses the system of remedies available to the Commission for the public enforcement of State aid rules – including the origin, legal basis, and logic of the remedies – and highlights the weaknesses that require reform to improve the system's effectiveness and coherence.

Part One of this book concerns the system of remedies that the Commission has at its disposal in the public enforcement of State aid rules. Building on past research on the topic, Part One analyses the origin, legal basis and rationale of the remedies before discussing the basic principles that constitute the backbone of the current system of remedies and emphasising the weaknesses that should be addressed through a reform of that system. This then leads to an analysis of some related recommendations for reform, among which the following are worth mentioning from the outset: (i) the reform must be based on a clarification of the concept of 'reestablishment of the *status quo ante*' and a differentiation of remedies depending on action needed in each case to achieve this objective; (ii) the reform must necessarily include, or serve as a prelude to, a revision of the role of third parties in State aid proceedings (in particular, beneficiaries should be closely involved in recovery proceedings); (iii) the recovery system should be better coordinated with insolvency procedures (which, at present, given the lack of harmonised rules, are governed by Member State's respective national legal systems); and (iv) convergence and uniformity should be sought in the system of remedies across all rules pertaining to public competition law.

The overview of the basic principles of the current system of remedies is followed by a detailed analysis of the Commission Notice on recovery ('*2007 Recovery Notice*'), amended in 2019 ('*New Recovery Notice*').[1] The 2007 Recovery Notice is analysed first, with the analysis then shifting to the preparatory works for the New Recovery Notice – including the public consultation carried out by the Commission[2] – and the interplay between this reform of the 2007 Recovery Notice and the modernisation process. This analysis concludes that the amendment of this important piece of soft law is necessary but insufficient if the proposed reform is to be comprehensive, coherent and conceptually satisfactory, and if it is to bring legal certainty.

The main brushstrokes of the proposed reform are thus put forward in a concise manner, with an explanation of how they would ideally complement the initiatives already taken by the Commission. Ultimately, however, this part of the book concludes by emphasising that an assessment of the private enforcement system of remedies is warranted before any conclusions can be reached on the need for, and scope of, the proposed reform.

1. EU Commission Notice on the recovery of unlawful and incompatible State aid of 22 July 2019. When the term '*Recovery Notice*' is used in this book (*i.e.*, without a date or 'New' before it), it refers to the notice in general.
2. Consultation on the Notice on the recovery of unlawful and incompatible State aid.

I THE BACKBONE OF THE RECOVERY SYSTEM: ESSENTIAL PRINCIPLES, ENFORCEMENT CRITERIA, AND BASIC SUBSTANTIVE AND PROCEDURAL RULES

This chapter explores the essential principles, enforcement criteria, and substantive and procedural rules that form the backbone of the recovery system for unlawful and incompatible State aid. It emphasises the basic principles and criteria developed over time mainly through case law and soft law. It also examines the system's ancillary remedies and related conceptual flaws.

A detailed analysis of all the rules of the State aid recovery system is contained in a book that this author published in 2018,[3] shortly before the public consultation launched by the Commission for the reform of the 2007 Recovery Notice.[4] That detailed explanation is repeated here only to a limited extent, *i.e.*, for the purposes of supporting the thesis as described above. This chapter summarises those rules and the enforcement policy principles that form the backbone of the system from both a substantive and a procedural standpoint. This provides the essential framework for the critical assessment and reform proposal that follows.

I.A Substantive Rules and Principles

I.A.1 Targeting the Abolishment of Unlawful and Incompatible Aid

The first element to consider in the recovery system is the idea that *if unlawful aid has been deemed incompatible with the internal market at the end of the investigation procedure regulated by Article 108(2) TFEU, recovery can be a means of 'abolishing' such aid.* Under Article 108(2), if the Commission finds that aid is incompatible with the internal market, it is competent to decide that the Member State concerned must abolish or alter it. If the unlawful aid is still being granted when the Commission decision is adopted (either because it is intended to last for a given or indefinite time, as in the case of tax rebates and exemptions - to give just one example - or because it is being granted in instalments), it must be discontinued. If instead all or part of the aid has already been disbursed, the Commission is competent to order repayment of the disbursed aid. The underlying reason is that to be of practical effect, the obligation to abolish or alter unlawful aid may include an obligation to repay aid granted in breach of the Treaty.[5]

3. M. Merola, *Rimedi per violazione delle norme sugli aiuti di Stato: misure repressive o di ripristino: Diritto positivo (post-modernizzazione) e scenari di riforma*, G. Giappichelli Editore, Torino 2018.
4. This author's ambition is, understandably, for the present book to help trigger an in-depth reassessment of the reform of the system of remedies from all the perspectives mentioned above, just as this author's previous work in the field helped raise awareness of the need for reform of the Recovery Notice.
5. Judgment of the Court of 12 July 1973, Case 70/72, *Commission of the EC v. The Federal Republic of Germany*, EU:C:1973:87, para. 13.

The recovery system thus stems from a concern about the effectiveness of State aid rules – and its sole objective is to abolish the aid. But what does 'abolish' mean in this context? Does this concept refer to the legal instrument used to grant the aid or to the aid itself, *i.e.*, the advantage obtained by the beneficiary? The only interpretation compatible with the level of attention that EU law (and more specifically, competition law) pays to economic substance rather than legal form is that the effects of aid should be eliminated if the aid has already been granted. There is no other way to give practical effect to the provision, as advocated for by the Court.

The principle of *effet utile* indeed played a crucial role in the Court's landmark judgment in *Kohlegesetz*.[6] The Commission had brought the Federal Republic of Germany before the Court for a declaration that Germany had failed to comply with a negative Commission decision and to abolish an aid measure that the Commission had held incompatible with the common market. Since Germany had continued to grant the aid after the Commission decision, the Commission argued that the Court should not simply declare that Germany breached the Treaty but should also order it to create the legal situation that would have existed had it complied with the decision. This could have been interpreted as entailing recovery of the aid granted after – and in breach of – the Commission decision.

At that point, not even the Commission advocated for the possibility of the decision having a retroactive effect, which would have meant recovery of aid granted *before* the decision's adoption. Indeed, although the aid was unlawful because Germany had extended the application of the aid scheme in question and informed the Commission thereof only after the extension, the Commission simply asked the Court to declare that Germany was obliged to recover the individual aid granted after the decision date, except for aid relating to applications submitted by beneficiaries ahead of the publication in the Official Journal of the Commission decision to open an investigation procedure.[7] However, the Court decided that:

> it is the aim of the Treaty to achieve practical elimination of infringements of Treaty provisions, and the consequences thereof, past *and* future (emphasis added).

It is true that, although the Court upheld the Commission's arguments on the admissibility of the infringement procedure and of the appeal, it then dismissed the Commission's application on the merits. However, in terms of legal statements, the Court went well beyond the Commission's request – by identifying the legal effect of both a final negative decision and a decision to open an investigation procedure. As to the former, the Court stated explicitly that if the power of the Commission to order abolition or alteration of an aid provision is 'to be of practical effect', this 'may include an obligation to require repayment of aid granted in breach of the Treaty'.[8] As to the

6. *See* footnote 2 in this Part One.
7. For a precise report on the case and enlightening comments, *see* R. Kovar, *Le régime des aides en droit Communautaire*, Journal Droit International, 1974.
8. Judgment of the Court of 12 July 1973, cited in footnote 5 of this Part One, para. 13. The Court then dismissed the Commission's arguments for lack of clarity in the Commission's position. Indeed, the Commission had continued to negotiate with the Member State after the decision's

latter, the Court seemed to accept that beneficiaries can no longer invoke a *legitimate expectation* to receive aid under the scheme after publication in the Official Journal of a decision to open an investigation procedure.[9]

As H. J. Brinkhorst put it, 'it may be assumed that the Court regards a decision taken by the Commission under Article 93, para. 2, EC [now Art. 108(2) TFEU] - at least in so far as it concerns an aid introduced after the coming into force of the Treaty - as *declaratory* and not as *constitutive*, and that the legal situation that may have to be redressed [through recovery] arises, in case new aid are concerned, after the aid itself has become effective'.[10]

Another important element of the system is, as mentioned, that the investigation procedure must lead to a finding of incompatibility with the internal market. *A finding that unlawful aid is incompatible with the internal market is thus a precondition for a repayment order and, more generally, a precondition for imposing remedies - except interim remedies.*[11] Interim remedies may be imposed before a final finding of incompatibility; their purpose is to prevent a distortion from materialising, to limit a

adoption, and the parties had eventually reached a consensus. However, the outcome of this specific case in no way diminishes the relevance of the Court's statements regarding the need to suppress the consequences - including in the past - of a breach of the Treaty.

9. The Court rejected the Commission's assertion that beneficiaries could no longer invoke the protection of their legitimate expectation to receive the aid granted under the scheme following publication in the Official Journal of the decision to open an investigation procedure. However, this conclusion was based on the specific circumstances of the case - not on the lack of legal effect of the decision to open an investigation procedure. Indeed, the opening decision's wording was considered insufficiently clear in the case in question. This implied that, with clearer wording, the opening decision could indeed have the effect of preventing arguments based on the beneficiaries' legitimate expectations. The Commission was quick to seize on this chance. A few months later, it informed Member States that in all opening decisions from that moment on, it would explicitly warn beneficiaries of the possible consequences of the investigation in terms of aid recovery (*see* Communication of the Commission of 1983, OJ C 318, 24 November 1983, pp. 3-4). For a complete analysis of the issue of legitimate expectation, *see* section I.A.2.6.c) of this Part One.
10. *See* H.J. Brinkhorst, *Note on Cases 77/72 (Capolongo) and 70/72 (Kohlegesetz)*, Common Market Law Review, n. 11, 1974, pp. 199-210.
11. Interim remedies that the Commission may impose in public enforcement proceedings are not examined in detail here, as they have no impact whatsoever on the assessment of the need for reform of the system of remedies. Moreover, interim remedies are very rare in practice. The Treaty does not refer to interim remedies. Based on Council Regulation (EU) No 2015/1589 ('Procedural Regulation'), however, three interim remedies exist: (i) the injunction decision that the Commission may adopt under Art. 12(2) of the Procedural Regulation to obtain all the information needed to carry out its compatibility assessment; (ii) the suspension injunction laid down under Art. 13(1) of the Procedural Regulation, which is intended to prevent the granting of aid or to discontinue the application of an aid scheme; and (iii) the provisional recovery order envisaged under Art. 13(2) of the Procedural Regulation. The Commission has the power to order provisional recovery for aid granted after the entry into force of the first Procedural Regulation (Regulation (EC) No 659/1999) if three conditions are fulfilled: (i) The Commission has no reason to doubt that the measure under examination is to be considered aid within the meaning of Art. 107(1) TFEU, and this conclusion is based on consolidated practice; (ii) there is an objective urgency to take action in order to prevent distortion of competition; and (iii) the damage for competitors inherent in the distortion is not only imminent but also significant and irreparable.

distortion's effects if it has materialised, or to provide the Commission with the means with which to complete its compatibility assessment.[12]

The principle according to which incompatibility is a precondition for recovery dates back to 1990 and was first stated in the *Boussac* judgment.[13] In this landmark judgment, the Court clearly rejected the Commission's argument that unlawfully granted aid should be held unlawful *per se* and, therefore, recovered without any need to assess its compatibility with the internal market.[14] According to the Court, the compatibility assessment is the key element in the system of State aid control enshrined in the Treaty. Indeed, the principle of incompatibility (or theory of the second best) is at the heart of the system and pervades every aspect of it.

This factor helps strengthen the idea that *effectiveness in public spending is the underlying objective* (or one of them) of the State aid control system. This again entails looking at the effects of the aid in question: Is it capable of incentivising investment and innovation in the common interest? Or does it distort these incentives and lead to a sub-optimal allocation of resources? If the effects are good (*i.e.*, in line with EU objectives) and the aid is proportionate, the system is working well and the aid cannot be recovered - irrespective of breaches of procedural rules under the Treaty, for which Member States can be held liable.

This is the key principle that emerged from the *Boussac* judgment. It was only to prevent Member States from feeling encouraged to neglect compliance with the procedural rules under Article 108(3) TFEU that the Court added a statement *that a finding of compatibility does not remedy an infringement of that provision*. The Court dismissed the French argument that the Commission, when faced with aid granted or altered by a Member State in breach of procedural rules, 'has only the same rights and obligations as those which it has in the case of aid duly notified at the planning stage'.[15] Consequently, the Court went on to elaborate on the Commission's powers and responsibilities in the analysis of unlawful aid,[16] which the EU legislator would codify several years later in the first Procedural Regulation.[17] It is therefore the crucial role given to the compatibility assessment that led first the Court, and later the EU legislator, to shape two procedures: one for notified aid and one for unnotified aid.

12. For a broader analysis of these conditions, *see* Merola, *Rimedi per violazione delle norme sugli aiuti di Stato: misure repressive o di ripristino: Diritto positivo (post-modernizzazione) e scenari di riforma*, cited in footnote 3 of this Part One.
13. Judgment of the Court of 14 February 1990, Case C-301/87, *French Republic v. Commission of the EU*, EU:C:1990:67, paras 9-24. France had granted aid under several forms to Boussac Saint Frères, a producer of paper, textile and clothing products.
14. The Commission had already put forward this argument in the XV Report on Competition Policy (1985, p. 150) and found support in the Opinions of the Advocates General Tesauro (Opinion of 19 September 1989, Case C-142/87, *Kingdom of Belgium v. Commission of the European Communities (Tubemeuse)*, EU:C:1989:335) and Jacobs (Opinion of 4 October 1989, Case 301/87, *French Republic v. Commission of the EU (Boussac)*, EU:C:1990:357).
15. Judgment of the Court of 14 February 1990, Case C-301/87, *French Republic v. Commission of the EU*, cited in footnote 13 of this Part One, para. 11.
16. *Ibid.*, paras 18-23.
17. Council Regulation (EC) No 659/1999 of 22 March 1999 laying down detailed rules for the application of Article 93 of the EC Treaty, OJ L 83/1999, p. 1.

Today, Articles 13(2) and 16(1) of the Procedural Regulation[18] clearly embody the principle that recovery is possible only for aid deemed to be both unlawful and incompatible. Article 20 further clarifies that recovery is possible also in a specific case of unlawfulness, *i.e.*, the 'misuse of aid' (when initially lawful aid is used by a beneficiary in a way that violates the approval decision or in breach of the conditions or obligations imposed in a conditional decision within the meaning of Article 9(4) of the Procedural Regulation). Aid initially deemed to be existing aid is also considered unlawful aid if it continues to be granted after a Commission decision declaring it incompatible with the internal market (following the procedure under Articles 108(1) and (2) TFEU).

I.A.2 Recovery of Unlawful and Incompatible Aid: Essential Features of the System

Having clarified the requirements for recovery, it is now possible to elaborate on the essential features of the system of remedies for unlawful aid. To do so, the main principles and criteria established in hard law, soft law and case law are described below in a logical, systematic order rather than analysing the relevant provisions one by one. Of course, wherever relevant, the source of the principles and criteria under discussion are mentioned.

I.A.2.1 Nature of the Remedies

It is worth clarifying from the outset that the system of remedies refers to both the recovery of unlawful aid and the suspension of granting any new aid to the same beneficiary for the entire time needed to achieve effective recovery of aid already granted. The latter remedy is known as the *Deggendorf* doctrine and stems from the Commission's practice and the creative case law of the Court of Justice. It is also worth mentioning the special (and derogating) infringement procedure established in the treaties for infringements of State aid rules and the Court's power to impose fines on Member States for non-compliance with Court judgments. All these instruments compose the system of remedies examined in the following pages.

No other remedies exist for violations of State aid rules, at least insofar as public enforcement is concerned. Indeed, a clear distinction must be drawn between prospective and restorative remedies. Prospective remedies are considered if the Commission deems it necessary, within the framework of compatibility assessments and take the form of conditions, obligations or commitments that go along with a decision approving State aid. By contrast, restorative remedies tend to neutralise an infringement of State aid rules.[19] Hence, the following sections address the three restorative remedies mentioned above (recovery orders, the suspension of granting any new aid, and fines

18. Council Regulation (EU) 2015/1589 of 13 July 2015, OJ L 248/2015, p. 9.
19. This classification of remedies will prove very important when outlining the reform scenarios in Part Four of this book.

for non-compliance with judgments declaring that a Member State failed to implement recovery orders) by analysing the essential features of each from both a substantive and a procedural standpoint.

I.A.2.2 Recovery as the Logical and Unavoidable Consequence of Granting Unlawful and Incompatible Aid

To start with, recovery is the logical and unavoidable consequence of the unlawful granting of incompatible aid, save for exceptional circumstances. This principle, laid down by the Court,[20] was codified in the first Procedural Regulation[21] and is reiterated in Council Regulation (EU) 2015/1589 (the Procedural Regulation currently in force),[22] where it is stated that:

> in cases of unlawful aid which is not compatible with the internal market, effective competition should be restored. For this purpose, it is necessary that the aid, including interest, be recovered without delay.[23]

Consequently, Article 16 of the same regulation states that 'the Commission *shall* decide that' aid be recovered (emphasis added). This implies that the Commission has no margin of discretion in this respect, except when it comes to the appraisal of exceptional circumstances (*i.e.*, whether recovery runs counter to a general principle of EU law, as mentioned in that provision).[24] This also implies that *no specific reasoning is required* for the recovery order other than the examination of the special circumstances invoked by the Member State or the beneficiary, if any.

Although a recovery order is necessarily embodied in a final negative decision, it is conceptually independent of the compatibility assessment and can be annulled by the EU courts without prejudice to the validity of the negative decision as such. Conversely, interested parties can challenge the absence of a recovery order when the Commission considers that, given the specific and exceptional circumstances of the case, recovery would conflict with a general principle of EU law (as the Commission is under an obligation to order recovery if its assessment of the existence of special circumstances is flawed).

However, interested parties are powerless if the Commission does not commence an infringement procedure against a Member State that fails to enforce a recovery order, as the general rule is that the Commission is not obliged to take legal action

20. Judgment of the Court of 24 February 1987, Case 310/85, *Deufil GmbH & Co. KG v. Commission of the EC*, EU:C:1987:96, para. 24, Judgment of the Court of 21 March 1991, Case C-305/89, *Italy v. Commission of the EC*, EU:C:1991:142, Judgment of the Court of 21 March 1990, Case C-142/87, *Kingdom of Belgium v. Commission of the EC*, EU:C:1990:125, and Judgment of the Court of 7 March 2002, Case C-310/99, *Italian Republic v. Commission of the EC (contratti di formazione e lavoro, CFL)*, EU:C:2002:143, paras 98-100. In particular, *see* the latter with respect to the concept of exceptional circumstances.
21. *See* footnote 17 of this Part One.
22. *See* footnote 18 of this Part One.
23. Recital 25 of Council Regulation (EU) 2015/1589, cited in footnote 18 of this Part One.
24. On this issue, *see* section I.A.2.6 of this Part One.

against a Member State for breach of Treaty rules. *There is a clear mismatch in the recovery system in this respect.* If the legislator chose a derogating system for a specific infringement (violation of State aid rules), this should logically extend to the commencement of infringement procedures if a Member State fails to comply with a Commission order. Of course, this is based on the assumption that recovery is the unavoidable consequence of granting unlawful and incompatible aid, as consistently held in case law (on the grounds that a level playing field should be restored).

I.A.2.3 Rationale of Recovery: Restoring Effective Competition by (Forfeiting the Financial Advantage and Thus) Re-establishing the Status Quo Ante

Recital 25 of the Procedural Regulation spells out the rationale of the recovery system: it refers (twice) to the need to restore effective competition. The European judicature, however, seems to prefer the expression 're-establishment of the *status quo ante*' and usually adds the idea that this objective is achieved by forfeiting the advantage granted by the aid. The Court started to refer to the re-establishment of the previously existing situation in the late eighties[25] and to use the concept of forfeiting the advantage shortly thereafter, in the mid-nineties.[26] The Court holds as follows:

> That objective [of restoring effective competition] is attained once the aid in question, increased where appropriate by default interest, has been repaid by the recipient ... By repaying the aid, the recipient forfeits the advantage which it had enjoyed over its competitors on the market, and the situation prior to payment of the aid is restored.

It is clear that the Court applies a syllogism: repayment of aid forfeits the advantage, the forfeiture restores competition, and hence repayment of the aid (plus interest) restores competition. The syllogism, however, is flawed because it relies on two different concepts of 'advantage'. The concept in the first sentence (repayment of aid forfeits the advantage) is that of financial advantage. Only by taking on this meaning does the sentence make sense: if the nominal value of the granted aid is withdrawn, the financial advantage disappears. The indication that default interest must be added to the nominal amount confirms this view. In the second sentence (forfeiting the advantage restores the pre-existing situation), by contrast, the term 'advantage' is necessarily used in the sense of 'economic advantage' or 'competitive advantage', *i.e.*, the competitive boost that the beneficiary obtained as a result of the aid. Only if the sentence is read in this way can one concur that the situation before the aid was granted is restored. Therefore, the syllogism is based on misleading terminology because the word 'advantage' (*i.e.*, the syllogism's middle term) is used in two profoundly different meanings.

25. Judgment of the Court of 21 March 1990, Case C-142/87, *Kingdom of Belgium v. Commission of the EC (Tubemeuse)*, EU:C:1990:125, para. 66.
26. Judgment of the Court of 4 April 1995, Case C-350/93, *Commission of the European Communities v. Italian Republic (ENI-Lanerossi)*, EU:C:1995:96, para. 22.

Many other judgments equally muddle the two concepts. A reference to the *SMI* case[27] is useful in this respect, as confusion arises from the inconsistent statements in paragraphs 74-76 thereof. First, the Court states that removing unlawful aid by means of recovery is the logical consequence of a finding that the aid is unlawful and adds that recovery seeks to re-establish the previous situation (paragraph 74). Second, in trying to better explain the rationale of the recovery and its application to the case at hand, the Court mixes up the two concepts when it holds the following (paragraph 75):

> [T]hat purpose is achieved once the aid in question, together where appropriate with default interest, has been repaid by the recipient ... or, in other words, by the undertakings which actually benefited from it ... By repaying the aid, the recipient forfeits the advantage which it had enjoyed over its competitors on the market, and the situation prior to payment of the aid is restored ... .

The reference to the *competitors* and the *market* seems to suggest that what matters is the competitive (not financial) advantage. This is clearly at odds with the idea of simply forfeiting the amount granted plus interest. The reasoning culminates in the statement contained in paragraph 76 (*i.e.*, the conclusion of the syllogism), where the contradiction becomes patent, as the Court states that:

> [c]onsequently, the main purpose of the repayment of unlawfully paid State aid is to eliminate the *distortion of competition* caused by the *competitive advantage* afforded by the unlawful aid [emphasis added].

Furthermore, the European judicature developed its approach well before the adoption of the first Procedural Regulation. However, the language used by the Court has remained exactly the same since the entry into force of the first Procedural Regulation. The codification of the obligation for the Commission to order the recovery of unlawful and incompatible aid and the rationale of this radical change as set out in recital 13 of that regulation (and more recently in recital 25 of Council Regulation (EU) 2015/1589, referred to above) do not seem to have prompted the Court of Justice to devote more attention to this issue.

Numerous judgments handed down in the early 2000s – but referring to cases decided before the adoption of the first Procedural Regulation – confirm that the language used by the Court of Justice has remained unchanged.[28] Nor did it change later on, not even after the enactment of Council Regulation (EU) 2015/1589.[29]

27. Judgment of the Court of 29 April 2004, Case C-277/00, *Federal Republic of Germany v. Commission of the EC*, EU:C:2004:238.
28. *See*, among others: Judgment of the Court of 7 March 2002, Case C-310/99, *Italian Republic v. Commission of the EC (contratti di formazione e lavoro, CFL)*, cited in footnote 20 of this Part One, paras 98-99; Judgment of the Court of 29 April 2004, C-277/00, *Federal Republic of Germany v. Commission of the EC*, EU:C:2004:238, paras 74-75; and Judgment of the Court of First Instance of 8 July 2004, T-198/01, *Technische Glaswerke Ilmenau GmbH v. Commission of the EC*, EU:T:2004:222, paras 132-133.
29. Judgment of the Court of 1 October 2015, Case C-357/14 P, *Electrabel SA and Dunamenti Erőmű Zrt v. European Commission*, EU:C:2015:642, paras 111 and 113, and Judgment of the Court of 21 December 2016, Joined Cases C-164/15 P and C-165/15 P, *European Commission v. Aer Lingus Ltd and Ryanair Designated Activity Company*, EU:C:2016:990, paras 89-92. This judgment is further analysed below. Although both these cases were decided by the Commission

Although the Court of Justice has never used the expression 'financial advantage'[30] thus far but simply 'advantage', it has become progressively clear that, when referring to the amount to be repaid, it does intend financial advantage as opposed to economic or competitive advantage.

The idea that recovery is intended to forfeit the advantage granted to the beneficiary through the aid leads to many other implications. One of these is that recovery should have retroactive effects (up to the moment the aid was made available to the beneficiary rather than the moment the aid measure was adopted or the aid was officially granted). However, the concept of 'advantage' also impacts how this retroactivity is to be interpreted. The immediate – *and minimum* – consequence of the need to forfeit the advantage is that the repayment obligation must include interest for the period between the receipt of the aid and the date of repayment,[31] as set out under Article 16(2) of Council Regulation (EU) 2015/1589. After some hesitation, the legislator clarified, under Commission Regulation (EC) No 794/2004,[32] that interest should be calculated by the compound interest method.[33]

However, the issue that remains unsolved is the following: Does the clear reference to financial advantage in Article 16(2) of Council Regulation (EU) 2015/1589 imply that the objective of recovery is merely to forfeit the financial advantage through repayment by the beneficiary of the nominal amount received plus interest? Or should it be understood that Article 16(2) sets out a minimum requirement, without prejudice to the Commission's freedom to calculate the amount of recovery under Article 16(1)

---

before the enactment of Council Regulation (EU) 2015/1589, nothing indicates that the Court might be revising its approach when confronted with cases decided after the entry into force of that regulation.

30. Notably, the expression 'financial advantage' can be found in the *Altmark* judgment (*see* Judgment of the Court of 24 July 2003, Case C-280/00, *Altmark Trans GmbH and Regierungspräsidium Magdeburg v. Nahverkehrsgesellschaft Altmark GmbH, and Oberbundesanwalt beim Bundesverwaltungsgericht*, EU:C:2003:415), though in that judgment it refers to the application of the 'compensatory theory' within the framework of compensation for public service obligations – not to the calculation of the amount to be repaid by the beneficiary. Indeed, the Court held as follows (para. 87):

    > [W]here a State measure must be regarded as compensation for the services provided by the recipient undertakings in order to discharge public service obligations, so that those undertakings do not enjoy a real financial advantage and the measure thus does not have the effect of putting them in a more favourable competitive position than the undertakings competing with them, such a measure is not caught by Article 92(1) of the Treaty.

31. Except for beneficiaries which have been declared insolvent, as in this case the debts of the undertaking cease to produce interest with effect from the date of the insolvency declaration if the applicable national legislation so provides. Such a rule, justified by the common interest of all creditors in not burdening the insolvent undertaking's assets with new debts likely to worsen the situation, applies to all creditors alike – be they private or public – in all insolvency procedures. *See* Judgment of 12 October 2000, Case C-480/98, *Kingdom of Spain v. Commission of the EC (Magefesa)*, EU:C:2000:559, para. 36.
32. Commission Regulation (EC) No 794/2004 of 21 April 2004, OJ L 140, pp. 1-134.
33. By contrast, up to the date of entry into force of Commission Regulation (EC) No 794/2004, the choice of the method to calculate interest was left to the Member State concerned (based on the principle of procedural autonomy). *See* Judgment of the Court of 3 September 2015, Case C-89/14, *A2A S.p.A./Agenzia delle Entrate*, EU:C:2015:537.

so as to achieve 'restoration of effective competition' as warranted by recital 25 of the preamble to the regulation and, therefore, remove the competitive harm caused by the aid?

The reference to the statutory interest rate in Article 16(2) suggests that the reason for applying interest is to cause the beneficiary to forfeit the financial advantage, not to measure the competitive harm caused by the aid. However, should this reading of the provision be retained, would it be consistent with the rationale of the upper norm? Or would it raise additional incongruity that the EU legislator should aim to remove within the framework of a reform of the remedies available under State aid law? This issue will be further analysed below when dealing with the criteria set out in the case law and in soft law concerning the determination of the amount to be recovered.[34]

Other incongruities also exist. Logically, the Commission should have the power to order the repayment of interest for the period between the moment the aid was made available to the beneficiary and the actual date of repayment, even in a decision declaring the aid unlawful but compatible. However, Article 16(2) does not mention this possibility, as it refers only to the decision ordering the recovery of the aid. In the absence of a clear legal basis, the Commission has thus far refrained from ordering the repayment of interest for compatible aid unlawfully granted.[35] Also, this question is further addressed below.[36]

The existence of so many uncertainties explains why, in the heading of this section, the objective of forfeiting the financial advantage was mentioned in parenthetical form next to that of re-establishing the *status quo ante*. Indeed, the first concept is not mentioned in the recitals of the Procedural Regulation or in Article 16 thereof. It is entirely a contribution of the case law, which, as mentioned, uses it merely as a predicate of the concept of re-establishing the situation existing prior to the granting of the aid – thus raising the inconsistencies discussed above.

I.A.2.4 Fading Procedural Autonomy and Recovery as an Obligation of Result

Article 16(3) of Council Regulation (EU) 2015/1589 sets out some procedural rules on recovery of unlawful aid, the most important of which is the principle of procedural autonomy of Member States for the execution of recovery orders. However, other rules in the same provision substantially limit the scope of procedural autonomy, and the case law has progressively lessened its relevance. All in all, it seems that the EU legislator – after having discarded the Commission's initial proposal to harmonise national procedures for the recovery of unlawful aid following a Commission's

34. *See* section II.A.3 of this Part One.
35. The Court retained a different solution within the framework of private enforcement. In its Judgment of 12 February 2008, Case C-199/06, *CELF et Ministre de la Culture et de la Communication c. SIDE (CELF I)*, EU:C:2008:79, the Court held that 'the national court must therefore, applying Community law, order the aid recipient to pay interest in respect of the period of unlawfulness' (para. 52). Furthermore, '[w]ithin the framework of its domestic law, it may, if appropriate, also order the recovery of the unlawful aid' (para. 53).
36. *See* section II.A.3 of this Part One.

recovery order in favour of applying the principle of procedural autonomy – has shaped this principle, with key support from the EU courts, in such a way that the result is not significantly different from what would have been achieved through the harmonisation of national laws.

First, Article 16(3) states that 'recovery shall be effected without delay' except in the case of any order of the EU Court of Justice under Article 278 TFEU. Article 16(3) clarifies that the national law of the Member State concerned must allow the *immediate* and *effective* execution of Commission decisions. This means that it is for the Member States to ensure effective recovery (within the prescribed time limit), if necessary by adapting national law accordingly. The case law confirms and even strengthens this approach without hesitation.[37] In *Olympic Airways* (among other cases), the Court held as follows:

> The application of national procedures should not ... impede the restoration of effective competition by preventing the immediate and effective execution of the Commission's decision. To achieve this result, Member States should take all necessary measures ensuring the effectiveness of that decision.[38]

According to the Court, recital 13 of the Procedural Regulation, which refers to the need to restore effective competition, offers sufficient legal basis in this respect. Following the judgment in *Scott*,[39] which came one year after *Olympic Airways*, the Court has confirmed the same approach several times, rejecting the attempts of the Member States concerned to confine their obligation to: (i) initiating the appropriate legal actions to obtain repayment of the aid by the beneficiary;[40] or, in the case of an aid scheme (ii) arranging and starting the investigation needed to establish the amount to be repaid by each beneficiary.[41]

The tension between the principle of procedural autonomy and the obligation to (effectively and timely) execute recovery orders surfaced in numerous cases brought before the EU courts. It is well established in the case law that only the absolute impossibility of obtaining repayment can justify the non-execution of the order, but this concept does not encompass difficulties arising from rules or principles of national legal systems. The *supremacy of the principle of effectiveness over that of procedural autonomy* reached its extreme consequences when the Court held that even the basic principle of *res judicata* should be set aside, at least under some circumstances, if its application obstructs the effective recovery of aid.[42]

37. Judgment of the Court of 12 May 2005, Case C-415/03, *Commission of the EC v. Hellenic Republic (Olympic Airways)*, EU:C:2005:287, paras 33, 34 and 44.
38. *Ibid.*
39. *See also* Judgment of the Court of 5 October 2006, Case C-232/05, *Commission of the EU v. French Republic (Scott)*, EU:C:2006:651, para. 50.
40. Judgment of the Court of 22 December 2010, Case C-507/08, *European Commission v. Slovak Republic*, EU:C:2010:802, paras 48-54.
41. Judgment of the Court of 17 September 2015, Case C-367/14, *European Commission v. Italian Republic*, EU:C:2015:611, paras 40-41.
42. Judgment of the Court of 18 July 2007, Case C-119/05, *Ministero dell'Industria, del Commercio e dell'Artigianato v. Lucchini SpA (Lucchini)*, EU:C:2007:434, paras 59-63. This issue is dealt with in more detail below, when discussing the application of the exception set out in Art. 16(1)

Likewise, regarding the choice of the most appropriate means to execute recovery decisions, the Court held that, in the absence of EU law regarding recovery procedures, a Member State:

> 'is free to choose the means of fulfilling that obligation' but only to the extent that 'the measures chosen do not adversely affect the scope and effectiveness of Community law'.

This clarifies that the measures chosen by Member States must have the same effect as that of repayment by way of a transfer of funds and that:

> any measure adopted in order to fulfil an obligation to recover illegal aid must be a suitable instrument for re-establishing the conditions of competition which have been distorted by the grant of that illegal aid, be capable of being identified as such by the Commission and other interested parties, and be unconditional and immediately applicable.[43]

Article 16(3), as presently construed, thus leads to an *obligation of result* for the Member States, *i.e.*, an obligation to ensure the effective, full and timely execution of recovery decisions.

As to the principle of procedural autonomy, it should be properly understood: it does not endow Member States with any room for manoeuvre in shaping the effects of the Commission's assessment regarding the unlawfulness and incompatibility of aid but is simply aimed at facilitating the effective execution of recovery decisions through *the most appropriate tools under national law*, in accordance with the general principle of *sincere cooperation*. Consequently, Member States may not invoke obstacles stemming from their own legal system to justify a failure to recover within the prescribed time limit,[44] and they should select the national procedures to achieve recovery in compliance with the consolidated principles of equivalence[45] and effectiveness.[46]

---

of Council Regulation (EU) 2015/1589 (exceptional circumstances due to the conflict between recovery and a general principle of EU law).

43. Judgment of the Court of 12 December 2002, Case C-209/00, *Commission of the EC v. Federal Republic of Germany (WestLB)*, EU:C:2002:747, paras 57-58. In this case, the Court rejected the two means of execution of the recovery order proposed by the Federal Republic of Germany because of their precarious character (*e.g.*, the right to receive an additional share of a company's surpluses in the event of its liquidation or of a change in the shareholders' holdings in the capital related to an uncertain future event). For a similar example – though one that concluded with a positive assessment – *see* Judgment of the Court of 8 December 2011, Case C-275/10, *Residex Capital IV CV v. Gemeente Rotterdam (Residex)*, EU:C:2011:814, para. 47, where the Court held that 'the cancellation of a contract, in so far as this is liable to lead to the mutual restitution of the services performed by the parties or the disappearance of an advantage for the future, may be better able to achieve the objective of restoring the competitive situation which existed before the aid was granted'.
44. Judgment of the Court of 20 March 1997, Case C-24/95, *Land Renania Palatinato v. Alcan Deutschland GmbH*, EU:C:C:1997:163, para. 24.
45. Judgment of the Court of 9 November 1995, Case C-465/93, *Atlanta Fruchthandelsgesellschaft mbH and others v. Bundesamt für Ernährung und Forstwirtschaft (Atlanta)*, EU:C:1995:369.
46. Judgment of the Court of 21 February 1991, Joined Cases C-143/88 and C-92/89, *Zuckerfabrik Süderdithmarschen AG v. Hauptzollamt Itzehoe and Zuckerfabrik Soest GmbH v. Hauptzollamt Paderborn (Zuckerfabrik)*, EU:C:1991:65.

However, it remains their competence to set the appropriate procedures. The Commission may not impose its choice in this respect, and although the principle of supremacy can impose a duty on national authorities to legislate, this cannot imply that general principles of national law must automatically be set aside. This limit has been vigorously recalled by German scholars[47] and, although clearly a nuance, it is not without effect: it implies that differences, even significant ones, can emerge between the solutions decided on by the various national legislators. This may bring the old question of the advisability of harmonising national laws on recovery procedures to the forefront again in reforming the system of remedies. Effective recovery is in any event - and in all respects - *a shared responsibility of the Commission and Member States.*

I.A.2.5 Analysis of the Effects of Aid Has No Bearing on Recovery

If the Commission is called on to investigate the actual and potential effects of aid when assessing its compatibility, its analysis has no relevance when ordering recovery of the aid.

Whether this is coherent is open to debate, but it is undeniable that the current recovery system leads to this conclusion. Indeed, the Commission is obliged not only to order recovery if the compatibility assessment is negative and the aid under scrutiny was unlawfully granted but also to do so irrespective of the time elapsed since the granting of the aid, provided that the ten-year time limit under Article 17 of the Procedural Regulation is not exceeded. Whether the aid has *actually* produced effects on the market - and, if so, whether *the effects are still perceptible and measurable* at the time of recovery - is irrelevant, as the Commission lacks the power to perform any qualitative assessment in this respect.

Under Article 17 of the Procedural Regulation currently in force (*i.e.*, Council Regulation (EU) 2015/1589), the ten-year period is called a 'limitation period', whereas in other linguistic versions, the words used correspond to the English 'prescription'.[48] The English version seems to better reflect the legislator's intentions at the time of the 2015 reform of the Procedural Regulation. The preparatory work to the first Procedural Regulation indeed shows that the basic reason underlying the ten-year rule was the presumption that, after such a long period, the aid was no longer capable of distorting competition or the level playing field.[49] The 2015 legislator eventually seemed to take a different view, emphasising simply the need to provide a limitation period after which no recovery can be ordered for reasons of legal certainty (recital 26). This approach is consistent with the obligation on the Commission to order recovery

47. *See* C. Arhold, *Recovery of Unlawful State Aid by the Member States: The New German Approach*, in European State Aid Law Quarterly (ESTaL), 2006, Issue 1, p. 9 https://doi.org/10.21552/estal/2006/1/73.
48. *See, e.g.*, the French (*prescription*), Italian (*prescrizione*) and Spanish (*prescripción*) versions.
49. *See* the Opinion of the Economic and Social Committee on the 'Proposal for a Council Regulation (EC) laying down detailed rules for the application of Article 93 of the EC Treaty', OJ C 284, 14.9.1998, p. 10.

irrespective of the actual distortive effects produced by the aid. Had the rationale of the first Procedural Regulation been maintained, it would have been necessary to allow the Commission to review the effects of the aid over time and mitigate the recovery obligation accordingly.

Furthermore, for the same reason, the limitation period affects solely the Commission's power to order recovery of the aid; it does not extend to the power to declare aid incompatible with the internal market. A statement of incompatibility is not at odds with the principle of legal certainty. Quite the contrary: it can help clarify the Commission's views on a given type of aid and provide guidance for the future. This solution also confirms that a finding of incompatibility and a recovery order are to be considered *two severable resolutions*, although simultaneous and contained in the same final decision.

Despite the clear approach taken in the new Procedural Regulation, the latent conflict between the two ideas of the recovery system remains. If recovery is aimed only at forfeiting the advantage by eliminating the financial advantage granted to the beneficiary, it is reasonable to conclude that no mitigation is warranted on the basis of a delay in adopting a final decision (within, of course, the limitation period). Likewise, it is coherent that the only acts capable of interrupting the limitation period are those adopted by the Commission, and that there is no need to notify the beneficiary of them, as the case law has clarified. However, it cannot be denied that the very concept of forfeiting the financial advantage and all the related formalistic solutions ensuing therefrom (*e.g.*, in relation to the calculation of interest and the limitation period) are at odds with the rationale indicated in the Procedural Regulation and reaffirmed in the case law, which is to remove the anticompetitive harm and to restore the level playing field. Anticompetitive harm is indeed not analysed or measured when ordering recovery.

The repayment of the nominal amount plus statutory interest in all cases of unlawful aid, irrespective of any effects analysis and of the time elapsed since the aid was granted, equates to the imposition of a sort of penalty on the beneficiary when the beneficiary has *de facto* not enjoyed any substantial competitive benefit. This approach has little to do with the re-establishment of the *status quo ante* from the standpoint of competition in the market.

Therefore, the doubt expressed when discussing the interest rule under Article 16(2) is also relevant here: Is full recovery of the nominal aid amount to be seen as the absolute rule? Or should it be understood as a minimum requirement, without prejudice to the Commission's freedom to calculate the recovery amount under Article 16(1) so as to 'restore effective competition'? Should the latter approach be retained, repayment of the nominal amount plus interest would merely serve a deterrence objective by penalising the beneficiary even in the absence of anticompetitive effects. However, the deterrent would be misplaced, as it would focus on the beneficiary only (not on the Member States – an approach that would be at odds with the representation of State aid rules as involving only, or primarily, the Member States) and would apply regardless of any analysis of the beneficiary's actual co-responsibility for breach of the Treaty. As mentioned, this issue is further analysed below.[50]

I.A.2.6 The Concept of Recovery as Phrased in the Case Law Minimises the Significance of the Derogation Based on Exceptional Circumstances

The EU legislator took care to state explicitly in Article 16(1) that the Commission may not order recovery 'if this would be contrary to a general principle of Union law'. This is the only derogation provided in the Procedural Regulation. Thus, the Commission is required to consider exceptional circumstances before ordering recovery only if such circumstances relate to the application of a general principle of Union law.

Despite this narrow but clear limit on recovery, the formulas used in the case law have enormous consequences on the scope of the statutory derogation. Reference in this respect is made to the definition of recovery as the logical and unavoidable consequence of granting unlawful and incompatible aid, and to the re-wording of the purpose inherent in recovery as the 're-establishment of the *status quo ante*' (rather than the restoration of conditions of effective competition). In brief, the scope of the derogation shrank radically as a result of developments in the case law. This can be seen by analysing the various general legal principles that may become relevant in this connection, *i.e.*, proportionality, *res judicata*, protection of legitimate expectations, and legal certainty.

a) Proportionality

First, the Court clarified that since forfeiting unlawful aid by means of recovery is the logical consequence of a finding that the aid is incompatible and merely seeks to re-establish the previously existing situation, full repayment by the beneficiary cannot breach the principle of proportionality.[51] This statement seems to have an absolute value, as the specific circumstances of every case are considered irrelevant in this respect. This conclusion, although never explicitly expressed in the case law, is confirmed by the fact that the principle of proportionality has never been successfully invoked to challenge a recovery order.[52]

---

50. *See* section II.A.3 of this Part One.
51. In its *ENI-Lanerossi* judgment (*see* footnote 26 of this Part One), the Court held that 'the recovery of State aid unlawfully granted for the purpose of re-establishing the previously existing situation cannot in principle be regarded as disproportionate to the objectives of the Treaty in regard to State aids' (para. 22). *See also* Judgment of the Court of 29 April 2004, Case C-277/00, *Federal Republic of Germany v. Commission of the European Communities*, EU:C:2004:238.
52. Not even in the case of the recovery of negligible amounts of individual aid from hundreds of thousands of Greek farmers during the darkest period of the financial and economic crisis, despite an initial suggestion in this sense by the President of the General Court. *See* Judgment of the General Court of 16 July 2014, Case T-52/12, *Hellenic Republic v. European Commission*, EU:T:2014:677, and Order of the President of the General Court of 19 September 2012, Case T-52/12 R, *Hellenic Republic v. European Commission*, EU:T:2012:447.

b) *Res Judicata*

Second, there is a general view, based on the landmark *Lucchini* case,[53] that the concept of general principles of Union law laid down in Article 16(1) does not encompass the *res judicata* rule as applied in national law. This view, however, should be nuanced. The Court held, in paragraph 63 of its judgment, as follows:

> Community law precludes the application of a provision of national law, such as Article 2909 of the Italian Civil Code, which seeks to lay down the principle of *res judicata* in so far as the application of that provision prevents the recovery of State aid granted in breach of Community law which has been found to be incompatible with the common market in a decision of the Commission which has become final.

It cannot be inferred from this statement that *res judicata* can never justify the application of the derogation under Article 16(1). Indeed, the judgment in *Lucchini* was not issued in an action for annulment against a recovery decision but as a preliminary ruling in very complex and unusual national proceedings. The main issue was whether the Italian Council of State was obliged to leave the principle of *res judicata* unapplied to ensure the effectiveness of the recovery decision. Under these circumstances, the Court could hardly take a different view, considering the basic principle of supremacy of EU law over national law, as constantly held in the case law.[54]

Several elements lead to the conclusion that the *res judicata* principle can fit, at least in some cases, in the definition of 'general principles of Union law' in Article 16(1) and, therefore, justify a derogation from the obligation to order recovery. Indeed, *res judicata* is an expression of the broader principle of legal certainty, whose relevance in the context of Article 16(1) is widely acknowledged. Moreover, the Court has often recognised - although in other fields of EU law - the need to keep the scope of the *res judicata* principle intact, given its importance in every legal system.[55] The case law also confirms that EU law does not require national courts to leave the national provisions on *res judicata* unapplied only because doing so would enable the courts to ascertain an infringement of EU law.[56] But above all, if a national judgment that has become *res judicata* concerns the lawfulness of the aid concerned (*i.e.*, compliance with Article 108(3) or with an exemption regulation), a Commission decision adopted afterwards could never negate that finding, which fell within the competence of that national

53. Judgment of the Court of 18 July 2007, Case C-119/05, *Ministero dell'Industria, del Commercio e dell'Artigianato v. Lucchini SpA*, EU:C:2007:434.
54. Judgment of the Court of 9 March 1978, Case 106/77, *Amministrazione delle finanze dello Stato v. Simmenthal SpA (known as Simmenthal)*, EU:C:1978:49, para. 17, and Judgment of the Court of 19 June 1990, Case C-213/89, *Factortame Ltd and others v. Commission of the EC*, EU: C:1990:257, paras 18-20.
55. In this respect, *see* Judgment of the Court of 16 March 2006, Case C-234/04, *Rosmarie Kapferer v. Schlank & Schick GmbH*, EU:C:2006:178, para. 21, and Judgment of the Court of 12 February 2008, Case C-2/06, *Willy Kempter KG v. Hauptzollamt Hamburg-Jonas*, EU:C:2008:78, para. 60. Among scholars, *see* G. Tesauro, *Diritto dell'Unione europea*, Cedam, 2010, p. 214, and S. Bastianon, *La tutela del legittimo affidamento nel diritto dell'Unione europea*, Giuffrè, 2012, pp. 66-72.
56. Judgment of the Court of 1 June 1999, Case C-126/97, *Eco Swiss China Time Ltd v. Benetton International NV*, EU:C:1999:269, paras 46-47.

court. In these circumstances, the Commission should refrain from ordering recovery by means of the derogation under Article 16(1).

The Court seems to have accepted this conclusion and to have drawn the limits of the *Lucchini* ruling in at least one case concerning Slovakia and decided in 2010.[57] Although the conclusion was that the Slovak Republic had failed to use all the means at its disposal to fulfil its obligation to recover the aid at issue, the Court underscored the importance of the principle of *res judicata* in both the EU and national legal systems. On this basis, it held as follows:

> In order to ensure stability of the law and legal relations, as well as the sound administration of justice, it is important that judicial decisions which have become definitive after all rights of appeal have been exhausted or after expiry of the time-limits provided to exercise those rights can no longer be called into question. Accordingly, European Union law does not in all circumstances require a national court to disapply domestic rules of procedure conferring the force of *res judicata* on a judgment, even if to do so would make it possible to remedy an infringement of European Union law by the judgment in question.

All things considered, it can thus be said that the reference to the general principles of Union law in Article 16(1) encompasses the *res judicata* principle only under very strict conditions, *i.e.*, when the national judgment asserts the lawfulness of the aid and becomes final before the Commission adopts a decision deeming the aid unlawful, and only within the limits of the specific (individual) aid that was the subject of the national proceedings. If the measure in question is an aid scheme of general application, the derogation does not apply beyond the aid covered by the national judgment and does not extend to other aid granted on the same basis, even more so if granted after the Commission decision.[58]

---

57. Judgment of the Court of 22 December 2010, Case C-507/08, *European Commission v. Slovak Republic*, EU:C:2010:802, paras 56-58. The case concerned aid – in the form of cancellation of a tax debt – granted by the Slovak Republic in 2004 to Frucona Košice, a producer of non-alcoholic beverages. The Commission found the measure to be incompatible with the common market and asked the Slovak Republic to recover the unlawfully granted aid (Commission Decision 2007/254/EC of 7 June 2006 – State aid C 25/2005). Frucona challenged the national administration's act adopted in execution of the decision to obtain repayment of the aid before the competent regional court, which held that Frucona was under no obligation to repay the aid. Hence, the Commission brought the Slovak Republic before the Court of Justice for failure to fulfil its obligations under the fourth paragraph of Art. 249 EC and Art. 2 of the decision. Before the Court, the Slovak Republic argued that Slovak tax law did not provide a legal basis for recovering a tax authority's claim that was subject to amnesty under an agreement, as in the case at issue. Therefore, the State could not 'annul' the regional court's decision, which in the meantime had become res judicata. The Court found that the measures taken by the competent Slovak authorities did not lead to the recovery of the wrongful aid and that normal conditions of competition were therefore not restored. It added that the documents before the Court and the observations made at the hearing by the Slovak Republic proved that means existed under national law that, if diligently used, could have ensured proper recovery of the aid at issue. Therefore, the Slovak Republic had failed to fulfil its obligation under the fourth paragraph of Art. 249 EC and Art. 2 of the decision.
58. It is a well-established principle in the case law, although in the field of indirect taxation, that extending the protection of res judicata to other cases that raise the same legal issues is incompatible with the principle of effectiveness of EU law provisions. *See* Judgment of the Court

c) Protection of Legitimate Expectations

Third, and above all, the declining weight of the derogation under Article 16(1) becomes clear when examining the application of the two general principles most often invoked, *i.e.*, the principles of protection of legitimate expectations and legal certainty.

The protection of legitimate expectations is a defence granted to beneficiaries of a public measure when enforcement of EU law would jeopardise the expectation created in the beneficiary by previous action taken by the Commission or another EU institution regarding that public measure's legality and, consequently, the stability of a given situation. The principle of protection of legitimate expectations must therefore be assessed with reference to the beneficiary's subjective position.

The statement so often repeated by the Commission in its pleadings before the EU courts that no legitimate expectation can exist if the aid was unlawfully granted (by violating the procedural rules) is based on a total misconception of this principle, which requires strict conditions for its application. Breach of the Treaty by a Member State does not imply that the conditions for the beneficiary to invoke the principle of protection of legitimate expectations cannot be met but simply that it cannot be invoked by that Member State. This principle indeed centres on the subjective position of the beneficiary of the aid measure and - despite the importance given to it by the legislator -would become meaningless (because a pre-condition for ordering recovery is that the aid must be unlawful) if infringement of procedural rules by a Member State were deemed sufficient to deprive the beneficiary of any protection.

Of course, in assessing the existence of legitimate expectations, *one of the factors* to consider is whether the beneficiary was or should have been aware, as a diligent business operator, that the aid was being granted unlawfully. However, this is but one circumstance to consider - along with all the other relevant facts - when assessing whether, from the beneficiary's standpoint, sufficient elements exist to create a legitimate expectation.

It is therefore deceiving that the General Court, even in recent case law, continues to mix Member States' responsibility for violation of their procedural obligations with the assessment of a beneficiary's legitimate expectation, whereas the Court of Justice seems more cautious in this respect.[59] This is all the more disappointing if one considers that, in recent cases, such as in *Volotea,* the General Court could have easily

of 3 September 2009, Case C-2/08, *Amministrazione dell'Economia e delle Finanze e Agenzia delle entrate v. Fallimento Olimpiclub Srl ('Olimpiclub')*, EU:C:2009:506, paras 22-31.

59. On the General Court's case law, *see* Judgment of the General Court of 13 May 2020 in Case T-607/17, *Volotea SA v. European Commission*, paras 221-226. The case concerned incentives granted by the Autonomous Region of Sardinia to airport operators for the increase of air traffic to the island (*i.e.*, reducing the seasonality of air routes and opening up new air routes) and promotional activities. The Commission considered that these measures did not involve State aid in favour of the airport operators but rather constituted indirect State aid in favour of some airlines, including Volotea. Because the aid had been put into effect by the Autonomous Region in breach of the standstill obligation, the Commission ordered Italy to recover it from the beneficiaries. Volotea challenged the decision by arguing, among other things, that the Commission had misidentified the beneficiaries of the aid scheme. In the applicant's opinion, there was indeed an absence of advantage for the airlines. Additionally, Volotea claimed that regardless of whether an advantage for the airlines could be identified, the Commission had

dismissed the beneficiary's legitimate expectation arguments by referring only to the absence of assurances given to the beneficiary and to the specific circumstances of the case, which should have made the beneficiary aware of the aid's unlawfulness. There was thus no need to refer to the Member State's violation of the notification obligation, let alone to mix this reference with other considerations (such as the absence of precise assurances given to the beneficiary and the commercial nature of its contractual relations with the airport operators) without clarifying how all these elements respectively contributed to the finding that no legitimate expectation existed.[60]

On top of this, it is easily predictable that circumstances giving rise to a legitimate expectation will arise more frequently in the post-modernisation landscape, given the huge increase in aid measures covered by block exemptions. There is no signal that the EU courts or the Commission have considered this factor thus far. Although the EU courts have, up to this point, consistently held that beneficiaries can have legitimate expectations only based on unambiguous assurances provided by EU institutions, they will likely soon be confronted with novel situations related to exempted aid. Given that, by definition, aid covered by block exemption regulations or decisions need not be notified to the Commission, the question is what the Commission's and courts' position

failed to consider its legitimate expectations, which rendered the repayment obligation ineffective under Art. 16(1) of the Procedural Regulation. *See also* Judgment of the General Court of 21 September 2022, Case T-95/21, *Portuguese Republic v. European Commission*, EU:T:2022:567. In this case, the General Court rightfully rejected the applicant government's argument based on the violation of the principle of protection of legitimate expectations as inadmissible and in any event unfounded (paras 196 and 203) but still tended to confuse the State's responsibility with that of the beneficiaries (*see* paras 196-197).

As to the Court of Justice's recent case law, *see* Judgment of 2 February 2023, Joined Cases C-649/20 P, C-658/20 P and C-662/20 P. EU:C:2023:60, para. 82, where the Court simply recalled that the protection of legitimate expectations and legal certainty can be granted only in exceptional circumstances in connection with unlawful aid.

60. In examining the third plea – which was based on an alleged violation of the principle of protection of legitimate expectations – the General Court started by recalling that, according to settled case law, the right to rely on the principle of the protection of legitimate expectations presupposes that an EU institution caused the beneficiary to have justified expectations; it also recalled that a breach of this principle cannot be invoked in the absence of specific assurances provided to the party by the administration (para. 220). Subsequently, in paras 221-225, the General Court went through various arguments raised by the applicant to rule out the existence of justified expectations in the case at hand. First, it stated that a diligent business operator must normally be in a position to confirm that the notification procedure has been followed and the standstill obligation complied with. Second, it found that at no point had the Commission given assurances to Volotea as to the aid scheme's compatibility with the internal market. Third, it held that, despite the commercial nature of the contractual relations between the airlines and the airport operators, the latter had never concealed the State origin of the funds used to enter into those contracts with the airlines; on the contrary, the financing mechanism of the incentives granted by the Cagliari-Elmas airport operator to Volotea (*i.e.*, the air carrier) was explicitly referred to in the contract (not to mention was referred to in the contract with the Olbia airport operator) and was in any case public knowledge, as the related provision was in a law that had been published in the Autonomous Region of Sardinia's Official Gazette. More interestingly, the General Court also dismissed Volotea's line of argument based on the difficulty of grasping the concept of indirect aid and of identifying the final beneficiary. The Court held that 'the indirect nature of the aid has no bearing on its recovery' and 'in no way constitutes an exceptional circumstance allowing it to escape the direct effect of the prohibition in Article 107(1)' – hence the application of the remedy (para. 225).

will be in relation to unlawful or abusive aid detected through *ex post* monitoring if beneficiaries claim that, to the best of their knowledge, the aid received was compliant with a block exemption.

Moreover, national courts are competent to assess compliance with block exemption regulations and decisions. In discharging this duty, they will have to determine whether the aid concerned has been lawfully granted, which implies that they will have to interpret the provisions of block exemption regulations and decisions, with the Court of Justice's help through preliminary rulings if needed. As a result, significant developments are to be expected in the field of legitimate expectations of aid beneficiaries, and the boundaries and scope of this limit on recovery will have to be redefined to factor in such developments.

For now, the requirements for the traditional application of the principle of protection of legitimate expectations are rigorous, in accordance with the case law. The principle has been applied in many areas of EU law, and the basic requirements that are valid in all those areas can be summarised as follows: (i) the expectation should be based on acts of EU institutions or, within certain limits, on the conduct of their members, representatives or (to a lesser extent) officials that led the beneficiary to have *reasonable* expectations (for a diligent operator); (ii) the act or conduct of the administration has given the beneficiary *precise* (not generic) assurances; (iii) the beneficiary should not be in a position to expect a change of position by the administration; and (iv) no superior Union interest exists that pre-empts recognition of the legitimate expectation.

In the field of State aid, these criteria are applied even more rigorously considering the unlawful nature of granted aid and the fact that Commission decisions concerning unlawful aid have retroactive effect by law. This stricter approach mainly affects the third condition, which is interpreted as requiring that the operator invoking the protection should not only be in good faith but should also have been unaware of (and incapable of ascertaining) the violation of the procedural rules by the Member State in question. A presumption exists that a diligent operator 'should normally be able to determine whether that procedure has been followed'.[61]

The result is that the beneficiary of aid can invoke the principle of protection of legitimate expectations only if precise assurances had been obtained from EU institutions that the measure in question was not State aid or that the aid was not subject to the notification obligation (because it was considered existing aid). If, by contrast, the assurances obtained by the beneficiary concern the aid's compatibility or other aspects but did not lead the beneficiary to believe that the advantage had been lawfully granted, the protection of legitimate expectations may be invoked only in exceptional circumstances, which the operator must prove. This seems to be the only consistent interpretation of the case law.

61. Judgment of the Court of 20 September 1990, Case C-5/89, *Commission of the EC v. Federal Republic of Germany*, EU:C:1990:320, para. 14.

The size of the beneficiary (whether a big, medium-sized or even small undertaking) has no bearing on the assessment of exceptional circumstances.[62] This seems to confirm that, for the derogation to be successfully invoked, the assurances on which the expectation is based should touch on the aid's lawfulness. It remains to be seen whether, in a post-modernisation era in which block exemptions and *ex post* controls abound, the European judicature will be prepared to apply the concept of exceptional circumstances at least when doubts exist on the correct interpretation of the block exemption regulation or other technically complex instruments of soft law.[63]

Despite the restrictive interpretation of the conditions for the application of the derogation, the EU courts have acknowledged the existence of legitimate expectations in some cases, although only very few. Among these, a distinction should be drawn between cases decided before and after the entry into force of the first Procedural Regulation. The *RSV* judgment handed down in 1987 is probably the only one belonging to the first category, and it is debatable whether it provides any guidance today.[64] However, it is certainly instructive in that it shows that the appraisal of the existence of legitimate expectations requires analysis of all the circumstances of a given case and that no specific element can be considered conclusive in itself.

This is still valid today, as not even a previous Commission decision not to raise objections against aid suffices to generate a legitimate expectation in the beneficiary if the decision has been appealed.[65] Nevertheless, it is submitted that the Commission could not adopt, without infringing the principle of protection of legitimate expectations, a less favourable approach than that retained in decisions subsequently annulled by the EU courts *if not strictly necessary for the proper execution of the ruling*.[66]

Situations in which the Court validated the application of the principle of protection of legitimate expectations after the entry into force of the Procedural Regulation are also extremely rare. These include cases in which assurances were provided to the beneficiary through previous Council and Commission decisions,

62. Judgment of the Court of First Instance (now General Court) of 15 June 2000, Joined Cases T-298/97, T-312/97, T-313/97, T-315/97, T-600/97 to 607/97, T-1/98, T-3/98 to T-6/98 and T-23/98, *Alzetta Mauro and others v. Commission of the EC*, EU:T:2000:151, paras 171-173.
63. Reference can be made here to texts of soft law that can impact the appraisal of the existence (not only the compatibility) of State aid. A good example can be found in the case of energy infrastructures within the Guidelines on State aid for environmental protection and energy 2014-2020 (Communication from the Commission – Guidelines on State aid for environmental protection and energy 2014-2020) (OJ C 200, 28.6.2014, pp. 1-55).
64. Judgment of the Court of 24 November 1987, Case 223/85, *Rijn-Schelde-Verolme (RSV) Machinefabrieken en Scheepswerven NV v. Commission of the EC*, EU:C:1987:502, paras 13-17. This case is still referred to as a benchmark by the EU courts in some cases (for a recent example, *see* Judgment of the General Court of 21 September 2022, Case T-95/21, cited in footnote 59 of this Part One, para. 213), but always to eventually reject the possibility of invoking that precedent in the case concerned.
65. Judgment of the Court of 14 January 1997, Case C-169/95, *Kingdom of Spain v. Commission of the EC*, EU:C:1997:10, para. 53.
66. In some national legal systems, this would be achieved through application of the estoppel principle. However, the Court has held that this principle is not recognised as a general principle of EU law and that situations characterised by a previous Commission decision must be assessed using the principles of protection of legitimate expectations and legal certainty. *See* Judgment of the General Court of 22 April 2016, Joined Cases T-50/06 RENV II and T-69/06 RENV II, *Ireland and Aughinish Alumina Ltd v. European Commission*, EU:T:2016:227, para. 56.

letters from the commissioner in charge of competition and from high officials, and commissioners' statements before the European Parliament, but these all related to exceptional circumstances in which all other relevant requirements were met - and in any case, such exceptional circumstances can apply only until the publication of the decision opening the investigation procedure under Article 108(2) TFEU.[67]

To conclude on the principle of protection of legitimate expectations, although the protection afforded by Article 16(1) is clearly limited to exceptional circumstances, it cannot be rendered useless by a misconception of its very nature, which is a variant of the principle of good faith (*bona fide accipientis*). While taking into account the overall system of State aid control, the conditions for application of the principle of protection of legitimate expectations should be construed consistently with its conceptual basis and with the interpretation they receive in other fields of EU law. Although Member States should certainly not be encouraged to infringe the Treaty's procedural rules, the focus must remain on the aid beneficiary's subjective position and the assurances provided by EU institutions, and any aim to punish the Member State for violation of the procedural rules must be refrained from.

Likewise, in analysing the circumstances of each case, it must be kept in mind that, at the present stage of development of EU competition law, beneficiaries are under no obligation to self-assess the compatibility of aid. Thus, adequate assurances regarding the lawfulness of aid suffice to generate legitimate expectations. It is submitted that omissive conduct by the Commission can also create a legitimate expectation if other circumstances concur, irrespective of whether the limitation period has expired.[68]

Moreover, a fair allocation of the burden of proof is crucial. This should be structured in two phases. First, the aid beneficiary needs to prove that exceptional circumstances exist and that they give rise to a legitimate expectation. The aid beneficiary should also prove that it acted in a diligent way *vis-à-vis* both the national authorities and the Commission. Second, if the Commission believes that some circumstances prevent the recognition of a legitimate expectation invoked by a beneficiary (*e.g.*, assurances given by EU institutions were not sufficiently precise or did not affect the beneficiary's position), or there are factors that call the beneficiary's good faith into question, the Commission should bear the burden of proof in this respect.

Finally, the period covered by legitimate expectations - in the event this defence is accepted -should extend from the moment the acts or behaviours that provide precise assurances to the beneficiary are put in place to the date of publication of the Commission decision opening the Article 108(2) procedure in connection with the aid in question. This would be coherent with the nature of the protection afforded by the

67. Judgment of 10 December 2013, Case C-272/12 P, *European Commission v. Republic of Ireland and Others*, EU:C:2013:812, paras 53-54.
68. If the limitation period has expired, the aid automatically qualifies as existing aid, and there is no need to invoke the protection of legitimate expectations because existing aid cannot be the subject of a recovery order. *See* the position expressed by the General Court in *WAM II* (Judgment of 27 September 2012, Case T-303/10, *Wam Industriale SpA v. European Commission*, EU:T:2012:505, para. 171, in connection with para. 101).

principle of protection of legitimate expectations, which looks at the beneficiary's subjective position and requires a causal link between the behaviours of the EU institutions and the expectation entertained by the beneficiary. Therefore, there is no need to grant retroactive protection to beneficiaries – *i.e.*, for the period preceding the acts or behaviours of the institutions – unless the legitimate expectation is based on an act or letter which explicitly refers to the past.

d) Legal Certainty

Analysis of the application of Article 16(1) of the Procedural Regulation with reference to the principle of legal certainty leads to similar results, *i.e.*, it confirms the very restrictive interpretation given to the derogation by both the Commission and the European judicature.

Depending on the perspective, the scope of application of the principle of legal certainty can be wider or narrower than that of protection of legitimate expectations. If the protection of legitimate expectations is considered a corollary of legal certainty, as largely held in the case law,[69] the latter is nonetheless broader, of course, as it can be invoked even if the requirements to establish legitimate expectations are not met.[70] However, if the two principles are examined separately, the scope of legal certainty is narrower because the circumstances of the case should be objectively exceptional, as no relevance is given in that context to the beneficiary's subjective position.[71]

For the same reason, while the principle of protection of legitimate expectations requires a dynamic appraisal because it takes into account the changing circumstances that can lead the beneficiary to entertain expectations at any given moment, the principle of legal certainty is static, in that it looks at the clarity of the legal framework only at the relevant moment.[72]

To successfully invoke protection based on legal certainty, several elements need to coexist, including one recurring factor in the case law: a long period of inactivity by the Commission despite its knowledge of the aid.[73] The most important factor, however, is a situation of objective uncertainty due to the lack of clarity as to the applicable rules or, more often, as to the Commission's practice.[74] The Commission's

69. *See, e.g.*, Judgment of the Court of 15 February 1996, Case C-63/93, *Fintan Duff and others v. Minister for Agriculture and Food and Attorney General*, EU:C:1996:51, para. 20.
70. *See* D. Grespan, *Recovery of Unlawful and Incompatible Aid*, in P. Mederer and V. Hoof, eds, 'EU Competition Law Volume IV: State Aid', Claeys & Casteels, 2008, para. 3.311.
71. *See* Opinion of Advocate General Dámaso Ruiz-Jarabo Colomer of 28 April 2005, Joined Cases C-346/03 and C-529/03, *Atzeni and Others v. Regione autonoma della Sardegna*, EU:C:2005:256.
72. *See* Opinion of Advocate General Cosmas of 15 February 1996, Case C-63/93, *Fintan Duff and others v. Minister for Agriculture and Food and Attorney General*, EU:C:1995:170.
73. *See, e.g.*, Judgment of the General Court of 22 January 2013, Case T-308/00, *Salzgitter AG v. European Commission*, EU:T:2013:30, para. 26, and Judgment of the General Court of 21 September 2022, Case T-95/21, cited in footnote 59 of this Part One, paras 204-214.
74. Judgment of the General Court of 22 April 2016, Joined Cases T-50/06 RENV II and T-69/06 RENV II, *Republic of Ireland and Aughinish Alumina Ltd v. European Commission*, EU:T:2016:227, para. 218.

lack of diligence in clarifying a situation after becoming aware of certain aid can be a reinforcing element.

Since the principle of legal certainty, unlike that of protection of legitimate expectations, can be invoked also by the Member State that granted the aid, the circumstances should be truly exceptional, *i.e.*, a blatant, or macroscopic, situation of uncertainty as to the applicable rules. The more pronounced exceptional nature required of a situation of legal uncertainty is reflected also in the limited period covered by the derogation, which certainly cannot have a retroactive effect. It therefore applies only to individual aid granted when a combination of several factors has already generated a macroscopic and objective uncertainty as to the applicable law and only until the Commission opens a formal investigation or the situation of uncertainty disappears as a result of the Commission's statements or decisions adopted in other cases.

In a nutshell, the EU courts adopt a very restrictive approach when considering the existence of circumstances that justify the application of the principle of legal certainty so as to prevent recovery of unlawful aid. It is therefore clear from the above review of the case law regarding the application of the derogation based on general principles of EU law under Article 16(1) of Council Regulation (EU) 2015/1589 that *the restrictive approach followed by the EU judicature combined with the prevailing formalistic concept of re-establishment of the* status quo ante *over the substantive concept of elimination of competition distortion greatly reduces the scope of the derogation.*

I.A.2.7 Very Narrow Scope of the Force Majeure Defence Due to Effective Recovery Being Considered an Obligation of Result on Member States

When the Commission adopts a negative decision, the only limit to recovery is the *absolute impossibility* of recovery. Absolute impossibility can also be partial (when the aid cannot be recovered in its entirety) or temporary (when it cannot be recovered by the deadline set out in the decision). The Procedural Regulation makes no reference to this limit, but this is without importance because absolute impossibility is a mere expression of the force majeure defence.

The idea expressed by Advocate General Whatelet in the *Montessori* case[75] (partially upheld by the Court, as further explained below) – according to which absolute impossibility is to be considered a general principle of law and thus falls within the derogation from the Commission's duty to order recovery under Article 16(1) – is unconvincing. Absolute impossibility is a matter of fact: it relates to the circumstances that may render a recovery decision unenforceable. In other words, it is a cause of non-enforceability. Consequently, it is not something the Commission should normally verify before adopting a recovery decision. It is only in exceptional circumstances when it is immediately evident at the time of adopting the decision that

75. Opinion of 11 April 2018, Joined Cases C-622/16 P and C-624/16 P, *Scuola elementare Maria Montessori v. European Commission*, EU:C:2018:229.

it could never be enforced, that the Commission should refrain from ordering recovery. For the same reason, a Commission recovery decision cannot be challenged for reasons of absolute impossibility except in the exceptional circumstances mentioned above.[76] In general, this is something that the Member State concerned should object to in the enforcement phase of the related decision.[77]

The Court of Justice's judgment in the *Montessori* case[78] mostly confirms this view,[79] despite the fact that the Court followed a different conceptual approach (based on absolute impossibility being considered a general principle of law in certain circumstances). Indeed, if one follows the Court's reasoning, it appears that a distinction must be drawn between: (i) 'pre-existing' absolute impossibility, which is, or should be, evident at the time of adopting the decision – in this case, it appears to have been considered a general principle of EU law and an inherent limitation on recovery; and (ii) absolute impossibility that arises after the decision's adoption, *i.e.*, only at the time of enforcement of a recovery order, and that, as such, is an extrinsic limitation on recovery.

In the former case, the Commission is obliged to consider absolute impossibility during the administrative phase, and both the Member State concerned and the interested parties may invoke its violation in an action for annulment before the EU courts. Conversely, the absolute impossibility of recovery that arises after the adoption of the decision cannot be so invoked; it can be used only as a defence in infringement proceedings brought by the Commission against a Member State for failing to enforce a recovery order.

76. *See*, among others: Judgment of the Court of 21 March 1990, Case C-142/87, *Kingdom of Belgium v. Commission of the EC*, EU:C:1990:125, para. 63; and Judgment of the Court of 14 September 1994, Case C-42/93, *Kingdom of Spain v. Commission of the EC*, EU:C:1994:326, para. 33, where the Court held that 'any procedural or other difficulties in regard to the implementation of the contested measure [*i.e.*, the recovery decision at issue] cannot have any influence on the lawfulness of that measure'. *See also*, more recently, Judgment of the General Court of 21 September 2022, Case T-95/21, cited in footnote 59 of this Part One, paras 221-222, where the General Court confirmed the distinction between absolute impossibility already existing at the time the Commission adopts a recovery decision and absolute impossibility arising later. Unfortunately, however, the General Court's judgment blurs the lines between the two scenarios when it refers, in para. 227, to the principle of sincere cooperation and to the Member State's failure to submit proposals to the Commission on how the difficulties could be overcome, as this requirement pertains to the execution phase of a recovery decision (*see* below in this section).
77. It has consistently been held in the case law that, after the expiry of the period in which an action for annulment can be brought against a Commission decision ordering the recovery of aid, a Member State which is the addressee of that decision may not call its validity into question within the framework of infringement proceedings brought by the Commission for non-enforcement of the decision. In those circumstances, the only defence left to the Member State in opposing the Commission's application for a declaration that the Member State failed to fulfil its obligation to enforce the decision would be to plead that it was absolutely impossible for it to implement the decision properly. *See, ex multis*, Judgment of the Court of 15 January 1986, Case 52/84, *Commission of the EC v. Kingdom of Belgium*, EU:C:1986:3, para. 13.
78. Judgment of the Court of 6 November 2018, Joined Cases C-622/16 P to C-624/16 P, *Scuola Elementare Maria Montessori Srl v. European Commission, European Commission v. Scuola Elementare Maria Montessori Srl and European Commission v. Pietro Ferracci*, EU:C:2018:873.
79. The opinion referred to in the preceding paragraph was expounded on by this author in the book 'Rimedi per la violazione delle norme sugli aiuti di stato: misure repressive o di ripristino. Diritto positivo (post-modernizzazione) e scenari di riforma', cited in footnote 3 of this Part One.

As mentioned, the practical outcome of the Court's approach is satisfactory, although the reasoning is logically flawed in that it considers absolute impossibility to be an *autonomous* general principle of law *in certain circumstances but not in others* (depending on the moment it can be ascertained). It would make more sense to consider absolute impossibility to be a situation of fact that falls within the legal concept (or general principle if this wording is preferred by the European judicature) of force majeure, *i.e.*, it arises when circumstances exist that make the decision unenforceable but do not affect its validity. As such, if the force majeure exists and has been represented to, or should have been known by, the Commission at the time of adopting the decision, the Commission should refrain from issuing a recovery order. Conversely, if force majeure arises later or, even if pre-existing, had not been brought to the Commission's attention during the administrative proceedings, it must be invoked by Member States during the execution phase. The circumstances in which, and the time when the defence is invoked do not change its legal nature.

The concept of force majeure (or, as the case law calls it, absolute impossibility) is interpreted in a very restrictive manner in the context of State aid recovery given the fact that effective recovery is considered an obligation of result for the Member State concerned. This is attributable to two factors.

First, any claim based on internal difficulties, whether legal, political, or economic - or even related to public order and security - is insufficient to constitute a case of absolute impossibility, as the Member State (a concept that includes not only the central government but also all related political and administrative branches and the national judiciary) is obliged to obtain effective recovery. Consequently, a Member State may not invoke provisions, practices or circumstances existing in its internal legal system to justify a failure to fulfil its obligations under Union law. The concept of absolute impossibility is therefore necessarily linked to *external constraints* and never linked to acts or omissions of whatever nature, be they direct or indirect, of the Member State concerned.[80]

Second, the force majeure defence is to be viewed in combination with the Member States' duty of sincere cooperation with EU institutions under Article 4(3) TEU. If unforeseen or unforeseeable difficulties arise in recovering aid, or if recovery would have undesirable consequences that were overlooked by the Commission, it is for the Member State concerned to inform the Commission and to present a proposal on how the difficulties can be overcome,[81] including, when necessary, alternative or indirect means of enforcing the order (*i.e.*, other than simple repayment).[82] Following that, the Commission and the Member State should work together in good faith to find the most appropriate solution that fully complies with the rationale of the recovery,

80. *See, ex multis*: Judgment of the Court of 13 November 2008, Case C-214/07, *Commission of the EC v. French Republic*, EU:C:2008:619; and Judgment of the General Court of 21 September 2022, Case T-95/21, cited in footnote 59 of this Part One, paras 223-226.
81. Judgment of the Court of 2 February 1989, Case 94/87, *Commission of the EC v. Federal Republic of Germany*, EU:C:1989:46, para. 9.
82. Judgment of the Court of 8 December 2011, Case C-275/10, *Residex Capital IV CV v. Gemeente Rotterdam*, EC:C:2011:814, para. 47.

which is (or should be) to eliminate distortion and restore the pre-existing competitive situation.[83]

To conclude, contrary to common opinion,[84] the legal concept of absolute impossibility is to be construed not as an additional derogation from the Commission's duty to order recovery of unlawful and incompatible aid but rather as an *extrinsic limit* to the effectiveness or binding force of recovery orders, which can *generally* be opposed only at the enforcement stage. However, the Commission should diligently examine it before the decision is adopted if the factual circumstances proving the existence of force majeure had been brought to its attention during the investigation. Furthermore, it implies not only an *objective element* (*i.e.*, the inability to fully or partially enforce the order) but also a *subjective element* (the diligent initiative of the Member State concerned, in conformity with the principle of sincere cooperation).

Although no link has yet been established in the case law between the absolute impossibility test and the basic goal of the recovery system, it seems clear that the concept of impossibility must be construed in light of the ultimate goal pursued by the recovery system. Hence, if the goal is solely to restore the pre-existing financial situation, with no reference to eliminating the competitive advantage, impossibility must be assessed also in financial terms: the test is satisfied any time the aid cannot be repaid (not even with the proceeds from liquidating the company). By contrast, if the goal is (essentially, or at least also) to eliminate the competitive advantage, *the range of situations that can be considered absolute impossibility is much wider* - but at the same time, it makes sense to delve more into alternative means of recovery when repayment in cash is either impossible or ineffective. Therefore, an additional inconsistency seems to exist in the case law in this respect.

Having clarified that absolute impossibility is not, except in exceptional circumstances, a limit to the Commission's power/duty to order recovery but rather a limit to enforcement of the recovery decision (or a *cause of non-enforcement*) - and that, as such, it is largely attributable to the notion of force majeure - the study of its application to specific cases in the case law reveals that the Court of Justice construes the absolute impossibility concept very narrowly. Only insurmountable difficulties, irrespective of the means necessary to enforce the decision and their political or administrative cost, can justify non-compliance with the recovery obligation. The limits of this book do not permit a detailed review of all significant cases. For what is relevant here, a few examples will suffice to illustrate the trend in the case law.

In *Commission v. Italian Republic*, Italy claimed that, among other things, recovery of the tax credit granted to the road haulage sector was technically impossible as it would require not only identifying more than hundred thousand beneficiaries but also checking the tax credits used by each over several years, the allocation of the total credit used by each beneficiary to the different tax headings, *etc.* Consequently, execution of the decision would have kept several tax departments scattered across the

83. Judgment of the Court of 2 February 1989, Case 94/87, *Commission of the EC v. Federal Republic of Germany*, cited in footnote 81 of this Part One, *ibid*.
84. *See, e.g.*, V. Rose and D. Bailey, *17 State Aids, 8 Judicial Remedies*, in Bellamy & Child, European Union Law of Competition, 2013.

national territory (tax offices, area offices, and direct taxation departments) busy for a long time, thus hindering the capacity of those services for carrying out other checks, which would prejudice the proper functioning of the tax system. In that regard, the Court, although admitting that recovery of the tax credit presented huge difficulties from an administrative standpoint, did not deem recovery to be technically impossible. As to the resulting burdens on the tax authorities, the Court simply held that the Italian Government had been informed - at the time of the decision to open an investigation into the aid - of the tax credit scheme's possible incompatibility and of the consequent risk of having to recover the credit. To acknowledge that recovery was impossible in those circumstances would call into question the effectiveness of EU State aid law.[85]

Moreover, this conclusion would be no different even if the aid had been granted (totally or partially) before the decision to open an investigation, and even if there had been thousands of recipients and the amount to recover from each (mainly individual farmers) had been insignificant, as in *Greece v. Commission*.[86] In a nutshell, the number of recipients and the resources that national authorities should devote to implementing recovery decisions are insufficient reasons to successfully invoke the absolute impossibility defence.

The same applies to difficulties linked to national legal systems, such as the length and complexity of national judicial proceedings,[87] the protection granted by the principle of protection of legitimate expectations or the principle of *res judicata* under national law (if wider than the corresponding protection guaranteed by EU law),[88] and even to situations in which contractual clauses (*e.g.*, clauses providing a public guarantee) are declared null by a national judge.[89]

During research for this book, only one case emerged in which the Commission and the Court admitted the absolute impossibility defence put forward by a Member State (France).[90] Recovery was held to be partially impossible (for the period of application of the tax regime at issue) because the data and information necessary to identify the beneficiaries and calculate the amount to be repaid by each were no longer available, and there was no way to retrieve them - they had been destroyed before the investigation commenced, in full compliance with French law (which requires tax data and information to be deleted after ten years). The Commission and the Court contented themselves with this finding and did not seek to ascertain the significance of

85. Judgment of the Court of 29 January 1998, Case C-280/95, *Commission of the EC v. Republic of Italy*, EU:C:1998:28, paras 23-26.
86. Judgment of the General Court of 16 July 2014, Case T-52/12, *Hellenic Republic v. European Commission*, EU:T:2014:677.
87. *See*, among others, Judgment of the Court of 27 June 2000, Case C-404/97, *Commission of the EC v. Portuguese Republic*, EU:C:2000:345.
88. *See*, among others, Judgment of the Court of 2 February 1989, *EC Commission v. Federal Republic of Germany*, EU:C:1989:46, para. 8. For the principle of res judicata, *see* section I.A.2.6.b) above and footnote 53 of this Part One.
89. Judgment of the General Court of 7 October 2010, *DHL Aviation SA/NV and DHL Hub Leipzig GmbH v. European Commission*, EU:T:2010:427, para. 42.
90. Judgment of the Court of 13 November 2008, Case C-214/07, *EC Commission v. French Republic*, EU:C:2008:619.

the distortive effects produced by the aid or the availability of alternative means of forfeiting those effects.

Given its peculiarity, the case is of little or no guidance when it comes to understanding whether the derogation can ever be applied for reasons other than the unavailability of data and information. However, the fact that this is the only case in which the defence was successfully invoked seems to indicate that the Court of Justice is unwilling: (i) to consider the effects of the aid concerned when assessing absolute impossibility arguments; and (ii) to impose alternative remedies on Member States if the information available prevents the amount of the financial advantage from being determined. If anything, this again proves that the Court of Justice applies a financial concept of the aid to be recovered, which is at odds with the rationale of the law and the non-formalistic approach of EU competition law.

In another case (involving Portugal), the Court - despite rejecting Portugal's absolute impossibility defence - considered the arguments put forward to that effect very seriously and provided two examples of circumstances that, had they been ascertained, would have warranted application of the derogation.[91] The first example relates to particularly serious and manifest flaws in the recovery decision such that it could be deemed non-existent. The second relates to inconsistencies in the decision's reasoning or between the reasoning and the operative part of the decision such as to create insurmountable doubts regarding proper execution. Clearly, both grounds could lead to the annulment of a decision in an appeal brought by the Member State concerned or an interested party; therefore, they must be classified as flaws (*i.e.*, causes of invalidity) of the recovery decision rather than as cases of absolute impossibility. Given the particularly severe nature of these flaws, the recovery decision would be unable to produce its effects. This explains why Member States could invoke the absolute impossibility defence even if they have not challenged the decision's validity by means of an action for annulment.

I.A.2.8 Absolute Impossibility in the Case of Insolvent Aid Beneficiaries and the Concept of Economic Continuity

A basic concept in the recovery system is that under no circumstances may the beneficiary's financial difficulties be deemed a case of absolute impossibility. This is the founding principle of one of the most complex issues in State aid remedies: the interplay between the rules on recovery, on the one hand, and the phenomenon of insolvency and all related national regulations and procedures on the other. Analysing the application of the rules on recovery to insolvent beneficiaries was key to the research behind this book, as time and time again it highlighted the shortcomings of the recovery system. Furthermore, although the case of insolvent beneficiaries is one of the main issues analysed in the Recovery Notice (as discussed in Chapter II of this Part

91. Judgment of 27 June 2000, Case C-404/97, *Commission of the European Communities v. Portuguese Republic*, EU:C:2000:345.

One), much remains unaddressed (despite the changes introduced in the New Recovery Notice).[92] It is therefore a topic that should be at the core of the reform.

The idea that the beneficiary's financial difficulties can never be seen as a case of absolute impossibility implies, first, that the elimination of the advantage generated by the aid must be obtained by winding up the recipient if repayment is impossible and, second, that alternative means of execution of the recovery decision can be considered (at the request of the Member State concerned) if they enable the objective of forfeiting the advantage to be achieved. The Court clarified these consequences back in the very first judgment dealing with recovery and insolvency in the mid-eighties.[93] Furthermore, the case law considers the winding-up of a beneficiary to be an alternative form of execution of the recovery decision rather than a case of absolute impossibility.

The underlying principle is that, with the winding-up of the beneficiary, its market share becomes available for the most efficient competitors damaged by the aid and the competitive harm is therefore removed. This implies that the elimination of the competitive advantage is the recovery system's ultimate objective - which is correct - and is always considered a fully satisfactory outcome. However, reference to the competitive advantage is necessary only when the financial advantage cannot be calculated with precision or repayment in cash is impossible for other reasons. In all other cases, a presumption exists in the case law, as has been shown above, that the system's objective is achieved if the amount granted by a Member State plus interest is paid back in its entirety. Therefore, the basic issue to be examined within the framework of a reform is whether this presumption is justified at this stage of development of EU law.

Moving on to analyse the interplay between recovery and insolvency more in-depth (although with the obvious limits for a book focused on remedies), the following set of requirements can be identified based on a global overview of the relevant case law:

(i) Member States must launch insolvency proceedings and pursue them diligently until the end.
(ii) They must choose the most suitable insolvency proceedings for ensuring repayment.
(iii) The Union's interest in the full execution of recovery decisions must be given full consideration throughout insolvency proceedings.
(iv) Member States may not accept: (a) subordination of the beneficiary's debt to the State to other debts of the same or lower seniority; (b) postponement of repayment in the case of liquidation without receivership (*in bonis*); or, *a fortiori* (c) partial relinquishment of their claim.
(v) Member States may not enter into creditors' agreements that imply a partial relinquishment of their claim, at least in insolvency proceedings that permit business continuity.

92. Section 4.8 of the New Recovery Notice, cited in footnote 1 of this Part One.
93. Judgment of the Court of 15 January 1986, Case C-52/84, *EC Commission v. Kingdom of Belgium*, EU:C:1986:3.

Only if all these requirements are fulfilled does the Member State escape liability for partial recovery or deferred recovery of the aid.

These principles cannot be found in a single judgment of the EU courts but are based on numerous statements made in different cases and summarised here in a logical order.[94] Do these principles form a coherent set of rules to address the interplay between recovery and insolvency? It is very doubtful. The Court itself showed some hesitation in that regard in a recent case involving a failing Greek textile undertaking that had benefitted from unlawful aid in the form of a State guarantee.[95] Following the Commission's recovery decision, the Greek authorities had the undertaking officially declared insolvent and notified the debts related to the aid to be recovered in the context of the insolvency proceedings. However, during the public auction of the failing undertaking's assets, the Greek authorities submitted a plan to the insolvency administrator to relaunch the undertaking's business and suspended the public auction for six months in order to examine this possibility more closely. They explained to the Commission that they intended to have the unlawful aid fully recovered before any relaunch of the undertaking's business. When the Commission brought an infringement action before the Court, it did not assess the Greek authorities' plan or the likelihood of repayment of the aid but simply submitted that Greece had not ensured the implementation of the recovery decision and, in any event, had not informed the Commission of the measures taken to implement the decision within the timeframe established in the decision.

It is apparent from the judgment that the Court hesitated in assessing the Commission's very formalistic grounds – and although the Court eventually decided that the Commission's pleas were well-founded, it did not entirely miss the opportunity to express its views on the substance of the case. The Court first restated the basic principle established in the case law whereby registration of State aid debt in the schedule of liabilities can satisfy the recovery obligation only if the full amount of the aid is then repaid or the insolvency proceedings result in the undertaking's winding-up. It went on to state that:

94. The key judgments covering the 1984-2018 period are referred to in footnotes 70-71 and 132-141 of the 2019 Recovery Notice (*see* section II.B of this Part One). The following are the landmark cases: Judgment of the Court of 15 January 1986, Case C-52/84, *Commission of the European Communities v. Kingdom of Belgium*, EU:C:1986:3; Judgment of the Court of 2 July 2002, Case C-499/99, *Commission of the European Communities v. Kingdom of Spain*, EU:C:2002:408; Judgment of the Court of 29 April 2021, Case C-277/00, *Federal Republic of Germany v. Commission of the European Communities ('SMI')*, EU:C:2004:238; Judgment of the Court (Grand Chamber) of 11 December 2012, Case C-610/10, *European Commission v. Kingdom of Spain ('Magefesa II')*, EU:C:2012:781; Judgment of the General Court of 21 October 2014, Case T-268/13, *Italian Republic v. European Commission*, EU:T:2014:900; and Judgment of the Court of 17 January 2018, Case C-363/16, *European Commission v. Hellenic Republic ('United Textiles')*, EU:C:2018:12. Since the 2019 Recovery Notice, the Court has addressed this topic mainly in the following judgments: Judgment of the Court of 29 April 2021, Case C-890/19 P, *Fortischem a.s. v. European Commission*, EU:C:2021:345 (appeal against the Judgment of the General Court of 24 September 2019, Case T-121/15, *Fortischem a.s. v. European Commission*, EU:T: 2019:684); and Judgment of the Court of 20 January 2022, Case C-51/20, *European Commission v. Hellenic Republic*, EU:C:2022:36.

95. Judgment of the Court of 17 January 2018, Case C-363/16, *European Commission v. Hellenic Republic*, EU:C:2018:12.

> the definitive cessation of the activities of the undertaking receiving aid is necessary only where the recovery of the entire amount of the aid remains impossible throughout the insolvency proceedings.[96]

This statement implies that, in the case of insolvent undertakings, aid should not necessarily be repaid in full before the continuation of the undertaking's activities (if that is envisaged) but rather only within the timeframe of the insolvency proceedings.

As to the time necessary to bring insolvency proceedings to an end, the Court noted that it is unlikely for the various steps in such proceedings to be completed within the four months usually set by the Commission for the recovery of unlawful aid. For this reason, in order to comply with the deadline set out in a recovery decision, it is sufficient to register the debt relating to repayment of the aid in the insolvent undertaking's schedule of liabilities within that period, provided that such a measure is actually followed either by the recovery of the full amount of the aid or by the winding-up of the undertaking and the definitive cessation of its activities if such recovery remains impossible throughout the insolvency proceedings.[97]

It is thus clear that the Court is distancing itself somewhat from the Commission's traditional approach, despite the latter being reaffirmed by the Commission in the New Recovery Notice.[98]

The Court's position, unlike that of the Commission, opens up the possibility that some forms of creditors' agreements allowing an insolvent undertaking to continue or relaunch some of its activities can be considered appropriate measures to ensure correct implementation of a recovery decision if they result in full recovery of the aid. This implies that the Member State that granted the aid and that is responsible for its recovery can, under some circumstances, legitimately enter into such agreements.

Furthermore, the Court seems inclined to accept that recovery of aid can be the decisive factor in triggering a beneficiary's insolvency only if no alternative exists to ensure implementation of the recovery decision. In this vein, the Court had already made it clear that the risk of insolvency can, under certain circumstances, justify the suspension of a recovery decision until a final judgment on the substance of the case.[99] The Court went even further in the abovementioned *Commission v. Hellenic Republic* case from 2018,[100] with the result that it now seems to accept that the possibility of a beneficiary maintaining its business continuity can justify the suspension of a recovery decision at least until the end of national insolvency proceedings.

This is certainly not enough to bring the recovery system in line with market realities and with the objective of effectively restoring the situation existing before the granting of a given aid measure, as stated in the preamble of the Procedural Regulation - but it is certainly an important step in the right direction.

Given that the elimination of the competitive advantage (or disadvantage for competitors) is the ultimate objective of the recovery system and that the winding-up

96. *Ibid.*, para. 39.
97. *Ibid.*, paras 41-42.
98. *See* Chapter II of this Part One.
99. *See* Order of the President of the General Court of 13 March 2020, Case T-603/19 R, *Helsingin Bussiliikenne Oy v. European Commission,* EU:T:2020:110.
100. *See* footnote 95 of this part One.

of the beneficiary fulfils that objective, the key questions are only whether: (i) the beneficiary exits the market that suffered competitive harm; and (ii) any benefit is transferred to other businesses in sectors open to competition and trade. It is submitted that, if the answer to the first question is yes and to the second no, the Commission should not interfere with national insolvency proceedings, in accordance with the principle of procedural autonomy. Deterrence objectives, if relevant, should therefore be pursued through different means, as better explained later.

A critical analysis of the whole set of rules governing the interplay between recovery and insolvency will have to be carried out before the recovery system can be effectively reformed. However, as already emerges from the few comments above, the recovery system needs to be entirely reshaped, simplified and codified in relation to insolvency, in order to ensure legal certainty and uniform application throughout the EU.

The conceptualisation of the repayment obligation as an obligation of result is at the root of most of the interpretative difficulties. The controversial application of the absolute impossibility defence in national rulings proves that this conceptualisation is unfit for a system of remedies based on the principle of procedural autonomy. Indeed, such a system must remain flexible enough to adapt to the wide kaleidoscope of cases seen in practice, with the objective of removing, *to the maximum extent possible*, the competitive harm caused by the aid in question. Is a Member State liable for infringement of the recovery obligation even when it has diligently brought the case to the last judicial level, but the national judge of last resort ultimately rejects its request? The case law shows hesitation and is indeed reasonable to doubt it, but at the same time this limitation of liability, if accepted, would appear to be at odds with the fundamental principle of EU law that the judiciary falls under the concept of 'Member State'. Difficulties of this kind are the direct and inevitable consequence of the rigidity of the remedies system.

The Italian legislation on insolvency - and more specifically the rules governing *concordato preventivo* (a pre-bankruptcy arrangement with creditors) - provides an excellent case study to illustrate the above considerations, including in view of the Italian rules' recent reform. Indeed, the way to restore an undistorted competitive situation varies based on the kind of *concordato preventivo* chosen.

According to the Commission's practice and the Court of Justice's case law, the recovery obligation should be considered duly fulfilled in the case of a *concordato liquidatorio*, which entails liquidation of the insolvent company's business, or a *concordato con continuità indiretta*, which entails the transfer of the insolvent company's business to a third party and the company's eventual liquidation, even if the State aid is not fully repaid by the company - on condition, however, that the beneficiary exits the market. This is considered to occur if the beneficiary's assets are liquidated or sold to third parties at market conditions following a competitive procedure, provided sufficient economic discontinuity exists between the beneficiary and the purchaser. Indeed, the application of the principle of *economic discontinuity* contributes to preserving the *effet utile* of State aid rules.

By contrast, in the case of a *concordato con continuità diretta* - where the business stays with, and continues to be run by, the insolvent company, which is eventually turned around and continues to operate on the market – the beneficiary remains on the market and should therefore be required to repay the full aid amount to the State.

This implies that during a *concordato* procedure, the Member State concerned – *i.e.*, Italy – has a duty to recover the full aid amount or to trigger the beneficiary's exit from the market. From this perspective, if it is impossible for the beneficiary to fully repay the aid, the Member State – as a creditor – should vote against the adoption of a business continuity plan and should insist on maximising the amount to be recovered and on obtaining the definitive cessation of the production activity benefitting from the aid. If the Member State fails to trigger the beneficiary's winding-up, it will be liable for non-fulfilment of the recovery obligation and will expose itself to an infringement procedure for violation of its obligations under the Treaty.

This example shows that the interplay between the recovery obligation and insolvency proceedings varies from one national system to another, depending on the nature of insolvency procedures and their regulation in national laws – and that it is thus necessary to clarify the basic common principles regulating the Member States' duty of recovery in the case of an insolvent beneficiary to ensure uniformity of the remedies across the EU.[101]

I.B Ancillary Remedies and Conceptual Flaws

The analysis of the additional remedies that are part of the EU State aid system confirms the conclusions reached in the previous sections on recovery. Additional or ancillary remedies are either the result of creative case law (as in the *Deggendorf* doctrine) or ensue from the application of the EU's general sanctioning system (the system of penalties under Article 260 TFEU) to the field of unlawful State aid. In short, a careful review of both the *Deggendorf* doctrine and the system of penalties demonstrates that the development of remedies in this field in recent years has been driven by concerns of effectiveness, with lesser attention devoted to the theoretical foundation of the system and its overall coherence. All changes, both in the Commission's practice and the Court's case law, can indeed be explained in light of enforcement objectives but lack a holistic view of the system. This has resulted in objectionable developments, which move away from the rationale of recovery. A comprehensive reform is thus necessary in this respect, too.

I.B.1 The Deggendorf Doctrine

Recovery is the only remedy in the field of State aid under EU legislation that has its direct source in primary law; however, the Court of Justice's case law (prompted by the Commission's initiative) has enriched the instruments at the Commission's disposal,

101. For a more detailed illustration of this example, *see* Merola, *Rimedi per violazione delle norme sugli aiuti di Stato: misure repressive o di ripristino: Diritto positivo (post-modernizzazione) e scenari di riforma*, cited in footnote 3 of this Part One.

with the objective of ensuring fulfilment by Member States of the recovery obligation. In the *Deggendorf II* case,[102] the Court of Justice held as follows:

> The Commission may order a Member State to suspend the payment of a new compatible aid to an undertaking that has at its disposal an unlawful and incompatible aid subject to an earlier recovery decision, and this until the Member State has reassured itself that the undertaking concerned has reimbursed the old unlawful and incompatible aid.[103]

The conceptual basis of this additional remedy is nothing more than the compatibility assessment of State aid entrusted to the Commission. Indeed, building on general criteria governing the compatibility assessment (*i.e.*, the Commission should take into account all elements of fact and law that it is aware of at the time of adopting its decision and that are relevant in measuring the competitive harm), the *Deggendorf* doctrine requires the Commission to factor in the effects produced by unlawful aid yet to be forfeited by means of recovery when conducting a compatibility assessment of new aid.

This empowers the Commission to adopt measures (such as freezing the new legal and compatible aid) if needed to avoid the beneficiary benefitting from an excessive and undue advantage. This undue advantage could result from the cumulation of the new aid with the previously unrecovered incompatible aid, thus affecting the balance of interests between the positive effects of the new aid and the distortion of competition and trade caused by the aforementioned cumulation.[104]

It follows that, at least in theory, failure to repay the old incompatible aid should not be seen as an automatic reason for the incompatibility of new aid to the same beneficiary, as this interpretation would be tantamount to providing the Commission repressive powers that would find no legal basis in primary law and would go far beyond the system of control enshrined in the Treaty.[105] Failure to repay old incompatible aid is therefore to be seen as a mere additional criterion of evaluation that the Commission is required to consider when reviewing new aid and that, as such, should be part of the compatibility assessment and the rules and parameters used in that assessment.[106]

---

102. Judgment of the Court of 15 May 1997, Case C-355/95 P, *Textilwerke Deggendorf GmbH (TWD) v. Commission of the European Communities and Federal Republic of Germany (Deggendorf II and III)*, EU:C:1997:241, which confirmed the Judgment of the Court of First Instance of 13 September 1995, Joined Cases T-244/93 and T-486/93, *TWD Textilwerke Deggendorf GmbH v. Commission of the European Communities*, EU:T:1995:160.
103. 2007 Recovery Notice, para. 75, cited in footnote 1 of this Part One.
104. This approach is compatible with the Treaties; conversely, a repressive approach aimed at preventing a beneficiary of unrecovered incompatible aid from benefitting from a new advantage – irrespective of any analysis of the distortive effects of this cumulation – would conflict with the Treaties.
105. In this respect, *see* Opinion of Advocate General Tesauro of 10 December 1996, Case C-355/95 P, *Textilwerke Deggendorf GmbH (TWD) v. Commission of the European Communities and Federal Republic of Germany (Deggendorf II and III)*, EU:C:1996:483, para. 17.
106. Therefore, the Commission should assess the presence of a cumulative effect, which should be real, or at least potential but supported by solid leads. Indeed, the Court of Justice clarified that a distortion of competition and trade must not be presumed. *See* Judgment of the Court of 23 February 2006, Joined Cases C-346/03 and C-529/03, *Giuseppe Atzeni and Others, Marco Scalas*

The Commission started applying the *Deggendorf* doctrine in a systematic manner in the second phase of State aid modernisation (SAM), which started with the 2005-2009 State Aid Action Plan (SAAP).[107] Consequently, leveraging on, among other things, the Court of Justice's statement that the doctrine applies to both individual aid and aid schemes,[108] the following measures have become common:

(i) The Commission requires that the Member State concerned undertakes, during the preliminary examination of a notified scheme, to suspend payment of aid to any beneficiaries under the notified scheme that previously received unrecovered incompatible aid.
(ii) The Commission, in the absence of this undertaking and if it considers the aid compatible, adopts a conditional decision under Article 9(4) of the Procedural Regulation, making authorisation of the scheme conditional on the suspension of payment of that aid to the beneficiaries of unrecovered incompatible aid.
(iii) The Commission has included a '*Deggendorf* clause' in all legislation,[109] soft law instruments[110] and decisions on aid schemes since the end of 2004.

Despite these developments, the practical application of the *Deggendorf* doctrine seems in many aspects to diverge from its conceptual basis (developed in the landmark 1997 case). This clearly emerges from the analysis of two critical issues: (i) the nexus between the quantification of the aid to be recovered and the analysis of the cumulative effect of multiple aid measures; and (ii) the review of cases in which the new aid is covered by an exemption to the obligation to notify.

As to the first issue, a precise and concrete rather than purely abstract evaluation of the cumulative effect - and therefore of the harm caused to competition - requires even just approximate knowledge of the amount of aid to be recovered. If lack of quantification is attributable to the Member State concerned (because the Commission decision delegated this task to the Member State and the latter failed to implement it), the *Deggendorf* doctrine clearly applies.[111] However, in other circumstances, rigid application of this remedy risks becoming a repressive instrument. This may happen: (i) when the lack of information on the amount of the unrecovered aid is not imputable to the Member State but is the consequence of other factors; and (ii) when the amount

---

and Renato Lilliu v. Regione autonoma della Sardegna, EU:C:2006:130, para. 74, and Judgment of the Court of First Instance of 6 September 2006, Joined Cases T-304/04 and T-316/04, *Italian Republic and Wam SpA v. Commission of the European Communities*, EU:T:2006:239, para. 62.

107. State Aid Action Plan - Less and better targeted state aid: a roadmap for state aid reform 2005-2009, 7 June 2005, COM/2005/0107.
108. Judgment of the Court of First Instance of 8 September 2009, Case T-303/05, *AceaElectrabel Produzione SpA v. Commission of the European Communities*, EU:T:2009:312, para. 96.
109. *See, e.g.*, Commission Regulation (EC) No 1628/2006 of 24 October 2006 on the application of Articles 87 and 88 of the Treaty to national regional investment aid, OJ L 302, 1.11.2006, p. 29, no longer in force.
110. *See, e.g.*, Communication from the Commission - Community guidelines on State aid for rescuing and restructuring firms in difficulty, OJ C 244, 1.10.2004, p. 2, para. 23, no longer in force.
111. Judgment of the Court of First Instance of 8 September 2009, Case T-303/05, *AceaElectrabel Produzione SpA v. Commission of the European Communities*, EU:T:2009:312.

to be repaid is so small - especially when compared with the new compatible aid - or affects totally different markets, or has clearly vanished over time, that speaking of a cumulative effect is nothing but an abstract assumption.

One example can be used to illustrate this: If the new aid is of great magnitude and importance for the beneficiary's business and in all respects is non-comparable with the small amount that remains unrecovered, logic suggests that a suspension of the new aid should affect at most the amount of the unlawful, unrecovered aid.[112] Only this approach is coherent with the theoretical foundation of the *Deggendorf* doctrine. However, a review of the Commission's practice reveals that it has always required suspension of the full amount of the new aid and has never taken into consideration a partial suspension. This confirms the tendency to diverge from the theoretical basis of the remedy and to turn it into a repressive instrument.

As to the second issue, if the new aid is exempted from the notification obligation because it falls within the *de minimis* safe harbour or is covered by the General Block Exemption Regulation ('*GBER*'), the Member State is not required to demonstrate that aid's compatibility. Therefore, applying the ancillary remedy (the *Deggendorf* doctrine) in the absence of any assessment of the cumulative effect whatsoever would equate to establishing a presumption of cumulative effect that has no legal basis in the Treaty or secondary legislation. Furthermore, it would have the same effect as obliging Member States to notify a measure that is, in principle, exempted by law, which would create additional inconsistency.

This position, which is apparently the Commission's position, once again amounts to giving the recovery remedy a repressive nature. Following this approach would at least require a legislative amendment, *i.e.*, to incorporate explicit provisions in the *de minimis* regulations and in the GBER requiring Member States to apply the *Deggendorf* doctrine even in those contexts. And even so, the compatibility of this hypothetical legislative change with primary law would likely give rise to debate.

A further problematic aspect, which confirms the tendency to convert the *Deggendorf* doctrine into a repressive instrument, concerns the relationship between this doctrine and the concept of absolute impossibility. More precisely, the issue is whether circumstances that constitute an absolute impossibility of recovery can be deemed to neutralise also the application of the ancillary remedy. This seems inevitable from a theoretical standpoint because if absolute impossibility is an appropriate defence against the main remedy, it must *a fortiori* be so against ancillary remedies. In other words, in the case of absolute impossibility, the force majeure justification should encompass the whole set of remedies, not just recovery. This means that Member States should be able to invoke the absolute impossibility defence against recovery orders and to oppose suspension decisions concerning new, compatible aid issued based on the *Deggendorf* doctrine. However, the paradox here lies in the fact that the adoption of this approach, which is entirely rational in itself, would be at odds with the rationale of recovery.

112. In this respect, *see* T. Joris, *The Concept of an 'Economic Unit' in State Aid Matters and the Deggendorf Principle*, in European State Aid Law Quarterly (ESTaL), 2012, Issue 1, p. 149 https://doi.org/10.21552/estal/2012/1/274.

An orthodox approach in the application of the *Deggendorf* doctrine - *i.e.*, one consistent with its theoretical justification - would imply objecting to the granting of new, compatible aid irrespective of whether the failure to recover previous aid is due to absolute impossibility. Indeed, even in this case, the old aid may generate a cumulative effect on the market when the new aid is granted. Nevertheless, if the absolute impossibility defence were considered irrelevant when applying the *Deggendorf* doctrine, it would lead to the beneficiary being indefinitely excluded from receiving compatible aid until the Commission or the Court of Justice officially acknowledged the existence of a case of absolute impossibility. As can be appreciated, a pragmatic and reasonable approach to this issue entails diverging from the theoretical basis of the system of remedies. *This paradox is an additional reason that prompts reflection on the entire system's rationality* and raises further doubts about the tendency to use the *Deggendorf* doctrine as a sanctioning tool.

To sum up, the Commission and the Court of Justice seem to diverge from the original conceptual basis of the *Deggendorf* doctrine. The Commission seems to acknowledge that the *Deggendorf* doctrine should at this point be considered part of the compatibility assessment. This situation mirrors what has been described with reference to recovery: namely, the existence of increasing discrepancies between the practical application of the remedy and its conceptual foundation. Beyond the system's theoretical flaws, the uncertainty is leading to repressive application of these tools, which conflicts with the non-punitive nature of recovery. Hence, in relation to this aspect too, a legislative reform is warranted to take a clear position and provide a solid legal basis for the application of the *Deggendorf* doctrine.

I.B.2 The System of Penalties

As clarified in the previous section, recovery of unlawful and incompatible aid does not constitute a penalty, since its objective is only to restore the competitive situation present before the aid was granted. Nevertheless, if a Member State fails to comply with a recovery decision within the prescribed time and has been unable to demonstrate the absolute impossibility of recovery, the general system of penalties that EU law provides to combat breaches of the Treaty applies.[113] This system is not, of course, designed for State aid cases. It is thus worth checking whether it is suitable to address violations of the recovery obligation, although this has never been questioned in the case law.

According to Article 260(1) TFEU:

> if the Court of Justice ... finds that a Member State has failed to fulfil an obligation under the Treaty, the State shall be required to take the necessary measures to comply with the judgment of the Court.[114]

---

113. Article 258 TFEU regulates infringement proceedings, namely the procedure whereby the Commission seeks to end a violation of the treaties by a Member State, including failure or delay in complying with a Commission decision. The liability of the Member State for violation of the treaties may derive from action/inaction not only on the part of the administrative authorities but also on the part of the national legislative and judiciary bodies.
114. Article 260(1) TFEU.

failing this, in light of Article 260(2) TFEU, the Commission may bring the Member State again before the Court, which may impose payment of a lump sum[115] and/or a penalty payment[116] on it. In its Communication on the application of Article 260(2), which in any case does not bind the Court of Justice, the Commission postulates three criteria for the calculation of the lump-sum and/or penalty payment, namely: (i) the seriousness of the infringement; (ii) its duration; and (iii) the need to ensure that the penalty is an effective deterrent to future infringements.[117]

In the field of State aid, the use of 'financial sanctions' – although at a second level (*i.e.*, for breach of the obligation to comply with a ruling upholding a recovery order and condemning the Member State for non-compliance) – has contributed significantly to increasing the effectiveness of recovery in recent years. However, the application of the general criteria for the quantification of 'sanctions' in the field of State aid raises several doubts. A review of the few Court of Justice judgments on the topic confirms that the application of the general criteria to the recovery of unlawful aid is the source of additional incongruencies.[118]

---

115. *See* Communication from the Commission on the application of Art. 228 of the EC Treaty (now Art. 260(2) TFEU), SEC/2005/1658, OJ C 126, 7.6.2007, p. 15. The Commission may impose payment of a lump sum with the objective of penalising the continuation of the infringement between the first judgment on non-compliance and a judgment delivered under Art. 260(2) TFEU. In the field of State aid, the Commission clarifies – in the 2007 Recovery Notice, para. 74 – that 'in view of the fact that the failure to implement the Commission recovery decision prolongs the distortion of competition caused by the granting of illegal and incompatible aid, the Commission will not hesitate to make use of this possibility if it appears necessary to ensure the respect of the State aid rules'.
116. The daily penalty payment is applied from the date of the second judgment until the date of the end of the infringement. The Commission has wide discretion in calculating the penalty payment amount, which it exercises by taking into consideration both the identified infringement and the behaviour of the Member State concerned. In this regard, *see* Judgment of the Court of 17 September 2015, Case C-367/14, *European Commission v. Italian Republic*, EU:C:2015:611, paras 86, 93 and 117. The daily penalty payment amount is calculated as follows: (i) multiplication of a standard flat-rate amount by a coefficient for seriousness and a coefficient for duration; and (ii) multiplication of the result obtained under point (i) by an amount fixed by country (the 'n' factor), which takes into account the Member State's capacity to pay and the number of votes it has in the Council.
117. Although the Commission – in its Communication on the application of Art. 260(2) TFEU – distinguishes calculation of the penalty payment from calculation of the lump-sum payment, the vast majority of the indicated criteria apply to both. Indeed, in many paragraphs, the Communication refers to 'financial sanctions' in general.
118. *See* Judgment of the Court of 7 July 2009, Case C-369/07, *Commission of the European Communities v. Hellenic Republic*, EU:C:2009:428, Judgment of the Court of 11 December 2012, Case C-610/10, *European Commission v. Kingdom of Spain (known as Magefesa)*, EU:C:2012:781, and Judgment of the Court of 17 November 2011, Case C-496/09, *European Commission v. Italian Republic*, EU:C:2011:740. In the latter judgment, the Court fixed the criteria for calculating the penalty and referred the calculation to the Commission. The Commission decision of 7 March 2013 was challenged by Italy and led to the Judgment of the General Court of 21 October 2014, Case T-268/13, *Italian Republic v. European Commission*, EU:T:2014:900. More recently, in *Larco* (Judgment of the Court of Justice of 20 January 2022, C-51/20, *European Commission v. Hellenic Republic*, EU:C:2022:36), the Court of Justice ordered Greece to pay a lump sum of EUR 5.5 million and periodic penalty payments of over EUR 4 million for each 6-month delay in complying with the Court's judgment of 9 November 2017, which had upheld the Commission recovery decision of March 2014. Notably, however, in a first judgment on the same matter, handed down on 26 March 2020, the Court of Justice had partially upheld the appeal brought by Larco against the recovery decision, referring the

As concerns penalty payments, some difficulties arise in, for instance, the application of the gravity parameter, *i.e.*, the seriousness of the infringement. Though the standard flat-rate amount[119] does not raise problems because it is completely independent of the nature of the initial infringement, the application of the seriousness coefficient is, by contrast, unfit for the recovery of State aid. This coefficient is based on two parameters, namely: (i) the importance of the EU rules breached; and (ii) the impact of the infringement on general and particular interests. Application of these two parameters in the field of State aid recovery can be problematic.[120]

In theory, a judgment is adopted on the basis of Article 260(2) TFEU not to penalise an infringement of Articles 107 and 108 TFEU but rather to penalise a violation of a previous judgment having ascertained the breach of a Commission decision ordering recovery. However, in practice, both the Commission and the Court of Justice tend to mix up the two levels of analysis when applying the seriousness-of-the-infringement parameter and thus link the quantification of the penalty payment to the type of aid measure concerned and to the seriousness of the violation of Articles 107 and 108 TFEU.[121]

The same confusion between the two levels of analysis arises when applying other factors, such as the financial sums involved in the infringement and the turnover

case back to the General Court for a new assessment of one of the measures concerned. And one month before that first judgment, Greece had put Larco under special administration and launched two public tenders to sell its assets and recover the aid. Eventually, despite the launch of those tenders, Larco would be placed into liquidation, and the debts owed to Greece relating to the recovery order would take precedence over other creditors. In this respect, the Court found that Greece had nonetheless failed to fulfil its obligations under Art. 260 TFEU, as each step undertaken to recover the aid occurred after expiry of the period prescribed by the Commission's letter of formal notice, *i.e.*, after 25 March 2019. Furthermore – and this is especially relevant here – the Court seized on the opportunity to clarify the criteria for calculation of the lump-sum payments due until full compliance with the judgment that concludes the infringement proceedings. Basically, the Commission is entitled to propose lump-sum payments following the method set out in its communication of 12 December 2005, as most recently amended in 2019 – with one caveat. Indeed, as indicated in footnote 116 of this Part One, that calculation method takes into account – along with other factors to consider, such as the infringement's seriousness and duration – the capacity to pay of the Member State concerned, expressed as the 'n' factor. The 'n' factor is currently calculated based on the Member States' GDP and 'institutional weight', *i.e.*, the number of representatives it has in the Council. In line with the Opinion of Advocate General Pitruzzella, the Court established the predominance of GDP and rejected 'institutional weight' as a criterion for calculating the lump sum under Art. 260 TFEU, thus reducing the amount proposed by the Commission from EUR 135 million to EUR 5.5 million.

119. The standard flat-rate amount is defined as the fixed basic amount to which the multiplier coefficients are applied. It penalises a violation of the principle of legality and a failure to comply with the judgments of the Court. At present, it is fixed at EUR 700 per day.

120. The seriousness of the infringement must refer to the non-compliance with the first judgment, not to the original infringement, namely the violation that caused the first infringement proceedings to be opened. In the field of State aid, this means that the characteristics of the aid should not be taken into account when determining the degree of seriousness.

121. On the contrary, they should refer to the Member State's non-compliance with the first judgment of the Court while taking into consideration some aspects of the violation, such as whether the judgment which the Member State has not complied with forms part of established case law, what efforts the Member State has made to comply with it, and whether any particular intrinsic difficulties hinder compliance.

or added value of the economic sector concerned in the Member State in question. These factors are mentioned by the Commission for application of the second parameter, namely the effects on general and particular interests, which again risks shifting attention to the type of aid. This confusion between two levels of analysis that should remain separate (*i.e.*, non-compliance with a judgment upholding the recovery order on the one hand, and violation of State aid rules on the other) yields a punitive factor, albeit indirectly, on recover orders. This is not in line with the basic principles of EU State aid law or the rationale of recovery.

A second issue concerns application of the duration coefficient. Indeed, the Commission introduces a multiplier in its Communication,[122] which is to be applied to the basic amount depending on the infringement's duration from the date the Court issues its first judgment until the Commission refers the matter to the Court. The issue, however, is that this coefficient is completely independent of the complexities of the case in complying with a given recovery decision. Luckily, the Court of Justice seems to have recognised, in the case of an aid scheme, this correlation between the duration of the recovery's implementation and the complexities of a given case. Therefore, if future case law confirms this interpretation, this issue will persist only with individual aid.[123]

As to the lump sum, the main issue is the same as discussed with reference to penalty payments, namely the confusion between violation of a first judgment of the Court ordering compliance with the recovery obligation and violation of Articles 107 and 108 TFEU, which should be irrelevant to the calculation of lump-sum payments. In proceedings based on Article 260(2) TFEU, the Court's case law gives great relevance to the need to obtain, by means of a lump sum, a deterrent effect - and this is not problematic as long as the deterrence concerns exclusively the non-compliance with the Court's judgment. However, the Commission's practice and the Court's case law show that the deterrent effect is oriented towards violation of Article 108(3) TFEU; indeed, when a Member State has a long history of non-compliance with decisions ordering recovery of unlawful, incompatible aid, it risks being treated more severely by the Court in its judgments under Article 260(2) TFEU.[124] This is completely irreconcilable with the system's theoretical basis and gives recovery a punitive nature.

To sum up, the practical application of penalty and lump-sum payments diverges from the fundamental principles of EU State aid law and, more precisely, from the

122. The multiplier varies between 1 and 3, calculated at a rate of 0.10 per month from the date of the Court's first judgment.
123. Judgment of the Court of 17 September 2015, Case C-367/14, *European Commission v. Italian Republic*, EU:C:2015:611, para. 104. However, in that case the Court did not explain how the complexity of the recovery criterion was considered; consequently, some doubts remain about the Court's view on this topic. Indeed, the Court has endorsed the Commission's approach in the past: *see* Judgment of the Court of 12 July 2005, Case C-304/02, *Commission of the European Communities v. French Republic*, EU:C:2005:444, paras 102 and 108.
124. *See, e.g.*, Judgment of the Court of 17 September 2015, Case C-367/14, *European Commission v. Italian Republic*, EU:C:2015:611, para. 119.

rationale of recovery. To overcome this discrepancy, the Commission and Court of Justice should avoid linking the calculation of these 'financial sanctions' to the seriousness, duration or recurrent nature of violations of Articles 107 and 108 TFEU and should refer exclusively to non-compliance with the Court's judgments condemning the Member State for non-implementation of recovery orders.

II MODERNISATION OF THE COMMISSION'S RECOVERY NOTICE: ACHIEVEMENTS AND LIMITS

The chapter analyses the successes and limitations of the modernisation of the 2007 Recovery Notice, highlighting unmet expectations and persistent issues. It discusses how the 2019 Recovery Notice has brought practical improvements but has not resolved the main conceptual flaws of the system.

The analysis conducted thus far has shown that the State aid system of remedies is based on a set of consolidated rules, the key concepts of which Chapter I goes through in a systematic order. However, the analysis has also revealed that no significant effort has been made to provide a solid theoretical basis for these rules and to build a coherent system. Many inconsistencies arise when these principles are translated into practice. As the credibility of the system of remedies is key to ensuring the effectiveness of State aid control, a reform is warranted and should not remain on the surface but be based on a reconsideration of the whole system.

The recovery system is regulated not only by the Procedural Regulation and the Court of Justice's case law but also by the Commission's New Recovery Notice (published in 2019),[125] which replaced the 2007 Recovery Notice.[126] The 2007 Recovery Notice complemented the procedural aspects of the second phase of the modernisation of State aid rules and was, as such, an important element of the 2005-2009 SAAP;[127] the New Recovery Notice, however, is part of the new modernisation efforts launched with the *SAM* Communication in May 2012.[128] The New Recovery Notice, like all instruments of soft law, sets out the Commission's policy and summarises the case law at the time of adoption.

For this book's purposes, it is certainly useful to examine the content of the Commission's communications on the subject and their evolution in order to understand how and to what extent they add - in terms of clarity and/or operational suggestions - to the essential principles stemming from positive law and related case law examined in Chapter I. Therefore, the examination below follows a chronological approach, with the New Recovery Notice consequently examined against the backdrop of the shortcomings identified in the application of the 2007 Recovery Notice. This method of analysis is justified by the need to highlight the expectations that surrounded the adoption of the New Recovery Notice and to show how and why these expectations were eventually not met. This exercise ultimately leads to an assessment of the merits of the 2019 reform and to an identification of the problems that remain unaddressed.

---

125. Communication from the Commission - Commission Notice on the recovery of unlawful and incompatible State aid, C/2019/5396, OJ C 247, 23.7.2019, pp. 1-23.
126. Commission Notice 'Towards an effective implementation of Commission decisions ordering Member States to recover unlawful and incompatible State aid', OJ 2007 C 272/4.
127. *See* footnote 107 of this Part One.
128. Communication from the Commission to the European Parliament, the Council, the European Economic and Social Committee and the Committee of the Regions on EU State Aid Modernisation (SAM) of 8 May 2012, COM/2012/0209/final.

II.A The 2007 Recovery Notice

This section starts by analysing the main principles enshrined in the 2007 Recovery Notice and identifying a number of shortcomings. This analysis follows the structure of the 2007 Recovery Notice, by addressing separately: (i) the division of competences between the Commission and the national authorities; (ii) the identification of the undertakings from which the aid must be recovered; (iii) the determination of the amount to be recovered; (iv) the implementation of the recovery; and (v) the role of national courts.

II.A.1 The Shared Responsibility Between the Commission and the National Authorities

The entire recovery system is based on cooperation between the Commission and national authorities, which have a 'shared responsibility' according to the 2007 Recovery Notice. Indeed, the Commission must be able to rely on the national authorities' full cooperation regarding State aid schemes and, even more so, fiscal aid schemes. These schemes might involve hundreds or thousands of beneficiaries, many of whom are small, meaning that the Commission would be unable to identify them (let alone quantify the respective amount to be recovered from each) without full cooperation from Member States' authorities.

This is perfectly in line with the principle of sincere cooperation, according to which Member States are expected not only to refrain from adopting measures that could jeopardise the achievement of the Treaty's objectives but also to facilitate the accomplishment by EU institutions of the tasks assigned to them.[129] In the field of State aid, this means that:

> in the context of the implementation of recovery decisions, the Commission and the Member States' authorities must ... cooperate to attain the objective of the restoration of *competitive conditions* in the internal market. (emphasis added)[130]

The precise reference to 'competitive conditions' is, of course, not without consequences when the task of calculating the amount to be recovered is delegated to national authorities. They rightfully stick to that rather than to the financial burden on the State budget in the case of indirect aid. Within the framework of a reform, the Commission was expected to make a choice as to the concept of recovery it considers in line with the upper norm and decide that this concept applies in a uniform manner irrespective of the authority in charge of implementing recovery orders.

Section 3 of the 2007 Recovery Notice was its core: it distinguished between the Commission's responsibilities and those of the Member States, clarifying that both the Commission and Member States 'have an essential role to play in the implementation of recovery decisions and may contribute to an effective enforcement of recovery

129. In the 2007 Recovery Notice, the Commission refers to Art. 10 of the EC Treaty; however, since the Treaty of Lisbon, the principle of sincere cooperation has been included in Art. 4(3) TEU.
130. 2007 Recovery Notice, cited in footnote 126 of this Part One, para. 27.

policy'.[131] More precisely, they share responsibility when it comes to three fundamental aspects: (i) identifying the undertakings from which aid must be recovered; (ii) determining the amount to be recovered; and (iii) implementing recovery.

However, the 2007 Recovery Notice failed to indicate precisely the respective boundaries of the Commission's and the Member States' prerogatives; nor did it set out the minimum requirements that Commission recovery decisions must ensure are met when identifying beneficiaries and determining the amount to be recovered. The following paragraphs examine these issues.

II.A.2 Identification of the Undertakings from Which Aid Must Be Recovered

The purpose of recovery - which includes interest - is to re-establish the situation that existed on the market before the aid was granted; thus, 'the unlawful and incompatible aid must be recovered from the undertakings that actually benefited from it'.[132]

Identifying the beneficiary of the aid - *i.e.*, the company (or undertaking)[133] exposed to the repayment risk - falls under the Commission's responsibility. This is because identifying the recipient of the advantage is *part of the substantive assessment of State aid*, which falls under the exclusive responsibility of the institution entrusted with enforcing Treaty rules. However, the Commission can delegate this power - under certain circumstances and by providing sufficient guidelines - to the authorities of the Member State concerned. More specifically, in State aid schemes, and even more so in fiscal aid schemes (which, by reducing the tax burdens on categories of taxpayers, can easily apply to a large spectrum of undertakings), the Commission is not in a position to assess the identity of all beneficiaries (and/or the individual amount granted to each).[134] Consequently, national authorities or national courts must conduct this assessment in the recovery phase.[135]

However, the 2007 Recovery Notice, while referring to this principle, failed to identify the minimum requirements that Commission recovery decisions must ensure

131. *Ibid.*, para. 30.
132. *Ibid.*, para. 32. *See also* Judgment of the Court of 21 March 1991, Case C-303/88, *Italy v. Commission*, EU:C:1991:136, para. 57, and Judgment of the Court of 29 April 2004, Case C-277/00, *Germany v. Commission* ('SMI'), EU:C:2004:238, para. 75.
133. The difference between 'company' and 'undertaking' is not a trivial issue in State aid law, though the case law generally fails to emphasise it. Although reference is normally made to an undertaking (*i.e.*, an economic group characterised by common or coordinated economic decision-making) in competition law, remedies for a breach of State aid law should be imposed on the business that benefitted from the advantage - whether it is a company (*i.e.*, a legal person) or not. This is without prejudice to the possibility for the Commission to have the remedy implemented by the group to which the business belongs in specific circumstances (especially if the remedy cannot be executed at the level of the business that benefitted from the aid). This issue is discussed further below in this section.
134. *See, ex multis*: Judgment of the Court of 12 October 2000, Case C-480/98, *Kingdom of Spain v. Commission of the European Communities (Magefesa)*, EU:C:2000:559, para. 25; Judgment of the Court of 8 December 2011, Case C-81/10 P, *France Télécom SA v. European Commission*, EU:C:2011:811, para. 102; and Judgment of the Court of 13 February 2014, Case C-69/13, *Mediaset SpA v. Ministero dello Sviluppo economico*, EU:C:2014:71, paras 21-22.
135. *See* Judgment of the Court of 7 March 2002, Case C-310/99, *Italian Republic v. Commission of the European Communities*, EU:C:2002:143, paras 89-91.

are met; nor did it examine the situations that might give rise to difficulties in identifying the beneficiaries, *i.e.*: (i) corporate changes between the granting of the aid and the recovery decision; (ii) indirect aid; and (iii) aid granted as part of a scheme. Consequently, these issues, which gave rise to heated debate and extensive case law in the years following the 2007 Recovery Notice, were expected to be at the core of the reform.

With regard to the first issue (*i.e.*, corporate changes), the 2007 Recovery Notice equated events that can affect beneficiaries after aid is granted to the transfer of the recovery obligation to a party other than the initial beneficiary (*e.g.*, when a company or branch that received aid is transferred during the implementation of the recovery order).[136] In this way, however, the Commission created confusion between the identification of the beneficiary (which is an ordinary task) and the exceptional situations that might arise in implementing recovery obligations. In any case, the general rule is that *a recovery obligation follows the branch of business that benefitted from the aid.*

The situation becomes more complicated when the entire beneficiary – or part of its share capital – is transferred outside the initial corporate group (share deals). It can become even more complicated when the transfer concerns all or part of the beneficiary company's production-related assets that contributed to the ongoing business that received the aid (asset deals). In these cases, specific criteria set out in the case law apply – but the Commission only briefly touched on these in the 2007 Recovery Notice.[137]

Clearly, this was one of the most complex issues to deal with when updating the Recovery Notice. However, given that this issue is conceptually very similar to that concerning the interaction between the rules on recovery and those on insolvency, and given that common principles apply to both the case of insolvent beneficiaries and the case of asset or share deals, it was going to be extremely difficult to adapt the criteria applicable in the case of share deals or asset deals without reviewing the parallel problem of insolvency and recovery, which might have required (or been better served by) legislative intervention to harmonise national laws.

Conversely, the other two situations – indirect aid[138] and aid granted as part of a scheme – were not examined in the 2007 Recovery Notice. The Commission was

136. 2007 Recovery Notice, cited in footnote 126 of this Part One, paras 32-34.

137. Specifically, para. 32 of the 2007 Recovery Notice addressed asset deals, clarifying that 'a transfer of the undue advantage may occur when the assets of the original aid beneficiary are transferred to a third party at a price that is lower than their market value', whereas para. 33 specified the general rule to be applied in cases involving share deals: 'the sale of shares in such a company to a third party does not affect the obligation of the beneficiary to reimburse such aid'. For a complete overview of this issue, *see* Merola, *Rimedi per violazione delle norme sugli aiuti di Stato: misure repressive o di ripristino – Diritto positivo (post-modernizzazione) e scenari di riforma*, cited in footnote 3 of this Part One, specifically Chapter VIII, pp. 191-268.

138. The advantage obtained from indirect aid might benefit a wide range of entities. An indirect advantage occurs when aid is granted to an entity or multiple entities (or even individuals) that use it for a specific purpose, with the result that the aid either is transferred totally or partially to other economic players or produces an economic advantage for the latter. As clarified in the Notice on the Notion of State aid (para. 115), a measure can also constitute both a direct advantage to the recipient undertaking and an indirect advantage to other undertakings, *e.g.*,

therefore expected to address these issues from scratch when reforming the recovery system.

II.A.3 Determination of the Amount to Be Recovered

Much like identifying beneficiaries, determining the amount to be recovered is based on close cooperation between the Commission and the national authorities. More specifically, the Commission's duty is not to quantify the precise amount, but only to include in its recovery decisions all the elements needed to allow the national authorities to determine and recover the correct amount.

Naturally, when the aid concerned is quite linear, the Commission specifies the exact amount to be recovered and the national authorities must simply enforce the recovery decision. In some cases, however, the aid element is more difficult to identify and quantify, such as in the case of aid schemes and indirect aid. In these cases, the Commission does not always have all the elements needed to calculate the amount to be repaid. As the 2007 Recovery Notice clarified, the Commission 'is legally not required to fix the exact amount to be recovered' and can perfectly delegate this task to national authorities.[139] It is sufficient for the Commission to include the information necessary in the recovery decision to enable the Member State concerned to determine the amount 'without too much difficulty'.[140]

However, clarification is needed regarding the notion of 'without too much difficulty', as neither the Commission nor the Court of Justice case law sheds any light on it. In some circumstances, the Commission - at the time of the decision - undoubtedly does not have all the elements needed to calculate the amount to be recovered from each beneficiary.[141] In other cases, even if the Commission does - in theory - have all the elements needed, in practice it may:

> legitimately confine itself to declaring that there is an obligation to repay the aid in question and leave it to the national authorities to calculate the exact amount of aid to be repaid where that calculation requires [applying] tax and social security

undertakings operating at subsequent levels of activity. *See, e.g.*: Judgment of the Court of Justice of 19 September 2000, C-156/98, *Germany v. Commission*, EU:C:2000:467, paras 26-27; Judgment of the Court of Justice of 28 July 2011, C-403/10 P, *Mediaset SpA v. Commission*, EU:C:2011:533, paras 73-77; Judgment of the General Court of 4 March 2009, T-445/05, *Associazione italiana del risparmio gestito and Fineco Asset Management v. Commission*, EU:T:2009:50; and Judgment of 17 December 2015, Joined Cases T-515/13 and T-719/13, *Kingdom of Spain and Others v. European Commission*, EU:T:2015:1004. On this last judgment, *see* S. Thomas, *The Spanish Tax Lease Case: Identifying the Beneficiary under the Selectivity Test in Fiscal Aid Schemes*, European Law Blog, 15 June 2016.

139. 2007 Recovery Notice, cited in footnote 126 of this Part One, para. 37.

140. *Ibid. See* Judgment of the Court of 12 October 2000, Case C-480/98, *Kingdom of Spain v. Commission of the European Communities (Magefesa)*, EU:C:2000:559, para. 25, and Judgment of the Court of 2 February 1988, Joined Cases C-67/85, C-68/85 and C-70/85, *Kwekerij van der Kooy BV and others v. Commission*, EU:C:1988:38.

141. This could happen in almost the same situations mentioned in the previous subsection (*Identification of the undertakings from which aid must be recovered*), namely aid schemes with several beneficiaries and indirect aid, which require extensive market analysis to determine the advantage enjoyed by each beneficiary.

> systems, the detailed rules of which are laid down in the applicable national legislative provisions.[142]

In other situations, the Commission can avoid calculating the amount and simply provide the parameters needed to that effect, even if the calculation does not involve any difficulties, *e.g.*, for soft loans or other kinds of preferential financing when it indicates the loan amount and the subsidy element in the interest rate.[143] On this basis, the notion of 'without too much difficulty' must be read in a qualitative way and, thus, in relation to the kind of calculations that national authorities are requested to perform.[144]

In short, Commission decisions must contain all the assessment and calculation criteria needed to enable the national authorities to determine the precise amount through factual verifications and mathematical operations - even complex ones. This must be done without leaving the national authorities any power to perform discretional evaluations. The Commission's practice concerning fiscal aid schemes is in line with this conclusion and offers some examples in which the Commission delegated the calculation of the recovery amount to national authorities, having explained in detail in its decision the method to be adopted.[145] The Commission was expected to leverage this experience to clarify the notion of 'without too much difficulty' when updating the Recovery Notice to improve cooperation with Member States.

Determining the amount to be recovered also involves another key issue, which is extensively explained in Chapter I and that the 2007 Recovery Notice failed to address properly:[146] the rationale of recovery. The issue concerns whether the concept of an 'advantage' to be recovered is to be understood in a financial/nominal way or in an economic way. According to the financial concept of advantage, the amount to be recovered is the nominal amount of the aid, equivalent to the financial burden borne by

142. Judgment of the Court of 12 October 2000, Case C-480/98, *Kingdom of Spain v. Commission of the European Communities (Magefesa)*, EU:C:2000:559, para. 26.
143. Judgment of the Court of 13 July 1988, Case C-102/87, *French Republic v. Commission of the European Communities*, EU:C:1988:391, para. 33. Sometimes, Member States confuse the 'without too much difficulty' requirement with the different issue of whether aid is impossible to recover, which is an extrinsic limit to recovery, as analysed in section I.A.2.7 above. *See* Judgment of the General Court of 21 September 2022, Case T-95/21, cited in footnote 59 of this Part One, where the General Court itself commits this error by examining the Portuguese Republic's argument in the context of its assessment of the absolute impossibility defence (para. 228).
144. For instance, in one case the Court of Justice ruled that determining the exact amount to be repaid may involve the obligation, on the Member State concerned, to collect the data needed to determine the relevant market. This means that determining the relevant market to enforce a recovery decision is deemed not to imply any difficult exercise for the national authorities, which can seem surprising. *See* Judgment of the Court of 6 May 2015, Case C-674/13, *European Commission v. Federal Republic of Germany*, EU:C:2015:302.
145. *See, e.g.*, Commission Decision of 17 July 2013, SA.21233, *Spanish Aid for the acquisition of ships - Spanish Tax Lease*, C(2013) 4426 final, OJEU L 114 of 16 April 2014.
146. The 2007 Recovery Notice contains only one reference to this issue, in para. 50:

> The Commission considers that in such cases, the national authorities will need to ensure that the beneficiary will not be able to enjoy a further tax deduction by claiming that the reimbursement has reduced his taxable income, since this would mean that the net amount of the recovery was lower than the net amount initially received.

the Member State. By contrast, according to the economic concept of advantage, the amount to be repaid corresponds to the actual improvement in the beneficiaries' market situation arising from the aid, which could be higher or lower than the nominal amount of the aid. As extensively discussed in Chapter I, neither the Commission nor the case law has an unequivocal position on this.

In the 2007 Recovery Notice, the Commission's wording seemed to refer to the financial concept of advantage, but its decisional practice does not appear to strictly adhere to this. More specifically, the Commission sometimes resorts to an economic concept of advantage: (i) when indirect aid exists; (ii) when the actual advantage is clearly higher than the nominal amount of the aid; and (iii) when the nominal amount cannot be determined.[147] For instance, in the *Mediaset I* case,[148] the Commission held that the amount of additional profit generated by the aid should be included when quantifying the amount to be recovered. In this regard, the Commission accepted that, when the economic advantage deriving from the aid is higher than the amount of the aid itself, the national authorities must take that into account in calculating the amount to be repaid.[149]

In that respect, the Court of Justice case law is as inconsistent as the Commission's practice, which further contributes to the confusion. For instance, in the *Mediaset II* case, the Court of Justice - in a preliminary ruling on a dispute between Mediaset and the Italian Ministry of Economic Development (*Ministero dello Sviluppo Economico*) relating to recovery of aid - confirmed the possibility for the national court to conclude that the amount of aid to be repaid was zero, as this conclusion derived from calculations made based on all the elements that the court was aware of (and was therefore consistent with the Commission decision). The economic concept of advantage is thus applied.

The General Court reached a similar conclusion in the *Aer Lingus* case.[150] However, following the Commission's appeal against the General Court decision, the

147. In that respect, *see* G. Biagioni, *Le modalità di calcolo dell'aiuto di Stato da recuperare e del risarcimento danni per violazione degli artt. 107 e 108 § 3 TFUE*, in L. Pace, 'Dizionario sistematico del diritto della concorrenza', Jovene, 2013.

148. Judgment of the General Court of 15 June 2010, Case T-177/07, *Mediaset SpA v. European Commission*, EU:T:2010:233, and Judgment of the Court of 28 July 2011, Case C-403/10 P, *Mediaset SpA v. European Commission*, EU:C:2011:533 (*Mediaset I* is used to distinguish this case from Judgment of the Court of 13 February 2014, Case C-69/13, *Mediaset S.p.A. v. Ministero dello Sviluppo Economico*, EU:C:2014:71, known as *Mediaset II*).

149. Commission Decision of 24 January 2007, C 52/2005 (ex NN 88/2005, ex CP 101/2004), implemented by the Italian Republic for the subsidised purchase of digital decoders, paras 193 and 195. On this case, *see* N. Niejahr, *It May Be Zero! CJEU Highlights National Courts' Authority to Review and Determine Amounts of Aid to Be Recovered*, in European State Aid Law Quarterly (EStAL), 2014, Issue 4 and M. Merola, *Mediaset III: The Recovery Revolution Deactivated*, in C. Buts and J.L. Buendía Sierra eds, 'Milestones in State Aid Case Law', Lexxion, 2017, p. 703.

150. Judgment of the General Court of 5 February 2015, Case T-473/12, *Aer Lingus Ltd v. European Commission*, EU:T:2015:78. The General Court, while sharing with the Commission its evaluation of the unlawfulness and incompatibility of the measure, partially annulled Art. 4 of the Commission's decision (which contained the recovery order), insofar as it specified the amount to be recovered. *See also* the judgment on Ryanair's appeal: Judgment of the General Court of 5 February 2015, Case T-500/12, *Ryanair Ltd v. European Commission*, EU:T:2015:73.

Court of Justice established – clearly but unsatisfactorily – that the fundamental criterion for recovery is the principle of equivalence between the nominal value of the aid and the amount to be recovered.[151] The Court recalled that the purpose of recovering unlawful aid is to restore the situation that existed before the aid was granted and held that this merely implies that:

> the recipient forfeits the advantage which it had enjoyed over its competitors on the market, and the situation prior to payment of the aid is restored.[152]

Apparently, according to the Court, any reference to the advantage enjoyed on the market and the situation existing before the granting of the aid is to be understood in financial terms rather than in economic terms or with reference to the competitive situation of the market.

However, unlike the *Mediaset II* case, this case concerned direct aid. The question is therefore whether the Court is prepared to depart from the financial concept of recovery only in the case of indirect aid. Not even this solution would be satisfactory, however, as the principle of equal treatment requires that, for infringement of the same provision of EU law, the same criteria should apply to determine the liability of the private parties involved, irrespective of the type of aid.

In short, great confusion exists on the notion of the advantage to be recovered, in both the Commission's practice and the case law – a confusion that continues to surface even in recent cases;[153] and a risk also exists that different concepts of recovery proliferate based on the different types of aid concerned. Nevertheless, the Recovery Notice was silent on this crucial issue. This exposes the Commission to criticism, as doubts could arise that the Commission applies one concept or another depending on the circumstances, using recovery as a means of punishment. The application of a single concept of recovery, be it nominal/financial or economic, would be useful to eradicate this concern – indeed, *this was deemed to be one of the main challenges the Commission was expected to take on when reviewing the Recovery Notice.*

151. Judgment of the Court of 21 December 2016, Joined Cases C-164/15 P and C-165/15 P, *European Commission v. Aer Lingus Ltd and Ryanair Designated Activity Company*, EU:C:2016:990.
152. *Ibid.*, para. 90. *See also* Judgment of the Court of 29 April 2004, Case C-277/00, *Germany v. Commission*, EU:C:2004:238, para. 75.
153. *See*, among others, the Commission decision in the Spanish tax lease case (decision No. 2014/200/EU of 17.7.2013, OJEU 2014, L 114, p.1) and the Judgment of the General Court of 8 May 2024, Joined Cases T-700/13 Joined Cases T-700/13, T-2/14, T-6/14, T-10/14, T-16/14, T-18/14, T-24/14, T-465/14, T-467/14, T-469/14, T-471/14, T-472/14, T-473/14, T-474/14, T-476/14, T-477/14, T-478/14, T-482/14, T-483/14, T-491/14, T-701/13, T-702/13, T-703/13, T-704/13, T-705/13, *Caixabank, SA and Vego Supermercados, SA v. European Commission*, EU:T:2024:295. The General Court held that a Member State to which a decision requiring it to recover unlawful aid has been addressed is obliged, under Art. 288 TFEU, to take all appropriate measures to ensure that the decision is implemented. It must achieve effective recovery of the sums due in order to eliminate the distortion of competition caused by the competitive advantage conferred by the unlawful aid. The contradiction between a State's obligation to strictly implement recovery decisions (which, as seen above, are generally based on a nominal concept of recovery, except in the uncertain case of indirect aid) and the stated objective of eliminating the *distortion of competition* caused by the *competitive advantage* conferred by the aid could not be clearer.

Of course, the choice of which concept should be applied is not without consequences, as it may heavily influence the need and type of other remedies that may be necessary to ensure deterrence and effectiveness of enforcement.

II.A.4 Enforcement of the Recovery Obligation

The recovery obligation is exclusively on national authorities. However, the Commission exercises a role of control over the timely and effective execution of recovery orders. On this point, the 2007 Recovery Notice amended the Commission's previous practice, which required:

> a single time-limit of two months, within which the Member State concerned was required to communicate to the Commission the measures it had taken to comply with a given decision.[154]

The 2007 Recovery Notice introduced two time limits that have appeared in all recovery decisions since the first is two months, within which the Member State must inform the Commission of the measures planned or taken, and the second is four months, within which the Commission decision must be implemented. The Commission is, naturally, allowed to grant one or more extensions. The Court of Justice case law has also indirectly confirmed the lawfulness of extensions, clarifying that the reference date 'is that provided for in the decision [sic] failure to implement which is denied or, where appropriate, that subsequently fixed by the Commission'.[155]

As recalled in paragraph 41 of the 2007 Recovery Notice, contact and negotiations between the Commission and the national authorities for the enforcement of Commission decisions cannot relieve national authorities from their duty to take all necessary measures to enforce decisions within the time limit. Nevertheless, in practice, even if the time limit expires, the Commission does not take any action (*e.g.*, bring infringement proceedings) against the Member State concerned if there is a dialogue on the difficulties encountered in the recovery. Conversely, the Commission does not endorse the use of delaying tactics by the Member States, and if it holds that the difficulties cited are specious and insubstantial, it immediately starts infringement proceedings.[156] Lastly, and importantly, the opening of a dialogue between the Commission and the national authorities on the difficulties of recovery does not obstruct or delay application of the *Deggendorf* doctrine.[157]

---

154. 2007 Recovery Notice, cited in footnote 126 of this Part One, para. 40.
155. *See*, to that effect: Judgment of the Court of 5 October 2006, Case C-232/05, *Commission of the European Communities v. French Republic*, EU:C:2006:651, para. 32; Judgment of the Court of 3 July 2001, Case C-378/98, *Commission of the European Communities v. Kingdom of Belgium*, EU:C:2001:370, para. 26; and Judgment of the Court of 2 July 2002, Case C-499/99, *Commission of the European Communities v. Kingdom of Spain*, para. 28.
156. This is what happened with the Judgment of the Court of 9 April 1987, Case C-5/86, *Commission of the European Communities v. Kingdom of Belgium*, EU:C:1987:198, paras 6-11.
157. Judgment of the Court of 15 May 1997, *Textilwerke Deggendorf GmbH (TWD) v. Commission of the European Communities and Federal Republic of Germany*, cited in footnote 102 of hits Part One.

In any case, the Commission's role is only to supervise compliance with the recovery obligation, which remains under the national authorities' responsibility. In enforcing recovery, they have a great degree of discretion in determining the internal procedure and the means of recovery. As to the internal recovery procedure, the 2007 Recovery Notice referred to the Study on the enforcement of State aid law at the national level,[158] according to which administrative procedures are generally more efficient than civil procedures because administrative recovery orders are immediately enforceable (except in the case of suspension orders issued by administrative courts). However, the Commission recognised that it is up to the Member State to determine the internal recovery procedure, 'subject to the condition that such procedure allows for the immediate and effective execution of the Commission's decision'.[159]

In practice, the choice is largely influenced by the nature of the measure concerned, and even more by the means of recovery chosen to enforce the recovery obligation. For instance, when the aid is granted through an administrative or legislative act, the natural means of recovery is an administrative/legislative act, and an administrative procedure applies. Conversely, when the aid is granted through a private contractual arrangement or other private instruments, the natural means of recovery is normally (in the absence of specific provisions) an act governed by private law, and civil procedure applies.

In any case, Member States must ensure that their recovery procedures are designed to enable them to obtain timely and effective recovery. If not, national authorities 'are under an obligation to set aside any provisions of national law, which might impede the immediate execution of the Commission decision'[160] and to adopt ad hoc measures to comply with the Treaty.

This part of the 2007 Recovery Notice did not require substantial amendments except for the definition of the time limit within which to execute recovery decisions. In that regard, however - given the consistent trend in the case law to construe Member States' obligation to recover aid as an obligation of result, in addition to the emphasis put on the need for cooperation between the Commission and the Member States - the reform could have addressed a key issue, namely to explain in which circumstances the four-month time limit can be extended or suspended. Clarification on this issue would foster both legal certainty and the system's credibility by making the Commission's behaviour more predictable in cases of failure to implement a recovery obligation or late implementation.

II.A.5 Role of National Courts

The role of national courts in the execution of recovery decisions constitutes part of the public enforcement concerning unlawful and incompatible State aid. It should not be

158. Study on the enforcement of State aid law at national level, Competition studies 6, Luxembourg, Office for Official Publications of the European Communities.
159. 2007 Recovery Notice, cited in footnote 126 of this Part One, para. 52.
160. *Ibid.*, para. 53. In that respect, *see* Judgment of the Court of 5 October 2006, Case C-232/05, *Commission v. France*, EU:C:2006:651.

confused with the role that national courts play within the framework of actions brought by private parties to challenge unlawful State aid, *i.e.*, unnotified aid or aid granted in violation of the standstill obligation (private enforcement, which is the subject of Part Two of this book).

As to the role of national courts in public enforcement cases, the 2007 Recovery Notice did not require significant changes in the context of the reform. It started off by underlining as follows:

> [T]wo main categories of recovery-related litigation can be distinguished: actions brought by the recovering authority seeking a court order to force an unwilling recipient to refund the unlawful and incompatible aid and actions brought by beneficiaries contesting the recovery order.[161]

The first category concerns situations in which national authorities cannot adopt an administrative act as a means of recovery because of the nature of the underlying measure or for other reasons.[162] The second category regards situations in which the aid beneficiary brings legal proceedings to challenge the administrative act of recovery. The latter is by far the most frequent situation and involves some issues relating to the length of proceedings. In this second case, it is important to distinguish between two scenarios, depending on whether the Commission decision has been previously challenged before the General Court.

In the first scenario, if the Commission decision has been challenged and the General Court has yet to issue its judgment, the beneficiary may claim the decision is invalid before national courts. However, the national court - if it holds that the applicant's arguments are not manifestly unfounded - may only stay the national proceedings and ask the Court of Justice for a preliminary ruling on the decision's validity, as the Court is the only body competent to ascertain the validity of acts issued by EU institutions. However, as the EU courts have already been seized of the proceedings, to avoid duplications, the national court may only stay the proceedings and simply await the General Court's judgment (and possibly that of the Court of Justice on appeal) rather than ask for a preliminary ruling on the validity of the contested decision. In this scenario, evident tension exists between the time limit for recovery and the principle of procedural autonomy[163] - a tension that should have been clearly addressed in a reform for reasons of legal certainty.

161. 2007 Recovery Notice, cited in footnote 126 of this Part One, para. 55.

162. For instance, in the United Kingdom it is common practice for competent national authorities to bring actions before the High Court to recover unlawful and incompatible State aid. In that respect, *see*, *ex multis*, the case *Department of Trade and Industry v. British Aerospace plc and Rover Group Holdings plc* [1991] 1 CMLR 165. In Italy, when national authorities cannot proceed through administrative proceedings (*e.g.*, because the aid is contained in a contractual provision), they may ask a national court to issue a payment order (*decreto ingiuntivo*). National authorities ground their request on the nullity of the contract in question because it contains a provision *contra legem*, as it is incompatible with EU law. Italian law also provides for an action for unjustified enrichment, though this is rarely resorted to.

163. Indeed, the Commission's recovery decision is immediately enforceable, and its effectiveness may be suspended only by the Court of Justice under Art. 278 TFEU. On the violation of this

In the second scenario (*i.e.*, the Commission decision has not been challenged before the General Court), the admissibility of the action brought before a national court – insofar as the validity of the Commission decision is concerned – depends on whether the applicant could have challenged that decision directly before the General Court.

In the first sub-scenario (*i.e.*, the applicant had standing to challenge the Commission decision before the General Court but failed to do so), the beneficiary cannot claim that the Commission decision is invalid in the national proceedings because this would circumvent the definitive nature of Commission decisions after expiry of the time limit under Article 263 TFEU for actions for annulment. This reasoning was endorsed by the Court of Justice in the *Deggendorf I* case[164] and has never been called into question. Moreover, in the *Georgsmarienhütte* case,[165] the Court of Justice went even further, stating that the principle established in *Deggendorf I* is also valid when the beneficiary relies, before a national court, on the invalidity of the Commission decision before the expiry of the time limit for challenging that decision before the General Court. It follows that, when a person who wants to challenge an EU measure undoubtedly has standing before the EU courts, that person is required to make use of the remedy provided for at the EU level by bringing an action before the General Court.

In the second sub-scenario, as the beneficiary cannot legitimately challenge the decision before the General Court, it may claim that the Commission's decision is invalid before the national court. The national court may reject the claim if it considers it manifestly unfounded. Conversely, if the national court has doubts as to the validity of the Commission decision (or any other act issued by an EU institution), it must refer the case to the Court of Justice for a preliminary ruling on its validity, in accordance with the *Foto-Frost* case law.[166] In the latter case, the national court stays the proceedings until the General Court hands down its judgment (or, in the case of an appeal, until the Court of Justice issues its judgment).

Nevertheless, this sub-scenario has become almost exclusively theoretical given the case law on the admissibility of appeals against recovery decisions that has developed since the *Deggendorf* case. Indeed, the Court of Justice has specified – based on the well-established criterion developed in the *Plaumann* case concerning the proof of the individual interest in bringing proceedings[167] – that actual beneficiaries of individual aid granted under a scheme the Commission declared unlawful and incompatible with the Treaty (and which it ordered to be recovered) are individually

principle, *see* Administrative Court of Lombardy (*TAR Lombardia*), Milan, Division III, Order of 22 May 2013, *Comune di Milano v. Presidenza del Consiglio dei Ministri*, Reg. Ric. No. 1084/2013.

164. In that respect, *see* Judgment of the Court of 9 March 1994, Case C-188/92, *Textilwerke Deggendorf GmbH v. Federal Republic of Germany*, EU:C:1994:90, paras 16-18.
165. Judgment of the Court of 25 July 2018, Case C-135/16, *Georgsmarienhütte GmbH and Others v. Bundesrepublik Deutschland*, EU:C:2018:582, paras 16-18.
166. Judgment of the Court of 22 October 1987, Case 314/85, *Foto-Frost v. Hauptzollamt Lübeck-Ost*, EU:C:1987:452.
167. Judgment of the Court of 15 July 1963, Case 25/62, *Plaumann & co v. Commission of the European Community*, EU:C:1963:17.

concerned under Article 230(4) TEC (now Article 263 TFEU) and can thus legitimately bring an action for annulment.[168] Doubts remain, at most, only in those cases where actual beneficiaries cannot be identified solely on the basis of the Commission decision, which does not contain all the criteria needed to that effect. Consequently, very few cases exist in which the beneficiary - when subject to a recovery obligation - cannot legitimately bring an action for annulment before the EU courts.

This being the status of the case law on admissibility, it is extremely unlikely that beneficiaries may challenge the validity of a Commission decision at the execution stage (by national authorities) of a recovery order. It is thus even more important that the system of remedies for breach of State aid rules be designed to ensure legal certainty, comply fully with the rights of defence, and be subject to full review by the EU courts.

II.B The New Recovery Notice

On 4 February 2019, the Commission launched a public consultation on the reform of the Recovery Notice. After examining the contributions received from eighteen Member States, six registered organisations and three individuals, the Commission published the New Recovery Notice on 23 July 2019.

This section first analyses whether the shortcomings identified in the 2007 Recovery Notice were addressed (section II.B.1). It then summarises the other main changes and discusses the shortcomings that remain in the New Recovery Notice (section II.B.2).

II.B.1 Little Progress in Addressing the Main Shortcomings

The New Recovery Notice is certainly more detailed and better structured than the previous version. In general, it appears to have been designed more as an instrument to drive Member States and practitioners in the recovery process than as a legal document on the foundations and main principles of recovery. It thus certainly offers more practical instructions than the 2007 version - but it substantially fails to address the main conceptual shortcomings mentioned above.

As to the division of competences between the Commission and the national authorities, the New Recovery Notice is a good step forward in the process of shaping the respective boundaries of the Commission's and the Member States' prerogatives. Section 3, for example, in recalling the principle of sincere cooperation, not only underlines the leading role of Member States in implementing recovery but also emphasises their crucial role in the phase of adopting recovery decisions. Indeed, in

168. *See* Judgment of the Court of 19 October 2000, Joined Cases C-15/98 and C-105/99, *Italy and Sardegna Lines v. Commission*, EU:C:2000:570, paras 34-35, Judgment of the Court of 29 April 2004, Case C-298/00 P, *Italian Republic v. Commission*, EU:C:2004:240, paras 38-39, and Judgment of the Court of 9 June 2011, Joined Cases C-71/09 P, C-73/09 P and C-76/09, *Comitato 'Venezia vuole vivere' and o. v. Commission*, EU:C:2011:368, para. 53.

providing accurate and complete information during the formal investigation, Member States contribute to the adoption of more easily enforceable recovery decisions and to the prevention or reduction of the risk that recovery is not immediate and effective.

Section 3 also contains a list of actions that the Commission may take to support Member States' fulfilment of their obligations. The list includes: (i) the provision of examples of spreadsheets for Member States to provide information on aid beneficiaries and aid amounts;[169] (ii) the evaluation of requests to extend the deadline to execute recovery decisions; (iii) the organisation of kick-off meetings;[170] (iv) the provision of a tool to calculate recovery interest and of examples of escrow agreements suitable for the provisional recovery of aid; and (v) the notice to Member States of the provisional or definitive closure of the recovery procedure. Moreover, according to paragraph 25, the Commission may elaborate, during the recovery phase, on the standard of proof and the type of evidence required for Member States to identify aid beneficiaries, the amount of aid subject to recovery, and the amounts recovered.

Despite these significant changes, the New Recovery Notice does not resolve the main (let alone all) shortcomings identified in the 2007 Recovery Notice. More precisely, it fails to set out any specific recovery procedure (or third parties' rights in that connection) and even fails to clarify the minimum requirements that Commission recovery decisions must ensure are met when identifying beneficiaries and determining the recovery amount. As to identifying the undertakings from which aid must be recovered, the New Recovery Notice is quite unsatisfactory. Indeed, not only does it fail to address the vast majority of the identified shortcomings but it also stretches some concepts that are not well-settled in the case law.

As to the first of the three situations that might give rise to difficulties in identifying beneficiaries – namely corporate changes that occur between when the aid is granted and when the recovery decision is issued – the new text makes little progress. Indeed, although it explains in more detail the conditions to be evaluated for both asset deals[171] and share deals,[172] it fails to overcome the confusion as to whether – and, if so, under which conditions and based on which rationale – certain events that can affect beneficiaries after aid is granted (before or after the Commission starts its investigation) entail the transfer of the recovery obligation to a party other than the initial beneficiary.[173] The same is true for the other situations that might give rise to difficulties in identifying the actual beneficiaries (*i.e.*, indirect aid and aid schemes).

In this connection, the New Recovery Notice does introduce a subsection on 'identification of the aid beneficiary belonging to a group of undertakings' (subsection 4.3.1), but this is where the Commission stretches some concepts that are not

169. For instance, according to para. 24 of the New Recovery Notice, cited in footnote 125 of this Part One, 'the Commission may also share mock calculations of aid to be recovered, based on the formulae or methodologies established in the relevant recovery decision'.
170. The New Recovery Notice, cited in footnote 125 of this Part One, dedicates an entire subsection (4.2) to the organisation of these meetings.
171. New Recovery Notice, cited in footnote 125 of this Part One, paras 91-92.
172. *Ibid.*, paras 93-94.
173. *See* section II.A.2 of this Part One.

well-settled in the case law. Indeed, the new text states that in cases involving a group of undertakings:

> the recovery decision may order the Member State concerned to recover the aid not only from the undertaking which directly benefitted from it but also from the whole group of undertakings forming an economic unit or from some of the legal entities belonging to it.

It follows that, according to the new text, the Member State concerned must prove that it has correctly recovered the aid either from its direct beneficiary or from the other undertakings subject to the recovery obligation.

To reach this conclusion, the Commission relies solely on the concept of economic unit as defined in competition law[174] and on the Court of First Instance judgment in the *DSG* case.[175] However, these two arguments seem insufficient to sustain a sort of joint liability of the group to which the undertaking belongs and even more to conclude that aid can be recovered from whichever company from within the beneficiary group; indeed, the concept defined in competition law applies only to antitrust and merger cases, and the Court of First Instance judgment in the *DSG* case - issued over twenty years ago - has never been confirmed by the Court of Justice. Thus, extending the recovery obligation to the multinational group to which the recipient company belongs is not a consolidated principle.

Although the Commission resorted to joint liability for recovery in a limited number of cases[176] - particularly in some recent cases regarding tax rulings - this principle simply constitutes an orientation of the Commission that has yet to be endorsed in the EU courts' case law. Consequently, room for doubt remains as to the lawfulness of joint liability, and this uncertainty will persist until the EU courts decide on a pending case in which the applicants dispute this very aspect.[177] The New Recovery Notice therefore seems to go a little too far on this point.

---

174. Judgment of the Court of Justice of 12 July 1984, Case C-170/83, *Hydrotherm Gerätebau GmbH v. Compact del Dott. Ing. Mario Andreoli & C. Sas.*, EU:C:1984:271, para. 11.
175. Judgment of the Court of First Instance of 29 June 2000, Case T-234/95, *DSG Dradenauer Stahlgesellschaft mbH v. Commission of the European Communities*, EU:T:2000:174, para. 124.
176. *See*: Commission Decision of 1 October 2014, SA 27339 (12/C) (ex 11/NN), aid implemented by Germany for Zweibrücken airport and airlines using the airport; Commission Decision of 15 October 2014, SA.26500 - 2012/C (ex 2011/NN, ex CP 227/2008), aid implemented by Germany for Flugplatz Altenburg-Nobitz GmbH and Ryanair Ltd; and Commission Decision of 30 March 2015, SA.38517 (2014/C) (ex 2014/NN), aid implemented by Romania - Arbitral award *Micula v. Romania* of 11 December 2013.
177. In two appeals against the Commission Decision on the Belgian excess profit exemption scheme, the recipients challenged the classification of the multinational groups as beneficiaries, claiming that the Commission wrongly found that the Belgian entities formed a single economic entity with the multinational group to which they belonged. The applicants also claimed that the companies were not subjected to the same taxation scheme, precluding the existence of a single economic unit. The General Court stated that in the context of decisions concerning aid schemes, the Commission is not required to carry out an analysis of the aid granted in individual cases under the scheme. It is only at the stage of recovery of the aid that it is necessary for the Member States to look at the individual situation of each undertaking concerned (*Italy v. Commission*, C-310/99; *Comitato 'Venezia vuole vivere' and Others v. Commission*, C-71/09 P, C-73/09 P and C-76/09 P; and *Copebi*, C-505/18). Moreover, according to the General Court, the Commission highlighted elements that supported its conclusion that,

Finally, it is important to mention a new subsection on the 'aid beneficiaries of tax measures' (subsection 4.3.3), in which the Commission clarifies that in identifying a beneficiary, it is irrelevant whether the undertaking in question applied the aid measure correctly in its tax declaration or instead breached the applicable national rules;[178] what is relevant is whether an undertaking enjoyed the tax advantage found to constitute incompatible State aid.[179] This statement is not entirely convincing, as cases of breach of a national tax system should be dealt with primarily at national level, at least if the tax system can be classified as an aid scheme.

As to determining the recovery amount, the New Recovery Notice fails to address the two main open issues, namely clarification on the notion of 'without too much difficulty' and whether the concept of an 'advantage' to be recovered is to be understood in either financial/nominal or economic terms. As to the notion of 'without too much difficulty', the new text is even more unsatisfactory than its predecessor, as it does not deal with the notion in the section dedicated to determining the recovery amount but merely mentions it in footnote 87 without further explanation.[180]

As to the concept of an 'advantage', even though the Commission's wording seems to continue to refer to the financial concept of advantage, in paragraph 125 the Commission makes a vague reference to an economic concept. Indeed, the new text specifies that one of the conditions to be met to be able to use alternative means of recovery is that the alternative means must be suitable for the purpose of re-establishing the *market conditions* that have been distorted by the unlawful aid measure. In this way, the Commission conveys the (wrong?) impression that its understanding of the concept of 'advantage' appears to be in the sense of 'economic advantage' or 'competitive advantage', *i.e.*, the competitive boost that the beneficiary obtained as a result of the aid. In any case, the Commission again fails to analyse all the case law on the matter or to take a clear position on the concept.

Despite this slow progress, the new text introduces some relevant changes and clarification as to calculating the amount to be repaid. More precisely, an important addition concerns the subsection dedicated to 'tax measures' (subsection 4.4.1). In that

in principle, links of control existed within the multinational corporate groups to which the Belgian entities that had obtained advance rulings belonged. The Belgian entities also performed some core functions for the whole group, and the choice to invest in Belgium was aimed at benefitting from the excess profit scheme (SA.37667). In light of this, the General Court confirmed the Commission's classification of the multinational groups as beneficiaries of the aid and stated that recovery may be ordered from all group entities if they form a single economic unit, regardless of their legal status and of the fact that they have a separate legal personality (*see* Joined Cases T-278/16, *Atlas Copco Airpower and Atlas Copco v. Commission*, T-370/16, *Anheuser-Busch Inbev and Ampar v. Commission*). The recipients appealed the decision on the point stating that recovery could be ordered from all group entities; the appeal is pending before the European Court of Justice (*see* Case C-755/23 P, appeal brought on 7 December 2023, *Atlas Copco Airpower and Atlas Copco and others v. Commission*, pending).

178. *See* Judgment of the Court of Justice of 14 July 2011, Case C-303/09, *European Commission v. Italian Republic ('Tremonti bis')*, EU:C:2011:483, para. 43.

179. New Recovery Notice, cited in footnote 125 of this Part One, paras 96-97.

180. For the sake of precision, it should be noted that in footnote 87 of the New Recovery Notice, the Commission uses slightly different wording (*i.e.*, 'without overmuch difficulty'), which is indeed the wording used in the only judgment referred to therein but not in previous case law.

subsection, the Commission first states – quoting the Court of Justice judgment in the *Unicredito* case – that in cases concerning tax measures:

> re-establishing the status quo ante means returning, as far as possible, to the situation which would have prevailed if the operations at issue had been carried out without the tax reduction.[181]

It then specifies that in calculating the 'advantage', the counterfactual situation – *i.e.*, the correct tax amount that an undertaking would have paid without the unlawful aid measure – must be based only on the choices made in the past, without considering alternative, hypothetical choices that would have been available absent the aid.[182] According to the Commission, only deductions that would have been applicable to the situation absent the aid, as envisaged by national and international law or by the recovery decision, can be taken into account. This new subsection might seem to go slightly too far given that this very issue, although raised in several cases on tax rulings recently decided by the EU courts, has never been explicitly addressed in the General Courts' judgments[183] and has never been questioned on appeal.

As to enforcement of the recovery obligation, the New Recovery Notice takes both steps forward and steps back. More precisely, although it is positive that the Commission eliminated all the previous version's references to the four-month time limit for recovery – indeed, experience shows (as emphasised above) that the time limit was rarely respected and was impossible to reconcile with the duration of national insolvency proceedings – the new text's generic reference to the duty to fulfil the obligation to recover the aid by the 'recovery deadline' determined by the Commission seems insufficient. Indeed, in substance, this change gives the Commission a large degree of discretion in determining the period for enforcing the recovery obligation on a case-by-case basis. This amendment does not contribute to fostering legal certainty or the system's credibility, but rather quite the opposite: it increases the level of uncertainty and reduces the predictability of the Commission's behaviour, thus ultimately penalising the interested parties.

A more efficient approach would have been to set a longer time limit that could reasonably be respected and then explain in detail the circumstances in which the limit may be extended or suspended. Regrettably, the New Recovery Notice makes very little progress on this point. Indeed, the new text requires that if difficulties arise in enforcing the recovery decision by the deadline, Member States must not merely report these difficulties – they also have a duty to provide proposals for suitable solutions,[184]

181. Judgment of the Court of Justice of 15 December 2005, Case C-148/04, *Unicredito Italiano SpA v. Agenzia delle Entrate, Ufficio Genova 1*, EU:C:2005:774, para. 117.
182. *Ibid.*, paras 118-119.
183. For instance, *see*, *ex multis*: Judgment of the General Court of 24 September 2019, Joined Cases T-755/15 and T-759/15, *Grand Duchy of Luxembourg and Fiat Chrysler Finance Europe v. European Commission*, EU:T:2019:670; Judgment of the General Court of 24 September 2019, Joined Cases T-760/15 and T-636/16, *Kingdom of the Netherlands and others v. Commission*, EU:T:2019:669; and Judgment of the General Court of 15 July 2020, Joined Cases T-778/16 and T-892/16, *Republic of Ireland and others v. Commission*, EU:T:2020:338.
184. *See* Judgment of the Court of Justice of 9 November 2017, Case C-481/16, *European Commission v. Hellenic Republic ('Larco')*, EU:C:2017:845, para. 29.

including a proposal to extend the recovery deadline if appropriate. The Commission clarifies that a deadline extension may be granted only in exceptional circumstances, namely when:

> 'the Member State demonstrates with conclusive evidence that all other possible measures that could lead to timely implementation of the Commission decision would not be effective'[185] – not when 'the delay in recovery is due to the ways and means chosen by the Member State, where faster options were available'.[186]

However, this clarification remains somewhat generic, as no concrete examples are provided and the Member State's burden of proof is particularly high.

Finally, as to the role of national courts and the tension between the timeliness of the recovery and the principle of procedural autonomy, the only amendment is the tautological clarification that when the conditions established by the Court of Justice in the *Zuckerfabrik*[187] and *Atlanta*[188] cases are not met, the Member State concerned cannot rely on interim measures granted by national courts to justify its failure to implement a decision. By contrast, the new text does not acknowledge the *Deggendorf/Georgsmarienhütte* case law, despite that case law being sufficiently clear in itself, albeit criticised by legal scholars from the perspective of effective judicial protection.[189]

II.B.2 Other Main Changes

In addition to the amendments described above, which concern the main shortcomings in the Recovery Notice, the new text includes some other significant changes. This subsection deals with these issues.

The first major amendment is the limitation to the recovery obligation, to which the New Recovery Notice dedicates a detailed subsection,[190] analysing in depth both the inherent and the extrinsic limitations to repayment. All in all, the addition of a subsection on this matter in the new text is certainly positive, as it clarifies the use of a procedural tool developed in the Commission's practice and envisages specific obligations on both sides in light of the principle of sincere cooperation.

More precisely, the new text contains an overview of the case law on the application of the general principles of Union law as a limitation to recovery, dealing

185. New Recovery Notice, cited in footnote 125 of this Part One, para. 76.
186. *Ibid.*, para. 77. In any case, recovery deadline extension requests cannot be granted once the deadline passes.
187. Judgment of the Court of Justice of 21 February 1991, *Zuckerfabrik Süderdithmarschen AG v. Hauptzollamt Itzehoe and Zuckerfabrik Soest GmbH v. Hauptzollamt Paderborn*, cited in footnote 46 of this Part One, paras 23 ff.
188. Judgment of the Court of Justice of 9 November 1995, *Atlanta Fruchthandelsgesellschaft mbH and others v. Bundesamt für Ernährung und Forstwirtschaft*, cited in footnote 45 of this Part One, para. 51.
189. For instance, *see* J. Derenne and C. Chilaru, *Renvoi préjudiciel en appréciation de validité et recours en annulation: quelle protection juridictionnelle effective en particulier en matière d'aides d'Etat?*, Revue des Affaires Européennes, 2, 2019.
190. New Recovery Notice, cited in footnote 125 of this Part One, subsection 2.4, paras 30-62.

with the principles of legal certainty, protection of legitimate expectations and *res judicata* – although several stakeholders emphasised during the public consultation that the case law reconstruction is one-sided.[191] The paragraphs devoted to the limitation period are also very detailed. Conversely, the section on the absolute impossibility of recovery appears weaker, as it does not take account of all the consequences arising from the Court of Justice judgment in the *Montessori* case[192] but merely states that the absolute impossibility of recovery *may* be established during the Commission's formal investigation.

Two other relevant additions regard the provisional implementation of recovery[193] and alternative means of recovery.[194] The Commission offers some examples of means of provisional implementation, such as payment of the full recovery amount into an escrow account or, when envisaged by national law, repayment under a special clause whereby the aid returns to the beneficiary if the beneficiary prevails in ongoing litigation. By contrast, the Commission clarifies that the provision of guarantees for the future payment of the recovery amount is an inadequate provisional measure because the aid is left at the beneficiary's disposal in the meantime. As to alternative means of recovery, the new text specifies the general cumulative conditions under which it accepts means other than cash payments, namely when: (i) the means are a suitable instrument for re-establishing distorted market conditions; (ii) the means can be identified as such by the Commission and other interested parties;[195] and (iii) Member States prove that they have an equivalent effect to a cash payment. Moreover, the Commission also reports the specific conditions required for repayments in kind and for the offsetting of claims.

Another major change concerns the internal practice of 'provisional closure' of recovery procedures developed by the Commission in the last few years. This practice applies to situations in which a recovery decision has been provisionally implemented but cannot be considered definitively enforced for various reasons, such as: (i) pending litigation at Union or national level; (ii) ongoing national administrative procedures that may still affect fulfilment of the recovery obligation; or (iii) pending insolvency proceedings in which the State aid claims have been properly registered at the appropriate rank. In any case, Member States must keep the Commission updated and continue to provide information and evidence at least once a year, and the Commission must continue to inform Member States of its assessment of the procedure status.

191. Indeed, several contributions submitted to the Commission during public consultation state that the Recovery Notice refers exclusively to cases in which the EU courts adopted a restrictive interpretation of those principles and pays little attention to cases that would be less supportive of the Commission's position.
192. Judgment of the Court of 6 November 2018, Joined Cases C-622/16 P to C-624/16 P, *Scuola Elementare Maria Montessori Srl v. European Commission, European Commission v. Scuola Elementare Maria Montessori Srl and European Commission, v. Pietro Ferracci*, cited in footnote 78 of this Part One.
193. New Recovery Notice, cited in footnote 125 of this Part One, subsection 4.6.
194. *Ibid.*, subsection 4.7.
195. Judgment of the Court of Justice of 12 December 2002, Case C-209/00, *Commission of the European Communities v. Federal Republic of Germany*, EU:C:2002:747, paras 57-58.

Finally, with regard to the service of recovery orders – also in light of several tax ruling cases involving large multinationals that were pending when the New Recovery Notice was issued – the Commission specifies that:

> for aid beneficiaries not having their seat or a permanent establishment in the territory of the Member State concerned, the service of recovery orders may be governed by the rules and procedures established in international agreements or private international law applicable in that Member State.[196]

By contrast, the new text is particularly unsatisfactory on two main themes: insolvency proceedings and ancillary remedies. Indeed, the insolvency proceedings section is almost identical to the 2007 version, with only some formal adjustments and new case law references. As to ancillary remedies, the new text not only fails to address the main shortcomings affecting them but also drastically reduces the subsection dedicated to the *Deggendorf* doctrine, thus raising additional suspicions about the uncertainty and debate existing within the Commission on how to use this remedy.

196. New Recovery Notice, cited in footnote 125 of this Part One, para. 114.

III REFORM OF THE PUBLIC ENFORCEMENT SYSTEM OF REMEDIES AND MODERNISATION

This chapter discusses the persistent shortcomings of the system of remedies under the New Recovery Notice and proposes a more comprehensive reform aligned with modernisation objectives. It examines the need for greater clarity and a more flexible and effective approach to recovery measures. It also looks at related opinions in legal scholarship on the system of remedies.

As shown so far in this book, the recovery system – as reflected in the Commission's practice following adoption of the first Recovery Notice in 2007 – is a very controversial area of State aid law. Statistics on the outcome of recovery proceedings offer little guidance in measuring the results achieved from both a quantitative and a qualitative standpoint.[197] Moreover, the system's conceptual basis has been questioned, and even more so the consistency between its conceptual basis on the one hand and the way the Commission is implementing its policy in practice on the other. The New Recovery Notice falls short of addressing, let alone overcoming, all the controversial issues.

Against this background, this chapter starts by recalling some relevant issues that are unsatisfactorily addressed in the New Recovery Notice or that remain unaddressed altogether. It then examines the crucial question of whether a more comprehensive reform of the system of remedies would fit well with the modernisation initiative and, if that is the case, how it should be conducted.

III.A Mapping the Persistent Shortcomings of the System of Remedies under the New Recovery Notice

The weaknesses of the current recovery system have already emerged with clarity from the analysis of the 2007 Recovery Notice and the insufficient changes introduced with the New Recovery Notice. This section simply summarises and breaks down those weaknesses to ease the discussion of possible reforms.

III.A.1 Failure to Indicate Precisely the Respective Boundaries of the Commission's and Member States' Prerogatives

As mentioned, one of the new trends characterising the recovery system is to seek national authorities' cooperation not only in the execution of the recovery decision but also in the precise delimitation of the recovery order. In most, if not all, cases concerning aid schemes, the Commission tends to delegate identification of all beneficiaries, or at least some of them, and calculation of the amount to be repaid by each, to national authorities. Moreover, when confronted with complex aid resulting

197. *See* DG Competition, State aid recovery statistics, 18 September 2023, available at state_aid-_recovery_statistics.xlsx (live.com). Recovery has been fully implemented with regard to only very few decisions; therefore, the real efficiency of the recovery mechanism cannot be estimated.

from the combination of several measures, the Commission tends to confine itself to describing and delimiting the aid elements without suggesting a precise methodology or providing examples of how to calculate the amount to be repaid. An initial controversial issue in this respect relates to the exact meaning of the 'without too much difficulty' requirement, as set out in the case law.[198] This is, of course, a crucial issue when allocating tasks and responsibilities between the Commission and national authorities - and thus crucial to avoiding delays in the execution phase of a recovery order.

Similarly, the Commission does not engage in in-depth discussions with Member States - and even less so with the undertakings subject to a given recovery order - before adopting the related recovery decision. It prefers to defer any such discussion to the execution phase of the recovery order - a phase which is, however, completely unregulated. In the absence of rules governing the execution phase, this practice is indeed a source of legal uncertainty. It is even questionable whether the Commission, when it refrains from identifying the aid beneficiaries and the amounts to be repaid under a given recovery decision, is actually empowered to impose a specific recovery method. Indeed, when these tasks are left to the execution phase and delegated to the Member State concerned, *it may be argued that the principle of procedural autonomy extends to such tasks*. But even if this argument is dismissed, the fact remains that the legal framework in such cases is limited to the application of the principle of sincere cooperation under Article 4(3) TEU.

It is therefore unquestionable that, given the recovery system's importance, it is time to regulate the sharing of competences and prerogatives between the Commission and the Member States more precisely, by: (i) laying down the *minimum requirements* that the Commission must comply with in recovery decisions or, in other words, the exact limits of the possibility to delegate tasks to national authorities; (ii) clarifying whether *procedural autonomy extends to the methods used for calculating amounts to be recovered*; and, even more importantly (iii) clarifying the *scope and limits of the execution phase*, including the procedure the Commission should follow when monitoring the remedies' implementation by Member States.

III.A.2 Lack of a Systematic Examination of Situations That Might Give Rise to Difficulties in Identifying Beneficiaries

The correct identification of beneficiaries is obviously essential both for reasons of substantive justice and for the effectiveness of the system of remedies. The case law of the Court confirms that this is a crucial issue. Indeed, there may be circumstances in which the establishment of new facts during the formal investigation procedure that lead to a change in the identification of the beneficiary may require that a supplementary or corrected opening decision be published.

As explained in section II.B.1 above, the New Recovery Notice touches on some of the situations that might give rise to difficulties in identifying beneficiaries but does

198. *See* section II.A.3 and footnote 140 of this Part One.

not deal with them in a systematic manner. For example, corporate changes in a recipient company that can occur between the granting of aid and a recovery decision are not precisely identified, let alone discussed in any detail. They continue to be confused with insolvency, and no distinction is drawn between events occurring before and those occurring after a recovery decision. For the sake of clarity, events that can affect beneficiaries after aid is granted (insolvency or winding-up) ought to be distinguished from events (*e.g.*, a transaction) that result in the transfer of the recovery obligation to a party other than the initial beneficiary.

Moreover, the New Recovery Notice does not contain a section relating to indirect aid, despite the specificities of recovery in these cases, which deserve to be examined in a methodological manner. The case law provides only very limited (and controversial) guidelines in this respect. Until very recently, the main reference was the 2009 judgment of the Court of First Instance (now the General Court) in the *Fineco Asset Management* case;[199] only in 2022, after the enactment of the New Recovery Notice, was it complemented by the Court of Justice's judgment in *Kingdom of Spain and others v. Commission* (the well-known tax lease case).[200]

In *Fineco Asset Management*, the Court of First Instance endorsed the Commission's choice to order repayment of the aid by the specialised investment vehicles or the fund managers (indirect beneficiaries) because they were the persons required by tax legislation to pay the substitute tax in question and, in their capacity as taxpayers, were the only possible interlocutors for the Italian Republic in the context of proceeding with the recovery. The Court of First Instance added that the specialised investment vehicles or the fund managers had the option of subsequently claiming repayment in turn from their investors or even from the State, in accordance with the provisions of national law. However, in the tax lease case, despite not referring explicitly to *Fineco Asset Management*, the Court held that the Commission (and the General Court) had erred in law by ordering Spain to recover the total aid amount from the investment vehicles and/or the investors after it had clearly emerged in the investigation – and the Commission had acknowledged in its reasoning – that most of the tax advantage had been compulsorily transferred to the shipping companies.

199. *See* Judgment of the Court of First Instance (Fifth Chamber) of 4 March 2009, Case T-445/05, EU:T:2009:50, paras 199-204. The judgment was not appealed before the Court of Justice and therefore became final. The measure under dispute envisaged amended tax treatment of certain undertakings for collective investment in transferable securities, which are specialised in shares in small- and medium-capitalisation companies listed on a regulated market of the EU ('specialised investment vehicles'). The capital revenue accruing to the specialised investment vehicles was to be subject to corporation tax at 5%, instead of at the standard rate of 12.5%. All Italian investment vehicles and the foreign undertakings for collective investment in transferable securities regulated by Council Directive 85/611/EEC could benefit from the reduced rate of 5%, provided that they were specialised in investing in stocks of small- and medium-capitalisation companies listed on a regulated European stock exchange ('small- and mid-caps'). The measure provided definitions of small- and medium-capitalisation companies and of specialised investment vehicles eligible for the aid.

200. *See* Judgment of the Court of Justice of 2 February 2023, Joined Cases C-649/20 P, C-658/20 P and C-662/20 P, cited in footnote 59 of this Part One, whereby the Court annulled the General Court's judgment under appeal and partially annulled the contested Commission's decision on the basis of an error in law when identifying the beneficiaries liable to repay the aid.

Although the implied refutation of the *Fineco Asset Management* ruling is, as mentioned, subsequent to the New Recovery Notice, in the latter the issue of identifying beneficiaries in cases of indirect aid is simply ignored. This shortcoming should be remedied as part of the reform by incorporating the most recent case law, especially the tax lease case. The latter, moreover, offers the possibility of further clarification concerning an issue once again ignored in the New Recovery Notice: that of contractual clauses intended to indemnify a party to a transaction from the economic consequences of a recovery decision addressed to several subjects, beneficiaries of indirect aid at different levels. In one of the General Court's judgments following the Court of Justice's ruling of February 2023, in the cases that were not selected as pilot cases,[201] the General Court clarified that national authorities must proceed with recovery from the actual direct or indirect beneficiaries and that, to this end, they must ensure that *the burden of restitution cannot be shifted to other parties by virtue of contractual clauses.*[202]

Moreover, the situation in other cases of indirect aid might very well be different from that examined in *Fineco Asset Management* and in the *tax lease* case in terms of the person required to pay a given tax, and the national authorities might have several interlocutors, not just one. Therefore, the solution endorsed by the Court of First Instance in *Fineco Asset Management* attracts criticism for several reasons. First, it is unclear how it would be possible to claim repayment from the State (as the Court affirms) given that the State, in effecting recovery, is only executing a Commission order and is therefore abiding by a duty under the Treaty. Second, the assumption that the legal persons required to repay aid in a given case can effectively sue other beneficiaries is often simply illusory and can give rise to disparities between beneficiaries of similar aid in different Member States depending on the national legislation, which is clearly unsatisfactory. Therefore, the solution to the problem of multiple beneficiaries at different levels of the economic chain is far from being clear and well-established – all the more reason why clarification and proposals from the Commission would be particularly welcome in that regard. In light of this, both an explicit refutation by the Court of the solution retained in *Fineco Asset Management* and a discussion of this issue in the New Recovery Notice would have been useful.

Similarly, the New Recovery Notice does not address issues related to aid granted as part of a scheme. Recovery of individual aid granted as part of a scheme deserves a methodological discussion, as it raises specific problems, which can differ depending on whether the unlawfulness of the individual aid stems from the unlawfulness of the scheme itself or from a misapplication of an existing (*e.g.*, previously approved) aid

---

201. *See* Judgment of the General Court of 8 May 2024, Joined Cases T-700/13 Joined Cases T-700/13, T-2/14, T-6/14, T-10/14, T-16/14, T-18/14, T-24/14, T-465/14, T-467/14, T-469/14, T-471/14, T-472/14, T-473/14, T-474/14, T-476/14, T-477/14, T-478/14, T-482/14, T-483/14, T-491/14, T-701/13, T-702/13, T-703/13, T-704/13, T-705/13, *Caixabank, SA and Vego Supermercados, SA v. European Commission*, EU:T:2024:295.
202. *Ibid.*, paras 96-127. The General Court rejected the applicants' argument that the Commission, in reminding the Spanish authorities of this principle in the contested decision, had exceeded its powers by declaring the clauses invalid. Instead, it is for the national authorities to determine the modalities (invalidity, nullity, ineffectiveness, *etc.*) by which the obligation to obtain restitution from all beneficiaries must be fulfilled.

scheme. The *Belgian excess profit* case[203] provides a clear example of the specific issues that the recovery of individual aid granted as part of a scheme can raise: How broad can the delegation of powers be? Who bears the burden of proof of the existence of a scheme?

Belgium contested the Commission's decision declaring the excess profit exemption scheme incompatible with the internal market and unlawful and ordering recovery of the aid from a list of beneficiaries that Belgium was required to submit to the Commission within two months from the date of notification of the decision. With its second plea, Belgium alleged an error of law and a manifest error of assessment, in that the Commission classified the measures as an aid scheme. Article 1(d) of Council Regulation (EU) 2015/1589 defines 'aid scheme' as follows:

> [A]ny act on the basis of which, *without further implementing measures being required* [emphasis added], individual aid awards may be made to undertakings defined within the act in a general and abstract manner and any act on the basis of which aid which is not linked to a specific project may be awarded to one or several undertakings for an indefinite period of time and/or for an indefinite amount.

In the case of an aid scheme, according to well-established case law, the Commission is not required to carry out an analysis of individual aid granted under the scheme. The Court held that:

> if individual aid awards are made without further implementing measures being adopted, the essential elements of the aid scheme in question must necessarily emerge from the provisions identified as the basis for the scheme.

Consequently, national authorities cannot have any margin of discretion as regards the determination of the essential elements of the aid in question and whether it should be awarded in a specific case.

National authorities may at most be vested with merely the power to carry out a technical assessment.[204] The Court noted that the existence of a margin of discretion could not be inferred from the mere fact that a prior request for approval had to be submitted to the competent tax authorities in order to benefit from an aid measure, as those authorities merely verified whether the applicant met the requisite criteria to become eligible for the aid. Given that the elements which, according to the Commission itself, constituted essential elements of the alleged aid scheme did not feature in the acts that supposedly constituted the legal basis of the scheme, the granting of the alleged aid necessarily depended on the adoption of implementing measures.[205]

Having found that the national tax authorities enjoyed a genuine margin of discretion - not merely a power to carry out a technical assessment - in deciding whether it was appropriate to grant the special tax treatment under discussion (downward adjustment of the normal tax rate), the Court concluded that the Belgian

203. Judgment of the General Court (Seventh Chamber, Extended Composition) of 14 February 2019, Cases T-131/16 and T-263/16, paras 79 and 90 ff.
204. *Ibid.*, paras 86-88.
205. *Ibid.*, para. 94.

excess profit system, as described in the contested decision, did not constitute an aid scheme.[206] This conclusion was further confirmed by the fact that the national tax authorities had a margin of discretion both in the determination of the amount to be exempted and in the definition of the beneficiaries – discretion which, based on statistical data, it appeared they actually exercised when granting or rejecting requests related to excess profit.[207]

The *Belgian excess profit* case implies that the Commission's power to order recovery by delegating to the national authorities the identification of the actual beneficiaries and the determination of the amount to be recovered from each is *not unlimited*. The Commission can confine itself to a general and abstract assessment of a given measure, without going into the details of each individual aid award, only if the measure qualifies as a genuine aid scheme because all the essential elements of the aid are pre-determined by the national law concerned and no margin of discretion whatsoever (other than that of a merely technical nature) is left to the national authorities applying the scheme.

In analysing the existence of a margin of discretion, it is irrelevant whether a request to obtain the aid award must be submitted to the tax authorities; the only key element is the margin of discretion that those authorities have with regard to essential features of the aid. Moreover, the Commission bears the burden of proving that no margin of discretion exists if it wants to order recovery in general and abstract terms and leave the identification of beneficiaries and determination of the recoverable amounts to the execution phase of the recovery decision – and thus to the national authorities concerned.

III.A.3 Clarification on the Possible Extension of the Recovery Obligation to the Multinational Group to Which the Aid Beneficiary Belongs

The New Recovery Notice introduces some clarification concerning situations in which beneficiaries belong to multinational (or, more precisely, diversified) groups of undertakings. In State aid law, and more generally in competition law, an undertaking's legal personality is irrelevant because what matters is the notion of economic unit and the ongoing business. This, however, does not mean that it is unnecessary to identify the actual beneficiary business. Quite the opposite: precise identification of the actual beneficiary is key to assessing the potential harm to competition and trade and to weighing the potential benefits that the aid may produce in terms of overcoming market failures or pursuing efficiency or equity objectives.

Likewise, precise identification of the actual beneficiary must drive the application of remedies: first and foremost, the recovery of unlawful and incompatible aid. Indeed, according to the case law discussed extensively above,[208] recovery is not a penalty but rather the natural consequence of the granting of an undue advantage, which needs to be forfeited to restore undistorted competition and trade. This marks a

206. *Ibid.*, para. 104.
207. *Ibid.*, paras 110-112 and 114-116.
208. *See* section I.A.2.6 and footnotes 47-48 of this Part One.

significant difference from other areas of competition law. When a competition law penalty is imposed in the form of a fine, it is unquestionable that, for the penalty to be effective, the liability for payment of the fine should be linked to the responsibility for the conduct being penalised. Hence, both the legal entity that engaged in the illicit conduct and the other legal entity or entities that exercised decisive influence over the former's business in the relevant period (*i.e.*, when the illicit conduct occurred) must be held liable for payment of the fine (joint and several liability). The EU courts have developed extensive and detailed case law to clarify when decisive influence exists, when it can be presumed, and who bears the burden of proof in this respect.

The situation is entirely different, however, when the amount to be paid is not a fine but the mere repayment of a previous grant, as in State aid law. In this case, the liability for repayment/reimbursement *is not linked to the responsibility for the given conduct but rather to the grant's destination.* What really matters is where (*i.e.*, in which business and market) the aid produced its effects, as these effects need to be forfeited. Notably, this issue is independent of the calculation of the aid recovery amount: even if, contrary to this author's opinion,[209] a formalistic approach were to be followed in determining the amount to be recovered (in accordance with the *Ryanair/Aer Lingus* case law),[210] this would not justify following a similarly formalistic approach when identifying the legal persons liable for repaying the aid.

It follows that, in principle, parental liability is possible for the recovery of unlawful aid only in very specific circumstances, *i.e.*, when there is documented evidence of a transfer of the advantage from the aid recipient to the holding company or parent group, or to related companies. But even in this case, each company should be liable for the part of the advantage that it gained - it would be meaningless to establish joint and several liability for all of them for the whole amount, at least in the framework of public enforcement. The clarification in the New Recovery Notice must be considered on this basis.

The New Recovery Notice indeed devotes a section to the identification of the aid beneficiary when it belongs to a group of undertakings, but it provides no conceptual guidance. The premise of this entire section ('where certain transactions occurred within a group of undertakings') is already unclear. This premise cannot be understood as referring to the case of aid elements that stem from intra-group transactions (*e.g.*, cross-subsidisation within a publicly owned group), as in such a case, the very opposite would be true: it would be imperative to recover the aid from the group entity that received it, and repayment would have to be made to the group's controlling entity, as recovering the aid from the controlling entity instead of from the subsidiary would be tantamount to granting the latter new aid to repay the previous one. Therefore, the only possible interpretation of the premise is that, if certain transactions occurred between the recipient entity and other companies within the same group *after the granting of the aid*, the Commission may either limit the scope of recovery to only one aid beneficiary within the group or conclude that the aid was transferred partially or totally to other

209. *See* sections I.A.2.5. and I.A.2.6. of this Part One.
210. *See* footnotes 29, 150 and 151 of this Part One.

companies belonging to the group and seek recovery from the latter.[211] This is perfectly logical and attracts no criticism.

However, in paragraph 87, the Commission adds that in the case referred to in paragraph 86, the recovery decision may order the Member State concerned to recover the aid not only from the undertaking which directly benefitted from it but also:

> from the whole group of undertakings forming an economic unit or from some of the legal entities belonging to it that also benefitted from the aid.

While the second part of this sentence is an unnecessary repetition of the concept in paragraph 86, the first part is flawed. It is hard to follow the Commission's reasoning on this point. The fact that a group of undertakings forms an economic unit has no bearing on the principles of recovery - namely, the objective of forfeiting the aid's effect - and is even at odds with the approach taken in the New Recovery Notice itself. Indeed, if recovery from the group was considered equivalent to recovery from the actual recipient, recovery could always be imposed on the group, and there would be no point in limiting this possibility to the circumstances described in paragraphs 85 and 86.[212] The case of aid in the form of cross-subsidisation within a publicly owned undertaking is particularly illustrative of the incongruity in paragraph 87, as in this case - and as mentioned above - the subsidiary would be ordered to repay the aid to the controlling entity that subsidised it.[213]

All in all, paragraphs 86 and 87 of the New Recovery Notice are not entirely clear and should be rephrased. However, what is more important is to clarify the relevance of the concept of economic unit in the field of recovery - which, as everyone knows, is a restorative remedy and is not considered a penalty. It is possible that the concept of economic unit has some relevance for ancillary remedies, but it is certainly of little help in the case of recovery, except in the very specific situation described above (*i.e.*, transactions between entities belonging to the same group of undertakings that occur after the granting of the aid) or in exceptional circumstances linked to the winding-up of the beneficiary.

As to ancillary remedies, a distinction must be drawn between application of the *Deggendorf* doctrine and the fines or other penalties levied under Article 260 TFEU for failure to comply with a final judgment confirming a recovery decision. As to cases in which the *Deggendorf* doctrine is to be applied, the limits that should be observed when

211. New Recovery Notice, cited in footnotes 125 of this Part One, paras 85-86.
212. It is true that the parent entity or holding company could always decide to capitalise the subsidiary for an amount equivalent to that of the aid to be repaid, thus nullifying the effects of recovery, but it is also true that, in the first place, such an operation is not always so immediate or easy - especially if there are other shareholders or if the parent entity or holding company is not in an optimal financial situation - and, in any event, there would be no reason to neutralise the effect of recovery on the business that actually benefitted from it through a Commission recovery decision rather than leaving the possible decision to inject new capital into the subsidiary to the parent entity or holding company's private discretion.
213. The case law offers numerous examples of this situation. *See, ex multis*: Judgment of the Court of Justice of 21 March 1991, Case C-305/89, *Italy v. Commission of the European Communities*, EU:C:1991:142; and Judgment of the General Court of 20 March 2015, T-456/13, *Sea Handling*, OJ C 155, 11.5.2015, p. 24.

referring to the concept of group have already been discussed (*see* section I.B.1). Conversely, the concept of group of undertakings can indeed be relevant in the case of levying fines or other penalties and, likewise, can be relevant in the case of penalties due to incomplete, elusive or misleading information provided during an investigation.

III.A.4 Failure to Address Some Conceptual Issues That Are Key to a Convincing Systematisation of Remedies

Three critical issues of a conceptual nature have emerged from the analysis carried out earlier in this book.

The first is whether the concept of an 'advantage' to be recovered is to be understood in a financial/nominal way or in an economic way. The New Recovery Notice, based on the recent case law, appears to endorse the first option, but hesitations and inconsistencies still surface from both the New Recovery Notice and the case law.[214] It is argued above that an economic concept of advantage to be recovered would be more in line with secondary law (recital 25 of the Procedural Regulation) and with the recovery system's underlying rationale. However, this controversy is too strictly related to the reform of the system of remedies for a position to be taken in abstract terms. Only once the main pillars of the reform have been shaped will it be possible to define the concept of advantage to be recovered in a manner consistent with the overall legal framework proposed. This issue is therefore at the heart of the debate in the final part of this book.

The second critical issue is the role to be played by ancillary remedies. Ancillary remedies, namely the *Deggendorf* doctrine and application of the system of penalties in the case of unrecovered aid, have developed over time as a response to specific circumstances that threatened the effectiveness of the system of remedies. However, this development - which, as mentioned, was driven by effectiveness-related concerns, and was without a systematic approach or a strong theoretical basis - resulted in several inconsistencies, as outlined in the previous sections. Here too, only once there is a precise view of the direction the reform is to take will the role of ancillary remedies become clear. Indeed, only on that basis will it be possible to assess the present status of the Commission practice and the case law.

The third critical issue concerns the limits to recovery, and in particular the distinction between external and internal limits and the consequences thereof. External (or extrinsic) limits to recovery refer to exceptions justified by the need to reconcile the application of remedies for breach of State aid law with other interests protected under EU law. The general principles of Union law referred to (though not enumerated) under Article 16(1) of the Procedural Regulation are the expression of such interests, which can be summarised as the stability and certainty of the legal system. It is intuitive that when these interests are at stake, application of the State aid system of remedies must give way to them.

214. *See* section II.A.3 of this Part One.

When a conflict arises between these interests and application of the system of remedies, the former prevails, and the legal system's response is that the aid should not be recovered. A recovery decision adopted in these circumstances would be invalid. However, the conflict might be only partial in nature or might not exist in relation to ancillary remedies. Furthermore, a conflict might arise if application of a given remedy slips toward becoming a penalty. Once more, it is necessary to first define the pillars and rationale underlying the reform of the system of remedies - only then will a consistent interpretation of the extrinsic limits to recovery become possible.

The situation is completely different for internal (or intrinsic) limits, which relate to the concept of absolute impossibility. Absolute impossibility - whether total or partial in scope and whether permanent or temporary in duration - is an expression of the force majeure defence. It refers to exceptional circumstances that make it impossible for the national authorities to obtain repayment of aid from the beneficiary. Absolute impossibility means that, because of circumstances inherent to the specific aid in question, the recovery order cannot be executed - but it is not a legal derogation. In other words, it is not the expression of a balance of interests but rather a mere finding of an exceptional situation. Only with these ideas in mind will it be possible in the final part of this book to define the boundaries and consequences of the absolute impossibility limitation within the framework of a reform of the system of remedies. This also entails a correct reading of the *Montessori* judgment, which has been subject to misleading interpretations so far.

III.A.5 Failure to Address the Procedural Shortcomings of the System of Remedies

The need for reform is no less felt when it comes to the procedural rules on recovery. The New Recovery Notice devotes little attention to procedural issues. It refers to the time limit for the execution of recovery decisions - which was the subject of debate during the public consultation - and makes it clear that this time limit can be adapted to the circumstances, but it does not even attempt to explain under which circumstances the four-month time limit for the execution of the recovery order can be extended or suspended. More importantly, the promptness in executing a recovery order is only one of the procedural issues related to the recovery system - and certainly not the most important one.

The main shortcoming of the present system from a procedural viewpoint is the lack of rules on the verification of the correct implementation of negative decisions. As negative decisions are increasingly not self-sufficient - *i.e.*, they increasingly rely on cooperation with national authorities in implementing the recovery orders (especially, but not only, in the case of aid schemes) - it is surprising that no effort has been made to develop the sincere cooperation principle and set out a procedural framework for this cooperation and for the Commission's verification of the correct execution of recovery orders by national authorities. A very significant loophole remains in this respect in the State aid *corpus juris* - this issue cannot be avoided when reflecting on a comprehensive reform of the State aid system of remedies.

An additional issue to be addressed concerning the effective enforcement/ execution of Commission decisions ordering the recovery of unlawful aid is the interplay between national and EU courts when the beneficiaries from which the aid must be recovered challenge the Commission's decisions – either directly before the General Court or indirectly before national courts. The *Deggendorf I* and *Georgsmarienhütte* judgments should prompt a clarification of the power of judicial review over the imposition of remedies. The judicial review should indeed embrace all aspects of the remedies, in respect of both their content and the decision-making that led to their adoption. A comprehensive reform of the system of remedies must necessarily include a check of the effective legal protection granted to beneficiaries and will require a systematisation and clarification of the principles stemming from the case law.

III.B Convergent and Dissenting Opinions on the Weaknesses of the Recovery System among Legal Scholars

Before analysing and discussing the various paths of reform to address all the shortcomings described above, it is worth looking at legal scholarship in the field to check whether there is consensus on the need for reform and, if so, on what the reform's extent should be. Although only a few articles have been published on the New Recovery Notice, all authors from outside the Commission acknowledge the existence of uncertainties and advocate for at least some clarification on specific aspects of the New Recovery Notice.

J. Blockx recalls that during consultation on the draft notice, several stakeholders requested that the Commission take more responsibility in identifying the beneficiaries and calculating the amounts to be recovered.[215] He states that the sharing of competences between the Commission and the Member States in this respect remains 'a thorny issue'. The same author refers to the concept of 'without too much difficulty' (or 'without overmuch difficulty', which is the expression used in the New Recovery Notice and referred to by Blockx) and observes that it 'can raise serious problems' and lead to 'protracted litigation which could have been avoided if the amount had been calculated more clearly in the recovery Decision'. Furthermore, the leeway that the Commission enjoys in the case of aid schemes, where early identification of beneficiaries might not be possible and is in any event not an obligation for the Commission, 'could create a temptation for the Commission to categorize an aid measure in its recovery Decision as a scheme rather than as one or more individual measures' – a practice that the General Court criticised in the recent *Belgian excess profit* case. Blockx also echoes the criticism that some stakeholders expressed during public consultation on the draft notice with respect to the 'one-sided' description of instances in which general principles of EU law prevent recovery under Article 16(1) of Council Regulation (EU) 2015/1589. He does not, however, put forward proposals as to the correct interpretative approach in applying this derogation.

215. J. Blockx, *New State Aid Recovery Notice (Obtaining a Pound of Flesh (Without a Jot of Blood?)*, in European State Aid Law Quarterly (EStAL), 2019, Issue 4, p. 540 https://doi.org/10.21552/estal/2019/4/10.

Similarly, although the author does not propose any way forward, he advocates for a revision, or at least a refinement, of the approach taken in the New Recovery Notice with respect to the interplay between recovery and insolvency proceedings. According to Blockx, Member States 'cannot choose to forego recovery of the aid in light of other considerations' (other than removal of the distortion of competition that the aid triggered). This applies even to their 'own financial interest' if that interest would be better served by preserving the beneficiary's ongoing business instead of pursuing the beneficiary's winding-up and the definitive cessation of its activities. This seems to imply that the activities of 'the original beneficiary cannot be transferred as a going concern to a third party'. This is problematic – Blockx argues – in light of the objectives of insolvency legislation, because 'insolvency proceedings are often understood as not merely aiming at the protection of individual creditors (which include the Member State recovering State aid), but also take into account the interests of the group of creditors as a whole and other stakeholders, such as the employees of the undertaking'.

Blockx further submits that this problem with the Commission's policy to pursue 'obstinate recovery of State aid' even in exceptional circumstances has become more acute with the entry into force of the new Directive on Restructuring and Insolvency.[216] Indeed, the directive introduces in EU law 'the idea that the rights of individual creditors ... cannot always take priority', as Member States now 'have to ensure that debtors have access to a preventive restructuring framework to avoid insolvency and ensure their viability, thereby protecting jobs and maintaining business activity'.

To sum up, Blockx advocates for a refinement or revision of the approach taken by the Commission in the New Recovery Notice, at least with respect to: (i) the interplay between recovery proceedings and insolvency; (ii) the limits to recovery; and (iii) the notion of 'without overmuch difficulty'.

Even before the adoption of the Directive on Restructuring and Insolvency, Advocate General Sharpston had already questioned the Commission's policy on recovery when it results in forcing undertakings that would otherwise be viable and could continue operating to wind up and exit the market.[217] Although the Advocate General did not go as far as suggesting a reform of the recovery system, she admitted that she found it 'inherently repugnant' that, within a system that aims at economic growth and full employment, 'undertakings that could otherwise be viable must cease operating, with the consequent loss of jobs'.[218] She, therefore, considered that 'in principle a Member State may envisage relaunching the activities of the beneficiary of an unlawful State aid' when a number of exceptional conditions are met: the first (and

216. Directive 2019/1023 of 20 June 2019 on preventive restructuring frameworks, on discharge of debt and disqualifications, and on measures to increase the efficiency of procedures concerning restructuring, insolvency and discharge of debt, and amending Directive 2017/1132, OJ L172/18.

217. Opinion delivered on 10 October 2017, Case C-363/16, *European Commission v. Hellenic Republic*, EU:C:2017:746. Although the Court does not echo the Advocate General's concerns in its judgment, its dismissal of the Hellenic Republic's defensive arguments is based on other grounds; the Court thus did not address the issue under discussion here.

218. *Ibid.*, para. 87.

most important) being that the aid can be repaid in full during the insolvency proceedings.[219]

The views expressed by Blockx and Sharpston concern specific aspects of the Commission's policy and do not aim to provide a comprehensive assessment of the recovery system, let alone an assessment of the whole system of remedies for breach of State aid rules. Nevertheless, they are worth considering and exploring further. Some indication that the criticism expressed by Blockx and Sharpston has not remained completely unheard can already be found in the recent case law. Indeed, the EU courts are not only willing to grant interim measures to suspend a recovery order when its implementation would trigger insolvency proceedings[220] but they also seem to accept that the winding-up of a beneficiary due to a recovery order is an acceptable and inevitable outcome only if full repayment of the unlawful aid cannot be obtained in the course of the insolvency proceedings.[221] This is perhaps only the first step and opens up interesting scenarios for business continuity, obviously under strict conditions and only if a beneficiary's insolvency is due solely to the execution of a recovery order.

However, the need for a thorough assessment of the interplay between insolvency and recovery goes even beyond the concerns expressed by Blockx and Sharpston, because the inadequacies of the present system do not stop there. For example, when Blockx argues that Member States cannot choose to forego recovery of the aid in light of other considerations, even their own financial interest as lenders or shareholders of the beneficiary, this necessarily implies that also the Market Economy Operator Principle ('*MEOP*') is inapplicable when assessing whether a Member State complies with a recovery decision. This might be a sound approach – but it is without a doubt something that needs to be deeply considered in light of the rationale of State aid law and that should have been clarified in the New Recovery Notice.

Opinions from inside the Commission Services should also be examined here. According to S. Donzelli, who has authored various contributions in the field, including for the State aid briefs published by the Competition Directorate-General of the European Commission,[222] the New Recovery Notice is 'a comprehensive tool to enforce State aid rules', which contributes 'to the correct recovery of unlawful aid'. It is, of course, understandable that the Commission Services involved in drafting the New Recovery Notice praise the achievement. Still, some of Donzelli's explanations of the position adopted by the Commission do nothing but emphasise the need to further analyse several topics related to the recovery system and to achieve a more complete reform of the system of remedies for breach of State aid rules.

219. *Ibid.*, paras 89-90.
220. *See* Order of the President of the General Court of 13 March 2020, Case T-603/19 R, *Helsingin Bussiliikenne Oy v. European Commission*, EU:T:2020:110, para. 26 and related case law.
221. *See* Judgment of the Court of 17 January 2018, Case C-363/16, *European Commission v. Hellenic Republic*, cited in footnotes 94 and 95 of this Part One.
222. S. Donzelli, *The 2019 Commission Notice on the Recovery of Unlawful and Incompatible State Aid*, Competition state aid brief: Occasional papers by the Competition Directorate-General of the European Commission, October 2019, Issue 1. By the same author, *see also The Commission's New Recovery Notice: A Handbook for the Recovery of Unlawful and Incompatible Aid*, European State Aid Law Quarterly (EStAL), 2019, Issue 4, pp. 528-539 https://doi.org/10.21552/estal/2019/4/9.

To cite just one example, Donzelli's recurring reference to the principle of sincere cooperation as the New Recovery Notice's underlying rationale and as one of the most important changes it introduces is perfectly in line with the message that the Commission wants to convey, *i.e.*, that sincere cooperation is one of the pillars of SAM. Nonetheless, there is no clear indication of the practical consequences of this approach - which is not surprising, as very little has changed in practice since the adoption of the New Recovery Notice when it comes to the sharing of competences and tasks between the Commission and Member States. Moreover, Donzelli does not explain why the Commission has not even attempted to elaborate on the principle of sincere cooperation in the New Enforcement Notice, especially when it comes to the verification of the correct implementation of recovery orders.

In any case, Donzelli does not miss the opportunity to recall that transparency and sincere cooperation can characterise only the bilateral dialogue between the Commission and the Member States. He underlines that 'there is no scope for a duty of sincere cooperation between the Commission and aid recipients' and concludes that 'the dialogue remains bilateral even during the recovery phase, as that is the way it has been designed by the Member States in the Treaties'. However, the author adds nothing to explain this surprising statement.[223]

Unfortunately, it is true that, thus far, the EU courts have endorsed the bilateral nature of all State aid procedures (which, to be clear, has no foundation in the Treaty beyond the mere fact that State aid rules are, obviously, addressed to the Member States and that the second sentence of Article 108(2) TFEU sets out an infringement procedure that derogates from the ordinary procedure)[224] and have not elaborated on the scope and limits of this bilateral nature. However, presenting this feature as a key component of 'a *modern system* of supervision of State aid' (emphasis added) appears to be almost provocative in nature and, in any case, is a totally unsupported statement. It certainly cannot be justified by fears that 'a specific cooperation between the Commission and a certain aid beneficiary may risk to unduly interfere [sic] with the autonomy of the Member State concerned' or that, because recovery is an obligation of result and an assessment of the execution of a recovery order requires cooperation between the Commission and the Member State concerned, 'a cooperation with an aid beneficiary ... may easily create controversy about ... the recovery measures taken by the Member State'.

How cooperation with an aid beneficiary would interfere with a Member State's autonomy is unclear. If the reference to autonomy is to be understood as the Member State's procedural autonomy under Article 16(3) of the Procedural Regulation, whatever the beneficiary might bring to the discussion regarding the execution of the recovery obligation would, of course, have no bearing on the application of national procedural rules. Typically, the beneficiary might have something to say on the

223. As is well known, recovery is not even mentioned as a remedy in the Treaty; therefore, nothing can be found in the Treaty as to the organisation of recovery procedures.
224. Since its landmark judgment in *Commission v. Italy* (better known as the 'Italian textile case'), Case C-173/73, EU:C:1974:71, the Court of Justice has acknowledged the autonomous nature of this provision with respect to the ordinary infringement procedure under Art. 258 TFEU.

methods of recovery, the calculation of the amount to be recovered, the identification of the legal person or persons liable for repayment of the aid and, in specific circumstances, on a claim of absolute impossibility, whether total or partial in scope and whether permanent or temporary in duration. No matter which of these arguments is used, the beneficiary's views would not prevent the Member State from choosing how to comply with its obligation to ensure recovery - nor the Commission from assessing the Member State's chosen method.

Even less clear is why the fact that recovery is an obligation of result and requires cooperation between the Commission and the Member State concerned should prevent the beneficiary from expressing its views, or how the beneficiary's views would create conflict between the Commission and the Member State.

Similarly, Donzelli's rebuttal of whatever criticism legal scholars have expressed on how the New Recovery Notice deals with the general principles of EU law does not obscure the need for a deeper analysis of this issue. Indeed, the New Recovery Notice's section on the general principles of EU law is arguably the weakest part of the document, for the reasons outlined above.[225] If anything, Donzelli acknowledges that the New Recovery Notice simply provides examples of circumstances that the EU courts found *insufficient* to support a claim for infringement of the principles of legal certainty and protection of legitimate expectations. For some reason, opposite examples are not provided - therefore, Donzelli's conclusion that the New Recovery Notice helps Member States and interested parties to better assess their situation is questionable.

As far as the principle of *res judicata* is concerned, Donzelli emphasises that the New Recovery Notice appears to have duly considered the comments submitted during public consultation, as the final wording is more nuanced compared to the draft wording. The fact remains, however, that the New Recovery Notice provides no clear and conclusive indication of how the application of the principle of *res judicata* can be reconciled with the primacy of EU law and the effectiveness of recovery decisions - in other words, under which circumstances national court decisions can no longer be called into question by State aid investigations under Article 16(1) of the Procedural Regulation.

More importantly, legal scholars, including scholars from inside the Commission, appear to unanimously agree that the goal of Article 16 is to remedy the distortion of competition in the internal market in a timely manner so as to avoid creating incentives for subsidy races and prejudicing the market's very functioning. It is sometimes difficult, however, to reconcile this approach with the position taken by the Commission in relation to specific circumstances. To give just one example: requiring a Member State to force an insolvent beneficiary to wind up by the recovery deadline, irrespective of the reasons for the insolvency and the length of insolvency proceedings (thereby making it impossible for the Member State to enter into any sort of arrangement with creditors), is a formalistic approach that takes no account of the economic reality or of the finding of actual competition distortions to be remedied.

225. *See* section II.B.2 of this Part One.

Additionally, this approach conflicts with other provisions of secondary EU law, such as Regulation (EU) 2015/848 on insolvency proceedings[226] and the Directive on Restructuring and Insolvency.[227] Justifying the Commission's formalistic approach to insolvency and recovery by simply saying that secondary law on insolvency proceedings and the rules on recovery of unlawful aid have different purposes and can coexist - on the assumption that the rules on recovery are *lex specialis*[228] compared to those on insolvency - completely misses the point. It is precisely because the two sets of rules pursue completely different objectives that no *lex specialis/lex generalis* relationship can exist between them.

Recovery is designed to remedy the distortion of competition caused by the granting of unlawful aid. As a redressive - not punitive - tool, it should target concrete distortions that negatively affect the common interest. Given that EU law sees insolvency proceedings as, among other things, a means to restore the viability of companies, this intended design can certainly not be ignored. The objective to achieve effective recovery should therefore prevail because it remedies a previous unlawfulness only when an actual distortion of competition exists that needs to (and can) be removed.

In light of the Commission's extremely conservative approach to the New Recovery Notice and the number of shortcomings and ambiguities concerning the position of third parties, it can only sound surprising that Donzelli, despite his valuable analysis, describes the New Recovery Notice's objective as that of not only providing guidance for Member States but also of assisting 'practitioners and interested parties' in effectively and timely implementing recovery decisions.[229] It is hard to see what kind of assistance practitioners or interested parties can draw from the New Recovery Notice given its conservative approach and its unilateral interpretation of case law. Furthermore, interested parties are excluded from the recovery procedure altogether and are prevented from accessing the case file - even in the recovery phase, when beneficiaries are clearly identified and subject to the repayment obligation.

Conversely, Donzelli is certainly right when he concludes that, given the dynamism of the regulatory framework that the modernisation process entails and the shift toward group exemptions and upstream assessments of State aid, 'very few arguments can be made to exclude or delay recovery'.[230] More precisely, it makes sense - given the number of exemptions available and the continuous effort the Commission is making to streamline notification procedures for the handful of cases that still need to be notified - for the recovery system (and, more generally, the system of remedies) to be designed and applied rigorously to unlawfully granted aid.

With that in mind, it is now time for a more in-depth examination of the interplay between the system of remedies and the modernisation process. As clearly emerges

226. Regulation (EU) 2015/848 of the European Parliament and of the Council of 20 May 2015 on insolvency proceedings, OJ L 141, 5.6.2015, p. 19.
227. Directive 2019/1023 of 20 June 2019, OJ L 172, 26.6.2019, p. 18.
228. *See* Donzelli, *The Commission's New Recovery Notice: A Handbook for the Recovery of Unlawful and Incompatible Aid*, cited in footnote 222 of this Part One.
229. *Ibid.*
230. *Ibid.*

below, legal scholars almost unanimously regret that modernisation has not sufficiently touched on procedural issues, including the system of remedies.

III.C Interplay Between the Modernisation Process and the Reform of the System of Remedies and Related Opinions in Legal Scholarship

There are both political and legal reasons for including a reform of the system of remedies in the SAM process. Until now, the only two initiatives the Commission has taken in this respect are the adoption of the New Recovery Notice, which is discussed in the previous sections, and the 2021 Notice on the enforcement of State aid by national courts, based on an April 2019 report on private enforcement,[231] which is examined in Part Two of this book.[232] Regardless of all the New Recovery Notice's weaknesses, these measures are insufficient. The Commission itself acknowledges that although private enforcement can certainly play a role, it 'remains marginal in the context of recovery policy'.[233]

All in all, the Commission's initiatives miss the chance of carrying out a comprehensive review of the recovery system and ancillary remedies. They do not address some of the crucial loopholes and ambiguities in the 2007 Recovery Notice and, more importantly, seem to lack a holistic view of the trends seen in State aid control. The Commission takes a conservative approach to assessing the need for reform and considers remedies in isolation, without exploring the current system's adequacy in dealing with new forms of State intervention, the new role of State aid control in the EU legal system, the new enforcement priorities or, ultimately, the new policy issues that are at the heart of today's debate. This inevitably results in a rearguard approach to reform.

With this criticism in mind, the present chapter first highlights the reasons for reform of the system of remedies in light of modernisation and explains why the alleged increase in transparency not only remains mostly unachieved but is also – and in any event – insufficient to serve modernisation objectives. It subsequently explains that the current procedural setting, with the very limited reforms introduced within the framework of the SAM initiative, is unsuitable for achieving those objectives. An excursus on the weaknesses inherent in the current enforcement paradigm, even beyond remedies, is then needed to help clarify the crucial nature of a reform of the system of remedies to ensure deterrence and effectiveness. That is followed by a discussion of whether increased cooperation with Member States' authorities and broader discretion given to the Commission in shaping the most appropriate remedies in connection with the circumstances of a given case can be suitable alternative means of promoting deterrence and effectiveness.

231. G. Monti et al., *Study on the Enforcement of State Aid Rules and Decisions by National Courts: Final Study*, Publications Office, 2019.
232. Communication from the Commission – Commission Notice on the enforcement of State aid rules by national courts, OJ C 305, 30.7.2021, pp. 1-28.
233. *Ibid.*

III.C.1 Political Reasons for Reform in Light of Modernisation

The political reasons in favour of a comprehensive reform of the system of remedies within the framework of SAM are threefold. First, a complete and solid system of remedies is part of the backbone of any legal system and essential to efficient enforcement – it should therefore necessarily evolve alongside the progress of the set of substantive rules in the given area of law. Second, the gap that has been created over time between a modernised *corpus juris* of substantive (and partly procedural) rules on the one side and an obsolete system of remedies on the other has made the latter totally inadequate to serve the new aims and mission that the legislator and policymakers have envisaged for State aid control. Third, the shift from *ex-ante* to *ex-post* control – which is an essential component of SAM's procedural side and is discussed in depth below – necessarily implies a change in the remedies enforcement paradigm employed thus far.

Now that national authorities are involved in determining the scope of a recovery order, as discussed above,[234] and even in detecting infringements or irregularities,[235] and now that the vast majority (above 95%, and increasing further) of granted aid escapes preventive screening and is subject only to sample-based, random *ex-post* review, it is meaningless to remain tied to a system of remedies designed for a completely different enforcement paradigm. National authorities can and should contribute to a precise determination of the effects of unlawful and incompatible aid and subsequently identify the most appropriate remedial actions. At the same time, when *ex-post* review provides a comprehensive overview of infringements and/or irregularities in a given market and it appears that they are recurrent or systematic, there are certain actions that serve the deterrence objective better than individual recovery – the latter remaining a possible tool for when a specific market distortion exists that should be removed.

The system of remedies has remained basically unchanged since the first two phases of modernisation, which took place in the late nineties and in the first decade of this century, respectively. Secondary law on recovery dates back to the first phase, with the adoption of the first Procedural Regulation.[236] Not even a word of the provision on recovery has changed in over twenty years. Soft law on recovery coincides with the second phase of modernisation, as it was implemented within the framework of the 2005-2009 *SAAP* with the adoption of the 2007 Recovery Notice. Though it was drafted twelve years later, the New Recovery Notice retains the same backbone, just as it retains most of the same crucial components. The New Recovery Notice puts forward only some (sometimes questionable) clarification and a limited number of slight adaptations. This lack of evolution contrasts with the huge developments in almost all other areas of State aid law. In the last twelve years, and even more if one considers the last twenty years, the underlying set of rules (secondary law and soft law, and partly

234. *See* sections II.A.2 and II.A.3.
235. *See* footnote 274 of this Part One.
236. *See* footnote 17 of this Part One.

also primary law) have gone through revolutionary changes, as have enforcement practice and case law.

This gap is even more evident if one looks at the new objectives of State aid control as shaped by the modernisation process. State aid rules are designed to prevent waste of financial resources and budgetary problems and to instead contribute to fostering investments in projects of common interest and concentrating resources on horizontal objectives in line with the Union's priorities. Nobody understands how a system of remedies that offers no protection to investors can ever contribute to attaining these objectives. Indeed, companies are not only excluded from review proceedings (even in the recovery stage), which remain bilateral between the granting Member State and the Commission but are also not allowed to submit proposals as to how to remove competition distortions, address competition concerns or forfeit the real advantage gained. They have no guarantee that the real market situation and the distortions the aid has (or has not) effectively caused will play any role in the Commission's assessment. Indeed, this happens only in very exceptional circumstances involving indirect aid: basically, when the Commission delegates powers to the Member State concerned not only to identify beneficiaries and calculate the amounts to be recovered but also to verify the aid's impact on competition and trade.

III.C.2 Legal Criticism of the Current Status of the System of Remedies in Light of Modernisation Objectives

Unsurprisingly, in light of the present status of the system of remedies, scholars consider the granting of State aid to be a win-win situation for the Member State concerned.[237] This observation dates back to the first phases of modernisation and is clearly even more justified today. Investors that contribute equity to an undertaking benefitting from aid - and the financial institutions that lend money to investors on the assumption of the advantage granted by the aid - are indeed more exposed to the risks entailed by a violation of State aid provisions than the Member States which are the target of those provisions, and which are responsible for their breach. Legal scholars have almost unanimously flagged this crucial issue.

C. Koenig and J. Lindner refer to this concern as the 'problem of enriching the malefactor'.[238] Indeed, the unlawful conduct of the Member State granting the aid results in its own enrichment given that the aid is repaid once its economic and social effects (which, from the Member State's perspective, are the objectives of granting the aid) have been achieved.[239] In an effort to address the problem of the lack of incentives

237. J. Lever, *The EC State Aid Regime: The Need for Reform*, in A. Biondi, P. Eeckhout and J. Flynn eds, 'The Law of State Aid in the European Union', Oxford University Press, 2004, p. 304.
238. C. Koenig and J. Lindner, *Criminal Liability: An Efficient Tool of EU State Aid Law Enforcement?* in European State Aid Law Quarterly (EStAL), 2015, Issue 1, p. 19.
239. *Ibid*. The authors note as follows:

> [T]here is a lack of effective incentives for Member States to prevent unlawful State aid *ex ante*, whereas the prospective State aid beneficiaries often do not even know that the aid they receive is non-compliant with EU State aid rules and, even if they know, there

for Member States to cooperate, the lamented J. Temple Lang, in his analysis of the need for substantive reform of EU State aid law (published in 2014), proposes two radical - yet impracticable today, absent a comprehensive reform - options. He suggests introducing an automatic fine to be levied on the Member State or the public entity responsible for the breach of State aid law or, alternatively, an explicit provision under EU law envisaging Member States' or public entities' general liability for damage to competitors of recipients of unlawful aid. All parties capable of proving damage would thus be able to seek and obtain compensation through private enforcement before national courts.[240]

J. Lever - to cite another very distinguished voice in the legal debate - takes it even a step further. In linking the inadequacy of the system of remedies to the many other deficiencies of the procedural framework in State aid law, he explains that this situation weakens the credibility of the entire State aid body of law.[241] Similar criticism is expressed by A. Sánchez-Graells, who also points to the need for a comprehensive rethinking of the procedural framework, which includes the application of remedies, to revitalise State aid control and adapt it to present times.[242] What is particularly interesting about Sánchez-Graells' analysis in connection with this book's topic is his critical assessment of the procedural framework in light of modernisation's objective, which he describes as that of revitalising State aid control. He considers the post-SAM procedural framework totally inadequate to support a scenario of stronger enforcement to overcome the previous relaxation due to the 2007-2008 financial crisis.

There is no need to take a position here on whether it is historically convincing to depict the SAM process as a strategy undertaken by the Commission 'to overcome ... the temporary rules resulting from the crisis and as an attempt to ensure the relevance and effectiveness of the EU State aid control regime in the post-crisis scenario'. It is at least one of the plausible explanations, considering the timing of the SAM Communication. However, irrespective of the answer to this question, it seems hard to dispute Sánchez-Graells' conclusion that the financial crisis further reduced whatever previous levels of effectiveness of non-crisis State aid control there were.

The author puts forward strong statistical and legal arguments to support his statement, especially as far as the 'structural inefficiency of State aid control' under the

is no possibility for them to notify the aid to the Commission, so that, in many cases, they rather take the risk associated with the granting of potentially unlawful and incompatible State aid than being left without any aid.

240. These options are impracticable today for political reasons, as it is highly unlikely that Member States would reach a consensus on enacting the appropriate legislation. The second option is also problematic from a legal standpoint without a legislative initiative on private enforcement of State aid law because, in the absence of a fully-fledged regulation of private enforcement actions that covers also the burden of proof, it is very difficult for competitors to prove a causal link between the granting of aid and the damage, save for exceptional circumstances (*e.g.*, in the case of public bids). This will be discussed in Part Two of this book.

241. J. Lever, *EU State Aid Law: Not a Pretty Sight*, European State Aid Law Quarterly (EStAL), 2013, Issue 12, p. 5 https://doi.org/10.21552/estal/2013/1/327.

242. A. Sánchez-Graells, *Digging Itself Out of the Hole? A Critical Assessment of the European Commission's Attempt to Revitalize State Aid Enforcement after the Crisis,* in Journal of Antitrust Enforcement, n. 1/2016, p. 157.

GBER mechanism is concerned.[243] First, he proves that the number of non-crisis-related enforcement decisions decreased sharply in the 2008-2013 period (roughly by the same number of crisis-related cases in that period). Second, he provides estimates of the volume of non-investigated unlawful State aid in the same period, showing an increasing trend. His purely legal arguments are no less compelling. The allegedly modernised system of State aid control, which is being rebuilt around the principle of 'trust and verify', is in fact 'premised on devolution of functions to the Member States or, more plainly, their outsourcing', thus undermining 'the last bastion of [the] Commission's enforcement monopoly in EU competition law'. This fundamental shift from *ex-ante* control to self-assessment based on an increasingly wider block exemption tool and on (thus far) extremely weak *ex-post* evaluations has not been followed by the reforms needed for the new system to work effectively.[244]

To conclude, all of the following constitute elements of a State aid control system that, according to Sánchez-Graells, 'is bound to fail': (i) the sharp decrease in *ex-ante* control, except for crisis-related cases; (ii) the lack of decentralisation in the enforcement of EU State aid rules; (iii) the reliance on self-assessments and voluntary compliance by Member States; and (iv) the *ex-post* evaluations left in the hands of the Member States themselves, albeit overseen by the Commission.[245]

III.C.3 The Alleged Increase in Transparency as an Insufficient Tool in Practice

The Commission's effort to ensure increased transparency is unlikely to remedy this situation for many reasons, but above all because interested parties – as direct, close competitors of beneficiaries or as trade organisations – were already able to identify and report breaches of State aid law before modernisation. Furthermore, they seldom take a belligerent approach given that, with substantially weakened and ineffective enforcement, they can hope to receive comparable State aid in the future. As the Commission has at the same time raised the bar for complainants by obliging them to substantiate their complaints much more than in the past, the overall result is unlikely to be a higher number of complaints by interested parties, and even more unlikely a higher number of non-crisis-related cases investigated by the Commission.

243. P. Nicolaides acutely observes in this respect that 'the opportunity cost of not using [the GBER] has increased significantly'. This is due, at least in part, to the limited deterrent effect of *ex-post* control, which is broadly due to the perception that the Commission has neither the resources nor the tools and techniques to monitor strict compliance with the GBER effectively. Sánchez-Graells concludes that, in all likelihood, 'the system will be reduced to a formal, box-ticking exercise'.
244. This deficiency and its implications are thoroughly discussed in Part Two of this book.
245. In this respect, the author refers to, among other things, a speech delivered by Vice-President Vestager at the High-Level State Aid Forum with Member States on 18 December 2014, in which she expressed worries that in the present paradigm of control 'serious negative effects' can be expected 'if Member States do not rank State aid self-assessment and compliance higher in their (economic) agendas'. Now, according to Sánchez-Graells, 'it seems unrealistic to expect Member States (or all of them; or under any circumstances) to self-regulate in this area and voluntarily comply with State aid rules'.

In this post-SAM procedural framework, the present level of development of the State aid system of remedies is extremely deceiving given the very conservative and limited reform achieved through the New Recovery Notice. As mentioned, the system of remedies has remained substantially unchanged since the adoption of the first Procedural Regulation in 1999. When the EU legislator eventually enacted a new Procedural Regulation in 2015, it left the provision on remedies entirely untouched. If one looks at the changes introduced in the Procedural Regulation with the SAM process, the only one that has a (very indirect) link with the system of remedies is Article 29, which concerns cooperation between the Commission and national courts within the framework of the private enforcement of State aid rules. This change is discussed in more detail in Part Two of this book. However, it is clear that its contribution to the overall effectiveness of State aid rules has been overestimated given the overall weakness of State aid private enforcement.

The other changes introduced in the Procedural Regulation - which, as mentioned, concern the handling of complaints[246] and the Commission's powers to investigate sectors of the economy and aid instruments[247] - mostly serve to facilitate the Commission's administration of the system. Again, they do not refer, directly or indirectly, to the system of remedies - and in general, their contribution to enhancing the effectiveness of State aid control is more than doubtful. Sánchez-Graells convincingly explains that the reform in the handling of complaints - with the introduction of the mandatory use of a standardised complaint form and the corresponding increased administrative burden on complainants, which must now provide the Commission with a significant amount of information - will hardly result in a higher number of complaints by interested parties.[248]

In the meantime, the Commission's new investigative powers have remained largely on paper. This is unsurprising if one considers the many limitations and constraints provided in Article 25 of the Procedural Regulation. First, the investigative powers are limited to sector inquiries or to the general application of given aid instruments.[249] Second, the effects on competition must be perceived across several Member States, such that global inquiries appear to be the most appropriate means for the Commission to deal with the issue efficiently and transparently. Third, the investigative powers are limited to addressing requests for information to Member States or undertakings and associations of undertakings. Fourth, the investigation's

246. *See* Art. 24(2) of Council Regulation (EU) 2015/1589.
247. *See* Art. 29 of Council Regulation (EU) 2015/1589.
248. Sánchez-Graells, *Digging Itself Out of the Hole? A Critical Assessment of the European Commission's Attempt to Revitalize State Aid Enforcement after the Crisis,* cited in footnote 242 of this Part One.
249. The wording of Art. 25 is unclear in this respect, as it refers to State aid measures in a given sector or 'based on a particular aid instrument'. The Procedural Regulation, however, contains no definition of what 'a particular aid instrument' is Recital 34 of the Procedural Regulation's preamble clarifies that the aim of the new investigative tools is 'to ensure that the Commission addresses similar issues in a consistent manner across the internal market'. The notion of 'aid instrument' should therefore be deemed to mean specific types (*e.g.*, tax rulings or, more generally, fiscal aid) or categories of horizontal aid (*e.g.*, aid for renewables or energy capacity mechanisms).

findings cannot be directly used in enforcement proceedings; rather, the Commission must previously summarise the findings in a report and invite Member States and interested parties to submit comments. Fifth, the Commission is bound by the principle of proportionality.[250]

When assessing the impact of the post-SAM procedural framework on the effectiveness of State aid control, some authors also refer to the increased transparency alleged by the Commission as one of the main changes introduced by the modernisation process. Transparency is certainly a mantra of modern times, but in the legal world (including, unfortunately, the EU legal system) it often remains wishful thinking or, at most, a declaration of principle. In an enlightening contribution on the evolution that State aid policy has undergone in just a few decades, A. Biondi and E. Righini refer to the new transparency requirement introduced with SAM[251] in enthusiastic terms.[252] They go so far as to say that this criterion, 'although apparently just an administrative requirement, has on its own the potential to revolutionise State aid control as we know it. From now on, in fact, all levels of the Member States' administration will be accountable to their citizens for how taxpayers' money is spent and who benefits'.

This prediction unfortunately turned out to be overly optimistic. Besides the fact that all national legal systems already have their own rules to control how the administration uses taxpayers' money, the ultimate goal of the transparency requirement seems to be to prompt increased monitoring of State aid spending by private operators. However, the new transparency rules will at most lead to a limited increase in the number of complaints or challenges against positive decisions. Indeed, competitors and trade organisations are generally well informed regardless of an official website. As to the general public, according to Sánchez-Graells, any effort to present

250. Recital 34 explains that 'in the light of the high administrative burden entailed by such investigations', they must be carried out only when the information available substantiates a reasonable suspicion that State aid measures in a given sector (or of a given type) could materially restrict or distort competition within the internal market in several Member States, or that existing aid measures in a given sector (or of a given type) in several Member States are not, or are no longer, compatible with the internal market.
251. *See* Communication from the Commission on EU State Aid Modernisation (SAM), COM (2012) 209 final, 8.5.2012, para. 18, where the Commission codifies seven common principles applicable to the compatibility assessment of all kinds of aid. The last criterion of this common assessment methodology is the transparency requirement for all State aid above EUR 0.5 million. This requirement has been implemented in several guidelines ever since. *See* the Communication from the Commission amending the Communications from the Commission on EU Guidelines for the application of State aid rules in relation to the rapid deployment of broadband networks, on Guidelines on regional State aid for 2014-2020, on State aid for films and other audiovisual works, on Guidelines on State aid to promote risk finance investments and on Guidelines on State aid to airport and airlines (C2014/ 198/02), OJ C 198, 27.6.2014, pp. 30-34, where it is stated that 'Member States shall, as a condition for granting aid ... in line with the relevant guidelines, establish comprehensive State aid websites, at regional and national level, for the publication of information on aid measures'. The information to be published includes the beneficiary's identity, the activity's location and sector, the amount granted, the aid's objective, and the aid's legal basis.
252. A. Biondi and E. Righini, *An Evolutionary Theory of State Aid Control*, in D. Chalmers and A. Arnull eds, The Oxford Handbook of European Union Law, July 2015.

the increased transparency requirement as an enabling mechanism to boost action against wastes of taxpayers' money is 'simply wishful thinking, if not deceitful'.[253]

Biondi and Righini concede that, in their attempt to present an overall picture of the evolution of State aid control, they 'perhaps constructed a rather optimistic model'. This is indeed the case when one considers the importance they give to the transparency requirement - though it is certainly important as a matter of principle, its actual contribution to enhancing the enforcement of State aid rules should not be overestimated, for all the reasons mentioned above.

III.C.4 Effectiveness-Related Weaknesses of the Procedural Setting Induced by Modernisation

To sum up, the effectiveness and efficacy of State aid enforcement overall under the SAM paradigm remains to be proved. For the time being, many concerns seem justified as to the capacity of a system that at this point relies to a very large extent on *ex-post* enforcement to consolidate and strengthen State aid control. The Commission deployed great efforts in presenting the SAM paradigm as a modern approach based on transparency, sincere cooperation with Member States and procedural simplification. This rhetoric, however, has short legs. State aid control has its peculiarities, and achieving the general goal pursued by the Commission (*i.e.*, to be 'bigger and more ambitious on big things, and smaller and more modest on small things')[254] is not an easy task. Combining this approach with the need to foster budgetary discipline and to concentrate financial resources on projects that can achieve equity and efficiency objectives through sustainable development (which is another of SAM's topical

253. *See* Sánchez-Graells, *Digging Itself Out of the Hole? A Critical Assessment of the European Commission's Attempt to Revitalize State Aid Enforcement after the Crisis*, cited in footnote 242 of this Part One. The author defines the Commission's discourse on transparency as 'a pointless gesture' and establishes a link between increased transparency and the Commission's restrictive approach in Commission Regulation (EU) No 372/2014 of 9 April 2014, OJ 2014 L 109/14, amending Regulation (EC) No 794/2004 as regards the calculation of certain time limits, the handling of complaints, and the identification and protection of confidential information. Both are Commission regulations implementing Council Regulation (EC) No 659/1999 (the first Procedural Regulation). Council Regulation (EU) 2015/1589 (the new Procedural Regulation) subsequently introduced new rules on complaints in Art. 24(2), basically following the Commission's approach. In the author's opinion, the Commission pursues a comprehensive strategy 'to regain control over its State aid enforcement docket' after the *Athinaïki Techniki* judgment (*Athinaïki Techniki AG v. European Commission*, C-521/06, EU:C:2008:422), as it 'does not want to find itself in a position where it formally has to conduct an investigation and issue a decision for each complaint it receives'. Even when one looks at the transparency requirement in isolation, the author submits that truly interested parties were already able to identify and report potential breaches of EU State aid law as part of their regular activities and that 'the problems they had to push their cases forward rarely related to lack of access to public information before filing a complaint, but rather depended on their ability to persuade the Commission to formally open investigation procedures'. He goes on to say that, in any case, 'the transparency added by SAM will only facilitate complaints by these parties in a marginal way, given that public information resulting from the SAM publication obligations will always be limited'.
254. Speech by J-C. Juncker, *A New Start: European Commission Work Plan to Deliver Jobs, Growth and Investment*, Strasbourg, 16 December 2014.

objectives) would require both credible *ex-post* monitoring/enforcement and efficient cooperation with Member States' authorities. At the moment, both objectives remain unachieved.

Sánchez-Graells already expressed this concern in the aftermath of the financial and economic crisis, noting that, in spite of public statements, the Commission 'seems to have already assumed that block-exempted aid is of low priority' in terms of surveillance and investigation, and adding that it is unlikely for the Commission to really prioritise *ex-post* enforcement and 'effectively engage in a proper audit' of what Member States do 'under the appearance of compliance with the 2014 GBER'. Even less will the Commission commit, let alone be able, to 'uncover in an effective manner a significant number of instances of undue application of the rules – which could eventually lead to a withdrawal of the block exemption under Article 10 of the 2014 GBER'.

In the absence of an effective, credible *ex-post* enforcement system, a high rate of flawed application of the GBER is to be expected – and this will inevitably encourage further deviation from a conventional interpretation of block-exempted aid categories and thus create a vicious circle of increasing non-compliance with the SAM objectives of budgetary discipline and concentration of resources on strategic and sustainable development.

Even the European Economic and Social Committee ('*EESC*') echoes these concerns in its comments on the SAM Communication.[255] The EESC refers to the (new) role of the Member States – one as 'judges in their own cause' – as the main problem associated with SAM. The EESC explains its concerns by raising the question of what legal and political means can be used to persuade Member States to cooperate fully in enforcing State aid law. According to the EESC, in the absence of effective means to achieve full and sincere cooperation with Member States, the higher responsibility conferred on them for the implementation of State aid control can only lead to subjective measurement and judgment in the application of the relevant rules, which increases legal uncertainty and can exacerbate economic nationalism. Several scholars support this view. C. Koenig and J. Lindner, to cite just one example, note that under the current legal framework, 'the only feasible way for the Commission to ensure effective State aid law enforcement at the national level is to increase the *ex-post* control of measures granted without prior notification. Yet, the effectiveness of the *ex-post* control depends on a large degree on the Member States' commitments to make their aid practice transparent'.[256]

Indeed, experience shows, even more so in recent years, that full and sincere cooperation from all Member States is a far-reaching – and perhaps chimerical – goal. Furthermore, it is unlikely that the Commission can improve its track record in terms

255. European Economic and Social Committee, 'Opinion on the Communication from the Commission to the European Parliament, the Council, the European Economic and Social Committee and the Committee of the Regions: European State Aid Modernisation (SAM)', 14 November 2012.
256. Koenig and Lindner, *Criminal Liability: An Efficient Tool of EU State Aid Law Enforcement?* cited in footnote 238 of this Part One.

of the number of enforcement actions (combining instances of *ex-ante* and *ex-post* control). This is an easy prediction to make, and it has a threefold basis.

First and foremost, though some progress has been made in *ex-post* monitoring in terms of the Commission's internal organisation and approach since the launch of the SAM process, no specific, transparent procedure has been put in place other than internal guidelines and the customary application of the principle of sincere cooperation with Member States. Consequently, neither the legal community nor stakeholders have the perception of credible *ex-post* enforcement. Second, Unit H4 – Enforcement and Monitoring was established in 2006 within the framework of the SAAP, for the *ex-post* monitoring of the correct implementation of aid schemes. Its competences now cover the *ex-post* monitoring of the application of several instruments, including the GBER,[257] but its role has not substantially changed – nor have its human resources. Third, and more importantly, no evidence exists of any specific monitoring targets established by the Commission or of the development of suitable monitoring methodologies, let alone specific procedures, as mentioned above.

Unit H4 has certainly developed some internal targets and guidelines in exercising its tasks, and this is, of course, laudable progress. The Commission follows a sample-based approach and apparently aims to review only a small percentage of individual aid measures granted under approved aid schemes or covered by the GBER but spanning as many objectives (horizontal and sectoral) as possible and covering many, though not all, Member States. To this end, the Commission annually selects a well-balanced (in terms of territory and type) sample of cases, including fiscal aid measures covered by the GBER.[258] When a case is selected for review, a comprehensive request for information is sent to the Member State concerned to gather all relevant information, as is usually done during official investigation procedures. For the selected cases, the Commission checks compliance with the legal framework in terms of both the legal basis used (*i.e.*, verification that GBER provisions have been correctly interpreted and that no unlawful extension or modification of existing aid measures has occurred) and the aid's practical implementation (*i.e.*, compliance with aid intensity thresholds and with compatibility requirements, such as the incentive effect).

257. The notion of *ex-post* monitoring refers to the verification of compliance of individual grants with previously approved or block-exempted measures. As such, it covers existing aid measures only. It does not cover follow-ups to conditional decisions; nor is monitoring linked to complaints brought against unlawful aid. Moreover, monitoring should not be confused with evaluations of existing schemes, which are compulsory under Art. 1(2)(a) of Commission Regulation (EU) No 651/2014 of 17 June 2014 declaring certain categories of aid compatible with the internal market in application of Arts 107 and 108 TFEU (OJ 2014 L 187/1), as amended by Commission Regulation (EU) 2017/1084 of 14 June 2017 amending Regulation (EU) No 651/2014 as regards aid for port and airport infrastructure, notification thresholds for aid for culture and heritage conservation and for aid for sport and multi-functional recreational infrastructures, and regional operating aid schemes for outermost regions, and amending Regulation (EU) No 702/2014 as regards the calculation of eligible costs (OJ 2017 L 156/1).

258. Article 12(2) of the GBER clarifies that the rules on monitoring apply also to fiscal aid measures. The peculiarity of fiscal measures from a monitoring perspective is that, because they are automatically applied, Member States are required to check compliance with the compatibility requirements on a sample basis. This means that the Commission's monitoring builds on checks that Member States are supposed to have already carried out on their own.

If a breach of relevant provisions is identified, the Commission typically distinguishes substantial infringements from purely formal ones. Substantial infringements are those with a financial impact (*e.g.*, the crossing of aid intensity thresholds, or the granting of aid in the absence of an incentive effect or other essential requirements), while formal infringements are those that have not led to grants exceeding the approved limits (*e.g.*, irregularities concerning the legal basis, or a lack of control or monitoring on the part of national authorities without proof that incompatible aid was granted).[259] Of course, the remedies are different depending on which of the two cases applies, as the Commission tends to flag formal infringements to the Member State without taking additional action (save for exceptional circumstances), whereas it requires recovery of unlawful aid in the case of substantial infringements. It appears that, in most cases, Member States resort to voluntary recovery and thus avoid triggering the opening of official investigations. If infringements are not occasional but rather repeat themselves and become systematic, the Commission may propose appropriate measures, such as administrative guidelines or even changes to the legal basis under national law to clarify the correct application of the State aid rules concerned.

Besides undertaking strict remedial actions when irregularities are detected in the implementation of existing aid, the Commission aims to accomplish the following through *ex-post* monitoring: (i) expand awareness of the need for compliance with EU State aid rules and the related need for correct reporting; and (ii) increase deterrence by showing that *ex-post* control can be just as effective as *ex-ante* control.[260] Last but not least, monitoring provides the Commission with useful data on the compatibility conditions that are most frequently misinterpreted or misapplied and thus helps improve legislative technique from a forward-looking perspective.[261] Overall, however, the mere internal reorganisation of the Commission Services is clearly insufficient to foster effectiveness and achieve modernisation's goals in this respect, as discussed below.

III.C.5 Ex-post Monitoring as an Insufficient Tool to Ensure Compliance with State Aid Rules

The above-described post-SAM progress in the way *ex-post* enforcement is organised and carried out should be checked against the objectives of the effectiveness of the State aid legal system and efficiency in enforcement. It must be kept in mind that under

259. For some statistical information on the relevance of infringement types, *see* M. Muñoz de Juan, *Monitoring of State Aid: From Ex Ante to Ex Post Control*, European State Aid Law Quarterly (EStAL), 2018, Issue 4, p. 483 https://doi.org/10.21552/estal/2018/4/5. More generally, the author clearly presents the Commission's *ex-post* monitoring methodology based on a selection of annual samples and related remedial actions.
260. *Ibid.*
261. *Ibid.* The author mentions the elimination of the requirement of providing a counterfactual scenario to prove the incentive effect for all aid granted to large undertakings under the GBER (Art. 9 of the 2008 GBER) as a significant example of changes triggered by the outcome of *ex-post* monitoring.

Article 108(1) TFEU, the Commission is required to keep existing aid measures under constant review. The Commission must ensure that this task is performed as efficiently as possible. The structure of the Treaty rules on State aid makes it very clear that the Treaty's authors considered this a crucial task to achieving effective enforcement. Indeed, it is explicitly mentioned at the beginning of Article 108(1), and the adjective 'constant' strengthens the impression of its central role. Its importance has increased dramatically with the shift from *ex-ante to ex-post* control following modernisation.

The Commission's obligation to review existing aid measures is complemented by the duty of sincere cooperation between the Commission and the Member States enshrined in Article 4(3) TEU, which, as is well known, plays an important role in State aid enforcement and policy. However, heavy reliance on cooperation from Member States in the field of State aid can be counterproductive. In any event, no reference to the need for sincere cooperation with Member States in policy documents, such as the SAAP or the SAM Communication, can prevent the Commission from carrying out its monitoring mission - nor can it release the Commission from its obligation to review existing aid measures on a constant basis in accordance with Article 108(1) TFEU.

In a case concerning the exemption regulation for SMEs,[262] Germany claimed that the Commission lacked competence to adopt an information injunction in accordance with Article 12(3) of the Procedural Regulation - *i.e.*, a decision ordering a Member State to provide information on projects exempted under the regulation - on the basis that the exemption regulation's wording suggests that the Commission's power of review is limited to cases in which doubts can be raised as to the compliance of individual aid with the conditions of that regulation. However, the General Court relied on the Commission's obligation under Article 108(1) TFEU and on the powers conferred on the Commission by Council Regulation (EC) No 994/98[263] to conclude that monitoring was an essential component of that (and in fact any) exemption regulation and that the power vested in the Commission to request information with a view to ensuring compliance with State aid rules cannot be limited to cases in which doubts of irregularities already exist.[264] Though this judgment clearly reinforced the Commission's position and released it from possible objections to its fact-finding activities, which is crucial for *ex-post* monitoring, it also increased pressure on the Commission to perform all the monitoring activities necessary to ensure efficient enforcement of State aid rules in the post-SAM era.

By the same token, in its 2016 report, the Court of Auditors expressed reservations about the actions taken by the Commission to ensure compliance with State aid rules.[265] The Court of Auditors found that almost 20% of cohesion policy projects with

262. Commission Regulation (EC) No 70/2001 of 12 January 2001 on the application of the State aid rules to small and medium-sized enterprises, OJ 2001 L 10, p. 33.
263. Council Regulation (EC) No 994/98 of 7 May 1998 on the application of Arts 92 and 93 of the Treaty establishing the European Community to certain categories of horizontal State aid, OJEU L 142, 14.5.1998, pp. 1-4.
264. Judgment of the General Court of 25 November 2009, Case T-376/07, *Federal Republic of Germany v. European Commission*, EU:T:2009:467.
265. *See* the Court of Auditors' Special Report No 24/2016, 'More efforts needed to raise awareness of an enforced compliance with State aid rules in cohesion policy', pp. 32-33.

State aid relevance were affected by various errors. Even more importantly, the Court of Auditors emphasised that audit authorities in Member States detected a significantly lower rate of errors. This can only mean that Member States' authorities, albeit an important part of the control chain, are still not entirely reliable when it comes to monitoring. The situation might have improved since the report's publication, but legal scholars largely agree that improvement is still needed and that monitoring is not a sufficient tool in itself to guarantee compliance.

P. Nicolaides, for instance, identifies several negative consequences of *ex-post* enforcement that might not have been taken into sufficient account.[266] Building on Nicolaides' comments, the following main areas of concern can be identified: (i) the number of infringements is likely to rise, and even assuming that the Commission detects the most important ones through *ex-post* monitoring, the fact remains that the cumulative impact of small errors will likely be significant; (ii) the extremely significant decrease in the number of non-crisis-related enforcement proceedings has led to a significant decrease in guidance and predictability concerning enforcement actions, which is not compensated for by the alleged increase in transparency; and (iii) legal certainty is also negatively affected by the resurgent use of comfort letters, which reduces even further the number of fully reasoned formal decisions that can provide guidance to stakeholders and the legal community. All this comes at a time when State aid spending is likely to increase even without counting genuine crisis-related measures, given, *inter alia,* that based on the common compatibility criteria set out by SAM, the Commission tends to consider any measure that is strictly needed for a given project to be completed (*i.e.*, to cover the funding gap) to be 'good aid'.[267]

Doubts about the suitability of the Commission's monitoring activities are also justified in light of the Court of Justice's case law. In one of the rare cases of preliminary rulings regarding the application of the GBER, the Court held that the conditions laid down by the GBER must be interpreted strictly.[268] It went on to say that only this approach is in line with the aims of GBERs, as set out in recitals 4 and 5 of Council Regulation (EC) No 994/98 (the Council's enabling regulation).[269] Indeed, 'while the Commission is authorised to adopt such regulations, with a view to ensuring efficient supervision of the competition rules concerning State aid and simplifying administration' this should not result in a weakening of the Commission's monitoring. Furthermore, 'the aim of such regulations is also to increase transparency and legal certainty',

266. *See*, among others: P. Nicolaides, *The EU State Aid Modernisation: Taking Stock of Its Initial Results*, CEPOB (College of Europe Policy Brief), July 2016, Issue 12.16; and Muñoz de Juan, *Monitoring of State Aid: From Ex Ante to Ex Post Control*, cited in footnote 259 of this Part One.

267. By comparing this approach to the more traditional 'balancing test', Nicolaides suggests that the opportunity cost of a given aid measure (which is equal to the forgone net gain in the best alternative use) is not taken into account. The mere fact that a project cannot be completed without aid does not prove that the aid benefits the economy at large. According to the author, this is at odds with some SAM objectives, such as strengthening budgetary discipline, improving the quality of public finances through better use of taxpayers' money, and achieving more effectiveness in public spending. Nicolaides suggests that a thorough cost-benefit analysis could help ensure that State aid does add value from a general economic perspective.

268. Judgment of the Court of 21 July 2016, Case C-493/14, *Dilly's Wellnesshotel GmbH/Finanzamt Linz*, EU:C:2016:577, para. 37.

269. *See* footnote 263 of this Part One.

which can only be achieved through rigorous compliance with 'all the conditions' laid down by those regulations.[270] This led the Court to conclude that even the breach of a purely formal requirement, such as the mere absence, in an aid scheme, of an express reference to the GBER (by citing its title and publication reference in the Official Journal of the EU) 'precludes that scheme from being considered to fulfil the conditions for exemption ... from the obligation to notify laid down in Article 108(3) TFEU'.[271]

Consequently, the Commission's approach to checking the suitability of a given aid measure's national legal basis and monitoring compliance with all compatibility conditions – whereby it gives conditions no ranking of importance but rather takes true remedial action only in the case of substantial infringements with a financial impact – is in itself questionable.[272] Building on the Court's judgment, it can be said that the Commission should instead draw all necessary consequences from the finding of an infringement, given that *any irregularity implies that the protection granted by the GBER does not apply*. It therefore appears that, even from this perspective, there is room to develop a *broader range of remedial actions than mere recovery* in order to take into account the nature of *ex-post* control and to best serve the deterrence and effectiveness objectives.

To conclude on the importance of *ex-post* monitoring as a tool to ensure compliance with State aid rules and on its link with the modernisation of the system of remedies, the following should be clarified: *ex-post* monitoring is necessary in a decentralised State aid control system, but stating that there are only gains from *ex-post* monitoring[273] entirely misses the point. The Commission can certainly not content itself with this partial achievement, regardless of the control system's overall efficiency, as the latter is very doubtful and can endanger the credibility and effectiveness of State aid policy as a whole. This is even more troublesome when the only additional tool the Commission seems to rely on is cooperation with Member States' authorities, whose limits are well known and have been confirmed by the statistics mentioned in the Court of Auditors' 2016 report. No evidence exists to show that the situation has significantly improved since then.

Therefore, the time is ripe to complete the modernisation toolkit with a reform of the system of remedies that internalises the post-SAM paradigm in terms of both an adaptation of the remedies to the new objectives of State aid control and a shift in the nature of control from *ex-ante* to *ex-post* review. Currently, very little of the *ex-post*

270. Judgment of the Court of 21 July 2016, *Dilly's Wellnesshotel GmbH/Finanzamt Linz*, EU:C:2016:577, cited in footnote 268 of this Part One, paras 38 and 45.

271. *Ibid.*, para. 52.

272. For a comprehensive illustration of the Commission's approach to remedies as a consequence of *ex-post* monitoring, *see* Muñoz de Juan, *Monitoring of State Aid: From Ex Ante to Ex Post Control*, cited in footnote 259 of this Part One. Muñoz de Juan clearly explains that different remedial actions are considered by the Commission depending on the importance and nature of the irregularity. In some cases, the Commission might simply draw a Member State's attention to unclear national provisions, request that the national legal basis be amended or, again, request that additional national monitoring be performed, or documentation gathered. If the irregularities affect the implementation of the aid and are substantial/have a financial impact, traditional remedies apply, and the Member State concerned may envisage taking voluntary action to recover unlawful aid or suspend future payments under a scheme.

273. *Ibid.*

review process and outcomes falls into public knowledge, and enforcement action as a whole in this field lacks transparency. Communication efforts by the Commission have also been very limited thus far.

III.C.6 Alternative Tools: Increased Cooperation and Increased Discretion in Determining the Appropriate Remedies

As discussed above, the adequacy of a system of remedies depends on, among other things, the degree of effectiveness achieved in the application of the substantive rules at issue. From this perspective, doubts have been expressed in the previous paragraphs on the current system's suitability when evaluated against the backdrop of modernisation objectives. This unsatisfactory situation is worsened by the fact that most of the Commission's resources are currently kept very busy with regulatory work, which includes not only the drafting of new proposals of both hard law and soft law but also – and more importantly – the periodic review, update and reform of the numerous existing frameworks, guidelines, communications and, of course, State aid secondary laws (regulations, directives and Article 106(3) decisions). This task is indeed burdensome if one considers that the Commission logically prepares every amendment carefully, through economic analysis, *ex-post* evaluation studies, multilateral dialogue with Member States and often extensive public consultations.

But there is more. Significant resources are periodically gathered to staff task forces entrusted with specific enforcement missions or emergency management. For example, this was the case with: (i) the implementation of the services of general economic interest (SGEI) package after the 2011 reform; (ii) some broad sectoral investigations, including in the energy and transport sectors; and above all (iii) the financial and economic crisis, in relation to the design, development and implementation of the temporary frameworks and the follow-up review of all banking cases. More recently, the Commission had to cope with the COVID-19 pandemic and the economic consequences of Russia's invasion of Ukraine. Consequently, it used a huge number of human resources to draft and update new temporary frameworks covering Article 107(3)(b) and (c) measures, develop guidelines for the application of Article 107(2)(b), and conduct a fast-track review of the numerous aid schemes and ad hoc aid notified by the Member States. *Emergency management is unfortunately evolving into a recurrent feature of State aid policy* and now cannot be ignored when assessing the Commission's overall enforcement capability. All this is indicative of the fact that *ex-post monitoring has never become a true political priority for the Commission.*

The outbreak of the COVID-19 pandemic and the war in Ukraine were obviously not events that could be foreseen at the time the SAM process was designed. Nonetheless, there was a clear perception at the time that exceptional circumstances could become fairly recurrent – and that perception is even clearer today. Though the nature of the next exceptional event – including its gravity, amplitude and characteristics – is totally unknown, the horizon of new emergencies is certainly fast approaching and becoming a factor that, logically and statistically, can and should be considered. An effort should be made to *internalise emergency management* in shaping the

State aid enforcement system for the years to come. Ineffective decentralisation or devolution of functions to Member States does not help address this problem. All efforts deployed thus far to implement the modernisation objective of increasing decentralisation have been minimal, to say the least. No modernisation tool has ever offered anything innovative in this respect.[274] Some proposals put forward by legal scholars (*e.g.*, on how to handle complaints) have remained unheard.[275] Constant reference to the principle of sincere cooperation is not the solution, for the reasons explained above - even less so if very little effort is made to translate this principle into specific procedures or best practices.

It is unquestionable that the exclusive power to assess the compatibility of aid with the internal market is, and should remain, with the Commission.[276] This, however, does not mean that decentralisation efforts should be limited to reminding Member States of the principle of sincere cooperation in complying with the transparency obligation, monitoring compliance with the GBER or other exemption tools, or assisting in the recovery of unlawful aid. Innovative avenues should be explored both in seeking cooperation with national authorities within the framework of public enforcement and in creating the conditions for more effective private enforcement.

The latter is left for Part Two of this book; what can be mentioned here is that much remains to be done to improve public enforcement. *National independent authorities* could be more closely associated with several aspects of enforcement while leaving the final word entirely to the Commission in ascertaining a breach of State aid

274. The idea of partial decentralisation surfaced for the first time in a clear and explicit manner in the SAAP (para. 51), in which the Commission acknowledged that, although the EU has the exclusive competence to adopt State aid rules, the successful implementation of these rules and the related procedures depends to a large extent on Member States. With that in mind, the Commission proposed examining whether independent authorities in Member States could play a role as regards facilitating the task of the Commission in terms of State aid enforcement, including based on the experience of independent authorities in candidate Member States. In particular, according to the Commission, Member States could contribute in terms of detection and provisional recovery of unlawful aid and execution of recovery decisions. Notwithstanding this clear message, the Commission did not explore this idea further during the period covered by the SAAP (2005-2009) and did not put forward concrete proposals. In the SAM Communication of 2012, the Commission appeared to drop the idea of cooperation on the enforcement of State aid law with independent authorities in Member States. Though the Commission clearly stated that one of the objectives of modernisation is to strengthen cooperation with Member States in State aid enforcement (para. 8), it made no reference to independent authorities and simply emphasised the increased responsibilities of Member States in the post-SAM era, given the increased volume of *de minimis* and block-exempted aid (para. 21). Once more, the Commission did not put forward any specific proposal.

275. *See* M. Merola and L. Armati, *Complainants' Rights in State Aid Matters: Lost in Modernisation?*, in I. Govaere and D. Hanf, eds, 'Scrutinizing Internal and External Dimensions of European Law: Liber Amicorum Paul Demaret', College of Europe and P.*i.e.* Peter Lang, 2013, pp. 569 ff.

276. In this respect, an even more rigorous approach could be justified. In particular, it is questionable that the Commission delegates Member States to assess the distortion of competition or effect on trade of individual aid measures granted under an unlawful aid scheme, which is what the Commission normally does when it orders recovery. It is appropriate for national authorities to check whether individual aid measures are covered by the *de minimis* rule, but it is not appropriate for them to establish on their own, directly on the basis of the Treaty, whether individual measures granted under unlawful aid schemes affect competition and trade.

rules. The typical example is the handling of complaints,[277] but other possibilities can be explored in the post-SAM control paradigm, for instance, within the framework of *ex-post* monitoring and related enforcement actions or in the monitoring of compliance with prospective remedies imposed in conditional decisions. Even more importantly, beneficiaries could be allowed to participate in recovery procedures in order to explore alternative and potentially more effective means of restoring undistorted competition.

Various forms of accountability could be considered in order to incentivise the Commission and national enforcers to take these needs and tasks seriously. Koenig and Lindner go so far as to propose that criminal liability be considered a possible tool of State aid law enforcement. They found that, over two years after the Commission set out the SAM initiative, no considerable progress had been achieved in increasing the efficiency of enforcement and in remedying the severe deficiencies at national level. In a paper published in 2015, they examine whether the granting of unlawful State aid potentially constitutes a crime under German law (and possibly under the laws of other Member States). If so, they argue, the efficiency of State aid enforcement could be significantly improved without any significant legislative changes in the EU legal system (which they consider highly unlikely to occur), as it could be achieved simply through interpretation and judicial action at national level.[278]

Koenig and Lindner's innovative proposal is meant to address the need to pursue new avenues in the systematic prevention of unlawful State aid and gives the issue greater relevance in the political agenda.[279] Quite obviously, if criminal liability can be

---

277. *See* footnote 286 of this Part One.
278. *See* C. Koenig and J. Lindner, *Criminal Liability: An Efficient Tool of EU State Aid Law Enforcement?* European State Aid Law Quarterly (ESTaL), 2005, Issue 1, p. 19. The authors refer to the *Commerz Nederland* case (Judgment of the Court of 4 December 2014, Case C-243/13, *European Commission v. Kingdom of Sweden*, EU:C:2014:2413), in which the Court held that a given aid measure is imputable to the State even if the State official involved in the granting of the aid is convicted of a criminal offence because 'he acted improperly, deliberately kept the provision of State aid in the form of guarantees secret and disregarded the undertaking's statutes'. The fact that the public authority would have opposed the provision of the guarantees had it been informed thereof does not undermine the classification of the measure as State aid. Based on this, they argue that, under German law, the granting of unlawful aid may be characterised as a crime of embezzlement if the deliberate unlawful spending of public money can be considered a breach of trust. In that regard, the authors observe that, as in many other Member States, budgetary law in Germany 'recognises the cardinal principles of efficiency and economy. According to the principle of efficiency, assets must be used in such a manner that they yield an optimal result (maximum principle). Furthermore, results have to be achieved with as little allocation of resources as possible (minimum principle)'. If these two budgetary postulates can be deemed to be enshrined also in Art. 107(1) – the authors argue – this would pave the way to classifying the granting of unlawful aid as a breach of trust and thus as a crime of embezzlement if the perpetrator is aware that his/her actions are clearly in breach of EU State aid law. The authors also submit that, to further increase the effectiveness of criminal liability as a State aid enforcement tool, the national criminal investigation procedure should be improved by facilitating cooperation between the criminal law enforcement authorities and the Commission. Public prosecutors should involve the Commission as *amicus curiae* when investigating State-aid-related embezzlement.
279. Indeed, their article cites a statement made by Vice-President Almunia when presenting the SAM initiative, in which he admonished Member States to reinforce their control mechanisms at all levels of their administrations in order to remedy the deficiencies of State aid law enforcement.

envisaged for breaches of State aid law in granting aid, their proposed solution can *a fortiori* be considered a way to force effective recovery or to implement other remedies when the Commission has already ascertained a breach. If this solution were adopted, public officials who disregard their monitoring duties and, in so doing, hinder the finding of irregularities, or who do not implement recovery obligations, could be exposed to criminal proceedings.

Suggestions like Koenig and Lindner's are indicative of the deficiencies of the State aid recovery system and of the widespread perception that effectiveness is a major problem in this area of EU law and that new avenues need to be explored to prevent the systematic breach of State aid law. However, it is not necessary to go as far as to design criminal liability. Rather, one of the keys to improved enforcement is undoubtedly a comprehensive reform of the system of remedies. Indeed, if effectiveness is the main problem, the solution is not to tighten the rules or to streamline procedures[280] but rather to demonstrate that any breach of the rules will be pursued and that remedies are appropriate and tailored to each situation.

It is therefore highly misleading (or, to use the albeit very strong words of Sánchez-Graells, 'deceitful') that the Commission puts so much emphasis on transparency in the post-SAM era when its enforcement policy and priorities, not to mention its own procedures, remain anything but transparent, and when absolutely no serious reform has been put forward when it comes to the system of remedies, which is the backbone of any enforcement action. The present status of the system of remedies within the post-SAM procedural framework is indeed extremely deceptive given the very conservative and limited reform achieved through the New Recovery Notice.

III.C.7 Concluding Remarks on the Link Between Modernisation and a Reform of the System of Remedies

Emphasis on the need for a comprehensive reform of recovery and of the whole system of remedies does not mean or imply weakening the remedies but quite the opposite: it means improving the system's effectiveness and credibility and, consequently: (i) strengthening the system's deterrent effect; and (ii) reinforcing the objective of forfeiting the market distortion by tailoring the restorative effect – *i.e.*, the re-creation of the situation existing before the unlawful aid was granted – to the specific circumstances of each case. The key issue with the system of remedies is not to make it more severe or to sharpen remedial actions, but rather – and quite simply – to adapt it to present times and, more precisely, to the post-SAM and post-crises enforcement paradigm.

This chapter has analysed the policy arguments in favour of a comprehensive reform of the system of remedies within the framework of modernisation. However, the link between the suggested reform and the modernisation process clearly emerges also from a strictly legal standpoint. Indeed, reference to the system's deterrent effect

280. As previously observed, streamlining procedures can even be counterproductive from an overall enforcement rate standpoint if it means that infringements of minor importance are not pursued at EU or national level, as this only fosters the creation of a sense of impunity.

helps highlight this link. A sufficient degree of deterrence is unquestionably tantamount to achieving the objective of focusing enforcement action on the most significant cases. It is crucial for State intervention to focus on projects capable of fostering economic development, but failure to ensure a sufficient degree of deterrence in enforcement policy could encourage Member States to devote resources to less important cases. The mere risk of recovery is insufficient to discourage undertakings – and even more insufficient to discourage public authorities – from trying to circumvent State aid rules when the risk of detection is low.

Similarly, the automatic application of the recovery obligation was introduced in State aid law well before the launch of the modernisation process and inevitably does not match with the idea that State intervention should be a means to foster economic growth – an idea that dates back to the SAAP and has been strengthened since then, while the system of remedies has remained unchanged for over twenty years. It would make sense to reinstate a *certain degree of discretion in the Commission's choice of suitable remedies*, based of course on clear and objective criteria, as this would enable a cost-benefit analysis of recovery to be integrated into State aid enforcement. A cost-benefit analysis would be able to capture the effects of recovery on competition by taking into account the market situation at the time remedies are ordered and implemented rather than at the time the aid was granted.

Along the same lines, a reform of the recovery policy would be consistent with the trend of redefining the sharing of competences between the Commission and the Member States, as envisaged in the SAM Communication. In this regard, Lever rightly points out that a substantial devolution of powers to national authorities goes hand in hand with a reform of the recovery mechanism.[281] Yet another argument can be added to the same line of reasoning, which has to do with the trend of devoting more attention to an economic analysis of the law across all fields of competition law. The determination of the amount to be recovered, especially in cases of multisectoral aid, indirect aid and the passing-on defence (to mention but the most controversial scenarios), is a clear example of a field that can be substantially affected by the sharing of competences that the Commission has definitively put forward within the framework of modernisation (both in the SAAP and in the SAM Communication). This makes it all the more necessary for the reform to include the provision of adequate and clear procedures, respectful of the principle of legal certainty and protection of the rights of third parties, for monitoring the correct application of remedies.

To conclude, given the inadequacies of the present system of remedies and the need for a comprehensive reform, *the principles underlying SAM are the best source for shaping the direction of a reform*. The modernisation process should involve procedural rules much more than has been the case to date and should extend to remedies for breaches of State aid rules. The system of remedies has remained unchanged since at least 1999 and is no longer suitable for fast-evolving State aid policy or even for the applicable rules and the enforcement trends seen since then. A reform of the system of remedies, with a focus on the design of innovative means of prevention and deterrence

281. Lever, *EU State Aid Law*, cited in footnote 241 of this Part One.

and including specific rules of procedure to monitor the correct implementation of remedies, would serve the objectives of reinforcing budgetary discipline and promoting the concentration of financial resources on projects of common European interest. It is therefore unsurprising that scholars point to a reform of Article 16 of the Procedural Regulation as the most important missing piece in the modernisation process.[282]

282. Y. Chevalier, *L'article 14 du règlement (CE) n. 659/1999, la réforme oubliée du droit des aides d'Etat,* thesis presented for a master's degree from the College of Europe, 2013.

Final Remarks on Part One

The final remarks emphasise that, despite the improvements brought by the New Recovery Notice, many conceptual weaknesses and unresolved practical issues remain. It reiterates the need for a complete and coherent reform of the State aid system of remedies – one that focuses on removing market distortions and enhancing the effectiveness of recovery measures.

The reform of the 2007 Recovery Notice is certainly a significant improvement and has clearly made a positive contribution to the overall reform of the recovery system. However, it fails to overcome most of the shortcomings and inconsistencies analysed in Part One. Moreover, it does not seem to be designed in a manner consistent with the modernisation objectives, and conversely, these objectives would have warranted a more far-reaching reform. Therefore, a long path still lies ahead to achieve a comprehensive and coherent reshaping of the system of remedies in State aid law.

Moreover, the New Recovery Notice, as a soft law instrument, has the advantage of being flexible and readily available, but it is probably insufficient given the number and relevance of problematic issues raised by the recovery system nowadays. Reform of soft law instruments, however thorough, does not permit all the problems identified in Part One of this book to be adequately addressed if the ambition is to modernise the system of remedies, which is clearly a fundamental component of the State aid *corpus juris*.

It is certainly understandable why the Commission has chosen the path it is pursuing, as its choice is largely conditioned by the political agenda – for example, at the time of the New Recovery Notice's adoption, the Commission logically prioritised projects that it could deliver before the end of President Juncker's mandate. However, the task left to the von der Leyen Commission[283] (and beyond) in this connection is undoubtedly challenging. The New Recovery Notice falls short of dealing with all the pending issues that could be addressed through soft law and, on top of that, is inherently limited. A more ambitious modernisation of the system of remedies needs to be built around a reform of the relevant provisions in the Procedural Regulation.

283. The second Von der Leyen Commission is in being formed at the time of writing.

From this perspective, a reform should be aimed at bringing the system of remedies back to its theoretical basis and key principles – and it should be based on two fundamental assumptions. First, in the case of unlawful and incompatible aid, the system of remedies is aimed at restoring the *status quo ante* in competition or market terms, *i.e.*, with respect to the economic and competitive advantage generated by the aid, not the mere nominal/financial advantage gained. If recovery is insufficient or inadequate, other remedies must be considered. Second, EU State aid law has a twofold objective: the protection of competition and the respect of the objectives of the internal market.[284] Indeed, recovery is justified not only by the necessity to restore a level playing field between undertakings but also by the need to re-establish an undistorted market and discourage Member States' unilateral measures affecting the market. It follows that it is always necessary to verify in practice whether a return to the *status quo ante* and the elimination of competitive distortion are possible and, if so, to what extent. A fully fledged and mature system of remedies – one that is coherent with the ambitions of the SAM process – can no longer be built on *mere presumptions* of unmeasured competition harm and of removal of the harm through the mere repayment of the financial benefit.

From a procedural standpoint, recovery procedures (obviously including procedures for alternative remedies to recovery) need to be reconsidered. The choice is between: (i) returning to the idea, shelved at the time of the Procedural Regulation's reform, of harmonising national administrative and judicial procedures to implement Commission decisions; and (ii) defining at least the essential elements of the procedure the Commission should follow when monitoring the correct execution of recovery decisions, in particular when they involve a margin of discretion on the part of the Member States, as in the case of multi-sectoral unlawful aid schemes with numerous beneficiaries. For this procedure, the same approach should apply *mutatis mutandis* as that taken in the well-known *Athinaïki* case, when the Court ruled out the admissibility of a phase of the review process during which the Commission would have full discretion and interested parties would have no rights.[285] If these unquestionable principles apply in the handling of complaints, there is no reason why they should not apply in the definition and monitoring of remedies.

---

284. In that respect, *see* J.L. Buendia Sierra, *EU State Aid Control: Competition Between Undertakings or Between Member States?*, in L. Rubini and J. Hawkins, eds, 'What Shapes the Law? Reflections on the History, Law, Politics and Economics of International and European Subsidy Disciplines', European University Institute ed., 2016, pp. 121-128.
285. Judgment of the Court of Justice of 16 December 2010, cited in footnote 253 of this Part One. In this case, which concerned the handling of complaints, the Court ruled out the admissibility of a 'phase 0', as advocated by the Commission, during which the Commission would enjoy full discretion in deciding whether to start a preliminary investigation into allegedly unlawful aid reported by complainants. The Court concluded that the Commission is bound either to initiate a preliminary review or to adopt a definitive decision rejecting the complaint, paving the way to the complainants bringing a challenge before the General Court. On this topic, *see also* the Opinion of Advocate General Bot of 3 April 2008, EU:C:2010:492. In legal scholarship, *see* F. Pastor Merchante, *The Status of Complainants in State Aid Cases: A Look Back into the Athinaïki Techniki Saga*, in C. Buts and J.L. Buendía Sierra, eds, 'Milestones in State Aid Case Law', European State Aid Law Quarterly (EStaL), Lexxion, 2017, pp. 209-2021.

Furthermore, for a reform of the system of remedies to be thorough and match the expectations explained above, it must be recognised that recovery as such cannot be a catch-all remedy. If it is reasonable for the post-modernisation era of the EU State aid system to have acquired ancillary tasks, such as supervision of public expenditure and deterrence against unilateral initiatives that lead to a waste of economic resources - tasks that may influence the compatibility assessment, given the Commission's discretionary power - at the same time, these new tasks should not affect the nature of recovery, whose legal and theoretical basis are precisely circumscribed.

Therefore, to take into account these new tasks, the Commission should use - and possibly enhance - all available remedies and means of action: from a diversification of remedies and more thorough consideration of alternative means of restoring undistorted competition, to a more targeted application of the *Deggendorf* doctrine and other ancillary remedies; from a development of private enforcement, which is discussed in Part Two of this book, to the use of the negotiated settlement mechanism by leveraging on experience in related fields of law, which is analysed in Part Three of this book; and from the setting up of appropriate procedures for remedies with beneficiaries' involvement, to an extension of the Commission's sanctioning power when incorrect, incomplete or misleading information is provided.

This conclusion has a twofold value: first, it solves the dilemma of the quantum of recovery, which ideally should match, to the extent possible, the distortion of competition, not the financial drain on the State budget; and second, it should prompt a reform of the entire system of remedies (not just recovery) with the aim of forfeiting the competitive distortion and contributing to the achievement of all the objectives of State aid enforcement.

In carrying out a comprehensive reform of the system of remedies based on a combination of several instruments, reconsideration of fundamental concepts such as absolute impossibility and legitimate expectations can also find a place. For instance, a modernised system of remedies can aim at a realistic (as opposed to abstract or purely presumptive) evaluation of the effectiveness of recovery for the purpose of restoring the *status quo ante*. The concrete possibility to do so, and therefore to fulfil the rationale of this remedy, should always be included in the Commission's assessment. Indeed, if recovery does not allow restoration of the undistorted competitive situation that existed before the aid was granted, the recovery obligation is inoperative. In other words, a situation of *absolute impossibility arises if recovery cannot achieve the objective of restoring the status quo ante*. Therefore, although the position taken by Advocate General Wathelet in the *Montessori* case - where he advocated for a review of absolute impossibility within the framework of administrative proceedings - is unconvincing under the present system of remedies, it would fit well in the new system which is advocated in this book.

In the circumstances just described (*i.e.*, the impossibility of the recovery remedy, as currently shaped and applied, to be effective), it should theoretically be left to the Member State concerned to decide whether to invoke the unlawfulness and incompatibility of the aid in order to recover, if possible, the granted amount. However, since it would be highly immoral to allow the Member State to incriminate itself to recover resources to the detriment of the beneficiary, especially if the latter was acting in good faith, EU law should provide a legal framework for the Member States to comply with in such cases.

These rules, even if set out in soft law, should be based on a political agreement with the Member States and should protect beneficiaries when they are acting in good faith and penalise them when their connivance with the Member State in breaching the Treaty is ascertained. The Commission, on its part, should instead focus on other remedies that better serve the objective of deterrence and that ensure the best possible use of available resources in the common interest. The establishment of the *complicity of aid recipients* (or the absence thereof) should become an element of the Commission assessment before ordering remedies.

This is particularly important because neutralisation of the financial advantage is not in itself sufficient in some cases to eliminate the distortion of competition and the harm caused to competitors, and one must therefore turn to other instruments or at least strengthen the complementary use of private enforcement (follow-on actions), whereas in other cases State aid does not generate significant market distortions but only financial inefficiencies.

This can be due to, among other reasons, administrative failures in the design or timing (in terms of when it was granted) of the aid. As is well known, State authorities tend to cluster resources in the interest of (among others, but at the very least) the ruling class and in pursuit of popularity rather than exclusively in the interest of maximising the economic effects of aid measures. Moreover, in other cases, the distortive effects may have been absorbed by the passage of time or may not be calculable with any reasonable certainty.

It follows that a dynamic - not static - economic analysis of the market, the supply structure of the aided products/services and the economic effects is necessary if market distortions are to be tackled. When the competitive distortion has not concretely materialised or has been absorbed by the evolution of the market, it remains only a violation of internal market rules: namely, the adoption of a unilateral measure of State intervention that is theoretically capable of affecting competition and trade. This infringement, however, can be addressed through the customary infringement procedure for unlawful aid rather than by imposing a recovery order on the beneficiary. Obviously, recovery would remain the rule, whereas cases in which recovery is inoperative would be the exception, but the entire EU State aid system would gain coherence, rationality and credibility.

These are nothing more than preliminary suggestions (which are elaborated on in the pages that follow)[286] for what a comprehensive and coherent reform of the system of remedies should take into account - suggestions that aim to feed the debate and avoid having EU institutions, under the pressure of national interest, content themselves with a reform that leaves the most crucial issues unaddressed, as was the case with the issuance of the New Recovery Notice.

286. *See* Part Four of this book.

Part Two

Private Enforcement of State Aid Rules

Introduction to Part Two

CONTENTS

This chapter gives an overview of Part Two, reflecting on the contribution that the enforcement of State aid rules by national courts can make to the overall effectiveness of EU State aid policy and whether it can compensate for the shortcomings of public enforcement. It also sets the stage for Part Two's analysis of the need for reform to improve the private enforcement of State aid rules.

Before expressing a final opinion on the best option for reform of the system of remedies in public competition law, it is worth reflecting on the contribution that State aid enforcement by national courts can bring to the effectiveness of the EU's State aid policy. If the private enforcement of State aid law can appropriately complement the Commission's action and result in a fully-fledged and perfectly suitable system of remedies, this will certainly affect the assessment of the need for reform and the breadth of any proposal to this effect. If, by contrast, the private enforcement of State aid rules is similarly ineffective and unsatisfactory, a proposal for reform will ideally encompass this instrument, too, and appropriately calibrate all the remedies available through public and private enforcement for the achievement of the ultimate objective of building a modern and effective system of remedies.

In theory at least, private enforcement is key to developing a cohesive enforcement standard of competition law in all sectors across Europe. Private enforcement is enshrined in the very core of EU law,[1] as it flows from the pivotal *Van Gend en Loos* case.[2] As EU law confers rights on individuals, which become part of their legal heritage, it also grants them - when the EU provision under discussion is clear and unconditional - the possibility to claim the direct protection of their rights stemming from that provision before national courts. Therefore, private claimants are to be considered active supervisors of the Commission's and Member States' diligence in enforcing the Treaty's provisions.

In the field of competition law, the Court of Justice case law has further elaborated on this basic feature of EU law. The possibility of seeking compensation for loss caused by conduct liable to restrict or distort competition is an essential element of the direct applicability of clear and unambiguous provisions of EU law. The full effectiveness of those provisions would be at risk if individuals were unable to claim damages for loss caused to them by conduct liable to restrict or distort competition in breach of competition law.[3]

Part Two of this book explores how these principles translate into practical means of contributing to the effectiveness of EU law in the field of State aid. The lack of a hard

1. *See* P. Adriaanse, *Public and Private Enforcement of EU State Aid Law*, in H.J. Blankel and S. Mangiameli, eds, 'The European Union after Lisbon: Constitutional Basis, Economic Order and External Action', Springer 2012, p. 456.
2. Judgment of the Court of 5 February 1963, Case 26/62, *NV Algemene Transport- en Expeditie Onderneming van Gend & Loos v. Nethderlands Inland Revenue Administration*, EU:C:1963:1.
3. Judgment of the Court of 13 July 2006, Joined Cases C-295/04 to C-298/04, *Vincenzo Manfredi v. Lloyd Adriatico Assicurazioni SPA, Antonio Cannito v. Fondiaria SAI SpA, and Nicolò Tricarico and Pasqualina Murgolo v. Aiitalia SpA*, EU:C:2006:461. *See also* Judgment of the Court of 20 September 2001, Case C-453/99, *Courage Ltd v. Bernard Crehan and Bernard Crehan v. Courage Ltd and others*, EU:C:2001:465.

law backbone to the private enforcement of State aid rules implies that the key role is played by the case law of the European courts and by the Commission's soft law. Against this background, Chapter I focuses on the role of the different sources of law, whereas Chapter II – in line with the structure of Part One of this book – identifies and examines the key principles of the private enforcement system. Chapter III then highlights the limits of the remedies that can be implemented in private enforcement and explores how and to what extent they can fill the gap left by the shortcomings of the current system of remedies in the public enforcement of State aid rules, as identified in Part One.

It has already been explained that the modernisation of State aid rules and practice has had little or no impact on the system of remedies available to the Commission in its enforcement action. But did it have a broader impact on the private enforcement of State aid rules? The answer to this question will emerge clearly at the end of Part Two, but it is worth keeping a few points in mind from the outset. The modernisation process resulted in a new attention to the sharing of competences between the Commission and Member States' authorities, including national courts. In theory, this could have led to rebalancing public and private State aid enforcement. One of the main concerns that has accompanied the modernisation of competition law from the outset, in both the private and the public sector, is the need to guarantee the uniform application of EU law across the Union. However, the key factors of the modernisation process in State aid law – from the inception and then the broadening of block exemptions and the related transfer of competences to national authorities and courts, to the Commission's approach whereby it focuses on the most significant cases – necessarily implies a certain degree of risk of different applications being seen at national level.

Chapter X of the Procedural Regulation, which is examined in detail later, was introduced in 2015 precisely with the objective of guaranteeing, as much as possible, the uniform application of State aid law across the Union. The provisions contained in this chapter codify and develop the approach that the Commission suggested in 2009 in its Notice on cooperation with national courts ('*Enforcement Notice*').[4] At that time too, the challenge was to combine administrative simplification (*i.e.*, streamlining procedures and implementing the 'bigger on big things, and smaller on small things' approach), which is another key factor of the modernisation process, with the effort to safeguard uniformity in the application of State aid rules, which are still characterised by the Commission's exclusive competence to assess compatibility. The analysis in Part Two clarifies whether this compromise has been successful. In doing so, it also answers the question raised above: whether the modernisation process fostered the effectiveness of the system of remedies and, more generally, whether it fostered the effectiveness of State aid rules through private enforcement more than it did through public enforcement.

4. Commission Notice on the enforcement of State aid law by national courts, OJEU 2009/C 085/01. This notice is also referred to herein as the 'Private Enforcement Notice'; the terms 'New Private Enforcement Notice' or simply 'New Enforcement Notice' are used to indicate the 2021 Enforcement Notice that completed, amended and replaced its 2009 predecessor. The first notice on cooperation with national courts, issued in 1995, is referred to herein as the 'Cooperation Notice' (*see* footnote 19 of this Part Two).

I ORIGIN AND SOURCES OF THE PRIVATE ENFORCEMENT OF STATE AID LAW

This chapter examines the origins and sources of private enforcement of State aid rules, analysing the role of creative jurisprudence and the limited legislative developments. It also discusses how these sources have shaped the current framework.

I.A Creative Case Law at the Origin of the Private Enforcement of State Aid Law

The EU institutions realised as early as the late seventies that effective enforcement of State aid rules could not be achieved without involving national courts in the task. The technique used is the same as in other areas of EU law: conferring individual rights on EU citizens related to the obligations that the Treaty provisions on State aid impose on Member States and entrusting national courts with the task of protecting them. By litigating their rights at the national level, private parties and national courts serve the common European interest of detecting State aid measures that would otherwise go unnoticed and thereby enhance the effectiveness of the Treaty provisions, despite the exclusive competence to assess State aid with which the Commission is vested.[5]

As long ago as in the late seventies, the Court of Justice paved the way for the application of State aid rules by national courts.[6] It acknowledged that these courts could act as decentralised courts of Union law by interpreting the relevant provisions on State aid, namely Article 107(1) TFEU, but only to the extent necessary to ascertain a breach of the procedural rules enshrined in the last sentence of Article 108(3) TFEU. When national courts are called on to assess whether the Member State granting the aid was in breach of the procedural rules, 'they may have cause to interpret and apply the concept of aid' under Article 107(1) TFEU and may also decide to stay the national judicial proceedings and make a reference for a preliminary ruling to the Court of Justice to obtain guidance on the interpretation of the relevant provisions on the concept of aid. This is the consequence of the 'direct effect' granted to those procedural rules.

---

5. *See*, among others, F. Pastor-Merchante and G. Monti, *The Functions of National Courts in the Private Enforcement of State Aid Law*, in P.L. Parcu, G. Monti, M. Botta, eds, 'EU State Aid Law', Edward Elgar Publishing Limited, 2020, p. 121; and F. Pastor-Merchante, *The EU Perspective on the Private Enforcement of State Aid Law*, in W. Wurmnest, F. Wollenschläger and T. Möllers, eds, *Private Enforcement of European Competition and State Aid Law: Current Challenges and the Way Forward*, Kluwer International, 2019. *See also* M. Merola and T. Ubaldi, *Il recupero degli aiuti illegali e incompatibili e le relative controversie dinanzi ai giudici nazionali*, in Dizionario sistematico del diritto della concorrenza, Lorenzo F. Pace ed., Jovene editore 2013, p. 799.
6. *See* Judgment of the Court of Justice of 22 March 1977, Case 78/76, *Steinike & Weinlig v. Federal Republic of Germany*, EU:C:1977:52, para. 14. Many other landmark judgments confirmed the position taken in *Steinike – see, e.g.*, Judgment of 21 November 1991, Case C-354/90, *Fédération Nationale du Commerce Extérieur des Produits Alimentaires and Others v. France*, para. 10; Judgment of 11 July 1996, Case C-39/94, *SFEI and Others*, EU:C:1996:285, para. 49; and Judgment of 5 October 2006, Case C-368/04, *Transalpine Ölleitung in Österreich*, EU:C:2006:644, para. 39.

Indeed, a few years earlier, in the landmark *Capolongo* judgment,[7] the Court of Justice held that the rules contained in the last sentence of Article 108(3) - namely the notification requirement for all aid projects and the standstill obligation - have a direct effect on national legal systems and can thus be invoked before national courts. Indeed, the Court clarified that the last sentence of Article 108(3) TFEU (the last sentence of Article 93(3) EEC at the time of the judgment), concerning new aid projects, establishes procedural criteria the national courts can appraise. A few months later, in the *Lorenz* judgment, the Court held that the immediately applicable nature of the provisions contained in the last sentence of Article 108(3) extends to the whole period to which it applies, *i.e.*, to the whole preliminary investigation and, when the Commission sets in motion the formal investigation, up to the final decision.[8]

Thus, the direct effect of the prohibition on implementing aid without previous authorisation applies not only to aid that has not been notified but also to aid implemented before the end of the Commission's preliminary or official investigation, depending on the situation. The Court added that:

> while the direct effect of the prohibition in question requires national courts to apply it without any possibility of its being excluded by rules of national law of any kind whatsoever, it is for the internal legal system of every Member State to determine the legal procedure leading to this result.[9]

With these statements, the Court 'fuelled' the private enforcement of State aid law before national courts.[10] In a nutshell, the direct effect applies to both the notification requirement and the standstill obligation - national courts must therefore uphold individual rights in cases of violation of these rules in accordance with the procedural rules of the Member State but regardless of any conflicting provision of national law.[11]

---

7. Judgment of the Court of Justice of 19 June 1973, Case 77/72, *Carmine Capolongo v. Azienda Agricole Maya*, EU:C:1973:65, para. 6, where the Court held:

> Whilst, for projects introducing new aids or altering existing ones, the last sentence of Article 93 (3) establishes procedural criteria which the national court can appraise, the same does not hold true for existing systems of aid referred to in Article 93 (1).With regard to such aids, the provisions of Article 92 (1) are intended to take effect in the legal systems of Member States, so that they may be invoked before national courts, where they have been put in concrete form by acts having general application provided for by Article 94 or by decisions in particular cases envisaged by Article 93 (2).

The matter involved a financial charge levied by a public body (ENCC) upon importation into Italy of packaging from a Member State.

8. *See* Judgment of the Court of Justice of 11 December 1973, Case 120/73, *Gebrüder Lorenz GmbH v. Federal Republic of Germany and Land Rheinland-Pfalz*, EU:C:1973:152.
9. *Ibid.*, at para. 9.
10. This expression is borrowed from Pastor-Merchante and Monti, *The Functions of National Courts in the Private Enforcement of State Aid Law*, cited in footnote 5 of this Part Two.
11. For a short summary of the origin and sources of the private enforcement of State aid law, *see*, among others, J. Derenne and C. Kaczmarek, *La recuperation des aides illegals: le role du juge national dans le* 'private enforcement' *du droit des aides d'Etat*, ERA Forum (2009) 10, pp. 251-268, in particular section 2.

Conversely, the substantive provision in Article 107(1) TFEU is not absolute and unconditional, as the Commission and the Council both have the power to authorise aid that they consider compatible with the internal market - and they enjoy wide discretion to that effect. Therefore, claimants in national proceedings cannot simply challenge a State measure as aid and claim its incompatibility with the Union rules, because national courts have no competence whatsoever to determine that a given measure infringes the rules on State aid and is to be deemed incompatible with the internal market. National courts can do so, however, where the provisions of Article 107 have been applied and implemented either by general provisions enacted on the basis of Article 109 or by decisions adopted in accordance with Article 108(2) TFEU.

Therefore, according to the *Capolongo* judgment, the same conclusion reached with respect to the last sentence of Article 108(3) in relation to aid projects (*i.e.*, new aid) holds true for aid that has become existing aid within the meaning of Article 108(1) TFEU following the Commission's exercise of its exclusive competence, *i.e.*, only where the provisions of Article 107(1) 'have been put in concrete form by acts having general application' provided for by Article 109 TFEU or 'by decisions in particular cases' envisaged by Article 108(2) TFEU.

In all other instances, finding State aid incompatible is the exclusive competence of the Commission, which acts by means of the appropriate procedures laid down in the Treaty and subject to review by the European courts.[12] In a nutshell, State aid is not prohibited under Article 107 TFEU; rather, it is declared incompatible with the common market unless necessary for reasons of economic efficacy (in the case of market failures) or equity and other common objectives (*e.g.*, social protection and cohesion). Consequently, no penalty of nullity exists for State administrative acts that grant aid,[13] and national courts have no power to declare incompatible aid void as they do with anticompetitive arrangements under Article 101 TFEU.

I.B Scarce Legislative Initiatives in Support of the Private Enforcement of State Aid Rules

As discussed above, the upper source of the private enforcement of State aid rules is in the TFEU itself, specifically the first sentence of Article 108(3) as interpreted by the Court of Justice. Through its case law, the Court of Justice has contributed to more precisely shaping the remedial strategy that national courts are supposed to adopt in State aid cases.[14] However, the EU legislator has done very little so far to develop this

12. *See* Judgment of the Court of Justice of 22 March 1977, Case 78/76, *Steinike & Weinlig v. Federal Republic of Germany*, cited in footnote 6 of this Part Two.
13. This would also clash with national legal systems, as State aid is most often granted by the public administration based on legislative provisions, which could never be declared void by the Commission.
14. Guidance based on case law, however, should not be overestimated. Moreover, private enforcement cannot be the catch-all solution to the weaknesses of the present system of remedies, as this book seeks to prove. On this specific point, therefore, this author does not concur with those scholars who consider that the Court of Justice has developed 'an increasingly exacting and precise set of rules regarding the remedies that national courts are bound to grant

particular aspect of State aid law in provisions with binding legal force. This may seem paradoxical if one considers that private enforcement harmonisation directives have been adopted since 2014 in the field of antitrust, in which the role of national courts, although crucial, is limited in scope compared to the variety of national court proceedings related to State aid matters, 'which go much beyond the strict definition of private enforcement and cover a wide variety of procedural settings'.[15]

The first wave of modernisation of State aid rules in the late nineties did not include provisions or actions related to private enforcement. The first Procedural Regulation adopted in 1999[16] was totally silent on the powers of national courts in the enforcement of State aid rules. The issue first came to light in the second phase of modernisation with the 2005-2009 SAAP,[17] when the Commission stressed that private litigation in national courts can contribute to improving both State aid monitoring and the enforcement of the relevant rules, thus ensuring increased discipline. In the Commission's view, the enhanced transparency (both in the granting of State aid and in State aid procedures), which is among the procedural objectives of the SAAP, should result in making it easier for firms, competition specialists and the public at large to take action against unlawful aid, particularly before national courts.

However, beyond this declaration of principle, very little has in fact been done to improve the transparency of State aid procedures, as discussed in Part One of this book.[18] And when it comes to concrete actions and proposals envisaged in the SAAP, no legislative initiative was included aimed at addressing the lack of private enforcement (the proposal for amendment of the first Procedural Regulation was included in the roadmap only as a possibility and was eventually left behind). In terms of soft law, by contrast, the SAAP foresaw the adoption of a communication on cooperation between national courts and the Commission in the State aid field, and the Commission accomplished the task by enacting the Enforcement Notice in 2009.[19]

This piece of soft law is examined in detail below but of course, cannot compensate for the lack of any binding provision intended to foster private enforcement. In the SAAP, the Commission also announced that it would engage in advocacy initiatives meant to encourage stakeholders to make full use of the possibilities offered by the direct effect of the last sentence of Article 108(3) TFEU. Similarly, the

in State aid cases' and that 'EU State aid law is quite specific when it comes to prescribing the outcome that national proceedings ought to produce' (F. Pastor-Merchante and G. Monti, *The Functions of National Courts in the Private Enforcement of State Aid Law*, cited in footnote 5 of this Part Two).

15. B. Brandtner, T. Beranger and C. Lessenich, *Private State Aid Enforcement*, in European State Aid Law Quarterly, 2010, Volume 9, Issue 1, pp. 23-32 https://doi.org/10.21552/estal/2010/1/168.
16. *See* footnote 17 of Part One.
17. 2005-2009 State Aid Action Plan, COM(2005) 107 final.
18. *See* Part One, section III.C.3.
19. Cited in footnote 4 of this Part Two. The 2009 Enforcement Notice replaced the 1995 Cooperation Notice (Notice on cooperation between national courts and the Commission in the State aid field, OJ C 312, 23.11.1995, p. 8), which was a first high-level attempt to enforce State aid rules via cooperation between the Commission and national judiciaries. The 1995 Cooperation Notice remained largely unapplied, basically because it lacked practical guidance for the Member States' national courts.

Commission reminded national courts of the role they can play in controlling whether measures deemed to fall under a block exemption or under the *de minimis* threshold – and which have therefore not been notified to the Commission – actually fulfil the requirements for exemption or are rather designed to circumvent the application of Article 107(1) TFEU.[20] Indeed, the role of national courts is expected to grow significantly due to the increasing volume of aid covered by the GBER[21] In this context, national courts have full competence to ascertain whether all the conditions, limitations and requirements of the exemption were actually complied with.[22]

Finally, the Commission called on company auditors, national market regulators and national courts of auditors to contribute to ensuring that State aid rules be fully respected. To help achieve these objectives, the Commission launched a study focusing on: (i) the role of national courts in the protection of individual rights of interested parties; and (ii) the enforcement of negative decisions at national level. Only the first aspect of the study is of relevance in this part of the book and is discussed at length below.

In terms of hard law, however, no provision affecting the private enforcement of State aid rules was adopted until the third phase of modernisation launched with the SAM Communication in 2012.[23] Although the SAM Communication was silent on private enforcement, it foresaw the proposal of amendment of the Procedural Regulation, as announced in the SAAP seven years before. The new Procedural Regulation was eventually enacted in 2015.[24] It included, in Chapter X, one single article (Article 29) concerning cooperation between the Commission and national courts. As clarified in recital 37 of the same regulation, consistency in the application of the State aid rules requires that arrangements be established to foster this cooperation. The arrangements referred to in recital 37 are to a large extent those that had already been foreseen as best practices in the 2009 Enforcement Notice.[25] Article 29 of the Procedural Regulation merely codified those arrangements and added a bit of practically relevant clarification.

Under Article 29(1), national courts may ask the Commission to send them information that they consider relevant for their assessment and can seek the Commission's opinion on points concerning the application of State aid rules. Conversely, under Article 29(2), the Commission may submit written observations to national courts on its own initiative. National courts must allow the Commission to submit written observations when the Commission believes this is necessary for the consistent application of State aid law. The Commission may also ask a national court's

20. State Aid Action Plan, cited in footnote 17 of this Part Two.
21. Commission Regulation (EU) No 651/2014 of 17 June 2014 declaring certain categories of aid compatible with the internal market in application of Arts 107 and 108 of the Treaty, amended by Commission Regulation (EU) 2023/1315 of 23 June 2023.
22. The specific requirements national courts must comply with in this context are analysed below (*see* Part Two, Chapter V.A).
23. Communication from the Commission to the European Parliament, the Council, the European Economic and Social Committee and the Committee of Regions, EU State Aid Modernisation (SAM), COM(2012) 209 final.
24. *See* footnote 18 of Part One.
25. *See* section 3 (Commission Support for National Courts) of the Commission Notice on the enforcement of State aid law by national courts, OJEU, C 85, 9.4.2009, p. 1.

permission to intervene orally at a hearing. The national court may grant the Commission leave to intervene orally but is not bound to do so and can freely determine whether its oral intervention may be useful in the specific case pending before it. Under the third sentence of Article 29(3), the Commission may also request the relevant court to access the file by sending documents it considers necessary to assess the case and prepare its observations.

This last provision is not entirely clear, but it seems rational to infer from it that the competent national court is bound to grant access to documents the Commission considers relevant for its assessment but is not obliged to grant it access to the whole file. When submitting information or opinions, either upon request from national courts or on its own initiative, the Commission should act exclusively in accordance with its duty to defend the public interest,[26] which can only mean that it should be very careful to avoid siding with either party in the proceedings and should therefore limit itself to supporting the national court without interfering with the court's assessment of the case.

In an article published in 2017, A. Scott reported a certain number of practical examples of application of the new cooperation tools envisaged by Article 29. The examples prove that Article 29 immediately attracted the interest of national courts in several Members States, which requested both information in the Commission's possession (or the sending of documents in the Commission's file) and opinions on how to interpret the notion of State aid, for instance, in cases involving public bank guarantees. Reliance on cooperation with the Commission seemed to be considered a useful tool by several national courts, even in Member States with significant experience in the field, such as Germany, Spain and France. However, Scott reports that in other cases national courts, when considering the possibility of adopting interim measures, have been frustrated by not receiving clear answers to their requests for assistance, especially when these requests concerned the expected timing of the Commission's decision on the compatibility of the aid under discussion.

The Commission, in turn, wasted no time in making use of its power to submit *amicus curiae* observations on its own motion. Scott reports that it did so in 2015 in several cases, spanning from cases related to the execution of recovery decisions to the finding of State aid elements in arbitration awards, and across different countries, such as France, Romania, Belgium and even the United States.

This albeit limited change, triggered by the modernisation process, can open avenues for a reform of the system of remedies. National courts are at liberty to draw from the violation of State aid procedural rules all the consequences available under national law, *i.e.*, to resort to all the remedies that national law puts at their disposal. Thus, the Commission may use the cooperation tools envisaged by Article 29 of the Procedural Regulation not only as a way to support national courts with its experience in the public enforcement of State aid law but also as an experimental field to elaborate on possible innovative remedies.

26. *See* recital 37 of the Procedural Regulation.

In this sense, cooperation between the Commission and national courts can pave the way to a sort of reciprocal fertilisation between State aid public and private enforcement, which can be very enriching in view of the proposed reform of the system of remedies. Part Four of this book examines these ideas further.

II THE 2009 COMMISSION NOTICE ON THE ENFORCEMENT OF STATE AID LAW BY NATIONAL COURTS: FOCUS ON REMEDIES

This chapter analyses the context and philosophy behind the 2009 Private Enforcement Notice, focusing on the cooperation tools and remedies available to national courts in enforcing State aid rules. It examines how the Enforcement Notice clarifies basic rules and provides guidance to national courts.

As mentioned, it is only with the SAAP that the Commission started reflecting on the need to enhance private enforcement as a complementary tool for improving the effectiveness of its enforcement policy in accordance with the principle of division of competences and cooperation between Member States and the Commission. The Enforcement Notice, *i.e.*, the Notice on the enforcement of State aid law by national courts, was thus first released in 2009 as a final achievement of the roadmap set out with the SAAP. As the basic principles of the Enforcement Notice have remained unchanged since, despite the adoption of the New Enforcement Notice,[27] these principles are recalled in detail here, whereas only significant changes will be highlighted when examining the New Enforcement Notice.

The aim of this chapter is not to provide a detailed description of the content of the Enforcement Notice - as this is examined later in the context of the hallmarks of private enforcement remedies[28] - but rather to explain its origins, general philosophy, and structure. Moreover, although reference is made, when necessary, to the overall system of private enforcement and to the contribution this system can bring to the effectiveness of State aid rules, the main focus is on the restorative remedies that national courts can order, with a view to assessing the necessity and urgency of a reform of the State aid system of remedies based on due consideration of public and private enforcement together. Similarly, the role of national courts in ensuring the execution of the Commission's recovery decisions is not covered by the analysis here. Indeed, in this case, national courts support the Commission in the execution of decisions it adopts;[29] therefore, they contribute to public enforcement and do not uphold the rights of private parties.[30] The same holds true for the role of national

27. *See* Part Two, section III.
28. The essential content of the Enforcement Notice in relation to remedies applied within the framework of private enforcement is organised around its essential substantive and procedural criteria and discussed in Chapters III and IV below.
29. *See* Part One, sections II.A.4 and II.A.5, in connection with the 2007 Recovery Notice and Part One, section II.B.1, last paragraph, in connection with the New Recovery Notice.
30. On this topic, *see* M. Merola and T. Ubaldi, *Il recupero degli aiuti illegali e incompatibili e le relative controversie dinanzi ai giudici nazionali*, in Dizionario sistematico del diritto della concorrenza, Lorenzo F. Pace ed., Jovene editore 2013, p. 799; Alain Ronzano, *Recovery of Aid: The EU Court of Justice Urges National Judges to Render Decisions on Illegal State Aid Recovery Requests Even When the State Aid Compatibility Is Still Being Debated (CELF)*, March 2010, Concurrences No. 2-2010, Art. 65434; and T. Lübbin and T. Morgan, *State Aid, National Courts and the Separation of Powers: Should Judges Be Bound to the European Commission's Unfinished State Aid Businesses?*, Journal of European Competition law & Practice, May 2014, Volume 5, Issue 5 https://doi.org/10.1093/jeclap/lpu013.

authorities when they find that they have granted aid in disregard of the procedural obligations enshrined in Article 108(3) TFEU. Although the *Eesti Pagar* and *Provinz Bozen* case law[31] holds that, in such circumstances, national authorities have the same duties, *mutatis mutandis*, as those incumbent on national courts - including that of recovering, on their own initiative, the unlawfully granted aid - they nonetheless act as public authorities to prevent a Commission recovery decision. Therefore, this kind of national enforcement belongs to the broad category of public enforcement rather than private enforcement, and while it can contribute to the effectiveness of State aid rules, it adds nothing in terms of the nature of remedies.

II.A The Context and Underlying Philosophy of the Enforcement Notice

The 2009 Enforcement Notice originates from its direct predecessor, the 1995 Cooperation Notice,[32] and the 2006 Study on the enforcement of State aid rules at the national level ('*2006 Enforcement Study*'), commissioned by the Commission within the framework of the SAAP. The 2006 Enforcement Study revealed that despite the increase of State aid legal proceedings at the Member State level, their contribution to enforcing compliance with State aid rules was relatively limited.[33]

Unsurprisingly, the study devoted particular attention to the remedies. First, it examined the various actions that could be brought before national courts and how these courts could contribute to the effective enforcement of State aid rules. It then focused on the recovery of unlawful State aid and analysed the enforcement practice in all Member States.

Consequently, the Enforcement Notice's main objective was to provide national courts guidance on the remedies available at the national level in the case of a breach of State aid rules and to introduce practical tools to support national courts dealing with this topic, in line with the Commission's commitment under the SAAP to a strict approach towards unlawful and incompatible aid.

The underlying philosophy of the 2009 Enforcement Notice is straightforward: The Enforcement Notice is one of the last initiatives taken by the Commission to implement the SAAP and, more specifically, the 'less and better targeted State aid' principle. A strict approach towards unlawful and incompatible aid is seen by the Commission as an essential component of this principle because all aid that goes unchecked inevitably clashes with the objective of redirecting public spending to

31. Cited in footnote 11 of the Introduction.
32. Notice on cooperation between national courts and the Commission in the State aid field, OJ C 312, 23.11.1995, p. 8, cited in footnote 19 of this Part Two.
33. Indeed, only 6% of the State aid litigation in the period 1996-2006 was through genuine private enforcement proceedings, *i.e.*, direct actions brought by competitors against aid beneficiaries, and only 19% concerned actions brought by competitors against a Member State authority to obtain damages, recovery or injunctions aimed at reducing the anticompetitive effect of the underlying State aid measures. The large majority of the legal proceedings concerned either actions brought by beneficiaries to challenge the recovery of unlawful and incompatible State aid ordered by the Commission or actions brought by taxpayers seeking relief from a discriminatory tax burden and therefore claiming application of the same undue tax advantage that was deemed to be State aid in their favour.

horizontal objectives of common interest. The Commission needs the support of national courts in discouraging the granting of unnotified and incompatible aid, even more so if one considers that the Treaty does not envisage penalties for the infringement of State aid rules and that the Commission can order only the recovery of the aid. Therefore, relying on remedies that can be imposed by national courts to uphold the rights of third parties (mainly competitors of aid recipients) is tantamount to the effectiveness of the 'less and better targeted State aid' principle.

II.B The 2006 Enforcement Study

The 2006 Enforcement Study commissioned by the European Commission's Directorate-General for Competition provided the Commission with a sufficiently clear picture of the contribution of national courts to the implementation of the effectiveness objective up to that point. The first part of the 2006 Enforcement Study gives a broad overview of the application of State aid rules by national courts, whereas the second part focuses on remedies, particularly on the recovery of unlawful State aid stemming from private enforcement proceedings.

The 2006 Enforcement Study's methodology is a comparative legal analysis of the cases inventoried in all fifteen Member States of the European Community (before the 2004 enlargement): the analysis is conducted according to the categories in which the individual cases fall. These categories are determined by reference to the economic goal pursued by the parties bringing the action before national courts rather than to the procedural setting in the Member State concerned. For each Member State, the 2006 Enforcement Study outlines the availability of judicial relief and a list of cases. The 2006 Enforcement Study's main findings can be summarised by focusing first on general aspects and then on remedies.

With regard to the general aspects (Part I), the 2006 Enforcement Study is divided into three sections. First, the authors explain that national courts apply State aid law in a wide variety of procedural settings (*e.g.*, actions by taxpayers for discriminatory legislation or by private parties against Member States). They note that the number of cases significantly increased and that parties progressively gained more experience in invoking State aid law in national proceedings. Second, however, the authors underline that in more than 50% of cases, private parties brought actions to seek relief from a burden not imposed on other parties (*e.g.*, tax exemption). Therefore, although the total number of cases sharply increased over time, only a limited number of direct actions were brought against competitors. Moreover, in the few cases of private actions against competitors, claimants typically only obtained the suspension and/or the recovery of the aid, as opposed to monetary damages, which were never awarded. The authors further observe that the uncertainty as to the legal basis to be used – exacerbated by the diversity of national rules – and the absence of uniform procedures likely contributed to the limited development of direct actions. Third, although recovery had improved over the previous few years, several obstacles still existed also in this respect. The authors list the following: (i) lack of clarity as to the national body responsible for issuing a recovery decision, the beneficiary required to repay, and the amount to be repaid; (ii) absence of a clear predetermined procedure; (iii) unavailability or no use of interim relief; (iv) stay of the recovery proceedings while an appeal is pending; and (v) administrative obstacles faced by governmental authorities of a Member State when recovering aid.

When it comes to examining remedies in detail (Part II), the 2006 Enforcement Study reviews the state of play in the field, summarises the main obstacles to efficient recovery, and proposes remedies. It also recommends adopting best practice guidelines. More specifically, the 2006 Enforcement Study analyses the practice of the five Member States with the largest total number of recovery cases as at 1 July 2005 (Germany, France, Spain, Italy and Belgium). For each one, the 2006 Enforcement Study examines the practice of administrative recovery and corresponding court decisions by highlighting the national authority responsible for recovery, the rules applicable, the possibility of interim relief, the extent to which the beneficiary's legitimate expectations can prevent recovery, and other obstacles to immediate and effective recovery. The 2006 Enforcement Study then briefly describes the situation in the other Member States, except for Ireland.

A series of common elements are outlined. For instance, in all the selected Member States, recovery is the responsibility of the same central or local authority that granted the aid. In most cases, the applicable rules are determined by the nature of the act: administrative law (if the aid was granted by an act of public law or in any event through the exercise of public authorities' prerogatives) or civil law (if the aid resulted from a civil transaction), or even a combination of both. The situation is reportedly different in Belgium, where the decision to order recovery is based on administrative law whereas the procedure to collect the amount is based on civil law. A similar situation exists in relation to the beneficiary's legitimate expectations as a means of preventing recovery: beneficiaries have less and less relied on the legitimate expectation defence successfully in all jurisdictions under review.

Recovery through administrative law is generally more efficient because the administrative order is immediately enforceable. If the recovery is sought through civil procedures, the authority seeking to recover the aid should generally request interim relief and comply with the requirements thereof, notably by proving urgency. Moreover, specific considerations apply when the obligation to repay unlawful aid interferes with the application of national insolvency procedures aimed at favouring the restructuring of insolvent companies rather than winding them up. However, the 2006 Enforcement Study simply flags the problem without examining it in detail or proposing specific measures.

II.C From the 2006 Enforcement Study to the Enforcement Notice

The 2009 Enforcement Notice supposedly relied extensively on the outcome of the 2006 Enforcement Study, but a closer examination reveals that it failed to address all the concerns the 2006 Enforcement Study raised and only partially followed the suggestions made by its authors. The 2006 Enforcement Study itself, as mentioned, did not contain an exhaustive inventory of all the issues related to the application of remedies in the private enforcement of State aid – as this was not its objective – let alone examine them in detail.

Rather than considering all the findings and recommendations contained in the 2006 Enforcement Study, the Commission only cherry-picked a few of them that corresponded to the desired approach of the Enforcement Notice and, of course, relied on the undeniable – albeit very basic and generic – indication that the private enforcement of State aid rules was insufficiently used and needed to be encouraged. In short, the Commission conceived the Enforcement Notice as an informative tool aimed at clarifying the basic rules and offering straightforward indications to national courts. Hence, its structure is very rational and didactic.

The Enforcement Notice starts by recalling the basic criteria that can assist national courts in the interpretation of Article 87(1) of the EC Treaty (now Article 107(1) TFEU),[34] as this is the preliminary check that national courts should invariably conduct before they consider possible remedies. If Article 107(1) does not apply, there can be no violation of the procedural rules (*i.e.*, prior notification and standstill obligations). As these rules are the only ones directly applicable in national legal systems, if no breach of procedural rules occurs, no remedial measure can be adopted at national level. The Enforcement Notice then briefly analyses the procedural rules by focusing on the notions of: (i) existing aid; and (ii) aid schemes in order to provide guidance to national courts on determining whether procedural rules have been breached.[35] It also reminds national courts that in case of doubt they can ask the Commission for an opinion on the applicability of the GBER or on whether the aid under scrutiny is granted in accordance with an existing aid scheme.

The Enforcement Notice also analyses the role of national courts in detail, starting with a distinction between the respective tasks of the Commission and national courts, as clearly defined in case law.[36] Only the first part of this analysis is relevant here, as it addresses the issue of national courts enforcing Article 108(3) TFEU in cases involving a breach of procedural rules (unlawful aid).[37] The Commission does not hesitate to state that dealing with legal actions brought by affected parties is one of the most important roles of national courts in the State aid field. The Commission even goes as far as to portray the role of national courts as that of protecting competitors' rights. In doing so, the Commission acknowledges that its own powers to protect competitors are limited, basically because it is obliged to conduct a full and typically lengthy compatibility assessment – regardless of any breach of procedural rules – before it can adopt a final negative decision to order recovery. Furthermore, the Commission's powers to issue recovery injunctions are subject to very strict legal requirements.

The Enforcement Notice briefly refers to the national courts' obligation to adopt preventive remedies to protect the rights of individuals affected by violations of the

34. Enforcement Notice, cited in footnote 4 of this Part Two, sections 8-13.
35. *Ibid.*, sections 14-18.
36. *Ibid.*, sections 19-22 and the case law cited in those sections.
37. *Ibid.*, section 2.2. Conversely, section 2.3 examines the role of national courts in the implementation of negative Commission decisions that order recovery.

standstill obligation and block the payment of unlawful aid. It then focuses on remedies, namely the recovery of the nominal amount of the unlawful aid, the recovery of interest, and the award of damages. The Enforcement Notice also contains a section on interim measures. Interim measures can indeed be appropriate when the unlawful aid has not yet been disbursed or when the issuance of a final judgment can take time and the competitive harm which stems from the aid's unlawfulness could increase in the meantime. The Commission goes as far as to suggest that national courts adopt a specific remedy, *i.e.*, to order that the unlawful aid and the unlawfulness period's interest be placed in a blocked account until the matter is resolved. The same remedy can be appropriate when national court proceedings run parallel to a Commission investigation and the national court wishes to await the outcome of the Commission's compatibility assessment before deciding whether to order recovery.

Although the section of the Enforcement Notice devoted to the role of national courts in the implementation of negative Commission decisions that order recovery is irrelevant here for the reasons mentioned earlier (*i.e.*, it is nothing more than a specific phase of public enforcement), the possibility to claim damages for the failure by the Member State authorities to comply with a Commission recovery decision is worthy of note. The Commission includes a paragraph in the Enforcement Notice to deal with this kind of legal action and essentially takes the view that infringement of the obligation to implement a recovery decision must be treated as a violation of the standstill obligation, thereby applying the principles set out in the *Francovich* and *Brasserie du Pêcheur* judgments.[38]

The last paragraph of the central section of the Enforcement Notice, which describes the role of national courts, is entitled 'Procedural rules and legal standing before national courts', but it in fact sets out the limits to the general rule of Member States' procedural autonomy. Procedural autonomy is already the general rule in relation to public enforcement for the implementation of Commission recovery orders under Article 16(3) of the Procedural Regulation.[39] This rule therefore applies even more so in private enforcement. The limitations or exceptions to this rule stem from some of the basic features of private enforcement of State aid rules, first and foremost the principles of equivalence and effectiveness.[40] All such features are examined in Chapter V below.

38. 2009 Enforcement Notice, para. 69. *See* Judgment of the Court of Justice of 19 November 1991, *Andrea Francovich and Danila Bonifaci and others v. Italian Republic*, in Joined Cases C-6/90 and C-9/90, EU:C:1991:428, and Judgment of the Court of Justice of 5 March 1996, *Brasserie du Pêcheur SA v. Bundesrepublik Deutschland and The Queen v. Secretary of State for Transport, ex parte: Factortame Ltd and others*, in Joined Cases C-46/93 and C-48/93, EU:C:1996:79.
39. The origin and meaning of procedural autonomy for the implementation of recovery decisions is discussed in Part One, section I.A.2.4.
40. The principle of effectiveness is of particular value in this respect: as mentioned in connection with public enforcement, it prevails over the principle of procedural autonomy and imposes an obligation of result on Member States. The nature of this obligation is different in public and private enforcement. In public enforcement, the result to be achieved is the enforcement of the Commission's recovery order or alternative/ancillary remedies. In private enforcement, the result is to safeguard the rights that individuals draw from State aid provisions. As observed by M. Köhler, the statement in case law that 'it is for the internal legal system of every Member State to determine the legal procedure leading to this result' simply enables the national legislator 'to

II.D The Enforcement Notice's Focus on Cooperation Tools

Section 3 of the 2009 Enforcement Notice deals with the support the Commission can offer national courts based on the duty of sincere cooperation enshrined in Article 4(3) TEU. This is in no way a new tool, as the duty of sincere cooperation has always existed in EU law, and the 1995 Cooperation Notice[41] offered national courts the possibility to seek the Commission's assistance. However, as the 2006 Enforcement Study revealed the very limited use of this tool by national courts, the Enforcement Notice reaffirms and elaborates on the benefits of the cooperation but leaves unchanged the two basic characteristics thereof: its voluntary nature for national courts and the utter[42] exclusion of private parties from the dialogue between national courts and the Commission. The Enforcement Notice also deals separately with the two main forms of cooperation: the transmission of information and requests for the Commission's opinion on specific issues of State aid law.

With regard to the transmission of information, national courts can ask the Commission for two different types of information that is relevant for their assessment: (i) information on the status of investigations pending before the Commission; and (ii) information and documentation in the Commission file that can be relevant for both the Commission and the national courts, *e.g.*, factual data, statistics, market studies commissioned by the Commission or provided by interested parties, and the like. These data can help national courts to classify a measure as State aid or existing aid because of previous Commission decisions or other elements or to determine the aid amount, *etc.*

In principle, the Commission is obliged to provide the given national court the information requested within one month from the request date. However, in transmitting information to national courts, the Commission will take into account its duty to protect professional secrecy. This may cause delays in sending the information because the Commission will first need to consult third parties. The Commission will also safeguard its own functioning and independence, which means that it may refuse to transmit internal documents or information concerning its decision-making process.

As to requests by national courts for the Commission's opinion concerning the application of State aid rules, these typically concern the classification of measures under scrutiny before the national courts as State aid or new/existing aid, particularly when one or more of the relevant requirements entail a detailed assessment.[43] Another typical situation that can lead national courts to seek assistance from the Commission

determine the way to arrive at a certain result – but the result has to be the same'. *See* M. Köhler, *Private Enforcement of State Aid Law: Problems of Guaranteeing EU Rights by means of National (Procedural) Law*, European State Aid Law Quarterly (ESTaL), 2012, Issue 2, Jubilee Issue: 10th Anniversary of European State Aid Law Quarterly (ESTaL), 2012, pp. 369-388 https://doi.org/10.21552/estal/2012/2/279.

41. Cited in footnote 19 of this Part Two.
42. Not only can private parties not ask the Commission to intervene, as the cooperation instrument is intended to serve the public interest only but they are also not given the possibility to submit comments or be heard by the Commission when its assistance is requested by the national court.
43. Cases of fiscal aid or measures administered by intermediate bodies are good examples of situations that can require the Commission's assistance, as they usually raise difficult questions

concerns the interpretation of block exemption rules or the classification of a measure as an aid scheme rather than individual aid. National courts can also ask the Commission to clarify the scope of a previous decision to determine whether individual aid is covered by it and therefore constitutes existing aid.

In addition, although national courts cannot question the Commission on issues related to the compatibility assessment because they have no competence in this respect, as mentioned above, they may nonetheless request information on whether an investigation is pending and when a decision is likely to be adopted. This can indeed provide national courts with relevant elements to facilitate their autonomous assessment of the best way to handle the case in compliance with national procedural rules. The Commission will try to assist national courts by giving indications as to the likely timeframe for the adoption of a decision.

Finally - and of particular relevance for this book - national courts can seek guidance from the Commission on the application of remedies. Hence, they can inquire about the quantification of aid, the calculation of interest, the existence of exceptional circumstances that would prevent a national court from ordering full recovery in accordance with EU law, and even the appropriate methodology for calculating damages if damages actions are brought before them.

From a procedural standpoint, the same duties of protecting professional secrecy and safeguarding the Commission's independence mentioned in relation to the transmission of information apply also to requests for opinions. Likewise, the Commission does not hear the parties to national proceedings before issuing its opinion. It is the national courts' responsibility to decide how to incorporate the Commission's opinion into their court files and how to take it into account in national proceedings. It is also the national courts' responsibility to protect individual rights during proceedings. The Commission's opinion, which is to be provided to a requesting national court within four months from the request, is not made public.

One issue the Enforcement Notice does not address with sufficient clarity is the interplay between a request for the Commission's opinion by a national court and the possibility or obligation of a request for a preliminary ruling under Article 267 of the TFEU. The Enforcement Notice states that matters concerning the interpretation of State aid law can obviously also lead national courts to ask for a preliminary ruling of the Court of Justice and that the use of the preliminary reference procedure is, in principle, mandatory when no further judicial remedy against a national court's decision exists under national law. It is also recalled that only the Court of Justice's authoritative interpretation of the law is binding on national courts, unlike the Commission's opinion.

Notwithstanding these obvious warnings, it is highly doubtful that presenting a request for the Commission's opinion as an alternative to the preliminary ruling procedure is the correct and most sensible approach. First, the Enforcement Notice should have stated more clearly that requesting the Commission's opinion on interpretative issues is not an option for national courts of last resort. It would be

in relation to the notion of selectivity or the use of public resources. However, national courts may seek assistance on any aspect related to the interpretation of Arts 107(1) and 108(3).

contradictory for any such court to consider itself not obliged to refer the case to the Court of Justice and then request the Commission's opinion. Indeed, if a national court seeks the Commission's advice, this is because: (i) the interpretative question raised is key to ruling on the case pending before it; and (ii) the question has not been sufficiently clarified in the Court of Justice's existing case law. Under these circumstances, a preliminary ruling is mandatory, and no alternative exists in EU law. Second, even for national courts of a lower level, the preliminary ruling procedure set out in the Treaty obviously remains the most appropriate option when a genuine interpretative problem of EU law arises before them.

Requesting the Commission's opinion on questions related to the interpretation of State aid rules is therefore to be seen only as a preliminary check to help national courts autonomously assess the need to submit a request regarding the interpretation of EU law to the Court of Justice. When seen from this perspective, there is a very narrow scope for requests for opinions to the Commission on genuine questions of interpretation of EU law. By contrast, the Commission can be asked to opine on issues concerning the scope of previous decisions, the expected timing of future decisions, the methodology to be used for recovery or calculating damages or interest, and similar matters.

III PREPARATORY WORKS LEADING TO THE ADOPTION OF THE NEW PRIVATE ENFORCEMENT NOTICE AND MAIN CHANGES INTRODUCED

This chapter describes the preparatory works leading to the adoption of the New Private Enforcement Notice in 2021, highlighting the proposals made to expand the competencies of national courts and the need for improved cooperation with the Commission.

Despite the indication in the Enforcement Notice that the Commission intended to carry out a review five years after its adoption, a comprehensive review was delayed several times and was performed only between 2018 and 2019 with the Study on the enforcement of State aid rules and decisions by national courts ('*2019 Enforcement Study*').[44] The 2019 Enforcement Study was aimed at offering a comprehensive overview of the enforcement of State aid rules by national courts in the then twenty-eight Member States and at analysing cases decided between 1 January 2007 and 31 December 2017 and thirty-three rulings decided in 2018.

In terms of methodology, the 2019 Enforcement Study had four main tasks. Task 1 was to analyse and classify the most relevant rulings issued by national courts on State aid matters in the reference period. Task 2 was to summarise the main qualitative trends in State aid enforcement at the EU level and compare them with the trends identified by the 2006 Enforcement Study in order to select the key issues to address in the New Enforcement Notice. Task 3 was to propose best practices for national courts. Finally, Task 4 was to review the use of cooperation tools envisaged in Article 29 of the Procedural Regulation by national courts.

Chapter 1 of the 2019 Enforcement Study is an introductory chapter that describes the legal background, the objectives and a summary of the methodology applied. Chapters 2-4 set out the findings, which can be analysed in relation to three main aspects: (i) State aid enforcement by national courts, which corresponds to Tasks 1 and 2 and is the focus of Chapter 2; (ii) best practices in State aid enforcement, which corresponds to Task 3 and is the focus of Chapter 3; and (iii) use of cooperation tools, which corresponds to Task 4 and is presented in Chapter 4. The three main aspects just mentioned are analysed in the following three sections.

III.A The 2019 Enforcement Study's Findings on the National Courts Competent to Hear State Aid Cases and Possible Classifications of State Aid Claims

When analysing the degree of application of State aid rules in EU Member States, the 2019 Enforcement Study observes a huge growth in the number of cases, which tripled in the reference period. This is attributed to multiple factors, some of which are

44. The Study was conducted for DG Competition by the Spark Legal Network, the European University Institute, Ecorys and Caselex and published under the reference COMP/2018/001.

country-specific (*e.g.*, cultural factors such as active participation in EU initiatives and the level of awareness of competition-related litigation), whereas some others are general in nature (*e.g.*, the impact of the 2008 financial crisis and the new procedural rules enshrined in Council Regulation (EU) 2015/1589).

With regard to the categories of courts that hear private enforcement cases, the 2019 Enforcement Study points out that the absence of specific EU rules results in a distribution of cases among civil and administrative courts: in most Member States, administrative courts are competent when a claimant challenges an act issued by a public authority, whereas civil and commercial courts are competent when the granting of the aid does not entail an administrative act and, *a fortiori* when a claimant is seeking damages.

When it comes to analysing the categories of aid measures challenged before national courts, the 2019 Enforcement Study finds that most cases concern specific measures in relation to which the fulfilment of the conditions under Article 107(1) TFEU is not self-evident and the debate revolves around whether the measures represent new aid subject to the notification obligation. Fiscal measures (tax breaks/rebates) represent 18% of this category and grants/subsidies 24%. The generic reference 'others' is used for 43% of cases because they do not fall into any of the typical categories but are very fact-specific. As to the economic sectors involved, financial and insurance activities, transport and storage, and energy are the sectors most prone to litigation. This is mainly due to the State legacy (as in these sectors, State intervention has had or still has a prominent role), the financial crisis, the increasing support for green technologies, and the impact of public services regulations ('*SGEIs*') on these sectors.

Interestingly, the 2019 Enforcement Study classifies claimants in private enforcement cases under several categories: of course, competitors contribute most to the enforcement of State aid rules (36%), but public authorities also hold a significant share (18%), followed by third parties (9%). Beneficiaries account for 14% of the cases, but these likely refer to applications for annulment of State measures that implement Commission negative decisions. In terms of defendants, public authorities are the most frequent (60%), followed by beneficiaries (21%), competitors (5%), and third parties (2%).

With regard to the characteristics of the reported private enforcement cases, several country reports point out that lodging a claim before a national court in State aid matters is not parallel to other types of remedies: when competitors file a complaint with the Commission or a national administrative body, they generally do not start actions before national courts. Even more importantly for the analysis carried out in this book, parties tend to submit a complaint to the Commission in relation to unlawful aid rather than bring legal action before national courts because remedies are rarely awarded in private enforcement cases. This trend has various causes: some factors are exogenous (*e.g.*, courts reject claims that are not based on very solid evidence), and others are endogenous (*e.g.*, interested parties are discouraged by the burden of proof).

Most cases of private enforcement are standalone actions, but Annex 3 to the 2019 Enforcement Study reports a few follow-on actions concerning damages claims brought by competitors after the Commission issued a decision. In some cases, the claimant succeeded in obtaining interim relief to suspend the implementation of an aid measure. Among the cases that resulted in remedies being imposed, recovery of unlawful aid prevails over damages actions. Finally, national courts are more likely to award remedies when the Commission has already opened a formal investigation or made informal communications. The rate of cases ending before the Court of Justice through preliminary reference is deceptively low, accounting for only 13 % of the cases brought before national courts.

In terms of legal issues raised before national courts, most cases concern the application of the legal notion of 'aid' in its various components, *i.e.*, the concept of 'undertaking', the existence of an impact on inter-State trade and the *de minimis* regulation, and the notion of advantage, particularly in relation to the application of the MEOP or the *Altmark* criteria.

III.B The 2019 Enforcement Study's Recommendations on Best Practices in State Aid Enforcement

The best practices presented in the 2019 Enforcement Study are aimed at embedding a culture of State aid enforcement among national stakeholders, with the objective of achieving the aims of the public and private enforcement of State aid rules. Seven best practices are identified and divided into three categories.

The first category corresponds to the best practices related to aid recovery and consists of three best practices: (i) compliance with the then recently adopted legal framework governing aid recovery,[45] which is considered essential to increase legal certainty and reduce litigation; (ii) the inclusion of recovery instructions about possible recovery proceedings in the administrative act that grants the aid; and (iii) the adoption of internal rules that envisage penalties for national administrative authorities that fail to properly and timely enforce Commission decisions. The second category of best practices concerns national screening mechanisms (divided into *ex-ante* and *ex-post* mechanisms) to ensure compliance with State aid rules. The third category addresses institutional practices, *i.e.*, the adoption of rules to clarify: (i) the jurisdiction and competence of national courts in State aid disputes, which should also make national courts more confident with the application of State aid rules; and (ii) the principle of investigation, which supports the claimant in bringing a claim in line with the remedies available under State aid rules.

As is apparent, this section of the 2019 Enforcement Study only partially concerns the application of remedies in private enforcement proceedings. Most best practices suggested in the 2019 Enforcement Study relate to the support that national authorities and courts are supposed to offer the Commission with the enforcement of its own decisions or with developing a national culture of compliance with State aid rules.

However, some recommendations included in the third category are intended to foster the private enforcement of State aid rules. These include the recommendation for

45. The New Recovery Notice discussed above (*see* Part One, section II.B and footnote 125).

a clear definition of the jurisdiction and competences of national courts (which is indeed key to encourage interested parties to have recourse to the remedies that national law can offer), and the recommendation for specifically tailored procedural rules based on the *principle of investigation*, as they allow private parties to bring legal actions before national courts under the assumption that they can rely on the courts' investigative powers – at least if they are able to show a solid *prima facie* case. Nevertheless, this last recommendation is all but easy to implement in several national legal systems, which are driven by the *principle of demand* – as opposed to the principle of investigation – in civil and administrative judicial proceedings.[46] It is therefore clear that, in this respect, only a legislative initiative at the EU level would create the conditions for such a significant change in national judicial proceedings applicable to State aid matters.[47]

III.C The 2019 Enforcement Study's Findings on the Use of Cooperation Tools by the Commission and National Courts

The last chapter of the 2019 Enforcement Study starts with the finding that national courts have only limited experience with the use of cooperation tools. The reasons for this are twofold: first, the cooperation tools have not proven to be very relevant in assessing individual cases, and second, a significant number of judges at national courts are unaware of the existence of the cooperation tools. More precisely, judges who deal with State aid matters form a diversified group because they differ in terms of work experience, the type of judiciary they belong to, and the type of cases they handle. Most are not specialised in State aid and have rarely been involved in State aid cases. Even when a judge is familiar with the cooperation tools and values the option of asking for the Commission's informative support or opinion in the case of need, that judge will typically try to draw up an answer to the legal questions involved without consulting the Commission or the Court of Justice.

Under these circumstances – and taking into account that: (i) the majority of the judges who had used the cooperation tools reported that the procedure is easy and effective (although some complained about the lack of clarity); and (ii) most judges who had not used any cooperation tool showed willingness to do so in the future if a suitable case were to be submitted to them – the 2019 Enforcement Study's authors concluded that it was worth enhancing the existing cooperation tools. They also put forward several suggestions for their improvement, including inviting the Commission to issue more practical guidelines. The extent to which the Commission followed this advice in the New Enforcement Notice is examined later in this chapter.[48]

---

46. The principle of demand in judicial proceedings implies not only that proceedings start on the initiative of interested parties (*i.e.*, claimant or applicant) but also that they are governed to a large extent by the initiative of the parties in terms of *petitum* and burden of proof.
47. The importance of a legislative initiative to harmonise national legal proceedings in actions for the private enforcement of State aid rules is discussed in Part Four of this book.
48. *See* this Part Two, Chapter IV.

III.D The EFTA Study on the Private Enforcement of State Aid Rules

Another study on the private enforcement of State aid rules by national courts was performed in 2019 by the EFTA Authority (*'EFTA Study'*),[49] which led to very similar conclusions to those expressed in the EU's 2019 Enforcement Study.

The EFTA Study covers the entire period from the entry into force of the EEA Agreement in 1994 until the date of the EFTA Study's issuance. Its structure mirrors that of the EU's 2019 Enforcement Study. The EFTA Study, after an introduction describing the EEA EFTA States' legal framework, focuses on the obstacles that weaken the effectiveness of the private enforcement of State aid rules before illustrating the available cooperation tools. A recommendation of best practices and reform patterns follows.

The EFTA Study also analyses the specific situation in the three EEA EFTA States (Iceland, Lichtenstein and Norway) in as many chapters. The main finding is that private enforcement in the three countries is anything but largely developed, with only six cases in total in the reference period (five of which were in Norway and one in Iceland). Given the small number of relevant cases, drawing any general conclusion as to the solidity and suitability of the EEA EFTA States' national legal systems for private enforcement and effective remedies is difficult, as is detecting trends.

Although the private enforcement of State aid rules is a rare phenomenon, a slight upward trend can still be seen in the frequency of State aid claims before EEA EFTA States' courts. A distinction should be made between judicial proceedings aimed at enforcing recovery orders contained in negative decisions of the EFTA Surveillance Authority and genuine private enforcement actions brought by private parties claiming a breach of the standstill obligation. The Constitutional Court of Lichtenstein and the Norwegian Supreme Court have observed that, despite a certain lack of clarity of the procedural rules, the respective legal systems do not contain major obstacles to the enforcement of recovery orders issued by the EFTA Surveillance Authority. However, no examples of recovery orders issued by national courts for breach of the standstill obligation or successful actions for damages or requests for interim measures were found.

State aid rules are largely invoked not in genuine private enforcement cases but *rather in support of another claim* or as a way to convince courts of a certain interpretation of a rule, scheme or contractual clause. The main obstacles to the development of private actions based exclusively on the breach of Article 108(3) TFEU are difficulties in the correct application of the notion of aid combined with the absence of clear procedural rules. Like within the EU, the use of cooperation tools (*e.g.*, requesting an advisory opinion from the EFTA Court) is considered potentially beneficial to overcome some of the difficulties identified.

49. EFTA Surveillance Authority, *Study on Private Enforcement of State Aid Rules by National Courts in the EEA EFTA States* of July 2019.

IV CHANGES INTRODUCED WITH THE NEW PRIVATE ENFORCEMENT NOTICE

This chapter examines the changes brought by the New Private Enforcement Notice compared to the 2009 version, with particular attention to the competencies of national courts and the available remedies, especially in the context of damages actions. It analyses how these changes may affect the effectiveness of private enforcement of State aid rules.

Following the results of the 2019 Enforcement Study concerning the situation of the private enforcement of State aid rules in the then twenty-eight Member States, in January 2021 the Commission launched a public consultation through the publication of a Draft New Notice on the enforcement of State aid rules by national courts, which ended on 16 April 2021. On 23 July 2021, the Commission released the New Enforcement Notice, which sets out the long-awaited reform of the cooperation tools with national courts.[50]

The expectations were inevitably very high, as the New Enforcement Notice was supposed to not only take stock of the results of the studies on the enforcement of State aid rules by national courts but also codify and build on twelve years of case law developments following the previous Enforcement Notice. Even more importantly, the new Enforcement Notice was expected to adapt to policy and legislative changes that had occurred in the meantime, including those of such a calibre as the SAM in 2012 and the new Procedural Regulation in 2015.

IV.A Changes Related to the Enforcement Notice's Approach, Rationale and Structure

The approach and rationale of the New Enforcement Notice differ partially from those of the previous Enforcement Notice. The concern about effective implementation of Commission recovery orders is no longer the main driver; the New Enforcement Notice instead focuses much more on private actions and builds on the recently adopted Recovery Notice for public enforcement.[51] Even more importantly, the objective is now to foster a State aid control culture in Member States, as this is of paramount importance to achieving effectiveness and guaranteeing a level playing field in the current landscape, which features a large majority of State aid measures (more than 96% at EU-wide level) covered by the GBER or the *de minimis* regulation.[52] This percentage is likely to increase following the release of the latest version of the GBER, which includes State aid granted through the financial resources made available under

50. Commission Notice on the enforcement of State aid rules by national courts (2021/C), OJ C 305/1 of 30 July 2021, pp. 1-28.
51. *See* section 4 of the new Enforcement Notice, cited in Part One, section II.B and footnote 125.
52. Commission Regulation (EU) No 651/2014 of 17 June 2014 declaring certain categories of aid compatible with the internal market in application of Arts 107 and 108 of the Treaty (OJ L 187, 26.6.2014) (GBER).

the Resilience and Recovery Fund (RRF), the main instrument of the Next Generation EU Fund.[53]

Against this background, it is clear that the Commission's *ex-ante* scrutiny will be reduced even further in the coming months and years.[54] Rather, the Commission will put increasing emphasis on *ex-post* control, which is (and will probably remain as such given the lack of sufficient human resources) based on samples and selected categories of cases.[55] Conversely, an increasingly heavier burden for State aid control will lie on the shoulders of national courts and perhaps national authorities alike. The Commission will necessarily rely on cooperation tools and the principle of sincere cooperation. Further progress in this direction is just around the corner.

The new protocol in State aid control will tend to be that of increased emphasis on national courts' role and, sooner or later, shared competences between the Commission and the Member States rather than the Commission's exclusive competence, despite all the legislative and practical adjustments that this shift may require. National courts will need to be equipped to deal with all sorts of cases arising on the correct interpretation of the requirements of block exemptions in addition to the typical controversies around the classification of measures as State aid under Article 107(1) or as existing aid under Article 108(1). The legal sources for their assessment are, and will increasingly be, more complex than in the past, as they include not only primary and secondary law and the related case law but also a boosting set of soft law, which includes even atypical and, until recently, unknown sources such as templates or assessment grids.[56]

The Commission only refers to the 2019 Enforcement Study in passing at the beginning of the New Enforcement Notice,[57] but basically draws from it only that the private enforcement of State aid rules is insufficient, given the very low number of damages actions brought and remedies awarded by national courts and the likewise insufficient use of the cooperation tools. No reference whatsoever is made to the more detailed findings of the 2019 Enforcement Study or the EFTA Study, let alone to the reform recommendations put forward by the authors.

---

53. Regulation (EU) 2021/241 of the European Parliament and of the Council of 12 February 2021 establishing the Recovery and Resilience Facility (OJ L 57, 18.2.2021), amended by Regulation (EU) 2024/795 of the European Parliament and of the Council of 29 February 2024 establishing the Strategic Technologies for Europe platform (STEP) (OJ L, 2024/795, 29.2.2024).
54. Prior scrutiny is already de facto limited to: (i) rescue and restructuring aid for undertakings in difficulty or for the resolution of failing financial institutions; (ii) very sizeable regional aid projects; and (iii) aid which does not comply with the ceilings and conditions set out under the GBER.
55. This issue has been extensively discussed in Part One, section III.C.4. *See* Muñoz de Juan, *Monitoring of State Aid: From Ex-Ante to Ex-Post Control*, cited in footnote 259 of Part One.
56. One can call this new source of law – which first appeared in response to the COVID-19 pandemic – 'super-soft law' because it does not take the form of communications, which are typical acts that, although not binding, are based on consultation with the Member States and political consensus, whereas the templates or assessment grids are atypical texts released by the Commission Services without any political endorsement. For example, *see* the Commission Impact Assessment accompanying the document *Communication from the Commission, Guidelines on State Aid for Climate, Environmental Protection and Energy 2022*, 27 January 2022, SWD(2022) 19 final.
57. New Enforcement Notice, cited in footnote 50 of this Part Two, paras 2-3.

Before describing the roles of the Commission and national courts, the Commission recalls the general principles underpinning the private enforcement of State aid rules, but the New Enforcement Notice contains no developments in this respect. However, the Commission also devotes a few paragraphs to explaining the interplay between the principle of procedural autonomy, on the one hand, and the principles of equivalence and effectiveness, on the other, particularly in relation to three issues: legal standing, jurisdiction and *res judicata*.[58]

This choice is questionable for two reasons. First, it is unclear why those three issues deserve more attention than others, such as the limitation period to impose remedies and the application of the legitimate expectation defence, to name but two examples. Second, although it makes sense to discuss the interplay between the principle of procedural autonomy and the principles of equivalence and effectiveness when dealing with the public enforcement of State aid rules - given that procedural autonomy is a choice of the EU legislator, which could have instead opted for the harmonisation of national laws - the situation is different when it comes to private enforcement. Indeed, the application of national procedural laws (*i.e.*, procedural autonomy) is standard for private enforcement: the default option, one might say.

As to the principles of equivalence and effectiveness, they apply in the State aid field just as in any other field of EU law and interact with national procedural rules in exactly the same way as in any other area. The sole justification for these paragraphs of the New Enforcement Notice is thus to recall the landmark case law on legal standing in relation to fiscal measures and *res judicata*, but this case law has little to do with the sharing of competences in private enforcement.[59] This issue is thus discussed later in

58. *See* section 2.2 of the New Enforcement Notice (cited in footnote 50 of this Part Two), paras 19-32.

59. Indeed, only the case law mentioned in para. 25 of the New Enforcement Notice (Judgment of the Court of Justice of 3 March 2020, *Vodafone Magyarország*, C-75/18, EU:C:2020:139, and Judgment of the Court of Justice of 26 April 2018, ANGED, C-233/16, EU:C:2018:280) relates to the private enforcement of State aid rules. Under this case law, taxpayers may be regarded as having an interest in bringing an action to obtain a refund of an amount levied to finance unlawful State aid if the fiscal measure concerned is adopted in breach of the standstill obligation. By contrast, taxpayers cannot rely on the unlawfulness of an aid measure that exempts certain undertakings from taxation to avoid payment of the same tax or levy, thereby triggering the extension of the aid measure to themselves, unless the tax revenue is earmarked entirely for funding the unlawful aid (*see* para. 26 of the New Enforcement Notice and the case law cited therein). However, contrary to the Commission's opinion, this is not a question of legal standing. Rather, it is a simple application of the principle that individuals should be given the possibility under national law to challenge all measures adopted in breach of EU law provisions that have a direct effect in the national legal system. It is for the national court before which the infringement of State aid rules is claimed to avoid adopting measures that may broaden, rather than eliminate, the application of the unlawful aid. Otherwise, they would be liable for a new violation of the Treaty rules according to the principle set out in the *Dimosia Epicheirisi* case (*see* Judgment of the Court of Justice of 26 October 2016, Case C-590/14 P, *Dimosia Epicheirisi Ilektrismou AE (DEI)*, EU:C:2016:797).
As far as the case law on *res judicata* is concerned (Judgment of the Court of Justice of 18 July 2007, *Lucchini*, C-119/05, EU:C:2007:434, discussed above, Part One, section I.A.2.6 and footnote 49), it concerns the implementation of a Commission decision that ordered recovery and therefore pertains to the role played by national courts in the field of public enforcement rather than *stricto sensu* to the field of private enforcement. Moreover, it must be noted that the Commission's explanation in paras 31-32 of the New Enforcement Notice is slightly one-sided.

this book when summarising the key principles governing private enforcement remedies.[60]

Following these introductory remarks, the structure of the New Enforcement Notice is rather straightforward. Section 3 deals with the role of the Commission and contains no significant improvements compared to the 2009 Enforcement Notice.[61] Section 4 deals with the role of the national courts and, as mentioned, is the most relevant part of the Private Enforcement Notice and the one that has been most significantly enhanced compared to the 2009 Enforcement Notice.

As a preliminary point, the New Enforcement Notice clarifies the delimitation of the competences of national courts as depending on the chronology of national court proceedings in relation to any investigation pending before the Commission.[62] In this respect, the main new element in the New Enforcement Notice is the clarification of the competences of national courts when they are seized after the Commission has adopted an opening decision but ahead of a final decision.

Even though the Commission's investigation is still pending at the EU level, the opening decision has legal consequences that national courts must consider. Specifically, to ensure the effectiveness of public enforcement under Article 108(3) TFEU, a

---

Although it is true that the principle of primacy of Union law can imply that national courts may have to set aside any conflicting provision of national legislation, 'including national rules enshrining the principle of *res judicata*', and that the existence of a national judgment - even delivered at last instance - 'cannot prevent the Commission from finding later that the measure at stake constitutes unlawful and incompatible State aid', the principle of effectiveness still does not go as far as affecting the principle of *res judicata* if the national judgment relates to a dispute that has the same subject matter and concerns the qualification of a measure as State aid under Art. 107(1) *and res judicata* pre-existed the opening of any formal investigation by the Commission. In other words, if the national judgment in question was handed down in a dispute with a different subject matter, the primacy of Union law prevails, 'even where national rules on *res judicata* extend to pleas in law that could have been, but were not, invoked in court proceedings'. However, as national courts are competent to interpret Art. 107(1) in disputes involving the claim of an infringement of Art. 108(3), a *res judicata* on this very issue before any action was taken by the Commission remains intangible.

As far as the allocation of jurisdiction is concerned, this is of course entirely a matter for the national legal system of each Member State to decide. Indeed, section 2.2.2, which deals with this topic, contains nothing relevant, as it simply refers to the fact that 'the structure of the Member States' judicial systems varies widely' (para. 29). This statement, if anything, proves that the harmonisation of national laws would be of great benefit to the effectiveness of State aid rules, but no such harmonisation is contemplated in the New Enforcement Notice.

60. *See* Part Two, Chapters V and VI.
61. The only addition to the 2009 Enforcement Notice is at the end of para. 39 and concerns the limitation period of ten years for the Commission to issue a recovery order, which had been introduced in the meantime by Art. 17(1) of the new Procedural Regulation. It is also clarified that this limitation period is to be counted from the day on which the unlawful aid was actually awarded to the beneficiary.
62. Section 4.1 deals with this issue and distinguishes the competences of national courts in the absence of a decision by the Commission (paras 43-44) and following a decision by the Commission (either a Commission decision that declares the aid compatible (section 4.1.1) or a decision that opens the formal investigation procedure (section 4.1.1.2)). Of course, nothing is said here of national court proceedings following a negative Commission decision, because in this case the role of national courts is to collaborate in implementing public enforcement decisions, which does not pertain to private enforcement.

national court cannot hold that a measure that is the object of an opening decision does not constitute aid within the meaning of Article 107(1).[63] Moreover, in this situation, a national court does not even have the option of simply staying the proceedings until the Commission issues a final decision.[64] The New Enforcement Notice also clarifies that the same constraints may apply to national courts when a final Commission decision has been annulled. From the standpoint of national courts, when a Commission decision is annulled, the situation is similar to that existing when proceedings are pending before the Commission and a final decision has yet to be adopted. The New Enforcement Notice therefore clarifies that in those circumstances:

> national courts are ... bound to ensure compliance with the standstill obligation resulting from the opening of the formal procedure, for instance preventing the recovered aid from being paid back

before the Commission adopts a new decision.

Nothing else is said to guide national courts in these difficult, although not unusual, circumstances. More attention is thus devoted to this issue in Chapter V below, which deals with the essential principles of the private enforcement system of remedies.

IV.B Changes Introduced in Relation to the Competences of National Courts and to the Remedies Available to Them, Especially Within the Framework of Damages Actions

Having delimited the competences of national courts in connection with the status of any proceedings before the Commission, the New Enforcement Notice goes on to examine national courts' competences in more detail. Hence, after briefly recalling the main competences of national courts in assessing the existence of aid[65] and the breach of the standstill obligation,[66] the New Enforcement Notice examines the most common remedies available to national courts.[67] In doing so, it lists and discusses the following remedies: (i) suspension or termination of the implementation of the aid measure;[68] (ii)

63. *See* Judgment of the Court of Justice of 21 November 2013, Case C-284/12, *Deutsche Lufthansa*, EU:C:2013:755, para. 38. Several scholars expressed criticism on this case law based on the principle of separation of powers, as it impinges upon the independence of national judiciary. *See* T. Lubbig and T. Morgan, *State Aid, National Courts and the Separation of Powers: Should Judges Be Bound to the European Commission's Unfinished State Aid Business?*, in Journal of European Competition Law & Practice, 2014, Volume 5, Issue 5, pp 256-260 https://doi.org/10.1093/jeclap/lpu013.
64. New Enforcement Notice, cited in footnote 50 of this Part Two, para. 60.
65. *Ibid.*, section 4.2.1.
66. *Ibid.*, section 4.2.2. In this respect, the Commission draws a distinction between the application of the conditions of block exemption regulations (section 4.2.2.1) and the assessment of the qualification of a measure as existing aid (section 4.2.2.2).
67. *Ibid.*, section 4.2.3.
68. *Ibid.*, section 4.2.3.1.

recovery orders;[69] (iii) adoption of interim measures;[70] and (iv) decisions that award damages.[71]

No significant improvement compared to the 2009 Enforcement Notice needs to be highlighted in relation to the remedies mentioned under points (i)-(iii) above. Conversely, the section on damages actions contains some material changes. To start with, the Commission takes a stand on the well-established *Asteris* case law that clarified in 1988 that:

> damages which the national authorities may be ordered to pay to individuals in compensation for the damage they have caused to those individuals do not constitute aid

within the meaning of Article 107(1) TFEU.[72] The Commission attempts to minimise the impact of this case law and argues that:

> when ruling on the compensation to third parties for the costs incurred as a direct result of an unlawful aid, national courts must be careful not to adopt decisions having the effect of granting [new] aid or enlarging the circle of beneficiaries.[73]

It goes on to state that the *Asteris* case law:

> does not concern cases where the applicant requests a national court to award to it previous State aid, which the applicant has not received for whatever reason.[74]

However, the authority referred to by the Commission to support these statements is unconvincing. In *Simet*, for instance, the General Court simply stated that the measure under examination (*i.e.*, compensation for the extra costs caused by public service obligations) could not be construed as the award of damages for the harm caused by public authorities and, even if construed as such, would not escape application of Article 107(1) because the compensation would be the result of the public obligations imposed on the beneficiary.[75] In other words, a formalistic reclassification of a given compensation as damages would change nothing from the perspective of application of Article 107(1) on the condition that the amount is paid to offset the charges caused by public service obligations. This of course does not deprive the principle stemming from the *Asteris* case law, *i.e.*, that damages which national authorities are obliged to pay to compensate for the harm caused to an undertaking do not constitute State aid, of its validity. The *Asteris* and *Simest* case law are referred to

69. *Ibid.*, section 4.2.3.2.
70. *Ibid.*, section 4.2.3.3.
71. *Ibid.*, section 4.2.3.4.
72. Judgment of the Court of Justice of 27 September 1988, *Asteris and others v. Greece and EEC*, Joined Cases C-106 to 120/87, EU:C:1988:457, paras 23-24. Although the *Asteris* case dates back to 1988, the Court of Justice referred to that case law more recently, without suggesting any modification thereto (Judgment of the Court of Justice of 21 December 2016, *Commission v. Air Lingus*, C-164/15 P and C-165/15 P, EU:C:2016:990, para. 72).
73. New Enforcement Notice, para. 96.
74. *Ibid.*, para. 97.
75. Judgment of the General Court of 3 March 2016, *Simet S.p.A. v. European Commission*, in Case T-15/14, EU:T:2016:124, paras 102-104.

here as they concern damages actions, but they are examined again in more detail below in relation to the role of arbitration proceedings.[76]

Similar considerations can be made with regard to the additional case law referred to in the New Enforcement Notice on this issue.[77] National courts cannot be

---

76. *See* Part Two, Chapter VI.D.

77. In footnote 137 (para. 97) of the New Enforcement Notice, the Commission refers to the Judgment of the Court of Justice of 29 June 2004, *Commission v. Council*, C-110/02, EU:C:2004:395, para. 43. However, this case concerned aid authorised by the Council in accordance with the last sentence of Art. 108(2) TFEU in favour of pig farmers in a situation in which exactly the same aid, for the same amount, had been previously declared unlawful and incompatible by the Commission. In those circumstances, the Court of Justice stated as follows:

> [T]o hold that a Member State is able to grant to beneficiaries of unlawful aid, which has previously been declared incompatible with the common market by a Commission decision, new aid in an amount equivalent to that of the unlawful aid, intended to neutralise the impact of the repayments which the beneficiaries are obliged to make pursuant to that decision, would clearly amount to thwarting the effectiveness of decisions taken by the Commission.

Obviously, given the very specific circumstances of this case, one cannot infer from the Court's statement any limitation whatsoever to the competences of national courts. Likewise, in the same paragraph and footnote, the Commission refers to the *Lucchini* and the *Klausner Holz Niedersachsen* case law, which add very little to the issue under discussion. In *Lucchini* (Judgment of the Court of Justice 18 July 2007, cited in footnote 59 of this Part Two, paras 59-63), the Court simply noted that the duty for a national court to give full effect to the State aid provisions of the Treaty – 'if necessary refusing of its own motion, to apply any conflicting provision of national legislation', such as the principle of *res judicata* – concerns not only 'pleas in law which have already been expressly and definitively determined but also precludes the examination of matters which could have been raised in earlier proceedings but were not'. In other words, the extent given to the principle of *res judicata* in the national legal system does not affect the application of Union law. However, the principle of effectiveness is not unlimited. Indeed, in *Fallimento Olimpiclub* (Judgment of the Court of Justice of 3 September 2009, Case C-2/08, EU:C:2009:506, para. 27), the Court held as follows:

> [E]very case in which the question arises as to whether a national procedural provision makes the application of EU law impossible or excessively difficult must be analysed by reference to the role of that provision in the procedure ... viewed as a whole, before the various national bodies. In that context, it is necessary to take into consideration, where relevant, the principles which lie at the basis of the national legal system, such as the protection of the rights of the defence, the principle of legal certainty and the proper conduct of the proceedings.

The application of this principle in the case of *res judicata* leads to the consequences discussed above (Part One, section I.A.2.6). Therefore, no general rule can be drawn from the *Lucchini* judgment as to the competence of national courts to award damages. The same can be said of the other judgment the Commission mentions in para. 97 of the New Enforcement Notice (Judgment of the Court of Justice of 11 November 2015, Case C-505/14, *Klausner Holz Niedersachsen*, EU:C:2015:742, paras 42-44). After recalling its *Fallimento Olimpiclub* case law on the interpretation of the principle of effectiveness, the Court of Justice goes on to find that a judgment of a German regional court obliging public authorities to continue implementing an aid measure contained in a supply agreement would lead to a circumvention of the obligation laid down in Art. 108(3) and would deprive the Commission's exclusive competence to assess the compatibility of State aid of any useful effect. Clearly, this statement is based on the specific circumstances of the case under examination, in which the national court had ordered the regional administration to continue performing a supply contract which had been considered in breach of the standstill obligation. Of course, even national courts – much like any national authority – can contribute to an infringement of State aid provisions at times (*see* Judgment of

prevented from awarding damages unless doing so enlarges the circle of beneficiaries of unlawful aid.[78] It would be paradoxical if competitors of aid beneficiaries could obtain the same aid by arguing before national courts that the aid is unlawful because it was not notified to the Commission. The same applies if the unlawful aid has since been declared compatible by the Commission, as a declaration of compatibility does not have the effect of regularising *ex post facto* implementing measures which, at the time of their adoption, were invalid because they were taken in disregard of the obligation referred to in the last sentence of Article 108(3) TFEU.

However, in some cases, the solution is not as clear as in the previous example. According to the Court of Justice, national courts must:

> strive to preserve the interests of individuals whilst taking the Community interest fully into consideration, taking particular care not to adopt a decision which would have the sole effect of extending the circle of recipients of the unlawful aid.[79]

While the abstract criterion is clear, its application can raise difficulties. The balance between the need to preserve the interests of individuals and the need to safeguard Union interests, with particular focus on the principle of effectiveness, is all but straightforward. This issue is thus examined in more detail in the next chapter,[80] which deals with the essential principles of the private enforcement system of remedies. Additional difficulties arise when considering the role of arbitral tribunals. Case law on this area is not yet consolidated, and clarification is warranted. Again, this matter is given detailed attention in the next chapter.[81]

A second significant improvement contained in the section that deals with damages actions concerns actions brought by aid beneficiaries ordered by the State to reimburse unlawful aid. Although the State usually acts to implement a Commission recovery order, beneficiaries sometimes hold the State responsible for the harm caused to them and claim damages from the State by arguing that its illegal conduct breached their legitimate expectations. The Commission bluntly rejects this possibility on the basis that, according to the Court of Justice case law:

> an unlawfully granted measure could not generate any legitimate expectation for the beneficiary, which should be able to determine whether the correct procedure for the granting of the aid has been followed.[82]

---

the Court of Justice of 26 October 2016, Case C-590/14 P, *Dimosia Epicheirisi Ilektrismou AE (DEI)*, EU:C:2016:797, especially para. 59; *see also* the more recent clarification given by the Court of Justice's Grand Chamber in *Dobeles Hes*, Judgment of 12 January 2023, Joined Cases C-702/20 and C-17/21, EU:C:2023:1, paras 73-76), but this has little to do with the national courts' competences in enforcing the State aid provisions and applying remedies under national law, let alone with the limits thereof.

78. The New Enforcement Notice, cited in footnote 50 of this Part Two, rightfully points out this specific aspect in para. 96 by referring to the Judgment of Court of Justice of 5 October 2006, Case C-368/04, *Transalpine Ölleitung in Österreich*, EU:C:2006:644, paras 57-59.
79. *Ibid.*, para. 59.
80. *See* Chapter V of this Part Two.
81. *Ibid.*
82. New Enforcement Notice, cited in footnote 50 of this Part Two, para. 98.

Although hastily reasoned, the Commission's statement in the New Enforcement Notice, which refers to the landmark *Eesti Pagar* judgment,[83] is certainly correct. This and the other significant contributions of the *Eesti Pagar* judgment are reviewed in the next chapter.

The New Enforcement Notice also deals with the related and more important issue of the damages actions brought by third parties that suffered losses because of the unlawful granting of aid to competitors. In this respect, the New Enforcement Notice refers to both actions brought against the Member State that granted the aid and actions brought against the beneficiaries. As to the former, it is certainly possible for third parties to seek damages from a Member State based on the violation of an EU law provision that has a direct effect on the national legal system, as is the case with Article 108(3) TFEU. Of course, a causal link between the violation and the damage must be proven to the extent required by national law. As always, the principles of effectiveness and equivalence must be fully respected.

Conversely, third parties cannot rely on the Treaty provisions on State aid to seek damages directly from beneficiaries. Indeed, 'Articles 107 and 108 TFEU do not impose any direct obligations on the beneficiaries'.[84] Therefore, a breach of that provision by Member States 'is not a sufficient basis for the recipient to incur liability where he has failed to verify that the aid received was duly notified to the Commission'.[85] National law on non-contractual liability, however, may stipulate that 'the acceptance by an economic operator of unlawful assistance of a nature such as to occasion damage to other economic operators may in certain circumstances cause him to incur liability'. If this is the case, 'the principle of non-discrimination may lead the national court to find the recipient of [unlawful] aid ... liable'.[86]

In other words, damages actions against beneficiaries are not required as a matter of EU State aid law and cannot find their legal basis in EU law. But of course, if national provisions on non-contractual liability can be used to that end, this is allowed under EU law (and probably welcomed by the Commission).[87] Whether this conclusion remains valid in light of the *Eesti Pagar* case law is something that deserves reflection (although it is not examined in the New Enforcement Notice) and is discussed in the next chapter along with all the other controversial issues identified above.

83. Judgment of the Court of Justice (Grand Chamber) of 5 March 2019, C-349/17, *Eesti Pagar AS v. Ettevõtluse Arendamise Sihtasutus and Majandus- ja Kommunikatsiooniministeerium*, EG, EU:C:2019:172, paras 98-104. In footnote 140 (para. 98) of the New Enforcement Notice, the Commission also refers to the Judgment of the Court of Justice of 15 December 2005, C-148/04, *Unicredito Italiano v. Agenzia delle Entrate*, EU:C:2005:774, para. 104, and Judgment of the Court of Justice of 19 March 2015, Case C-672/13, *OTP Bank Nyrt. v. Magyar Állam and Magyar Államkincstár*, EU:C:2015:185, para. 77.
84. New Enforcement Notice, para. 99, and Judgment of the Court of Justice of 11 July 1996, C-39/94, *Syndicat français de l'Express international (SFEI) et autres contre La Poste et autres*, EU:C:1996:285, paras 72-74.
85. *Ibid.*
86. Judgment of the Court of Justice of 11 July 1996, C-39/94, *Syndicat français de l'Express international (SFEI) et autres contre La Poste et autres*, cited in footnote 84 of this Part Two, para. 75.
87. New Enforcement Notice, cited in footnote 50 of this Part Two, para. 99.

The New Enforcement Notice contains no other improvement on the fundamental issue of damages actions or, more generally, on the remedies available to national courts beyond those just discussed.

IV.C Changes Introduced in Relation to Cooperation Tools

IV.C.1 Introductory Remarks

The remainder of the New Enforcement Notice (sections 5 and 6) focuses on the cooperation tools available to the Commission and national courts and the consequences of the failure to implement State aid rules and decisions. As far as section 6 is concerned, it also refers to: (i) the appropriate measures that national courts are called on to take in order to ensure that Commission recovery decisions are effectively implemented; and (ii) the consequences that the failure to adopt these measures can give rise to for the Member State concerned. As these issues concern the role of national courts in the prolongation of public enforcement rather than genuine private enforcement; as such, they have already been examined in Part One of this book. Logically, indeed, the Commission itself refers to the Recovery Notice in this respect.[88]

Section 5 is divided into two subsections, which deal with the Commission's assistance to national courts (section 5.1) and national courts' assistance to the Commission (section 5.2). The basis for this approach is the idea that the obligation stemming from Article 4(3) TEU is mutual and, as far as Member States are concerned, applies to all national bodies, including the judiciary. This means that 'the Commission assists national courts when they apply Union law, and that, conversely, national courts assist the Commission in the fulfillment of its tasks'.

Although section 5.1 is by far more complete than the corresponding section of the 2009 Enforcement Notice,[89] material changes are few and essentially concern the Commission's intervention as *amicus curiae* before national courts. Indeed, the New Enforcement Notice deals separately with three means of assistance that the Commission can offer to national courts: the transmission of information,[90] the transmission of an opinion on the correct application of State aid rules,[91] and the submission of *amicus curiae* observations.[92] As far as the first two means of cooperation are concerned, the New Enforcement Notice contains no substantial changes compared to the 2009 Enforcement Notice. It simply adds a reference to the new Procedural Regulation (Article 29), restructures the presentation of the topic, and rephrases certain concepts.

The paragraphs that deal with the respect of professional secrecy also remain substantially unchanged. When dealing with the transmission of information, mention is no longer made of the possibility for national courts to ask the Commission, in the

88. *Ibid.*, para. 135.
89. 2009 Enforcement Notice, cited in footnote 4 of this Part Two, section 3, paras 77-96.
90. New Enforcement Notice, cited in footnote 50 of this Part Two, section 5.1.1.1.
91. *Ibid.*, section 5.1.1.2.
92. *Ibid.*, section 5.1.1.3.

absence of a decision, to clarify when it is likely to adopt one. The reason for this change is probably to avoid any statement that could be read as encouraging national courts to wait for the Commission to complete its investigation, as, on the contrary, they are required to uphold the rights of individuals even when proceedings are pending before the Commission. However, this change alone is unlikely to lead to national courts taking a more proactive approach.

When it comes to the transmission of opinions on the application of State aid rules, the Commission obviously reminds national courts of the possibility of seeking the Court of Justice's opinion through a reference for a preliminary ruling. In doing so, however, the Commission uses less clear language than in the 2009 Enforcement Notice, perhaps mindful of the normal duration of the procedure before the Court of Justice.[93] This is an odd choice, given that the preliminary ruling is a pillar of EU law. As mentioned in relation to the 2009 Enforcement Notice, stronger encouragement to prioritise preliminary rulings when genuine interpretative issues are at stake would have been welcomed. Beyond this, one minor change can be spotted in the list of matters that can arise in national proceedings, which national courts may want the Commission to clarify. This relates to the calculation of the aid to be recovered.

While both the 2009 Enforcement Notice and the New Enforcement Notice include the amount of the aid in the list of matters on which the Commission's assistance can be requested, a slight difference exists when it comes to calculating the amount to be recovered, as only the New Enforcement Notice refers to the calculation of the amount to be recovered and not only to the interest calculation and the interest rate to be applied. Whether this change is appropriate is debatable, as national courts which uphold the rights of individuals arising from a breach of the standstill obligation apply the remedies offered by national law, not EU law remedies, as they do when they assist in implementing a Commission recovery decision. They must of course identify the aid element based on the requirements of Article 107(1), but the remedies – including the assessment as to whether recovery is the most appropriate remedy to re-establish the *status quo ante* and, if it is, whether it can be equivalent to the aid element – is entirely a matter of national law, on condition that the principles of equivalence and effectiveness are complied with. Equivalence, however, in this context means only that the ordinary remedies of national law must be applied; and effectiveness binds national courts to uphold the rights conferred on individuals by directly applicable provisions of EU law in the case of a breach of these provisions but does not extend such that it dictates specific remedies to those same courts.

93. Indeed, the New Enforcement Notice includes only the following words as a simple aside in the sentence that refers to the possibility to seek the Commission's assistance: 'Without prejudice to the ultimate interpretation of the Treaties by the Union Courts ...'. Instead, the 2009 Enforcement Notice more explicitly stated as follows:

> Matters concerning the interpretation of Community law can obviously lead the national court to ask for a preliminary ruling of the ECJ under Article 234 of the Treaty. Where no further judicial remedy exists against the court's decision under national law, the use of this preliminary reference procedure is, in principle, mandatory.

IV.C.2 The New Section on the Amicus Curiae Mechanism

As mentioned, the New Private Enforcement Notice includes a new section on the third means of cooperation between the Commission and national courts, *i.e.*, the submission of *amicus curiae* observations. The new section is based on the provisions of Article 29(2) of the Procedural Regulation,[94] which empowers the Commission to: (i) take the initiative to submit written observations to a national court; (ii) ask the national court's permission to submit oral observations; (iii) request the relevant court to transmit documents at that court's disposal which are necessary for the Commission's assessment of the matter; and (iv) oblige the Commission to inform the Member State concerned of its intention to submit observations before formally doing so.[95]

By building on the experience gained between 2015 and 2019 (*i.e.*, from the date the Procedural Regulation came into force until the New Enforcement Notice was adopted),[96] the New Enforcement Notice provides clarification and explanations on how national courts can have recourse to this cooperation tool and on how the Commission will abide by its duties. As a preliminary point, the Commission elaborates on the indication in the first paragraph of Article 29(2) that the Commission is empowered to submit written observations to the national court (or to ask the national court for authorisation to submit oral observations) *on its own initiative*. Giving the Commission the possibility to act on its own initiative does not mean that the Commission is prevented from acting upon request from national courts or even from parties to national proceedings. However, the decision to do so falls entirely within the Commission's discretion because this specific cooperation tool – unlike the other two (transmission of information and transmission of opinions) – is an 'exclusive prerogative' of the Commission.

Moreover, the Commission acts in the public interest (*i.e.*, to ensure coherent application of Articles 107(1) and 108(3) TFEU), which means that even when intervening upon request of a party or parties involved in national proceedings, it will not hear any of them before submitting its observations. This is presented as being part of the Commission's more general duty – which applies regardless of the cooperation means used – to remain neutral and objective when fulfilling its duties under Article 4(3) TEU. This is a questionable choice. The Commission must of course remain neutral, and even more obvious is that it must endeavour to be objective, but this does not necessarily imply that it should not hear interested parties. Neutrality and objectivity are the Commission's duties in all procedures, whether pending before the Commission itself, other European institutions, or national courts.

94. Article 29(2) is divided into three subparagraphs, which are discussed in detail in Chapter I of this Part Two when dealing with the sources of the private enforcement of State aid rules in secondary law.
95. This provision can be understood only in the sense that the information should be given to the governmental authorities of the Member State concerned, in addition to the relevant court. The New Enforcement Notice confirms this reading in para. 123 and clarifies that the Commission informs the Member State concerned 'by sending a letter to its Permanent Representation to the Union'.
96. As reported in the 2019 Enforcement Study, cited in footnote 44 of this Part Two.

Therefore, the reason underlying the choice not to hear the parties to the proceedings is certainly not to be found in the Commission's neutrality or objectivity or in the fact that it acts in the public interest. Rather, the choice is probably based on practical considerations related to the need to streamline the process.[97] Considerations of this kind should be balanced with the need to offer parties the opportunity to present their views, also considering that the Commission's position is likely to determine the outcome of the case. It is hard to see any inconvenience in leaving maximum flexibility to national courts and the Commission on how to organise their cooperation in each case, depending on its relevance, the technicality of the issues involved, and the timing considerations related to the specific case under discussion.

Further, the New Enforcement Notice lists several criteria that are expected to guide the Commission Services in deciding whether to submit *amicus curiae* observations. Unsurprisingly, all but one of the criteria revolve around the case's significance from a State aid policy perspective and the contribution that the Commission's intervention as *amicus curiae* can bring to this policy.[98] As the Commission is expected to intervene in cases that raise substantial and new issues of general interest, it will endeavour to make its observations known to the public. To this effect, it will: (i) report on its cooperation with national courts in its annual report on competition policy; and (ii) ask the relevant national court to authorise the publication of its observations on the Directorate General for Competition's website and, when available; (iii) publish the judgment rendered by the national court concerned.

As to the fourth and last criterion, it is expressed as follows: 'whether the case is pending before a court whose judgment cannot be subject to further appeals'. The rationale of this criterion is not entirely clear. If the case presents new legal issues of a general nature, which in addition to their novelty in the case law, are not covered by soft law or the Commission's practice, the relevant national court of last instance is under an obligation to refer the case to the Court of Justice for a preliminary ruling. Under these circumstances, the Commission – for reasons of institutional respect – should carefully avoid playing a role in the interpretation of State aid rules in connection with the case pending before the national court. Therefore, its intervention as *amicus curiae* should be limited to explaining the relevance of the case and recommending the national court to abide by its duty to seek the interpretation of the Court of Justice.

97. More specifically, one could argue that the Commission's objective in introducing this rule in the New Enforcement Notice is to keep the procedural dispute before the national court as simple and speedy as possible and to help reconcile this external intervention with national procedural rules.

98. Indeed, the first criterion is whether the case involves a general question of State aid law and is therefore expected to provide clarification which can be relevant much beyond the case at hand. The second criterion is even broader and refers to the contribution that the Commission's observations can bring to the effectiveness of State aid enforcement. The third criterion completes the first two by making clear that the general question of State aid law involved must be new, *i.e.*, it is not already covered by the Commission's soft law or by its decision-making practice.

Having clarified the criteria that guide the Commission in evaluating the necessity and appropriateness of its intervention before national courts, the New Enforcement Notice turns to the legal value of the Commission's observations.[99] It goes without saying that the Commission's observations are not binding for national courts, as the Commission must respect their independence. However, the independence of national courts logically relates to the application of State aid rules to the case that they must adjudicate - not the legal principles themselves. Indeed, should a national court fail to apply EU law provisions correctly, it would expose that Member State to a breach of the Treaty. As national courts are expected to forward to the Commission - without delay - a copy of the written judgment handed down following the submission of *amicus curiae* observations,[100] the Commission is of course vigilant on the correct application of Union law.

As far as the procedure is concerned, the Commission must (naturally) respect the functioning of national courts, and since no harmonised procedural framework for the submission of *amicus curiae* observations exists, the Member States' procedural rules and practices fully apply (principle of procedural autonomy).[101] As usual, it is the Member State's responsibility to ensure that the applicable national rules enable compliance with Article 29 of the Procedural Regulation, which empowers the Commission to submit *amicus curiae* observations. Therefore, the national procedural framework should be adapted when necessary to comply fully with the principles of effectiveness and equivalence.[102]

The New Private Enforcement Notice specifies in this respect that the principle of procedural autonomy applies also to the rules and practices which safeguard parties' rights. This clarification, however, brings up an additional question: if national procedural rules or national judicial practices envisage the broadest possible application of the rights of defence, thereby granting parties the possibility to comment on whatever expert opinion is added to the judicial filing, this would imply that parties to the proceedings are given the opportunity to comment on the Commission's observations. Under these circumstances, it would be much more effective and expeditious to organise a hearing of the parties by the Commission before the Commission submits its final observations. In any event, the national court remains free to proceed in this manner - *i.e.*, to give the parties to proceedings the opportunity to comment on the Commission's observations - despite any provision to the contrary in the New Enforcement Notice.[103]

IV.C.3 The Reverse Side of Cooperation

Section 5 ends with a few paragraphs on the reverse side of the principle of sincere cooperation, which envisages a mutual duty of assistance between the Commission

99. New Enforcement Notice, cited in footnote 50 of this Part Two, paras 123-124.
100. *Ibid.*, para. 132.
101. *Ibid.*, para. 125.
102. *Ibid.*, para. 126.
103. *Ibid.*, para. 101, cited and commented on above.

and Member States' authorities.[104] The latter are expected to facilitate the achievement of the Union's tasks, which include protecting competition and preventing State intervention that is not compatible with the internal market.

Although these paragraphs are entirely new, they contain nothing new of any significance. Rather, they put forward a few practical recommendations for more effective cooperation and communication with national courts and for the dissemination of a culture of State aid prevention and control.[105]

As mentioned, the principle that the obligation of sincere cooperation enshrined in Article 4(3) TEU applies to all national bodies, including the judiciary, means that national courts are under a duty to cooperate with the Commission in its task of ensuring the effectiveness of the Treaty's State aid rules. To do so, national courts must draw the appropriate consequences from breaches of Article 108(3) TFEU and safeguard the rights of individuals damaged by unlawful State aid. Failure to do so may result in infringement proceedings being initiated by the Commission and potentially give rise to liability for the Member State concerned.[106]

However, the duty of sincere cooperation also implies that national courts must refrain from issuing decisions which could jeopardise attainment of the objectives of the Treaty's State aid provisions. As with any other national body, their decisions can render the Member State liable for breach of the Treaty. These aspects are examined in section 6 of the New Enforcement Notice, which is entirely new compared to the 2009 Enforcement Notice. It builds upon the Court of Justice case law in the period between the 2009 Enforcement Notice and the New Enforcement Notice.[107] Hence, the Commission explains that national courts may, by their judgments, grant new aid in breach of the standstill obligation and that this can lead the Commission to initiate an

104. *Ibid.*, section 5.2. *See also* section 2.1 on the general principle of sincere cooperation.
105. Indeed, para. 132 merely invites national courts to forward to the Commission without delay a copy of any judgment issued in cases in which the Commission has intervened as *amicus curiae* or provided information or an opinion. If one of the parties lodges an appeal against that judgment, the Commission will of course continue following the case. Likewise, national courts are invited to authorise that the judgment be published on the Commission's website, but again, they cannot be obliged to do so because of the principle of procedural autonomy. Furthermore, the Commission encourages the Member States to set up 'coordination points for national judges dealing with State aid issues', although it clarifies that these coordination points 'should match with the administrative structure of the Member States and respect the independence of the judicial authority' (New Enforcement Notices, para. 133). Finally, the Commission also encourages the 'creation of formal or informal networks of judges dealing with State aid matters, either at national or European level', which it considers 'particularly important for knowledge sharing' (same paragraph).
106. New Enforcement Notice, cited in footnote 50 of this Part Two, paras 140-142 and case law referred to therein (*see* especially Judgment of the Court of Justice of 30 September 2003, Case-224/01, *Köbler*, EU:C:2003:513).
107. Reference is made here in particular to: Judgment of the General Court of 8 October 2014, Case T-542/11, *Alouminion v. European Commission*, EU:T:2014:859; Judgment of the Court of Justice of 26 October 2016 rendered on appeal in the same case, Case C-590/14 P, *Dimosia Epicheirisi Ilektrismou AE (DEI)*, cited in footnotes 59 and 77 of this Part Two, which annulled the General Court judgment and sent the case back to it; the subsequent Judgment of the General Court of 13 March 2018, Case T-542/11 RENV, *Alouminion tis Ellados VEAE v. European Commission*, EU:T:2018:132; and finally the second Judgment of the Court of Justice in the same matter, Case C-332/18 P, *Mytilinaios Anonymos Etairia – Omilos Epicheiriseon v. European Commission*, EU:C:2019:1065.

investigation procedure in accordance with Article 12 of the Procedural Regulation.[108] Although the New Enforcement Notice does not contain a catch-all definition of this situation, the Commission's practice shows that this can be the result of judgments that order the public administration, public entities, or State-owned undertakings to pay a given amount to an economic operator or to apply a given contract, or conclude a given transaction, which entail an aid element.

Only one example is mentioned in the New Enforcement Notice in this respect. The example refers to the case in which 'the interpretation of a contract or an aid-granting decision has the effect of prolonging the original duration of an aid measure', as in the *DEI* case.[109] In a situation like this, national courts must comply with Article 108(3) just as any other State body must. They must therefore notify the Commission of any judgment or order that results in amending or prolonging an act that grants State aid ahead of its implementation.[110]

In *DEI*, the Court of Justice overturned a General Court judgment which had annulled a negative Commission decision and recovery order concerning the aid element contained in the electricity supply agreement concluded between DEI, a State-owned electricity company, and Alouminion, an energy-intensive aluminium producer in Greece. The main legal issue under debate was the possibility of classifying as State aid a judicial decision that had ordered DEI by interim measure to continue applying the preferential tariff envisaged in the supply agreement beyond the termination date.[111]

108. New Enforcement Notice, cited in footnote 50 of this Part Two, para. 134. However, the structure of section 6 is not entirely clear, as it mixes up issues related to private and public enforcement. The first three introductory paragraphs (134-136) briefly recall the roles that national courts may be called on to cover when applying Art. 108(3) directly - and, incidentally, Art. 107(1) - in their national legal systems. These roles are respectively: (i) to adjudicate cases that affect the implementation of an act that grants State aid (para. 134); (ii) to support the Commission in ensuring that recovery decisions are effectively implemented (para. 135); and (iii) to safeguard the rights of individuals faced with a possible breach of the standstill obligation. Then, in subsections 6.1 and 6.2, the Private Enforcement Notice deals with the consequences that the failure by national courts to implement State aid rules and decisions can entail. Obviously, however, the national courts' roles mentioned under points (ii) and (iii) above are nothing new, and failure to comply with these tasks may result in typical infringement proceedings against the Member State concerned, as explained in subsection 6.2. By contrast, the new contribution of this section of the New Enforcement Notice lies in the possibility that national courts might inadvertently directly infringe the Treaty's State aid provisions when adjudicating on cases that affect the granting of State aid. Indeed, according to the New Enforcement Notice, in doing so national courts might de facto grant new aid themselves and thus infringe Arts 107(1) and 108(3) TFEU.

109. *See* footnotes 59, 77 and 107 of this Part Two.

110. Private Enforcement Notice, cited in footnote 50 of this Part Two, para. 138.

111. In February 2004, DEI informed Alouminion tis Ellados ('*AtE*') of its intention to terminate the contract on its natural expiry date, without letting it automatically renew. In the meantime, the Commission had examined the preferential tariff granted to AtE in 1992 and classified it as compatible State aid. However, the market situation and the cost of electricity had considerably changed since then, leading DEI to send a termination notice to AtE. AtE challenged the termination before the competent national court and obtained an interim order that suspended the termination effects. The national court held that that termination did not comply with the contract and the applicable domestic legal framework. DEI challenged the interim order before the competent appeal court, which - also in interlocutory proceedings - granted DEI's application to terminate the supply contract (and the related preferential tariff) by order of 6 March 2008. However, the appeal order had effect *ex nunc*. Thus, during the period between

Setting aside the legal technicalities of the case,[112] the *DEI* judgment sets out three fundamental points of clarification which portray the national courts' responsibility when adjudicating cases that concern the application of State measures granting aid.[113]

First, national courts that adjudicate cases concerning a dispute on the application of a measure that can contain an aid element (*i.e.*, a public act or a contract or transaction that involves a public undertaking or a public entity) might directly

---

the first interim order and the appeal order (approximately fifteen months), AtE continued to benefit from the preferential tariff. Shortly thereafter, the Commission received complaints that challenged the application of the preferential tariff during that fifteen-month period. The Commission thus opened a formal investigation procedure and eventually adopted the contested decision, whereby it held that the Hellenic Republic had granted AtE unlawful State aid through the preferential tariff during the period in question. Given that that aid granted in contravention of Art. 108(3) TFEU was now deemed incompatible with the internal market, the Commission ordered the Hellenic Republic to recover the aid from AtE. AtE consequently brought an action for annulment of the contested decision before the General Court, which upheld the first plea in law - which disputed the classification of the measure at issue as new aid - and annulled the contested decision without ruling on the other pleas in law in that action.

112. As indicated, the case originated from an electricity supply agreement entered into between DEI and AtE in 1960. The supply agreement stipulated that it was to be renewed automatically every five years until the expiry date (31 March 2006). Following DEI's termination notice, served on AtE in 2004, AtE challenged the termination before the competent national court and obtained an interim order that suspended the termination effects, which was the subject of the contested Commission decision. The dispute brought by AtE before the General Court for the annulment of that decision raised several interesting issues of law, which basically hinged on the applicability of the principles of Member States' responsibility for violation of EU State aid provisions to the national judiciary, and the possible limits thereon. The General Court based its assessment on the idea that the competent national court, when issuing the interim order under discussion, had interpreted only the relevant provisions of the agreement. Therefore, in its view, the consequence of that interpretation, *i.e.*, the extension of the agreement term (and of the preferential tariff envisaged therein) was to be ascribed to the true meaning of the contractual provisions and therefore to the parties' will, not to the national court. This idea underpins all the General Court's findings in relation to the three parts of the first plea in law submitted by AtE. Once the Court of Justice rejected that idea, it could only overturn the General Court's findings. Consequently, the Court of Justice upheld the first ground of appeal in its entirety. With this ground of appeal, DEI - supported by the Commission - complained that the General Court had infringed Art. 108(3) TFEU and Art. 1(b) and (c) of the Procedural Regulation. As explained later (*see* footnotes 112-115 of this Part Two), this ground of appeal is in fact divided into three different pleas in law, which the Court of Justice examined one by one to conclude that the General Court had made errors in law in examining each of them.

113. The summary in the text is based on this author's understanding of the judgment. However, the case has been the subject of several comments in legal scholarship, including the following: O. Peiffert, *Le juge national des référés octroyant une nouvelle aide d'État: syllogisme ou sophisme dans la jurisprudence de la Cour de justice?* in Revue Lamy de la Concurrence: droit, économie, régulation 2016 n° 56, pp. 38-42; L. Idot, *La suspension, par un juge des référés, de la résiliation d'un contrat, qui était le support juridique d'une aide existante, conduit à une modification de cette dernière et peut être qualifiée d'aide nouvelle,* Europe 2016 Décembre Comm. n° 12 pp. 36-37; A. Metaxas and S. Spyrou, *Alteration of Existing State Aid and New Aid: On the Criteria of this Legal Categorisation*, European State Aid Law Quarterly 2017, pp. 73-76 (which focuses exclusively on the distinction between new aid and existing aid); M. Kekelekis, *DEI v. European Commision • C-590/14 P • Annotation by Mihalis Kekelekis,* European State Aid Law Quarterly 2017, pp. 291-294 https://doi.org/10.21552/estal/2017/2/16 (which, again, focuses on the distinction between new aid and existing aid); and P. Nicolaides, *Existing v. New Aid and Role of National Courts,* StateAidHub.eu, 20 December 2016.

infringe, under certain circumstances, Articles 107(1) and 108(3) TFEU.[114] Second, the mere fact that the Commission considered the aid in question compatible with the internal market in a previous decision is not in itself sufficient to prevent the infringement of State aid rules if: (i) the judicial decision entails an extension, prorogation or other substantial modification of the measure; and (ii) the compatibility assessment can evolve depending on market circumstances.[115] In the case under discussion, the Court of Justice held that the mere extension of the period of application of the preferential tariff due to the first interim order entailed a reclassification of the measure as new aid.[116] Third, national courts might infringe State aid rules even when they adopt interim measures within the framework of interlocutory proceedings.[117]

114. Judgment of the Court of Justice of 26 October 2016, *Dimosia Epicheirisi Ilektrismou AE (DEI)*, cited in footnotes 59 and 77 of this Part Two, paras 80-81. In the judgment under appeal, the General Court had concluded that 'it was not the purpose of the first order for interim measures to amend the legal framework of the preferential tariff' and had inferred from this that the legal basis of the aid at issue was not that order, but the supply agreement itself and the relevant national law, as interpreted by the competent national court. The Court of Justice rejected this reasoning and held that 'by extending the application of the preferential tariff' during the period between the first order for interim measure and the order for interim measure adopted on appeal, the national court had altered the ordinary time-limit of the supply contract and, accordingly, the time-limit of the preferential tariff. It therefore concluded that 'the legal basis of the aid during the period at issue was the first order for interim measures'.

115. The General Court found that the first interim order had not altered the aid that the Commission had previously declared compatible with the internal market. The General Court relied on the *Namur-Les assurances de crédit* case law (Judgment of the Court of Justice of 9 August 1994, Case C-44/93, EU:C:1994:311) to conclude that 'the extension of the period of application of existing aid does not, in itself, lead to the grant of new aid'. In other words, the suspension order adopted by the first-instance Greek court within the framework of interim proceedings was based on an interpretation of the supply agreement based on Greek law and, consequently, had not modified (and could not modify), according to the General Court, the aid authorised by the Commission, which therefore continued to qualify as existing aid. However, the Court of Justice overturned this assessment and stated that 'contrary to the General Court's findings in the judgment under appeal, by reinstating the application of the preferential tariff during the period at issue, the first order for interim measures had the effect of altering the time limits of application of that tariff ... and therefore the time limits of the aid scheme, as authorised by the Commission'. It therefore concluded that the first order for interim measures had to be regarded as constituting an alteration of existing aid and, as such, subject to the notification obligation under Art. 108(3) TFEU (paras 58-60).

116. This is the part of the *DEI* judgment that has attracted most attention from legal scholars (*see* footnote 113 of this Part Two). Kekelekis, to mention but one, expresses criticism of the Court of Justice's decision to overturn the General Court judgment, which was based on a substantialist approach. According to Kekelekis, only substantial changes to existing aid have the effect of reclassifying it as new aid and thus trigger a new notification obligation. To consider whatever extension, even minor (for the duration of the interlocutory proceedings), of the period of application of existing aid to be a change that triggers a notification obligation would be overly formalistic (M. Kekelekis, *DEI v European Commission C-590/14 P • Annotation by Mihalis Kekelekis*, European State Aid Law Quarterly 2017, pp. 291-294 https://doi.org/10.21552/estal/2017/2/16).

117. In the judgment under appeal, the General Court had considered that an order for interim measures cannot constitute the grant or alteration of aid, under Art. 108(3) TFEU, for the following reason:

> [This] would ... be tantamount to requiring, in law and in fact, the national court hearing the application for interim measures in a dispute relating to a contract ... to notify to the Commission and submit for its preventive review ... all [judicial] measures

The subsequent judgments adopted first by the General Court upon referral back by the Court of Justice and second by the Court of Justice do not alter these basic principles or add anything significant to the role of national courts[118] and are therefore not referred to in the New Enforcement Notice.

> which affect the interpretation and implementation of a contract that may have an impact on the functioning of the internal market, on competition or simply on the actual duration, over a specific period, of aid which continues to exist.

However, the Court of Justice held as follows:

> [The General Court] erred in law by holding that, because it is ruling in interlocutory proceedings, a national court seised of a dispute relating to a contract does not have to notify to the Commission, in accordance with Article 108(3) TFEU, 'all measures which affect the interpretation and implementation of that contract that may have an impact on the functioning of the internal market, on competition or simply on the actual duration, over a specific period, of aid which continues to exist'.

Thus, the Court of Justice once more overturned the General Court's assessment and unequivocally stated as follows:

> [T]o make it possible for national courts hearing an application for interim measures to escape the obligations incumbent upon them in the context of the control of State aids introduced by Articles 107 and 108 TFEU would lead those courts to disregard the limits of their own jurisdiction, intended to guarantee the observance of EU State aid law.

In a nutshell, the duty of sincere cooperation with the institutions of the Union applies also to national courts judging within the framework of interim proceedings, and these courts must therefore abide by the obligations imposed on Member States' authorities under Art. 108(3) TFEU if their decision has the effect of extending or widening the application of State aid (paras 103-108). Commenting on this point of the judgment, Kekelekis emphasises that the Procedural Regulation and especially Art. 29 is silent on the application of the notification obligation to national courts. In this context, Kekelekis raises the question as to whether this broad interpretation of the notification requirement needs to be reflected in a specific provision of the Procedural Regulation as a new feature of the State aid procedure. However, Art. 29 refers solely to the means of cooperation between the Commission and national courts, and in particular to the *amicus curiae* tool. It would not be appropriate to refer to the notification obligation applicable to national courts in this context, as that obligation stems directly from the concept of 'State' applicable across all State aid provisions, which includes all decentralised administrative authorities and all legislative and judicial organs. The EU courts' case law has been developing the principle of unity of Member States since at least the mid-nineties. Member States are therefore legally responsible to the Union for breaches of the Treaty regardless of the body that causes the infringement. Likewise, the principle of State liability holds good for any case in which a Member State breaches Community law, whatever the body of the State may be whose act or omission was responsible for the breach (Judgment of the Court of Justice of 5 March 1996, Case C-46/93, *Brasserie du Pêcheur SA contre Bundesrepublik Deutschland et The Queen contre Secretary of State for Transport, ex parte: Factortame Ltd et autres*, EU:C:1996:79, better known as *Brasserie du Pêcheur*). As the principle applies also to the last-instance courts of the Member States (*see* Judgment of the Court of Justice of 30 September 2003, C-224/01, *Köbler*, and Judgment of the Court of Justice of 13 June 2006, C-173/03, *Traghetti del Mediterraneo*, EU:C:2019:51, para. 61), there is no need to amend the Procedural Regulation to hold the State liable for a violation of the standstill obligation by the judiciary.

118. The General Court's second judgment on this matter, after the Court of Justice's annulment of its first one and referral back to it, was handed down on 13 March 2018, Case T-542/11 RENV, cited in footnote 107 of this Part Two. This judgment applies the principles set out by the Court of Justice and contains no new developments on the application of the principle of sincere cooperation to national courts. Nevertheless, it reiterates the Commission's and the EU courts' approach to the calculation of the aid to be recovered. This formalistic approach is questioned

Having clarified that national courts can directly infringe Article 108(3) by granting new aid in proceedings pending before them, the New Enforcement Notice adds a warning that 'if the national court does not ensure compliance with the standstill obligation and the new aid is not notified', the Commission may initiate an investigation procedure either on its own initiative or following a complaint lodged by any interested party.[119]

It must be clarified that while the changes introduced in the New Recovery Notice in this respect (*i.e.*, the national courts' liability as potential grantors of new aid when adjudicating disputes pending before them) are already outdated following the Court of Justice's Grand Chamber's judgment in *Dobeles Hes*,[120] the key issue concerning the

---

in Part One of this book, and this is one of the main aspects that deserves to be reconsidered in the recommended reform of the system of remedies in State aid law. The applicant had challenged the calculation of the amount to be recovered as stated in the judgment, which was based on the gap between the ordinary tariff as applied to other users and the preferential tariff set out in the contract between AtE and DEI. According to the applicant, the tariff applied to other users was not a reliable proxy of the tariff that would have been applied in AtE's case based on market terms in a liberalised market. The General Court might have ultimately considered this argument to be factually wrong, but it deserved to be examined on its merits. Instead, the General Court rejected it on purely formalistic grounds, by holding that the Commission, having found that the preferential tariff granted the beneficiary an advantage, had rightfully determined the amount to be recovered based on the difference between the preferential tariff and the ordinary tariff. The General Court's second judgment was again appealed before the Court of Justice. Although one of the pleas in law submitted in the new proceedings before the Court of Justice was based on the finding of an advantage granted to the beneficiary based on the difference between the mandatory standard tariff and the preferential tariff during the period between the first interim order and the second interim orders on appeal, the applicant did not challenge the calculation of the amount to be recovered under the principles of the recovery system. The Court of Justice thus did not have to examine this argument any further once it rejected the applicant's plea based on the alleged mistake in finding the existence of an advantage. *See* Judgment of the Court of Justice of 11 December 2019, Case C-332/18 P, *Mytilinaios Anonymos Etairia – Omilos Epicheiriseon (formerly Alouminion tis Ellados) v. European Commission*, cited in footnote 107 of this Part Two.

119. New Enforcement Notice, cited in footnote 50 of this Part One, para. 139.

120. Judgment of the Court of Justice (Grand Chamber) of 12 January 2023, Joined Cases C-702/20 and C-17/21, *Dobeles Hes*, EU:C:2023:1. The key question in this case was whether the payment ordered by the national court following a claim based on a support scheme for producers of electricity from renewable energy sources constituted State aid per se. Interestingly, the Court seemed to imply in its reasoning that it was the first time that it had dealt with this question, rejecting the relevance of case law cited by the parties. The Court explicitly stated that 'no conclusion can be drawn from previous case law concerning the possibility of a national court granting State aid' (*ibid.*, para. 73). Thus, the Court, departing from the Opinion of Advocate General Rantos (Opinion of 14 June 2022, EU:C:2022:465), rebutted the Commission's argumentation regarding the relevance of previous case law and held that, although:

> the national court may, where appropriate, deliver a judgment from which it follows that one of the parties must, in accordance with national law, receive a sum corresponding to State aid, that does not mean that it itself grants that aid. Such a judgment has the sole effect, by virtue of the principle of *res judicata*, of requiring the other party, generally the competent administrative authority, to pay that aid.

Furthermore, the Court of Justice clarified that 'the establishment of State aid entails a decision as to the appropriate course of action which falls outside the scope of a court's powers and obligations' and added that 'a different outcome would also go against the principle of separation of powers'. On the significance of this judgment and the change of approach with respect to the case law mentioned in the New Enforcement Notice, especially the *DEI* case, *see*

national courts' duty of sincere cooperation with the Commission remains intact. Indeed, in *Dobeles Hes,* the Court acknowledges that if the referring court classifies the measure under scrutiny as State aid following its check of relevant facts,[121] it may grant a request for payment of a sum due on the basis of a support measure for renewable energy production on condition that the payment is made subject to prior notification of the aid to the Commission and to the latter's consent. As national courts are bound by the obligation of sincere cooperation, they:

> 'must take all the necessary measures, whether general or specific, to ensure fulfilment of the obligations under EU law and refrain from taking those which may jeopardise the attainment of the objectives of the Treaty'.

This point is illustrative of the responsibility that national courts bear in order to comply with State aid provisions.

IV.C.4 Changes Related to the Limits to Recovery

As to the limits to recovery (or other remedies for that matter), the New Enforcement Notice merely refers to the limitation period to clarify that national limitation periods apply (rather than the ten-year limitation period envisaged by the Procedural Regulation, which applies solely to the Commission) regardless of whether they are longer or shorter than the limitation period applicable to the Commission. This is of course the case within the framework of private enforcement, whereas national limitation periods cannot obstruct the execution of a recovery order contained in a Commission decision.[122] In

M. Merola and G. Theodorakopoulous, *Brève chronique des developpements en matière d'aides d'Etat en 2023,* in Annuaire de Droit de l'Union européenne 2023, Editions Panthéon-Assas, Paris 2024.

121. The case concerned two Latvian undertakings that operated hydroelectric power plants and had benefitted until 7 June 2005 from the right to sell their surplus electricity production to the approved electricity distributor at a preferential price amounting to twice the average electricity sale tariff, as determined by the Latvian regulatory authority. Though a law went into in force on 8 June 2005 seeking to amend the rules applicable to the sale of surplus production by renewable electricity producers, it included an exemption for producers that had already commenced their activity at the date of the entry into force of the amendment and allowed them to continue benefitting from the previous - more favourable - conditions. Following the entry into force of the aforementioned law, the Latvian regulatory authority interpreted the latter as having the effect of blocking, for these producers, the average electricity sale price at its value in force on 7 June 2005, in the sense that the term 'prices' used in the law was to be understood as a fixed price, not a price-fixing mechanism. As a result, as of that day, the authority ceased to update that price.
After the Latvian Constitutional Court invalidated the regulatory authority's interpretation, the producers submitted a claim to the regulatory authority for payment of 'damages' as compensation for the losses incurred as a result of the blocking of the tariff. The regulatory authority refused to grant those claims, but the Latvian administrative courts partially upheld the action brought by the producers and made the payment of the sums charged to the regulatory authority, as payment of State aid, contingent on the adoption of a decision of the Commission authorising such aid. Following an appeal by the regulatory authority against these judgments, the Supreme Court of Latvia sent 13 preliminary questions to the Court of Justice.

122. Judgment of the Court of Justice of 18 December 2008, Case C-384/07, *Wienstrom GmbH/Bundesminister fuur Wirtschaft und Arbeit,* EU:C:2008:747, para. 82.

other words, the limitation period under Article 17(1) of the Procedural Regulation does not apply to remedies ordered by national courts.[123]

This principle was again confirmed and further elaborated on by the Court of Justice in a recent preliminary ruling case.[124] The peculiarity of this case stems from the fact that the Czech national court, in referring the question to the Court of Justice, classified the contested aid as 'existing aid'.[125] The national court reasoned that after the expiry of the limitation period under Article 17(1) of the Procedural Regulation, aid becomes existing aid in accordance with Article 1(d) of that regulation, and existing aid is subject to permanent scrutiny by the Commission. However, since existing aid is no longer unlawful and therefore cannot be recovered, the question arises as to whether the classification as existing aid and the related limit to recovery also bind national courts.

The Court reiterated that it is only the Commission's power to order the recovery of unlawful and incompatible aid which is covered by Article 17(1) of the Procedural Regulation. This regulation sets out rules applicable to all administrative State aid proceedings pending before the Commission and does not contain provisions concerning the powers and obligations of national courts, which remain governed by primary law only. Hence, the Court held that expiry of the limitation period under Article 17(1) of the Procedural Regulation cannot have the effect of retroactively regularising unlawful State aid merely because it becomes existing aid and, consequently, depriving of any legal basis actions (whether actions for damages or actions intended to obtain recovery of the contested aid) brought against the Member State concerned by competitors or private individuals harmed by the granting of the unlawful aid.

Clearly, the notion of existing aid is contained in the Treaty, which also sets out the basic feature of the rules of procedure applicable to this category of aid.[126] However, the indication that unnotified aid for which the limitation period has lapsed

---

123. In para. 82 of the New Enforcement Notice, the Commission recalls the *Fallimento Traghetti del Mediterraneo* case law (Judgment of the Court of Justice of 23 January 2019, C-387/17, EU:C:2019:51, para. 61), which clarified that national limitation periods longer or shorter than ten years bind national courts, as they do not conflict with the ten-year limitation period, which applies solely to the Commission, or to national courts but only when they cooperate in implementing a Commission decision (Judgment of the Court of Justice of 20 March 1997, *Land Rheinland-Pfalz v. Alcan Deutschland*, C-24/95, EU:C:1997:163 paras 34-37, confirmed by Judgment of the Court of Justice of 29 March 2012, *Commission v. Italy*, EU:C:2012:182, para. 35, and Judgment of the Court of Justice of 30 April 2020, *Nelson Antunes da Cunha*, C-627/18, EU:C:2020:321, para. 60). This of course creates tension between private enforcement and public enforcement, as a uniform limitation period applies for the latter but not for the former.
124. Judgment of the Court of Justice of 7 December 2023, Case C-700/22, *Regiolet a.s. and Student Agency k.s./České dráhy a.s. and others*, EU:C:2023:960, paras 17-20.
125. The applicants before the national court claimed that, when concluding a contract with the National Railway Administration, Ceské had obtained a price capable of constituting State aid within the meaning of Art. 107(1) TFEU and that that aid was unlawful because it had not been notified to the Commission prior to implementation. The Czech Supreme Court asked the Court of Justice to clarify whether, in the context of a procedure initiated at the request of a third party, a national court must order the beneficiary to repay unlawfully granted aid even though the limitation period under Art. 17(1) of the Procedural Regulation has expired and, consequently, the aid under dispute is considered existing aid within the meaning of Arts 1(b) and 17(3) of the Procedural Regulation.
126. Article 108(1) TFEU.

also falls within this category is contained in the Procedural Regulation, which governs public enforcement procedures before the Commission and therefore binds the Commission only, not national courts. This conclusion cannot be extended to the other categories of existing aid, because although they are also the subject of Article 1(b) of the Procedural Regulation, they find their basis directly in the Treaty, as interpreted by the Court of Justice's case law prior to the Procedural Regulation's enactment.[127]

As to the remaining limits, the New Enforcement Notice merely insists on the need to take into account the non-payment of the interest related to the aid principal during the period of unlawfulness and how national courts should calculate illegality interest (*i.e.*, in accordance with national law, as neither Article 16(2) of the Procedural Regulation nor Articles 9 and 11 of the Commission Implementing Regulation[128] apply to a recovery ordered by national courts in the absence of a Commission recovery decision).[129]

IV.D Conclusions on the Legal Bases for Private Enforcement Remedies

Before analysing the main principles underpinning the system of remedies in private enforcement, it is worth drawing some conclusions from the review of the legal sources and the comparison between the 2009 Enforcement Notice and the New Enforcement Notice examined in this chapter. These conclusions will help reflect on the genuine results achieved with the modernisation initiative in this specific area of State aid law.

Although the New Enforcement Notice is far more elaborate and precisely structured than its 2009 predecessor, it contains no breakthrough change of approach. Only section 6, concerning the application of the principle of sincere cooperation to national courts and the implications of a violation of State aid rules by national courts, is entirely new. However, this section is basically an explanation of the Court of

127. These categories are: (i) aid granted before the entry into force of the Treaty, which is obviously not unlawful (*see* Judgment of the Court of Justice of 12 January 2023, *'DOBELES HES' SIA and Sabiedrisko pakalpojumu regulešanas komisija*, in Joined Cases C-702/20 and C-17/21, EU:C:2023:1, para. 99); (ii) individual aid granted in application of an aid scheme authorised by the Commission, which likewise is not unlawful (*see* Commission Decision of 16 August 1991 concerning aids granted by the Italian Government to the Italgrani S.p.A. company for the setting-up of an agri-foodstuffs complex in the Mezzogiorno) (91/474/EEC, 11/09/1991); (iii) aid granted after the expiry of the 2-month preliminary review period if the Commission has not opened a formal investigation procedure (*see* Judgment of the Court of Justice of 11 December 1973, *Gebrüder Lorenz GmbH v. Federal Republic of Germany*, cited in footnote 8 of this Part Two); and (iv) aid granted before the liberalisation of the sector concerned, which was therefore not subject to the notification obligation at that time but then became aid within the definition of Art. 107(1) as a result of the liberalisation (*see* Judgment of the Court of First Instance of 15 June 2000, *Alzetta and Others v. Commission*, Joined Cases T-298/97, T-312/97, T-313/97, T-315/97, T-600/97 to T-607/97, T-1/98, T-3/98 to T-6/98 and T-23/98, EU:T:2000:151). Unlike these four categories, the fifth one – *i.e.*, aid for which the limitation period expired – obviously remains unlawful despite the time passed since it was granted. It is therefore not rigorously existing aid within the meaning of the Treaty but is likened to existing aid by the Procedural Regulation as far as the Commission's powers are concerned.
128. Commission Regulation (EC) No 794/2004 of 21 April 2004, which implemented Council Regulation (EC) No 659/1999, which laid down detailed rules for the application of Art. 93 of the EC Treaty (OJ L 140, 30 April 2004, p. 1).
129. Private Enforcement Notice, cited in footnote 50 of this Part Two, paras 77-81.

Justice's *DEI* judgment and has been partially superseded by the Grand Chamber's judgment in *Dobeles Hes*. Likewise, the new subsection on the application of the *amicus curiae* instrument is merely a repetition and clarification of the new cooperation tool introduced by Article 29 of the Procedural Regulation. The subsections devoted to the other means of cooperation remain substantially unchanged.

Even more significantly, when it comes to the backbone of private enforcement, *i.e.*, the competences of national courts within the framework of the various types of proceedings which can be pending before them, the changes compared to the 2009 Enforcement Notice are minor. Beyond a clarification concerning the limitation period based on recent case law, and a reference to the principle that aid beneficiaries cannot invoke a violation of the principle of the protection of legitimate expectations to claim damages equivalent to the aid they have been asked to reimburse, the New Enforcement Notice adds only a couple of points of clarification concerning damages actions that were not already contained in the 2009 Enforcement Notice.[130]

In a nutshell, the New Enforcement Notice falls far short of achieving a significant step forward in terms of remedies for breach of State aid provisions. It basically limits itself to an orderly recap of the developments in secondary legislation and case law in the decade 2009-2019, with some additional clarification. In essence, the New Enforcement Notice reveals a lack of ambition altogether by the Commission when it comes to modernising the system of remedies. This conclusion is corroborated by an analysis of both the preparatory works (notably the 2019 Enforcement Study and the EFTA Study) and the declared goals of the New Enforcement Notice itself. The gap between the weaknesses highlighted in these preparatory works and the changes introduced by the New Enforcement Notice is indeed huge.

As discussed, the 2019 Enforcement Study found that, in terms of the number of cases, the private enforcement of State aid rules now prevails over the public enforcement of State aid rules, and this represents a drastic change witnessed in the last decade. Moreover, the 2019 Enforcement Study stressed the importance of adopting a specific legal framework for aid recovery in several Member States. Despite the lack of uniformity due to the absence of harmonisation at the EU level, this is a major difference from the findings of the 2006 Enforcement Study. Recovery legislation

130. Indeed, in section 4.2 – on the competences of national courts – only four paragraphs contain some relatively significant improvements compared to the 2009 Enforcement Notice: (i) para. 82, which is on the inapplicability of national limitation periods to prevent recovery and is based on the *Fallimento Traghetti del Mediterraneo* case law (*see* footnotes 77and 123 of this Part Two); (ii) para. 96, which is based on the *Asteris* case law and sets out a warning to national courts that they must be careful not to adopt decisions that have the effect of granting aid or enlarging the circle of beneficiaries when ruling on compensation to third parties for costs incurred as a direct result of unlawful aid (*see* footnote 72 of this Part Two); (iii) para. 97, which, in the same vein as the previous one, clarifies that a potential beneficiary of unlawful aid that has not received the aid cannot claim the amount of the non-received aid as compensation for damage, as this would constitute an indirect grant of unlawful aid; and (iv) para. 98, which is based on the *Eesti Pagar* case law and precludes beneficiaries from putting forward arguments concerning the alleged breach of their legitimate expectations to obtain damages from the granting Member State if they are obliged to repay unlawful State aid previously received (*see* footnote 83 of this Part Two).

typically specifies the public authority in charge of recovery proceedings and the procedural steps to be followed.

Nevertheless, the 2019 Enforcement Study also flags several shortcomings of the present system of private enforcement remedies, such as (to name but a few): the fragmentation of competent courts in State aid proceedings, with an inefficient sharing of competences between civil and administrative courts in several Member States; the large recourse to private enforcement to extend the application of beneficial tax regimes rather than tackle the granting of unlawful aid; the insufficient use of interim measures in interlocutory proceedings; the low number of cases in which remedies are actually applied compared to the overall number of private enforcement cases (which is mainly due to the high standard of proof required from claimants, the complexities related to quantifying damage and the causal link between the damage and the lack of a State aid notification); the lack of familiarity of market players with private enforcement remedies; and the reluctance by national courts to award damages for unlawful aid while the Commission is reviewing the aid's compatibility in parallel proceedings. The New Enforcement Notice fails to address many of these shortcomings and does not analyse - let alone implement - most of the suggestions contained in the 2019 Enforcement Study in terms of best cooperation practices.

The lack of sufficient improvements (beyond the customary reference to new case law) or original suggestions and, more generally, the Commission's unambitious approach to the reform of the system of remedies available to national courts is surprising considering that the modernisation objectives stated at the beginning of the New Enforcement Notice are profoundly different from those stated in the 2009 Enforcement Notice.

Even more deceiving is the fact that the New Enforcement Notice makes absolutely no attempt to elaborate on the interplay between private and public enforcement and, more precisely, on how to exploit the possible synergies and complementarity between the two sets of remedies in a modernised system of remedies. The Commission has shown a considerable capacity for innovative thinking within the framework of the modernisation initiative in other fields of State aid law. By contrast, it has been very conservative and unambitious when dealing with the system of remedies altogether, first in the field of public enforcement with the New Recovery Notice[131] and then also in the field of private enforcement with the New Private Enforcement Notice. It will be important to reflect on the reasons that might have led to this uneven approach when discussing reform avenues in Part Four of this book.

The second conclusion that can be drawn from the above analysis of the changes introduced by the New Enforcement Notice compared to the 2009 Enforcement Notice concerns the question of legal basis. The national courts' competences to cooperate with the Commission in the enforcement of State aid rules find their legal basis in primary law (Article 108(3) TFEU and Article 4(3) TEU, as interpreted by the European courts) and in secondary legislation solely for the application of the means of cooperation, *e.g.*, the *amicus curiae* tool. The Commission thus has a very broad

131. *See* Part One, section II.B.

margin of manoeuvre and could build up a rather modernised system of private enforcement remedies through soft law (or even better through harmonisation as will be illustrated in Part Four), as *the upper norms impose very few constraints*. It is true - and this will become clear when discussing the reform avenues in Part Four of this book - that an ambitious and complete reform should start from public enforcement and would strongly benefit from a few amendments to the Procedural Regulation, but this is, of course, no excuse for refraining from enhancing the private enforcement system of remedies consistently with the modernisation objectives rather than clinging to a system that has not undergone significant reform for decades.

V BACKBONE PRINCIPLES OF THE PRIVATE ENFORCEMENT SYSTEM OF REMEDIES: SUBSTANTIVE CRITERIA

This chapter delves into the substantive legal principles that underpin the enforcement of State aid rules by national courts. It highlights the principle of autonomy of national courts and the complementarity between national courts and the Commission, emphasising the importance of a coherent and systematic approach. The section discusses the need for a wide array of remedies to address the harm caused by unlawful aid.

In light of the above-examined sources of law for the private enforcement of State aid rules,[132] this chapter now aims to thoroughly and systematically analyse the substantive legal principles stemming from those sources of law and underpinning the national courts' exercise of their competences in the enforcement of the rules on State aid. Although some repetitions are inevitable, this chapter is structured around the legal principles stemming from the law sources and related case law, with an attempt to put them in a logical order while also considering the interlinks between them and the relative importance, regardless of chronology.[133] This methodology mirrors that used in Part One of this book with reference to public enforcement, with the view of making the argumentation more coherent and easily understandable.

V.A Complementarity Between National Courts and the Commission

The role of national courts, which stems from the direct effect of Article 108(3) TFEU,[134] is seen as complementary to that of the Commission.[135] This is of course the

132. *See* Part Two, Chapters I-III.
133. To the best of this author's knowledge, no attempt has been made in legal scholarship to date to systematically identify and classify all the legal principles that underpin the private enforcement of State aid rules. The scholars' contributions on private enforcement reviewed as part of the research for this book focus on specific case law or take a didactic approach based on the explanation of the origins of national courts' competences. The origins and rationale of the role of national courts in State aid enforcement are covered above, in Chapter I of this Part Two.
134. The Court held that 'the immediate enforceability of the prohibition on implementation referred to in that article extends to all aid which has been implemented without being notified and, in the event of notification, operates during the preliminary period, and if the Commission sets in motion the contentious procedure, until the final decision' (Judgment of the Court of Justice of 21 November 1991, Case C-354/90, *Federation Nationale du Commerce Extérieur des Produits Alimentaires, Syndicat National des Négociants et Transformateurs de Saumon (Saumon)*, EU:C:1990:440, para. 11).
135. *Ibid.*, para. 14, and Opinion of Advocate General Jacobs of 3 October 1991 (EU:C:1991:371), particularly points 23-24. Although in that case the Advocate General emphasised the complementary roles of the Commission and national courts with specific reference to the case of aid implemented prematurely and on which the Commission is required to examine the substance and assess the compatibility of the aid with the internal market, the principle applies to other situations as well. Indeed, the Advocate General rejected the idea that the Court's judgment in *Boussac* (Judgment of 29 October 1980, Case 22/80, *Boussac Saint-Frères SA/Brigitte Gerstenmeier*, EU:C:1980:251) could be construed as an attempt to qualify or relativise earlier case law on the direct effect of Art. 108(3). Quite the contrary, the Advocate General considered that the

consequence of the exclusive competence vested in the Commission for its compatibility assessment of new aid. As national courts cannot replace the Commission in the compatibility assessment, their competence is limited to enforcing the standstill obligation set out in Article 108(3) TFEU. However, the concept of complementarity clearly goes beyond this. Complementarity means that national courts have something to add to the Commission's competences. In other words, they can do something that the Commission cannot, or they are better placed than the Commission to adopt certain measures to enforce State aid provisions.

What national courts can do better than the Commission is to safeguard the rights of individuals, as clarified in case law.[136] The Commission's role is basically to protect competition and trade, and in the modernisation era, to foster the optimal use of resources and channel them towards the objectives of common interest. In doing so, the Commission only indirectly protects competitors of aid recipients and pursues only the public interest, whereas national courts must rule on cases brought by individuals and can use all the measures they are empowered to adopt under the national legal system. As the Court held, national courts:

> offer to individuals entitled to rely on disregard of the obligation of notification that all appropriate conclusions will be drawn, in accordance with national law, with regard to both the validity of the acts giving effect to the aid and the recovery of financial support granted in disregard of that provision or possible interim measures.[137]

One could say that the role of national courts is more to protect competitors than to ensure the undistorted functioning of the market.

The experiential truth, however, is that the distinction between the Commission's role and that of national courts is much deeper than what the mere legal framework reveals. Policy considerations are indeed an increasingly strong factor in the public enforcement of State aid provisions, especially in times of emergency and in certain strategic or sensitive sectors. Moreover, public enforcement of State aid provisions is typically under the strain of political considerations due to the pressure national governments exert on the Commission. This often impacts at least the timing

Boussac judgment emphasises not the parallel but the distinction between the Commission's position and that of the national court. He went on to say that the two functions of the Commission and national courts 'are, while distinct, nevertheless complementary, since the exercise by the national court of its power to declare unlawful measures which are not notified, or which are implemented prematurely, will help to ensure that Member States comply with their obligations and will facilitate the Commission's task of examining the substance of proposed aid'. Hence, he reaffirmed the full validity and importance of the case law concerning the direct effect of Art. 108(3) and its consequences on national courts' competences (Opinion, points 25-26).

136. *See* the *Saumon* judgment, cited in footnote 134 of this Part Two, and the related Opinion of Advocate General Jacobs, and the Judgment of 5 October 2006, Case C-368/04, *Transalpine Ölleitung in Österreich GmbH and Ohers v. Finanzlandesdirektion für Tirol and Others (Transalpine Ölleitung)*, EU:C:2006:644, especially para. 47. *See also* the Opinion of Advocate General Jacobs delivered on 29 November 2005, EU:C:2005:724.

137. *See* the *Transalpine Ölleitung* judgment, cited in footnote 136 of this Part Two.

and even the effectiveness of State aid control, although the Commission struggles to always ensure coherence in its actions and decision-making.

Against this background, which no-one could seriously dispute, private enforcement not only safeguards the rights of individuals in specific cases but also, from a broader perspective, limits the possibility and scope of political arrangements in the application of State aid rules, thereby ultimately helping ensure their effectiveness.[138] Moreover, private enforcement can contribute to the uniformity of application of these rules, at least if national courts rely on the preliminary reference tool under Article 267 TFEU any time this is compulsory or appropriate.

V.B No *Ex-post* Regularisation to Prevent Breaches of Procedural Obligations

A second fundamental principle of private enforcement is that unlawful aid cannot be regularised *ex post* in the case of a compatibility decision. If the Commission completes its investigation as required by the *Boussac* case law[139] and concludes that the aid in question, although unlawful, is compatible with the internal market, this does not change the classification of the unnotified measure as unlawful State aid. Consequently, national courts are required to draw the consequences of such unlawfulness in accordance with national law. As the Court of Justice held in *Transalpine Ölleitung*,[140] a Commission decision that finds that unnotified aid is compatible with the common market does not have the effect of regularising *ex post facto* measures taken in disregard of the prohibition laid down by the last sentence of Article 108(3) TFEU:

> since otherwise the direct effect of that provision would be impaired and the interests of individuals, which are to be protected by national courts, would be disregarded. Any other interpretation would have the effect of according a favourable outcome to the non-observance of that provision by the Member State concerned and would deprive it of its effectiveness.

This solution is considered indispensable to safeguard the effectiveness of the procedural obligations because, as explained by Advocate General Jacobs in his opinion in the *Transalpine Ölleitung* case:[141]

> if ... failure to comply with such obligations carried no greater risk or penalty than compliance, the incentive for Member States to notify and await a decision of compatibility would be greatly diminished – as would, consequently, the scope of the Commission's control.

---

138. It is true, as is discussed later in this chapter, that national courts must take into full consideration the Union's interest, which implies that they must avoid conflicts with compatibility decisions adopted by the Commission; still, they always have certain prerogatives and should not allow a breach of procedural provisions to go without consequences.
139. *See* footnote 133 of this Part Two.
140. Cited in footnote 136 of this Part Two. *See also* Judgment of the Court of Justice of 21 July 2005, Case C-71/04, *Administración del Estado v. Xunta de Galicia*, EU:C:2005:493, para. 31.
141. Cited in footnote 136 of this Part Two.

The reference to the necessity of a greater risk or penalty for Member States than mere compliance as a means to prevent breaches of procedural obligations is of particular interest, including from the perspective of a reform of the system of remedies. The message that the Advocate General and the Court of Justice[142] wanted to convey is twofold: first, some sort of penalty or other negative consequence would act as a significant deterrent and thus tackle non-fulfilment of procedural obligations; and second, measures adopted by national courts can complement public enforcement remedies (at least so long as EU law does not envisage fines or other penalties).

Additionally, the principle of non-*ex-post* regularisation of unlawful aid applies regardless of whether an interested party brings an action before the competent national court *before or after* the Commission adopts a decision that declares the aid compatible with the internal market. Even if the action is brought after the Commission's decision, this does not relieve the competent national court from its duty to draw the appropriate consequences, in accordance with its national law, from the unlawfulness of the aid.[143]

It is worth pondering the huge implications of this principle in terms of disincentivising breaches by Member States of their procedural obligations. In a nutshell, Member States which have granted unlawful aid to serve their economic objectives but have then immediately started cooperating with the Commission and provided all the information and arguments necessary to prove the aid's compatibility can no longer rely on the Commission's diligence in timely reviewing the case or on the Commission focusing on the case's substance. Conversely, the Commission is deprived of the full control of the enforcement process, as it does not necessarily have the last say on whether the aid can eventually be granted; by contrast, it cannot be blamed for the economic consequences of recovery if the aid must eventually be reimbursed.

Given the importance of the powers granted to national courts in cases involving a breach of procedural rules, the question arises as to what the ultimate purpose is of the requirement for the Commission to reach a decision on the compatibility of unnotified aid, in accordance with the *Boussac* case law,[144] considering that a compatibility decision can in no way cure the initial unlawfulness. Advocate General Jacobs raised this very question in *Transalpine Ölleitung*, and his reply was threefold. First, if the case refers to an aid scheme or to individual aid which has not yet been entirely paid out, the decision - whatever it may be - will produce full effects for the future. Second, an assessment by the Commission of a particular type of aid will be of assistance to Member States in determining whether future planned aid of the same type is permissible. Third, the consequences of the unlawfulness could still change as a result of the Commission's decision, even for the period before it was adopted. Indeed, although national courts must draw the appropriate conclusions from that

142. The Court made express reference to the Advocate General's opinion on this specific issue in para. 42 of the *Transalpine Ölleitung* judgment (cited in footnote 136 of this Part Two).
143. Judgment of the Court of 5 October 2006, *Transalpine Ölleitung*, cited in footnote 136 of this Part Two, paras 53-56.
144. Cited in footnote 135 of this Part Two.

unlawfulness, they must also take the Union's interest into full consideration, including by avoiding depriving a Commission decision of any effect and thereby rendering it useless.

The Advocate General does not delve deep into this issue in his opinion, but the subsequent case law has shed light on the full meaning of his comment, as is discussed in detail below.[145] For the time being, it is worth keeping in mind the breadth of the competences conferred on national courts even when a Commission decision on the compatibility of aid under scrutiny is adopted before the national court's judgment or order is delivered.

V.C The Principle of the Autonomy of National Courts Is Given Priority over the Risk of Conflicting Decisions

National courts' duty to adjudicate the case pending before them and to protect the rights of individuals is given priority over the risk of conflicting decisions. This key principle of the private enforcement of State aid rules, however, should be applied differently depending on whether the investigation before the Commission is still pending when the national court adopts a decision or the investigation has already ended with a compatibility decision. These two situations are examined separately below.

V.C.1 National Courts' Competences Ahead (or in the Absence) of a Commission Decision

Although national courts are bound to respect the sincere cooperation principle, putting a remedy in place while the Commission is still assessing aid is not a breach of that principle. This question was raised in *CELF III*. The *CELF II* and *CELF III* judgments are preliminary rulings which were rendered upon requests from the French *Conseil d'Etat* (Council of State) and which clarify national courts' competences and duties. The Court of Justice's decision in *CELF III*, due to the general interest of the issues raised, featured the intervention of five Member States and the EFTA Surveillance Authority and led to a landmark judgment from the Court of Justice's Grand Chamber, which followed and supplemented the important indications that the Court of Justice had already given to the competent national court in *CELF II*, which is discussed in the next section.[146] Interestingly, these cases are characterised by parallel proceedings

145. *See* Part Two, section V.C.2, which deals with the *CELF II* case law.

146. Judgment of the Court of Justice (Grand Chamber) of 12 February 2008, Case C-199/06, *Centre d'exportation du livre français (CELF) et Ministre de la Culture et de la Communication v. Société internationale de diffusion et d'édition (SIDE)*, EU:C:2008:79; and Judgment of the Court of Justice (Grand Chamber) of 11 March 2010, Case C-1/09, EU:C:2010:136. The cases concerned a French book export centre, which from 1980 to 2002 received operating subsidies from the French Government to offset the extra costs of handling small orders placed by booksellers established outside France. These measures were the subject of a long, complex legal battle that lasted almost a decade. The *CELF I* judgment is of no particular interest for private enforcement – in September 1995, the Court of First Instance (now General Court)

brought by a competitor before the Commission and national courts,[147] which explains why the *Conseil d'Etat* submitted two requests for a preliminary ruling to the Court of Justice: one before and one after the General Court's annulment of the third Commission decision declaring the aid compatible.

In *CELF III*, the Court of Justice - in replying to the second request - focused on, among other issues, the competence of national courts when a Commission compatibility decision has been annulled. This situation can be considered similar to cases in which a national court adopts a decision ahead of a Commission decision, *i.e.*, while the investigation procedure at the EU level is pending. Indeed, when an action for annulment is deemed well-founded by the EU courts, the judicature declares the contested act void - and the annulment decision leads to the disappearance of the contested act retroactively. Hence, at the time of annulment of a positive decision, the aid under scrutiny is deemed not to have been declared compatible by the annulled decision and is (still and again) subject to the Commission's review.

Therefore, the dilemma the Court had to solve was how to reconcile: (i) the necessity to guarantee the *effet utile* of a Commission decision in an area where the Commission has exclusive competence, with (ii) the national court's obligation not to defer the examination of the case brought before it and to safeguard the rights of individuals in cases of a breach of the notification and standstill obligations. Clearly, the interest in respecting the autonomy of national courts when they contribute to the

annulled a decision whereby the Commission had rejected a complaint brought by SIDE in 1992 and decided not to raise objections, as the aid was deemed to be prima facie compatible with the internal market. Later, in 1998, the Commission declared the aid under discussion unlawful but again concluded that it was compatible with the internal market. In early 2002, however, the General Court upheld the application brought by SIDE and annulled the Commission decision due to a manifest error in the definition of the relevant market (Judgment of the General Court of 28 February 2002, Case T-155/98, 2002:53). The General Court reached the same conclusion again in 2008, following the Commission's readoption, for a third time, of a compatibility decision (Judgment of the General Court of 15 April 2008, Case T-348/04, *Société internationale de diffusion et d'édition (SIDE) v. Commission CE*, EU:T:2008:109). In short, after each re-adoption, the General Court annulled (three times) the decision whereby the Commission declared the aid compatible with the internal market. Meanwhile, however, the proceedings brought before the French courts had led to an appeal before the *Conseil d'Etat* in which CELF and the Minister for Culture and Communication argued that the Paris *Cour administrative d'appel* had erred in law by not holding that the mere fact that the Commission had recognised the aid's compatibility with the common market precluded the obligation to repay the aid. The *Conseil d'Etat* decided to refer this matter to the Court of Justice for a preliminary ruling, and this led to the *CELF II* judgment, which was handed down in February 2008. Only two months later, the General Court annulled the Commission's compatibility decision for the third time. This led the *Conseil d'Etat* to stay the national proceedings again and ask the Court of Justice for a second preliminary ruling, this time regarding the calculation of interest. The Court of Justice therefore adopted the *CELF III* judgment, which specifically concerns national courts' competences when they are called to take action ahead of a Commission decision.

147. Appeals were brought before the *Conseil d'État* by CELF and the French Minister of Culture and Communication against a judgment of the *Cour administrative d'appel de Paris* (Administrative Court of Appeal of Paris) of 5 October 2004 whereby the French State was ordered, at SIDE's request, to recover, within three months of the judgment's notification date, the aid paid to CELF for handling small orders for books placed by foreign booksellers and, in default, to pay a EUR 1,000 penalty for each day of delay.

effectiveness of State aid provisions by safeguarding the rights of individuals prevailed in the Court's assessment.

The Court has consistently confirmed this approach ever since. In *Deutsche Lufthansa*, for instance, it held that national courts must ensure that all appropriate action is taken, in accordance with their national law, to address the consequences of an infringement of the last sentence of Article 108(3) TFEU 'as regards both the validity of measures giving effect to the aid and the recovery of financial support granted in disregard of that provision ..., so that the aid does not remain freely available to the beneficiary until such time as the Commission's decision is made'.[148] In *Eesti Pagar*, the Court analysed the role of national courts in ensuring that all consequences be drawn from a misapplication of block exemption regulations, as aid that does not clearly and fully comply with the conditions laid down in the applicable regulation remains subject to the notification requirement laid down in Article 108(3) TFEU.[149] The Court held that such conditions must be interpreted strictly and must be clear and easily enforceable by national authorities.[150] Therefore, nothing authorises national authorities to carry out their own assessment of whether the aid compatibility requirements (*e.g.*, the incentive effect) are met, as the Commission did not transfer the task of determining whether a genuine incentive effect exists to the national authorities by adopting the exemption regulation concerned; rather, the task of national authorities is limited to verifying that all the conditions laid down in the exemption regulation (or in the Commission guidelines implementing the regulation) are met. In other words, national authorities do not have any administrative discretion in applying the compatibility criteria; their role is to ensure, *under the control of national courts*, that all conditions laid down in the exemption regulation are complied with. If that is not the case, national courts are called on to take all necessary measures, just as they are called on to do in all other instances in which they ascertain an infringement of the notification or standstill obligations.[151]

148. Judgment of the Court of Justice of 21 November 2013, *Deutsche Lufthansa*, C-284/12, EU:C:2013:755, paras 30-31. *See also* Judgment of the Court of Justice (Grand Chamber) of 5 March 2019, C-349/17, *Eesti Pagar AS v. Ettevõtluse Arendamise Sihtasutus and Majandus- ja Kommunikatsiooniministeerium, EG*, cited in footnote 83 of this Part Two, para. 89.

149. *See* Judgment of the Court of Justice of 21 July 2016, C-493/14, *Dilly's Wellnesshotel*, EU:C:2016:577, paras 37-38.

150. *Ibid.*, paras 60-64. In *Eesti Pagar*, the controversy revolved around the incentive effect and the specific criterion that any application to benefit from aid must precede the work on the aided project in order to ensure that the aid is necessary and acts as an incentive to develop further activities or further projects, and therefore to ensure that the regulation concerned should not apply to aid for activities in which the beneficiary would already engage under market conditions alone. According to the Court, the 'criterion that the aid application must precede the start of work on the investment project is simple, pertinent and adequate, enabling the Commission to presume that the proposed aid has an incentive effect'.

151. As to the other aspects of the controversy, the *Eesti Pagar* judgment examines, in connection with the obligation to recover unlawful aid, whether EU law must be interpreted as meaning that it is the task of the national authority that granted the aid to recover on its own initiative aid granted pursuant to a block exemption regulation 'when it finds, subsequently, that the conditions laid down by that regulation were not satisfied'. This issue pertains to the scope of public national enforcement rather than to genuine private enforcement and is touched on in this book's Introduction and Part One, section II.

V.C.2 *National Courts' Competences When the Commission Has Already Adopted a Decision*

National courts' competences when they are called on to adjudicate a case for breach of procedural obligations and the Commission has already adopted a final decision declaring the aid compatible with the internal market slightly differ, although not substantially, from their competences in the previous scenario, *i.e.*, when they must rule ahead of a Commission decision. At least, the same basic principles on which their competences are based apply in both cases: they are required to safeguard the rights of individuals without delay and to draw all the consequences that would generally be drawn under their national law for a breach of a provision conferring rights on individuals.

The Court of Justice has gradually developed its approach in relation to this scenario. Initially, in the 2006 *Transalpine Ölleitung* judgment, when considering a case brought before a national court after the Commission had adopted a decision declaring the aid compatible with the common market, the Court simply held that:

> it is of little consequence whether an application is made before or after adoption of the decision declaring the aid compatible with the common market, since that application relates to the unlawful situation resulting from the lack of notification.[152]

and consequently concluded as follows:

> [D]epending on what is possible under national law and the remedies available thereunder, the national court may thus ... order recovery of unlawful aid from its recipients, even if that aid has subsequently been declared compatible with the common market by the Commission. In the same way, a national court may be required to rule on an application for compensation for the damage caused by reason of the unlawful nature of the aid.[153]

Only fifteen months later, however, in the 2008 *CELF II* judgment, the Court held that when a national court rules on the recovery of financial support granted in breach of the procedural obligations stemming from Article 108(3) TFEU, it is indeed required – even if the aid in question is declared compatible by the Commission in the meantime – to order the measures *most appropriate to remedy* the consequences of the unlawfulness as effectively as possible.[154] However, the Court added that in this scenario:

> even in the absence of exceptional circumstances, Community law does not impose an obligation of full recovery of the unlawful aid.[155]

Notably, until then national courts had been expected to order the recovery of unlawful aid (principal plus interest) except in exceptional circumstances in which

152. Judgment of the Court of Justice of 5 October 2006, *Transalpine Ölleitung*, cited in footnote 136 of this Part Two, para. 55.
153. *Ibid.*, para. 56.
154. Judgment of the Court of Justice (Grand Chamber) of 12 February 2008, *CELF II*, cited in footnote 146 of this Part Two, para. 45.
155. *Ibid.*, para. 46.

recovery would conflict with general principles of law, in a way that was analogous to the obligation imposed on the Commission under Article 14(1) of Council Regulation (EC) No 659/1999 (now Article 16(1) of Council Regulation (EU) 2015/1589). However, the analogy was flawed because: (i) the conditions of recovery are different in public and private enforcement; and (ii) national courts' autonomy in assessing the most appropriate manner to restore the situation existing before the aid was granted must be safeguarded. The Commission can order recovery only when the aid is declared incompatible, whereas national courts have no competence to scrutinise the aid's compatibility, yet still have a duty to adopt all the remedies available under national law to forfeit the advantage caused by the breach of Article 108(3) TFEU. This fundamental difference justifies *the softening of the recovery obligation* when a given aid measure, despite being unlawful, has been deemed compatible with the internal market by the Commission by way of a final decision.

Conscious of the novel issue raised before it and of the significance of its statement that national courts are not under an obligation to order the full recovery of unlawful aid even in the absence of exceptional circumstances, the Court went on to explain that the last sentence of Article 108(3) TFEU is based on 'the *preservative purpose* of ensuring that an incompatible aid will never be implemented' (emphasis added).[156] That purpose, the Court added:

> is achieved first, provisionally, by means of the prohibition which it lays down, and, later, definitively, by means of the Commission's final decision, which, if negative, precludes for the future the implementation of the notified aid plan.

Given that the intention of the Treaty's authors in drafting Article 108(3) was that solely compatible aid can be implemented, the premature disbursement of aid does not frustrate the *effet utile* of that provision if the Commission deems the aid compatible with the internal market.[157]

With this reasoning, the Court provides a theoretical basis for its (essentially pragmatic) solution that national courts are not under an obligation to order full recovery even in the absence of exceptional circumstances if the Commission has ascertained the compatibility of the aid plan under scrutiny. Rather, if the Commission declares the aid compatible, national courts are merely obliged to 'order the aid recipient to pay interest in respect of the period of unlawfulness'. Whether the competent national court can still order full recovery of the aid under these circumstances depends on national law, but *no such requirement is imposed by EU law*.

As to the obligation to order the recovery of interest, the Court explains that this obligation is justified regardless of whether the aid is declared compatible by the Commission and that national courts thus need not await the Commission compatibility decision before ordering recovery. Indeed, even if a beneficiary reimbursed the amount of unlawful aid following a national court decision but the Member State concerned was subsequently authorised to reimplement the aid following a positive compatibility decision, the beneficiary could still have obtained a financial advantage

156. *Ibid.*, para. 47.
157. *Ibid.*, paras 48-49.

if the period between the initial granting of the aid and the compatibility decision is longer than the period running from repayment of the aid and the reimplementation.[158] Conversely – though the Court does not mention this – the Member State should have the possibility to indemnify the beneficiary for the delay in disbursing the aid amount, even more so if one considers that the delay is due to the Member State's infringement of the procedural rules.

In a nutshell: (i) if a national court is called on to adjudicate a case, it must do so without delay to safeguard the rights of individuals in the case of breach of the procedural obligations stemming from Article 108(3) TFEU;[159] (ii) if, by the time the national court has ruled, the aid under discussion has not been the subject of a final Commission decision regarding its compatibility, recovery will have to be full (principal plus interest) to comply with EU law requirements;[160] (iii) if a Commission decision declaring the aid compatible is adopted later on, the Member State concerned will have the possibility to reimplement the aid;[161] (iv) if, by contrast, the Commission has already declared the aid compatible through a final decision, the national court will be obliged, under EU law, only to order the recovery of interest running from the moment the aid was made available to the recipient up to the date of the Commission's decision; and (v) if the scenario in the previous point applies, the national court may still order full recovery if national law empowers it to do so, but in this case, too, the Member State concerned will have the possibility to reimplement the aid.

V.D Taking the Union Interest into Consideration to Prevent Enlargement of the Circle of Fiscal Aid Beneficiaries

As explained above, although the Court acknowledged and even emphasised the national courts' autonomy in adopting all measures envisaged under national law to draw the consequences of a breach of the procedural obligations and safeguard the rights of individuals, it also clarified that national courts are bound to fully consider the Union interest when ordering remedies.

This statement acquires practical significance when it comes to determining remedies related to unlawful aid that takes the form of a (partial or total) tax exemption or deferral. In this respect, the Court has consistently held that the remedies imposed by national courts should not result in broadening the category of beneficiaries of an unlawful tax measure, as this would only aggravate the breach of Union law. National courts are thus prevented from ordering the extension of tax exemptions or benefits, as this would lead to an increase in the effects of unlawful aid.[162] Therefore, operators liable to pay a tax cannot rely on the argument that the exemption enjoyed by other

158. *Ibid.*, para. 54.
159. Judgment of the Court of Justice of 5 October 2006, *Transalpine Ölleitung*, cited in footnote 136 of this Part Two, para. 38.
160. *See* footnote 148 of this Part Two.
161. Judgment of the Court of Justice (Grand Chamber) of 11 March 2010, *CELF III*, cited in footnote 146 of this Part Two, paras 53 and 63.
162. *See* Judgment of the Court of Justice of 15 June 2006, Joined Cases C-393/04 and C- 41/05, *Air Liquide Industries Belgium SA v. Ville de Seraing et Province de Liège*, EU:C:2015:403, paras

businesses constitutes State aid in order to avoid payment of that tax.[163] Indeed, the fact that tax exemptions or benefits may constitute unlawful aid does not affect the legality of the tax itself, save for exceptional circumstances (*i.e.*, when the tax's revenues are earmarked for the financing of the exemptions or benefits in question).[164]

In stating this, the Court obviously disregards the distortion of competition that the granting of unlawful aid might cause and instead focuses on the formal infringement of procedural rules only. Moreover, the Court seems to imply that the enlargement of a measure does not result in it losing its selective nature and thus falling outside the scope of State aid rules. Theoretically speaking, this position is not entirely convincing in light of recent developments concerning the selectivity requirement, whereby a given measure's sectoral nature is considered insufficient to prove that the selectivity requirement is met and thus prompts application of the three-step test whenever it can be applied (based on the circumstances of the case); that said, it is consistent with the Commission's policy to reduce the overall amount of aid granted

44-45. *See also* Judgment of the Court of Justice of 5 October 2006, *Transalpine Ölleitung*, cited in footnote 136 of this Part Two, paras 49-50.

163. *See* Judgment of the Court of Justice of 20 September 2001, Case C-390/98, *H.J. Banks & Co. Ltd v. The Coal Authority et Secretary of State for Trade and Industry*, EU:C:2001:456, in particular para. 80. This judgment concerned Art. 4(c) of the ECSC Treaty and the general decisions (better known as 'steel codes') adopted by the High Authority or the Commission to implement it (in this case, Decision 3632/93, which expired on 23 July 2002). First, the Court held that national courts must afford individuals in a position to rely on a breach of an implementing decision, such as the breach of Art. 9 of Decision 3632/93, the prospect that all the necessary inferences will be drawn, in accordance with national law, as regards not only the validity of measures giving effect to the aid but also the adoption of remedies and, whenever necessary, of interim measures (para. 73). Regarding possible remedies, the Court added that 'withdrawal of an unlawful aid measure by way of recovery is the logical consequence of a finding that it is unlawful' (para. 74). With these statements, the Court applied – within the framework of the ECSC Treaty's State aid provisions – the exact same principles it had developed in the context of the EC Treaty. However, when examining the potential consequences of the direct effect of the relevant provision (*i.e.*, Art. 9(4) of Decision 3632/93), the Court observed that the claimant in the national proceedings was not claiming that aid should be repaid or that similar restorative measures should be adopted but was merely asking to be exonerated from the payment of royalties, given that the contested aid element was precisely the exoneration of British Coal from the same royalties. Moreover, the Court concluded that, given the case's specific circumstances, the situation that existed before the aid was granted could not be restored by repayment of the aid. Indeed, one reason was that the purchasers of the State companies which succeeded British Coal had acquired those companies under non-discriminatory competitive conditions; another reason was that the aid could not be recovered from the seller, as the State was both seller and aid provider. Despite these difficulties and the impossibility to recover the aid from the beneficiary, the Court held that the exoneration of other operators from the same royalties was not a suitable alternative to repayment of the aid. Instead, it left the door open to the possibility, for British Coal's former competitors, to bring an action under national law (if the conditions were met) to claim compensation for the damage caused to them by the competitive advantage enjoyed by British Coal and the State companies which succeeded it (paras 76-80).

164. If the tax's revenues are earmarked for the aid measure under the applicable national rules – in the sense that they have a direct impact on the amount thereof – the tax and the envisaged exemption are considered to constitute an integral part of the aid measure; in other words, the tax serves only to cover the benefit granted to beneficiaries. However, the revenues of a given tax cannot be earmarked for the financing of an exemption from payment of that same tax for a category of businesses, as the benefit would be limited to the non-payment of the tax itself (*ibid.*, para. 45).

unilaterally by Member States, *i.e.*, aid unrelated to specific horizontal objectives of common interest or to EU policies.

Interestingly, in the landmark *Banks* case,[165] the Court did not seem to think that recovery of the aid or equivalent restorative remedies always had to be available and appropriate. Quite the opposite: the Court stated that 'the national court must examine, in the light of the circumstances, whether it is possible to uphold the individuals' claims so as to help restore the situation' that existed before the aid was granted and thus preserve the effectiveness of the Treaty provisions.[166] Similarly, the Court consistently adopted an economic perspective in carrying out this analysis and explicitly referred to the need to offset or compensate the competitive advantage enjoyed by the beneficiaries (*see* paragraph 80).[167] There is no reason why this approach should be considered valid in the context of the ECSC Treaty but should instead be rejected within the framework of the TFEU.

More generally, building on the legacy of the *Banks* case, if one accepts that: (i) national courts can conclude that repayment of aid is practically impossible under the circumstances of a given case; (ii) equivalent remedies might not be available to restore the previous situation from an economic perspective; and (iii) national courts cannot consider broadening the category of aid beneficiaries to be an alternative remedy, it would be reasonable to conclude that situations might arise in which a national court can conclude, under its own responsibility, that no remedies (at least restorative remedies) must be ordered.

V.E Wide Array of Remedies Available to National Courts (Interim Remedies, Restorative Remedies, and Compensatory Remedies), with the Sole Exception of Prospective/Regulatory Remedies

The Union law provisions which govern the direct application of the last sentence of Article 108(3) TFEU do not indicate the types of remedies that should be ordered by national courts. Nor has the case law elaborated on this aspect,[168] in keeping with the principle of procedural autonomy, which is enunciated in Article 16(3) of the Procedural Regulation for the execution of public enforcement remedies but which can be applied by analogy (and *a fortiori*) in the context of private enforcement.[169]

In a nutshell, procedural autonomy means that the regulatory instruments giving effect to claims based on EU law are to be provided by national laws. The case law

165. *Ibid.*
166. *Ibid.*, para. 75.
167. *Ibid.*, paras 79-80.
168. A similar opinion is expressed by T. Jaeger, *The CELF Judgment: A Precarious Conception of the Standstill Obligation*, European State Aid Law Quarterly, 2008, Volume 7, Issue 2, pp. 279-289. Jaeger explains that the Court has left the content of the right afforded by Art. 108(3) TFEU 'practically open' and has deliberately provided only 'a basic set of claims' drawn from this provision, without elaborating any further.
169. On the concept of procedural autonomy in the enforcement of rights and obligations stemming from EU law, *see*, among others: Judgment of the Court 14 December 1995, Case C-312/93, *Peterbroeck, Van Campenhout & Cie SCS v. Kingdom of Belgium*, EU:C:1995:437, para. 12; and Judgment of the Court of 21 February 2008, Case C-426/05, EU:C:2008:103, para. 51.

simply requires that all inferences be drawn, in accordance with national law, from breaches of the procedural provisions enshrined in Article 108(3) TFEU. In other words, national courts are required to fully exploit the possibilities offered under their national law to remedy the consequences of a breach. Put in yet another way, national courts are bound solely to ensure that the measures they take with regard to the validity of aid measures enable achieving the objective of restoring 'the competitive situation existing prior to the payment of the aid in question'.[170] This explains why a wide array of remedies can indeed be used by national courts.

This section reviews the principles that can be drawn from the EU's soft law and case law in connection with at least the most common types of remedies. By contrast, a systematic analysis of the decisions adopted by national courts falls outside this book's scope, which mentions only a few examples to better illustrate the panoply of remedies available in the private enforcement of State aid rules. A systematic analysis of remedies in national laws is contained in the 2006 and 2019 studies commissioned by the Commission for that very purpose. The Commission itself reviews the main types of private enforcement remedies in section 4.2.3 of the New Private Enforcement Notice, which covers the means of 'safeguarding the rights of individuals faced with the breach of the standstill obligation'[171] and which are broadly referred to in the sections below.

V.E.1 Interim Measures

The duty of national courts to draw the necessary legal consequences from breaches of the last sentence of Article 108(3) TFEU is not limited to their final decisions. Since the very first judgment referring to the private enforcement of State aid law, the Court of Justice has clarified that national courts can and should consider interim measures when assessing the remedies they can offer, in accordance with their national law, to individuals claiming a breach of the last sentence of Article 108(3) TFEU in order to fully protect their rights.[172]

170. *See* Judgment of the Court of Justice of 8 December 2011, Case C-275/10, *Residex Capital IV CV v. Gemeente Rotterdam*, EU:C:2011:814, para. 45. It is worth noting that: (i) the objective set by the case law for national courts in the private enforcement of State aid rules is, once again, to restore the competitive situation that existed before the aid was granted; and (ii) national courts are given a broad degree of discretion in assessing the most appropriate measures to that effect.
171. *See* Part Two, section V.B.
172. Judgment of the Court of Justice of 21 November 1991, *Fédération nationale du commerce extérieur des produits alimentaires and Others v. France*, cited in footnote 134 of this Part Two, para. 12, where the Court states as follows:

> National courts must afford individuals in a position to rely on such breach the certain prospect that all the necessary inferences will be drawn, in accordance with their national law, as regards the validity of measures giving effect to the aid, the recovery of financial support granted in disregard of that provision and possible interim measures.

This statement is consistently recalled in the case law in exactly the same terms (*see*, among others: Judgment of the Court of Justice of 20 September 2001, Case C-390/98, *H.J. Banks & Co. Ltd and the Coal Authority*, cited in footnote 163 of this Part Two, para. 73; Judgment of the

Among the factors that the competent national court may consider in deciding whether it is necessary to order interim relief, the case law mentions: (i) how much time is expected to elapse before the final decision,[173] taking into account, among other things, the potential need to consult with the Commission or to refer the case to the Court of Justice for a preliminary ruling; (ii) whether a formal investigation is pending;[174] and (iii) what degree of risk exists that new aid amounts will be granted.[175] Other relevant factors include the risk of reiteration of the infringement and the need to avoid irreversible competition distortions, such as in the case of participation in tender procedures or similar situations.

Interim measures can be ordered by national courts before or after the implementation of the aid measure. If a State aid authority has not yet granted the aid when the national court is called on to ascertain a breach of Article 108(3), it must use all means at its disposal to prevent implementation of the unlawful measure.[176] Of course, in most cases, if a national court finds that the procedural obligations have been breached, this implies that the aid has already been granted, at least partially. Even so,

Court of Justice of 8 November 2001, Case C-143/99, *Adria-Wien Pipeline GmbH and Others v. Finanzlandesdirektion fur Karnten*, EU:C:2001:598, para. 27; Judgment of the Court of Justice of 21 November 2013, Case C-284/12, *Deutsche Lufthansa v. Flughafen Frankfurt-Hahn GmbH*, EU:C:2013:755, para. 30; Judgment of the Court of Justice of 11 November 2015, Case C-505/14, *Klausner Holz Niedersachsen GmbH v. Land Nordrhein-Westfalen*, EU:C:2015:742, para. 24; Judgment of the Court of Justice of 26 April 2018, Case C-233/16, *Asociación Nacional de Grandes Empresas de Distribución (ANGED) v. Generalitat de Catalunya*, EU:C:2018:280, para. 71; Judgment of the Court of Justice (Grand Chamber) of 3 March 2020, Case C-75/18, *Vodafone Magyarország Mobil Távközlési Zrt. V. Nemzeti Adó- és Vámhivatal Fellebbviteli Igazgatósága*, EU:C:2020:139, para. 23; and Judgment of the General Court of 10 November 2021, Case T-678/20, *Solar Electric Holding and Others v. European Commission*, EU:T:2021:780, para. 30).

173. Judgment of the Court of Justice of 11 July 1996, Case C-39/94, *SFEI and Others*, EU:C:1996:285, para. 52.

174. As indicated above, the fact that an investigation is ongoing does not release the national court from its obligation to safeguard the rights of individuals claiming a breach of the last sentence of Art. 108(3) TFEU and to thus take a position on the allegedly unlawful aid measure, but it can be taken into account when deciding whether it is appropriate to order interim relief. Indeed, the adoption of interim measures can be useful to safeguard not only the interests of the parties concerned but also the effectiveness of the Commission's decision to initiate a formal investigation. *See* Judgment of the Court of Justice of 21 December 2016, Case C-524/14 P, *European Commission v. Hansestadt Lübeck*, EU:C:2016:971, para. 29. Legal scholars have underlined that interim measures, such as interim recovery, can be 'a very effective instrument in cases where national court proceedings run parallel to a Commission investigation' (*see* A. Knade-Plaskacz, *Enforcement of State Aid Law at National Level. The Relationship Between National Courts and the European Commission*, Juridical Trib., 2013, Volume 3, p. 116). Despite this opinion and the clear statement in the judgment, it is doubtful whether national courts are really required to take into account a decision by the Commission to initiate a formal investigation/the effectiveness of an ongoing formal investigation, as the Commission has its own powers to adopt interim measures to safeguard the effectiveness of its (public) enforcement of State aid rules.

175. Judgment of the Court of Justice of 26 October 2016, C-590/14 P, *DEI and Commission v. Alouminion tis Ellados*, EU:C:2016:797, para. 101.

176. This situation is not included in the section of the New Enforcement Notice on interim measures but in a specific section entitled 'Suspension or termination of the implementation of the measure' (section 4.2.3.1.); nonetheless, it is clear that in such a situation, national courts will seriously consider the adoption of interim measures to prevent the granting of the aid.

the adoption of interim measures can be appropriate to avoid disbursement of the remaining part of the aid.[177] Moreover, it is also possible that an infringement can be ascertained but that the aid has not yet been disbursed at all. Indeed, Member States are required to notify any new aid project, even before the adoption of the related legislative measure or the enactment of the related administrative act. It is thus possible that a breach can be ascertained ahead of the aid's actual disbursement. Likewise, it is possible that a measure has been adopted or enacted but not yet implemented by the time the case is brought before a national court.

Some authors believe that this is the first mission that national courts must accomplish, *i.e.*, 'to prevent State aid measures from deploying their potentially distortionary effects until the moment the Commission has assessed the risks that the measure entails via the compatibility assessment under Article 107(3) TFEU'.[178]

The New Enforcement Notice merely confirms that:

> Union law does not impose any specific conclusion that the national courts must necessarily draw about the validity of the act granting the unlawful aid.[179]

Rather:

> it solely requires that they take effective measures to prevent the disbursement of the unlawful aid to the beneficiary.

This also implies that Union law leaves national courts free to order the remedies that they consider most appropriate to prevent implementation of the unlawful measure and disbursement of the aid (or part of it).[180]

In other words, as Pastor-Merchante and Monti emphasise, national courts must use all the 'toolkit that they derive from their respective national laws, picking the right instrument to achieve the goal mandated by EU law ... . Suspension orders stand out as one of the most obvious tools through which this goal may be achieved, but other remedies may be appropriate too'. In other words, EU law does not oppose the adoption of stronger remedies, such as the nullity of the act granting State aid, 'if national administrative law treats the violation of the notification and standstill clause

177. National experience shows that interim measures can be a very effective means in this situation, according to A. Knade-Plaskacz, *Enforcement of State Aid Law at National Level. The Relationship Between National Courts and the European Commission*, Juridical Trib., 2013, Volume 3, p. 116.
178. F. Pastor-Merchante and G. Monti, *The Functions of National Courts in the Private Enforcements of State Aid Law*, in P.L. Parcu, G. Monti, M. Botta, eds, 'EU State Aid Law', Edward Elgar Publishing Limited 2020, p. 121. The authors call this mission 'prophylactic' because the objective is to impede unlawful State aid measures from having an impact on the market.
179. New Enforcement Notice, cited in footnote 50 of this Part Two, para. 73.
180. In para. 73, footnote 101, of the New Enforcement Notice, the Commission refers to the *Residex* case (cited in footnote 170 of this Part Two) to illustrate that 'there may be situations under national law where the unlawful implementation of the measure can be suspended by annulling the granting act'. However, the implications of the Court's judgment in *Residex* go far beyond the issue dealt with in section 4.2.3.1. of the New Enforcement Notice (*i.e.*, unlawful measures that have not yet been implemented). Therefore, *Residex* is further examined below (Part Two, section V.E.3).

as a procedural flaw that affects the validity of unlawful State aid measures'.[181] Legal scholars unanimously agree that wide discretion must be left to national courts. Jaeger underlines that the various remedies available in national proceedings 'have not been elaborated in the case law at all'.[182]

If, contrary to the scenario discussed above, the unlawful aid measures have already been implemented and the aid disbursed by the time a national court is called on to ascertain a breach of Article 108(3) TFEU, the national court's role is to verify whether interim measures can be useful to remove the aid's anticompetitive effects on a provisional basis, with account again taken of the principles of equivalence and effectiveness.[183] The aim of interim measures in this scenario is to 'ensure that the advantage does not remain further at the disposal of the beneficiary'.[184] National courts may therefore consider adopting interim measures 'as a way to address the consequences of a potential infringement of the standstill obligation'[185] and regardless of whether a Commission investigation is ongoing.

As mentioned above, this circumstance 'does not release the national court from its obligation to protect rights of individuals under Article 108(3)'.[186] Therefore, interim measures can be adopted even when a Commission investigation is pending. If anything, an ongoing Commission investigation can be an additional reason that leads the national court to consider the adoption of interim measures appropriate.

For instance, if the national court considers there to be sufficient evidence of unlawful aid, it may decide, after carefully evaluating the balance of interests, to order the temporary suspension of the aided investment in order to prevent irreversible competition distortions until the Commission reaches a conclusion on the aid's compatibility. If the aid has already been disbursed and the national court intends to await the outcome of a parallel Commission investigation (which it is clearly not obliged to do, as clarified above), it must safeguard competitors' rights in the interim. Therefore, in this scenario, it may – as suggested by the Commission – order payment of the aid (plus interest) into a blocked account or adopt other interim measures that it considers appropriate in that specific case.[187] The Commission's suggestion is only one of several options and does not appear to be endorsed by EU case law. As Buendía Sierra and Bolsa Ferruz put it, the measure suggested in the New Private Enforcement

181. Pastor-Merchante and Monti, *The Functions of National Courts in the Private Enforcements of State Aid Law,* cited in footnote 178 of this Part Two.
182. Jaeger, *The CELF Judgment: A Precarious Conception of the Standstill Obligation,* cited in footnote 168 of this Part Two.
183. New Enforcement Notice, cited in footnote 50 of this Part Two, para. 83.
184. *Ibid.*, para. 84.
185. *Ibid.*
186. *Ibid.*, para. 85.
187. The Commission explains that depending on the outcome of its investigation, this amount can then either be reimbursed or withheld by the granting authorities. *See* B. Brandtner, T. Beranger and C. Lessenich, *Private State Aid Enforcement,* European State Aid Law Quarterly, 2010, Volume 9, Issue 1, pp. 23-32 https://doi.org/10.21552/estal/2010/1/168. For a diverging opinion on the same issue, *see* J.L. Buendía Sierra and M.Á. Bolsa Ferruz, *State Aid Assessment: What National Courts Can Do and What They Must Do,* European State Aid Law Quarterly, 2017, Volume 16, Issue 3, pp. 406-415 https://doi.org/10.21552/estal/2017/3/9.

Notice, *i.e.*, placement of the aid amount plus interest in a blocked account, 'does not seem to garner the support of the majority of the case law'.

More generally, the main question that arises in this respect is whether national courts must adopt interim measures when certain conditions are met. The Commission answers in the affirmative and, referring to the *CELF III* judgment,[188] enumerates the following conditions that national courts should verify: '(a) there is no doubt regarding the existence of State aid; (b) the aid is about to be, or has been, implemented; and (c) no exceptional circumstances have been found, which would make recovery inappropriate'.[189] In *CELF III*, the Court of Justice clarified from the outset that the national court's 'obligation to give a ruling without delay on the application for safeguard measures does not require the court before which that application is brought actually to adopt such measures'.

It was in that context that the Court of Justice enumerated the conditions justifying the adoption of such measures and, in so doing, made sure to leave a significant degree of discretion to national courts. Indeed, the expression 'no exceptional circumstances have been found, which would make recovery inappropriate' should be understood as meaning what common sense would have it mean – not as recalling the wording of Article 16(1) of Council Regulation (EU) 2015/1589, especially given that no reference is made to that legal basis.

This is confirmed by the word 'inappropriate', which implies a subjective assessment, not a strict legal test. This interpretation, which is primarily based on the principle of the procedural autonomy of Member States' judicatures in the private enforcement of State aid rules,[190] is all the more convincing in the context of interim measures, as the adoption of such measures presupposes a 'balance of interests' test, which is a typically discretionary exercise. What is more, *CELF III* is not the sole judgment that supports this view: *Klausner Holz*,[191] *Airport Handling*[192] and *Lübeck*[193]

188. Judgment of the Court of Justice of 11 March 2010, *CELF III*, cited in footnote 146 of this Part Two, para. 36. The New Enforcement Notice also refers to Order of the General Court of 3 March 2015, Case T-251/13, *Gemeente Nijmegen v. European Commission*, EU:T:2015:142, para. 45, where the General Court recalls the conditions for the adoption of interim measures in the private enforcement of State aid rules to reject the applicant's claim that the contested Commission decision had paved the way to the adoption of interim measures by the Dutch courts. The applicant was seeking annulment of a Commission decision opening an investigation into aid granted to some football clubs in the Netherlands.
189. *Ibid.*, CELF III Judgment, cited in footnote 146 of this Part Two, para. 86.
190. As always, procedural autonomy is constrained by the principles of effectiveness and equivalence, but this is a common feature to all situations in which national courts act as decentralised judicial bodies of the EU legal system. Furthermore, although the notion of equivalence is self-explanatory, the notion of effectiveness requires a value judgment, which necessarily implies a certain degree of discretion, subject only to verification of manifest error by the Commission as the Treaty's guardian.
191. Judgment of the Court of Justice of 11 November 2015, Case C-505/14, *Klausner Holz Niedersachsen GmbH v. Land Nordrhein-Westfalen*, EU:C:2015:742. The case concerned a reference for a preliminary ruling submitted by a German court in the context of a dispute between German authorities and the potential beneficiary of incentives envisaged in a contract that the competent authorities had initially signed but had later reconsidered because they claimed the incentives were unlawful State aid. Buendía Sierra and Bolsa Ferruz observe that in this judgment, the Court emphasised the need for national courts to reconcile the interests of both the alleged aid beneficiary and its competitors when determining the content of interim

have also been cited by some authors as pointing in the same direction. Based on an analysis of these three judgments, Buendía Sierra and Bolsa Ferruz conclude that national courts should 'read the Commission guidelines with prudence and scrutinise them in light of the caselaw'.[194]

However, some concrete examples exist across Europe of a stricter view of national courts' obligations when it comes to the adoption of interim measures. One interesting example is reported by J.J. Piernas López and M. Munoz de Juan. It concerns the position taken by the Spanish Supreme Court in the long-lasting litigation involving the aid granted by the Spanish Government to finance the transition from analogue to digital terrestrial television in remote areas.[195] According to the Spanish Supreme Court, when a Commission investigation is ongoing, national courts are required to take the *most proactive approach possible* under national law to effectively protect the rights of interested parties until the Commission adopts a final decision, regardless of whether interested parties in national proceedings have requested such protection.[196] As a matter of fact, they must consider all the possibilities at their

measures, in addition to the effectiveness of the Commission final decision that might ultimately find the aid to be compatible (this latter point has already been discussed above).

192. Order of the President of the Fourth Chamber of the General Court of 2 September 2015, Case T-688/14, *Airport Handling SpA v. European Commission*, EU:T:2015:588.

193. Order of the Court of Justice (Grand Chamber) of 4 April 2014, Case C-27/13, *Flughafen Lübeck GmbH v. Air Berlin plc & Co. Luftverkehrs KG*, EU:C:2014:240.

194. *Klausner Holz* is indeed a good example of the Court's approach, which seems to lean towards allowing wide discretion to national courts as to the content of interim measures and their appropriateness in a given case. *Airport Handling* and *Lübeck*, by contrast, concern the consequences to be drawn from a Commission decision to open an investigation and thus provide lesser support in this context. It is true, however, that the view of the German court - which was not convinced of the existence of State aid in *Lübeck* and therefore sought the Court of Justice's opinion on the options at its disposal - was ultimately confirmed by both the General Court and the Court of Justice. Therefore, leaving a degree of discretion to the national court to decide on the most appropriate interim measures turned out to be the best option in *Klausner Holz*.

195. J.J. Piernas López, *Enforcement of State Aid Law at the National Level: Recent Trends in Spain*, in P.L. Parcu, G. Monti, M. Botta, eds, 'EU State Aid Law', Edward Elgar Publishing Limited 2020, p. 218; and M. Muñoz de Juan, *National Courts and Interim Measures*, in European State Aid Law Quarterly, 2013, Volume 12, Issue 2, pp. 421-423.

196. A Luxembourg-based provider of satellite communication and transmission services challenged an administrative act implementing the national plan of transition to digital terrestrial television (DTT) before the *Audiencia Nacional* (the Spanish National Court) and, in light of the Commission's opening of an investigation, asked the court to order interim measures: namely, suspension of the administrative act until the Commission adopted its final decision. When the *Audiencia Nacional* rejected this claim on the basis that the contested aid had already been disbursed, the applicant brought the case before the Spanish Supreme Court, which annulled the *Audiencia Nacional's* decision and referred the case back to the latter. The Spanish Supreme Court upheld the lower court's conclusion on the point that a suspension of the administrative act would have been ineffective given that the aid had already been disbursed, and it rejected the applicant's request for the provisional recovery of the State aid already granted, but it concluded that the *Audiencia Nacional* should have been more proactive in protecting the rights of the affected parties, for instance, by ordering the placement of the contested funds in a blocked account until the Commission concluded its investigation into the aid's compatibility. The Spanish Supreme Court based its reasoning on the 2009 Enforcement Notice, which explicitly mentions this remedy as appropriate to protect the individual rights of affected parties when a national case runs parallel to an ongoing Commission investigation, as

disposal, especially those recommended in the Commission Notice on cooperation with national courts (the 2009 version at the time of the judgment). Indeed, although the Enforcement Notice is not legally binding for national courts, it is 'undoubtedly an authoritative criterion on the legal effects derived from Article 108(3) TFEU'.

The approach taken by the Spanish Supreme Court sharply contrasts with that of other judicatures across Europe, for instance, in Germany. As reported by J. Weinzierl, both the German Federal Court of Justice and the German Supreme Administrative Court have denied binding force to the Commission's preliminary assessments in decisions opening an investigation.[197] Piernas López praises the Spanish Supreme Court and considers its commitment to a proactive approach for national courts when considering the most appropriate interim measures while a Commission investigation is pending – regardless of whether interested parties request such measures – to be a positive sign. He also advocates for a more uniform approach across Europe – one based on the Spanish Supreme Court's example.

Of course, the fact that national courts try to prevent competition distortions during Commission investigations by adopting interim measures is a positive thing from the standpoint of cooperation between Member States and the Commission; however, from a strictly legal standpoint, the principle of sincere cooperation enshrined in Article 4(3) TEU does not imply that national courts should go beyond their role as set out in EU case law. *National courts are not entrusted with ensuring the effectiveness of the Commission's public enforcement* through the adoption of interim measures, as the Commission is itself empowered to issue interim measures if it considers them necessary.[198] The role of national courts is limited to safeguarding the rights that individuals are afforded under the directly applicable EU law provisions (*i.e.*, the last sentence of Article 108(3) TFEU for what concerns State aid rules).

---

this circumstance does not release the national court from its obligation to protect individual rights granted by Art. 108(3) TFEU.

197. J. Weinzierl, *Recent Developments in German State Aid Jurisprudence: A Scrutiny from the Perspective of the Preliminary Reference Procedure (Art. 267 TFEU)*, in P.L. Parcu, G. Monti, M. Botta, eds, 'EU State Aid Law', Edward Elgar Publishing Limited 2020, p. 194.

198. On this point, Pastor-Merchante and Monti (*see* footnote 181 of this Part Two) argue that national courts have an important role to play in neutralising the effects of unlawful State aid measures pending a Commission decision because, although the Commission has the power to order provisional recovery so as to avoid unlawfully implemented State aid measures continuing to deploy their effects while the Commission carries out its assessment, the following is also true:

> [T]he Commission power is subject to stringent conditions: the Commission can adopt interim measures to stop the implementation of an aid measure during the compatibility assessment only when there is no doubt that the measure constitutes State aid, there is urgency and there is a risk of substantial and irreparable damage to a competitor.

However, these conditions are rather standard for interim measures, and the Commission's choice to order recovery almost exclusively by final decision is based purely on practical convenience, or at most on policy reasons; it does not change the role and function of national courts, which is to safeguard the rights of individuals, as the Court of Justice masterfully illustrated in the landmark *Capolongo* and *Saumon* cases (*see* footnotes 7 and 134, respectively, of this Part Two) and has consistently reiterated thereafter in its settled case law.

In doing so, they are supposed to exploit all the remedies available under their national law and to assume their responsibilities regardless of possible investigations pending before the Commission. From this perspective, the Spanish Supreme Court's reliance on the 2009 Enforcement Notice - especially its idea of deriving specific duties for competent national courts therefrom - is unconvincing. Moreover, as appropriately pointed out by Muñoz de Juan, the reasoning of the Spanish Supreme Court's decision is far from flawless, as it does not analyse the notion of aid or consider the applicability of block exemption regulations.[199]

V.E.2 Recovery

It has already been shown that, in the context of public enforcement, recovery of the aid amount (the 'aid principal') is possible only when the Commission has ascertained that the aid is both unlawful (for the State infringed the standstill obligation) and incompatible with the internal market. This rule has been codified only in relation to State aid public enforcement, however;[200] in the context of private enforcement, aid incompatibility is not a pre-condition for recovery, although a compatibility assessment precludes recovery. Indeed, recovery cannot be ordered (at least not on the basis of EU law) if the Commission has found the aid compatible ahead of the national court's decision. This is because the principle of sincere cooperation applies, which prevents national courts from adopting measures based on directly applicable EU law provisions that conflict with previous Commission decisions. However, this general rule must be reconciled with the other well-established principle that an infringement of the notification and/or standstill obligations cannot be retroactively regularised, as State aid screening would otherwise lose its deterrent effect and thus be made ineffective. Only full compliance with the notification and standstill obligations exempts the Member State concerned from liability for infringements of EU law.

Therefore, although national courts cannot order recovery of the aid principal based on EU law in the case of compatible aid (assuming, of course, that the Commission has officially ascertained the aid to be compatible), they may do so if national law autonomously provides them that power. By contrast, they are in any case obliged to forfeit the financial advantage that the beneficiary unduly obtained in the period before the Commission's positive decision. They can do so by ordering repayment of the 'illegality interest', *i.e.*, the interest that the undertaking would have paid had it had to borrow the aid amount on the market during the period of

199. Muñoz de Juan emphasises that the Spanish Supreme Court decision lacks an assessment of the measure, which should have been included in the analysis of whether there was a prima facie case justifying the adoption of interim measures. Moreover, in her opinion, the Spanish Supreme Court should have asked itself whether the measure - if it constituted State aid - might have been covered by the GBER or by the Art. 106(3) TFEU exemption decision, as in either case the alleged aid could not have been regarded as unlawful.
200. *See* Art. 16(1) of Council Regulation (EU) 2015/1589, which refers to the Commission's negative (*i.e.*, incompatibility) decisions adopted in relation to unlawful aid.

unlawfulness.[201] In the absence of a compatibility decision, breach of procedural rules is a sufficient reason to order recovery of unlawful aid (both the aid principal and the illegality interest), given the obligation to enforce directly applicable EU law provisions such as the last sentence of Article 108(3) TFEU.[202]

That said, the crucial question here is whether national courts are *not only empowered but also obliged*, in the absence of a Commission decision declaring the aid compatible, to order the full recovery of the unlawfully paid amount plus the related interest. Such an obligation would hypothetically follow on from the idea, constantly relied on in the case law, that recovery is the logical consequence of unlawfulness. The alternative solution would be to rely on national courts' independent assessments, based solely on the direct effect of Article 108(3). This would entail giving national courts the responsibility to *assess every case on its own merits* and to *autonomously determine* what the most effective and appropriate remedies allowed under national law are, in order to restore the situation existing before the aid was granted.

Some confusion exists both in soft law and in legal scholarship on this issue. Scholars often refer to the *FNCE*[203] and *SFEI*[204] judgments, in which the Court mentioned recovery as one of the normal consequences that, in principle, should be drawn from an infringement of the last sentence of Article 108(3).[205] However, the exact meaning of this statement has given rise to controversy. The confusion reached its height in the 2009 Enforcement Notice, in which the Commission, after recalling that national courts must draw all legal consequences available under national law from the unlawfulness of the aid, immediately drew the conclusion that they 'must therefore in principle order the full recovery of unlawful State aid from the beneficiary'.[206] To

201. *See* the 2008 *CELF II* judgment, cited in footnote 146 of this Part Two and extensively discussed when dealing with the power of national courts after the adoption of a compatibility decision by the Commission (Part Two, section VI.C).

202. *See* the *Capolongo* judgment, cited in footnote 7 of this Part Two.

203. Judgment of 21 November 1991, Case C-354/90, *Fédération Nationale du Commerce Extérieur des Produits Alimentaires and Others v. France*, cited in footnote 134 of this Part Two, para. 11.

204. Judgment of the Court of Justice of 11 July 1996, Case C-39/94, *Syndicat Français de l'Express International (SFEI) and Others/La Poste*, EU.C:1996:285, paras 40 and 68.

205. *See, e.g.*, B. Brandtner, T. Beranger and C. Lessenich, *Private State Aid Enforcement*, in European State Aid Law Quarterly (EStaL), 2010, Issue 1, pp. 23-33 https://doi.org/10.21552/estal/2010/1/168. These authors not only claim that national courts are obliged to order recovery simply because a State aid measure has not been notified, irrespective of any other circumstances but also go further by arguing that the legal consequences of a national court's recovery order are similar to those of a Commission decision, without further explanation. More importantly, they dismiss the important caveat in the *FNCE* and *SFEI* judgments (*i.e.*, the words 'in principle') as referring solely to the limits to the recovery obligation under the Procedural Regulation with respect to public enforcement. In other words, the authors consider the national courts' obligation to order recovery to be much broader than the Commission's but at the same time consider the exceptions to this obligation to be just the same for the national courts and the Commission. This conclusion not only lacks a clear legal basis but is also illogical from an economic and practical perspective, as it would make more sense to grant national courts a broader margin of appraisal of the actual economic effects of a given measure (and therefore greater discretion in determining how to better restore the competitive situation existing before its adoption) if it has not been found incompatible with the internal market.

206. *See* the 2009 Enforcement Notice, para. 30.

substantiate this conclusion, the Commission referred to case law that in no way supported its views.

In *Xunta de Galicia*,[207] for instance, the question submitted to the Court of Justice revolved around the notification obligation in the case of a modification of an aid scheme for shipbuilding and ship conversion falling outside the scope of the EEC Directive on aid to shipbuilding, which was in force at the time the aid was granted. No question was asked in respect of the remedies that national courts could or ought to impose. Admittedly, the Court stated that the finding that aid had been granted in breach of the procedural obligations ought to lead, in principle, to its repayment in accordance with the procedural rules of domestic law. However, the Court fell short of putting a clear obligation on national courts to order recovery of the aid and, in the very same paragraph, explained that:

> it is for the national court ... to draw the necessary consequences, in accordance with their national law, with regard to both the validity of the acts giving effect to the aid and the recovery of financial support granted.[208]

Therefore, the Court mentions recovery of the aid as the most obvious consequence of unlawfulness but takes care to add the words 'in principle' to clarify that it is merely providing an example of what a national court may do.[209] It is true that the

207. Judgment of the Court of Justice of 21 July 2005, Case C-71/04, *Administracion del Estado/Xunta de Galicia*, EU:C:2005:493.
208. *Ibid.*, para. 49.
209. Similar conclusions can be drawn from the analysis of the two (older) judgments referred to in this respect in the 2009 Enforcement Notice:

    (i) In *SFEI* (Judgment of the Court of Justice of 11 July 1996, Case C-39/94, *Syndicat Français de l'Express International (SFEI) and Others/La Poste*, EU.C:1996:285), the Court held that 'national courts must offer to individuals the certain prospect that all the appropriate conclusions will be drawn from an infringement of Art. 93(3), last sentence, of the Treaty, in accordance with their national law, as regards the validity of measures giving effect to the aid, the recovery of financial support granted in disregard of that provision and possible interim measures' (para. 40). In para. 68 of the same judgment, the Court held that a finding of the breach of procedural rules 'must in principle lead to its repayment in accordance with the procedural rules of domestic law'. Beyond the words 'in principle', which are already examined above in connection with the *Xunta de Galicia* case, with this statement the Court was replying to the Spanish Government's claim that a breach of the procedural obligations could give rise only to interim measures and that a recovery order could not be ordered until it was found that the measure concerned constituted incompatible aid. Therefore, once more, the Court did not go as far as imposing an obligation on national courts to choose repayment instead of other remedies when drawing the available consequences of infringements under national law.
    (ii) In the landmark Saumon case (Judgment of the Court of Justice of 21 November 1991, Case C-354/90, Federation Nationale du Commerce Extérieur des Produits Alimentaires and Syndicat National des Négociants et Transformateurs de Saumon/French Republic, referred to in footnote 134 of this Part Two), the Court likewise clarified that national courts 'must offer to individuals in a position to rely on such breach the certain prospect that all the necessary inferences will be drawn, in accordance with their national law, as regards the validity of measures giving effect to the aid, the recovery of financial support granted in disregard of that provision and possible interim measures' (para. 12). Once more, the concept of 'recovery' is used here as the typical example of remedy, but there is no clear indication of an obligation imposed on national courts to prioritise

Commission reproduces the words 'in principle' in the 2009 Enforcement Notice - but only two paragraphs later, when explaining why 'the national court's recovery obligation is not absolute', it refers to the limits to the recovery obligation under the Procedural Regulation, *i.e.*, to the 'external' limits to the Commission's duty to order recovery of unlawful aid.[210] In doing so, the Commission conveys the wrong impression that national courts are bound by the same rules that regulate the Commission's powers in the public enforcement of State aid law.

When working on the New Private Enforcement Notice, the Commission supposedly identified the problem and endeavoured to work it out by eliminating the reference to the Procedural Regulation and referring to case law that emerged after issuance of the 2009 Enforcement Notice. Building on a statement repeatedly found in the case law of the last decade (*i.e.*, 'removal of the aid by means of recovery is the logical consequence of its unlawfulness'),[211] the Commission now maintains that:

> national courts must, in principle, and in the absence of a Commission decision declaring the aid compatible, order the full recovery of the unlawfully paid amount.[212]

However, this time the Commission clarifies that, more generally, national courts:

> must abolish completely the advantage unlawfully conferred on the beneficiary,

as the objective is:

> to restore the situation existing before the aid was granted.[213]

Hence, recovery is correctly framed as a means (indeed the most typical one) whereby the competent national court can ensure restoration of the situation existing before the aid was granted - it being understood that, as the words 'in principle' indicate, the national court might consider another remedy to be more effective and/or appropriate in a given case.

This peculiarity of recovery in the context of private enforcement has not escaped some scholars. Jaeger is one of the authors who has delved more deeply into the issue, specifically as concerns the recovery obligation from a private enforcement

---

recovery over other possible remedies offered by national law that they might consider more appropriate in the circumstances of a given case.

210. *See* the 2009 Enforcement Notice, para. 32. The external limits are compliance with general principles of law and the limitation period, as set out under Arts 14 and 15 of the Procedural Regulation in force at the time of the *Xunta de Galicia* judgment (Arts 16 and 17 of the currently applicable Procedural Regulation).
211. *See*, among others, Judgment of the Court of Justice of 21 December 2016, Case C-164/15 P and C-165/15 P, *Commission v. Air Lingus*, EU:C:2016/990, para. 116.
212. *See* the New Enforcement Notice, cited in footnote 50 of this Part Two, para. 76 and footnote 103, where the relevant case law is mentioned.
213. *Ibid.*, para. 77.

perspective.[214] The starting point of his analysis is that in light of the national courts' autonomous competences under the standstill obligation, their duty is to protect the right afforded to individuals by Article 108(3) TFEU, which, as termed in *SFEI*, is the right to receive protection 'against the consequences of unlawful implementation of aid'.[215] This is, of course, the correct perspective. He then observes that the Court of Justice sketched out these rights only in very broad terms when referring to the possibility of obtaining suspension of a State aid measure, recovery, damages, or interim measures. The Court - he concludes - does not elaborate further on these rights because national courts are expected to draw from their domestic law whatever consequences they deem necessary to give effect to the protection granted by Article 108(3) TFEU. For instance, 'the Court has never prescribed a specific means to curtail the legal force of (civil or public law) acts in contravention of the standstill obligation. Instead, the wide range of possible consequences ... (*i.e.*, absolute nullity, relative nullity, provisional nullity, *etc.*) is left to national law'.

It is thus clear that, as argued above, the Court mentions recovery, along with interim measures and damages, only in a very generic manner. And it is at least debatable that its intention is to impose an *absolute and automatic* obligation on national courts to order full recovery of the aid amount regardless of the specific circumstances of each case and of any other remedy available under national law.

Other authors take a less conclusive position. J. Derenne and C. Kaczmarek, for instance, refer to the *SFEI* judgment[216] to underline that, according to the Court, recovery may turn out to be inappropriate in exceptional circumstances.[217] The authors, just like the Court, make no attempt to clarify the notion of exceptional circumstances (though it is clearly up to the national court concerned to give substance to the notion in its assessment of the case);[218] and despite the reference to circumstances that may justify departing from a repayment order, they submit that the obligation to recover unlawful aid is unconditional. However, no authoritative sources are cited to support this statement, and the authors do not elaborate on their reasoning behind it.

A. Knade-Plaskacz,[219] on her part, recalls Advocate General Kokott's opinion in the *Residex Capital IV* case[220] to emphasise that EU law requires national courts 'to

214. Jaeger, *The CELF Judgment: A Precarious Conception of the Standstill Obligation*, cited in footnote 168 of this Part Two.
215. Judgment of the Court of Justice of 11 July 1996, Case C-39/94, *SFEI*, cited in footnote 204 of this Part Two.
216. *Ibid.*
217. *See* Derenne and Kaczmarek, *La recuperation des aides illegals: le role du juge national dans le* 'private enforcement' *du droit des aides d'Etat*, cited in footnote 11 of this Part Two.
218. Arguably, had the Court wanted to rely on the limits to the recovery obligation under the Procedural Regulation, it would have explicitly done so. It can thus be assumed that the Procedural Regulation's provisions on recovery do not apply to national courts and that the notion of exceptional circumstances is not necessarily limited to a breach of general principles of law, as it is in Art. 16(1) of the Procedural Regulation.
219. A. Knade-Plaskacz, *Enforcement of State Aid Law at National Level. The Relationship Between National Courts and the European Commission*, Juridical Tribune, December 2013, Volume 3, Issue 2, pp. 116-125.
220. Judgment of the Court of Justice of 8 December 2011, Case C-275/10, *Residex Capital IV CV/Gemeente Rotterdam*, EU:C:2011:814, and Opinion of Advocate General Kokott of 26 May 2011, EU:C:2011:354.

order those measures which [or, more correctly, whichever measures] are appropriate effectively to remedy the consequences of the unlawfulness of an aid measure', *i.e.*, the most appropriate measure to ensure that at least the recipient forfeits the unduly obtained economic advantage so that the previously existing situation is re-established. The author then underlines, by reference to the *Wienstrom* case,[221] that the situation is different when the Commission has already declared the aid compatible, as in this case EU law still requires national courts to order the appropriate measures to effectively remedy the consequences of the unlawfulness but, 'even in the absence of exceptional circumstances ... does not impose an obligation of full recovery of the unlawful aid'.

It is difficult not to concur with these statements. However, Knade-Plaskacz's opinion can no longer be followed when, in her attempt to clarify the notion of exceptional circumstances, she refers solely to the concept of protection of the aid recipient's legitimate expectations, whereas national courts are free to consider other circumstances, too, as explained above. Besides, reference should be made, if considered relevant, to the notion of the protection of legitimate expectations as developed under national law - not to the EU law notion.

Other scholars opine that, notwithstanding the lack of harmonisation of the State aid remedies available at national level, EU law 'actually constrains rather tightly the remedial strategy that national courts are supposed to adopt *vis-à-vis* well-founded State aid claims'.[222] However, it is difficult to understand on what authority this conclusion is based. Even the definition of the national courts' function - once they are seized after the implementation of an aid measure - as being merely 'restorative' in nature (in the sense that they 'should aim at bringing the market back to the situation in which it would have been in the absence of the unlawful State aid measures')[223] is debatable. Indeed, national courts are bound only to safeguard the individual rights conferred on EU citizens by the Treaty provisions that create obligations for Member States (such as the notification and standstill obligations) - all the more reason why the appropriate means to restore the *status quo ante* are a matter for national courts to consider.

It is true that Article 108(2) TFEU states that Member States must 'abolish or alter' incompatible aid and that doing so retroactively in the case of unlawful aid entails the adoption of restorative remedies. However, this refers to the Commission's powers within the framework of public enforcement administrative procedures. Although the remedies that national courts can impose will most likely also seek to undo the effects of unlawful aid and therefore fall under the definition of restorative remedies, national courts are under no binding obligation to order recovery, as they may select the remedies that they consider the most suitable in a given case to abide by their mission.

221. Judgment of the Court of Justice of 18 December 2008, Case C-384/07, *Wienstrom GmbH/Bundesminister fuur Wirtschaft und Arbeit*, cited in footnote 122 of this Part Two.
222. Pastor-Merchante and Monti, *The Functions of National Courts in the Private Enforcement of State Aid Law*, cited in footnote 178 of this Part Two. *See also* footnote 194 of this Part Two, where the opinion of these authors is more extensively reported.
223. *Ibid.*

It is therefore worth defining that mission. As observed by Jaeger,[224] the case law on the aims of the standstill obligation that are relevant for national courts 'remains sketchy'. Yet – Jaeger adds – two aims seem sufficiently established in the case law: to protect individuals from the consequences of the unlawfulness and to contribute to ensuring the effectiveness of the notification obligation (*i.e.*, to enhance compliance with that obligation). Whereas the first aim is beyond a doubt the typical task of national courts, it is less intuitive to think that they have the additional mission of enhancing compliance with the standstill obligation.

Even if one assumes that, to abide by their mission to protect individuals from the consequences of the unlawfulness, national courts must necessarily pursue the aim of restoring the situation that existed before unlawful aid was granted, this does not mean they must stick to recovery of the aid regardless of the specific circumstances of a given case. Indeed, they could well go beyond a recovery order if they consider that recovery would not be sufficient to erase all the harmful effects caused by the aid. For instance, they may order that all taxes paid to finance unlawful State aid be the subject of restitution to taxpayers. Moreover, they may order the recipient to pay compensation for damage suffered by competitors and other third parties as a result of the aid measure's unlawful implementation if it can be considered responsible for the damage under national provisions on non-contractual liability (which usually implies that the damage was foreseeable and avoidable).

Likewise, national courts should also be permitted to partially or totally replace recovery with other measures if they consider that recovery (or full recovery) would be an inefficient remedy in the case under consideration. The same should be possible if the competent national court believes that recovery is useless to erase the distortive effects and restore the situation existing before the unlawful aid was granted.

Although EU law does not require national courts to play any specific role in ensuring effective deterrence against the infringement of the standstill obligation,[225] the adoption of more effective measures by national courts would go in the direction indicated by the Court of Justice.[226] Conversely, national courts may not replace recovery or equivalent remedies with a positive remedy, such as the extension of the advantage to any further beneficiary, because this would conflict with the common EU interest in avoiding massive recourse to State aid and thus with the principle of sincere

224. Jaeger, *The CELF Judgment: A Precarious Conception of the Standstill Obligation*, cited in footnote 168 of this Part Two.

225. Jaeger expresses a different opinion on this issue by recalling the *Transalpine Ölleitung* judgment, cited in footnote 136 of this Part Two, para. 42 of which states that if failure to comply with Art. 108(3) TFEU 'carried no greater risk or penalty than compliance, the incentive for Member States to notify and await a decision on compatibility would be greatly diminished – as would, consequently, the scope of the Commission's control'. However, the phrase 'no greater risk or penalty than compliance' seems to refer to compliance with a compatibility decision, *i.e.*, that compliance with such a decision cannot have the effect of regularising the violation of procedural obligations.

226. This is indirectly confirmed by, among others, the *CELF II* case law (cited in footnote 146 of this Part Two). Indeed, the Court's reasoning in that case seems to imply that if national law envisages the possibility of ordering full recovery despite a compatibility decision by the Commission, national courts are in principle obliged to do so (or at least to go beyond the mere requirement imposed by EU law, which is to order payment of illegality interest).

cooperation. EU State aid law clearly bans national courts from granting this kind of remedy. However, it can be the object of debate whether broadening the advantage to the point that the measure under consideration is deprived of its selective nature would also be banned as a way of restoring effective competition.

One could therefore conclude that *national courts have the liberty to determine the most suitable remedies for restoring the situation that existed before unlawful aid was granted, on condition that the remedies do not amplify the scope of the infringement by adding other recipients*. In the absence - at the present stage of development of EU State aid law - of harmonised rules, national law governs not only purely procedural issues such as standing, time limits, and the determination of the competent judicial body but also the nature of the remedies available and the required standard of proof to grant each of them.

A situation in which a national court believes that recovery would be ineffective or disproportionate given the unlawful aid's effects raises more doubts. Based on the case law to date, it is reasonable to consider that, in such cases, recovery would be a *minimum requirement*, as it would be the natural consequence of the unlawfulness according to the EU courts. However, it could also be argued that this position would confer a task on national courts (assure effective deterrence) that goes beyond the mission they are entrusted with by the Treaty.

Pastor-Merchante and Monti acknowledge that national courts are not required to discharge any specific duties *(e.g.*, to order damages, payment of illegality interest, recovery, restitution of taxes, or other measures) in every single case. As they rightly point out, '[w]hich task is appropriate depends, among other things, on the factual background and on the remedies requested by the applicants in each case'. It can be added that the 'factual background' should be understood as including an *assessment of the efficacy of every single remedy against the specific circumstances of the case*, including the effect that the unlawful aid generated and the economics of the relevant market. However, even these authors ultimately consider any departure from the recovery remedy to be exceptional in nature and point to legitimate expectations and absolute impossibility as the sole scenarios in which national courts may refrain from ordering recovery.

This conclusion once more transfers criteria that the legislator set out when shaping the Commission's powers to the different field of private enforcement, and unduly limits the autonomous assessment of national courts. National courts are bound only to pursue the objective of safeguarding the rights of individuals in the manner permitted by national law that they consider the most suitable in every single case. Their role is not to protect the market's integrity but rather to uphold private parties' demands if they are 'procedurally sound and substantively well-founded'. Indeed, although their opinion diverges from the one expressed above,[227] Pastor-Merchante and Monti themselves correctly point out as follows:

227. *See* Pastor-Merchante and Monti, *The Functions of National Courts in the Private Enforcement of State Aid Law*, cited in footnote 178 of this Part Two.

> [T]he capacity of national courts to fulfil [their] function depends on the initiatives taken by third parties ... National courts are powerless if third parties fail to bring to their attention allegedly unlawful State aid measures. More importantly, it is the time and content of these applications which determine the exact remedies that national courts may take in each case.[228]

Therefore, the effects of the breach of EU law are not necessarily entirely removed with a successful national action because they extend to the applicants only - but this is inherent to the nature of private enforcement. The same opinion is expressed by M. Köhler.[229]

Köhler proposes an interesting perspective to explain the constraints imposed on national courts by EU law in determining the appropriate remedies: the close link that must be ensured between 'rights' and 'remedies'. The *substantive rights* that national courts must safeguard are derived from Union law, whereas it is for the Member States to legislate the procedural rules or to select the most appropriate ones between those existing in national law, *including the necessary remedies* which enable the competitors of beneficiaries of unlawful aid to secure their rights.

The most controversial issue in this respect, as correctly pointed out by Köhler, is whether the internal legal system of every Member State is responsible solely for determining the legal procedure to be followed in order to achieve a given result (*i.e.*, to safeguard the rights of individuals derived from Article 108(3) TFEU) - it being understood that the result should be exactly the same in all EU jurisdictions - or whether instead the concept of procedural autonomy includes the competence of national courts to determine the most appropriate remedies to achieve that result.

According to Köhler, one might understand from the *Lorenz* case law that it is acceptable to have differences in Member States' legal systems with regard to the consequences in civil law of a breach of Union law provisions. This might especially be the case, he adds, with respect to 'interferences as regards the validity of measures'. Indeed, '[p]rivate enforcement ... might (only) lead to different consequences in the different Member States by combining the immediate (and compulsory) effect of the *Lorenz* caselaw with the respective remedies under national law'.

This opinion is faultless, as some degree of divergence in the enforcement of EU rules across Member States - especially in competition law - is inherent to the system, and the EU legislator is responsible for eliminating or reducing it by means of harmonisation if it deems it necessary. For the time being, in the absence of harmonisation of national laws, national courts are bound solely to comply with the minimum requirements set out under EU law. In matters of State aid, currently, these minimum requirements are only to adjudicate on the recovery of financial support granted in accordance with national law upon requests from interested parties, with no specific constraint as to the content of their decision.

---

228. *Ibid.* These statements, however, seem to reinforce the conclusion that, contrary to Pastor-Merchante and Monti's view, the role of national courts is not to protect the market's integrity but simply to safeguard third parties' rights in the most efficient manner possible in accordance with national law.
229. Köhler, *Private Enforcement of State Aid Law: Problems of Guaranteeing EU Rights by Means of National (Procedural) Law,* cited in footnote 40 of this Part Two.

Köhler further argues (and, on this aspect, his opinion coincides with Jaeger's) that the reference to the national legal system must not be understood as a reference to national substantive law as far as the content of competitors' rights is concerned because the aid's unlawfulness derives directly from Union law and from the competitors' right to obtain restoration of the previously existing situation. However, restoration of the previous situation can be achieved in many ways under national law depending on, among other things, the kind of measure constituting the aid. Indeed, remedies available under national law can differ substantially depending on whether the aid is granted through an administrative act or through measures issued by an authority or a public enterprise under civil law.

This leads Köhler to observe as follows: '[T]he court confronted with a claim of a competitor might have to decide whether it should set aside parts of its procedural rules and accept the claim to avoid that the Member State does not fulfil its obligations under the Treaty. As long as no settled caselaw has been developed by the various courts that might be competent for different remedies (remedies according to different domestic regulations), this might prove to be a very tricky task.'

Buendía Sierra and Bolsa Ferruz also emphasise that the case law offers no clear answer to the question of whether national courts are bound to order the recovery of unlawful aid, and they criticise the Commission for its *tendency of subjecting national courts to allegedly automatic and absolute obligations that have no clear basis in EU law.* Although their analysis focuses essentially on situations in which parallel proceedings are pending before the Commission,[230] especially when a decision opening a formal investigation has already been adopted, some of their observations are valid also when it comes to situations in which no investigation is ongoing at EU level or an EU-level investigation is only at a very early stage.

First, the authors argue that the Commission adopts a maximalist stance in the New Private Enforcement Notice because although its opinion that national courts should automatically and in all instances order recovery whenever they find that a State measure constitutes unlawful aid is perhaps supported by some judgments, 'there does not appear to be unanimity in the caselaw in this respect and this may not always seem to be the most logical interpretation'. As the reader knows by now, the analysis carried out in this section has led to exactly the same conclusion on this point.

Second, Buendía Sierra and Bolsa Ferruz add that 'a systematic reading of the regulations and the caselaw does not seem to give support to the Commission's position'. Although this statement must be nuanced,[231] the authors' main argument is

230. Indeed, the starting point in their analysis is that because two fora (European and national) exist before which State aid measures can be reviewed from a State aid perspective, it is important to study the exact allocation of tasks between them.

231. This statement indeed deserves further commentary. Whereas the argument that the case law is not unanimous and offers no clear and consolidated indication in support of the Commission's position is certainly correct, to state that this conclusion can be drawn from the Procedural Regulation – in particular from the fact that it empowers the Commission to order recovery before aid is declared incompatible only in exceptional circumstances – is debatable. This is in fact the direct consequence of the different roles given to the Commission and to national courts. The fact that national courts are not bound to automatically order recovery is not due to the fact that they should await a decision on the aid's compatibility but simply to the

certainly flawless: EU law does not oblige national courts to order recovery of the funds automatically and without any further inquiry, and 'it does not seem appropriate for the Commission to seek to impose on national courts "through the back door" the obligation to exercise a power that is not granted to itself, even as a possibility, apart from a limited number of exceptions'.

Clearly, the authors are referring to interim recovery (when an investigation is pending before the Commission) as an alternative to the adoption of interim measures. However, the basic principle – whereby the imposition of automatic obligations on national courts is to be avoided in favour of leaving the courts the possibility of assessing the specific circumstances of a given case – applies also to the consequences to be drawn from a given aid measure's unlawfulness whenever it has not (yet) been declared incompatible by the Commission (regardless of whether an investigation is pending). Therefore, the authors' conclusion that the case law appears to be more cautious than the Commission is valid across the whole field of private enforcement remedies.

Ultimately, the objective of the tasks conferred on national courts is 'to pronounce measures appropriate [(without determining them beforehand)] to remedy the unlawfulness of the implementation of the aid, in order that the aid does not remain at the free disposal of the recipient during the period remaining until the Commission makes its decision'. If the Commission has already found the aid incompatible, national courts are called on to cooperate in the enforcement of the Commission's decision, and an autonomous assessment is no longer necessary under national law in connection with the aid recovery (but national courts may consider additional remedies if their national law allows them to do so).

Another topic which needs to be addressed in this context concerns the interplay with national insolvency proceedings. This book has already dealt with the broader topic of insolvency in the case of a recovery decision adopted by the Commission – a scenario specifically examined in the Recovery Notice.[232] National courts could be called on to rule in the context of the enforcement of a Commission decision, in which case they must of course apply the criteria developed in the case law and summarised in the Recovery Notice.[233] The issue here, however, is slightly different: namely, whether a national court called on to adjudicate a private action that is brought by interested parties and based on Article 108(3) TFEU should act any differently if insolvency proceedings are pending or if a substantial risk of insolvency exists.

This question should be answered in the negative. In such cases, the national court is bound to adjudicate the claim brought by private parties by determining whether: (i) the measure at issue constitutes State aid; and (ii) the standstill obligation

fact that they are free to assess the specific situation brought to their attention and to select the restorative remedies that they consider most appropriate in the case. That said, what matters here is the authors' clear position that the case law 'generally appears to be more cautious than the Commission', as it 'grants national courts the 'possibility' (not the obligation) of requesting recovery of the funds if this is the best solution in the light of the specific circumstances of the case'.

232. *See* Part One, sections I.A.2.7 and I.A.2.8.

233. Although not in an impeccable manner, as discussed above (*ibid.*).

has been infringed. If the determination in both cases is affirmative, the national court must order the measures that it considers most appropriate to restore the competitive situation that existed before the aid was granted, irrespective of any other factor. If the national court were to order recovery of the aid, the situation would mirror that which would exist in the case of a recovery order adopted by the Commission, and the same criteria regarding the possible interplay with insolvency proceedings would apply, *i.e.*, in a nutshell: (i) the fact that the aid recipient is insolvent or subject to insolvency proceedings has no effect on its obligation to repay unlawful aid; and (ii) national insolvency rules can apply only to the extent they take into account the EU interest and comply with EU law.

Reference is often made to the principles of effectiveness and equivalence to argue that national courts have no option but to order recovery in the absence of a compatibility decision.[234] However, these principles should be correctly understood. They certainly apply when national courts are called on to execute a Commission recovery decision. But in the context of private enforcement, what is the obligation that needs to be made effective? It is certainly not the obligation to ensure recovery but rather the obligation to safeguard the rights of individuals, which is broader and less specific. National courts might have to show initiative and creativity in figuring out effective legal paths in order to safeguard the rights of individuals stemming from Union law and prevent their Member State from being held liable for infringements of its obligation to ensure the effectiveness of EU law provisions that have a direct effect in national legal systems.

In this respect, Köhler reports the solutions found by the German Federal Court of Justice (*Bundesgerichtshof*) and the Austrian Supreme Civil Court to overturn decisions from lower courts and thus guarantee the effectiveness of the last sentence of Article 108(3) TFEU.[235] Both the German and the Austrian courts identified the

234. *See*, for instance, Derenne and Kaczmarek, *La récupération des aides illégales: le rôle du juge national*, cited in footnote 11 of this Part Two. These authors, however, refer to the principles of effectiveness and equivalence in the context of the national court's cooperation in the execution of a recovery decision adopted by the Commission. Hence, they rightfully recall (as an example) the rules relating to the standard of proof, as clarified by the Court of Justice in *Boiron* (Judgment of the Court of Justice of 7 September 2006, Case C-526/04, *Laboratoires Boiron*, EU:C:2006:528), or the obligation to leave unapplied a conflicting decision of domestic law, as clarified in *Scott* (Judgment of the Court of Justice of 5 October 2006, Case C-232/05, EU:C:2006:651). *See also* F. Pastor-Merchante and G. Monti, *The Functions of National Courts in the Private Enforcement of State Aid Law*, cited in footnote 5 of this Part Two. The latter authors recall that domestic law applies to the private enforcement of State aid law, based on the principle of procedural and institutional autonomy, 'so long as it complies with the principles of equivalence and effectiveness'; however, they immediately add that 'EU law has not harmonised *the remedies* [emphasis added] through which national courts are supposed to protect the rights that private parties derive from the rules on State aid'.

235. In both the Austrian case and the German case, the competitors sought injunctive relief under the respective national codes against unfair competition. Moreover, both countries' courts were confronted with decisions from lower courts that denied that all the requirements under domestic law for the injunction were met. As reported by Köhler (*see Private Enforcement of State Aid Law: Problems of Guaranteeing EU Rights by Means of National (Procedural) Law*, cited in footnote 40 of this Part Two), the German court reached the opposite conclusion by classifying Art. 108(3) TFEU as a *Schutzgesetz* (norm of protection) within the meaning of Art. 823(2) of the German Civil Code, which states that a person can be held liable for damage

domestic substantive provision that could govern competitors' claims based on Article 108(3) TFEU, but they left some of the requirements of that provision under domestic law unapplied because their application would have made it impossible to safeguard the rights of competitors and would have thus made the related TFEU provision ineffective. Indeed, they argued that the substance of each claim was based on EU law, not domestic law - as the latter provided merely the procedural means to fulfil the obligations stemming from EU law. In other words, national courts must apply the domestic legal system in a way that enables competitors to enforce the standstill obligation. However, under no circumstances does the duty to make the standstill obligation effective and enforceable extend to the kinds of remedy that national courts must order to achieve that objective.

Advocate General Jacobs expressed the same concept neatly: whatever action is taken before national courts, he wrote,[236] 'should be such as to achieve the aim of negating the unlawfully granted aid or at least its effects, of guaranteeing the effectiveness of Article 88(3) EC [now Art. 108(3) TFEU] and protecting the rights of affected third parties'. As can be seen, Sir Jacobs had a very clear and strong opinion on what should be achieved, and he imagined very ambitious objectives for the private enforcement of State aid rules. Yet he made it clear that 'the appropriate consequential measures to be taken by national courts are not dictated by Community [*i.e.*, Union] law but depend on the kinds of remedy available under national law' and may depend on, among other things, the nature of the aid, *i.e.*, how it is categorised in the domestic legal system concerned.

Hence, the choice of remedy falls within the competence of national courts and is governed by national law, whereas EU law sets the goals that should be targeted. Even more importantly, this implies that whereas Member States have an obligation of result in executing a Commission recovery decision, *no such obligation can be considered to arise when they act within the framework of private enforcement.* Indeed, nothing in the EU courts' case law supports the view of an obligation of result in such a context.

Rather, Member States are bound by: (i) the principle of effectiveness, in the sense that the national legislator must determine appropriate legal paths to allow individuals to bring claims for infringements of the last sentence of Article 108(3) TFEU, and national courts must order the remedies that they consider most appropriate to achieve these aims (*see* the broad definition of those aims proposed by Advocate General Jacobs); and (ii) the principle of equivalence, in the sense that all the legal paths available for claims similar to State aid-related claims based on substantive provisions of national law must also be at the disposal of individuals claiming an infringement of State aid rules.

---

caused to third parties by his/her conduct if he/she consciously infringes a provision (fault) and the damage was foreseeable and avoidable; the Austrian court, however, classified the breach of the standstill obligation (or more correctly, the recipient's awareness of the breach of the standstill obligation) as *sonstige unlautere Handlung* (other unfair behaviour) within the meaning of Art. 1(1)(1) of the Austrian code against unfair competition.

236. Opinion of Advocate General Jacobs of 29 November 2005, Case C-368/04, *Transalpine Ölleitung*, cited in footnote 136 of this Part Two, EU:C:2005:724.

Although the principle of effectiveness limits the principle of procedural autonomy within the framework of public enforcement, that is not so much the case within the framework of private enforcement – at least given the current status of EU law. The adaptation and flexibility of the principle of effectiveness in the field of private enforcement can be seen not only when it comes to the choice of the most suitable remedy by national courts but also when it comes to the application of general principles of national procedural law. This issue is explored further when examining the key features of private enforcement from a procedural perspective.[237]

To conclude on the issue of recovery:

- National courts are bound to safeguard the rights granted to individuals by the last sentence of Article 108(3) TFEU.
- The basic right granted by Article 108(3) is that no State aid is to be put into effect without the Commission's scrutiny (whatever form that scrutiny takes); if State aid is put into effect without the Commission's scrutiny, the rights that individuals draw from Article 108(3) must be safeguarded, which means that the competitive situation that existed before the aid was granted must be restored so long as the aid is not declared compatible with the internal market.
- National courts – to accomplish this task – must ensure that all the necessary consequences are drawn from breaches of the standstill obligation enshrined in Article 108(3), in accordance with their national law.
- Procedural autonomy in this context means that national law must provide (or be interpreted as providing) the necessary means to deliver the result mentioned in the previous bullet point.
- National procedural law must thus offer the appropriate legal instruments to enforce substantive EU law provisions.
- National courts have autonomous competence to apply those instruments, and no automatic obligation can be imposed on them.
- It is reasonable to assume that the minimum requirement ensuing from the principle whereby recovery is the natural consequence of infringement of State aid rules is for national courts to order full recovery plus interest, but only if no other more appropriate remedy (in their independent view) is available under national law – save for exceptional circumstances, of course (*i.e.*, absolute impossibility and/or conflict with general principles of the national legal system).

The above is what can be inferred from EU positive law and related case law as developed to date. However, much remains to be discussed on the issues raised in the last bullet point in terms of consistency with the overall system of EU law – a topic that is addressed in Part Four of this book.

237. *See* Part Two, Chapter VI.

V.E.3 *Alternative Remedies at the Disposal of National Courts*

The panoply of measures at the disposal of national courts is broader than mere recovery as a restorative remedy and suspension of the aid measure (or equivalent interim measures) as a preventive remedy. Of course, huge differences can exist in this respect among the various national legal systems. Although claims brought by a beneficiary's competitors can generally be based on rules on non-contractual liability existing in all jurisdictions - in combination with rules on unfair competition - the requirements thereof can vary significantly.

To provide just one example, as early as 1995 a claim brought before the Brussels *Tribunal de commerce* by virtue of Article 1382 of the Belgian Civil Code (Aquilian liability) led the Belgian court to order the aid beneficiary (the Italian company Breda) to discontinue the unfair practice of using State aid to submit an offer below cost. Breda was obliged to withdraw its bid in a tender procedure for railway supplies in Belgium.[238] No damages were awarded, but the discontinuation order turned out to be an effective remedy, as the tender was eventually awarded to another bidder.

In general, a given aid measure's unlawfulness, if ascertained by a national court, results in all civil law transactions concluded in connection with the granting of the unlawful aid to be considered null and void and all related administrative acts to be considered invalid and ineffective. The nullity/invalidity of contracts/administrative acts indissolubly linked to the granting of the aid is a first response of national legal systems to infringements of directly applicable EU law provisions. This response - which can be construed as an *automatic remedy* - is twofold, as it can work both as a preventive and as a restorative remedy depending on the circumstances and, in particular, on the nature of the remedy.[239]

How this remedy works depends on the provisions available under national law. Indeed, situations might arise in which the unlawful implementation of a given measure can be suspended by annulling the granting act. In *Residex IV*, it was established that EU law does not impose any specific conclusion that national courts must draw regarding the validity of acts relating to the implementation of aid. However, since national courts must adopt the most appropriate measures to restore the competitive situation existing before the aid was granted, nullity of the underlying contract could be an effective means to achieve that goal.[240] Likewise, Advocate General Kokott observed that 'the validity of acts entailing implementation of aid measures is affected by failure, on the part the national authorities, to observe the prohibition on implementing aid without Commission authorization'.[241]

---

238. Président du tribunal de commerce de Bruxelles, 13 February 1995, *Breda Fucine Meridionali/Manoir Industries*, J.T.- dr. eur., 1995, p. 72.
239. If, for instance, the aid takes the form of a guarantee or a long-term loan or supply agreement, nullity of the related contracts has the effect of discontinuing the granting of the aid and preventing the distortion of competition from materialising.
240. Judgment of the Court of Justice of 8 December 2011, *Residex Capital IV*, C-275/10, ECLI: EU:C:2011:814, paras 44-47. *See also* footnote 220 of this Part Two.
241. Opinion of Advocate General Kokott in Case C-275/10, *Residex Capital IV CV v. Gemeente Rotterdam*, cited in footnote 220 of this Part Two, paras 29-32 and the case law cited therein.

Similarly, as mentioned above, Advocate General Jacobs - in his opinion on the *Transalpine Ölleitung* case - stated that the measures to be taken by national courts are not governed by EU law but depend on the kinds of remedy available under domestic law,[242] and that 'the appropriate course of action depends on the nature of the aid'.[243] Regardless of the action taken, the goal should always be 'to negate the unlawfully granted aid or its effects', guaranteeing the effectiveness of Article 108(3) TFEU and protecting the right of affected third parties.[244]

The Commission develops its views on the invalidity of acts and the nullity of contracts in the New Private Enforcement Notice. These views are based on case law, such as *Residex IV*, that developed after publication of the 2009 Enforcement Notice. Therefore, the Commission emphasises that national courts are allowed to annul the act granting the aid or to declare the contract by which the aid is granted null and void without any condition having to be fulfilled other than a breach of the standstill obligation.[245] Indeed, if aid is granted in breach of the duty to notify, it must be ensured that the recipient forfeits the advantage so that competition is not distorted. And as stems from *Residex IV*, the Court of Justice considers nullity to be the natural consequence of the contract's illegality in any case. This view has been accepted by national courts: the German *Bundesgerichtshof*, for instance, as reported by Köhler, has accepted the nullity of contracts concluded in breach of the standstill obligation.[246]

V.E.4 Compensation for Damage

Beyond the automatic nullity of contracts/invalidity of acts, the most typical alternative (or even additional) remedy under national law is liability for damage caused to competitors because of the unlawful implementation of State aid measures. Compensation for damage aims at forfeiting the negative effects produced by the unlawful implementation of State aid measures on competitors of beneficiary undertakings.[247] Claims for compensation for damage have the advantage that, when successful, they provide claimants with direct financial compensation for the loss suffered.

Compensation for damage is not necessarily an alternative to more traditional remedies such as recovery,[248] because it would be possible - in theory, at least - for the claimant to prove that it suffered damage that cannot be entirely remedied by obtaining

See also Knade-Plaskacz, *Enforcement of State Aid Law at National Level. The Relationship Between National Courts and the European Commission*, cited in footnote 219 of this Part Two.

242. Opinion of Advocate General Jacobs of 29 November 2005, Case C-368/04, *Transalpine Ölleitung*, cited in footnote 136 of this Part Two, para. 61.
243. *Ibid.*, para. 62.
244. Opinion of Advocate General Jacobs 29 November 2005, Case C-368/04, *Transalpine Ölleitung*, para. 66, cited in footnote 136 of this Part Two. *See also* Köhler, *Private Enforcement of State Aid Law: Problems of Guaranteeing EU Rights by Means of National (Procedural) Law*, cited in footnote 40 of this Part Two.
245. New Enforcement Notice, cited in footnote 50 of this Part Two, paras 73-74.
246. Köhler, *Private Enforcement of State Aid Law: Problems of Guaranteeing EU Rights by Means of National (Procedural) Law*, cited in footnote 40 of this Part Two.
247. F. Pastor-Merchante and G. Monti, *The Functions of National Courts in the Private Enforcement of State Aid Law*, cited in footnote 5 of this Part Two.
248. New Enforcement Notice, cited in footnote 50 of this Part Two, para. 87.

repayment of the aid. Compensatory damages protection constitutes, together with direct effect and the obligation of conforming interpretation, one of the pillars of private enforcement. Although the first judgment on the subject (the famous *Francovich* case)[249] concerned pecuniary damage suffered in the absence of direct effect of the rules invoked by a private individual, the Court soon made it clear that a damages claim may be brought also for the violation of rules having direct effect.[250] In the field of State aid, the Court has clearly characterised compensatory protection as a remedy that does not have an alternative nature to direct effect but can be cumulated with it.[251]

Moreover, in several legal systems, tort law liability is somewhere between a restorative remedy and a penalty (and is therefore ontologically different from recovery): it aims not only at compensating for loss suffered by the claimant but also at enhancing deterrence and, to some extent, punishing the tortfeasor for his/her illegal conduct.

A difference exists also between the broad range of persons that may invoke the direct effect of Article 108(3) TFEU and the more limited subjective scope of compensatory protection. The possibility of relying on the invalidity of an administrative measure granting aid or of a contract in which the aid element is inherent does not in itself imply a right to compensation. Only operators that directly suffered adverse effects of a distortion of competition caused by the aid and the resulting pecuniary damage have this right.

In its case law, the Court of Justice has held that affected third parties can bring actions for damages before national courts, in accordance with national law, which in turn must comply with the principles of equivalence and effectiveness.[252] Although the unlawfulness of the aid stems directly from the breach of the Treaty, the legal basis for damages compensations is again to be found under national tort law or State liability rules.

In this context, compliance with the principles of effectiveness and equivalence means that national law must provide the necessary means, whether specific to State aid or not, which allow competitors to claim damages and that these means should not be less favourable than similar instruments available for damage caused by violation of national law provisions – in other words, liability for damage caused by a violation of the last sentence of Article 108(3) *must not be subject to additional requirements*. This explains why a limitation on the nature of compensable damage (*i.e.*, exclusion of loss

249. Judgment of the Court of Justice of 19 November 1991, *Francovich and Bonifaci v. Italy*, C-6/90 and C-9/90, ECLI:EU:C:1991:428.

250. *Brasserie du pêcheur v. Bundesrepublik Deutschland and The Queen/Secretary of State for Transport, ex parte Factortame and Others*, C-46/93 and C-48/93, ECLI:EU:C:1991:428.

251. *See* New Enforcement Notice, cited in footnote 50 of this Part Two, para. 88 and case law cited therein. In particular, *see*: Judgment of the Court of Justice of 5 October 2006, *Transalpine Ölleitung in Österreich*, cited in footnote 136 of this Part Two, para. 56; and Judgment of the Court of Justice of 23 January 2019, *Fallimento Traghetti del Mediterraneo*, cited in footnote 123 of this Part Two, para. 56.

252. *Ibid. See also* F. Bestagno, *L'azione risarcitoria come strumento di* private enforcement *della disciplina di diritto dell'UE sugli aiuti di Stato*, Diritto del Commercio internazionale, 2013, Volume XXVII, Issue 3, pp. 623 ff. The author explains that compensatory protection concerns the pecuniary content of the private party's claim and can be added to the protection that direct effect offers with regard to the substantive claim.

of profit), would be incompatible with EU law: it would indeed be contrary to the principle of effectiveness, given that loss of profit is precisely the type of pecuniary damage that competitors of a beneficiary of unlawful aid most commonly claim they have suffered.

Damages awarded to third parties represent a significantly small portion (1 %) of the overall remedies awarded by national courts in cases of private enforcement of State aid rules.[253] The number of rulings issued by national courts in which damages were successfully awarded is even smaller, as *only six relevant rulings fell within this category* until 2019 – all of which involved French courts.[254] These data are reported in the 2019 Enforcement Study, which confirms the conclusions drawn in the previous Enforcement Study (2006): damages for violation of State aid rules remain rather hypothetical. The Commission believes that the main reasons behind the unsuccessful history of this remedy can be attributed to market players' lack of familiarity with this type of remedy (unlikely, in this author's opinion) and the complexity related to proving a causal link between the harm suffered and the lack of State aid notification (a real and often discouraging obstacle based on practical experience; *see also* below).[255]

Notwithstanding this low success rate, the concept of State liability is slowly developing before national courts, at least in some Member States. In France, several cases have ended with significant damages awarded to competitors of aid beneficiaries, with the *CELF* and *SNCM* cases probably among the most emblematic.[256] In Italy, in the famous *Traghetti del Mediterraneo* case,[257] the Italian Supreme Court upheld the court

253. Final Study on the enforcement of State aid rules and decisions by national courts (COMP/2018/001), Publications Office of the European Union, Luxembourg, 2019, p. 77, fig. 25.

254. *Ibid.*, p. 81.

255. *Ibid.*, p. 90. *See also* Bestagno, *L'azione risarcitoria come strumento di* private enforcement *della disciplina di diritto dell'UE sugli aiuti di Stato,* cited in footnote 252 of this Part Two, in particular section 7, where the author describes the obstacles that can arise in connection with the proof of the causal link in several scenarios.

256. *See*, respectively, Conseil d'Etat Judgment No. 434446 of 22 July 2020, *SIDE*, and Administrative Court of Appeal of Marseille Judgment No. 17MA31582 of 22 February 2021, *Collectivité de Corse,* followed by Conseil d'Etat Judgment No. 450892 of 29 September 2021, *Collectivité de Corse v. Sté Corsica Ferries*, as cited by J. Derenne and D. Jouve, in *State Aid & National Enforcement: An Overview of EU and National Case Law,* Concurrences, 2 March 2023, fns 45-46, available at https://www.concurrences.com/en/bulletin/special-issues/state-aid-national-enforcement/aides-d-etat/state-aid-national-enforcement-an-overview-of-eu-and-national-case-law.

257. *See* Italian Supreme Court Judgment No. 22631 of 16 October 2020, *Presidenza del Consiglio dei Ministri v. Fallimento Traghetti del Mediterraneo S.p.A.*, commented on by M. Merola, D. Gallo, A. Cogoni and G. Bellenghi, in *The Italian Supreme Court Decides, Following a Preliminary Reference to the EU Court of Justice, That Aid Which Predated EU Market Liberalisation Can Constitute State Aid,* e-Competitions, October 2020, Art. 107757. For the Court of Justice's judgment in the same case, *see* footnote 123 of this Part Two. *See also* P. Nicolaides, *The EU Court of Justice Holds That EU Rules Do Not Impose Time Limitation Rules When National Courts Deal with a Claim for Damages Arising from Non-Notified Aid,* e-Competitions, 23 January 2019, Art. 89736, and F. Viana and S. Petit, *The EU Court of Justice Clarifies the Concept of 'Existing Aid' in a Private Enforcement Case and Holds That Unlawful Aid Cannot Be Retroactively Legalized under a Limitation Period That Has Lapsed,* e-Competitions, 23 January 2019, Art. 90591.

of appeal's decision to hold the State liable for compensation of a competitor of the aid beneficiary following a preliminary ruling of the Court of Justice on the classification of the measure as new aid capable of affecting trade between Member States as a result of the liberalisation of the economic sector concerned.

The main distinction to be drawn when dealing with actions for damages is between actions brought against the Member State granting the aid and claims brought against the beneficiary undertaking(s). These two kinds of actions are examined separately below.

V.E.4.1 Actions Against the Member State

Although competitors have been awarded monetary compensation in only very limited actions for damages against Member States, no major obstacle to a successful action seems to exist in EU law other than the need to prove a causal link between the aid and the damage. Determining which legal basis can be used under national law to award damages and whether the related requirements are met is a different issue, however. While EU law is self-sufficient when it comes to determining the liability of granting Member States, national law is needed - based on the principle of procedural autonomy - to govern the actual award of monetary compensation. These two issues are examined below.

a) State Liability

National courts need not identify a national legal basis on which to establish unlawful conduct of the State because State liability is based directly on EU law: EU courts' case law confirms that a breach of the standstill obligation constitutes a 'serious enough' breach of a superior provision of EU law and that third parties have the right to seek compensation for damage suffered because of such a breach.[258] As a reminder, according to the landmark case law on State liability for breaches of EU law,[259] individuals are entitled to compensation for damage when: (i) the breached provision is meant to confer rights on individuals; (ii) the breach is sufficiently serious; and (iii) a causal link exists between the breach of the State's obligation and the damage sustained by the injured parties. The first two conditions are automatically met in cases in which the standstill obligation is breached, in accordance with consolidated case law and as recalled by the Commission in the New Enforcement Notice.

The third condition - namely, that the breach of Union law must have caused actual and certain financial damage to the injured party - represents the major

258. Judgment of the Court of 11 July 1996, Case C-39/94, *Syndicat français de l'Express international (SFEI) and others v. La Poste and others*, cited in footnote 204 of this Part Two.
259. Judgment of the Court of Justice of 19 November 1991, *Francovich and Bonifaci v. Italy*, cited in footnote 249 of this Part Two, paras 30-46. *See also* Judgment of the Court of Justice of 5 March 1996, *Brasserie du pêcheur v. Bundesrepublik Deutschland and The Queen/Secretary of State for Transport, ex parte Factortame and Others*, cited in footnote 250 of this Part Two, para. 51.

challenge faced by claimants. According to the 2019 Enforcement Study, national courts are reluctant to award damages as 'the quantification of the damage and the establishment of the causal link between the harm and the unlawful aid represent major obstacles'. It is indeed likely that the fact that claimants must prove a causal link between the two aforementioned elements constitutes one of the reasons, if not the most important reason, why so few actions for damages are seen across the Union.[260]

State aid claims generally entail a rather heavy burden of proof on the claimant, as illustrated by numerous cases brought before national courts, such as the well-known *Corsica Ferries* case, which is a rather atypical follow-on action for damages before a national court following a Commission recovery decision.[261] Even if a claimant can rely on a Commission decision, proving a causal link between aid and damage suffered by a competitor is difficult given the many outside factors that can impact the competitor's market position in the period concerned. It is also extremely complex to quantify the impact of aid on interested parties' market position over time – especially if the aid covers a long period, as was the case in *Corsica Ferries*.[262] Therefore, damage quantification and the establishment of a causal link remain major obstacles for claimants.

b) The Legal Basis under National Law to Claim Compensation for Damage

As observed above, the legal basis on which to establish State liability in breaches of the standstill obligation is to be found directly in EU law. Conversely, based on the principle of procedural autonomy, national courts must identify the national law whereby injured parties can claim financial compensation for damage caused by State misconduct and check whether the related requirements are met. However, as previously mentioned, those requirements should not outrightly preclude the possibility for injured parties to obtain compensation (principle of effectiveness) and should not be more onerous than those applicable to cases of liability caused by a breach of a national law provision (principle of equivalence). In the New Private Enforcement Notice, the Commission merely refers to these principles but does not delve any deeper into the requirements that are set under national law.

260. Final Study on the enforcement of State aid rules and decisions by national courts (COMP/2018/001), Publications Office of the European Union, Luxembourg, 2019.
261. Marseille Administrative Court of Appeal, 12 February 2018 (an appeal against ruling no. 1500375 of the Bastia Administrative Tribunal). From 2007 to 2013, Corsica granted aid to Société nationale maritime Corse-Méditerranée (SNCM) to guarantee the regularity of ferry connections on the Toloun-Ajaccio and Toulon-Bastia routes. The Commission found that the aid was unlawful and incompatible with the internal market, ordering recovery of the aid. Corsica Ferries (*i.e.*, SNCM's main competitor) sought damages before the Bastia Administrative Court, alleging that the aid had led to a sharp decrease in its market shares. The national court relied on the Commission's decision and awarded damages based on an expert assessment submitted by Corsica Ferries. On appeal, however, the Marseille Administrative Court partially quashed the previous ruling by the Bastia Administrative Court in relation to the quantification of damage.
262. *See* the 2019 Enforcement Study, p. 81.

Usually, three conditions should be met under national law to successfully invoke State liability: an objective condition, an intentionality condition, and a causal link condition. The objective condition (*i.e.*, proving the damage itself) does not raise major issues. The intentionality condition is usually deemed to be twofold: the infringement must be deliberate, and the resulting damage must be foreseeable by the infringer. The infringement of State aid procedural rules is certainly deliberate, as Member States are expected to know the breadth of the notification obligation and are required to notify even in the case of doubts regarding the classification of a measure as State aid. Foreseeability, in turn, is easily established if the sector concerned is open to competition and trade, as in that case, it is inherent in the measure's selectivity. This condition should thus not be problematic, either, in most cases.

When it comes to the causal link condition, it is imperative to avoid confusion with the analogous condition under EU law when establishing a Member State's liability. Under EU law, for liability to arise, the unlawful aid must be the direct cause of the damage suffered by competitors. Under national tort law, the causal link condition is slightly different, as a damages claim can be brought if the aid's unlawfulness caused the damage. In other words, in cases in which the standstill obligation was breached, a damages claim can be brought if *the claimed damage would have been avoided had the standstill obligation been complied with.*[263]

This condition can give rise to several problems. For avoidability to be proven, it should not be required to demonstrate that the damage would not have materialised had the aid not been granted. Rather, it must be sufficient to prove that the State could have reasonably anticipated the potential effects of the unlawfulness and that it consciously accepted the possibility that they would occur. Likewise, it is not necessary to prove that the granting authority was conscious of all the consequences that the aid then produced - such as a claimant's insolvency - and for which compensation is sought. The granting authority might not have wanted that consequence to occur, but that is irrelevant if it accepted that damage (such as a loss of market share or of commercial opportunities) could ensue from the granting of unlawful aid.[264]

Nevertheless, unlike the foreseeability condition, the avoidability condition requires - as a matter of practice - unlawful aid in a given case to be considered at least *prima facie* incompatible. Indeed, only in this case can it be assumed that the unlawfulness (*i.e.*, the breach of the procedural rules) was decisive; conversely, if the aid was *prima facie* compatible, compliance with the rules would not have prevented the damage from materialising - though the damage would have been delayed until the end of the Commission investigation. This means that, in most cases, damages can be claimed only for the expected duration of Commission investigations; for the remainder, national courts might have to use the cooperation tools made available by the Commission to ascertain whether the aid was *prima facie* incompatible.

263. This means that, had the aid been notified, the Commission would not have approved it or would have imposed conditions.
264. This distinction is well known in national legal systems - such as Italy's - which acknowledge the concept of potential wilful misconduct (*dolo eventuale*) and accept that it can give rise to liability.

In essence, the avoidability condition risks creating a clash between national law and the EU law principle that all consequences must be drawn from the aid's unlawfulness, irrespective of the compatibility analysis. In the case of conflict, national courts would have to leave the avoidability criterion unapplied. However, it is debatable whether such a conflict can be deemed to exist only because the application of national law would restrict the damage that can be compensated for the loss that occurred during the (actual or expected) time of the compatibility assessment (in the case of compatible aid, of course), even if traditional remedies (interim orders and recovery) remain available under national law. In a nutshell, the conditions for a successful damages claim are a fair amount more complex than as explained by the Commission in the New Private Enforcement Notice. Failing to acknowledge and address these complexities does not help increase stakeholders' awareness and the system's effectiveness.

That said, in most cases in which unnotified aid is also *prima facie* incompatible, the avoidability condition (like the foreseeability requirement) would in principle likely be satisfied, as the State can never claim that it could not avoid the unlawful conduct because it was bound to comply with other provisions. Indeed, whatever provision of national law the State might argue it was bound by would have to be left unapplied by virtue of the primacy of Union law over national law. Therefore, the damage would generally be considered avoidable, and compensation would have to be awarded (if a causal link is established) - unless the award of damages would breach general principles of law (similarly to what happens with the recovery of unlawful aid).

A final note concerns actions for damages being brought against a Member State by a beneficiary that was required to repay unlawful aid following a Commission decision. This scenario brings two difficult-to-overcome obstacles: (i) the action, if successful, would most likely be read as a way of circumventing the obligation to recover, similarly to what is stipulated in the New Enforcement Notice with regard to arbitration awards (*see* section VI.D below); and (ii) the beneficiary of the unlawful aid would have great difficulty in proving that it was totally unaware that the aid was unlawful and had no way of becoming aware of this, even acting with the utmost diligence; this would make it difficult to prove a direct causal link between the State's conduct and the damage claimed. It is thus unsurprising that there are no known cases of such actions with a favourable outcome, to the best of this author's knowledge.

V.E.4.2 Damages Claims Against Beneficiaries

As the standstill obligation applies to Member States, a claim for damages against the authorities that granted the aid is the most obvious course of action for competitors and other interested parties. Member State authorities cannot argue that they were unaware of the standstill obligation, as extensive case law and Commission guidance exists on the application of Articles 107(1) and 108(3) TFEU.[265] Nevertheless, a damages claim

265. Judgment of the Court of 11 July 1996, Case C-39/94, *Syndicat français de l'Express international (SFEI) and others v. La Poste and others*, cited in footnote 204 of this Part Two, para. 74.

can also be brought through an action against the beneficiary. In this case, however, the legal basis on which to claim the unlawfulness of the conduct must be found in national law, as the Treaty envisages no legal basis for such a *horizontal effect of the standstill obligation*. In fact, the notification and standstill obligations are addressed to Member States, and Article 108(3) does not impose any direct obligation on beneficiaries,[266] as confirmed in the *SFEI* judgment. Therefore, a *breach of that provision is not a sufficient basis for aid beneficiaries to incur liability*.[267]

Moreover, as acknowledged by the Commission in the New Private Enforcement Notice, actions for damages against aid beneficiaries *are not required* as a matter of EU State aid law. Consequently, if a given national legal system offers competitors no legal paths that would allow them to bring a claim for damages against beneficiaries, the Member State will not be found in violation of EU law for that reason. Nevertheless, according to the principle of equivalence, if the national legal system envisages the possibility of characterising an aid beneficiary's conscious acceptance of an unlawful economic advantage granted by a public body as illegal conduct in itself, which can give rise to civil liability, the beneficiary's competitors must be given the possibility to bring an action for damages against the beneficiary.

Indeed, if it can be proven that the beneficiary was aware or should have been aware, as a diligent economic operator, that the aid was being granted without prior notification to the Commission, or that it had been implemented before the Commission's approval,[268] its liability for damages cannot be excluded *a priori* and must be ascertained in light of all relevant provisions of national law.

However, the truth is that the chances of bringing a successful claim for damages against a beneficiary are extremely slim even in jurisdictions where the possibility of such an action exists. Indeed, beyond the difficulty of proving the causal link between the aid and the damage (discussed earlier), other serious obstacles arise. First, it is highly problematic to characterise the alleged conscious acceptance of an economic advantage granted by a public authority as an unlawful act, as unlawfulness generally presupposes a legal obligation, which in this case would be a non-existent obligation on beneficiaries to prevent damage to competitors.[269] Second, even in the unlikely situation of national law offering solid ground on which to base such a legal obligation, liability in national tort law is often restricted to cases in which an intentionality condition is also met, in the absence of which the damage is not imputable to the beneficiary.[270]

Likewise, other obstacles could arise, such as difficulties in: (i) proving the beneficiary's awareness of the public authorities' misconduct (or demonstrating

266. New Enforcement Notice, cited in footnote 50 of this Part Two, para. 99.
267. Judgment of the Court of Justice of 11 July 1996, *SFEI and Others*, cited in footnote 204 of this Part Two, para. 75.
268. B. Derenne, *State Aid and Private Enforcement: An Overview of EU and n*, e-Competition State Aid Private Enforcement, May 2020, Art. 9521.
269. It is doubtful whether such an obligation can be rooted in national provisions on unfair competition, at least in most jurisdictions (Italy being one example).
270. This would be the case in Italy. *See*, *ex multis*, Italian Supreme Court, Division 3, Judgment No. 3294 of 3 February 2022.

beyond a doubt that it should have been aware thereof); and (ii) proving that the beneficiary could have avoided the damage caused to the claimant without incurring liability to the shareholders and/or Member State concerned (consider, *e.g.*, the case of State aid in the form of a concession agreement or other kind of contract between the beneficiary and public authorities, or a situation in which the beneficiary had already undertaken to perform certain activities or carry out a given investment).

In a nutshell, many legal obstacles – related to both the characterisation of the beneficiary's alleged unlawful conduct and the beneficiary's liability (*i.e.*, the intentionality condition and the causal link condition) – make the option of bringing an action for damages against the beneficiary ('horizontal effects') largely theoretical at the present stage of development of the private enforcement of State aid rules. Though it is a well-established principle that beneficiaries cannot successfully invoke their good faith against Member States when procedural obligations are violated (*i.e.*, diligent economic operators are supposed to be able to ascertain such a violation),[271] it is much more difficult to construe their alleged lack of diligence as unlawful conduct in itself.

V.E.4.3 Conclusion on Actions for Damages

In light of all the difficulties inherent in successfully pursuing actions for damages as a remedy, it is unavoidable to acknowledge that this remedy, which would constitute the real added value that private enforcement could bring to the effectiveness of State aid provisions, remains largely theoretical. Against this background, as discussed in the previous chapter, the New Private Enforcement Notice failed to bring significant improvements. Although the Commission pursued its goal of fostering actions for damages, it did not put forward any significant new proposals or analyses compared to the 2009 Enforcement Notice. The main addition is the suggestion that national courts should apply a presumption whereby the first two requirements of the test developed in *Francovich* and *Brasserie du Pêcheur* are met if the claimant can prove the existence of the aid and its unlawfulness. Therefore, according to the Commission, claimants must only demonstrate the causal link between the first two requirements in order to be entitled to compensation for damage.

This statement lends itself to various interpretations and raises perplexities: if it is to be understood as referring to the avoidability condition discussed above, it is certainly to be endorsed but would require legislative harmonisation, in the absence of

271. A good example of this can be found in Italian case law (both the Italian Supreme Court and the Italian Constitutional Court). *See* Italian Supreme Court, Division 3, Judgment No. 16870 of 10 August 2016, in which the Italian Supreme Court held that beneficiaries of unlawful aid cannot claim legal protection against the State responsible for the violation of procedural obligations. Similarly, the Italian Constitutional Court held that beneficiaries are required to diligently check the State's compliance with its procedural obligations and, consequently, cannot invoke the protection of legitimate expectations against a Member State liable for violation of those obligations (Italian Constitutional Court Judgment 36/2009).

which the principle of procedural autonomy would prevail; if, however, it is to be understood as referring to the causal link, it would entail a reversal of the burden of proof that would not only require legislative intervention but also have little chance of garnering the necessary consensus for its adoption, as it would run counter to Member States' common legal rules on Aquilian liability.

Moreover, the Commission emphasises that claimants should be allowed to seek experts' advice for the purpose of determining the actual amount of damage to be compensated. Moreover, the Commission provides guidance to national courts for cases in which a claimant argues that aid directly caused a loss of profit. When assessing whether loss of profit was directly caused by aid, the following criteria should be applied: (i) in all cases, national rules cannot outrightly exclude a Member State's liability for loss of profit (*i.e.*, if a national law provision contains such an exclusion, national courts must leave that provision unapplied as regards damages claims for breach of Article 108(3) TFEU); (ii) in cases in which the beneficiary won and executed a contract or a specific business opportunity by means of unlawful aid, the damage should be easily quantified by referring to the value of that contract; (iii) in cases in which the damage must instead be calculated by reference to a loss of market share, the claimant's actual income situation should be compared with the hypothetical income situation had the unlawful aid not been granted; and (iv) in cases in which the damage suffered by the claimant exceeds the lost profit, it must be considered whether the claimant was forced out of business as a consequence of the unlawful aid.

Finally, the Commission recalls that actions for damages cannot be used to circumvent the ban - based on the Union interest criterion - on enlarging the circle of beneficiaries of unlawful aid through private enforcement. Therefore, although the *Asteris* judgment[272] held that 'State aid is fundamentally different in its legal nature from damages that national authorities may be ordered to pay to individuals in compensation for damages they have caused', this case law does not mean that claimants in a damages action can request a national court to order that they be awarded the same State aid granted to other beneficiaries that they had not received for whatever reason.[273]

Although these improvements and guidance are useful, they are unlikely to increase the rate of successful claims to any significant extent. A more thorough analysis of the difficulties arising in national laws would have been of help, but above all, the intrinsic limitations in the private enforcement of State aid provisions must be openly acknowledged and used to foster a reform of the system of remedies, as advocated in Part Four of this book.

272. Judgment of the Court of Justice of 27 September 1988, *Asteris and others v. Greece and EEC*, cited in footnote 72 of this Part Two.
273. New Enforcement Notice, cited in footnote 50 of this Part Two, paras 96-97, where the Commission explains that 'individuals who might be entitled under national law to receive aid which has not been notified to and approved by the Commission, but who have not received such aid, cannot claim as compensation for damages the equivalent of the sum of the non-received aid, since this would constitute an indirect grant of unlawful aid'.

V.E.5 Reimbursement of Taxes

Before concluding on the kind of remedies available in the private enforcement of State aid rules, reference must be made to the reimbursement of taxes paid for financing an unlawful aid measure. Aid can indeed be indissolubly linked with means of financing based on levies imposed on companies, which can seek reimbursement if it is eventually established that the aid was unlawful.

This is an extremely rare remedy in cases of private enforcement of State aid rules. It is only briefly discussed in the 2019 Enforcement Study, whereas the Commission does not even mention it in the 2009 Enforcement Notice or in the New Enforcement Notice. Overall, based on the data in the 2019 Enforcement Study, the reimbursement of taxes paid for financing unlawful aid represents less than 1 % of the 34 % of cases in which remedies were awarded by national courts.[274]

In the *Streekgewest* judgment, the Court of Justice stated that a third party can challenge its tax burden when the tax payment 'forms an integral part of the unlawful State aid measure whether or not the person is affected by the distortion of competition resulting from that aid measure'.[275] Consequently, a third party is entitled to challenge the unlawful aid even if it is not a competitor of the beneficiary or is not directly affected by the unlawful aid. By contrast, a third party cannot obtain from a national court an exemption from payment of a tax which is equivalent to the unlawful aid. Although, under certain circumstances, such an exemption could be sought by a competitor under national rules on unfair competition,[276] this remedy is precluded if it leads to a broadening of the number of beneficiaries rather than reducing it.[277]

The reason why this type of action is particularly rare is probably to be found in the interpretative difficulties involved in assessing the requirement of non-severability between the aid and its method of financing, which should be indissolubly linked. Indeed, this is one of the thorniest issues within the notion of aid, and it is likely that neither interested parties nor national courts are familiar with the case law referring to it.[278]

---

274. Final Study on the enforcement of State aid rules and decisions by national courts (COMP/2018/001), Publications Office of the European Union, Luxembourg, 2019, p. 77, fig. 25.
275. Judgment of the Court of 13 January 2005, Case C-174/02, *Streekgewest Westelijk Noord-Brabant v. Staatssecretaris van Financiën*, ECLI:EU:C:2005:10, para. 21.
276. Final Study on the enforcement of State aid rules and decisions by national courts (COMP/2018/001), Publications Office of the European Union, Luxembourg, 2019, p. 19.
277. Judgment of the Court of Justice of 5 October 2006, *Transalpine Ölleitung*, cited in footnote 136 of this Part Two, para. 49.
278. For an overview of the problem in the light of recent case law, *see* M. Merola and G. Theodorakopoulou, *Chronique of the 2023 Main Developments in State Aid*, in C. Blumann and F. Picod, *Annuaire de droit de l'Union européenne*, Brulyant, 2024, where all the relevant case law, including the landmark *Iannelli* case (Judgment of the Court of 22 March 1977, Case C-74/76, *Iannelli & Volpi SpA v. Ditta Paolo Meroni*, EU:C:1977:23), is discussed.

VI BACKBONE PRINCIPLES OF THE PRIVATE ENFORCEMENT SYSTEM OF REMEDIES: PROCEDURAL RULES

This chapter examines the procedural rules governing the private enforcement of State aid rules, including criteria for the allocation of domestic jurisdiction and the proper delimitation of the national procedural framework. The section also addresses the legal status of beneficiaries and the difficulties inherent in using arbitration as a private enforcement tool.

Most of the key procedural issues surrounding the private enforcement system of remedies have already been touched on in previous sections and thus need only to be briefly recalled here. Moreover, reference is made here to purely procedural issues, whereas the requirements that the various actions should comply with were examined in the previous chapter.

Thus far, the recognition of third parties' rights to bring legal actions before national courts in the case of violation of the notification and standstill obligations has not led to harmonisation of the procedural rules that govern those actions. Pastor-Merchante and Monti emphasise that EU State aid law is silent on issues such as standing (*i.e.*, who is entitled to bring an action based on State aid law before national courts), time limits (*i.e.*, what is the deadline by which these actions must be brought) and competence (*i.e.*, which courts have jurisdiction to hear these actions).[279] Thus, in accordance with the principle of procedural autonomy, all these issues and many others are governed by national law. National legislators are supposed to check and ensure that the applicable domestic provisions comply with the principle of effectiveness and are not less favourable than those applied to similar actions for breaches of national law. Likewise, the judicature must ensure that less favourable or ineffective provisions are left unapplied - totally or partially - to safeguard the rights that individuals are afforded under the last sentence of Article 108(3) TFEU.

Even if private parties' claims are based on EU State aid law, they must be crafted in light of the remedies available under the domestic law of the country where they litigate, and national courts must refer exclusively to that law to identify the remedies they consider most appropriate to each case. Moreover, the protection that national courts owe to third parties can vary from one legal system to another, and even within the same jurisdiction, as different types of State aid measures can be subject to different legal regimes. Indeed, Pastor-Merchante and Monti explain as follows:

> [G]iven the breadth of the EU concept of State aid, the national laws of Member States often lack a transversal regime for State aid litigation. Thus, third parties may need to take a different route and apply for different remedies depending on the nature of the measure that they wish to contest, which may be a subsidy, a tax advantage, a public procurement procedure, a commercial transaction, and so on.[280]

279. Pastor-Merchante and Monti, *The Functions of National Courts in the Private Enforcements of State Aid Law*, cited in footnote 178 of this Part Two.
280. *Ibid.*

Against this background, the key procedural issues surrounding the private enforcement of State aid rules can be summarised as follows: existing aid versus new aid; allocation of domestic jurisdiction and procedural framework; legal status of beneficiaries; and arbitration as a private enforcement tool. This chapter analyses these issues in as many sections.

VI.A Existing Aid Versus New Aid

The last sentence of Article 108(3) TFEU requires Member States to notify aid projects prior to their implementation. Article 2 of the Procedural Regulation reiterates that any plans to grant new aid must be notified to the Commission in due time by the Member State concerned, save as otherwise envisaged in regulations adopted under Article 109 TFEU or under other relevant provisions of the TFEU. Article 3 of the Procedural Regulation adds that notifiable aid cannot be put into effect before the Commission has taken, or is deemed to have taken, a decision authorising such aid.

Existing aid is instead governed by Article 108(1) TFEU and is not subject to the notification and standstill obligations. Consequently, the classification of a given State aid measure as unlawful presupposes that the measure has been found to be new (a 'project' or 'plan') and thus not existing. Hence, in both public and private enforcement, the classification of aid as new aid is, in principle, an inherent part of the assessment before any remedies can be ordered.

As to public enforcement, the case law has clarified that if a complaint is lodged before the Commission, the latter is required to either open a formal investigation or adopt a definitive decision rejecting the complaint - even when the Commission or the Member State concerned has classified the contested measure as existing aid.[281] Any other interpretation would be in stark conflict with Article 24(2) of the Procedural Regulation, which stipulates that the right to submit complaints concerns all cases of 'alleged' unlawful aid.

Therefore, even if the Commission finds that the contested measure constitutes existing aid, it should adopt a definitive position in this respect, reject the complaint and thus give the complainant the chance to challenge its decision before the EU courts. Conversely, it cannot refuse to take a position on a complaint by merely arguing that it constitutes existing aid.

Likewise, in the context of private enforcement, national courts must examine claims brought before them regardless of whether the alleged unlawful aid is classified as existing aid. The mere fact that the Member State concerned considers the aid to be existing aid does not release the national court from the obligation to carry out its own assessment. In doing so, the national court can of course stay the proceedings and seek the Court of Justice's opinion through a reference for a preliminary ruling on the

281. *See* Judgment of the Court of Justice of 18 November 2010, *NDSHT Nya Destination Stockholm Hotell & Teaterpaket AB v. European Commission*, in Case C-322/09 P, EU:C:2010:701. In the judgment, the Court clarifies how the Commission is obliged by Art. 13(1) of Council Regulation (EC) No 659/1999 to close the preliminary examination either by rejecting the complaint or by opening a formal investigation.

interpretation of the relevant provisions of EU law. It may also use the cooperation tools under Article 29 of the Procedural Regulation to ask the Commission about any investigations pending before it or any relevant piece of information at the Commission's disposal.

Moreover, the same holds true even when national courts are hearing a case that is also under the Commission's scrutiny and the Commission is dealing with the case according to the procedure for existing aid. This can happen in two instances: either the Commission is conducting a preliminary examination of the aid according to the procedure under Article 108(1) TFEU or it has opened a formal investigation under Article 108(2) TFEU and, in doing so, has classified the aid as existing aid. Although, to the best of this author's knowledge, no case law exists on this issue, there should be no doubt that in this case, the national court cannot simply await the Commission's final decision but must instead timely adjudicate the claim brought before it.[282] Hence, the national court can and must make its own assessment regarding the classification of the measure under scrutiny as existing aid or new aid, because this classification – just as the application of the notion of aid – *is essential to the finding of a breach of the procedural rules enshrined in Article 108(3) TFEU.*

Only if the Commission has already adopted a final decision and has considered the measure under discussion to be existing aid (whether compatible or incompatible) should the national court in principle avoid adopting a conflicting decision and either: (i) conclude its own assessment by dismissing the applicant's claim on the basis that the aid is indeed existing aid and that, as such, no breach of the procedural obligations can have occurred; or (ii) stay the proceedings if in doubt and submit a request for a preliminary ruling to the Court of Justice.

However, even in this case, the national court must assess the circumstances of the case and check whether the aid was indeed unlawful when it was granted and became existing aid later because the Commission issued a compatibility decision or did not open an investigation procedure within the prescribed time limit.[283] Indeed, in this case, the aid's unlawfulness cannot be regularised by a subsequent decision (or lack thereof), and the national court must draw all the consequences from the unlawfulness under national law.

The Commission has several ways in which it can decide to classify a measure as existing aid: (i) by dismissing a complaint brought by a third party for an alleged infringement of procedural obligations; (ii) by adopting a decision under Article 9(2) of the Procedural Regulation;[284] (iii) by recording the acceptance of proposed measures by the Member State concerned and informing the Member State accordingly under Article 23(1) of the Procedural Regulation (as this will have the effect of making the

282. This conclusion is based on an application by analogy of the principles enunciated by the Court of Justice in *CELF III* (*see* footnote 146 of this Part Two).
283. *See* Part Two, section III.3.4, and footnote 123 of Part Two.
284. Although Art. 9(2) merely refers to a finding by the Commission that the notified measure does not constitute aid, it must be understood as encompassing also a finding that the notified aid is in fact existing aid and need not have been notified. This is possible, at least in theory, if the Member State concerned submitted a formal notification without any pre-notification check with the Commission.

appropriate measures binding on the Member State); and (iv) by adopting a final decision under Article 23(2), in combination with Article 9, of the Procedural Regulation. If any of these final decisions have been adopted, it seems reasonable to consider that the classification of the measure as existing aid can no longer be questioned unless the lawfulness of the Commission's final decision is challenged. In this respect, the principles developed by the Court of Justice in *Deggendorf I* apply by analogy.[285]

This implies that the lawfulness of a Commission decision can be questioned – by means of a request for a preliminary ruling on the decision's validity – only if the claimant before the national court did not have standing to timely challenge the decision before the General Court under Article 263(4) TFEU. To allow interested parties to challenge a decision after expiry of the mandatory time limit under Article 263 TFEU in cases in which they could have brought an action for annulment before the General Court would be at odds with the principle of legal certainty.

Nevertheless, the analogy with *Deggendorf I* doctrine – which concerns the challenge of a Commission recovery decision before national courts – cannot be pushed too far. Indeed, given the evolution of the case law on admissibility of actions for annulment brought by interested parties before the General Court against a recovery decision,[286] in most cases a party that has an interest in challenging the lawfulness of the recovery decision before national courts also has standing to challenge the decision directly before the General Court. This is certainly not the case, however, when third parties invoke a breach of procedural obligations before national courts and the measure under dispute has been classified as existing aid in a previous Commission decision.

It is all but certain that, in the above scenario, a claimant before a national court would be recognised as having standing before the General Court to apply for an action for annulment of the Commission's decision, as standing depends on several factors, such as evidence of direct competition between the applicant and the aid beneficiary, classification of the contested measure as individual aid or an aid scheme, and the contested measure's immediate applicability (*i.e.*, no need for national authorities to adopt implementing acts).[287] *In the case of doubts on the admissibility* of an action for

285. Judgment of the Court of 9 March 1994, *TWD Textilwerke Deggendorf GmbH v. Federal Republic of Germany*, in Case C-188/92, EU:C:1994:90, in which the Court ruled as follows:

> The national court is bound by a Commission decision adopted under Article 93(2) of the Treaty where, in view of the implementation of that decision by national authorities, the recipient of the aid to which the implementation measures are addressed brings before it an action in which it pleads the unlawfulness of the Commission's decision and where that recipient of aid, although informed in writing by the member State of the Commissions' decision, did not bring an action against that decision under the second paragraph of Article 173 of the Treaty, or did not do so within the period prescribed.

286. For a recent review of the case law on this matter, *see* V. Noël and S. Thomas, *Locus Standi in State Aid Litigation after Montessori*, in European State Aid Law Quarterly, 2021, Volume 20, Issue 4 https://doi.org/10.21552/estal/2021/4/7.
287. On competitors' *locus standi*, *see*, among others: Judgment of the Court of Justice of 28 January 1986, *Compagnie française de l'azote (Cofaz) SA and Others v. Commission of the European Communities*, in Case 169/1984, EU:C:1986:42; Judgment of the Court of Justice of 27 April

annulment brought by an interested party before the General Court, *the interested party must be given the right to argue* before national courts that the Member State concerned infringed a procedural obligation because the contested measure, albeit classified as existing aid by the Commission, was in fact new aid.

VI.B Allocation of Domestic Jurisdiction and Correct Delimitation of the National Procedural Framework

The basic principle that Member States have autonomy in regulating the private enforcement of State aid extends to the allocation of domestic jurisdiction.[288] It is for the domestic legal system of each Member State to designate the courts that have jurisdiction over actions brought on the basis of EU State aid rules and intended to safeguard the rights which individuals derive from them and to determine the detailed procedural rules governing those actions.[289] This implies not only an allocation of jurisdiction within the judiciary (*i.e.*, determining which civil or administrative court – or both, depending on the form of aid – have jurisdiction over actions brought by individuals based on Article 108(3) TFEU) but also clarification of the form of remedy available and the procedural framework.

However, Member States' autonomy is not unlimited. In exercising its domestic autonomy, each Member State encounters the two limits that invariably restrain Member States' discretion whenever the EU legislator opts for the principle of procedural autonomy as the method of implementation of EU rules at national level: the principle of equivalence and the principle of effectiveness. As discussed above with respect to aid recovery,[290] the Court indeed applies the usual criteria in the context of the private enforcement of State aid rules: national rules should not be less favourable than those governing rights which originate in domestic law (principle of equivalence)

1995, *ASPEC and Others v. Commission*, in Case T-435/93, EU:T:1995:79; Judgment of the Court of Justice of 25 June 1998, *British Airways and Others v. Commission*, in Joined Cases T-371/94 and T-394/94, EU:T:1998:140; Judgment of the Court of Justice of 21 October 2004, *Lenzing AG v. Commission*, in Case T-36/99, EU:T:2004:312; and Judgment of the Court of Justice of 31 January 2023, *Commission v. Braesch and Others*, in Case C-284/21 P, EU:C:2023:58.

288. *See, e.g.*, Judgment of the Court of Justice of 5 October 2006, *Transalpine Ölleitung*, cited in footnote 136 of this Part Two, para. 38 of which states that 'it is for the national courts to ensure that the rights of individuals are safeguarded where the obligation to give prior notification of State aid to the Commission pursuant to Article 88(3) of the Treaty is infringed', and para. 44 of which reaffirms that 'it is for the national courts to safeguard the rights of individuals against possible disregard, by the national authorities, of the prohibition on putting aid into effect before the Commission has adopted a decision authorising that aid'. More recently, *see* Judgment of the Court of Justice of 23 January 2019, *Fallimento Traghetti del Mediterraneo*, in Case C-387/17, cited in footnote 123 of this Part Two, para. 55.

289. *See, e.g.*, Judgment of the Court of Justice of 5 October 2006, *Transalpine Ölleitung*, cited in footnote 136 of this Part Two, para. 45 of which affirms that 'since there is no Community legislation on the subject, it is for the domestic legal system of each Member State to designate the courts having jurisdiction and to determine the detailed procedural rules governing actions at law intended to safeguard the rights which individuals derive from Community law'.

290. Part One, section I.A.2.4.

and should not render impossible or excessively difficult in practice the exercise of rights conferred by the EU legal system (principle of effectiveness).[291]

More specifically, the principle of equivalence in the context of private enforcement procedural rules means that, when Member States identify the action and procedure available to interested parties, they should either refer to the rules governing similar actions based on national law or set up new rules that are at least as favourable as those applicable to actions based on national law. The *Laboratoires Boiron* case provides a useful illustration of this principle, as the Court held that national courts – when protecting rights derived from EU State aid law – must make any procedural instrument existing in the domestic legal framework available to private parties to produce the evidence needed to sustain their claim. The message behind the *Laboratoires Boiron* case will be further discussed when examining the issue of evidence in view of a possible harmonisation initiative in Part Four of this book.[292]

Just like the principle of equivalence, the principle of effectiveness is deeply rooted in the EU legal system (*effet utile*) and is applied in a very broad range of cases. When it comes to State aid matters, the *Scott and Kimberly Clark* case enabled the Court to clarify that this principle requires Member States not to jeopardise the scope and effectiveness of State aid rules.[293] The *Scott* judgment refers to the role of national law and national courts in ensuring full implementation of Commission recovery decisions;

---

291. *See, e.g.*, Judgment of the Court of Justice of 5 October 2006, *Transalpine Ölleitung*, cited in footnote 136 of this Part Two, para. 45. *See also* Judgment of the Court (Grand Chamber) of 12 September 2006, *M. G. Eman and O. B. Sevinger v. College van burgemeester en wethouders van Den Haag*, in Case C-300/04, EU:C:2006:545, para. 67, and Judgment of the Court (Grand Chamber) of 19 September 2006, *i-21 Germany GmbH (C-392/04) and Arcor AG & Co. KG (C-422/04) v. Bundesrepublik Deutschland*, in Joined Cases C-392/04 and C-422/04, EU:C:2006:586, para. 57. More recently, *see* Judgment of the Court of Justice of 23 January 2019, *Fallimento Traghetti del Mediterraneo*, in Case C-387/17, cited in footnote 123 of this Part Two, para. 72.

292. The reference to 'all procedures available ... under national law' derives from reasoning based on the principle of equivalence, even though the Court refers only to the principle of effectiveness. *See* Judgment of the Court of 7 September 2006, *Laboratoires Boiron SA*, in Case C-526/04, EU:C:2006:528, paras 55 and 57, which state as follows:

> [I]n order to ensure compliance with the principle of effectiveness, if the national court finds that the fact of requiring a pharmaceutical laboratory such as Boiron to prove that wholesale distributors are overcompensated, and thus that the tax on direct sales amounts to State aid, is likely to make it impossible or excessively difficult for such evidence to be produced, since inter alia that evidence relates to data which such a laboratory will not have, *the national court is required to use all procedures available to it under national law, including that of ordering the necessary measures of inquiry, in particular the production by one of the parties or a third party of a particular document* [emphasis added].

293. *See* Judgment of the Court of 20 May 2010, in Case C-210/09, *Scott SA and Kimberly Clark SAS v. Ville d'Orléans*, EU:C:2010:294, para. 21, which states as follows:

> In accordance with the principle of effectiveness, as consistently applied specifically to State aid in the case-law, a Member State which, pursuant to a decision of the Commission, is obliged to recover unlawful aid is free to choose the means of fulfilling that obligation, provided that the measures chosen do not adversely affect the scope and effectiveness of Union law.

as such, it is not directly relevant to the private enforcement of State aid law, *i.e.*, the enforcement of State aid rules based on the direct applicability of Article 108(3) TFEU.[294] However, it illustrates well the importance of the principle of effectiveness in this area of EU law and is thus relevant also to private enforcement.

As long as the *effet utile* of EU law is ensured, national legal systems are free to choose the means to fulfil their obligations deriving from the direct effects of EU law provisions such as Article 108(3) TFEU. The Court further clarified in which regard national courts must ensure compliance with the principle of effectiveness, namely with regard to the procedural rules set out to safeguard the rights of individuals claiming a breach of Article 108(3) and the duty to restore, to the maximum extent possible, the situation that existed before the unlawful aid was granted.

Moreover, the principle of effectiveness not only restrains the discretion of Member States' legislators in shaping the procedural rules and remedies to enforce the direct applicability of Article 108(3) but also limits the national courts' discretion in handling State aid claims brought before them. Indeed, as discussed above, it was on the basis of the principle of effectiveness that the Court held that a Commission decision declaring aid compatible does not regularise *ex post facto* a breach of procedural rules;[295] and it is again on the basis of that very principle that the Court held in *CELF II* that national courts cannot stay proceedings for violation of Article 108(3) pending the Commission's decision on the compatibility of the aid concerned.[296]

Nevertheless, the EU courts are always very clear and firm in underlining the autonomy of the domestic legal system in choosing the means to abide by duties stemming from EU State aid law - and this is particularly true in the field of private enforcement. Consider a case in which, for instance, the principle of effectiveness might collide with another basic principle or feature of a national legal system. The outcome of this conflict might change depending on the role that national courts are called to play. Within the framework of national courts' cooperation in the enforcement of Commission recovery decisions, the principle of effectiveness generally prevails;

294. Unfortunately, legal scholars and even case law are not always careful in distinguishing the two areas, as illustrated below.

295. *See* Judgment of the Court of 21 November 1991, *FNCE*, Case C-354/90, cited in footnote 134 of this Part Two, para. 16; Judgment of 5 October 2006, *Transalpine Ölleitung*, cited in footnote 136 of this Part Two, para. 41; and, most recently, Judgment of 23 January 2019, *Fallimento Traghetti del Mediterraneo*, cited in footnote 123 of this Part Two, para. 59, which states as follows:

> [C]oncerning the level of independence of the national courts, a Commission decision finding aid that was not notified to be compatible with the internal market does not have the effect of regularising ex post facto implementing measures which were invalid because they were taken in disregard of the prohibition laid down by the last sentence of Article 93(3) of the EEC Treaty, since otherwise the direct effect of that provision would be impaired and the interests of individuals, which are to be protected by national courts, would be disregarded. Any other interpretation would have the effect of according a favourable outcome to the non-observance of that provision by the Member State concerned and would deprive it of its effectiveness.

296. *See* Judgment of the Court, 11 March 2010, in Case C-1/09, *CELF III*, cited in footnote 146 of this Part Two, paras 30-33.

indeed, the peculiarities of a given national legal system cannot justify the non-execution of a Commission decision unless recovery is absolutely impossible or would conflict with a general principle of law.

When it comes to private enforcement, however, a national legal system's autonomy is naturally broader, and the principle of effectiveness does not require a specific outcome to be achieved, such as recovery of the aid. What really matters is that national courts do whatever is in their power to safeguard the rights that individuals draw from Article 108(3) by restoring the pre-existing situation (*i.e.*, the situation that existed before the breach of the procedural obligations) as much as possible - though again, there is no predefined result to be achieved as is instead the case when the Commission imposes remedies. Therefore, one should be very cautious in transposing solutions developed within the framework of public enforcement to the field of private enforcement.

To provide just one example, the case law on public enforcement provides criteria as to how to deal with a conflict between the principle of effectiveness and the principle of *res judicata* in the *Lucchini* and *Frucona Košice (Commission v. Slovak Republic)* cases.[297] Although some authors tend to recall this case law when discussing the private enforcement of State aid rules, the teachings of those judgments - which focus on whether a Commission recovery decision already exists when the case is brought before national courts - are clearly not transposable as such to the field of private enforcement. Therefore, based on the current status of EU law in the field of the private enforcement of State aid rules, it would be difficult to ground an infringement procedure against a Member State on a national court's decision to dismiss a claim because of the existence of *res judicata* under national law.

VI.C Legal Status of Beneficiaries

An additional key aspect of the private enforcement system from a procedural rules standpoint is the very weak position of beneficiaries. From this perspective, beneficiaries before national courts find themselves in a situation similar to that they experience in proceedings before EU institutions, as they are essentially deprived of effective protection in cases of conflicting interests with the Member State concerned.

The recent *Solar Electric* case offers a good illustration of this,[298] as it concerns an aid scheme duly implemented by the Member State concerned for several years until the French *Cour de Cassation* (Supreme Court) while hearing claims for compensation, found that the aid scheme had not been notified to the Commission before implementation.[299] The beneficiary energy producers - despite their attempts to obtain a

297. For a detailed analysis of these judgments, *see* Part One, section I.A.2.6, and footnotes 49 and 53 of Part One.

298. Judgment of the General Court of 10 November 2021, Case T-678/20, *Solar Electric Holding and others v. European Commission*, EU:2021:T:780.

299. The case concerned a legislative measure intended to encourage the development of renewable energy in France that had been adopted back in 2000. Based on this measure, a purchase obligation at a price set by ministerial pricing orders was imposed on energy distributors. The costs borne by the latter as a result of the purchase obligation were fully compensated through

statement from the Commission (first) and from the General Court (subsequently) that would prove the aid's compatibility and therefore bind the national judge, limiting in some way the consequences of the *Cour de Cassation*'s judgment - eventually had to accept what had become obvious, *i.e.*, that they lack protection when the State's position changes and their interest becomes conflicting with that of the State. This is yet another consequence (a harmful one when one considers the logic of the State aid system) of the misconception of the bilateral relationship between the Commission and the Member State under Article 108(3) TFEU.

In a nutshell, private entities have only a severely limited possibility to turn to national courts to obtain compliance by Member States with the procedural rules. Indeed, if a potential beneficiary wants to obtain an order from a national court for the Member State to notify the measure concerned to the Commission, even if only for reasons of legal certainty and to avoid being exposed to the risk of repayment, its request is likely to be inadmissible. Based on the General Court's reasoning in *Solar Electric*, the beneficiary would not have a legitimate interest since EU law does not grant beneficiaries any right to obtain confirmation of a measure's compatibility (or of the fact that it does not constitute aid).[300]

In this respect, the General Court's reasoning appears contradictory in that, on the one hand, it denies beneficiaries any right to obtain clarification as to the compatibility of a measure with the Treaty, but on the other hand, it appears to hold that beneficiaries may bring an action before a national court against an implied or express refusal to notify. Nor is it clear on what basis a beneficiary can ask a national court to impose a penalty on the Member State concerned in order to have it comply with the notification obligation.[301]

In essence, if one wants to stay on the practical ground and avoid purely theoretical debates, the reality is that in all cases in which a private party's interest

---

an offset mechanism financed by a contribution to the public electricity service, which was levied, directly or indirectly, on electricity consumers. Pricing orders were adopted in 2006, 2010 and 2017. The purchase price of electricity set in the orders was applicable during the whole duration of the purchase contracts concluded in accordance with the measure under discussion, *i.e.*, twenty years. Later, however, compensation claims arose - probably as a consequence of the French authorities' intention to do away with a mechanism which was no longer consistent with the new energy market situation. Hence, in September 2019 the *Cour de Cassation* held that the pricing orders that implemented a purchase obligation mechanism at a price higher than the market price constituted unlawful State aid in that they had not been notified to the Commission. Some renewable energy producers reacted by submitting a complaint to the Commission against the unlawful aid, with the aim of obtaining a declaration of the measure's compatibility and thus avoiding the detrimental consequences of the judgment issued by the *Cour de Cassation*, such as termination of the purchase contracts. The Commission, however, rejected the complaint - in a nutshell, it did so on the ground that the complaint filed by the renewable energy producers could not be considered a complaint in the technical sense (under Art. 24(2) of the Procedural Regulation), because it was aimed at obtaining a declaration of compatibility. The complaint therefore performed a function similar to that of a notification - which, however, according to the Treaty's system, is reserved for Member States.

300. Judgment of the General Court of 10 November 2021, Case T-678/20, *Solar Electric Holding and others v. European Commission*, cited in footnote 298 of this Part Two, paras 26-29.

301. *Ibid.*, para. 31.

conflicts with that of the State, the instrument of private enforcement proves useless.[302] This is not only unsatisfactory from both a practical and a theoretical standpoint but it is also paradoxical when one considers that an aid recipient is then not allowed to oppose an order to repay aid by alleging its good faith with respect to the choice – by the State, and only by the State – not to proceed with notification. Likewise, according to the case law, whatever assurance the beneficiary received from the State as to the measure's compatibility or its classification as non-aid is insufficient to generate any legitimate expectation that can be validly invoked to oppose a recovery order.

What is more, it seems clear that this situation profoundly undermines the effectiveness of State aid procedural rules insofar as it encourages Member States not to comply with them in the event of doubts as to a measure's legitimacy, especially when the public interest is to obtain implementation of the investment in any event and without delay.

VI.D Arbitration as a Private Enforcement Tool

VI.D.1 General Remarks and Status Quo

The use of arbitration as a tool for private enforcement of State aid rules has not been studied in depth; rather, the opposite is true.

As explained in the chapter on the New Enforcement Notice,[303] the latter contains an appropriate reference to the issue but limits itself to very general explanations. First, the New Enforcement Notice specifies that arbitral tribunals are not considered courts or tribunals within the meaning of Article 267 TFEU, as parties are under no obligation to refer their disputes to arbitration, and the public authorities of Member States are neither involved in the decision to opt for arbitration nor required to intervene in the proceedings before the arbitrator. However, the New Enforcement Notice refers also to the Court statement in *Merck* confirming that a preliminary question referred to the Court by an arbitral tribunal is admissible if that tribunal was established by law, its decisions are binding on the parties, and its jurisdiction does not depend on the parties' will.[304]

Second, the New Enforcement Notice refers to the *Asteris* case law,[305] recalling that State aid is intrinsically different in legal nature from damages that national

302. A similar situation arises when a Member State grants aid to a beneficiary, deeming it not to be State aid or not to be notifiable, but then decides, once the beneficiary has carried out the aided investment, not to defend the aid's lawfulness before the Commission and to execute the recovery order without reservation. To delve deeper into this issue, *see* Merola, *Rimedi per violazione delle norme sugli aiuti di Stato: misure repressive o di ripristino*, cited in footnote 3 of Part One.
303. *See* Part Two, Chapter V.
304. Order of the Court of Justice of 13 February 2014, C-555/13, *Merck Canada*, EU:C:2014:92, paras 17-18.
305. Judgment of the Court of Justice of 27 September 1988, C-106 to 120/87, *Asteris and Others v. Hellenic Republic and European Economic Community*, cited in footnote 72 of this Part Two, para. 23; and Judgment of the Court of Justice of 21 December 2016, C-164/15 P and C-165/15 P, *Commission v. Aer Lingus*, EU:C:2016:990, para. 72.

authorities may be ordered to pay to individuals in compensation for the damage the authorities have caused. Still, when ruling on the compensation to third parties directly related to the granting of unlawful aid,[306] national courts must be careful not to adopt decisions having the effect of granting new aid or enlarging the circle of beneficiaries.[307]

The New Enforcement Notice contains no further information or suggestions beyond these meagre indications, yet it reports sufficiently comprehensively on case law, which itself does not go much further. Indeed, the case law on arbitration and State aid has only incidentally touched on the issue of private enforcement.

In the *Asteris* case, the Court simply held that the payment by the State of compensation for damage ordered by a national court as a consequence of an infringement of EU law does not, as such, constitute State aid within the meaning of Article 107(1) TFEU. In *Simet*,[308] which is also mentioned in the New Enforcement Notice,[309] the Court simply rejected the applicant's argument based on equating compensation for public service obligations with compensation for damage, in order to avoid circumvention of EU rules on the financing of SGEIs.

In *Transalpine Ölleitung*,[310] the Court added that, when a national court is asked by a competitor of the beneficiary to award damages caused by aid's unlawful nature, it 'must strive to preserve the interests of individuals while also taking the EU interest into full consideration, taking particular care not to adopt a decision which would have the sole effect of extending the circle of recipients of the unlawful aid'.

In *Achmea*,[311] which concerned the enforcement of an arbitration award by which Slovakia had been ordered to compensate the damage caused to a Dutch investor in the insurance sector, the German *Bundesgerichtshof*, hearing the case on appeal, referred several questions to the Court of Justice for a preliminary ruling on the arbitration clause's compatibility with EU law.[312] The Court first recalled that, based on settled case law, an international agreement cannot affect the allocation of powers fixed by the Treaties or the EU legal system's autonomy, and that the principle of

306. This could be the case when the applicant seeking damages incurred investment costs as a result of the aid (*i.e.*, because it relied on a commercial relationship with the aid recipient in its capacity as, for instance, a supplier of technology or equipment for the aided investment).
307. New Enforcement Notice, cited in footnote 50 of this Part Two, para. 96 and footnote 134.
308. Judgment of the General Court of 3 March 2016, Case T-15/14, *Simet SpA v. European Commission*, EU:T:2016:124, paras 102-104.
309. New Enforcement Notice, cited in footnote 50 of this Part Two, footnote 134.
310. Cited in footnote 136 of this Part Two and in the New Enforcement Notice, footnote 136.
311. Judgment of the Court of Justice (Grand Chamber) of 6 March 2018, Case C-284/16, *Slowakische Republik v. Achmea BV*, EU:C:2018:158 (with Opinion of Advocate General Wathelet of 19 September 2017, EU:C:2017:699).
312. More precisely, the Court had to rule on the request of the *Bundesgerichtshof* to assess the compatibility with EU law of the arbitration clause in the bilateral treaty entered into in 1993 by the then Czech and Slovak Federative Republic and the Netherlands. The Slovak Republic claimed that the clause conflicted with EU law and was no longer applicable after Slovakia's accession to the EU in 2004. The arbitral tribunal, seated in Frankfurt, had instead ruled that the clause was valid and ordered Slovakia to compensate Achmea for damage. After the Frankfurt Higher Regional Court (*Oberlandesgericht Frankfurt*) upheld the arbitration award at first instance, the *Bundesgerichtshof* referred questions to the Court on the validity of the bilateral treaty's arbitration clause following the entry into force of the EU Treaties in Slovakia.

sincere cooperation requires Member States to ensure the application of EU law in their respective territories. The Court also noted that the arbitral tribunal established by the bilateral treaty cannot be classified as a court of a Member State within the meaning of Article 267 TFEU and is thus not entitled to refer a case for a preliminary ruling and that the arbitration award is subject to a limited review that does not include questions of compatibility with EU law. This meant that the signatories of the bilateral treaty under consideration (*i.e.*, the Netherlands and Slovakia) had agreed to remove from the jurisdiction of their own courts any disputes concerning the application or interpretation of EU law.

On this basis, the Court concluded that the mechanism established by that treaty for settling disputes between an investor and a Member State could prevent those disputes from being resolved in a manner that ensures the full effectiveness of EU law. Hence, the treaty's arbitration clause called into question both the autonomy of EU law and the principle of sincere cooperation.[313]

VI.D.2 The Debate Surrounding the Micula *Case*

The most controversial case concerning the interplay between arbitration and State aid is *Micula*,[314] which was decided – it must be acknowledged – after the release of the New Enforcement Notice, and in which the issue examined by the EU courts stemmed from an arbitration award that had ordered Romania to pay the applicants damages for breaching their legitimate expectations to receive incentives in support of their investment in the country.[315] The applicants' main pleas were: (i) the Commission's

313. Judgment of the Court of Justice (Grand Chamber) of 6 March 2018, Case C-284/16, *Slowakische Republik/Achmea BV*, cited in footnote 311 of this Part Two, paras 51-56.

314. Judgment of the General Court of 18 June 2019, Case T-624/15, *European Food and others v. European Commission*, EU:T:2019:423, overturned by the Judgment of the Court of Justice (Grand Chamber) of 25 January 2022, Case C-638/19 P, *European Commission v. European Food and others*, EU:C:2022:50 (with the Opinion of Advocate General Szpunar of 1 July 2021, EU:C:2021:529). The Court of Justice referred the case back to the General Court, which recently handed down its second judgment on the case, rejecting the application for annulment in its entirety (Judgment of the General Court of 2 October 2024, Case T-624/15 RENV, T-694/15 RENV and T-704/15 RENV, *European Food SA and others v. European Commission*, EU:T:2024:659). Only the Commission Decision is mentioned in the New Enforcement Notice, as the case before the General Court was pending when the New Enforcement Notice was released.

315. In its award of 11 December 2013, the arbitral tribunal ordered Romania to pay approximately EUR 178 million in damages. According to the tribunal, Romania had violated the applicants' legitimate expectations that those incentives would be available, in substantially the same form, until 1 April 2009, and therefore failed to 'ensure fair and equitable treatment of the investments'. The fairly complex background to the case can be summarised as follows. Just as any other Europe agreement, the Europe agreement between the EEC and Romania, which came into force in 1995, included a provision that mirrored the Treaty's substantive rules on State aid. In 1998, the Romanian authorities adopted a regional aid scheme granting certain investors in disadvantaged regions that had obtained permanent investor certificates a series of incentives. The scheme was amended in 2000 to align it with EU legislation. In 2002, Sweden and Romania concluded a bilateral investment treaty ('*BIT*') on the promotion and reciprocal protection of investments. Under the BIT, each contracting party committed to ensuring fair and equitable treatment of the investments by investors of the other contracting party. Art. 2(3)

alleged lack of competence and abuse of power, given that all the Romanian Government's actions and omissions causing the damage occurred before Romania's accession to the EU and that Article 351 TFEU protects Romania's international obligations arising from agreements concluded before its accession and still in force against any possible post-accession effects of EU State aid rules; (ii) the alleged lack of proof that the measure fulfilled the requirements to be classified as State aid under Article 107(1);[316] and (iii) the alleged violation of the principle of protection of legitimate

---

of the BIT stipulated, among other things, that 'each Contracting Party shall at all times ensure fair and equitable treatment of the investments by investors of the other Contracting Party and shall not impair, by means of arbitrary or discriminatory measures, the administration, management, maintenance, use, enjoyment or disposal thereof by those investors'. Disputes between investors and the contracting countries were to be settled by an arbitral tribunal. Based on the BIT, some companies owned by Swedish nationals carried out certain investments in one of Romania's disadvantaged regions. In 2004, Romania repealed most of the incentives provided under the regional aid scheme at issue within the framework of the accession talks ongoing at that time with the EU, on the basis that 'to complete the negotiations under Chapter No 6 – Competition Policy, it [was] necessary to eliminate all forms of State aid in national legislation incompatible with the *acquis communautaire*'. The repeal took effect as of 2005. The aid scheme in question was not referred to in the Accession Act among the State aid measures that would be considered existing aid at the time of Romania's accession, as it had been repealed by the Romanian authorities. Given that Romania had breached its obligation under the BIT by repealing the incentives scheme, the beneficiaries requested the establishment of an arbitral tribunal to obtain compensation for the damage resulting from that breach. While the arbitration proceedings were pending, Romania acceded to the EU (on 1 January 2007). The accession treaty did not include the disputed incentives in the list of existing State aid. Despite the Commission's intervention as *amicus curiae* in the arbitration proceedings, the proceeding ended with the arbitral tribunal's decision to award the applicants approximately EUR 178 million in compensation payable by Romania. Romania then filed an application for the annulment of the arbitral award before an ad hoc committee, but the applicants simultaneously brought court proceedings with a view to enforcing the arbitral award. After the Regional Court of Bucharest ruled that the arbitral award was enforceable, an executor started the procedure to enforce the arbitral award. Despite the Commission's request to the Regional Court of Bucharest to suspend and annul the forced enforcement of the arbitral award and to refer preliminary questions to the Court of Justice in accordance with Art. 267 TFEU, the enforcement procedure proceeded to offset a portion of the compensation awarded to the applicants by the arbitral tribunal against taxes owed by one of the applicants (European Food) to the Romanian authorities. The Commission reacted by adopting Decision C(2014) 3192, which obliged Romania, under Art. 11(1) of Council Regulation (EC) No 659/1999, to immediately suspend all action that could lead to the implementation or enforcement of the arbitral award – on the ground that any such action appeared to constitute unlawful State aid – until the Commission could issue a final decision on the compatibility of that State aid with the internal market. The Commission also decided to initiate the formal investigation procedure laid down in Art. 108(2) TFEU in relation to Romania's partial implementation of the arbitral award, which led to the adoption of the contested decision. When the decision was adopted, the arbitration award had already been fully implemented according to the Romanian authorities. The Commission ordered Romania to recover the amounts paid to enforce the arbitral award (principal and interest). *See* Commission Decision (EU) 2015/1470 of 30 March 2015, SA.38517 (2014/C, ex 2014 NN), on State aid implemented by Romania through arbitral award (OJ L 232, 4 September 2015, p. 43).

316. More specifically, the beneficiaries claimed that the Commission had failed to demonstrate fulfilment of several requirements under Art. 107(1), notably the economic advantage requirement (as the award was intended solely to compensate for damage and therefore met the conditions of the *Asteris* case law), the selectivity requirement (as the bilateral treaty established a system that was equally applicable to any investor) and the imputability requirement (as Romania had no margin of appreciation to execute the arbitration award).

expectations, as the EU authorities, by actively encouraging the conclusion of bilateral agreements to foster intra-EU investments, allegedly caused the beneficiaries to entertain legitimate expectations that an effort to enforce an arbitration award based on such a treaty would not be blocked under State aid rules.

The General Court upheld the first plea and the first part of the second one; it did not go on to examine the remaining pleas.[317] The General Court held that the Commission erred in applying its powers retroactively to events predating Romania's accession to the EU.[318] It based its conclusion on the principle that State aid must be considered granted at the time the right to receive it is conferred on the beneficiary under the applicable national rules. Therefore, according to the General Court, *the repeal of the incentives in 2005, well ahead of Romania's accession to the EU, constituted the event giving rise to the damage for which compensation was awarded by the arbitral tribunal.* As the arbitral tribunal confined itself to determining the exact damage suffered by the applicants, its award was merely an ancillary element of the compensation and was therefore not severable from the earlier tax incentives and could not be classified as new aid.[319] As to the first part of the second plea, the General Court held that, since the incentives granted before Romania's accession to the EU did not constitute State aid within the meaning of Article 107(1) for the reasons explained above, the *Asteris* requirements were met, *i.e.*, the award of damages could not be regarded as compensation for the withdrawal of aid which is unlawful and incompatible with EU law.[320]

However, the Court of Justice (Grand Chamber) took a different approach.[321] It recalled that the concept of 'advantage', which is intrinsic to the classification of a measure as State aid, is an objective one, irrespective of the reasons underlying the granting of the aid. Therefore, even if the repeal of the tax incentives scheme at issue constituted the event giving rise to the damage, the right to compensation was granted solely by the award issued by the arbitral tribunal, which not only ascertained the applicants' right to receive compensation but also quantified the amount thereof. Furthermore, the accession treaty granted the Commission the power to review the aid even if one were to consider that the aid had been granted before the Treaty's entry into force.

Lastly, the Court also quashed the General Court's statement that the *Achmea* case law was irrelevant to the case at issue. The Court specified that, with effect from Romania's accession to the EU, the system of judicial remedies provided for by the TEU and the TFEU necessarily replaced the arbitration procedure of the bilateral agreement

317. Judgment of the General Court of 18 June 2019, Case T-624/15, *European Food and Others v. Commission*, cited in footnote 314 of this Part Two.
318. *Ibid.*, paras 91-92.
319. *Ibid.*, paras 76-77.
320. *Ibid.*, paras 103-107.
321. Judgment of the Court of Justice (Grand Chamber) of 25 January 2022 in Case C-638/19 P, *European Commission v. European Food and Others*, cited in footnote 314 of this Part Two.

between Sweden and Romania,[322] which implies that the consent given to that effect by Romania, from that time onwards, lacked any force.[323]

The Court therefore upheld the beneficiaries' first plea (without examining the second one, concerning the lack of an advantage), set aside the General Court's judgment[324] and referred the case back to the General Court to adjudicate the pleas raised before it concerning the merits of the contested decision.[325]

Despite the Court's judgment in *Micula*, it is still far from clear whether investor-State arbitration is compatible with the EU legal system when applied in an intra-EU context to disputes involving compensation for damage related to previously granted State aid measures which are then repealed or modified. Recently, the question was raised again in *Antin*, concerning a 2018 international arbitration award based on

322. Otherwise disputes which might concern the application or interpretation of EU law would be resolved outside the EU system of judicial remedies, thus putting the full effectiveness of EU law at risk (*Ibid.*, para. 139).

323. Judgment of the Court of Justice (Grand Chamber) of 25 January 2022, *European Commission v. European Food and others*, cited in footnote 314 of this Part Two, para. 145.

324. *Ibid.*, paras 123-127.

325. *Ibid.*, para. 154. The General Court ruled in October 2024 on all pleas raised by the applicants at first instance that had not been examined by the Court. In doing so, it ought to check whether the Court's ruling on the first plea impacted the solution to be given to the other pleas. This was indeed the case for several grounds of appeal, which were based, directly or indirectly, on the incorrect premise that the Commission was not competent to adopt the contested decision. The main issue the General Court needed to consider was whether State aid rules can be used to prevent the implementation of a remedy envisaged in an international agreement without impinging on the beneficiaries' rights to obtain compensation for damage – or in other words, whether there are means of awarding that compensation which do not create market distortions. The General Court (Judgment of the General Court of 2 October 2024, Case T-624/15 RENV, T-694/15 RENV and T-704/15 RENV, *European Food SA and others v. European Commission*, cited above at footnote 314) first held that the ICSID Convention could not be interpreted as having created 'rights' within the meaning of the first paragraph of Art. 351 TFEU in favour of third States signatory to that convention that correspond to obligations on the part of Rumania to execute the arbitral award. Further, the General Court held that 'the Commission was fully entitled to define, contrary to what the applicants have claimed, the aid measure at issue as the payment of the sums at issue in order to ascertain, in its assessment of the existence of State aid, within the meaning of Article 107(1) TFEU, whether that payment represented an economic advantage from which the applicants would not have benefited under normal market conditions'. More importantly, the General Court stated that 'an action for damages, such as that brought by the arbitration applicants before the arbitral tribunal, cannot lead to circumvention of the effective application of the rules on State aid' and that damages paid as 'compensation for any loss resulting from the repeal of an aid scheme' cannot escape classification as State aid where those damages meet the definition of an economic advantage for the purposes of those rules. In analysing the existence of State aid, the Commission is not bound by the legal classification of the sums as 'damages' adopted by the arbitral tribunal.
For the sake of completeness, it should be pointed out that the *Micula* case also had a second front at national level (more precisely in Belgium, where one of the beneficiaries of the compensation awarded by the arbitral tribunal had requested the seizure of amounts that Romania owed to Eurocontrol, which had offices in Brussels, in order to obtain full enforcement of the award), which ended with a preliminary reference to the Court of Justice by the Brussels Court of Appeal. On 21 September 2022, the Court of Justice handed down an order based on Art. 99 of the Rules of Procedure of the Court whereby it held that the answer to the questions referred to the Court was already implicit in the Grand Chamber's judgment of 25 January 2022. The Court held that the Belgian court could under no circumstances execute the arbitral award without infringing EU law and was therefore obliged to set it aside. *See* Order of the Court of Justice of 21 September 2022, Case C-333/19, *Romatsa and Others*, EU:C:2022:749.

the Energy Charter Treaty, a multilateral agreement concerning the protection of investment in the energy sector. The award had granted compensation for damage to two investors whose investment projects benefitted from a 2007 Spanish renewable support scheme, which was later amended and approved by the Commission as compatible aid in 2017.[326] Upon notification from the Spanish authorities, the Commission is currently reviewing the compatibility of the compensation for damage with EU State aid rules.[327]

Although no final decision has been issued yet, the opening decision contains many references to *Micula*. The Commission preliminarily considered that the notified award to Antin constitutes aid because it: (i) has the effect of compensating for the withdrawal of unlawful aid, *i.e.*, the unnotified 2007 scheme; (ii) is granted to one undertaking only and is therefore selective; (iii) is imputable to the State because Spain entered the Energy Charter Treaty and adopted the support scheme; (iv) is granted through State resources; and (v) is likely to distort competition and trade.

The key issue the Commission will now have to examine is whether the 2007 aid scheme is compatible with EU law when taking into account the State aid guidelines applicable to operating aid to energy from renewable sources (the 2008 State aid guidelines for environmental protection and the guidelines on State aid for environmental protection and energy 2014-2020, respectively), and whether it leads to discrimination based on nationality since Spanish investors are precluded from bringing an action before an arbitral tribunal in relation to modifications to the 2007 scheme. If the Commission's conclusion is in the affirmative, the compensation ordered by the arbitration award will very likely be considered incompatible aid based on the *Micula* case law. In that case, the Commission will prohibit Spain from enforcing the award.

VI.D.3 Conclusions on Arbitration as a Private Enforcement Tool

As is evident from the abovementioned case law that has developed over the years on the relationship between State aid rules and arbitration procedures, the issue of

326. The background to the case can be summarised as follows. In 2007, Spain established a scheme to support the production of electricity from renewable sources. This scheme was not notified to the Commission for approval under State aid rules. Antin Infrastructure Services Luxembourg S.à r.l. and Antin Energia Termosolar B.V. ('*Antin*'), incorporated in Luxembourg and the Netherlands, respectively, had invested in renewable installations in Spain, which benefitted from this support scheme. In 2013, Spain modified the terms at which renewable installations could receive support, which involved also the installations that had started to receive incentives under the 2007 scheme. On 10 November 2017, the Commission adopted a decision (SA.40348) that classified the 2013 aid scheme as compatible aid. Antin initiated an arbitration procedure to be compensated for the support it would have received on the basis of the 2007 scheme but was forced to forgo. When an arbitral award, issued on 15 June 2018, found that Spain had infringed the Energy Charter Treaty and ordered Spain to compensate Antin for losses suffered, with the compensation amounting to over EUR 100 million, Spain notified the arbitration award to the Commission in accordance with Art. 108(3) TFEU.
327. Spain notified the arbitration award to the Commission on 17 April 2019; on 19 July 2021, the Commission notified Spain of its decision to initiate the procedure laid down in Art. 108(2) TFEU and expressed its preliminary doubts about the measure's compatibility with the internal market. The non-confidential version of the Commission's decision is available under the case number SA.54155 in the State aid register on the Commission's competition website.

arbitration as a tool for private enforcement has not really been addressed thus far. The case law has focused essentially on questions of an institutional nature, such as the relationship between the EU legal system and international treaties, and on whether compensation for damage determined by an arbitral tribunal can be classified as State aid under Article 107(1) TFEU.

Only the judgments cited by the Commission in the New Enforcement Notice have some (modest) bearing on the above question: *Asteris* excludes, as a general rule, that compensation for damage is tantamount to an advantage within the meaning of Article 107(1); *Simet* circumscribes this rule by excluding the possibility of equating compensation for damage with compensation for public service obligations; *Transalpine Ölleitung* sends a warning[328] about the need to avoid a situation in which compensation for damage suffered by a competitor of a beneficiary of unlawful aid might lead to the enlargement of the circle of beneficiaries of an unlawful measure; and finally, *Micula* assumes that compensation for damage can constitute aid if it is the direct consequence of unlawful aid, as the Commission stated in the New Enforcement Notice, whereas Article 107(1) is inapplicable in all other cases of compensation for damage. Furthermore, by recalling that the notion of advantage is objective, *Micula* warns that the motive underlying the payment of a sum by the State, *i.e.*, the enforcement of an arbitral award concerning facts that predate the entry into force of the Treaty, is not sufficient to exclude the applicability of Article 107(1).

Even these rulings, however, do not reach the heart of the matter of the relationship between the private enforcement of State aid rules and arbitration. Indeed, they do not help answer the two essential questions in that regard: Is arbitration a useful tool for an aid beneficiary (who wants to acquire absolute legal certainty of the aid's lawfulness before making a related investment) to obtain State compliance with the notification obligation? And similarly, is arbitration a useful tool for a competitor of the aid beneficiary to invoke an infringement of Article 108(3) TFEU and obtain enforcement of the appropriate remedies more quickly and effectively than it could before a national court? In a nutshell, is arbitration a useful tool for the private enforcement of State aid rules, both for beneficiaries and for competitors?

As far as beneficiaries are concerned, the answer can only be negative. If the aid is granted directly on the basis of a legislative measure, *e.g.*, under a tax scheme or other instrument that does not require the adoption of an administrative act, beneficiaries have no possibility of having an arbitration clause inserted (unless it is envisaged under international treaties as in the *Micula* and *Antin* cases – but even then, given the outcome of those cases, it would not be a sufficient guarantee). A similar situation arises when aid is granted by an administrative act, because even in that case the granting of aid is generally based on a mere verification of the beneficiary's

328. The warning in *Transalpine Ölleitung* is addressed to national courts, not to arbitral tribunals, but applies equally to the latter. Though it is true that an arbitral tribunal is not a State body, the implementation of an arbitral award by the State may well fall within the scope of Art. 107(1) TFEU if it is the direct consequence of unlawful aid, as rightfully noted by the Commission in para. 96 of the New Enforcement Notice, cited in footnote 50 of this Part Two.

fulfilment of legal requirements, without any real negotiation between the State and the beneficiary.

In the (infrequent) cases in which beneficiaries can instead negotiate an aid package with the granting Member State (which is likely to be the case only for very large investment projects receiving individual aid), they might be able to obtain an arbitration clause allowing them to claim damages in the event of a subsequent modification or repeal of the measure or a recovery order. However, such a clause would be totally ineffective in the case of unlawful aid because it would be incompatible with EU law and therefore unenforceable, regardless of whether the damage resulted from a recovery order issued by the Commission or from an autonomous decision of the State, as in *Micula* and *Antin*.

The clause could therefore only be effective if the aid was notified and authorised or was covered by a block exemption (which the beneficiary would have an interest in having confirmed by an independent expert). If aid is not block exempted, beneficiaries should in theory make their acceptance of the aid (and execution of the aided project) conditional on prior notification of the aid to the Commission, although anyone with any experience in business affairs will immediately understand how unrealistic this usually is.

As far as competitors are concerned, arbitration is not a tool they can use because they are obviously not contractually tied to beneficiaries by agreements that might include an arbitration clause for damage arising from unlawful aid. As for other interested parties, arbitration may play a role in the sale and purchase of shares or assets of companies that have benefitted from aid. In business practice, it is indeed common for a share or asset sale and purchase agreement to include an arbitration clause under which any disputes arising between the parties are to be submitted to (and resolved by) arbitration. In these cases, one of the events that might trigger the arbitration clause could be when, after completion of the sale, the company whose shares have been transferred (in the case of a share deal) or the buyer of the assets (in the case of an asset deal) is confronted with the consequences of an order to repay unlawful aid from which the acquired company or business benefitted before the acquisition. This would cause damage to the buyer; and if the buyer had obtained precise assurances in this regard in the purchase agreement, it may seek recourse against the seller by appealing to the arbitral tribunal.

Moreover, in certain circumstances, the recovery of unlawful and incompatible State aid can affect not only the direct beneficiaries of the aid measure but also companies not among the initial recipients. This can occur precisely when the direct beneficiary of the aid sells all or part of its business to another company after receiving the aid. If these sales take place before the Commission adopts a recovery decision, the Commission generally examines them and sets out in its decision the name of the actual and ultimate beneficiary from which the aid must be recovered by the national authorities. However, this is not what normally happens when aid is granted under an aid scheme: in these circumstances, the Commission normally examines the aid scheme only in abstract and general terms.

Consequently, the national authorities responsible for implementing the recovery order must investigate whether the advantage formally given to the beneficiary was passed on to the purchaser. This entails ascertaining whether economic continuity exists between the two parties to the transaction. This assessment can lead to an extension of the recovery obligation if it is necessary to 'forfeit' the actual competitive advantage granted with the aid by imposing the financial burden entailed by recovery on the party that actually benefitted from the aid.[329] When the purchaser is identified as the ultimate beneficiary and exposed to the repayment obligation, it may, again, seek recourse against the seller by invoking the arbitration clause in the purchase agreement.

It is apparent from these considerations that all the practice and case law on the interplay between arbitration and State aid control essentially serves to *neutralise arbitration as a means by which recipients of unlawful aid can protect the stability of the economic advantage deriving from that aid.* The contribution of practice and case law to developing arbitration as a tool for achieving the fundamental objectives of the private enforcement of State aid rules is therefore nil. As things stand today, arbitration can play a role only in certain situations and is limited to relationships arising from commercial transactions. But again, it is not – or if it is, it is only very indirectly – a means of enforcing a Member State's breach of the duty to notify and of safeguarding the rights arising from such a breach.

All in all, it seems clear that arbitration plays no role, or at least no important role, in ensuring the effectiveness of the notification obligation or in safeguarding the rights that individuals or companies may derive from a breach of that obligation. This conclusion is obviously relevant for the purposes of this book's analysis and will have to be considered when discussing possible avenues for reform.

329. *See* Judgement of the Court of Justice of 16 January 2025, Case C-588/23, *Scai Srl v. Regione Campania*, EU:C:2025:23 commented by P. Nicolaides, *Incompatible State Aid May Be Recovered from an Undertaking other than the Direct Recipient*, Lexxion, 2025, available at https://www.lexxion.eu/en/stateaidpost/incompatible-state-aid-may-be-recovered-from-an-undertaking-other-than-the-direct-recipient-when-there-is-economic-continuity-between-the-two-undertakings-an-undertaking-may-challenge-a-commission-re/.
The CJEU clarified that the recovery of incompatible State aid is not limited to the beneficiary identified in a Commission decision but may extend to any entity that continues its economic activity and retains the competitive advantage derived from the aid. The existence of economic continuity is assessed upon several factors, including asset transfers, transfer price, and ownership links between the original and acquiring undertakings. The Court also clarified that although the Commission's 2019 Notice on aid recovery is not binding, it should nonetheless be taken into account by national courts. Furthermore, the Court reaffirmed that the actual beneficiary of the aid must have the opportunity to seek judicial review of the Commission decision declaring the aid unlawful and incompatible, by a national court, thereby safeguarding their rights under Articles 41 and 47 of the Charter.

Final Remarks on Part Two

The final remarks assess whether the system of remedies for violations of State aid rules is adequately complemented by the solutions available in private enforcement of those same rules. Possible avenues for reform are suggested to improve the overall effectiveness of the system of remedies.

Part Two of this book has sought to determine whether the system of remedies for violations of the Treaty's State aid rules - which, as reflected in the conclusions reached in Part One, is currently very deficient - is adequately complemented by solutions available in the private enforcement of those same rules. Of course, this analysis could only be carried out based on an examination of the overall characteristics of private enforcement - but this book does not claim to delve into every aspect of it, as it focuses instead on the specific topic of remedies.

To conclude this analysis and set the basis for a reflection on the avenues for reform, it is necessary to consider the conclusions reached thus far against the backdrop of the modernisation objectives, which are expected to spread across all areas of State aid law, and more specifically the objective to adequately complement the public enforcement system of remedies.

This is the goal of the present chapter, which first briefly recalls the essential role of national courts in State aid enforcement (section I), delves into the impact of modernisation on the private enforcement of State aid rules (section II), examines the persistent shortcomings of the system of remedies after the adoption of the New Private Enforcement Notice (section III), and then draws conclusions (section IV).

I THE ROLE OF NATIONAL COURTS IN STATE AID ENFORCEMENT, IN A NUTSHELL

Broadly speaking, the role of national courts in safeguarding the rights of individuals when the notification and standstill obligations are breached encompasses the following tasks: (i) ascertaining the existence of aid; (ii) assessing the aid's classification as existing aid or new aid;[330] (iii) checking compliance with all GBER conditions;[331] and (iv) ordering the appropriate remedies.

In terms of remedies, whereas the Commission can only issue injunctions and order recovery of incompatible and unlawful aid, national courts, as discussed above, have a wider range of remedies at their disposal - in fact, all those allowed under national law (recovery, suspension, termination, interim relief, damages, and possibly others). In performing their function of safeguarding the rights of individuals, national courts enjoy a degree of independence in relation to the Commission. This degree of independence implies, among other things, that a Commission decision finding aid compatible does not have the effect of regularising the aid's unlawfulness *ex post facto*.[332]

More precisely, if no Commission decision has been adopted before a case is brought before a national court, the latter must determine on its own whether the contested measure falls within the scope of Article 107(1) TFEU (if necessary, by activating the cooperation mechanism or referring the case to the Court of Justice for a preliminary ruling) and take all possible measures to safeguard the interest of individuals. If the Commission has adopted an opening decision, this creates a presumption of existence of aid that national courts must consider. However, national courts cannot stay proceedings to await the Commission's final decision, as the opening of a formal investigation does not release them from their duty to safeguard the rights of individuals faced with a possible breach of Article 108(3) TFEU.[333] They can order provisional placement of the funds on a blocked account and/or adopt interim measures preventing the disbursement of presumably unlawful aid if they consider it

330. Notably, according to the Court of Justice, the definition of the concept of existing aid in EU secondary law (Art. 1(b) of the Procedural Regulation) is not always applicable in actions for damages pending before national courts. The Procedural Regulation contains rules which apply to all administrative procedures concerning State aid pending before the Commission, but it does not contain any provisions relating to the powers and obligations of national courts, which continue to be governed by the provisions of the Treaty as interpreted by the Court. In particular, the Court held that Art. 1(b)(iv) of the Procedural Regulation does not prevent national courts from awarding damages for a breach of Art. 108(3) TFEU. *See* Judgment of the Court of 23 January 2019, Case C-387/17, *Fallimento Traghetti del Mediterraneo*, cited in footnote 123 of this Part Two, paras 65-67.

331. In discharging this task, national courts must comply with the principles laid down by the Court of Justice in the *Eesti Pagar* case law (cited in footnote 83 of this Part Two) concerning the strict interpretation of GBER conditions and the consequences of a breach thereof.

332. *See* Judgment of the Court of 23 January 2019, Case C-387/17, *Fallimento Traghetti del Mediterraneo*, cited in footnote 123 of this Part Two, paras 57-59, and Opinion of Advocate General Wahl of 13 September 2018, EU:C:2018:712.

333. Judgment of the Court of 21 November 2013, Case C-284/12, *Deutsche Lufthansa*, cited if footnote 63 of this Part Two, para. 31.

appropriate.[334] If the Commission has adopted a final compatibility decision, national courts must draw the consequences of the unlawfulness by ordering the payment of at least interest with respect to the period of unlawfulness.[335]

It is also reasonable to assume that, beyond the interplay with Commission decisions, national courts' degree of autonomy extends to other fields of private enforcement, including the choice of the most effective remedies. Case law has already clarified that EU law does not impose any conclusion that national courts must necessarily draw on the validity of acts implementing unlawful aid,[336] insofar as the objective of restoring the *status quo ante* is achieved by removing the full advantage enjoyed by the beneficiary[337] (unless it is absolutely impossible to do so).

Among the actions that can be brought before national courts, actions for damages are of particular interest in this context. Damage compensation is an exclusive remedy of private enforcement that the Commission and the Court of Justice tend to encourage, though they set precise limitations on the scope of these kinds of actions when the action is brought by potential aid beneficiaries.[338] Given the current status of EU law, however, this remedy is available only against the Member State that granted the aid,[339] unless a legal basis to bring the action against the actual beneficiary is available under national law. EU law offers no support for direct action against the actual beneficiary of the aid. Given the absence of harmonisation in this area, the principle of procedural autonomy fully applies.

This has many implications in terms of legal standing, allocation of competence, standard of proof and admissible means of proof, among other things. The only limitations derive from the principles of equivalence and effectiveness – though the principle of effectiveness is to be construed as related to the obligation to safeguard the rights of individuals, not to achieve a specific outcome. Conversely, if national law offers better protection to the interested parties, for instance, in terms of *res judicata* and limitation periods or legal standing (*e.g.*, actions are open to holders of non-economic interests), no objections can be raised, as this is a desirable situation from the standpoint of the effectiveness of State aid rules.

334. Judgment of the Court of 26 October 2016, Case C-590/14 P, *Dimosia Epicheirisi Ilektrismou AE /DEI*, cited in footnote 59 of this Part Two.
335. Judgment of the Court of 12 February 2008, Case C-199/06, *CELF II*, cited in footnote 146 of this Part Two.
336. Judgment of the Court of 8 December 2011, C-275/10, *Residex Capital IV*, cited in footnote 220 of this Part Two.
337. Judgment of the Court (Grand Chamber) of 5 March 2019, Case C-349/17, *Eesti Pagar AS*, cited in footnote 83 of this Part Two, para. 141.
338. *See* the *Asteris* case law, cited in footnote 72 of this Part Two.
339. Based on the *Francovich* and *Brasserie du Pêcheur* case law, cited in footnote 249 and 250 of this Part Two.

II THE IMPACT OF MODERNISATION ON PRIVATE ENFORCEMENT OF STATE AID RULES

In line with the analysis in Part One of this book with reference to the system of remedies in the field of public enforcement, it is worth asking whether modernisation has led to significant development of private enforcement tools or, from a different perspective, whether recent developments in these tools have been shaped by the objectives and characteristics of the modernisation initiative.

Reflection of the sort must start with the consideration that the first Private Enforcement Notice dates back to 2009, *i.e.*, well before the start of the third phase of the modernisation process. The strong, modernisation-triggered expansion of the GBER's scope, and the objective of reinforcing cooperation between the Commission and Member States, are certainly likely to have influenced the development of private enforcement. The introduction of Article 29 of Council Regulation (EU) 2015/1589 fits into this pattern. So does the 2019 Enforcement Study, which flagged that the cooperation tools were underused and the award of remedies fairly rare at national level, and which led to the adoption of the New Enforcement Notice.

As to the latter's purpose and scope, the following key points have emerged in this book's analysis: (i) the New Enforcement Notice offers useful clarification on general principles based on updated case law (2009-2019); (ii) it seeks to provide more concrete guidance on specific aspects of the various types of cases in which private parties seek remedies against the unlawful implementation of aid; (iii) it provides some clarification on the Commission's and national courts' respective roles; and (iv) it elaborates on the reinforced cooperation mechanisms introduced by Article 29 of the Procedural Regulation.

Mutual cooperation based on the duty enshrined in Article 4(3) TEU is articulated in various ways in the New Enforcement Notice, in implementation of Article 29 of the Procedural Regulation. All these ways of cooperation are, of course, independent of the possibility or obligation for national courts to refer preliminary questions to the Court of Justice, which alone is competent to interpret provisions of Union law. The analysis in this part of the book has noted the New Enforcement Notice's contribution to the proper understanding and use of the various instruments envisaged under the Procedural Regulation, namely: (i) requests for opinions from the Commission, which are essentially to be used when soft law instruments provide insufficient guidance or doubts exist as to the calculation of aid or as to the conditions for implementing approved schemes or implementing aid under previous conditional decisions;[340] (ii) requests for information on the status of proceedings pending before the Commission; and (iii) autonomous decisions by the Commission to intervene in proceedings before national courts.

It can thus be concluded that, on balance, the New Enforcement Notice – which is linked to the amendment of secondary legislation and to the New Recovery Notice,

340. It was explained in detail that this tool must not be an alternative to preliminary references to the Court of Justice and must therefore be limited to the topics indicated above or, alternatively, used as a means to better evaluate the need to address a request for interpretation to the Court.

and which represents the culmination of modernisation with regard to private enforcement – has little overall impact on the effectiveness of the system of remedies. It does not seem to have changed the percentage of successful private enforcement actions to any significant extent since its adoption.[341] It does provide useful clarification and specification but, on the whole, seems to be of little significance and innovation compared to the benchmark of modernisation. Above all, from another perspective, the changes introduced (and induced by modernisation) do not solve the problems surrounding private enforcement of State aid rules, as listed below.

341. Although no official statistics post-2019 exist, the data collected in individual jurisdictions do not seem encouraging. In Italy, the Itaca portal shows that in the period 2018-2023, 376 private enforcement actions were brought but only one concerned State aid, and was rejected because the national courts considered, at first instance and on appeal, that the contested measure did not fall within the scope of Art. 107(1) TFEU for lack of effect on trade (*see* https://itaca.europeanlitigation.eu/it/p1).

III THE PERSISTENT SHORTCOMINGS OF THE SYSTEM OF REMEDIES AFTER ADOPTION OF THE NEW ENFORCEMENT NOTICE

It has clearly emerged that private enforcement of State aid law, as currently regulated, cannot adequately compensate for the shortcomings of the system of remedies available to the Commission and cannot adequately serve the modernisation objectives. First, private enforcement does not currently offer uniform opportunities to individuals across Member States and is unlikely to develop in that direction in the near future without legislative intervention. A substantial reason for the fragmentation of private enforcement is the legal basis on which national courts adjudicate, which is usually not a specific legal basis for the purpose of private enforcement but rather administrative or civil actions conceived for other situations or general actions for non-contractual liability concerning compensation for damage. This has caused a startling lack of uniformity in the case law on State aid across the EU.[342]

Even the modernisation process has not introduced decisive changes to the regulation of private enforcement at the EU level and, reciprocally, *the evolution of private enforcement in practice has fallen short of achieving modernisation's objectives.*

The New Enforcement Notice contains no original suggestions to address the main causes of inefficiency, such as the burden of proof, the sharing of competences between civil and administrative courts, or the insufficient use of interim remedies. Moreover, the New Enforcement Notice does not fully consider, let alone leverage, the findings of the 2019 Enforcement Study, which highlighted the need for reform.

Indeed, despite the *natural progressive development* of private enforcement due to the decreasing number of individual cases examined by the Commission and the broadening of block exemptions, the number of national proceedings in which remedies are actually applied remains very limited. The Commission continues to stick to an unambitious approach: it invests in the training of national judges but fails to take legislative initiatives or at least provide clear indications capable of encouraging interested parties to start legal proceedings at national level, and it shows no attempt to develop an innovative system of remedies that takes inspiration from the synergies between private and public enforcement.

When it comes to specific remedies, legal scholars – including Pastor-Merchante, Monti and Jaeger – acknowledge the wide degree of discretion granted to national courts in choosing the adequate interim measure. In *CELF III*,[343] the Court of Justice indicated the conditions under which national courts are required to adopt interim measures but confirmed the discretionary power of national courts. Concerning recovery, neither case law nor soft law undermines national courts' procedural autonomy. Although recovery is the natural consequence of the breach of the standstill

342. Derenne and Jouve, *State Aid & National Enforcement: An Overview of EU and National Case Law*, cited in footnote 256 of this Part Two. The national reports used to compile the aforementioned article have yet to be published. They include a report on State aid private enforcement in Italy co-authored by this author (*see* footnote 256 of this Part Two).

343. Judgment of the Court of Justice (Grand Chamber) of 12 February 2008, *CELF III*, cited in footnote 146 of this Part Two.

and notification obligations and is meant to restore the situation existing before unlawful aid was granted, there is no absolute obligation for national courts to select that remedy instead of others, as there is for the Commission. As confirmed by most scholars,[344] the specific circumstances and factual background of a given case could lead national courts to order a different remedy.

But there is more. As experience in some countries shows,[345] national courts are not limited to choosing between restorative and preventive remedies; they may also order alternative or complementary redressive measures, depending on the procedural and substantive rules of the national legal system concerned.

Although this wide degree of discretion is a positive thing - as in the current situation, national experience can only enrich private enforcement solutions - the lack of ad hoc provisions in national laws weakens the system of remedies. In choosing a remedy, national courts should identify the most suitable one to accomplish the only duty they have under EU law: to safeguard the individual rights conferred on EU citizens by the Treaties.[346] As things stand, the current EU case law and legal framework merely suggest that a Member State's response to a violation of Article 108(3) TFEU should be appropriate to fulfil the above duty in a way that is consistent with the principle of effectiveness and equivalent to the same level of safeguards granted to national claims.

344. *See* Part Two, section V.E.
345. Derenne and Jouve (cited in footnote 256 of this Part Two, pp. 2-3) emphasise the great diversity of national means of recovery and the related divergencies in State aid enforcement across the EU. To provide just one example of this variety, reference can be made to a situation in which a competitor of beneficiaries of an aid scheme who does not satisfy the requirements to be granted the same aid challenges the unlawfulness of the State measure addressed to numerous beneficiaries. The national court would not dispose of sufficient information and means to order recovery from each and all the beneficiaries but could draw inspiration from the Italian Supreme Court Judgment of 20 November 2020 (commented on by M. Merola, D. Gallo, A. Cogoni and G. Bellenghi, in e-Competitions November 2020, Art. No. 107762, as cited by Derenne and Jouve, cited in footnote 256 of this Part Two, p. 15) and order that repayment be sought by means of ad hoc legislation or regulation providing for financial penalties against recalcitrant beneficiaries.
346. *See also* the Opinion of Advocate General Jacobs of 29 November 2005, *Transalpine Ölleitung*, cited in footnote 136 of this Part Two.

IV CONCLUSIONS

Substantive State aid rules are enshrined exclusively in the competition provisions of the Treaty, at least when inter-State trade is affected. Therefore, only EU law - not national law - defines the aim, scope and content of the protection afforded by State aid rules. Conversely, national law - based on the principle of procedural autonomy - establishes the legal instruments to enforce directly applicable State aid rules at national level. But, as the analysis carried out thus far shows, the distinction between EU law and national law is not that clear when it comes to understanding the consequences of an infringement of State aid rules.

Should the consequences to be drawn from the infringement be considered inherently related to the content of the substantive rules, which would imply that EU law can considerably restrain the autonomy of national courts in this field, and should procedural autonomy be confined within strict limits, as the Commission - in the New Private Enforcement Notice - seems to infer from EU case law? Or should the consequences of the infringement be considered strictly linked to the applicable enforcement procedures and tools set out at the national level? This would imply that EU law can provide guidance limited to defining substantive rules' object of protection (*i.e.*, its aim, scope and content), but that the manner through which the protection is achieved, or at least pursued, should be freely assessed by national courts based on their domestic procedural laws.

Whatever the answer to these questions, it is clear, as Jaeger puts it, that recourse to substantive national laws for the enforcement of EU law 'is not a consequence of, and cannot be justified by, the principle of national procedural autonomy' nor by any considerations related to subsidiarity in the enforcement of EU law. Hence, only two possibilities remain: either: (i) EU law merely indicates the object of protection (or the goals), and the manner of pursuing it is left to national law when Article 108(3) is invoked before national courts; or (ii) EU law indicates also the instruments by which the protection or the goal is to be pursued.

When put this way, it is undeniable that EU law does not currently indicate the instruments to use - and this gap cannot be filled by the Commission through policy acts such as the New Private Enforcement Notice or by proposing its own interpretation of the notion of procedural autonomy. And as far as case law is concerned, as demonstrated above, no conclusive indications can be drawn regarding the interpretation of the latter notion.

If this is so, it is the EU legislator's duty to have the final word on this issue. Indeed, if the EU courts push their search for effectiveness and deterrence too far, they risk going beyond what the division of competences justifies. This risk has not escaped some scholars. Jaeger is once more the most thoughtful in this respect. He observes that the case law on the private enforcement of State aid rules 'incorporates a conceptual and a practical problem'. From a conceptual perspective, national substantive law cannot determine the scope of substantive EU law, and only a uniform definition of the scope of protection in accordance with EU law can mitigate the differences in the application of State aid law in the various national jurisdictions. From a practical perspective, if national courts must draw all possible inferences from the breach of the standstill obligation in accordance with their domestic law, as held by the EU courts, this can lead national courts to interpret EU law along the lines of national law or even to bend EU law to the requirements of national law, which should not be allowed. Principles of national law might then act as a potential limit to the remedies that would be most in line with EU law.

The principle of *dolo agit qui petit quod statim redditurus est* can help illustrate this view:[347] in some jurisdictions, where this principle is applied, if a beneficiary was aware of an aid measure's unlawfulness but applied for it anyway, a claim for damages or other measures against that beneficiary before domestic courts could be upheld because of the mere fact that the beneficiary applied for the aid, regardless of any other conduct (such as the submission of an unfair bid, as in the *Breda* case), whereas this would not be possible in other jurisdictions.

Jaeger is certainly right in pointing out both the conceptual incongruencies and the undesirable consequences of the present status of EU case law and the lack of uniformity in the application of State aid rules at national level. Thus far, the dilemma has resulted only in far-from-unambiguous guidance from the EU courts and in the Commission's unfortunate attempt to bend case law in favour of its own vision.

No optimal solution for interpreting the principle of procedural autonomy exists at the moment, as either: (i) the uniform application of EU law is strengthened (especially the principle of restoring the *status quo ante* as interpreted in the EU courts' case law), with the result being that the wealth of solutions that national law can offer is lost, as is the possibility of applying the law in a way that is closer and more appropriate to a given situation; or (ii) the independence of assessment enjoyed by national courts is preserved, with the result being that a certain fracture, or at least distancing, between the substantive State aid rules and the system of remedies is accepted.

Either way comes up short. To sum up, the uniform application of State aid rules is likely to collide with the EU courts' drive to pursue the effectiveness of State aid rules, leading to unsatisfactory conceptual and practical results. As indicated above, the discretion left to national courts and the wide range of measures that the experience of national jurisprudence can offer are elements that the EU institutions should keep in mind and promote in order to *exploit the complementarity between public enforcement and private enforcement* and ultimately improve the overall effectiveness of the system of remedies.

Given the complexity of this issue and the difficulty in providing a timely, comprehensive and systematic solution through preliminary rulings, it would be extremely helpful if the EU legislator took up the challenge of reshaping the system of remedies in this field in relation not only to public enforcement but also to private enforcement. Before putting forward ideas in view of a possible reform, it is worth turning to strictly related fields of EU public competition law in search of a model to mirror – or at least some examples of alternative systems of remedies. As far as public

347. 'He who requests that which he will have to return acts by deceit'. This is a maxim originating in Justinian's *Digest* (44.4.2). *See also* Jaeger, *The CELF Judgment*, cited in footnote 168 of this Part Two.

enforcement is concerned, the most obvious reference in this regard is the recently adopted regulation on foreign subsidies, to which most of Part Three of this book is devoted. As far as private enforcement is concerned, the harmonisation achieved in public procurement law and in antitrust law deserves to be briefly analysed.

Part Three

Comparative Analysis

Introduction to Part Three

CONTENTS

This chapter introduces Part Three's comparative approach in seeking alternative models for the reform of remedies in the field of State aid. It explains how Part Three analyses the EU's recently adopted FSR and other relevant pieces of secondary law in order to identify potential avenues or models for reform.

As indicated, Part Three examines whether existing systems of remedies in the EU legal order could serve as a model or at least offer insights for a reform of the system of remedies in the field of State aid. Since foreign subsidy control is evidently the closest benchmark for State aid control, this will be the main focus, starting with an explanation of how the discipline originated and what its objectives are – a fundamental premise for understanding whether its system of remedies can serve as a valid model – and then going into detail on the founding principles of such a system and its provisions.

Faced with China's competitive pressure and economic colonialism, the Union has made a conscious choice to reject a drift of the European system towards the Chinese model of shaping competition law and policy based on political choices and geopolitical objectives. The Union has indeed favoured the harmonisation of competition systems at a global level, the export of the European model, and the limitation of public interest assessments to strategic sectors (with precise limits), while rejecting proposals to downgrade competition law. This precise rationale underpins the '*FSR*' and must guide the interpretation of the entire body of law – including the part on remedies, whose lessons can easily spill over to the contiguous area of State aid control.

It could be debated whether this precise choice to preserve the role of competition law within the Union – the consequence of, among other things, not only the economic function but also the political function of this branch of EU law[1] – has been betrayed later, when, in a world deeply marked by the war in Ukraine, the Chinese challenge was followed by the entry into force of the 2022 Inflation Reduction Act in the US.[2] Indeed, under pressure from the German and French governments, the Commission announced a relaxation of State aid policy up to 2025 to respond to the American initiative and target similar objectives.[3] Similarly, other forms of State control of the economy have been introduced or proposed. The debate surrounding the Commission's announcement, however, goes far beyond the bounds of this book, which refers

1. Competition law has indeed played a political role in European integration since the founding Treaties, serving objectives such as economic democracy, economic and social cohesion, the social dimension of the market economy and, most recently, environmental sustainability. Thus, in the EU, the protection of competition is not exclusively aimed at economic efficiency and better market structures.
2. The Inflation Reduction Act of 2022 is the most significant climate legislation in US history, offering massive funding and incentives (worth USD 369 billion) to US-based companies to accelerate the transition to a clean energy economy. The full text of the act is available at https://www.congress.gov/bill/117th-congress/house-bill/5376/text.
3. *See* the Special Address by Commission President Ursula Von der Leyen at the 2023 World Economic Forum in Davos, followed by the Speech by Executive Vice-President Margrethe Vestager in the State aid High Level Forum of Member States on 25 January 2023, available at https://ec.europa.eu/commission/presscorner/detail/en/speech_23_232 and https://ec.europa.eu/newsroom/comp/items/itemType/1067, respectively.

to foreign subsidy control only as a possible model for reform of remedies in the field of State aid.[4]

Against this backdrop, this part of the book first addresses the FSR model and then considers other potential models within the EU legal framework (specifically, in the fields of public procurement and antitrust) before embarking on a study of the possible directions a reform of the system of remedies should take. To this end, the FSR's structure and the essential features of the new control system are first briefly described following a synoptical approach, followed by an in-depth examination of the part of the FSR that addresses remedies. The similarities and differences with the State aid system of remedies are then considered, including reflections on how the two could converge and whether convergence is desirable. As regards public procurement and antitrust, a similar approach is adopted, although logically, as these areas are traditional elements of the EU system for many years, the analysis is limited to highlighting the similarities and differences with the State aid system of remedies.

4. On top of that, from a historical perspective, it is probably too early to judge the new course of aid policy announced in Vice-President Vestager's speech and to understand whether it represents a new paradigm shift in aid policy after those resulting from: (i) the 2008 financial and economic crisis; (ii) the modernisation of State aid rules; (iii) the management of the COVID-19 health crisis; and (iv) the response to the energy crisis triggered by Russia's invasion of Ukraine.

I THE FSR's STRUCTURE AND A SUMMARY OF ITS MOST SALIENT FEATURES

This chapter provides an overview of the FSR's structure and most salient features. It highlights to what extent the FSR differs from – or instead closely mirrors – State aid rules, offering insights on a possible convergence of the system of remedies in public competition law.

Before addressing the issues relevant to this book's analysis, which are those concerning enforcement and remedies, some background and contextual information is necessary to understand why the FSR is an appropriate model.

Published in the Official Journal of the EU on 23 December 2022,[5] the FSR is the final leg of a journey that began in June 2020 with the Commission issuing a white paper on the topic. Strong political support characterised this new instrument throughout the entire law-making process.[6] Based on Articles 114 and 207 TFEU,[7] the regulation has been applicable since 12 July 2023 – except for the new notification obligations, which came into effect on 12 October 2023. The FSR is considered the missing piece in the EU legal system to preserve the internal market. Indeed, through the FSR, the EU aims to bridge the regulatory gap whereby only funding granted by a Member State to undertakings operating in the internal market was subject to the Commission's scrutiny, whereas funding granted by non-EU countries escaped all scrutiny, even when it benefitted undertakings that operated in the internal market and thus produced effects within that market.

This asymmetry had long been tolerated for at least two reasons. First, the dominant view at the EU level was that State aid rules were an advantage for European companies because they ensured a fully competitive market, which in the long run would favour the emergence of the most efficient companies in Europe – companies that could be competitive also on the global market. Second, the EU's interest in attracting foreign investments played a significant role in accepting the asymmetry. Indeed, the Union has historically adopted a trade policy with a low degree of protectionism in order to create an 'open' economy capable of attracting foreign

5. Regulation (EU) 2022/2560 of the European Parliament and of the Council of 14 December 2022 on foreign subsidies distorting the internal market, OJ L 330/1, 23.12.2022, pp. 1-45.
6. Alain Alexis rightly observed that the strong political support by national governments is well illustrated by the unusual speed of the legislative process, despite the politically sensitive nature of the proposal. The Commission indeed adopted its proposal on 5 May 2021, and a final political agreement was reached on 30 June 2022. *See* A. Alexis, *The Control of Foreign Subsidies Distorting the Internal Market: The Main Amendments Introduced by the Co-legislators*, Concurrences No. 1/2023, p. 1. By the same author, *see also Foreign Subsidies Control: The New European Commission Proposal*, Concurrences No. 4/2021, p. 210.
7. Article 114 deals with the approximation of laws and belongs to Title VII of the TFEU (Common rules on competition, taxation and approximation of laws). It sets out the legislative procedure applicable to measures of approximation and harmonisation intended to establish or ensure the functioning of the internal market. Art. 207 sets out the principles applicable to the common commercial policy of the Union and the legislative procedure thereof. For a critical analysis of the legal bases of the FSR, *see* J. Smela Wolski, *Legal Basis of the Proposal for a Regulation on Foreign Subsidies Distorting the Internal Market*, European State Aid Law Quarterly (ESTaL), 2002, Issue 2, p. 153 https://doi.org/10.21552/estal/2022/2/6.

investments. Thus, the encouragement of investments from non-EU countries was one of the reasons that had held back the extension of State aid rules to foreign subsidies until the FSR's adoption.

The FSR is built around four stages of substantive legal assessment: (i) analysis of whether financial contributions fall within the notion of foreign subsidy; (ii) assessment of a given foreign subsidy's potential market distortion, whether related or unrelated to concentrations or public procurement procedures; (iii) a balancing test that examines the subsidy's negative and positive effects; and (iv) the offering of commitments or the determination of the most appropriate redressive measures to effectively remedy the distortion.

The starting point – and primary issue – of any assessment is the notion of foreign subsidy.[8] This notion has been rightfully described as an *autonomous notion of the EU legal system*,[9] and it indeed results from a combination of various elements and is thus of a hybrid nature. More in detail, it reflects, on the one hand, the definition of subsidy in the Agreement on Subsidies and Countervailing Measures ('*SCM Agreement*') concluded within the framework of GATT[10] and, on the other hand, the concept of State aid within the meaning of Article 107(1) TFEU. The legislator opted for a broad definition of foreign subsidy that covers any financial contribution from a third country that is capable of conferring an advantage to one or more undertakings or industries engaging in an economic activity in the internal market. For the FSR's purposes, it is irrelevant whether the undertaking concerned is established in an EU Member State or in a third country – as long as it is active in the internal market.[11] Indeed, the only relevant elements are the financial contribution's origin and the effects thereof within the internal market.

Despite the terminology used, which derives from Article 1 of the SCM Agreement, the concept of foreign subsidy takes its inspiration mainly from State aid law, in that it requires all the following conditions to be met: (i) a financial contribution must exist (in the very broad sense explained above); (ii) the financial contribution must be – directly or indirectly – of a public nature; (iii) the financial contribution must grant an economic advantage not achievable under market conditions to undertakings operating in the internal market; and (iv) the advantage must be selective, *i.e.*, the financial contribution targets – *de facto* or *de jure* – a limited number of undertakings or sectors.

The concept of financial contribution is illustrated through several examples, such as capital injections, grants, loans, loan guarantees, fiscal incentives, the setting

8. *See* Art. 3 FSR in combination with recitals 11-16.
9. *See* A. Becquet, *Analyse du Règlement subventions étrangères à la lumière du droit des aides d'Etat: Contexte, Objectifs, Contenu et Mise en Œuvre*, thesis presented for a master's degree in European Legal Studies from the College of Europe, 2023-2024 academic year, under the supervision of Prof. Massimo Merola, available at the College library.
10. *See* Art. 1(1.1) of the SCM Agreement, World Trade Organization (1994), available at https://www.wto.org/english/docs_e/legal_e/24-scm.pdf.
11. Consider the following examples of the FSR's application to EU companies: (i) a public holding company in a third country provides an interest-free loan to a subsidiary established in the internal market; or (ii) an EU company invests in a new business in a third country and benefits from incentives, such as temporary tax exemption.

off of operating losses, compensation for financial burdens imposed by public authorities, debt forgiveness, debt to equity swaps or rescheduling, supplies at below market price or purchases at above market price, the foregoing of revenue that is otherwise due, acceptance of liabilities, and even inadequately remunerated special or exclusive rights.[12]

All foreign subsidies that have an impact on the internal market are subject to the regulation, regardless of whether the beneficiaries are State-owned or private foreign or EU companies and, as mentioned, regardless of where their headquarters are located, on condition that they operate in the internal market. As to the link between the financial contribution and a third country, the second point (b) of Article 3(2) FSR provides the criteria for directly or indirectly attributing a financial contribution to a foreign authority. Foreign government action can be concealed behind the behaviour not only of public entities but also of private operators; therefore, State origin can be established by taking into account the *peculiarities of the legal and economic framework in place in the third country concerned.*

The FSR is a key instrument of the European trade strategy that pursues the 'open strategic autonomy' model, according to which the EU will continue to support the development of an open global economic system while protecting the internal market from commercially invasive intervention by third countries.

Until the adoption of the FSR, only the instruments envisaged under the GATT were available to address foreign subsidies (mainly the SCM Agreement) - but their scope and effectiveness are limited. The SCM Agreement applies to the import of goods into the territory of a signatory party at a dumped price due to the benefit of subsidies granted by the undertaking's country of origin but does not encompass subsidies granted to third countries' undertakings established in the internal market. Moreover, it only covers goods to the exclusion of services. The FSR (both the notification procedures and the ex-officio procedure) cannot apply to remedy alleged subsidies that would fall within the scope of WTO instruments. The strict limits of the WTO rules have been emphasised by the emergence of a new global economic landscape. Globalisation has in fact led free-market systems to compete with economies that use market instruments but that are, in reality, pervasively directed and subsidised by public authorities. It has therefore become increasingly necessary to respond to the competitive distortions caused by States 'planning' the economy behind the façade of a competitive market.

At the same time, the development of a level playing field in the global market has come to a standstill in the face not only of China's economic expansionism and the reactions it has provoked in the US and elsewhere but also of the return of protectionist tendencies fostered by populist and nationalistic movements. All this has led to a stalemate in the WTO's functioning and the failure of bilateral negotiations between the EU and some third countries. Moreover, the economic turmoil provoked by the COVID-19 pandemic - and, subsequently, by the Russian invasion of Ukraine - has

12. The reference to inadequately remunerated special or exclusive rights was added through an amendment by the European Parliament.

rendered many European companies more vulnerable, exposing them more than in the past to the risk of hostile takeovers supported by subsidies from third countries.

That said, the FSR is not meant to overlap with international trade rules but rather to complement them, with the objective of contributing to the proper functioning of the internal market and ensuring a level playing field, as clarified in Article 1 FSR.[13] Likewise, the FSR does not overlap with the foreign direct investment ('*FDI*') screening carried out by Member States and coordinated by the Commission based on Regulation (EU) 2019/452[14] – though clearly the same transactions might require notification under both the FSR and one or more national FDI rules. Moreover, recital 10 of the FSR clarifies that the regulation is without prejudice to Article 346 TFEU and the Member States' right to protect their essential security interests. Consequently, Article 28(3) FSR excludes procedures for the award of contracts covered by Directive 2009/81/EC (concerning public procurement in the fields of defence and security) from application of Chapter 4 of the FSR.[15]

Despite its undeniable specificities, the FSR mirrors the substantive and procedural rules on State aid to the widest extent possible. It introduces three instruments: (i) a preventive control procedure based on an obligation to notify concentrations (creation of joint ventures, acquisitions, and mergers) in EU territory for undertakings

13. Article 1(1) FSR delineates the subject matter of the regulation. It reads as follows:

> The purpose of this Regulation is to contribute to the proper functioning of the internal market by establishing a harmonised framework to address distortions caused, directly or indirectly, by foreign subsidies, with a view of ensuring a level playing field. This Regulation lays down rules and procedures for investing foreign subsidies that distort the internal market and for redressing such distortions. Such distortions can arise with respect to any economic activity, and in particular in concentrations and public procurement activities.

14. Regulation (EU) 2019/452 of the European Parliament and of the Council of 19 March 2019 establishing a framework for the screening of foreign direct investments into the Union, OJ L 791, 21.3.2019, pp. 1-14 ('*FDI Screening Regulation*'). Notably, however, the FDI Screening Regulation is not a suitable instrument to eliminate the asymmetry between the control of State aid within the Union and the absence of control over aid granted by third countries. The FDI Screening Regulation merely sets the framework on the basis of which Member States that have a screening mechanism in place (in accordance with the Commission's recommendations) coordinate with each other and with the Commission for coherent and more effective supervision. Moreover, its scope is limited to strategic sectors, assets and activities, such as infrastructure, critical technologies, defence, and national security. Lastly, non-investment-related subsidies fall completely outside the scope of FDI, which indeed, from a more general perspective, is not related to the notion of a level playing field.
15. Directive 2009/81/EC of the European Parliament and the Council of 13 July 2009 on the coordination of procedures for the award of certain works contracts, supply contracts and service contracts by contracting authorities or entities in the fields of defence and security, and amending Directives 2004/17/EC and 2004/18/EC, OJ L 216, 20.8.2009, pp. 76-136. Despite this exclusion, subsidies granted by third countries to defence companies with civil activities in the EU might fall within the scope of the FSR, at least in the absence of clearly separated accounts. *See* the presentation given by Alain Alexis at the 130th Global Competition Law Centre ('*GCLC*') Lunch Talk of 3 March 2023, available on the GCLC's website (https://www.coleurope.eu/research/global-competition-law-centre).

that received foreign subsidies above certain thresholds in the previous three years;[16] (ii) a preventive notification obligation for bids submitted within the framework of procurement procedures in the EU for undertakings that received foreign subsidies above certain thresholds in the previous three years; and (iii) an investigation tool that the Commission may use *ex officio*.

However, the notification obligation is triggered only if two thresholds are exceeded: the first concerns the undertaking's turnover (or in the case of public procurement, the contract value) and the second concerns the amount of foreign financial contributions, which must be analysed by the Commission to determine whether they are to be classified as foreign subsidies.

The turnover threshold is set at EUR 500 million for concentrations,[17] which, depending on the type of concentration at stake (joint venture, acquisition or merger), refers to the joint venture, the acquired undertaking (target) or one or more of the merging undertakings. For public procurement procedures, the threshold is EUR 250 million in terms of the value of the contract to be awarded. The financial contribution threshold for concentrations is set at EUR 50 million in the three years before the related agreement is entered into and refers to the aggregate amount of contributions received from third countries by the merging undertakings, by the acquirer(s) and the acquired undertaking, or by the undertakings creating the joint venture and the joint venture (*i.e.*, all the undertakings concerned taken together).

For public procurement procedures, the financial contribution threshold is set at EUR 4 million per non-EU country in the three years before a bid is submitted and refers to the economic operator concerned, including, where applicable, its main subcontractors and suppliers involved in the tender. Where the procurement is divided into lots, a notification obligation arises if: (i) the overall estimated value of the procurement net of VAT exceeds the EUR 250 million threshold; and (ii) the value of the lot or the aggregate value of all the lots to which the tenderer applies is equal to or greater than EUR 125 million.

As with State aid, filing a notification triggers a standstill obligation on the parties involved until the Commission's decision. Although the thresholds are quite high, the FSR also empowers the Commission to require undertakings involved in sub-threshold mergers to file a notification if it suspects that an involved undertaking has received foreign subsidies, and the Commission thus deems it necessary to assess possible distortive effects in the internal market. Interestingly, as to public procurement procedures that do not trigger a notification obligation, bidders must submit a statement to the contracting authority or entity in which they list all foreign financial

16. The FSR requires notification procedures for concentrations under the EU's Merger Regulation and under the FSR to run in parallel. However, a different timeline might result from potential procedural circumstances or from different theories of harm identified by the Commission.
17. This is twice the threshold envisaged for target undertakings under the EU's Merger Regulation. The cutoff for mergers under the FSR will certainly be the turnover threshold given that the second threshold – *i.e.*, the one referring to the value of the financial contribution – is not that high (EUR 50 million). This will result in only the most relevant mergers (a few dozen per year based on statistics) falling under the FSR's scope.

contributions received in the previous three years and confirm that those contributions are not notifiable.[18]

When the notification obligation applies,[19] the Commission must first ascertain the existence of a foreign subsidy within the meaning of the FSR and then, if existence is confirmed, determine whether it generates a direct or indirect distortion in the internal market.[20] Contrary to Article 107(1) TFEU, which includes distortion of competition among the constituent elements of State aid, Article 3 FSR does not include distortion of the internal market in the definition of the notion of foreign subsidy, nor are the concepts of foreign subsidy or distortion of competition included in the definitions of Article 2 FSR. Instead, distortion of the internal market is envisaged as a requirement for the Commission to intervene.[21] This choice is not without practical consequences, as explained in the next section.

18. The control of foreign subsidies in the context of public procurement procedures is justified because although the public procurement regulations in force at European level are aimed at maintaining a level playing field and full competition in tenders, they do not contain provisions preventing companies supported by foreign subsidies from being awarded European contracts. Art. 69(4) of Directive 2014/24/EU is an emblematic provision in this respect: it allows contracting authorities to reject an excessively low tender for the sole reason that it is supported by unlawful State aid, but it does not appear to envisage the possibility of tenders supported by foreign subsidies. Therefore, regulatory asymmetry can be found here, too.
19. The post-filing phase consists of a two-step process: (i) a preliminary examination phase of 25 business days for concentrations and 20 business days (which can be extended by 10 business days) for public procurement procedures; and (ii) an in-depth investigation phase of 90 business days for concentrations (which can be extended by 15 business days if the undertakings involved propose commitments) and 110 business days for public procurement procedures (which can be extended by 20 business days in exceptional situations).
20. Reference also to the distortions caused 'indirectly' by foreign subsidies was added during the debate before the European Parliament. Recital 9, introduced by the co-legislators, clarifies that the FSR should be applied and interpreted in light of the relevant Union legislation, including that relating to State aid, mergers and public procurement. Therefore, the concept of indirect distortion can be interpreted in light of the Commission's practice in the field of State aid (*see* recital 9 of the FSR).
21. In order to determine whether a given subsidy is distortive, the FSR provides some indicators as to whether the subsidy strengthens the competitive position of the undertaking concerned. These indicators are related to the subsidy's characteristics (amount and nature), the undertaking's situation, the market(s) concerned, and the purpose for which the subsidy was granted and is used.

II ENFORCEMENT-RELATED FEATURES OF THE FSR

This chapter examines the enforcement-related features of the FSR, including the submission of notifications, investigations and fact-finding, and the submission of commitments to address potential distortions of the internal market. It then discusses how these features can influence the effectiveness of remedies.

II.A Introductory Remarks

The approach followed by the EU legislator in the FSR when it comes to the assessment of the distortion of competition plays a role in shaping enforcement methods and the effectiveness thereof. First, State aid falls within the definition of Article 107(1) TFEU only if it distorts competition, whereas the concept of foreign subsidy is broader in this respect because it does not require a test of a foreign subsidy's distortive nature; in any case, the difference in practice is negligible from this perspective, as the distortive nature of State aid is largely presumed under Article 107(1). On the contrary, the fact that an analysis of a given foreign subsidy's distortive nature lies outside the very notion of foreign subsidy is likely to result – and, in the first months of application of the FSR, has indeed resulted – in a more thorough test than is normally the case for State aid: a test more akin to that carried out for the purposes of antitrust enforcement.

Second, foreign subsidies are not *prima facie* incompatible with the Treaty precisely because, contrary to the case with State aid, a test for distortive effects is not part of the notion of foreign subsidy. This implies that it will be more difficult for national courts to play a role in applying the new framework. They could theoretically ascertain a breach of a notification obligation when applicable, but no remedy would be applicable given that: (i) a foreign subsidy is not, as such, incompatible with the Treaty; and (ii) national courts lack the power to ascertain distortive effects or to impose fines for breach of procedural requirements. These issues are examined in more detail in section III.B.5 below.

Under the FSR, one of the factors that can exclude the existence of a foreign subsidy's distortive effects is if it does not exceed the EUR 5 million threshold in three consecutive tax years (*de minimis* rule of a substantive nature). This rule does not, however, legitimise foreign subsidies whose amount remains below the threshold; rather, it takes the form of a rebuttable legal presumption. Therefore, the Commission can intervene in cases in which foreign subsidies total under EUR 5 million if evidence of distortive effects exists.

If the existence of a foreign subsidy and an ensuing market distortion is established, the Commission – as it does with the compatibility test for State aid – balances that distortion against any positive effects (including certain policy objectives, *e.g.*, supporting the development of remote regions or addressing climate change). Through this balancing test, referred to as the 'EU interest test', the Commission can further promote its policy objectives, such as job creation, climate neutrality and digital transformation. The broad scope of such a balancing test could allow the Commission to apply criteria similar to those envisaged under Article 107(2) and (3) TFEU in order to exclude certain categories of foreign subsidies from the application of remedies.[22] This includes the possibility of considering foreign subsidies granted during economic crises to be legitimate if they are temporary and proportionate to the event being addressed.[23]

In any case, it is to be expected that this balancing test will be particularly complex in light of recent developments in State aid enforcement within the Union, which have led to a clear relaxation of control. The traditional rigorous control seen in the application of derogations established in the Treaty has in fact been tainted by the consideration of interests linked to crisis management and the resilience of the economy as a whole. Furthermore, these interests are not necessarily specific or targeted; indeed, they are sometimes traceable to general economic policy considerations. One of the main challenges posed by the FSR will therefore be how to adapt the control of foreign subsidies to the changing degree of rigour that characterises modern enforcement of the EU's State aid rules if the rationale of eliminating the asymmetry between the control of aid granted by Member States and that granted by third countries is to be kept unchanged.

Likewise, another main challenge will be how to prevent different instruments from overlapping in a way that ends up discriminating against operators that benefit from foreign subsidies. One example is the rule in the Temporary Crisis and Transition Framework ('*TCTF*')[24] that allows the Commission to authorise aid to offset advantages granted by a third country. Coordination between the two instruments – *i.e.*, the FSR and the TCTF – will be necessary to avoid a situation in which FSR remedies are applied to foreign subsidies that have already been offset through aid authorised under the TCTF.

If the Commission decides that a foreign subsidy's distortive effects prevail, it may: (i) prohibit the transaction or the award of the contract under scrutiny; (ii) accept the commitments proposed by the parties; or (iii) impose remedies of various kinds (examined in detail in the next chapter). The Commission may also impose fines for breaches of procedural requirements: up to 10% of the aggregate turnover of the undertakings involved for breach of the standstill requirement or failure to notify; and

22. *See* R. Luja, *The Foreign Subsidies Regulation*, in European State Aid Law Quarterly: European State Aid Law Quarterly (ESTaL), 2021, Issue 2, p. 191 https://doi.org/10.21552/estal/2021/2/3, where the author underlines that the vague concept of balancing in Art. 6 could lead the Commission to be guided by the State aid framework or other key policy objectives and thus allow foreign subsidies that stimulate economic activities supported by the EU and that contribute to reaching certain goals set by the Union, such as the Green Deal objectives. *See also* N. Cunha Rodrigues, *Filling the Regulatory Gap to Address Foreign Subsidies: The EC's Search for a Level Playing Field Within the Internal Market*, in *Extraterritoriality of EU Economic Law*, 2021, 224, where the author points out that the different treatment of State aid and foreign subsidies could result in a violation of the principle of non-discrimination established in WTO rules.
23. *See* European Commission, *White Paper on Levelling the Playing Field as Regards Foreign Subsidies*, COM/2020/253 final, p. 16, where it is stated that 'subsidies granted to remedy a serious national or global disturbance of the economy do not fall in this category, if they are limited in time and proportionate to remedy the respective disturbance'.
24. Temporary Crisis and Transition Framework for State aid measures to support the economy following the aggression against Ukraine by Russia, OJ C 101, 17.3.2023, pp. 1-17.

up to 1 % of the total turnover of the undertaking(s) involved, plus default interest for each working day of delay, for incorrect, incomplete or misleading information.

As to ex-officio procedures, the Commission may initiate an investigation if it suspects that an undertaking operating in the EU received a foreign subsidy that distorts the internal market – regardless of whether the foreign subsidy relates to a notifiable concentration or public procurement procedure – but the notification obligation was not complied with, or the suspected foreign subsidy distorts the market in other ways unrelated to concentrations or public procurement procedures. Ex-officio procedures are thus supplementary and residual in nature, but they encompass whatever distortions remain unaddressed by other procedures – their scope is therefore very broad. An ex-officio investigation may cover foreign subsidies granted up to five years before the FSR came into effect if the market distortion persists at the time of the review.[25]

Several enforcement-related aspects were clarified with the adoption of the FSR's implementing rules in July 2023 ('*FSR Implementing Regulation*').[26] The FSR Implementing Regulation set out detailed procedural rules concerning: (i) submission of notifications (*see* section II.B below); (ii) conduct of inspections and interviews in the context of in-depth investigations (section II.C); (iii) submission of commitments to address potential distortions of the internal market (section II.D); and (iv) access to the Commission's file and, more generally, rights of defence (section II.E). Since these rules are only very partially and indirectly relevant for this book's purposes, they are examined here only to the extent strictly necessary, *i.e.*, in relation to the aspects that appear to be directly or indirectly relevant for the assessment of the system of remedies discussed in the next chapter. This very focused examination concerns the four main areas indicated in points (i)–(iv) above.

II.B Submission of Notifications

The thresholds over which prior scrutiny is required for mergers and public procurement procedures are defined directly in the FSR in terms of financial contribution amount and the merger or contract value. Nonetheless, the Implementing Regulation sets out – by means of notification forms[27] – which types of financial contributions must be disclosed to the Commission upon notification and above which threshold. Therefore, whereas the FSR sets the notification thresholds in terms of the volume of financial contributions received, the rules of procedure provide details on which

25. As usual, the procedures comprise two stages: a preliminary examination and an in-depth investigation. However, there are no time limits for completing them.
26. Commission Implementing Regulation (EU) 2023/1441 on detailed arrangements for the conduct of proceedings by the Commission pursuant to Regulation (EU) 2022/2560 of the European Parliament and of the Council on foreign subsidies distorting the internal market, OJ L 177, 12.7.2023, pp. 1-44.
27. The notification forms can be found in Annexes I and II to Commission Implementing Regulation (EU) 2023/1441 on detailed arrangements for the conduct of proceedings by the Commission pursuant to Regulation (EU) 2022/2560 of the European Parliament and of the Council on foreign subsidies distorting the internal market, respectively Form FS-CO and Form FS-PP.

financial contributions must be taken into account and reported when notification is required.

Specifically, in the case of mergers, the form requires disclosure of foreign financial contributions equal to or in excess of EUR 1 million that fall into any of the categories under points (a)-(d) of Article 5(1) FSR (*i.e.*, categories of foreign subsidies most likely to distort the internal market, for which a presumption of distortion applies, as clarified in Article 5(2)).[28] In the case of public procurement procedures, the form requires an assessment of the distortion by foreign subsidies by evaluating indicators of distortion and whether the tender is unduly advantageous in relation to the works, supplies or services concerned.[29] Only financial contributions falling within the scope of points (a)-(c) and (e) of Article 5(1) FSR must be reported by parties under this section of the form. For foreign contributions not falling into these categories (for which no presumption applies), the FSR Implementing Regulation requires an overview of foreign financial contributions equal to or in excess of EUR 1 million granted to the notifying parties in the three years preceding notification.[30] Additionally, for public procurement procedures meeting the thresholds in Article 28(1)(a) and 28(2) FSR in which foreign financial contributions reportable under Article 28(1)(b) FSR have been granted to the notifying parties in the three years preceding notification, each party must indicate whether they have individually been granted foreign financial contributions equal to or in excess of EUR 1 million.[31]

The scope of information required is very broad, even when compared with merger control or FDI screening. Indeed, in merger control and FDI screening, the scope of information required is – rightfully – limited to the information relevant for the substantive test (*i.e.*, in merger control, information to determine whether the merger concerned constitutes a significant impediment to effective competition; and in FDI screening, information to determine the likelihood of the investment affecting national security or public order/policy). For instance, under merger control rules, notifying parties must submit extensive information on affected markets only, *i.e.*, relevant information to assess the merger's unilateral and coordinated effects. Under FDI screening rules, information requirements touch on the target's activities, the identity

28. Point 5.1 in Annex I (Form FS-CO) to Commission Implementing Regulation (EU) 2023/1441 on detailed arrangements for the conduct of proceedings by the Commission pursuant to Regulation (EU) 2022/2560 of the European Parliament and of the Council on foreign subsidies distorting the internal market. On this point, it is worth noting that the draft FSR Implementing Regulation required disclosure of all financial contributions exceeding EUR 200,000 individually and EUR 4 million in aggregate per third country and per year.
29. Point 3.1 in Annex II (Form FS-PP) to Commission Implementing Regulation (EU) 2023/1441 on detailed arrangements for the conduct of proceedings by the Commission pursuant to Regulation (EU) 2022/2560 of the European Parliament and of the Council on foreign subsidies distorting the internal market. On this point, it is worth noting that the draft FSR Implementing Regulation required disclosure of all financial contributions exceeding EUR 4 million in aggregate per third country in the three years preceding notification.
30. *Ibid.*
31. Point 3.1 in Annex II (Form FS-PP) of Commission Implementing Regulation (EU) 2023/1441 on detailed arrangements for the conduct of proceedings by the Commission pursuant to Regulation (EU) 2022/2560 of the European Parliament and of the Council on foreign subsidies distorting the internal market.

and control chain of purchasers, and the target's relationship with public entities, *i.e.*, relevant information to assess the strategic nature of the assets/activities concerned. Conversely, under the FSR implementing Regulation, the substantive test for foreign subsidies is so broad that no workable delimitation of the information requirement can be drawn from it.

As a result, notifying parties need to report all foreign financial contributions granted by whatever entity to the purchaser or target in the previous three financial years, except for contributions falling below the threshold mentioned above (*i.e.*, below EUR 1 million). For each financial contribution, the notifying parties must indicate its purpose and economic rationale, the granting authority, the conditions attached to it, the resulting benefit, the contribution's selectivity, information and supporting documents on the third country providing the contribution, the contribution amount, and the main elements related to the contribution (*e.g.*, interest rates and duration in the case of a loan). Additional information is required in relation to bidding processes, financial contributions linked to concentrations, and financial contributions to ailing undertakings.[32] In the latter case, notifying parties must also indicate whether the undertaking – in the period in which it was ailing – received any foreign financial contributions that may have contributed to restoring its long-term viability; and if a restructuring plan is in place that is capable of contributing to the undertaking's long-term viability and entails a significant own contribution by a notifying party, it is required to provide details thereof.[33] Document production requirements are equally broad and invasive.[34]

The burden on notifying parties is obviously high, and stakeholders have to a large extent considered it inappropriate;[35] although it is true that there is the possibility

32. Stakeholders have criticised several aspects of the information requirements, such as the difficulty for purchasers or bidders to obtain information on targets and/or on other bidders early enough in the pre-notification or notification process.
33. Point 3.1 in Annex II (Form FS-PP) of Commission Implementing Regulation (EU) 2023/1441 on detailed arrangements for the conduct of proceedings by the Commission pursuant to Regulation (EU) 2022/2560 of the European Parliament and of the Council on foreign subsidies distorting the internal market.
34. To provide just one example, the FSR Implementing Regulation requires notifying parties to provide all due diligence reports and external assessments of whatever nature (*e.g.*, economic, legal, tax, market and strategic consultancy reports).
35. Criticism has focused first and foremost on the legislator's choice to require information concerning all financial contributions, rejecting the option of putting any self-assessment burden on the notifying companies concerning the classification of a financial contribution as a foreign subsidy. The notification burden is expected to be especially heavy for private equity firms, and indeed it would be worth having special rules to alleviate this burden for them. In fact, not only will they be subject to scrutiny in several transactions but they will also need to notify financial contributions provided to all their portfolio companies. Stakeholders have also advocated – as a second-best option if notifying parties are not entrusted with a self-assessment to determine which financial contributions are to be considered foreign subsidies – that at least some categories of financial contributions that would make the notification obligation particularly intrusive (*e.g.*, tax incentives, tax exemptions, and transactions with public entities) be excluded from the notification obligation, with these categories left to the parties' self-assessment (obviously under their own responsibility, since the Commission could fine them for providing partial, deficient or misleading information). It has also been noted that while the thresholds might appear clear on paper, in practice it will likely be challenging to ascertain that a party has not exceeded the threshold of EUR 4 million over three years in a given country – even more so

of obtaining waivers from the Commission during the pre-notification phase, it remains to be seen whether the possibility for the Commission to grant waivers will represent an adequate (and uniformly applied) solution to this problem.[36] Given their nature and scope, the information and documentation requirements risk being especially burdensome for big companies (including EU companies) and private equity firms with global activities.[37] All this burden, which has prompted criticism of the FSR,[38] is at first sight hardly reconcilable with Article 47(1)(a) FSR and recital 40, which both require the utmost account to be taken of the goal of limiting administrative burden for notifying parties.[39] One possible reading of the choice made by the Commission in setting out the

if all financial contributions need to be included, even if they are unrelated to the concentration/bid concerned. Finally, many stakeholders have contested the type of information required for each financial contribution, which includes the contribution's purpose and economic rationale and any conditions attached to the contribution's use. *See* the contribution submitted by the European Competition Law Forum (ECLF) on the Draft Implementing Regulation Concerning Foreign Subsidies, available at https://www.europeancompetitionlawyersforum.com/submissions. *See also* the contributions submitted by Mayer Brown and WilmerHale (among others), available on their websites at https://www.mayerbrown.com/en/insights and https://www.wilmerhale.com/en/insights-and-events, respectively.

36. The Commission may indeed dispense with the obligation to provide information or documents if compliance is unnecessary for the case assessment or is not reasonably available. However, in the absence of 'safe harbours' and definitions of what is 'unnecessary' or 'not reasonably available', not to mention an absence of best practices, no guarantee exists of a reasonable and expeditious granting of waivers and, even more importantly, of a uniform approach. To prevent this, DG Comp should urgently make its waiver practice public.
37. *See* footnote 35 of this Part Three.
38. *See* U. Solstész, *Foreign Subsidies Control: A Bureaucratic Monster?* European State Aid Law Quarterly (EStaL), 2023, Issue 2, p. 175 https://doi.org/10.21552/estal/2023/2/7. The author emphasises that the Commission has tried to alleviate the information burden 'by striving for convergence between the EUMR and the FSR tracks as far as jurisdictional questions are concerned (notion of concentration, control, ownership, notifying parties, *etc.*)' and by 'granting some (limited) exemptions from the notification obligation' but considers these efforts insufficient. In addition to contesting the breadth of information required by the FSR Implementing Regulation, Solstéz conveniently points out that the FSR Implementing Regulation 'does not address the relationship between the FSR and free trade agreements with non-EU States (FTAs)'.
39. *See* Art. 47(1)(a) and recital 40 FSR.
    Article 47(1)(a) states as follows:

    > The Commission is empowered to adopt implementing acts concerning … the form, content and procedural details of notifications of concentrations pursuant to Article 21, including a possible simplified procedure, *taking utmost account of the goal of limiting administrative burden for notifying parties pursuant to Article 21 of this Regulation and Article 4 of Regulation (EC) No 139/2004* [emphasis added] … .

    Recital 40 states as follows:

    > The need to address foreign subsidies distorting the internal market is especially salient in public procurement, given its economic significance in the internal market and the fact that it is financed by taxpayer funds. The Commission should have the power, upon notification prior to the award of a contract, to examine information on foreign financial contributions to the participating economic operator in the context of a public procurement procedure. Prior notifications should be mandatory above a threshold set in this Regulation to capture economically significant cases *while minimising the administrative burden and not hindering the participation of SMEs in public procurement.* … The Commission also has the right to request the prior notification of a foreign

information requirements in the FSR and in the FSR Implementing Regulation is that identifying which financial contributions are to be classified as foreign subsidies is far from easy, especially in the initial phase of application of the regulation, in view of (among other things): (i) the absence of established practice or interpretative filters deriving from case law; and (ii) the hybrid nature of these notions, which lie at the crossroads between State aid rules and international trade law.

However, stakeholders' criticism in the aftermath of the publication of the draft FSR Implementing Regulation focused essentially on the information/administrative burden but often failed to consider the new rules' overall benefit in terms of levelling the playing field and the need to offset undue and often concealed advantages. Therefore, an appropriate balance between opposite interests will have to be struck, and the Commission is expected to be as transparent as possible and to make its enforcement policy public with respect to, among other things, the granting of waivers.[40] Nonetheless, it must be recognised that the information and documentation requirements - which were confirmed and to some extent even broadened in the definitive FSR Implementing Regulation - will allow the Commission to carry out an independent assessment of subsidy amounts and address, as much as possible, concerns about the possibility to gather sufficient information for the FSR's enforcement. This is particularly important because accurate fact-finding is key to setting out appropriate and proportional remedies.

For this reason, the FSR Implementing Regulation's rules are more substantive than formal in nature. They are intended to *deter circumventing behaviour* and thereby reinforce the equal treatment of State aid and foreign subsidies, in view of the greater difficulty for the Commission to autonomously gather information on the latter in view of its decision on potential remedies. It is also true, however, that once experience is gathered in the enforcement of the FSR and the FSR Implementing Regulation, it should not be impossible to reach a compromise that can alleviate the administrative burden - so broadly and harshly criticised by stakeholders - while reassuring the Commission that it will be able to use the necessary tools and information to accomplish its new task, for effective enforcement is in everyone's interest.[41]

> financial contribution during a public procurement procedure despite its estimated value being below the notification thresholds. *The Commission should endeavour to limit interference with public procurement procedures, by taking into account how close the date of the award of the contract is when deciding whether to request such prior notification* [emphasis added].

40. Nina Niejahr has suggested setting out objective criteria to make the concession of waivers more transparent and predictable. For instance, except in exceptional circumstances, waivers could apply to financial contributions to entities belonging to the same group as the notifying party but with no activities in the notifying party's NACE codes or in related markets. Likewise, waivers could apply to financial contributions resulting from sales to/purchases from a single third country up to a given threshold (safe harbour) and to tax incentives/exemptions not directly benefitting the notifying parties or their controlling companies. *See* the presentation given at the 130th GCLC Lunch Talk of 3 March 2023, available on the GCLC website at https://www.coleurope.eu/130th-gclc-lunch-talk-draft-foreign-subsidies-implementing-regulation-path-enforcement.
41. *See* M. Merola and A. Cogoni, *Foreign Subsidies and Financial Contributions: Much Fine-Tuning Ahead*, in Competition Law & Policy Debate, 2023, Volume 8, Issue 1, where a possible solution

II.C Investigations and Fact-Finding

The Commission encourages notifying parties to engage in pre-notification discussions based on a draft notification form, as it is good practice in the context of merger control.[42] Albeit not mandatory, pre-notification contact is considered extremely valuable for both the notifying parties and the Commission. To incentivise companies to pre-notify, the Commission underlines that pre-notification could result in a significant reduction in the amount of information required. Indeed, as discussed above, the Commission can grant waivers and dispense with the obligation for parties to submit certain information early in the process. This is a potentially important tool to focus notifying parties' efforts on information that is truly necessary for examination of their case.

These rules do not have a direct impact on the system of remedies but, if anything, could be relevant for the submission of commitments and thus for redressive measures to be negotiated during review procedures. Indeed, the pre-notification phase is not meant to carry out an early assessment of the foreign subsidy's impact on

---

is considered. The article focuses on what appears to be the most controversial issue in this current phase: the quantity and type of information required in the notification process with regard to financial contributions received by notifying parties in the previous three years. It analyses the rationale and related risks of the Commission's choice to require the notification of foreign financial contributions rather than foreign subsidies, evaluates the possible alternative paths proposed during the public consultation, and concludes by proposing a solution for the reduction of administrative burden on undertakings based on two fundamental requirements: first, undertakings should be required to notify only foreign subsidies - not financial contributions - when they relate to concentrations (alternatively, the self-assessment should concern only certain kinds of measures, *e.g.*, the provision and purchase of goods and services, and certain tax measures); and second, as a counterbalance to this autonomy granted to undertakings, they should be required to provide a general description of financial contributions that cannot be classified as foreign subsidies. This approach could be further fine-tuned in the future with the adoption of exemptions based on the Commission's practice, *e.g.*, by introducing: (i) instruments like the GBER or 'safe harbours'; (ii) 'whitelisted' subsidies (*i.e.*, subsidies granted by non-EU countries with effective State aid control mechanisms); and (iii) an *ex-post* assessment with the involvement of national authorities and courts.

Another key contribution to alleviating burden on both companies and the Commission will be the Commission's indication of priority areas/cases on which the Commission will focus its scarce resources, especially in the initial period. However, a clear definition of priorities might reduce administrative burden and make the system easier to administer only with regard to the handling of complaints submitted by companies. Indeed, the Commission has no flexibility with regard to complaints submitted by Member States and mandatory notifications: in those cases, it will have no choice but to take a decision.

Finally, as Solstéz rightly pointed out, another means of alleviating burden for both companies and the Commission would be to draw up a safe harbour list of third countries that have signed some sort of free trade agreement (FTA) with the EU. According to Solstéz, this list should include at least EEA Agreements, the EU-UK Trade and Cooperation Agreement, and Stabilisation and Association Agreements containing an explicit prohibition on State aid similar to that under EU law and an institutional enforcement mechanism. *See* Solstész, *Foreign Subsidies Control: A Bureaucratic Monster?*, cited in footnote 38 of this Part Three.

42. Overall, the process set out in the FSR Implementing Regulation mirrors EU merger control rules to some extent: the timelines and pre-notification phase are aligned, and the notification form is modelled, to the extent possible, on that used for merger control. However, the information required is substantially different from what parties must submit under the EUMR.

competition in the internal market, but rather to ensure a smooth information-gathering process and dispel doubts on jurisdictional issues, as well as to coordinate FSR proceedings with other pending reviews concerning merger control and FDI screening. Therefore, pre-notification rules are not relevant for assessing the effectiveness of enforcement and remedies, which is the subject of this book, except for the fact that skilful use of the pre-notification tool will allow notifying parties to *identify, at an early stage of the process, the commitments that might be necessary to obtain clearance.*

II.D Submission of Commitments to Address Potential Distortions of the Internal Market

The topic of commitments is obviously very relevant when examining the effectiveness of enforcement and the related system of remedies. In this respect, a fundamental difference exists between State aid rules and the FSR.

In the field of aid, remedies are essentially restorative measures provided for in the case of unlawful and incompatible aid (primarily recovery and alternative remedies in the limited cases where they are possible, as well as ancillary remedies, all of which are examined in Part One of this book; together with remedies which may be ordered by national courts, mainly of a preventive or compensatory nature, examined in Part Two). Remedies of this kind clearly differ from the measures (*i.e.*, conditions or prospective remedies) which may be imposed in the context of a compatibility assessment ('*conditional decisions*'). In fact, the latter measures are often negotiated between the Member State concerned and the Commission, but it is ultimately in the Commission's power to impose any measures concerning the method of granting the aid or the aided project which it considers necessary to ensure the aid's compatibility. Moreover, the Commission is not bound by any pre-defined list of possible conditions, as no list is provided under the Procedural Regulation or its implementing rules.[43]

Moreover, the FSR provides a list of remedies (examined in detail in the next chapter) and substantially blurs the distinction between restorative remedies and other remedies (redressive and even prospective remedies to some extent). Moreover, again as better explained in the next chapter, the same remedies apply across all types of procedures, whether notification-based or *ex officio*. Nevertheless, the FSR Implementing Regulation regulates the submission of commitments only in relation to procedures under Chapters 3 and 4 of the FSR, thus excluding ex-officio procedures. Conversely, in the field of State aid, conditional decisions - *i.e.*, decisions imposing prospective remedies - can be adopted also within the framework of *ex officio* investigations concerning unlawful aid.

This is a significant feature of the FSR because it can only mean that the legislator has seen the remedies under Article 7 FSR as a full set of remedies, which are restorative or redressive/prospective in nature according to the circumstances. The same measures are typically those that the undertakings concerned can propose as

43. Council Regulation (EU) No 2015/1589 of 13 July 2015, OJ L 248/2015, p. 9, and Commission Regulation (EU) No 2015/2282 of 27 November 2015 amending Regulation (EC) No 794/2004 as regards the notification forms and information sheets, OJ L 325, 10.12.2015, p. 1.

commitments within the framework of notification procedures for concentrations or public bids. For the rest, the FSR Implementing Regulation deals only with purely procedural matters, such as the time limit and the procedure for proposing commitments with a view to remedying a distortion in the internal market, which are of no relevance to this book's purposes and are thus not examined here.

II.E Access to the Commission's File and Rights of Defence

Article 20 of the FSR Implementing Regulation contains provisions concerning the right to access the Commission's file (under Article 42(4) FSR) during investigations governed by the FSR. Article 20(2) specifies that this right does not concern internal documents exchanged between the Commission Services and authorities of Member States/third countries and related correspondence.

Under Article 20(3) and (4), the Commission must provide: (i) a non-confidential version of all documents mentioned in the statement of grounds on which the Commission intends to adopt a decision; (ii) a list of all documents in the Commission's file; and (iii) all documents on its file submitted by information providers,[44] without any redactions, but under terms of disclosure to be set out in a Commission decision.[45] The terms of disclosure must entail that access to documents be granted only to a limited number of specified external legal, economic and technical experts, which/who must be undertakings, employees of undertakings or in a situation comparable to that of undertakings' employees. Additionally, Article 20(4)(c) includes further provisions for when specific external legal or economic counsel or external technical experts subsequently enter into an employment relationship with the undertaking under investigation, either while the investigation is ongoing or in the three years following the end of the Commission's investigation.

Disclosure is also subject to stricter safeguards.[46] During public consultation on the draft FSR Implementing Regulation, the access-to-file provision was widely criticised for the very broad exclusion under Article 20(2) and for its inconsistency with Article 42(4) FSR, which excludes only Commission documents and correspondence with Member States but not correspondence with third countries.[47] Moreover, some stakeholders considered the proposed limitation concerning external legal and economic counsel unjustified and the procedure under Article 20(6) and (7) too

44. The Commission may decide not to disclose certain documents or to disclose partly redacted documents if it determines that non- or partly redacted disclosure is needed to duly take into account the harm the information provider would likely suffer from disclosure.
45. The draft FSR Implementing Regulation envisaged compliance only with terms of disclosure which could appropriately safeguard the protection of business secrets and other confidential information; it did not indicate terms of disclosure to be set out in a Commission decision.
46. However, under Art. 20(6) and (7), the specified external legal and economic counsel and technical experts may make a reasoned request to the Commission for access to non-confidential versions of certain documents, with a view to making the documents available to the undertaking under investigation.
47. *See* the contributions submitted by ELCF and Association des Avocats pratiquant le droit de la concurrence, March 2023, p. 4, available at https://www.apdc.fr/.

complex.[48] Despite the extensive criticism, the broad exclusion is seemingly confirmed in the definitive FSR Implementing Regulation.

In addition to the access-to-file provision, the FSR Implementing Regulation contains a few provisions on rights of defence. Especially relevant here are the provisions concerning ex-officio investigation procedures. Article 8 allows undertakings under investigation and third parties (including Member States and the third country that granted the foreign subsidy) to submit their views in writing to the Commission within the time limit fixed by the Commission, which is generally one month from the opening of an in-depth investigation; Article 17(1) provides undertakings under investigation the same opportunity after the Commission informs them of the grounds on which the Commission intends to adopt its decision. The latter provision also requires the Commission to set a time limit of no less than ten working days for the undertaking under investigation to submit its observations in writing.[49]

During the public consultation, it was pointed out that these rights of defence are inadequate to enable the Commission to consider all relevant aspects of a case, let alone safeguard an investigated undertaking's rights of defence.[50] Interestingly (for this book's purposes), the Commission was asked to replicate the rights-of-defence provisions found in antitrust and merger control rules rather than those found in State aid rules: specifically, it was suggested that the FSR Implementing Regulation include the possibility to request oral hearings and state-of-play meetings and to introduce the role of a Hearing Officer.[51] However, stakeholders' criticism concerning the draft FSR Implementing Regulation's content did not lead to any amendments in the final text as to the shortcomings identified.

An experienced and attentive reader cannot fail to notice the discrepancy between, on the one hand: (i) Article 7 FSR, which lists a panoply of remedies and is inspired by merger control and antitrust experience; and, on the other hand (ii) the FSR's - and, even more so, the FSR Implementing Regulation's - provisions on rights of defence and the right to access the Commission's file, which instead refer to the (much criticised) regulation of the rights of interested parties in State aid proceedings, with the only difference being the right to submit observations (within as few as ten working days) on the grounds on which the Commission intends to adopt its decision under Article 17 of the FSR Implementing Regulation (as indeed no similar provision exists in the State aid Procedural Regulation).

There is no doubt that this discrepancy constitutes a serious weakness in the newly introduced rules on foreign subsidies. This deficiency needs to be corrected through an overall reform aimed at harmonising the system of remedies in public

48. *See* the contributions submitted by McDermott Will & Emery and Clifford Chance, respectively (McDermott Will and Emery, *A Global Law Firm* (mwe.com) and Clifford Chance | International Law Firm | Global Law Experts?).
49. Notably, this provision on specifying a time limit was not included in the draft Implementing Regulation but was included in the final text.
50. *See* the contributions submitted by the American Chamber of Commerce to the European Union and the European Federation of Pharmaceutical Industries and Associations, July 2023, p. 4, available at https://www.amchameu.eu/.
51. *See* the contributions submitted by ELCF and Association des Avocats pratiquant le droit de la concurrence, March 2023, p. 2, available at https://www.apdc.fr/.

competition law, as discussed in Part Four of this book. Nevertheless, a positive aspect from a rights-of-defence perspective is that the Commission has the power to adopt restorative or redressive measures[52] only at the end of in-depth investigations, in accordance with Article 11(2) and (3) FSR – even if the redressive measures are based on commitments offered by the parties concerned. This should at least guarantee interested third parties that they will be granted the possibility to submit observations in accordance with Article 10(3)(d) FSR.

52. Although the FSR refers to the whole list of measures under Art. 7 as redressive measures, there is no doubt that Art. 7 enumerates also a number of measures, such as the repayment of distortive subsidies, that would be more precisely classified as restorative measures. This aspect is illustrated in the next chapter.

III THE FSR's SYSTEM OF REMEDIES

This chapter analyses the system of remedies envisaged under the FSR (both primary and ancillary remedies), highlighting the system's coherence, originality and flexibility and its anchoring on the principles of effectiveness and proportionality. It compares the FSR's system of remedies with that of State aid rules, highlighting potential areas for improvement and convergence.

III.A General Remarks

To understand the FSR's system of remedies, it is first necessary to dive into some basic ideas underpinning the enforcement of the regulation's substantive rules.

First, the FSR is meant to complement the existing set of rules to prevent distortions of the internal market. Thus, it should be interpreted and enforced in light of the relevant EU legislation, especially that relating to State aid, mergers and public procurement.[53] This principle extends to the field of measures (referred to as 'redressive measures' under Article 7 FSR) intended to remedy distortions caused by foreign subsidies. The combination of Union traditions, enforcement policies and expertise in applying remedies in these three areas of EU law is liable to produce a stimulating and, in a certain sense, innovative system of remedies.

Second, since the Union cannot require third countries granting foreign subsidies to recover them from the beneficiary, the FSR departs significantly from the intra-Union model centred on the absence of penalties and on the recovery of unlawful aid as the natural consequence of unlawfulness.[54] However, taken alone, this pragmatic consideration does not seem to explain the innovative features of the FSR's system of remedies. A much more straightforward solution would have been to refer to the well-known alternatives to recovery in State aid law or to extend the use of countervailing duties, or even to establish that subsidised undertakings must prove that they have repaid the aid back to the granting authority if they want to continue doing business in the EU. In other words, the difficulty in monitoring effective repayment is

53. *See* recital 9 of the FSR.

54. EU law has no effect on third countries that provide a subsidy. Therefore, EU law cannot guarantee recovery of a subsidy from the body or authority that granted it, as is the case for State aid. In this respect, *see* N. Cunha Rodrigues, *Filling the Regulatory Gap to Address Foreign Subsidies: The EC's Search for a Level Playing Field within the Internal Market*, Extraterritoriality of EU Economic Law, Springer, Cham 2021, p. 219. Moreover, an order to repay a subsidy might not be effective against companies with their head office in a third country – all the more so if the company is under State control in that country. Furthermore, transnational enforcement of EU law has already shown its limits in the application of antitrust penalties to foreign companies and can create significant political tension with the third country concerned. *See* R. Luja, *The Foreign Subsidies Regulation*, in European State Aid Law Quarterly (EStAL), 2021, Issue 2, pp. 187-199 https://doi.org/10.21552/estal/2021/2/3. However, a restitution order or other restorative remedies imposed on companies might be effective because, in this way, the companies concerned are given the opportunity to avoid structural measures that could jeopardise their activity in the EU's internal market through commitments aimed at eliminating distortion of competition.

not the only reason that prompted the EU legislator to design a varied and sophisticated system of remedies in the FSR.

Besides, the usefulness of such a system of remedies with respect to aid granted by Member States had already been tested by the Commission in the context of some sectoral rules, in particular in the air transport sector, which Article 7 FSR mirrors, systematises and develops.[55] These regulatory references are particularly relevant because they concern provisions that pertain to restorative remedies - not to conditions, corrective measures or burdens that might be established during an investigation for the purpose of rendering a corporate transaction or State intervention compatible with the Treaty.

Interestingly, the Commission's final proposal and the FSR's definitive text make instead no reference to the examples of remedies stemming from the Rescue and Restructuring Guidelines[56] and the Broadband Guidelines[57] - nor to those stemming from the important projects of common European interest (IPCEI) Communication[58] and the GBER,[59] which were referred to several times during preparatory works.[60] The

55. The rules referred to here are those set out in the regulations mentioned in recital 71 of the FSR. The most important and closest precedent is Regulation (EU) 2019/712 of the European Parliament and the Council of 17 April 2019 on safeguarding competition in the air transport sector, OJ L 123, 10.5.2019, pp. 4-17, Arts 11 et seq. of which empowers the Commission to impose redressive measures against third-country air carriers benefitting from competition-distorting measures adopted by the third country to the detriment of Union air carriers. Such measures may take the form of financial obligations or operational constraints - such as the suspension of concessions, licences or other rights - of equivalent or lesser value to the benefit enjoyed. Redressive measures must not exceed what is strictly necessary to offset the harm to European carriers and may be limited in time or to a specific geographical area. The other two regulations mentioned in recital 71 are: (i) Council Regulation (EEC) No 4057/86 of 22 December 1986 on unfair pricing practices in maritime transport, OJ L 378, 31.12.1986, pp. 14-20, which empowers the Commission to impose countervailing duties on foreign shipowners which are found liable for unfair injurious practices (and which might be supported by subsidies from their home countries); and (ii) Regulation (EU) 2016/1035 of the European Parliament and of the Council of 8 June 2016 on protection against injurious pricing of vessels, OJ L 176, 30.6.2016, pp. 1-20, which empowers the Commission to impose border fees or equivalent alternative measures on shipbuilders from third countries which are found liable for unfair pricing that is detrimental to European industry.
56. Guidelines on State aid for rescuing and restructuring non-financial undertakings in difficulty, OJ C 249, 31.7.2014, pp. 1-28.
57. Guidelines on State aid for broadband networks, OJ C 36, 31.1.2023, pp. 1-42.
58. Communication from the Commission on the criteria for the analysis of the compatibility with the internal market of State aid to promote the execution of important projects of common European interest, OJ C 528, 30.12.2021, pp. 10-18.
59. Regulation (EU) 2023/1315 of 23 June 2023 amending Regulation (EU) 651/2014 declaring certain categories of aid compatible with the internal market in application of Articles 107 and 108 of the Treaty and Regulation (EU) 2022/2473, OJ L 167, 23.6.2023, pp. 1-90.
60. European Commission, *White Paper on Levelling the Playing Field as Regards Foreign Subsidies*, COM/2020/253 final, p. 19; and Impact Assessment in Commission Proposal for Regulation (EU) 2022/2560 on foreign subsidies distorting the internal market, COM/2021/223 final, 5.5.2021, p. 9. Legal scholars have referred to other pieces of soft law which allegedly could likewise have inspired the EU legislator when drafting Art. 7 FSR. M. Schonberg, for instance, refers to the bail-out aid to financial institutions during the financial crisis (Commission Communication on the return to viability and the assessment of restructuring measures in the financial sector, OJ C, 19.8.2009, pp. 9-20) and to the emergency recapitalisation measures during the COVID-19 pandemic (Temporary Framework for State aid measures to support the economy in the COVID-19 outbreak, OJ C 91I, 20.3.2020, pp. 1-9, as amended).

reason seems obvious: the legislator, having chosen to erase the difference between restorative remedies and redressive measures and thereby provide a single list of remedies that can be used also in the case of *ex officio* procedures, preferred to refer only to precedents that are of substantive relevance from this perspective - not to others that concern aid compatibility assessments.

Third, the legislator took a more cautious approach to foreign subsidies compared to the Treaty's approach to State aid. Indeed, as highlighted in the previous sections, the FSR itself clarifies that - unlike State aid granted by a Member State, which is in principle incompatible with the internal market unless a derogation applies - foreign subsidies are not generally prohibited.[61] Although this statement oversimplifies the legal approach, it is true that the extent of the harm caused by foreign subsidies to the internal market must be carefully ascertained, which is not the case for State aid.[62] This approach is also reflected in the balancing test. Indeed, the Commission, having precisely ascertained the harm to the internal market, can more precisely weigh this factor against the positive effects of a given foreign subsidy; what is more, the positive effects to be taken into account relate not only to the Union's policy objectives, such as environmental protection, the promotion of research and development and regional development but also to the strengthening of subsidised economic activities within the common market. Here too, the economic analysis of the subsidy's effects will presumably be more sophisticated than in the case of State aid because the balancing test applies in all cases as opposed to only some particular exemptions, as in the case of State aid.[63]

61. *See* recital 17 of the FSR.
62. The statement oversimplifies the legal approach because, in reality, the conditions related to the impact on the market that a State support measure must meet to be considered State aid - *i.e.*, that it must distort competition and must affect trade between Member States - are already laid down in Art. 107(1) TFEU. Thus, an aid measure falls within the definition of State aid in the Treaty only if it produces distortive effects; if this condition is not met, the measure does not fall within the definition and is not considered incompatible. However, as is well known, EU practice and case law have greatly simplified the standard of proof in relation to this condition, which is presumed to be met whenever the aid concerned impacts a sector open to competition. Conversely, although the FSR envisages a non-exhaustive set of indicators/assumptions to determine the existence of distortion when it comes to foreign subsidies (essentially because of the lack of transparency that comes with foreign subsidies, which can make it difficult to identify and quantify a subsidy's impact on the internal market), the Commission must normally prove such distortion. Certain categories of foreign subsidies, just like certain types of State aid, are likely to create distortions in the internal market because of their very nature, and this entails a presumption of distortion. For instance, this is the case with unlimited guarantees (*i.e.*, guarantees without any limitation as to their amount or duration) and export financing aid (*see* recital 20 of the FSR). In normal cases, however, the Commission must consider several indicators - *e.g.*, the subsidy amount compared with the target's purchase price (in the case of a concentration) or the contract value (in the case of a public procurement procedure), the type of subsidy, and the market's characteristics, including the existence of barriers to entry or overcapacity - and has the burden to prove distortion of the internal market. Foreign subsidies to a single undertaking that do not exceed EUR 4 million over three consecutive years or fall below the threshold set for SGEIs by Art. 3(2) of Regulation (EU) No 1407/2013 per third country over the same period are considered not to distort the internal market within the meaning of the FSR (recital 19).
63. *See* recital 21 of the FSR. Furthermore, unlike State aid rules, the FSR entitles any natural or legal person to submit information on a given foreign subsidy's positive effects, and the Commission

Lastly, the precise determination of the (hypothetically) negative result of the balancing test is considered the starting point in determining 'redressive measures' within the meaning of Article 7 FSR – which in reality includes, as explained in detail below, not only redressive measures in the exact meaning of the word but also restorative measures. Once again, such an approach diverges from that adopted in the field of State aid, where the assessment of possible remedies is restricted by the almost absolute obligation to repay the financial advantage (and only the financial advantage, except for indirect aid) gained by the beneficiary.

In short, redressive measures are part of the FSR's balancing test.[64] Indeed, when assessing the appropriateness of redressive measures and determining how invasive they should be, the Commission needs to balance a foreign subsidy's negative effects in terms of market distortion with the potential boost to economic activities in the EU and other relevant Union policy objectives.[65] This more flexible and economically more sophisticated approach is confirmed by the fact that, even if the subsidy recipient commits to repaying it, the Commission is obliged to accept that commitment only if it can ascertain that repayment will: (i) remedy the distortion in full; (ii) be executed in a transparent and verifiable manner; and (iii) be effective in practice.

A final preliminary issue worth mentioning here is the interplay between merger control rules and the FSR when it comes to subsidies related to acquisitions of stakes in the EU. Situations in which an acquisition is prohibited or cleared without commitments under merger control rules do not raise difficulties, as: (i) in the former situation, application of the FSR would be of no use; and (ii) in the latter situation, there is no doubt that redressive measures could be imposed under the FSR if deemed appropriate, even if merger clearance was granted without conditions. Indeed, the test under the FSR is different from that under the EU's merger control regulation ('*EUMR*'). In other words, there is a double barrier (arising from the EUMR plus the FSR) that a prospective deal must comply with in order to be considered compatible with the internal market. Merger clearance with commitments is a more problematic situation, as the possibility to cumulate remedies under the FSR and under merger control rules can give rise to controversy.

---

should take due account of these views when carrying out the balancing test. Hence, even from a procedural standpoint, the FSR is characterised by more openness and a greater focus on the objective of achieving the best possible assessment of each case.

64. This can clearly be inferred from recital 21 of the FSR, which also states that the 'balancing can lead to the conclusion not to impose redressive measures where the positive effects of the foreign subsidy outweigh its negative effects'. Furthermore, the recital clarifies that positive effects are not only those related to the development of the relevant subsidised economic activity on the internal market but also 'broader positive effects in relation to the relevant policy objectives, in particular those of the Union. Those policy objectives can include, in particular, a high level of environmental protection and social standard, and the promotion of research and development'. This clarification was added during the trialogue at the initiative of the European Parliament, which advocated expanding the benefits to be considered so as to include environmental and social policy objectives.
65. *See* recital 16 of the FSR. W. Weiß expresses the same opinion in his article *Ex Officio Third Country Subsidies' Review*, European State Aid Law Quarterly (ESTaL), 2022, Issue 2, p. 136 https://doi.org/10.21552/estal/2022/2/4, written before the FSR's enactment (while debate in the trialogue was pending).

For instance, it has been observed that given the 'level playing field' and 'fair competition' imperatives underlying the FSR, one might query whether a different threshold for intervention and a different calibration of remedies from what is envisaged under the EUMR should apply. Nevertheless, a cumulation of remedies cannot be excluded, as the applicable standard under the FSR seems to be one based on effects on rivals rather than on potentially significant impediments to effective competition (which is associated with the consumer welfare standard under merger control rules).[66]

Without having to take a position on this issue here, it seems logical that in enforcing the FSR, the balancing test – and thus the calibration of remedies – must take into account the commitments entered into by the undertakings concerned in the context of merger control. Some commitments might well be insufficient or even ineffective for the FSR's purposes, but others may affect the balancing of interests or even entirely eliminate the market distortion that justifies the adoption of remedies under the FSR.

Similar considerations apply to the interplay between foreign subsidy control under the FSR and FDI screening. Again, it seems logical that the calibration of remedies under the FSR take into account, whenever possible, any conditions already imposed on the undertakings concerned in the context of FDI screening in one or more Member States. Some conditions might well be ineffective or insufficient for the FSR's purposes, but others may affect the balancing of interests or be relevant when considering the most appropriate redressive measures under the FSR. Indeed, it might well happen that commitments accepted, or redressive measures imposed, when reviewing a concentration under the FSR lead to a different evaluation of the same concentration under FDI screening mechanisms and *vice versa*.[67]

The cooperation mechanism established by the FDI Screening Regulation can provide the Commission the opportunity to flag the existence of previously imposed redressive measures to the Member State(s) reviewing a given transaction under national FDI regulations; and *vice versa*, undertakings involved in an FSR procedure might very well flag to the Commission that conditions have already been imposed at national level which, in their opinion, can be relevant for the assessment of competition distortion or for the balancing test under the FSR.

It is worth noting in this respect that recital 36 of the FDI Screening Regulation stipulates that, for investments in the form of a concentration falling within the scope of the EUMR, FDI screening should be without prejudice to the application of Article

66. M. Schonberg, *The EU Foreign Subsidies Regulation: Substantive Assessment Issues and Open Questions*, European State Aid Law Quarterly (ESTaL), 2022, Issue 2, p. 152 https://doi.org/10.21552/estal/2022/2/5.
67. F. Genoni, in his thesis presented for a master's degree in European Legal Studies from the College of Europe, 2023-2024 academic year, expresses the same opinion and warns of the risk of antinomies in the parallel application of the FSR and national FDI screening mechanisms. The paper is available at the College library. *See also* C. Dackö, C. Brodin and A. Arlebo, *The FDI Screening Mechanisms and the Draft EU Foreign Subsidy Regulation: Potential Conflicts of Interests and in Application*, ZEuS, 25, No. 3 (2022), pp. 505-518.

21(4) EUMR[68] and that the two regulations should be applied in a consistent manner.[69] Although the extent of this obligation is anything but clear, as observed by legal scholars,[70] at least the legislator expressly stated that a coherent interpretation of legitimate interests within the meaning of the third paragraph of Article 21(4) and of the grounds for screening set out in Article 1 of the FDI Screening Regulation is warranted. No similar provision exists to regulate the relationship between the latter and the FSR, especially when it comes to the imposition of redressive measures under Article 7 FSR.

Having made this clear, an in-depth examination of the mutual interference between the remedies envisaged in different regulations belonging to public economic and competition law merits independent research; it is indeed not addressed here, where the remedies envisaged in the FSR and in other regulations are discussed only for comparison purposes in advocating for a reform of remedies in State aid law. From this perspective, what is interesting to emphasise is the adaptability of the system of remedies envisaged by the FSR, which allows the Commission – when calibrating remedies – to logically take into consideration both the possible conditions imposed within FDI screening frameworks and the possible measures justified by overriding national interests under Article 21(4) EUMR (despite such measures not being expressly envisaged therein).

---

68. Article 21(4) EUMR states that, notwithstanding paras 2 and 3 of that same Art. 21, which stipulate that the Commission has sole jurisdiction to take the decisions provided for in the EUMR and that no Member State may apply its national legislation on competition to any concentration that has an EU dimension, 'Member States may take appropriate measures to protect legitimate interests other than those taken into consideration by this Regulation and compatible with the general principles and other provisions of Community law.' Furthermore, it states that '[p]ublic security, plurality of the media and prudential rules shall be regarded as legitimate interests within the meaning of the first subparagraph' and that '[a]ny other public interest must be communicated to the Commission by the Member State concerned and shall be recognised by the Commission after an assessment of its compatibility with the general principles and other provisions of Community law before the measures referred to above may be taken.'
69. Recital 36 states as follows:

> When a foreign direct investment constitutes a concentration falling within the scope of Council Regulation (EC) No 139/2004, the application of this Regulation should be without prejudice to the application of Article 21(4) of Regulation (EC) No 139/2004. This Regulation and Article 21(4) of Regulation (EC) No 139/2004 should be applied in a consistent manner. To the extent that the respective scope of application of those two regulations overlap, the grounds for screening set out in Article 1 of this Regulation and the notion of legitimate interests within the meaning of the third paragraph of Article 21(4) of Regulation (EC) No 139/2004 should be interpreted in a coherent manner, without prejudice to the assessment of the compatibility of the national measures aimed at protecting those interests with the general principles and other provisions of Union law.

For the sake of clarity, the current consolidated version of the FDI Screening Regulation (https://eur-lex.europa.eu/legal-content/EN/TXT/?uri=CELEX%3A02019R0452-20211223) does not appear to have recitals, whereas the initial legal act (https://eur-lex.europa.eu/legal-content/EN/TXT/?uri=CELEX%3A32019R0452) does.
70. *See* G. Pitruzzella, *Foreign Direct Investment Screening in the EU*, in Foreign Direct Investment Screening. Il controllo sugli investimenti esteri diretti, ed. G. Napolitano, Il Mulino, Bologna, 2020, in particular pp. 63-69.

III.B Exegesis of the FSR's Provision on Remedies

This chapter is structured as follows: first, it identifies and discusses three key features of the system of remedies in the FSR (sections III.B.1 to III.B.3) and then carries out an in-depth examination of the various types of remedies envisaged in the regulation (section III.B.4).

III.B.1 The Same Remedies Apply Across All Kinds of Procedures

The first point to be noted from an analysis of Article 7 FSR is that it is part of Chapter 1, which sets out the general provisions applicable to all procedures governed by the regulation. This is extremely relevant, as Article 7's particularity lies precisely in the fact that it considers the restorative and redressive measures usually envisaged for notification procedures, *i.e.*, within the framework of a negotiated enforcement model between Member States and the Commission, applicable to *ex officio* procedures and to the related system of remedies.

In commenting on this provision, M. Schonberg goes even further and reasons that, when it comes to determining what redressive measures are suitable to address distortions of competition if the latter affects a concentration or a competitive tender procedure, 'it is difficult to envisage how anything short of prohibiting that concentration and public contract award would be sufficient to address those distortions'.[71] According to the author, the application of the kinds of structural and behavioural remedies set out in the FSR 'seems appropriate in the context of the ex-officio tool, where the Commission is investigating the broader competition and trade distortions caused by a foreign subsidy'.[72]

In essence, Schonberg relies on this argument to infer that assessment of the effects of a given subsidy 'must necessarily go beyond the specific market for the acquisition or the competitive tender procedure concerned'[73] and thus extend to all markets in which the undertakings concerned operate within the internal market. Otherwise, the structural and behavioural remedies set out in the FSR would become superfluous in relation to concentrations and public procurement procedures. The same argument can be used in the opposite sense to conclude that the structural and behavioural remedies set out in Article 7 are particularly well suited for other market distortions examined during *ex officio* procedures.

More generally, unlike in State aid procedures, negotiated enforcement is the rule within the framework of foreign subsidies, as redressive measures are imposed only if the Commission considers that the commitments offered do not fully and effectively remedy the distortion. Thus, an order of priority exists in the FSR, with commitments taking priority over restorative or redressive remedies imposed by the Commission. This is entirely new in EU competition law for an *ex officio* procedure.

71. Schonberg, *The EU Foreign Subsidies Regulation: Substantive Assessment Issues and Open Questions*, cited in footnote 66, p. 149.
72. *Ibid.*, p. 151.
73. *Ibid.*, p. 149.

One important reason that might explain this divergence from State aid investigation procedures is that the FSR *ex officio* procedure applies, first and foremost, to cases that are not covered by any notification obligation but that are nevertheless deemed liable to distort the internal market. Indeed, the *ex officio* procedure is essentially intended for this reason - whereas recourse to the *ex officio* procedure for non-notified foreign subsidies in breach of the obligations laid down in the FSR is not expressly envisaged in the FSR and may be inferred only by way of interpretation.[74]

In essence, the FSR *ex officio* procedure combines some features typical of the administrative procedure for unlawful aid with others more characteristic of merger control, such as the possibility of offering commitments. If a foreign subsidy beneficiary offers commitments and the Commission deems them appropriate and sufficient to fully and effectively remedy the distortion, the Commission may adopt an implementing act, in the form of a decision, in order to make the commitments binding on the beneficiary undertaking.[75]

On this point, the FSR *ex officio* procedure is similar to the procedure for existing State aid. In the latter context, the Commission has permanent monitoring power, which can lead to the opening of an *ex officio* investigation. When this happens, the preliminary investigation can end either with the opening of a formal investigation under Article 108(2) TFEU or, if the Member State concerned agrees on the appropriate measures proposed by the Commission to make the existing aid compatible with the internal market, with a decision that makes these measures binding on the Member State.

When it comes to foreign subsidies, however, the preliminary investigation is a negotiated procedure which, for obvious reasons, involves the beneficiary undertaking - not the third country concerned - and in which the initiative of proposing commitments (or appropriate measures to eliminate the distortion of competition) lies with the undertaking itself, not with the Commission. Nevertheless, the monitoring power vested in the Commission and the final decision whereby the commitments are made binding on the country concerned mirror the rules on existing aid.

This similarity between the possible outcome of the first phase of FSR *ex officio* procedures and the first phase of existing aid procedures is not surprising given that foreign subsidies, unlike new aid (or aid projects), are not in principle incompatible with the internal market. In other words, just as existing aid, they benefit from a presumptive or provisional legitimacy, which can be reversed only by a finding of distortive effect in an investigation and/or a finding of a lack of sufficient contribution to the common interest.

74. Indeed, Art. 26 FSR (Fines and periodic penalty payments applicable to concentrations) stipulates that - in addition to the penalties envisaged under Art. 17 for intentionally or negligently supplying incomplete, incorrect, or misleading information in replying to requests for information or for other cases of non-cooperation in investigations or failure to comply with a Commission decision - the Commission may impose fines on undertakings that intentionally or negligently supply incorrect or misleading information in a notification. The same rules apply in the context of public procurement procedures (Art. 33 FSR).

75. Article 7(2) FSR.

In this regard, it must also be pointed out that foreign subsidy procedures involve the undertakings concerned - not third countries, over which the Commission lacks enforcement powers.[76] Indeed, one must ask whether this difference between State aid control and foreign subsidy control justifies or even necessarily entails a different setup of the system of remedies.[77] Of course, a clear difference exists between a Commission procedure against (or upon the initiative of) a Member State, in which the interested parties are considered third parties, and a procedure involving companies as the main parties. This difference requires a different setup of the various procedural steps that can lead to the application of remedies. However, when it comes to the nature of such remedies, there is no compelling reason why the remedies should be substantially different, let alone outright divergent. On the contrary, various elements can be made in support of an objective of convergence.

First, there is no reason Article 108(2) TFEU should be interpreted as allowing the Commission to order recovery of aid but not to order different measures, as long as they are related to the subsidised project or aimed at framing its effects.[78] Indeed, Article 108(2) simply sets out the objective of altering or abolishing incompatible aid. Second, from a practical standpoint, nothing would prevent the Commission from ordering a subsidised undertaking, at the end of a State aid investigation, not to repay the aid but to take steps to neutralise its distortive effects.[79] And conversely, from a theoretical standpoint, nothing would have prevented the FSR's legislator from limiting the Commission's discretionary power in adopting remedies by referring to recovery or restorative measures alone.

76. During the preparatory works that led to the FSR's enactment, the issue of which parties could be involved in a review of third-country subsidies was raised. Unlike State aid reviews, in which basically only the granting Member State is involved in the review, foreign subsidy reviews cannot involve third countries granting subsidies, as the Commission has no power over them. Conversely, as pointed out in the Impact Assessment (cited in footnote 60 of this Part Three), the EU has jurisdiction over companies operating in the EU's internal market. Thus, the Commission is competent to impose redressive measures on them, irrespective of their ownership or establishment, as is the case in EU competition law (*see* Weiß, *Ex Officio Third Country Subsidies' Review*, cited in footnote 65 of this Part Three).
77. This aspect is very useful to bear in mind for Part Four of this book, which examines the prospects for reforming the State aid system of remedies with a view to achieving convergence between the rules on State aid and the rules on foreign subsidies - thereby progressing towards a single system of remedies in public competition law.
78. This issue is especially relevant when it comes to discussing the avenues for reform of the State aid system of remedies; it is therefore examined in greater detail in Part Four.
79. Some authors express a different opinion: Weiß, for instance, considers that the difference in decision-making between State aid control and foreign subsidy control can be easily explained non only 'by the different subjects of the proceedings', but also by the different aim, namely by the fact that the aim of State aid rules is to approve or prohibit national aid, whereas the FSR is concerned with offsetting the adverse effect of foreign subsidies on competition in the internal market (Weiß, *Ex Officio Third Country Subsidies' Review*, cited in footnote 65 of this Part Three). This is a debatable issue, which is discussed in more detail in Part Four when the potential avenues for reform are examined and the grounds for a differing conclusion are set out. In any event, all authors, including Weiß, concur that redressive measures 'must be tailored precisely to the distortion of competition triggered by the subsidy'.

III.B.2 The Concept and Role of Repayment under the FSR

Another factor of particular analytical importance is the inclusion in Article 7 FSR of a closing provision - not by chance positioned as the last paragraph - whereby the Commission accepts (or more correctly, must accept) repayment of a foreign subsidy with interest as a remedy only if the following requirements are met: the repayment is transparent, verifiable, effective and able to mitigate the risk of circumvention.

Given the difficulty in monitoring effective recovery and in avoiding the risk of circumvention in relation to foreign subsidies, it is reasonable to expect that repayment will seldom meet the requirements under the last paragraph of Article 7. Even more interestingly, subsidy repayment - despite retaining priority over other remedies when offered by the recipient concerned - is placed on the same footing as other remedies. Thus, *no conceptual difference exists between them*. This clearly indicates that repayment is not seen as the natural and unavoidable consequence of granting a distorting subsidy, unlike - once again - the case of unlawful and incompatible State aid.

As to the requirements with which an offer to repay a subsidy must comply for it to be binding on the Commission (*i.e.*, transparency, verifiability, and ability to prevent or mitigate the risk of circumvention), the first two are self-explanatory and represent a need for clarity with respect to both the outside world and the Commission, which must be able to carry out its checks. As to the requirement that the offer must be able to prevent or mitigate the risk of circumvention, upon closer inspection it appears to be a form of the verifiability requirement: indeed, it requires verifying that the burden of restitution/repayment is not placed on parties that do not operate in the market (or operate in a different market from the one in which the distorting effects occurred) or that are unable to comply with it, which would nullify its effects. Given that the FSR departs from the State aid principle of repayment as the natural and unavoidable consequence of the granting of unlawful and incompatible aid, the Commission should be put in a position to carry out this verification effectively.[80]

80. State aid practice has shown just how ineffective the principle that recovery of aid is the natural and inevitable consequence of its unlawfulness is. Two examples, among many others, serve to illustrate this. The first can be taken from the restructuring of large companies of national interest in distress in the air transport sector. The most recent Commission decision in this respect was adopted on 29 March 2023 in relation to Alitalia. The Commission concluded that a State loan of EUR 400 million granted by Italy in 2019 to Alitalia Società Aerea Italiana S.p.A. and its wholly owned subsidiary, Alitalia CityLiner S.p.A., was unlawful under EU State aid rules. Italy was therefore required to recover the unlawful aid, plus interest, from Alitalia. However, Alitalia had been placed into special bankruptcy proceedings under Italian bankruptcy law back in 2017, following which its main assets had been divested. Moreover, the Commission had already found in September 2021 that ITA Airways, which had acquired most of Alitalia's assets in 2021, could not be considered Alitalia's economic successor and therefore was not liable for repayment of the unlawful aid received by Alitalia. Hence, the Commission concluded that Alitalia - not ITA - was liable for repayment of the aid. This is a recurrent finding when it comes to the recovery of State aid in the air transport sector. Many other examples of the same approach exist in the Commission practice. Recovery from the company being liquidated is of course a purely formalistic solution, as it has no impact on market conditions - and, in most cases, the company will be unable to repay the aid. A second example can be taken from the determination of the amount to be reimbursed in the case of indirect aid. After some hesitation

Additionally, all redressive measures imposed must be proportional to the distortion allegedly caused by the foreign subsidy concerned. This again differs from the State aid domain, where repayment of the full aid amount is presumed to be proportionate and no proof to the contrary is accepted.[81] Along the same lines, under the FSR, unlike in the State aid domain, the Commission has an obligation to choose the remedies which are least burdensome for the undertaking under investigation. Its assessment in this respect is also subject to judicial review, with the EU courts arguably holding full jurisdiction in that regard.

Interestingly, the flexibility and sophistication of the FSR's approach to redressive measures does not at all entail a wavering or softening of enforcement; on the contrary, it is the result of a concern for effectiveness which pervades the whole foreign subsidy control system, given the difficulties inherent in dealing with measures adopted by third countries rather than Member States. However, this concern for effectiveness is opportunely balanced with a concern for proportionality in remedies, with a view to not discouraging investments in the Union and to preserving the openness of the internal market.[82]

It can be inferred from the above that, when dealing with the FSR's system of remedies, the EU legislator decided to discard the principle of absolute impossibility developed by the case law and soft law on State aid.[83] Absolute impossibility is linked with the idea that recovery is the natural consequence of the unlawful nature of the aid. As such, it is therefore irreconcilable with proportionality. This is illustrated by the fact that the case law on State aid recovery has invariably refused to recognise any role whatsoever for the principle of proportionality, as it would be illogical to consider recovery disproportionate no matter the specific circumstances of a given case. The underlying reason for this is that recovery is not a penalty but the mere consequence of the need to restore the conditions that existed before the aid was granted. A large part of the case law on State aid recovery – including all the developments concerning the relation between recovery and insolvency – is based on these ideas.[84]

In the same vein, proportionality is also difficult to reconcile with the idea that Member States that receive a recovery order are bound by an obligation of result – at least if the result to achieve is rigidly equated with offsetting the financial amount of the

---

in the case law, the EU courts have clearly opted to calculate reimbursement based on the aid's nominal amount. This trend is discussed at length in Part One of this book; *see* Part One, section I.A.2.8.

81. This approach is only but strengthened by the fact that, after a period of uncertainty, the Court of Justice eventually opted for a nominal concept of repayment, corresponding to the financial burden borne by the State plus interest (*see*, among others, Judgment of the Court of 21 December 2016, Case C-164/15 P, *European Commission v. Aer Lingus Ltd and Ryanair Designated Activity Company*, EU:C:2016:990).

82. This is clear from the FSR's general structure and several specific provisions that strengthen the Commission's decision-making power when it comes to imposing penalties (*see*, *e.g.*, recitals 32-33 of the FSR).

83. *See* Part One, sections I.A.2.7 and I.A.2.8.

84. To avoid useless repetitions, *see* Part One, sections I.A.2.6, I.A.2.7 and I.A.2.8 for a complete overview of the State aid case law related to proportionality and absolute impossibility.

aid.[85] The decision to depart from these established principles in the system of remedies for foreign subsidies represents the EU legislator's precise choice to have a different concept of effectiveness and a different definition of the result to achieve when compared to the State aid *acquis*. In essence, the result to achieve is forfeiture of the economic advantage caused by the foreign subsidy and restoration of undistorted market conditions. Alternatively, if the foreign subsidy under investigation generated efficiencies, the result to achieve is the best economic setup from a Union interest standpoint, taking into account that the market's proper functioning is considered the primary mechanism to that effect (first-best approach).

In short, the rationale is to re-establish a level playing field from a more substantive rather than formal perspective, including by taking due account of the consumer welfare standpoint – and therefore at no cost. From a substantive standpoint, one must look at the subsidy's concrete effects on the market. Additionally, one must consider the possibility of eliminating those effects or re-establishing conditions as equivalent as possible to those prevailing before the subsidy was granted (only in this way can one explain the decisive downgrading of the remedy of recovery in a strict sense). The consideration of 'at no cost' can be explained by the fact that the Commission, in weighing the remedies against the Union interest, is expected to also seek to preserve the possible beneficial effects of a given subsidy (as a subsidy could give rise to economically virtuous conduct even when its negative effects outweigh its positive effects).

Arguably, if the undertaking concerned is at risk of insolvency, the Commission must assess on a case-by-case basis whether the insolvency is due to: (i) repayment of the subsidy; or (ii) imposition of remedies that seriously jeopardise the undertaking's economic equilibrium and its possibility of remaining on the market. Furthermore, all factors must be weighed against the Union's interest. The concept of effectiveness must therefore be duly analysed in this context: the Commission will give preference to remedies that most effectively achieve the desired objective – as determined on a case-by-case basis following the balancing test – and that are transparent and verifiable.

To achieve this concept of effectiveness, the EU legislator swept away any difference between prior authorisation procedures initiated upon notification and *ex post* procedures initiated *ex officio* when it comes to the determination of remedies. In other words, the system of remedies envisaged under the FSR is a combination of restorative and redressive or even prospective remedies, jointly referred to in Article 7 FSR as redressive measures, whereas in the field of State aid, prospective remedies are applied only in authorisation procedures in the case of notified aid, and restorative remedies – primarily recovery – are the only remedies available in the case of *ex officio* procedures for unlawful aid, to the exclusion of other redressive measures.

It should be noted right at the outset that the existence of unlawfulness, which is the basis of *ex officio* procedures for State aid, is not sufficient to explain this difference. In fact, the *ex officio* procedures regulated by the FSR apply not only to non-notifiable

85. Once more, *see* Part One, section I.A.2.4, which also provides a full overview of the obligation of result as developed in the case law.

subsidies but also to non-notified subsidies, irrespective of any penalties imposed for failure to notify under Article 26 or Article 33 FSR.

This precise choice by the EU legislator, which certainly cannot be the result of carelessness, is to be welcomed and is fully in line with the non-punitive nature of foreign subsidy control procedures (and of State aid remedies, for that matter). The only penalty procedures that can be initiated are those for breach of the information or cooperation obligations under Articles 17, 26 and 33 FSR.

Based on the foregoing, it should now be clear that, whereas the foreign subsidy control system draws inspiration from the State aid control system from several standpoints and will largely rely on the decades-long State aid enforcement practice in its practical application, it also displays features that can become a model for State aid. In other words, the opportunity offered by the work done in designing foreign subsidy control, in particular its system of remedies, must not go unexploited; rather, it should be combined with the long-awaited reform of procedural rules in State aid law (especially, but not limited to, remedies) and with the reflections and proposals already put forward by scholars in that respect *to foster a more ductile, varied, effective and tailored system of remedies, in line with the modernisation approach*. This reform would then most likely extend to State aid procedures altogether and result in a largely unified procedural and remedial system applicable across all fields of public competition law.

This highly desirable development would also help shed light on the contradiction that has instead been consolidated over time in the system of remedies for violations of State aid rules. Indeed, on the one hand, case law has consistently reaffirmed the principle of the non-punitive nature of recovery of unlawful and incompatible aid.[86] On the other hand, however, this approach has been ill-matched by the rigidity of secondary legislation[87] and the Commission's practice in imposing recovery orders and ancillary remedies (both the *Deggendorf* doctrine and the penalties envisaged in Article 260(2) TFEU) – and even more so by the lack of attention paid to alternative remedies to recovery, even in cases in which alternative remedies would be more effective in restoring undistorted competitive conditions.

In a nutshell, the FSR's provisions – namely: (i) that undertakings under investigation can offer to repay the subsidy, together with appropriate interest; (ii) that the Commission is bound to accept repayment offered as a commitment only when it can ascertain that repayment fully remedies the distortion, is executed in a transparent and verifiable manner, is effective in practice, and does not entail the risk of circumvention;[88] and (iii) that the Commission can otherwise impose the remedies that it considers most suitable to the case at hand, including dissolution of the deal

86. The procedure for controlling unlawful aid is in fact an infringement procedure that derogates from ordinary infringement procedures; like any infringement procedure, it ends with the moral/political condemnation of the Member State for breach of the Treaty, but without penalties (except in the case of subsequent non-compliance with the Court's judgment).
87. Indeed, Art. 16(1) of the Procedural Regulation leaves no choice to the Commission but to order recovery any time unlawful aid is found to be incompatible with the internal market and recovery does not clash with any general principle of law.
88. *See* recital 24 of the FSR.

concerned or reduction of the subsidised business or the beneficiary's market presence - can only mean that recovery is nothing more than *one of the many measures to achieve re-establishment of a level playing field*. The reason it is given priority over other possible remedies is simply that it is the easiest to implement and the most accurate and effective in restoring the *status quo ante* whenever a subsidy has not yet created irreversible distortions or a subsidy's effects have not vanished because of evolving market conditions or other reasons.

III.B.3 The Focus on the Effectiveness of Remedial Action

A third and final feature of the FSR's system of remedies that is of particular analytical importance in view of the reform of the State aid system of remedies has to do with the requirement that whichever remedy is imposed under the FSR, it must comply with the principle of effectiveness.[89] This emphasis on effectiveness can be read in two ways: referring to either the implementation of repayment or the elimination of the distortion caused by the foreign subsidy. At first sight, Article 7(6) FSR could justify some doubts about the correct reading, as it states that the Commission must verify that repayment of the subsidy is transparent, verifiable and effective. However, a closer examination leaves no doubt as to the legislator's intention to refer to the elimination of the distortion of competition in the internal market as the real - and sole - parameter of effectiveness.

Indeed, if effectiveness were to refer to repayment, regardless of the subsidy's and repayment's effects on the market, it would add nothing to the verifiability requirement. Moreover, Article 7(3) FSR, which relates in general to all commitments or remedies, expressly ties a given remedy's effectiveness to the actual or potential distortion caused by the related subsidy in the internal market.[90] Finally, recital 24 of the FSR clarifies that repayment must fully remedy the distortion.[91]

Therefore, it is beyond doubt that under the FSR, the EU legislator is looking at the remedies' suitability to address market distortions or at least to limit market distortions to the extent strictly necessary to achieve the overall Union interest referred to under Article 6 FSR. Article 6(2) itself confirms this approach, as it stipulates that the Commission:

89. *See* recital 24 and Art. 7(3) FSR.
90. 'Commitments or redressive measures shall be proportionate and fully and *effectively remedy the distortion* [emphasis added] actually or potentially caused by the foreign subsidy in the internal market'; *see* Art. 7(3) FSR.
91. Recital 24 states as follows:

> The undertaking under investigation could offer to repay the subsidy, together with appropriate interest. The Commission should accept a repayment offered as a commitment if it can ascertain that the repayment fully remedies the distortion, is executed in a transparent and verifiable manner and is effective in practice, while taking into account the risk of circumvention of the objectives of this Regulation.

The expression 'effective in practice' can only be understood as referring to the elimination of the foreign subsidy's effect, as the same recital expressly mentions the need to fully remedy the distortion.

> 'shall take into account the outcome of the balancing test when deciding whether to impose redressive measures or to accept commitments, and the nature and level of those redressive measures or commitments'.

The concept of Union interest in turn can only be interpreted as referring to the Union's long-term economic/industrial objectives and total welfare, given the very broad wording of Article 6(1).[92]

III.B.4 Analysis of the Various Remedies Envisaged under Article 7 FSR

Article 7(4) FSR enumerates various remedies, which can take the form of commitments offered by the undertaking concerned (and made binding by the Commission) or redressive measures imposed by the Commission when the undertaking has not offered suitable commitments. It is explicitly stated that the list is not exhaustive, which is yet another element of flexibility that characterises the system of remedies established by the FSR. There is therefore no limit whatsoever to undertakings' or the Commission's creativity in modelling remedy packages that are transparent, verifiable, and effective but that at the same time do not cause undue constraints on the implementation of the market strategy of the undertakings concerned.

A first type of redressive measure available to the Commission[93] can be used when a company, thanks to a foreign subsidy, finds itself in a *de facto* monopoly situation because it comes to own infrastructure that cannot be replicated, at least not in the short term. In such a case, the company may be obliged to offer third-party access to the infrastructure under fair, reasonable and non-discriminatory conditions, unless such access is already envisaged by sectoral legislation.[94] The notion of infrastructure is explicitly broad and includes research facilities, production capabilities and essential facilities.

Next, Article 7(4) refers to an even broader remedy, *i.e.*, reduction of capacity or market presence, including by means of a temporary restriction on commercial activity.[95] Here the degree of flexibility envisaged by the legislator reaches its highest point because *the remedy is expressed as an objective to be attained, not as a specific form of conduct.* There are therefore no limits to the measures or initiatives through which undertakings may reduce their market presence. The divestment of certain

92. Indeed, Art. 6(1) stipulates as follows:

> The Commission may, on the basis of information received, balance the negative effects of a foreign subsidy in terms of distortion in the internal market ... against the positive effects on the development of the relevant subsidised economic activity on the internal market, while considering other positive effects of the foreign subsidy such as the broader positive effects in relation to the relevant policy objectives, in particular those of the Union.

93. *See* Art. 7(4)(a) FSR.
94. In the field of State aid, a similar requirement is envisaged in the EU Guidelines for the application of State aid rules in relation to the rapid deployment of broadband networks; *see* para. 80 of the Guidelines, OJ C 25, 26.1.2013, pp. 1-26. It is therefore applied as a prospective remedy in compatibility assessments.
95. *See* Art. 7(4)(b) FSR.

assets or business operations is a typical example but, quite surprisingly, is mentioned only later (and separately) in Article 7.[96] However, other measures are conceivable, such as (to name but a few): (i) a temporary reduction of the rate of utilisation of production facilities; (ii) an obligation to comply with an output growth ratio below the growth rate of the relevant market; or (iii) a commitment to refrain from promotional initiatives.

The Commission obviously has a very wide margin of discretion in assessing the foreseeable impact of proposed measures; the only constraint appears to be that they must not be discriminatory or lead to market foreclosure or segmentation.[97]

Looking at possible similarities with the remedies used in State aid law, the only example that can be recalled is to be found in the Guidelines on State aid for rescuing and restructuring non-financial undertakings in difficulty,[98] wherein it is stated that beneficiary undertakings may be forced to divest assets or to reduce their production capacity or market presence in order to eliminate a distortion of competition. A comparison with these Guidelines confirms, first of all, that in the FSR the legislator wished to enrich the system of redressive remedies by integrating the experience gained from the use of prospective remedies in the context of State aid compatibility assessments. Second, it further highlights the creativity and flexibility shown by the FSR's legislator, given that the remedy envisaged under Article 7(4)(b) FSR is even broader than its predecessor and, above all, leaves the choice of the measures to be proposed to the undertakings concerned.

Finally, experience with the Guidelines' application indicates that, for the abovementioned remedy to be effective, it should not lead to deterioration in the market's structure. This means that the divested ongoing business should be viable on a standalone basis and competitive in the long term if operated by a suitable purchaser. Alternatively, the aid/subsidy beneficiary should carve out adequate activities and assets to create a new entity that should be able to compete. Divestments of assets alone that do not involve the creation of a viable competitor are less effective and therefore generally unsuitable to remove distortions of competition. Thus, they are acceptable only in exceptional cases in which the undertakings concerned demonstrate that no other remedies would be feasible.

A similar remedy is for the subsidy beneficiary to commit to refraining from certain investments.[99] Conceptually, this remedy in fact constitutes a more specific version of the previous one, but one which the legislator preferred to indicate separately, perhaps in order to give it greater prominence. In any event, the same considerations highlighted above concerning measures to reduce a foreign subsidy beneficiary's market presence apply to the waiver or prohibition of certain investments.

96. *See* Art. 7(4)(f) FSR.
97. It would thus not be admissible to propose not to target certain categories of customers or not to sell in certain geographical areas, as this would be contrary to the proper functioning of the internal market.
98. Guidelines on State aid for rescuing and restructuring non-financial undertakings in difficulty, OJ C 249, 31.7.2014, pp. 1-28.
99. *See* Art. 7(4)(c) FSR.

An additional remedy is envisaged for cases in which a foreign subsidy has enabled the recipient concerned to acquire a capital asset, such as the right to exploit a certain telecommunications frequency or to develop a certain technology. In this scenario, too - just as in cases in which a foreign subsidy made it possible for the recipient to develop or obtain rights to infrastructure (including research infrastructure) located in the Union territory - the envisaged solution consists of the granting of licences on fair, reasonable and non-discriminatory terms as an alternative to the repayment of the subsidy.[100]

Similarly, if foreign subsidies that come under the Commission's scrutiny were used to support R&D&I activities that led to results that are likely to enhance the recipient's competitive capacity, publication of those results - thereby enabling other market players to exploit or replicate them - could be a way of removing the competitive advantage. Also in this case, the specific remedy envisaged - *i.e.*, the sharing of the results of illegally financed research[101] - is preferable to both repayment of the subsidy (because it is presumably more effective, given its specific nature) and divestment of the R&D&I results (because it is capable of preserving the innovative capacity of the company concerned).

This explains why the legislator preferred to treat this remedy separately from remedies entailing a reduction in the market presence of the undertaking concerned. The remedy envisaged under Article 7(4)(e) is in line with the experience of the prospective remedies aimed at ensuring aid compatibility developed within the framework of IPCEIs and the R&D&I State aid guidelines and the related provisions of the GBER.[102] Once more, *the FSR bridges the gap between prospective remedies, which are typical of compatibility assessments, and restorative/redressive remedies*, as it empowers the Commission not only to accept and make binding redressive measures proposed by notifying companies participating in mergers or public procurement procedures in the EU but also to impose the most appropriate structural or behavioural remedies within the framework of *ex officio* procedures.

Article 7(4) then mentions two typical cases of remedies: an order to dissolve the concentration under scrutiny[103] and repayment of the subsidy plus interest.[104] The former obviously applies only to *ex officio* procedures, whereas the latter can be imposed by the Commission but also proposed by companies during the notification process. In the Commission proposal that led to the adoption of the FSR, recital 17 contained a specific indication that redressive measures ordered by the Commission

100. *See* Art. 7(4)(d) FSR.
101. *See* Art. 7(4)(e) FSR.
102. *See* Communication from the Commission - Criteria for the analysis of the compatibility with the internal market of State aid to promote the execution of important projects of common European interest, OJ C188, 20.6.2014, p. 2. *See also*: Communication from the Commission - Framework for State aid for research and development and innovation, OJ C 198, 27.6.2014, para. 119; and Art. 25(6)(b) of Regulation (EU) No 651/2014 (GBER), which links increases in admitted aid intensities to proof that 'the results of the project are widely disseminated through conferences, publication, open access repositories, or free or open-source software'.
103. *See* Art. 7(4)(g) FSR.
104. *See* Art. 7(4)(h) FSR, which, for the calculation of interest, refers to Commission Regulation (EC) No 794/2004 (implementing the procedural rules on State aid).

should include the option to repay the foreign subsidy and prioritise behavioural over structural remedies. Although this wording was deleted from the final version of the FSR,[105] it still seems appropriate to consider that, according to the FSR's rationale, an order to dissolve a concentration can be imposed only in exceptional circumstances and as a remedy of last resort, *i.e.*, if no other measure is available or suitable. It presupposes not only that the Commission finds repayment of the subsidy to be ineffective in the case concerned but also - and more importantly - that no other remedy, be it behavioural or structural in nature, is available. The unwinding of a concentration is in fact the most invasive structural remedy conceivable. Indeed, the last sentence of recital 22 of the FSR states that when several redressive measures can be envisaged that are capable of fully and effectively remedying the distortion, the Commission should choose the measure which is least burdensome for the undertaking under investigation.[106]

The last type of remedy envisaged is requiring the undertakings concerned to adapt their governance structure.[107] The rationale for this atypical remedy - which was introduced at the European Parliament's request[108] - is unclear, and no reference to it can be found in either the FSR's recitals or in the preparatory works, including the comments submitted by stakeholders during the public consultation. Notably, this measure is not commonly used as a prospective remedy when assessing compatibility under State aid rules. Even in merger control practice, although it is possible for companies to change the governance initially envisaged during pre-notification contacts in order to facilitate the granting of clearance, it is not common practice for such a measure to be included among commitments offered during the formal notification

105. The reasons underlying this change are probably twofold. As far as repayment is concerned, it is rational not to oblige the Commission to offer it, as the Commission is instead free to assess the appropriateness of repayment and whether it can prove more effective than alternative remedies in the case at hand; as to the choice between structural and behavioural remedies, once more the legislator's choice was to leave the Commission free to assess the most appropriate remedies on a case-by-case basis, as clearly indicated in recital 17, which now reads as follows:

> Once the existence of a foreign subsidy is established, the Commission should assess on a case-by-case basis whether it distorts the internal market. Unlike State aid granted by a Member State, foreign subsidies are not generally prohibited.

106. The last sentence of recital 22 reads as follows:

> Where the Commission considers alternative redressive measures, which would each fully and effectively remedy the distortion, the Commission should choose the measure which is least burdensome for the undertaking under investigation.

The adjective 'alternative' can only be read as referring to repayment as the normal benchmark. Therefore, even if the explicit reference to an obligation to prioritise repayment of the subsidy was deleted from the final text of the FSR, the underlying idea remains that repayment is the ordinary remedy and that all other measures are alternatives to repayment.

107. *See* Art. 7(4)(i) FSR.
108. The European Parliament proposed this amendment during its first reading of the legislative proposal; unfortunately, no statement of reason is available in the preparatory works. The Committee on the Internal Market and Consumer Protection and the Committee on International Trade expressed their support for the introduction of the amendment but did not provide their reasons for doing so, either.

procedure. In any case, it seems unlikely that the Commission will have recourse to this remedy during *ex officio* procedures.

One can imagine that the legislator wanted to leave open the possibility for undertakings to grant certain powers to European shareholders in the case of joint ventures or to amend a buyer's articles of association in order to eliminate golden shares or other powers granted to representatives of a non-EU country, in the hope that this could affect the balancing of interests that the Commission is called on to carry out when examining the effects of foreign subsidies. However, only practical experience will tell whether this remedy can be of real significance and, if so, under which circumstances.

III.B.5 Sanctions Intended to Complete the System of Remedies

Enforcement of all the redressive measures analysed in the previous section is ensured in the FSR's system through a set of safeguards and penalties. First, under Article 7(5) FSR, the Commission may impose reporting and transparency requirements to facilitate the monitoring of compliance with remedies and the detection of infringements. The penalties envisaged for non-compliance with remedies are considerable: the Commission may order the undertaking to pay a fine of up to 10% of the aggregate turnover generated in the year preceding the infringement (*see* Article 17(5)(a)). The Commission also has penalty payments at its disposal: for each day of non-compliance, the infringing undertaking may be ordered to pay up to 5% of its average daily turnover (*see* Article 17(5)(b)).

Furthermore, to the extent proportionate and necessary, undertakings under investigation may be required, for a certain period, to inform the Commission of participation in mergers or public procurement procedures, even if they do not cross the financial thresholds set out in the FSR. All penalties for non-compliance with redressive measures must, of course, be proportionate and appropriate to the nature, seriousness and duration of the infringement concerned.

In terms of enforcement, it is also worth emphasising that Article 16(1) and (3) empowers the Commission to adopt a decision based on the facts available when an undertaking under investigation or a third country that granted a subsidy fails to cooperate.[109] The Commission is given the same power in all three enforcement procedures: *ex officio*, merger-related, and public-procurement-related. This marks a significant difference from State aid procedures, according to which the Commission's power to adopt a decision based on the information available is limited to unlawful

109. Article 16(1)(a)-(d) enumerates various forms of non-cooperation in very broad terms: provision of incomplete, incorrect or misleading information in response to a request for information; failure to provide the information requested within the time limit prescribed by the Commission; refusal to submit to inspections within or outside the Union; and whatever other impediment or obstacle to the Commission's investigation, be it during the preliminary review or during the in-depth investigation.

aid[110] and, even in that context, has been somewhat restrained by the case law, at least when the MEOP is applied.[111]

Even more important from the standpoint of effective enforcement is Article 18 FSR, which empowers the Commission to revoke a decision containing redressive measures or making commitments binding on the undertaking concerned and replace it with a new decision - not only when the revoked decision was based on incomplete, incorrect or misleading information or when the undertaking acts contrary to its commitments or fails to comply with redressive measures but also when the commitments or redressive measures turn out to be ineffective. The latter provision is indeed very intrusive and unusual: it confers considerable power on the Commission, which will in essence be able to correct in self-defence any decision based on what it considers an erroneous assessment of the effectiveness of imposed remedies and to adapt the remedies to the relevant market's changing conditions.

Two comments are immediately called for in this regard. First, a provision of this nature further supports the legislator's choice to favour a *substantive view* of the concept of re-establishment of the competitive conditions that existed before a given subsidy was granted, the aim of which is to eliminate the competitive advantage gained by the beneficiary. Second, it is reasonable to expect that the application of this provision will give rise to controversy and that the EU courts will be called on to more precisely delineate what the conditions and limits of a revocation decision are and whether it can be justified solely by a change in circumstances, without entailing any liability on the part of the undertakings involved. In particular, it will be interesting to see how undertakings' legitimate expectations will be protected and how their right to defence will be guaranteed through implementing measures or creative case law, including in the spirit of ensuring the respect of general principles of law and fundamental rights.

III.B.6 Limited Scope for Private Enforcement Remedies

When comparing the system of remedies in the field of State aid to that in the FSR, one element in particular cannot be overlooked: while the State aid remedies that can be applied by the Commission are complemented by those available under private enforcement, this is not the case for foreign subsidies, or at least it remains to be seen whether private enforcement can play any significant role in that context. The possibility of private enforcement of the FSR's rules cannot be ruled out in principle,

110. Articles 14 and 15(1) of Council Regulation (EU) 2015/1589 stipulate that, if the Member State concerned fails to cooperate, the Commission is entitled to examine the substance of an unlawful aid measure and to adopt a final decision based on the information available. However, this applies only if the Commission has adopted a suspension injunction or a provisional recovery injunction under Art. 13(1) or (2) of the regulation, respectively, and the Member State failed to comply with that injunction.

111. According to recent case law on the burden of proof in relation to the application of the MEOP, the Commission must gather all information available from all sources at its disposal in order to carry out its assessment of the MEOP's applicability. *See* Judgment of the General Court of 14 June 2023, *Ryanair DAC and Airport Marketing Services Ltd v. Commission*, T-79/21, EU:T:2023:334.

but the scope and relevance of the FSR's private enforcement seems modest, at least at the current stage of development. A full analysis of the scope of private enforcement in the field of foreign subsidy control goes beyond the limits of this book. The few considerations that follow have the sole objective of explaining that the limited scope of private enforcement remedies for FSR rules has no impact on the suitability of the FSR's system of remedies as a model for the reform of State aid remedies.

The Commission is the sole public authority competent to enforce the FSR (as is the case with State aid), but of course this does not prevent individuals from invoking the FSR's directly applicable provisions before national courts. These provisions, like those of any EU regulation, have direct effect on national legal systems and can be invoked before national courts by interested parties if they are suitable for direct application, without any need for the Commission's prior action. However, the FSR was enacted based on Articles 114 and 207 TFEU and is aimed at ensuring the proper functioning of the EU's internal market and common commercial policy. It therefore comes as no surprise that the FSR has no explicit rules on private enforcement.

Whereas the absence of specific rules is, as mentioned above, not preclusive of FSR provisions being invoked before national courts,[112] the absence of a prohibition on foreign subsidies is instead a serious obstacle to that effect. Indeed, although the FSR targets distortive foreign subsidies, it does not prohibit them. Furthermore, the FSR lacks a State-aid-like general notification obligation. Notifications are required only for specific above-threshold transactions or bids in public procurement procedures, and foreign subsidies that do not meet those thresholds are subject only to *ex officio*, *ex-post* monitoring.

Therefore, in principle, no general standstill obligation that could be enforced by third parties is envisaged by the FSR. However, undertakings that cross the FSR thresholds under the M&A and public procurement tools are required to notify the Commission thereof. Additionally, a standstill obligation applies to notifiable concentrations and to the awarding of contracts in public procurement procedures to undertakings benefitting from notifiable financial contributions. The notification and standstill obligations are distinct but complementary and both sufficient to establish direct applicability, at least in principle.

Despite this, FSR-related actions before national courts might in practice entail only claims for cease-and-desist orders (especially in the case of alleged breaches of the standstill obligations) and claims for specific performance (*e.g.*, claims seeking to force the defendant to notify a notifiable concentration). Conversely, it is difficult to imagine that claimants can seek the adoption by national courts of redressive measures such as those listed under Article 7 FSR, as the adoption of such measures would require national courts to carry out a substantive assessment for which they lack competence. It cannot be ruled out that, in some national systems, the mere violation of the

112. The experience in antitrust law helps illustrate this. Prior to Directive 2014/104/EU, there were no EU rules on private enforcement of competition law; nevertheless, the Court of Justice clarified in the landmark *Courage and Crehan* case that Arts 101 and 102 TFEU can be enforced also by private parties before national courts (Judgment of the Court of 20 September 2001, Case C-453/99, EU:C:2001:465).

procedural obligations stemming from the FSR can entail the nullity of the merger agreement or public procurement concerned and therefore make it unenforceable between the parties, but this would of course not be an effective remedy for third parties.

Claims might also be brought seeking the adoption of an order of recovery of financial contributions by third countries. However, such claims are unlikely to be successful, as no general standstill obligation applies to the granting of foreign subsidies, and on top of this, compliance with a recovery order imposed on a third country would be difficult, if not impossible, to verify or enforce.

Despite these difficulties in attributing a significant role to private enforcement in the application of the FSR at the current stage of regulatory development, it does not appear that this shortcoming is in any way related to the way remedies have been modelled under the FSR. First, no link between the two aspects emerges from an analysis of the preparatory works. Second, if a link existed, it would have justified a stricter and tougher modelling of remedies for foreign subsidies compared to remedies for State aid, given that private enforcement remedies are available for the latter. Instead, as described above, Article 7 FSR is characterised by *greater flexibility and more focus on the substantive effects of State intervention* than is the case in the field of State aid based on the Commission's case law and practice. Lastly, it would make no logical sense to make the nature of remedies dependent on the possibility of private enforcement: if the latter can play a complementary role with respect to public enforcement, it will help alleviate the administrative burden on the Commission and, at the same time, offer broader guarantees of the regulation's effectiveness - but in no case does it impact the nature of the remedies.

Hence, the conclusions reached in comparing the system of remedies under the FSR with that envisaged for State aid remain valid regardless of the difficulty in foreshadowing a role for private enforcement of the FSR at the current stage of regulatory development.

III.B.7 Final Remarks on the FSR's System of Remedies

A final consideration concerning the overall nature of the FSR's system of remedies stems from the one-by-one examination of the redressive measures conducted above. Now that it has been clarified that *the system's objective is not punitive*[113] *but rather functional in nature* (*i.e.*, to preserve the proper functioning of the internal market and the attainment of the maximum benefit therefrom for EU citizens), it appears that remedies under the FSR (*i.e.*, redressive measures within the meaning of Article 7) can be classified into two categories:

113. Although, under State aid rules, aid repayment is similarly not considered a punitive measure but the normal consequence of the unlawfulness of the aid, the non-punitive nature of redressive measures under Art. 7 FSR is to be understood differently, as foreign subsidies are not prohibited (more precisely, no incompatibility principle exists, save for the derogations envisaged in the Treaty, as is the case for State aid under Art. 107 TFEU). This is explicitly clarified in recital 22 of the FSR.

(i) remedies aimed at penalising a foreign subsidy recipient in terms of its market position based on the assumption that it gained that position thanks to the subsidy (*e.g.*, reducing capacity or market presence, restricting commercial activity, refraining from certain investments, or divesting certain assets); and
(ii) remedies aimed at stimulating competition by re-establishing a fair balance (*e.g.*, offering access to infrastructure at FRAND conditions, licensing technology at FRAND conditions, and publishing R&D&I results).

The combination of these two categories is already a clear indication that the FSR's system of remedies is far not only from having punitive intentions but also from instituting a rigid *restitutio in integrum* mechanism based on the nominal value of the foreign subsidy concerned. Rather, by empowering the Commission *to ascertain the subsidy's distortive nature* regardless of the context in which the distortion materialises (corporate transactions, tenders or normal market operations), and regardless of the rules of procedure applicable in a given case (notification-based or *ex officio*), the FSR gives the Commission the discretionary power to adopt *the most appropriate corrective measures* (from among those generically set out by the law) in order to strike a fair balance, in the interest of Union citizens, between re-establishing the correct competitive dynamics in the internal market and preserving the virtuous effects of subsidised activity for the internal market.

This applies irrespective of any penalties imposed for breach of cooperation obligations (be it related to notifications, responses to requests for information, or cooperation in the conduct of an investigation), which, if penalties are in fact applicable, are the subject of a separate penalty procedure and in no way interfere with the choice of the most appropriate remedies.

In a nutshell, the logic underpinning the system prioritises a remedy's effectiveness in addressing ascertained distortions of competition that are not overcompensated by the related benefits for the EU citizens over formal forfeiture of the subsidy through repayment of its nominal value.

It is clear that the Commission must be accorded broad discretionary power for the purposes of the aforementioned balancing test, which must be carried out with the aim of ensuring that the remedy is suitable and effective in relation to the distortion identified,[114] not to mention proportionate. Moreover, this discretionary power is framed by two unfailing principles: (i) consideration of proposals made by the undertaking concerned,[115] as the Commission is obliged to choose the measure which is least burdensome for the undertaking under investigation;[116] and (ii) compliance with the criteria of transparency, verifiability and effectiveness of the redressive measures eventually imposed.

114. *See* again recital 22 of the FSR.
115. As already indicated, this especially applies when a recipient undertaking proposes repayment of the subsidy, as such a proposal may be rejected only if repayment would prove inadequate to remedy the distortion caused or if it would prove difficult to ascertain whether repayment occurred – with the burden of proof being clearly on the Commission.
116. Once again, *see* the last sentence of recital 22 of the FSR.

As to judicial review of the Commission's assessment, this is of course shaped by the broadness of the Commission's prerogatives. Consequently, the Court's review will necessarily be limited when it comes to assessing the appropriateness of corrective measures taken by the Commission, as the EU courts cannot replace the Commission's assessment with their own. That said, the Court will be able to examine not only: (i) whether the Commission correctly reasoned its position and did not commit errors of law or an abuse of power, whether it breached procedural rules and whether it disregarded or misinterpreted the facts at its disposal; but also (ii) whether all those facts are capable of supporting the Commission's conclusions.[117] Of course, the Court will also be able to detect possible violations of the criteria of transparency, verifiability and effectiveness and exercise full control over compliance with those criteria.

117. The *Scott* case law can be applied by analogy in this context; *see* Judgment of the Court of 2 September 2010, *Commission v. Scott SA*, C-290/07 P, ECLI:EU:C:2010:480, paras 81-85.

IV OTHER POTENTIAL MODELS FOR THE REFORM OF REMEDIES IN THE FIELD OF STATE AID

This chapter explores how the FSR can provide potential models for the reform of private (i.e., not just public) enforcement remedies in the field of State aid, drawing inspiration from other areas of competition law and internal market rules. It discusses whether these models can offer innovative solutions and improve the effectiveness of the system of remedies.

IV.A Introductory Remarks

This part of the book cannot close without a question: if the FSR is the natural and indispensable model when thinking about a reform of the system of remedies in the public enforcement of State aid law, what can be the model for private enforcement? To answer this question, one should look at legislative measures in the field of market regulation and competition aimed at achieving the harmonisation of dissimilar national systems at the private enforcement level. On this basis, two legal frameworks are the closest from the standpoint of the subject matter and the objectives pursued by the legislator. They both concern areas where, like in the private enforcement of State aid law, national systems differed to such an extent as to prevent the internal market from developing properly and in accordance with the principles it is inspired by.

The first legal framework that needs to be considered is the legislation on remedies in public procurement, specifically Directive 2077/66/EC ('*Remedies Directive*').[118] The second legal framework is Directive 104/2014/EU ('*Damages Directive*')[119] in the area of competition law. In both cases, the lack of homogeneity between national laws did not allow the internal market to function properly, as the rights arising for individuals from the EU legal system's rules did not receive effective protection in all Member States, creating incompatible disparities of treatment across the Union. In addition to reducing differences between Member States, these directives are aimed at ensuring legal certainty by guaranteeing effective protection for undertakings harmed by the infringement of Union rules.[120]

118. Directive 2007/66/EC of the European Parliament and of the Council of 11 December 2007 amending Council Directives 89/665/EEC and 92/13/EEC with regard to improving the effectiveness of review procedures concerning the award of public contracts, OJ L 335, 20.12.2007, p. 31.
119. Directive 2014/104/EU of the European Parliament and of the Council of 26 November 2014 on certain rules governing actions for damages under national law for infringements of the competition law provisions of the Member States and of the European Union, OJ L 349, 5.12.2014, p. 1.
120. *See, ex multis*: E. Chiti, *Directive 2007/66 and the Difficult Search for Balance in Judicial Protection concerning Public Procurements*, Italia Journal of Public Law, 2010, Volume 2, Issue 1, pp. 144-172; R. Carvalho, *The Remedy of Ineffectiveness: Reform Perspectives*, European Procurement & Public Private Partnership Law Review, 2017, Volume 12, Issue 4, pp. 374-382 https://doi.org/10.21552/epppl/2017/4/4; and W-J. Barends, *Judicial Protection in the Field of Public Procurement: The Transposition into Dutch Law of Directive 2077/66/EC, Amending the Remedies Directive*, Utrecht Journal of International and European Law, 2010, Volume 26, Issue

These directives are briefly examined in this chapter. However, the analysis is necessarily limited and very selective, geared solely towards understanding whether and, if so, to what extent these directives can be taken into consideration in Part Four of this book, which attempts to outline a precise proposal for reforming the system of remedies in State aid law. Although neither of the two directives can truly serve as a model for remedies in the field of State aid for reasons that become clear below, their examination offers more food for thought in view of drawing conclusions from the research conducted thus far.

IV.B Directive 2007/66/EC

IV.B.1 Background

The Remedies Directive, which is based on Articles 53(1), 62 and 114 TFEU, supplements the rules on judicial protection in the field of public procurement – the origin of which dates back to 1989[121] – and is aimed at enhancing the potential for private enforcement of EU public procurement rules.[122] More specifically, the directive's purpose is to harmonise national legislations both for reasons of uniformity and with the aim of ensuring that the principles of equality and transparency, to be balanced with the principle of efficient administrative action, are respected in all Member States.

To this end, the Remedies Directive sets minimum national review standards to ensure that rapid and effective means of redress are available in all EU countries when an economic operator that has an interest in a public procurement procedure believes that it has been run without proper application of the EU Public Procurement Directives. The Remedies Directive thus grants access to review procedures to any person having or having had an interest in obtaining a particular contract and who has been or risks being harmed by an alleged infringement.[123] The directive thus extends the right to review to all undertakings that are in a position to claim harm in the context of a procedure for the award of a contract, so as to prevent possible discrimination against economic operators by virtue of different national laws.

IV.B.2 Remedies

To enhance the effectiveness of individual rights stemming from EU public procurement rules, the Remedies Directive contains various provisions intended to encourage

71, pp. 17-25 https://doi.org/10.5334/ujiel.ac. *See also*: M. Honoré and N.E. Jensen, *Damages in State Aid Cases*, European State Aid Law Quarterly (ESTaL), 2011, Issue 2, pp. 265 ff. https://doi.org/10.21552/estal/2011/2/227, who refer to the Remedies Directive in dealing with the private enforcement of State aid rules; and C. Jadot, *Damages Actions and State Aid: Time for Action at EU Level?*, Market and Competition Law Review, April 2022, Volume VI, Issue 1, who examines one by one the provisions of the Damages Directive to analyse their value as a model for a harmonisation directive in the field of State aid.

121. *See* Directive 89/665/EEC, OJ L 395, 30.12.1989, p. 33, later amended by Directive 92/12/EEC, OJ L 076, 23.3.1992, p. 1.
122. *See* recitals 3 and 4 of the Remedies Directive.
123. *See* Art. 1(3) of the Remedies Directive.

undertakings that consider themselves harmed by a violation of EU market-opening rules to pursue judicial protection at national level.

The Remedies Directive distinguishes between remedies available before the conclusion of a contract and those available after. The first shortcoming it proposes to remedy is in fact the absence in several national legal systems of a time limit - between the award of a tender and the signing of the contract - within which tenderers have the possibility to bring an action. This shortcoming constituted a serious impediment to effective judicial protection since any appeal is certainly more effective if introduced before the contract is signed.[124]

The Remedies Directive requires the contracting authority to wait at least ten days after an award before concluding the contract.[125] It also lays down information obligations on the part of the contracting authority, which must promptly inform interested parties of the outcome of the tender.[126] This gives interested parties sufficient time to challenge the contracting authority's decision and thus allows the legal system to intervene to correct any violations before the contract takes effect.[127] If interested parties seek judicial protection, the contracting authority must refrain from signing the contract before a decision is taken either on the application for interim measures or on the merits of the case. This provision is intended to guarantee the effectiveness of 'bottom-up' actions and access to competition procedures. The above-mentioned time limit indeed translates into a standstill obligation for the contracting authorities before signing a contract.[128]

As to remedies available once the contract is signed, the Remedies Directive requires Member States to impose 'effective, proportionate and dissuasive' sanctions if directly applicable provisions of the directive are breached. Hence, if the contract is concluded unlawfully (*i.e.*, before the expiry of the standstill period), national courts must be granted the power to declare it ineffective, in order to re-establish a level playing field and restore economic and commercial opportunities to those who have been deprived of the possibility to compete.[129]

More generally, a public contract concluded in violation of the rules in Directives 89/665 and 92/13 (as amended by the Remedies Directive) is to be declared ineffective by a national court and thus cannot produce its effects.[130] The consequences resulting from a contract being considered ineffective should be determined by national law. National law may therefore determine whether the contract becomes ineffective *ex tunc* (this would imply the cancellation of all contractual obligations arising from the

124. *See* recital 28 of the Remedies Directive.
125. *See* Art. 2a(1) and (2) of the Remedies Directive.
126. *See* Art. 2a(2) and 2(c) of the Remedies Directive.
127. Chiti, *Directive 2007/66 and the Difficult Search for Balance in Judicial Protection concerning Public Prosecutions*, cited in footnote 120 of this Part Three.
128. *See* recital 4 of the Remedies Directive. *See also* Chiti, cited in footnote 120 of this Part Three. The directive distinguishes between a substantive standstill, which consists of a minimum period of ten days between the award of the tender and the conclusion of the contract, and a procedural standstill, which requires contracting authorities not to conclude the contract before the competent judicial body has decided *at least* on the application for interim measures.
129. *See* recital 14 of the Remedies Directive.
130. *See* Art. 2d(1) and (2) of the Remedies Directive.

contract since the beginning) or conversely *ex nunc* (thus limiting the scope of the cancellation to those obligations which would still have to be performed).[131]

If obligations under a contract have already been fully performed or if the protection of general interests is at stake, Member States can impose alternative penalties.[132] In addition, the directive requires Member States to put in place suitable procedures to award damages to stakeholders harmed by unlawful tender procedures.[133] Such a provision has enabled national courts to effectively implement - at a private enforcement level - Community rights in the field of public contracts.

In a nutshell, to achieve effective private enforcement, the Remedies Directive establishes an obligation for Member States to put in place effective, proportionate and dissuasive remedies for a breach of directly applicable EU provisions and even directly identifies the standard suitable remedy to ensure full protection for individuals in the case of a breach of the standstill obligation. Some comments can be made in this regard.

First, the remedy envisaged for violation of the standstill obligation, although openly defined as a 'sanction', is similar to that envisaged for State aid (given that depriving a contract - concluded following its award - of its effects is equivalent to restoring the previous situation from a competitive dynamics standpoint, which is the same objective pursued with the recovery of aid), but the analogy applies more in form than in substance. Indeed, for the party harmed by the infringement, the remedy imposed by the Remedies Directive is capable of restoring the opportunity to compete on equal terms; on the contrary, aid recovery, especially in the formalistic interpretation that has prevailed since the 2016 *Ryanair/Air Lingus* judgment,[134] restores the *status quo ante* from a financial perspective only, but not necessarily from an economic or competitive dynamics perspective.[135]

Interestingly, the Remedies Directive encourages Member States to seek alternative remedies whenever the obligations under a public contract have already been performed or public interest considerations prevent the contract from being declared ineffective, whereas no similar provision exists in State aid law. Furthermore, current practice tends to prioritise a formalistic implementation of the recovery obligation rather than a search for alternative and more effective means to re-establish a situation of undistorted competition.

Second, the result to be achieved is imposed by the directive (*i.e.*, ineffectiveness of any contract awarded in breach of the standstill obligation), but the legal instruments may differ from one legal system to another, and it is up to the national courts to identify them. Finally, since the remedy must be not only effective and proportionate but also dissuasive, the national legislator should also aim to go beyond the mere re-establishment of the *status quo ante*.

131. *See* recital 21 of the Remedies Directive.
132. *See* recital 22 of the Remedies Directive.
133. *See* Art. 1(2) and 2(2) of the Remedies Directive.
134. *See* Part One, section III.A.3 and footnote 146.
135. *See* Part One, section IV.

As to the interlocutory remedy, the obligation to wait for a certain period after the award of the tender in order to enable the injured party to initiate a judicial review - in combination with the consequent obligation, if a review is initiated, to refrain from signing the contract until at least the ruling of the court with jurisdiction over the interlocutory application - is undoubtedly an interesting and effective remedy which at present has no correspondence in the State aid system of remedies.

IV.C Directive 2014/104/EU

IV.C.1 Background

The Damages Directive[136] was adopted to address procedural differences between national laws across the EU when it comes to safeguarding individual rights stemming from violations of Articles 101 and 102 TFEU.[137] These differences had a strong impact on the way in which damage resulting from a breach of EU competition law could give right to compensation across the Union.[138] Here again, the uneven conditions existing in national laws inevitably affected the internal market and its proper functioning.[139] Therefore, the Damages Directive's objectives are to ensure a level playing field for European companies by granting effective judicial protection across the EU,[140] at least in connection with one of the ways (perhaps the most important one) in which Articles 101 and 102 TFEU can be invoked in litigation between private parties.

Articles 101 and 102 TFEU may indeed be invoked also as a defence against a contractual claim brought because of non-performance of obligations under a contract or against claims brought as intellectual property infringement actions; moreover, they can be used as a basis to claim injunctive relief, including interim relief, for instance, in the form of a cease-and-desist order.[141] However, antitrust actions different from, or

136. Directive 2014/104/EU of the European Parliament and of the Council of 26 November 2014, cited in footnote 119 of this Part Three.
137. Recitals 1 and 2 of the Damages Directive. *See also*: M. O'Regan, *Private Enforcement of EU Competition Law: The Impact of the Damages Directive*, Competition Law Journal, 2019, Volume 18, Issue 1, pp. 51-53; and P. Iannuccelli, *La Responsabilità Civile Antitrust delle Imprese e la Direttiva 104/2014*, La Responsabilità delle Imprese nel Diritto della Concorrenza dell'Unione Europea e la Direttiva 2014/104, Chapter 4, Giuffrè, 2017, pp. 107-156.
138. Recitals 8 and 12 of the Damages Directive. *See* Judgment of the Court of 20 September 2001, *Courage ltd v. Bernard Crehan*, C-453/99, EU:C:2001:465, and Judgment of the Court of 13 July 2006, *Vincenzo Manfredi v. Lloyd Adriatico Assicurazioni Spa*, C-295/04, EU:C:2006:461, which affirmed the existence of a right to damages, in the form of compensation, arising from breaches of EU competition law.
139. Iannuccelli, *La Responsabilità Civile Antitrust delle Imprese e la Direttiva 104/2014*, cited in footnote 137 of this Part Three. *See also* recital 54 of the Damages Directive.
140. Recitals 5 and 9 of the Damages Directive.
141. For a complete analysis of private enforcement in antitrust law, *see*, among many others, W.P.J. Wils, *Private Enforcement of EU Antitrust Law and Its Relationship with Public Enforcement: Past, Present and Future*, World Competition: Law and Economics Review, 2017, Volume 4, Issue 1, pp. 3-46 https://doi.org/10.54648/woco2017002. The article provides a short history of private enforcement of EU antitrust law and its relationship with public enforcement, from the 1957 EEC Treaty over Regulation 17 and Regulation 1/2003 until the

unrelated to, damages claims are relatively rare, and indeed an action for damages remains the most typical private enforcement remedy in that field.

Actions for damages are of two types: (i) follow-on actions, whereby private parties – after a competition authority has concluded proceedings with a finding of an infringement of Articles 101 or 102 TFEU – seek damages before a national court against the undertakings found to have committed the infringement; and (ii) standalone actions, *i.e.*, actions for damages that do not directly rely on a finding of infringement following public enforcement proceedings, although in certain cases they might still be less directly related to public enforcement proceedings.

The Damages Directive – which is based on Articles 103 and 114 TFEU and is inspired by the principles of legal certainty,[142] good administration,[143] loyal cooperation[144] and effectiveness[145] – builds upon the creative case law of the Court of Justice[146] and represents a landmark evolution in the field of private enforcement, precisely because of its express purpose of not only harmonising national procedures but also encouraging private enforcement of competition law as an essential component of modernisation. As apparent from its Articles 1, 2(1) and (3), the Damages Directive covers actions for damages relating not only to infringements of Articles 101 and 102 TFEU but also to parallel infringements of similar provisions of national competition law.[147] The directive seeks to grant all persons harmed as a consequence of a breach of competition rules full compensation of that harm, covering compensation for actual loss and for loss of profit, plus the payment of interest.

However, Article 3(3) of the Damages Directive, in rejecting the US model, clarifies that full compensation 'shall not lead to overcompensation, whether by means of punitive, multiple or other types of damages'. In line with this approach of rejecting the US conception of private actions for damages as an instrument of deterrence and punishment, Articles 12-14 of the Damages Directive stipulate that defendants must be able to invoke the passing-on defence, that indirect purchasers also have a right to full compensation, and that overcompensation must be avoided at any level of the supply chain.[148]

IV.C.2 Remedies

As indicated by its title, the Damages Directive deals with one remedy only (*i.e.*, a request for damages), and introduces several requirements that national laws must comply with in order to facilitate the implementation of this remedy and improve the chances of a positive outcome of well-grounded requests. Leaving aside the articles

Damages Directive and the current outlook. Readers can find all the most important bibliography related to this topic cited in that same article.

142. Recitals 9, 10 and 34 of the Damages Directive.
143. Recital 21 of the Damages Directive.
144. Recital 15 of the Damages Directive.
145. Recitals 3, 4, 6, 11, 22, 26, 34, 46, 47, 48 of the Damages Directive.
146. *See* footnote 139 of this Part Three.
147. *See* Wils, *Private Enforcement of EU Antitrust Law and Its Relationship with Public Enforcement: Past, Present and Future*, cited in footnote 141 of this Part Three.
148. *Ibid.*

devoted to the amicable settlement of disputes,[149] which are of little use for the purposes of this book, the directive introduces important novelties on *locus standi*, mainly with reference to the role of indirect purchasers, the disclosure of evidence, and joint and several liability.

IV.C.2.1 Locus Standi

The Damages Directive extends legal standing to all parties who have suffered harm[150] from cartels or abuses of dominant position - even to those who have suffered it indirectly. The latter is defined as the parties to which overpricing previously suffered by undertakings that purchased goods or services directly from undertakings that infringed Articles 101 and 102 TFEU was transferred. This significantly broadens the possibility of damages in competition law (especially in the case of cartel infringements) and therefore offers an important compensation tool to undertakings and individuals indirectly harmed by an infringement, in addition to strengthening deterrence.

However, the value of this provision as a model for the development of private enforcement in the field of State aid is minor, if not negligible. When it comes to State aid, actions for damages are typically brought by competitors, not direct or (even less so) indirect customers. Moreover, for the latter, it would be extremely difficult, if not impossible, to prove the harm derived from unlawful aid, also considering the difficulty inherent in distinguishing the direct consequences of the economic advantage (direct or even indirect) granted through the aid measure and the broader consequences of the measure on the economy, at different levels of the production chain, which need not be addressed by remedies.

IV.C.2.2 Gathering of Evidence

The Damages Directive emphasises the fundamental importance of information in judicial proceedings aimed at the award of damages. It envisages the possibility for national courts to impose an obligation of disclosure on defendants and third parties, including by injunction.[151] Article 5 stipulates that, upon request of a claimant who has presented a reasoned justification containing reasonably available facts and evidence sufficient to support the plausibility of its claim for damages, national courts must be able to order the defendant or a third party to disclose relevant evidence which lies in their control, subject to a proportionality requirement. In the event of a refusal, the courts should be given the power to apply effective, proportionate and dissuasive penalties.[152]

Disclosure of evidence can be ordered from competition authorities, too. This is especially relevant for follow-on actions and actions indirectly related to public

149. Chapter VI of the Damages Directive.
150. *See* Art. 12 of the Damages Directive.
151. *See* Art. 5 of the Damages Directive.
152. *See* Art. 8 of the Damages Directive.

enforcement proceedings. However, in accordance with Article 6(10) of the Damages Directive, national courts may order disclosure from competition authorities only if no party or third party is reasonably able to provide that same evidence. When evidence is sought from private parties, confidential information must also be disclosed if relevant to the action for damages, but such information must be effectively protected - and those from whom disclosure is sought must have an opportunity to be heard before the national court orders disclosure.

The provisions on evidence are particularly relevant for proceedings in which the defendant is a monopolist or a member of a cartel, as such defendants are necessarily in a position to have better knowledge of the facts of the case than the claimant.[153] The provisions seek to eliminate (as far as possible) the information asymmetry between parties, allowing them to have the same tools[154] at their disposal to obtain effective judicial protection of their rights under EU competition law. This provides an incentive to bring actions before national courts.

The Damages Directive also contains provisions intended to protect leniency statements and settlement submissions.[155] This is a typical necessity of antitrust enforcement and is not directly relevant for the purposes of this book, as no similar situation arises in State aid proceedings. More generally, however, the protection of confidential information can be relevant in State aid proceedings in connection with written observations submitted by aid recipients to the Commission within the framework of an official investigation procedure or even during a preliminary investigation procedure, to prove compliance with the MEOP or the fourth condition of the *Altmark* test. Within these limits, experience gathered in the application of the Damages Directive can be of help to shape a reform of State aid private enforcement.

The Damages Directive also stipulates - again on the gathering of evidence in support of an action for damages - that until a competition authority has closed its proceedings, national courts cannot order disclosure of documents submitted to the authority by a natural or legal person within the framework of the proceedings or documents that the authority has drawn up and sent to the parties in the course of the proceedings.[156] Indeed, information contained therein cannot be used in actions for damages until the competition authority has closed its proceedings if it has been obtained solely through access to the file of a competition authority.[157]

This provision - which is clearly aimed at discouraging actions for damages that run parallel with public enforcement proceedings - could be of some relevance in the field of State aid, too. Indeed, although a positive final decision by the Commission does not have the effect of regularising *ex post facto* the unlawfulness of a given State aid measure, the nature of a Commission final decision can help national courts better identify the harm and determine whether it is neutralised by the repayment of the nominal amount plus interest (in the case of negative decisions) or the repayment of

153. *See* S. Peyer, *Compensation and the Damages Directive*, European Competition Journal, 2016 Volume 12, Issue 1, pp. 87-112 https://doi.org/10.1080/17441056.2016.1221168.
154. *See* recital 15 of the Damages Directive.
155. *See* recitals 26 and 27 and Arts 6(6) and 7(1) of the Damages Directive.
156. *See* Art. 6(5) of the Damages Directive.
157. *See* Art. 7(2) of the Damages Directive.

interest (in the case of positive decisions).[158] This would be even more so if the reform of remedies advocated for in this book was eventually adopted, as the Commission would be given the possibility of adapting the remedy to the specificities of a given case based on the competition distortion detected.

In addition, the possibility of relying on the Commission's final assessment in follow-on actions for damages (although very rare in the field of State aid) would give national courts the opportunity to consider the potential negative effect on market structure of the cumulative effects of repayment and liability for damages, especially in cases in which the aid beneficiary is a maverick or a small or medium-sized enterprise and the claimant for damages is the largest competitor. There would thus be an interest in discouraging actions for damages that run parallel with public enforcement proceedings, if the latter have been initiated.[159]

More generally, State aid has its specificity in that public enforcement proceedings entail exchanges of information and opinions between the Commission and Member States. The temporary protection of information drawn from public enforcement proceedings should therefore be strengthened to shield the exchanges between the Commission and the Member State concerned so long as the case is pending or the decision is subject to judicial review.[160] Waiting until the end of the public enforcement proceedings would not impair the rights of harmed interested parties because the case law clarified that the time limit under Article 17 of the Procedural Regulation applies only to the Commission's enforcement powers (*i.e.*, it does not preclude national courts from drawing all consequences from the unlawfulness of the aid) – and in any event, if public enforcement proceedings conclude with an infringement decision, damages claimants will be able to rely on that decision, which would likely qualify as a new fact under national tort law.

IV.C.2.3 Joint and Several Liability

Given the ultimate aims of the Damages Directive, another key provision is Article 11(1), which establishes joint and several liability for undertakings that 'have infringed competition law through joint behaviour'. This provision allows those who have suffered harm because of the infringement to sue even only one of the infringers and to

158. *See* Part One, section I.A.2.4 and footnote 33, and Part Two, section 5.3.2.
159. This corresponds to the concern – expressed in relation to the application of the Damages Directive – about the impact on market structure of the cumulative effects of fines and damages in cartel cases in which the largest competitor receives immunity under a leniency programme. *See* Wils, *Private Enforcement of EU Antitrust Law and Its Relationship with Public Enforcement: Past, Present and Future*, cited in footnote 141 of this Part Three. *See also* S. Davies, P.L. Ormosi & M. Graffenberger, *Mergers After Cartels: How Markets React to Cartel Breakdown*, University of East Anglia Centre for Competition Policy (CCP) Working Paper 14-1 (20 March 2014).
160. *See* Art. 4.2 of Regulation (EC) No 1049/2001 of the European Parliament and of the Council of 30 May 2001 regarding public access to European Parliament, Council and Commission documents, OJ L 145, 31.5.2001, p. 43, and the related case law (among others, *see* Judgment of the Court of 5 May 2024, *Public.Resource.Org and Right to Know v. Commission and Others*, C-588/21 P, EU:C:2024:201, and Judgment of the Court of 8 June 2023, *Council of the European Union v. Pech*, C-408/21 P, EU:C:2023:461).

claim full compensation from that infringer. This not only facilitates the exercise of legal action but also increases the chances that the claimant will actually be awarded compensation for the harm suffered.[161] Moreover, the fact that all cartel participants are considered jointly and severally liable for the entire harm caused provides an incentive for undertakings to cooperate with competition authorities in leniency programmes in exchange for immunity or at least a reduction in penalties if they report useful information.

The Damages Directive envisages three exceptions to the general rules on joint and several liability:[162] for immunity recipients, *i.e.*, undertakings or individuals that have been granted immunity from fines by a competition authority under a leniency programme;[163] for small or medium-sized enterprises;[164] and for co-infringers that have reached a consensual settlement with harmed parties.[165] Just like the rules on the interplay between evidence-gathering and leniency or settlement procedures, these exceptions are very specific to the field of antitrust and are of little use within the framework of State aid.

As a corollary, the Damages Directive gives binding effect to decisions on infringements of Articles 101 and 102 TFEU taken by the Commission[166] or the national competition authority of the country where the action for damages is lodged.[167] Indeed, an infringement ascertained in a final Commission decision, in a final decision of a national competition authority, or in a judgment handed down by a national court reviewing the decision of the national competition authority must be deemed to be irrefutably established for the purposes of an action for damages brought before a court in the same EU Member State.

This implies that, when settling a dispute between private individuals, national courts may not adopt judgments contrary to the decisions issued by the aforementioned authorities. Thus, a private party may rely on these decisions and need not prove the infringement or its ability to harm competitors and customers, but only the

161. Peyer, *Compensation and the Damages Directive*, cited in footnote 153 of this Part Three.
162. For a complete examination of these exceptions, *see* Wils, *Private Enforcement of EU Antitrust Law and Its Relationship with Public Enforcement: Past, Present and Future*, cited in footnote 141 of this Part Three.
163. Immunity recipients are jointly and severally liable to: (i) their direct or indirect purchasers or providers; and (ii) other injured parties only when full compensation cannot be obtained from the other undertakings that were involved in the same infringement.
164. Under certain conditions, small and medium-sized enterprises are liable only to their own direct and indirect purchasers if their market share in the relevant market was below 5 % at any time during the infringement and the application of the normal rules of joint and several liability would irretrievably jeopardise their economic viability and cause their assets to lose all their value.
165. *See* Art. 19(2) and (3) of the Damages Directive stipulates that co-infringers that have not settled their dispute are not permitted to recover contribution for the remaining claim from the co-infringer that did settle, except when the non-settling co-infringers cannot pay the damages that correspond to the remaining claim of the settling injured party.
166. The binding effect of a finding of infringement by the Commission in follow-on actions for damages in the national courts of all EU Member States already flows from Art. 16 of Regulation 1/2003 and the *Masterfoods* case law (Judgment of the Court of 14 December 2000, *Masterfoods v. HB Ice Cream*, C-344/98, EU:C:2000:689).
167. *See* Art. 9 of the Damages Directive. *See also* recital 34.

causal link and the harm suffered.[168] More precisely, the binding effect in follow-on actions for damages of a finding of infringement made in public enforcement proceedings covers the nature of the infringement and its material, personal, temporal and territorial scope as determined by the competition authority or review court in the exercise of its jurisdiction.[169] Moreover, for cartel infringements, Article 17(2) of the Damages Directive adds a rebuttable presumption that cartel infringements cause harm.

Decisions adopted by a national competition authority in another Member State - *i.e.*, in a different Member State from that in which a given action for damages is brought - are conferred *prima facie* evidentiary authority, thus favouring the recognition of harm suffered in a Member State other than that of residence.[170]

IV.C.3 Conclusions

In a nutshell, the Damages Directive has certainly played a prominent role in the harmonisation and development of private enforcement of EU antitrust law. Not only has it simplified the bringing of legal claims for compensation of harm suffered as a result of breaches of EU competition law but also - by stipulating disclosure requirements and giving binding effect to national decisions - it has increased the chances of obtaining compensation. However, its potential role as a model for private enforcement in the field of State aid seems limited for the reasons explained below.

To start with, the most important intended effect of the Damages Directive on the practice of private enforcement in antitrust law is 'an increase in the number of (purely compensatory) follow-on actions for damages. Significant change as to the frequency of standalone actions for damages was not intended by the legislator and is most unlikely to result from the Directive'.[171] Now, follow-on actions for damages in the private enforcement of State aid law are an exceptional occurrence and would likely become even less attractive if the reform advocated for in this book is eventually implemented and the Commission is given the power to consider the effects of unlawful and incompatible aid when ordering restorative or redressive measures. Moreover, the question of the binding force of Commission decisions on national authorities regarding proof of infringement does not arise in State aid law, as: (i) the Commission has exclusive competence; and (ii) State aid case law has already very precisely defined the obligations of national courts, both when a Commission decision has been issued and when proceedings before the Commission are pending or were never started.[172]

As to actions for damages, they are a decisive element of a successful private enforcement system in antitrust cases, but their importance - although not to be

168. *See*, among others, Peyer, *Compensation and the Damages Directive*, cited in footnote 153 of this Part Three.
169. *See* recital 34 of the Damages Directive.
170. *See* Art. 9 of the Damages Directive.
171. *See* Wils, *Private Enforcement of EU Antitrust Law and Its Relationship with Public Enforcement: Past, Present and Future*, cited in footnote 141 of this Part Three.
172. *See* Part Two, sections V.C.1 and V.C.2.

underestimated - is not comparable in State aid cases. Indeed, in State aid cases, national courts are mainly expected (based on EU case law) to adopt remedies capable of restoring, to the extent possible, a level playing field, *i.e.*, the market situation existing before the aid was granted.[173] Damage compensation can become important mainly as a dissuasive means but is not the main objective of enforcement. All these aspects will have to be duly considered in shaping a reform of the system of remedies in State aid law, which is the subject of the final part of this book.

Furthermore, of the three pillars of the Damages Directive (*locus standi*, evidence, and joint and several liability), only the second one could play a significant role in a directive on remedies for violations of State aid rules. Indeed, in the context of State aid, actions for damages are typically brought by competitors, not direct or indirect customers. As already explained, it would be extremely difficult, if not impossible, for the latter to prove harm deriving from unlawful aid. As to the joint and several liability of cartelists, this obviously does not apply to the aid sector, although one could imagine, within the limits of liability for damages, that an aid beneficiary could be held jointly and severally liable with its parent or other group companies.

Finally, when it comes to evidence, an important difference is that in the private enforcement of State aid rules, actions for damages are typically brought against the granting Member State because, as EU law currently stands, there is no legal basis for a damages claim against a recipient undertaking (horizontal direct effect) unless envisaged at national level.[174] Some disclosure obligations under the Damages Directive could be useful for a claimant in an action for damages concerning unlawful aid against a defendant Member State. For example, obliging the Member State to disclose the assessments carried out to consider the MEOP test satisfied could facilitate the proving of the existence of aid. Similarly, having to disclose assessments concerning the incentive effect or compliance with other GBER requirements could help a damages claimant prove the harm caused to competitors if the GBER is eventually considered not applicable by the court hearing the case.

That said, the context is obviously very different between antitrust and State aid damages cases; indeed, the provisions that could be helpful in facilitating damages claims in cases of unlawful aid are quite different - including with regard to the means of proof - from those needed in a case between private parties based on antitrust laws. Overall, the role that the Damages Directive can play as a model for a hypothetical directive harmonising private enforcement of State aid law can only be limited.[175]

173. *See* Part Two, section V.E.2.
174. *See* Part Two, sections V.C.1 and V.C.2.
175. Some scholars express a different opinion, which is discussed in Part Four of this book when drawing conclusions on the analysis conducted and reflecting on the avenues for reform of the current system of remedies in State aid law.

Final Remarks on Part Three

The final remarks emphasise the importance of a convergent system of remedies in public competition law. It is suggested that the FSR could serve as a model for the reform of remedies in the public enforcement of State aid – one that promotes greater coherence and effectiveness – and that private enforcement would also naturally evolve as a consequence of such a reform.

Before proposing practical and sufficiently detailed guidelines for a reform of the system of remedies in State aid law, it seemed necessary to verify the extent to which a model for such a possible reform could be found in secondary EU law – or, if not truly a model, at least some starting points from which a reform could depart. Logically, the focus has been on legal frameworks most akin to that of State aid law in terms of inspiration and objectives, namely those that have the task of protecting the conditions for the proper functioning of the internal market, guaranteeing the healthy competitive dynamic that constitutes its necessary corollary – and indeed its real driving force.

The greatest attention has fallen on the system of remedies in the control of foreign subsidies, because the rules in the FSR are the logical complement to the rules on the control of State aid and, together with the latter, form a single branch of law. With the addition of the rules on public undertakings and on the liability of States for antitrust violations, this single branch has been defined as 'public competition law'.[176] An examination of the FSR and, in particular, the system of remedies envisaged therein has confirmed this initial impression.

The FSR is rich in insights because it starts precisely from the experience of applying State aid rules but then adapts and develops it along two lines: on the one hand, since the FSR rules are addressed to companies directly as opposed to States, the FSR combines the experience in the field of aid with that in private competition law; on the other hand, it moves on terrain less constrained by ideological conditioning, such as the principle of the second best (*i.e.*, the principle of incompatibility of State aid) and the need to affirm the exclusive competence of the Commission and to avoid circumvention. These two elements allow the FSR to freely pick up on the most promising

176. *See* Introduction, p. 1.

aspects of the various frameworks in order to combine them in the best possible way for the sole purpose of ensuring the effectiveness of control and the Union's interest.

This is not to deny the obvious differences between State aid control and foreign subsidy control - differences that remain intact despite the complementary nature of the two frameworks. Instead, it is a question of determining whether and, if so, to what extent:

(i) these differences justify a completely different approach to the system of remedies, thus precluding a convergence between the two;
(ii) the State aid system of remedies cannot be deprived of the objective of deterrence, which can be pursued by more effective means than mere recovery of the nominal aid amount regardless of the circumstances of a given case and the distortive effects produced by the aid; and
(iii) it is not logical and perhaps even desirable, in a post-modernisation era, to lighten the legalism that characterises the State aid system of remedies. This even more so considering the general context of substantive law, which is instead increasingly bending towards an analysis of the actual effects of aid measures (substantialist approach). Under this paradigm, the original principle of the second best has been largely emptied of content by the recurring use of State aid to cope with crises of various kinds and by the fact that European institutions themselves encourage a judicious use of State aid to achieve the increasingly precise horizontal objectives defined at Union level.

These are clearly rhetorical questions, and in fact, in Part Four of this book, the question is raised of precisely how to achieve a long-overdue real modernisation of the State aid system of remedies to bring it into line with developments in substantive law, now that the adoption of the FSR has helped chart the way forward.

The analysis carried out in this Part Three also reveals that no other pieces of legislation can serve as a true model for the reform of remedies in the field of State aid. Neither the Remedies Directive in the field of public procurement nor the Damages Directive in the field of antitrust law can fulfil this role, although for different reasons. Still, they do provide useful insights and food for thought in view of the modernisation of State aid private enforcement advocated for in Part two of this book.

The Remedies Directive regulates a situation that is not so different from that of State aid, since it is addressed to Member States and concerns infringements committed by contracting authorities or contracting entities, with the aim of setting minimum requirements that national regulations must comply with in order to contribute to the effectiveness of EU rules. The obvious difference is that private enforcement in the field of public procurement is even more crucial for the effectiveness of the relevant EU law provisions, as the Commission does not have exclusive competence and can only have recourse to the ordinary infringement procedure. Furthermore, giving interested parties a window of time in which to react before aid is implemented would risk being ineffective because, unlike in public procurement, interested parties are not necessarily - let alone timely - informed of contested State aid measures.

Nevertheless, the idea that national procedural laws must comply with certain minimum requirements and that remedies in cases of violation of the standstill obligation must be effective, proportionate and dissuasive can be of interest. Likewise, the idea that national courts must at least consider a contract ineffective if it has not already been fully performed and if this does not run against imperative public interests is a valuable one, especially considering the numerous cases of State aid in the form of project or investment agreements or other forms of State aid contractualisation.

Furthermore, the fact that the Remedies Directive encourages Member States to seek alternative remedies whenever the obligations under the contract concerned have already been performed or public interest considerations prevent the contract from being declared ineffective can also be a source of inspiration for the reform of the State aid system of remedies.

As to the Damages Directive, it clearly builds upon the role of national competition authorities, which thus far have no competence in the field of State aid. Moreover, the antitrust legal framework is relatively different from that of State aid because its provisions are addressed to undertakings, meaning the latter are directly liable to harmed parties. These are very significant differences when compared to the State aid framework. If a harmonisation directive is adopted in the field of the private enforcement of State aid rules, it should be shaped around the peculiarities of the State aid framework and should target the specific weaknesses of State aid private enforcement, as described in detail in Part Two of this book.

Despite all these significant differences, some basic principles of the Damages Directive can be a source of inspiration. This is the case with the joint and several liability rule, although this rule would have different content in the field of State aid. First, the possibility of Member States and aid beneficiaries having parallel liability could be explored. This would imply giving relevance to the 'intent' factor: whether the aid beneficiary was aware - or should have been aware based on the information at its disposal - of the aid's unlawfulness; in other words, whether it was complicit with the Member State in the violation of the procedural rules. Intent is, in any event, relevant when applying national provisions of tort law.

This approach would also have the advantage of serving as a deterrent. Furthermore, if this approach were retained, it would become possible to give harmed undertakings the opportunity to seek damages, not only from the legal person that directly benefitted from the aid but also from the group to which it belongs.[177]

In addition, both directives provide interesting insights from an evidence-gathering standpoint. In State aid matters, the gathering of evidence to prove a causal link between the granting of aid and harm suffered is particularly problematic because the causal link is twofold (upstream causation and downstream causation), as explained earlier in this book.[178] Thus, the harmonisation of national laws could prove

177. The concept of 'economic unit' is of relevance in the field of State aid but not in all circumstances and not in relation to all aspects of State aid law. For instance, it has been argued that it has a limited role to play when it comes to the repayment of aid (*see* Part One, sections III.A.2 and II.A.3). However, it seems appropriate to apply it in relation to damages claims.
178. *See* Part Two, section V.E.4.

helpful to developing private enforcement by giving national courts the necessary tools to request Member States and/or aid beneficiaries to submit non-confidential information suitable to demonstrate the result achieved through the aid and any change in the beneficiary's financial or market position.

In damages actions in which the defendant is (or the defendants include) an aid beneficiary (if such a possibility is envisaged in a would-be harmonisation directive), national courts' power to request information could extend to the aid beneficiary's knowledge of the aid's unlawfulness. National courts should of course be required to check that the damages claim is sufficiently well grounded and that requests for information are proportionate and precisely targeted to what is strictly relevant for the case.

These ideas and others are examined in Part Four with the aim of sketching out the main lines of a reform of the remedies system in the field of State aid - without, however, assuming that a harmonisation directive is an indispensable condition of whatever reform of the State aid remedies system, as the goal of this book is to formulate various conduits for reform with a view to maximising the chance that a long overdue and necessary reform for the system's coherence and credibility is eventually implemented.

Part Four

Scope of Reform

Introduction to Part Four

CONTENTS

This chapter summarises what is covered in the first three parts in preparation for Part Four, which endeavours to propose various options for a comprehensive reform of the system of remedies through secondary law, soft law and creative jurisprudence and discusses how these options can overcome the limitations of the current system.

State aid law has always undergone constant – sometimes groundbreaking – developments, most of which are closely linked with the evolution of Member States' role in the economy and EU institutions' increasing use of State aid control as leverage for establishing industrial and macroeconomic objectives for the Union as a whole. Nonetheless, the State aid system of remedies has remained surprisingly stable, at least since the enactment of the first Procedural Regulation in 1999. Even then, the only noteworthy change was the introduction of an obligation for the Commission to order recovery except in very limited circumstances (*i.e.*, when recovery clashes with fundamental principles of Union law). Apart from that, the case law developments that have contributed to shaping remedies can be described as nothing more than quite ordinary.

Against this background, in introducing the final part of this book, focused on specific and pragmatic suggestions for the reform of the State aid system of remedies, it is worth summarising the research conducted and the conclusions reached in the previous three parts.

The first two parts of this book conduct a detailed investigation into the limitations and shortcomings of the current system of remedies. Part One, which is devoted to public enforcement, identifies and discusses the key principles of the post-modernisation recovery regime.[1] The analysis reveals at least two extremely relevant weaknesses in the current system of remedies in public enforcement. First, a blatant inconsistency exists between the statements of principle regarding the remedies' objectives and their practical application. Whereas the stated objectives are to effectively offset market distortions and re-establish the competitive situation existing before unlawful aid was granted (*see* both the recitals of the Procedural Regulation and the case law discussed in detail in Part One), in practice the Commission and the EU courts content themselves with a blind recovery of the nominal aid amount. Second, the current system of remedies is markedly rigid and formalistic, which is ill-suited to the substantialist approach of competition law and EU law in general. What is this formalism rooted in? It is rooted in the gap between assessing the compatibility of a given aid measure and determining the appropriate remedies.[2] Although a compatibility assessment is indispensable for the issuance of a recovery order, in practice it never

1. Part One is largely based on this author's previous book on remedies in State aid public enforcement, published by Giappichelli in 2018 (*see* Part One, footnote 3). However, not only does it significantly summarise and update that book's content but it also takes a completely different slant in presenting the topic, as it does not follow a chronological or exegesis-based order but rather identifies and discusses – one by one – the key principles that can be inferred from case law and soft law.
2. Pastor-Merchante refers to this gap as a 'bifurcation' between the substantive and the procedural assessments in State aid law. *See* Part Two, footnotes 5 and 174.

seems to affect the remedy, which always remains the same: recovery of the nominal amount plus interest.

This rigidity plays out in two directions: on the one hand, it can lead to *overenforcement* when the aid's effects on competition in the market have vanished; on the other hand, it can lead to *underenforcement* when the aid has brought about a significant change in competition dynamics. Several examples of this mismatch exist in relation to, first and foremost, indirect aid. There is indeed some uncertainty and incoherence on the amount to be recovered in relation to this kind of aid, as the Commission and the EU courts appear to derogate from the nominal amount approach, but without openly acknowledging it or providing any reasoning for doing so. The mismatch also arises in relation to insolvency proceedings and, more generally, as a result of the lack of differentiation between forms of aid – despite the fact that different forms of aid affect the market differently, as the Commission itself acknowledges in its post-modernisation compatibility criteria.[3]

Overall, the analysis conducted in Part One proves that numerous incongruities and weaknesses exist in the current public enforcement system of remedies, which extends to ancillary remedies. The analysis also proves that a reform of the system of remedies – which has remained inexplicably stable despite the evolution of State aid law and policy – would be coherent with the objectives and principles that inspired the modernisation of State aid rules. Nevertheless, it is also suggested that an assessment of the private enforcement system of remedies is highly advisable before reaching conclusions on the design of such a reform. This leads to an examination of the private enforcement system of remedies in Part Two.[4]

In Part Two, the research question is whether the private enforcement of State aid rules, in its current form and stage of development, suitably complements public enforcement and forges an adequate overall system of remedies. To answer this question, it first recalls the basic principles underpinning private enforcement in the field of State aid, from both a substantive and a procedural standpoint, and then reviews the changes introduced with the modernisation efforts – notably with the new Enforcement Notice in 2021. Although private enforcement is less rigid on paper than public enforcement – as national courts are, in principle, free to appraise the market situation and decide on the most suitable remedies to restore the situation existing

3. As early as in the Commission Communication on State Aid Modernisation (cited in footnote 128 of Part One), emphasis is put on the actual impact of the aid on the single market, on the distortive effect of specific measures, including fiscal aid, and on the need for Member States to design aid measures appropriately (*see* para. 19). This concept is further developed in the Commission Communication on Compatibility Criteria (OJ C 528, 30.12.2021, pp. 10-18), in which the Commission clarifies that Member States must provide evidence that the proposed aid measure constitutes the appropriate policy instrument to address the objective of the project concerned. An aid measure is not considered appropriate if other less distortive policy instruments *or* if *other less distortive types of aid instruments* make it possible to achieve the same result (*see* para. 42).
4. It is important to remember that Part Two does not aim at providing an exhaustive analysis of the State aid private enforcement system as a whole. Although an overview of the full enforcement system is necessary to discuss remedies, Part Two makes no claim of an exhaustive overview, as the attention remains focused on remedies throughout this book.

before the aid was granted – the role of national courts in practice is hindered in several ways, as follows:

- The case law is anything but clear when it comes to the obligation of national courts to order recovery[5] and the methods to be used to calculate the amount to be recovered.
- The notion of aid is likewise anything but clear from several angles, which is discouraging for national courts.
- The new Enforcement Notice, although more complete and better structured than its predecessor, does not offer sufficient guidance and does not resolve the most common uncertainties (*e.g.*, on the interplay between enforcement and insolvency proceedings, on economic continuity, and on the suitability of alternative remedies and the quantification thereof).
- A great deal of uncertainty surrounds the interplay between private enforcement and the Commission's decisions and pending investigations.
- National law only rarely provides specific rules or procedures for the enforcement of State aid rules,[6] and the general provisions of national legal systems are not easily adjustable to the peculiarities of State aid law, for instance, when it comes to the causal link between aid granted and damage caused to the market or the limits of Member State liability for damage under national tort provisions (*e.g.*, the application of the foreseeability requirement).[7]

5. It is indeed not uncommon, as seen in Part Two, to find conflicting indications in the same judgment: *e.g.*, one instance might affirm that national courts are free to assess the most suitable remedies, whereas another instance might suggest that recovery is the unavoidable consequence of the aid's unlawfulness.
6. Only a few Member States (*i.e.*, Belgium, Estonia, Finland, the Netherlands and Spain) have enacted a specific legal framework on aid recovery. Even in these cases, the legal framework generally envisages specific procedural rules to be followed for the implementation of Commission recovery decisions but does not address the issue of private actions brought by competitors or other interested parties to have State aid provisions enforced by national courts. Exceptions are very limited: Estonia, for instance, amended the Estonian Competition Act such that the granting authority is required to recover unlawful aid even in the absence of a recovery decision following the procedure provided for in the act; and Ireland has attributed exclusive jurisdiction to the Competition List of the High Court to hear competition law disputes, including State aid cases (both public and private enforcement). Likewise, in Italy, the administrative courts have been attributed nearly exclusive jurisdiction to hear cases concerning public and private enforcement of State aid rules, although civil courts have kept their jurisdiction over certain types of proceedings and actions, such as those brought within the framework of insolvency procedures – *see* Art. 133(1)(z-*sexies*) of the Italian Code of Administrative Procedure (*Codice del processo amministrativo*). *See also* L. Iera, *Il quadro regolatorio italiano sul recupero degli aiuti di Stato nell'ambito delle regole di public enforcement*, available at the following link: Giustizia Amministrativa – 12-13 giugno 2023 – Corso di formazione e aggiornamento – 'Il regime degli aiuti di Stato' – Piattaforma Teams 12-13 giugno 2023 (giustizia-amministrativa.it).
   No other Member States have modified their court systems and assigned exclusive jurisdiction to a single court in State aid disputes or set out specific procedures for the private enforcement of State aid rules. *See* the Final Study on the Enforcement of State aid rules and Decisions by National Courts (cited in footnote 44 of Part Two (Chapter III)).
7. On this requirement and the uncertainties that its application might entail in relation to State aid, *see* Part Two, section V.E.4.1.b).

All these findings reported in Part Two lead to the conclusion that: (i) nowadays private enforcement is insufficiently developed to adequately supplement public enforcement; and (ii) a harmonisation initiative would be needed to achieve satisfactory results overall, at least in the absence of a reform of public enforcement, whereas it would be not absolutely unavoidable if a reform of public enforcement is implemented (although, as explained below, the combination of both reforms, of private and public enforcement, would give a pivotal contribution to the achievement of a modernises system of remedies in State aid law). Moreover, private enforcement today is intrinsically limited in at least two ways: (1) it can hardly offer protection to the aid beneficiary *vis-à-vis* the Member State granting the aid; and (2) it can hardly be used to effectively remove the market distortion when the aid has been effective and generated a multiplier effect, considering that, absent a legislative initiative, EU law does not offer a legal basis for actions for damages against beneficiaries.

In a nutshell, when one considers the conclusions of Part One and Part Two together, the need for a reform of the State aid system of remedies emerges with even more clarity.[8] A huge misunderstanding lies at the heart of the system of remedies as a whole, which characterises both public enforcement and private enforcement. It is, in a broad sense, a *problem of accountability*, due to the fact that the State is solely (or at least primarily) responsible for the violation of procedural rules. The reality, however, is that the State faces no consequences whatsoever – it is not affected in the least by remedies, apart from evanescent hits to its prestige. Quite the contrary: in some cases, which are more numerous than one might think, the recovery of the aid is to the State's advantage.

Indeed, the granting Member State could theoretically be affected by a recovery order in two ways: (1) recovery could generate social reprobation or turmoil; and/or (2) recovery could lead to a loss of a benefit for the national economy or consumer welfare. However, from the first standpoint, the popularity of a State's ruling class – which is an aspect that plays an important role when granting aid, as it often translates into decisions that appear to lack economic rationality (*institutional failure*) – is at most only marginally at stake at the moment of recovery, if at all. Indeed, the social disapproval that can in theory accompany an order to recover unlawful aid actually affects the Commission much more directly than the State concerned. From the second standpoint, too – *i.e.*, the national economy or collective interest standpoint – there are no major consequences: typically, the investment project concerned will have already been executed by the time recovery is ordered, and in that case recovery affects only the recipient undertaking; if, conversely, the project has not been completed yet, in most cases the fact that the aid was declared incompatible means that it did not serve the common interest very effectively or, in any case, gave rise to negative repercussions (*e.g.*, a subsidy war).

8. However, as discussed below, a reform of public enforcement is the unavoidable initial step which, if achieved, could lead to satisfactory results also in the private enforcement of State aid rules with a simple update and further elaboration of the Enforcement Notice, *i.e.*, even in the absence of a harmonisation directive.

This paradox is due to the fact that beneficiaries are not closely associated with the procedure, and their possible *co-responsibility is not considered* – with these two aspects being strictly interrelated, of course.[9] If co-responsibility were considered, this would pave the way for very different scenarios, including co-liability in some instances. Indeed, if companies were co-responsible, alternative redressive measures would become meaningful with a view to effectively and completely offsetting the competitive advantage gained. The risk of underenforcement would be eliminated, and the risk of overenforcement – again, if companies were co-responsible – would be tolerable, as it would be considered a sort of (potential) penalty. Conversely, as long as the State is solely responsible, recovery will remain the rule, as it is a (formalistic) tool that aims at preventing Member States from taking advantage of infringements of procedural rules and (allegedly) acts as a deterrent.

Even with the present system of sole responsibility of the State, nothing stands in the way of going beyond recovery of the nominal amount if necessary to avoid underenforcement or, conversely, of not proceeding with recovery if recovery would risk putting the State in a better situation than in the case of non-recovery. A change in the paradigm of absolute impossibility would be necessary, however, as explained below. Additionally, EU law (at least the Private Enforcement Notice) should be adapted to establish a principle that could underpin actions for damages by beneficiaries against the granting State, to prevent the latter from benefitting from recovery while at the same time ensuring that the beneficiary is not put in a better situation than that in which it was before the unlawful aid was granted.

Emphasising the current paradox and all the system's weaknesses would remain fruitless if it were not translated into concrete suggestions with a view to the system's much desirable – and long overdue –modernisation. In making any suggestions, though, it seems only appropriate to: (i) consider the current state of development of the State aid control system overall; and (ii) delve into whether it is possible to draw inspiration from other regulations in the European legal system that provide their own system of remedies.

As to the first point, the current state of the State aid control system is characterised by what has now become an overt impoverishment of economic liberalism (not to mention the ordoliberalism that marked the early years of European integration's economic history) so deeply intertwined with the European project. In a nutshell, the current trend's main feature is that State intervention is back. Public powers now have a massive presence in European economies. Moreover, State aid expenditure is just one of the many phenomena heading in the same direction: more regulation, an increasingly greater role for public investment corporations, and greater FDI control, to name but a few.[10] Overall, the current economic system is clearly increasingly closer to the regulated model than to the liberal one.[11]

9. Opening up to a co-responsibility paradigm would indeed make it necessary to enhance aid beneficiaries' rights of defence in accordance with general principles of EU law.
10. On 20 June 2023, for instance, the Commission announced its intention to introduce – by the end of the year – a mechanism to control outbound investments as part of a new economic security

In this context, it is of paramount importance – for the future solidity of the State aid system and the survival of the internal market – to avoid continuous recourse to emergency legislation and to stick to the recently developed interpretation and implementation of the emergency legal bases existing in the Treaty, thereby limiting Member States' discretion and, consequently, inequalities and distortions of competition. Likewise, procedural guarantees and third-party rights ought to be reinforced in parallel, ideally by amending the Procedural Regulation so as to avoid leaving undertakings at the mercy of Member States and their new interventionism, which, although understandable in the current circumstances, carries the risk of abuses and distortions – abuses and distortions that the Commission alone does not seem prepared, let alone equipped, to halt. Nevertheless, the road ahead still appears to be long and blocked by the dominant intergovernmental approach.[12]

Now, given the above, the question is whether the impoverishment of the original liberal approach could have an impact on the system of remedies. In the short term, the increased role of Member States in the economy and the growing relaxation of State aid control – whereby it is increasingly becoming mainly a tool to tackle recurring crises – could lead to a further tightening of the application of existing remedies (with essentially recovery being used, in the formalistic manner in which it is currently implemented) in the dwindling number of cases in which aid is declared incompatible; in the long term, however, the loss of credibility of State aid control risks making even this form of remedy less effective and less politically acceptable.

Conversely, the development of a new, modernised system of remedies – one that focuses on the effects of unlawful aid on the market and is sufficiently adaptable so that the most appropriate instruments can realistically be used to affect the competitive dynamic in order to achieve the objective of re-establishing the *status quo ante* – may help restore credibility and realistic efficiency for the entire control system, thereby halting the current drift.

As long as the system of remedies remains unchanged – with no penalties (formally speaking) but rather solely the non-adaptable, rigid, blind (and therefore often disproportionate in practice) and blunt remedy that is full recovery – State aid will become more and more politicised and less and less predictable, and the related rules less and less reliable from the perspective of ensuring a true level playing field.

The air transport sector is a prime example: in several cases, recovery orders have been addressed to companies no longer active on the market and undergoing liquidation proceedings (making the orders totally ineffective),[13] accompanied by compatibility decisions addressed to the purchaser of the going concern or of the valuable assets

strategy. The Commission's focus is on emerging technologies that could be used for military purposes ('dual use'). Here too, the model for this new legislative initiative is likely to be the dual-use export control system.

11. M. Merola and A. Cogoni, *Chronique of the 2022 Main Developments in State Aid*, Annuaire de Droit Européen, Editions Panthéon-Assas, Paris 2023.
12. *Ibid.*
13. One of the latest examples is the Commission decision concerning the setting up of a new airline called ITA (subsequently acquired by Lufthansa), which had purchased numerous assets that previously belonged to Alitalia Società Aerea Italiana S.p.A. (Alitalia). The Commission adopted two recovery decisions – one in 2021 and the other in 2023 – ordering Italy to seek repayment

that remain. In other cases, conditional decisions are issued, imposing significant prospective remedies on the buyer to ensure economic discontinuity with the aid recipient.[14] Clearly, the recovery order's effects in such cases are limited to reducing the body of receivables which creditors of the failing company can use to recover their claims, while undeservedly rewarding the State by giving it the possibility of recovering a certain amount of capital precisely at the expense of non-preferential creditors.

As to the second point (*i.e.*, the possibility of drawing inspiration from other European regulations), the analysis conducted in Part Three shows the FSR (which recently came into force) to appear quite interesting – worthy of an examination of its innovative system of remedies in detail. Thus, after a general introduction to the FSR's framework, most of Part Three is devoted to explaining the system of remedies it envisages, highlighting its differences from the State aid framework. Part Three emphasises the special features of the FSR's system, which is based on a deliberate convergence between the traditional prospective and restorative remedies in State aid law and the redressive measures in competition law, and which applies the same remedies irrespective of the kind of procedure (*i.e.*, whether notification-driven or *ex officio*).

Clearly, aid unlawfulness is a concept that cannot be replicated in the field of foreign subsidies, and the procedure in the case of unlawful aid is an atypical

---

of two bridge loans from Alitalia, which had been placed into special bankruptcy proceedings back in 2017. Indeed, to keep Alitalia operating, Italy had granted the company loans of EUR 900 million in 2017 and EUR 400 million in 2019, neither of which were ever repaid. *See* Commission Decision of 10 September 2021, C(2021) 6659 final, OJ L 141, 20.5.2022, p. 53, and Commission Decision of 27 March 2023, C(2023) 1713 final, OJ L 2160, 20.10.2023. *See also* footnote 80 of Part Three.

14. *See* Commission Decision of 10 September 2023, C(2021) 6665 final, OJ C 177, 29.4.2022, which found that: (i) ITA's purchase of Alitalia in liquidation's tangible and intangible assets did not involve the granting of State aid to the buyer because the purchase had taken place as a result of a competitive procedure or against consideration certified by independent experts; and (ii) ITA did not qualify as a beneficiary of the bridge loans granted to Alitalia in 2017 and 2019 and was therefore not under an obligation to repay them, provided that a number of conditions were met, failing which the economic discontinuity between ITA and Alitalia would be deemed to cease to exist and ITA would qualify as Alitalia's successor. These conditions included – to name but a few – a ban on ITA participating in the tender for the purchase of the 'MilleMiglia' frequent flyer programme, a limitation whereby ITA could bid only for a minority shareholding in Alitalia's maintenance business, limitations relating to the possibility of ITA bidding for Alitalia's handling business, a ban on transferring Alitalia client information to ITA, and an obligation on ITA to hire new staff or to negotiate new employment contracts with existing staff for a given number of employees. It is immediately clear that several of these conditions do not actually relate to the need to avoid aid elements in the asset purchase transaction – nor are they strictly necessary to avoid ITA being held liable for the old aid granted to Alitalia, as discontinuity could have been ensured by other means (*e.g.*, by simply requiring all assets to be sold in tender procedures or at a price certified in advance by independent experts appointed in agreement with the Commission). The conditions in fact aim at *ensuring achievement of a result which the repayment of the aid to Alitalia in liquidation cannot ensure, namely the elimination of the competitive advantage enjoyed as a result of the aid.* In other words, they aim at ensuring that competitors benefit at least in part from the freeing-up of market shares that would have resulted from the liquidation of Alitalia under ordinary procedures. Had the rigidity and formalism of the current system of remedies not been standing in the way, it would have been much more straightforward and transparent – as is always the case in such situations – to impose the conditions as remedies in the negative decision concerning unlawful aid granted to Alitalia.

infringement procedure that cannot apply to foreign subsidies. Furthermore, as subsidy recipient companies are liable in the event of an infringement of procedural rules, the penalties envisaged for this purpose complete the system of remedies and complement redressive measures, thus ensuring deterrence. However, this does not rob the FSR's innovative content of its significance, for two reasons: first, the Commission could have stuck to the concept of repayment of the financial advantage (not necessarily repayment to the third country but perhaps to an earmarked fund, given the difficulty in monitoring repayment to granting third countries), but instead it significantly downgraded it; and second, useful lessons for State aid can likely also be found in: (i) the emphasis placed on the actual degree to which the competitive advantage is eliminated; (ii) the priority to be given to less intrusive remedies; and (iii) the possibility of combining measures of different nature.

Consequently, while the *acquis communautaire* in the field of State aid will certainly be crucial for the effective implementation of the newly introduced framework on foreign subsidies, the latter framework could itself serve to relaunch the process of State aid reform, mainly in areas - such as remedies and procedures in general - where the experience of modernisation has thus far been most disappointing. Furthermore, as far as private enforcement is concerned, inspiration can be drawn - although only marginally, and despite the obvious differences - from other systems of remedies existing in EU law, namely the harmonisation directives adopted in the field of public procurement (Remedies Directive) and antitrust law (Damages Directive). With respect to both directives, the gathering of evidence is certainly the most important aspect (although not the only one) from which inspiration can be drawn to formulate a proposal of harmonisation of national laws to foster State aid private enforcement.

Part Three therefore closes, in reference to public enforcement, with the hope for a progressive convergence between the system of remedies in the field of State aid and that in the field of foreign subsidies, which can lead to a comprehensive system of remedies for public competition law altogether. Moreover, a convergence seems entirely consistent with the objective of a level playing field between economic operators active in the internal market, which is indeed what inspired the FSR. As to private enforcement, Part Three closes with the hope of a true modernisation of the current tools, including the need to seriously consider the potential for a harmonisation directive.

I TOOLS OF REFORM: THE DIFFERENT OPTIONS - HOW TO ACHIEVE A SUBSTANTIAL REFORM OF THE SYSTEM OF REMEDIES THROUGH SOFT LAW AND CREATIVE JURISPRUDENCE

This chapter discusses whether a substantial reform of the system of remedies can be achieved only through soft law tools and creative jurisprudence. It analyses how these tools can improve the system's flexibility and effectiveness, while also highlighting the limits of this option.

When reflecting on how to best translate the suggestions of amendment or development of the public enforcement system of remedies into reform proposals, two major alternatives must be considered: (i) propose a substantial reform of the new Procedural Regulation - despite its relatively recent enactment (in 2015) - within the framework of the last phase of SAM; or (ii) stretch the existing provisions as much as possible through soft law instruments and creative jurisprudence.

The third alternative - *i.e.*, a reform of primary law - is not considered here because the reform proposed in this book is conceived as the missing leg of SAM (which has not involved any reform of the Treaty);[15] therefore, it should be easy to enact and should be able to contribute to shaping State aid policy in the near future. Ideally, the two avenues indicated above (*i.e.*, reforming the Procedural Regulation and adapting soft law) could be combined to achieve the best possible outcome in terms of both content and timing of the reform. However, it is also worth considering the second option as a standalone avenue, given the political difficulties that could indefinitely delay a substantial reform of the procedural rules.

Therefore, this chapter first goes through the reform option based on new soft law instruments and creative jurisprudence. This will provide the background needed to then analyse the added value that the alternative/supplementary reform option - *i.e.*, the one based on legislative initiative - could bring about.

As indicated in Part Three,[16] it seems reasonable to reflect on the influence of the recently adopted FSR when considering the changes that can be made to the State aid system of remedies. However, some authors consider that 'the Commission has quite a broad leeway when it comes to the substantive content of a decision in third country subsidies' review'.[17] This is because the FSR requires the distortion of competition caused by a subsidy in the internal market to be completely and effectively eliminated. While State aid law is supposedly concerned with approving or prohibiting national aid, third-country subsidy review is concerned with offsetting the adverse effect of

15. The last reform of primary law in the field of State aid dates back to the Treaty of Lisbon, when some changes were introduced in both Art. 107(2) and Art. 108(2). Although at that time the first wave of the modernisation process - broadly understood - was already ongoing, the reform did not touch on any aspect of modernisation but basically codified changes that had already emerged in practice (in relation to the reunification of Germany and to the scope of group exemptions, including for *de minimis* aid).
16. *See* Part Three, Chapters II-IV.
17. *See*, among others, Weiß, *Ex Officio Third Country Subsidies' Review*, cited in footnote 65 of Part Three.

subsidies on competition in the internal market. According to the same authors, this alleged difference, which translates into the different powers given to the Commission in relation to State aid and foreign subsidies, can be easily explained by the different subjects of the respective procedures. As the reimbursement of a foreign subsidy to a granting authority in a foreign country is almost impossible to monitor, and as recovery orders would be impossible to enforce outside the EU, the EU legislator was obliged to give more prominence to structural and behavioural remedies that are used only rarely in State aid law.

Although this reconstruction is not wrong, it has many weaknesses, some of which have been already highlighted in Part Three.[18] The difference in objectives between State aid control and foreign subsidy screening needs to be very much downplayed: in fact, if one looks carefully at the statements of principle in both the preamble to the Procedural Regulation and the Court of Justice's case law, as extensively examined in Part One,[19] the differences are reduced to nuances. Even more importantly, the impossibility of enforcing a recovery order outside the EU explains why the FSR takes a different path when it comes to shaping remedies but says nothing about the suitability of similar remedies in the field of State aid – and certainly does not explain why, in the latter field, similar remedies should remain confined to exceptional situations. Therefore, it is anything but useless to explore whether lessons for the reform of State aid remedies can be drawn from the FSR – even more so given that the progressive approximation between State aid control and foreign subsidy screening is a reasonable step forward and should be considered by itself an objective to be pursued.

Instead, the first problem to be addressed when it comes to exploring this avenue of reform (*i.e.*, the approximation to the FSR's system of remedies) is the interpretation of primary law: namely of Article 108(2) TFEU. This issue is examined in the next section.

I.A Interpreting Primary Law in an Innovative, yet Literal, Way

The interpretation of Article 108(2) is crucial for the purposes of this book insofar as it states that, if the Commission, when examining unlawful aid, comes to the conclusion that the aid is incompatible, it shall decide that the State concerned shall abolish or alter such aid within a period determined by the Commission. The question must therefore be asked whether the expression 'abolish or alter' allows for the State aid system of remedies to develop towards the use of redressive measures, alternative to recovery, and also in the context of (restorative) remedies. For the sake of clarity, it is worth recalling that the term 'abolish' underlies the entire remedies policy as it has developed from the early 1970s to the present day, for the Court held, in the famous *Kohlegesetz* judgment,[20] that this wording in Article 108(2) allowed (and indeed required) the Commission not only to order States to abolish existing aid deemed incompatible with

18. *See* Part Three, section IV.B.1.
19. *See* Part One, section I.A.2.3.
20. *See* Part One, footnote 5.

the internal market (and thus to stop granting it) but also to recover aid already illegally paid if it was also incompatible.

In the context of the permanent monitoring of existing aid, altering incompatible aid means modifying certain aspects of the scheme (rate, budget, duration, eligibility criteria, and/or other aspects) that are sufficiently substantial to convert incompatibility into compatibility. The Union legislature has in fact clarified and supplemented these rules by means of the Procedural Regulation, which not only identifies the elements characterising an aid scheme[21] but also brings alterations to existing aid within the scope of control.[22] In this way, *the Commission is assured control without loopholes*: incompatible existing aid may become compatible if some essential element of it is changed; and any aid thus changed becomes new aid and must therefore be authorised in advance by the Commission before payments can be resumed (though the Commission's decision may take the form of a decision that records the Member State's acceptance of the necessary alterations and that is aimed at making those alterations compulsory in accordance with Article 23(1) of the Procedural Regulation – not a decision in accordance with Article 9(4) of the same regulation). However, if the aid is then granted as it was in the past (*i.e.*, without the alterations), recovery becomes possible as of the date the alterations should have been applied.

In summary, if an existing aid measure is or becomes incompatible, the solution advocated by Article 108(2) is that it be abolished or altered – and both possibilities are indeed implemented in practice. When it comes to new aid, however, traditional interpretation tends to emphasise only the possibility of abolition of the aid, not that of alteration. Alteration is envisaged in the case of notified aid because, during the compatibility procedure, the Commission may accept or propose alterations and impose conditions that make the aid compatible and thus come to an authorisation decision or a conditional decision. In contrast, for unlawful aid, practice and case law totally disregard the possibility of alteration, which in practice is equivalent to discarding a specific provision of primary law. Undoubtedly, this view presupposes a broad and innovative interpretation of the term 'alteration' insofar as it refers to the subsidised project and not to the aid as such. However, this type of reading of Article 108(2) TFEU is already currently applied in the examination of the compatibility of aid, where the alterations or conditions that make the aid compatible can perfectly relate, and often do relate, to the characteristics of the subsidised investment project. In other words, aid and subsidised investment are two aspects of the same reality, which are usually examined together.

---

21. Article 1(d) of the Procedural Regulation, cited in Part One, footnote 18.
22. Article 1(c) of the Procedural Regulation. *See also* Art. 4 of the Implementing Regulation (Commission Regulation (EC) No 794/2004 of 21 April 2004, OJ L 140, 30.4.2004, p. 1, as amended), which sets out a simplified procedure for the following alterations of existing aid: (i) increases in the budget of an authorised aid scheme exceeding 20% (smaller increases are considered unlikely to affect the Commission's original compatibility assessment, as explained in recital 4); (ii) prolongation of an existing authorised aid scheme by up to 6 years, with or without an increase in the budget; and (iii) tightening of the criteria for the application of an authorised aid scheme, a reduction of aid intensity or a reduction of eligible expenses.

The fact that the aid has already been disbursed - and is therefore classified as unlawful - in theory, does not exclude the possibility of intervening *ex post* to change its effects and bring it back into line with the Treaty's objectives. The only difference would be that such intervention would take place in the context of a negative decision, through which an infringement of the Treaty and the incompatibility of the aid granted are established and restorative (or redressive) measures for competition and the internal market are imposed (no longer proposed). Of course, the possibility of proceeding in this way depends on the circumstances of each case, which means that the Commission would have to be granted some discretionary power. But this is exactly what happens in the field of foreign subsidies.

I.B Interpreting Article 16(1) of the Procedural Regulation in Line with the Proposed Interpretation of Article 108(2) TFEU

Article 16(1) of the Procedural Regulation, which identifies recovery as the natural (and in fact sole) remedy in the case of unlawful aid, is anchored in concepts dating back more than thirty years.[23] However, upon a closer look, imposing a single method to achieve the objective of removing incompatibility or altering incompatible aid in the case of unlawful aid does in fact give substance to the very outcome that the Court rejects, *i.e.*, a sanctioning concept of recovery.

Furthermore, it is simply not a convincing argument that forcing a State to recover unlawful aid *without concern for the related effects on the market* serves as an effective deterrent - on the ground that, if recovery was not imposed under all circumstances, Member States would have no incentive to comply with their procedural obligations. Indeed, this argument does not take into account that in the case of unlawful aid the Commission, if the reform is implemented, would be allowed to go beyond mere recovery if necessary to restore the competitive situation that existed before the aid was granted. And even for those redressive measures that could mirror the kind of prospective measures that the Commission could impose in the framework of a compatibility assessment for notified aid, different procedural rules would apply. It is not the same for the Commission to negotiate with a Member State within the framework of a notification procedure - during which it evaluates the State's proposals and potentially authorises them with conditions - on the one hand, and to impose the remedial measures it considers most appropriate within the framework of a negative decision on the other hand. The judicial review would also be different, and the effects of non-compliance with conditions would likewise differ.

In the case of notified aid - to mention but one difference - the Commission has a duty to explain why it imposed certain measures to make the aid compatible and why those measures are proportionate (*i.e.*, why compatibility could not be assured by less invasive means), whereas in the case of unlawful aid, should the Commission be

23. Judgment of 21 March 1990, *Kingdom of Belgium v. Commission of the European Communities (Tubemeuse)*, Case C-142/87, EU:C:1989:125, para. 66, and Judgment of 21 March 1991, *Italian Republic v. Commission of the European Communities (Alfa Romeo)*, C-305/89, EU:C:1991:142, para. 41.

allowed to order redressive measures as an alternative to recovery, the proportionality argument could be put forward only by the State and/or the beneficiary challenging the remedies if they prove that the redressive measures are heavier than full recovery of aid principal plus interest, and heavier than what would be needed to restore the situation that existed before the granting of the aid.

As to the consequences of non-compliance with remedies: In the case of notified aid, the Commission would normally be open – if duly informed of the difficulties in complying – to discussing possible amendments to the remedies with the Member State concerned, as it usually does with prospective remedies;[24] and it would resolve to open an investigation in accordance with Article 20 of the Procedural Regulation (*i.e.*, for misuse of aid), only if the conditions on which the compatibility assessment was based have been infringed since the assessment was issued – and only in this case would its decision have retroactive effect. Even in this case, the Commission would have to give the State and interested parties the possibility to submit observations based on Article 108(2) TFEU.

Conversely, in the case of unlawful aid, in case of breach of a final decision, the Commission could bring the case immediately to the Court, the aid would have to be recovered retroactively, and the Member State would be exposed to penalties if it did not comply with the Court's judgment. Furthermore, based on *Deggendorf* case law,[25] the Commission would never allow a Member State to grant any new aid to the same beneficiaries so long as the advantages of the unlawful aid have not been entirely forfeited, and the Member State would be obliged to refrain from relying on the GBER or other exemption instruments until the Commission acknowledges that the effects of the unlawful aid have been entirely removed.

Therefore, no major problem would ensue from a *revirement* in the interpretation of Article 16(1) of the Procedural Regulation (or a change in the wording of the provision, for that matter) aimed at granting the Commission broader discretion in assessing the most appropriate remedies in a given case to restore the situation existing before the unlawful aid was granted (*i.e.*, restorative remedies) or in imposing adequate remedial measures, whether retrospective or prospective if the restorative goal cannot be attained – or cannot be attained through recovery (*i.e.*, redressive measures).

I.C Revisiting Traditional Case Law on the Concept of Absolute Impossibility

Although a change of the wording used in Article 16(1) of the Procedural Regulation – which sets out recovery as the natural remedy against unlawfully granted aid – would be of great help, a revision or at least softening of the traditional case law on the concept of absolute impossibility would already be a decisive contribution to the development of a more flexible and effective system of remedies.

24. *See*, for example, Commission Decision of 12 September 2019, C(2019) 6525 final, OJ C 7, 10.1.2020 and Commission Decision of 2 August 2022, C(2022) 5536 final, OJ C 387, 7.10.2022.
25. *See* Part One, section I.B.1 and footnote 98.

In a nutshell, as things currently stand, redressive measures alternative to recovery can be considered only when it is absolutely impossible to recover the full amount of the aid plus interest - but the concept of absolute impossibility is construed so narrowly[26] that, in practice, no alternative proposal can be considered except the winding-up of the recipient undertaking. To the best of this author's knowledge, no successful claim of absolute impossibility has ever been brought since the Procedural Regulation came into force, except for cases in which the recipient undertaking was wound up; but even if a case of absolute impossibility had been established in any of those unsuccessful claims, the only acceptable alternative remedy would have been, again, the winding-up of the undertaking.

This outcome is meaningless both conceptually and in practice. Conceptually, not only does it lead to confusion between the pathology and the remedy, but more importantly it is also at odds with the true meaning of absolute impossibility. Indeed, it is a general principle of EU law that nobody can be held to the impossible - as the Court recalls in the *Montessori* judgment[27] - and here the concept of impossibility should be seen in connection with the stated objective of recovery, *i.e.*, the restoration of the competitive situation existing before the aid was granted. Hence, absolute impossibility should be acknowledged any time it can be anticipated that a recovery order would fail to achieve that objective.

Similarly, from a practical perspective, it is certainly no guarantee of effectiveness to regard the winding-up of the recipient undertaking as the sole cause of impossibility and at the same time the sole acceptable alternative remedy. Indeed, if the undertaking has become or is becoming insolvent despite the aid, the effects generated by the aid in the past will not be cancelled by its liquidation; whereas if the liquidation is prompted by recovery, it will offer competitors a possibility to obtain compensation by increasing their market share - but whether this would actually re-establish the *status quo ante* depends on the circumstances of each case. Therefore, a relaxation of the inflexible interpretation of the concept of absolute impossibility would not only more accurately reflect the intrinsic meaning of the general principle of law that is at stake but it would also lead to more appropriate outcomes tailored to the specificity of each case.

If it were accepted that, at least in the case of absolute impossibility construed as explained above, the Commission could order restorative measures aimed at altering the aid in order to remove its distortive effects other than or in addition to recovery, national courts - which already have the power to impose the measures they consider most appropriate to restore the situation that existed before the aid was granted - would follow suit, with one difference: since they cannot evaluate the aid compatibility, national courts would be allowed to consider only measures that remove the aid and remove its effects, either by abolishing or neutralising the measure retroactively or by ensuring that the measure no longer qualifies as aid (within the limits, however, of the *Transalpine* case law).[28]

26. *See* Part One, section I.A.2.7.
27. *See* Part One, section I.A.2.7 and footnote 71.
28. *See* Part Two, section V.D and footnotes 158 and 159. The national court could not eliminate selectivity by extending the effects of the aid because that would have meant disregarding the

Furthermore, it would be helpful if the Commission, in the context of a negative decision, could impose – again retroactively, to eliminate the effects of the unlawfully granted aid – remedies that would make the aid compatible and not necessarily remove it altogether. This would be possible if the jurisprudence took note of the fact that granting the Commission this greater discretion in determining remedies against unlawful aid would not encourage Member States to violate the procedural rules and thus would not, for the reasons mentioned above, lead to a relaxation of deterrence, or if additional remedies were used to ensure deterrence (such as a correct implementation of the *Deggendorf* doctrine, as explained in the next section).

I.D Fully Exploiting the Potential of Soft Law

Further significant progress towards a more flexible and effective system of remedies could be achieved through simple soft law interventions that would build upon a less entrenched, more creative jurisprudence, in line with present times. For example, no codified rules exist for the applicable remedies in cases of insolvency of a beneficiary undertaking, and even case law – traditionally formalist and rigid on the matter – has recently opened up some leeway.[29] It appears there is thus room for innovative intervention through soft law instruments, with the aim of giving the Commission the power to adopt (and to suggest that national courts adopt) measures that are more tailored to each case and that are suitable for removing the concrete distorting effects identified in relation to a given beneficiary's situation and the relevant market.

As to the ancillary remedy known as the *Deggendorf* doctrine, here too it would suffice to go back to the doctrine's theoretical basis, as enunciated by Advocate General Tesauro,[30] in order to bring also this remedy more in line with the times and make it more effective from a deterrence standpoint. If recovery or another restorative measure were more tailored to remove the concrete effects and market distortion caused by the aid, the remedy's non-execution would fully justify the ban on granting new aid to the same beneficiary, *i.e.*, any entity that is part of the beneficiary's group or is under the same management and control as the recipient within the group.[31] Furthermore, the *Deggendorf* doctrine would not be seen as being used in an unduly penalising manner in cases of total or partial absolute impossibility of recovery, understood in the sense explained above.

Union's interest in circumscribing State intervention in the economy to the greatest possible extent. However, the court could take other measures. For example, in the case of compensation for public service obligations, a national court could not only reduce the amount of compensation to the point of eliminating, even retroactively, any overcompensation, but also impose reparation for the breach of those obligations to customers or similar measures.

29. *See* Part One, section I.A.2.8 and footnote 95.
30. *See* Part One, section I.B.1 and footnote 105.
31. *See* Part One, section II.A.2 and footnote 133. *See also* Part One, section III.A.3, on the possible extension of the recovery obligation to the ultimate beneficial owner. For a wider analysis of this issue under the *de minimis* rules and, by way of comparison, in other areas of State aid law, *see* M. Merola, *De Minimis Principle and State Aid, European Union Law*, report presented at the symposium 'De minimis non curat praetor', European Law Centre at Panthéon-Assas Paris University, 8 December 2022 – Symposium series, Bruylant, publication forthcoming.

An element of *accountability* could then be added to this ancillary remedy, taking into account the recipient undertaking's possible liability in the non-execution of a recovery order or other restorative measures. If such liability was established by national authorities administering an approved or exempted scheme, by a national court, or by the Commission in the context of the notification of new aid, the beneficiary undertaking could be precluded from access not only to new ordinary aid but also to extraordinary aid envisaged for crisis situations.[32]

Similarly, a simple innovative spirit – one that is at the same time attentive to the rights of third parties – would suffice for the Commission to draw up, with soft law instruments, a procedure or best practices to be followed when Member States have difficulties in executing a recovery decision (*e.g.*, due to the difficulty of quantifying the aid, as in the *Mediaset* case)[33] and for the proposal, in agreement with the aid beneficiary, of alternative measures. The same applies to the establishment of a procedural framework for the Commission's verification of the correct implementation of recovery orders by national governments or courts, and for the assessment – at the request of the Member State concerned or the acquiring company – of economic discontinuity in cases in which shares or assets are acquired from a former aid beneficiary.

Quite logically, the establishment of procedural rules concerning the proper application and enforcement of remedies should entail the recognition of procedural guarantees for third parties. As one of the most acute scholars put it, State aid procedures 'still [breathe] the spirit of times long gone [or that should be long gone] in terms of bilateralism, narrow procedural participation, limited legal protection …'.[34] In particular, the aid recipient should be closely involved in all these procedures, as they would no longer concern the examination of the State measure – which could involve complex negotiations with the Member State concerned – but only the more precise and effective implementation of the Commission's decision or the consequences to be drawn in the context of subsequent corporate transactions. Moreover, the recipient's involvement would in many cases make it possible to prevent subsequent challenges at national level, which often considerably delay the implementation of remedies, and would prevent the State, which is primarily responsible for the granting of unlawful aid, from exploiting the situation to its advantage given the latent conflict of interest in which it finds itself in the aid recovery phase.[35]

---

32. Conversely, the Commission has thus far tolerated the disapplication of the preclusion of new aid under the *Deggendorf* doctrine in emergency situations, such as that caused by the COVID-19 pandemic. For example, the Commission authorised the Italian framework scheme, which expressly envisaged disapplication of the *Deggendorf* ban (*see* Art. 53 of Italian Law Decree No. 34 of 19 May 2020).
33. *See* Part One, section II.A.3 and footnote 148.
34. *See* T. Jaeger, *The Future of State Aid*, Editorial, European State Aid Law Quarterly (EStaL), 2022, Issue 2, p. 117 https://doi.org/10.21552/estal/2022/2/2.
35. *See* Part One, section III.C.2. *See also* Jaeger, *The Future of State Aid*, cited in footnote 34 of this Part Four.
    It is especially worth recalling Jaeger's opinion that the time would be ripe to 'do away with the dogma that State aid is a sanction-free area with recovery of illegal aid limited to nullifying the advantage' and that 'an infringing Member State always walks away free'. Nevertheless, contrary to what Jeager suggests, an amendment of primary law is not strictly necessary, and

The recognition of rights of defence would be even more necessary if the reform opened up the possibility of holding the beneficiary co-responsible (more precisely complicit with the State) for breach of procedural rules, as this would (as explained earlier) translate into potential co-liability for the harm caused to competitors. In other words, the finding of the aid recipient's complicity in the public enforcement investigation could lead to co-liability in private enforcement, and this in turn would strongly contribute to increasing the number of follow-on damages actions in a post-reform landscape.

I.E Clarifying the Concept of Recovery

Although the approach of the reform suggested and advocated for in this book would lead to moving past recovery as essentially the sole remedy against unlawful aid, recovery nonetheless remains a central element of the system of remedies. It is therefore appropriate to clarify from the outset what concept of recovery the reform should be inspired by. In this regard, the proposal analysed in this book remains rooted in a merely restorative concept of recovery. The analysis explained thus far has in fact shown that it would be inappropriate to confuse redressive with restorative aims. This would give rise to various problems (the grounds for exclusion from recovery, to cite but one example) that would be detrimental to legal certainty. Preserving a purely restorative concept of recovery does not mean, however, that alternative redressive measures and ancillary remedies for deterrence cannot be envisaged. More importantly, as mentioned, there is no less a need for definitive clarification of the concept of recovery.

As submitted by this author in the past,[36] it is generally assumed that the concept of recovery corresponds to that of re-establishment of the *status quo ante*. This assumption, however, remains unproven and in any case presupposes - to verify its validity - that it is specified what is meant by the re-establishment of the *status quo ante*. For this objective to have a theoretical basis, it must be read consistently with primary law, *i.e.*, the second sentence of Article 108(2) TFEU. As explained above, the dieresis constituted by the 'abolition or alteration' of aid found to be incompatible shows that the focus of the Treaty's authors was on substantive effects: they aimed to eliminate the distortion of the competitive balance caused by the aid, either by bringing it into conformity with the Treaty's objectives whenever possible or by eliminating it altogether.

This choice can only be seen as having been strengthened by the evolution that has characterised EU competition law, namely one towards an increasingly less formalistic approach with a focus on economic effects instead. The modernisation of State aid law towards an increasingly sophisticated economic approach also points in the same direction, as does the deterrence objective consistent with modernisation (set out in the preamble to the Procedural Regulation). To sum up, re-establishing the

other solutions are possible, as advocated for here.

36. Merola, *Rimedi per violazione delle norme sugli aiuti di Stato: misure repressive o di ripristino*, cited in footnote 3 of Part One, pp. 369-371.

status quo ante can only mean - even more so in a post-modernisation scenario - reinstating, to the extent possible, the market situation existing before the aid was granted, or if that is not possible, seeking to neutralise the aid's economic effects and to remove the distortion of competition.

Against this background, the real issue is which concept of recovery - and more generally, which restorative measure - best corresponds to the stated objective. The Court has unfortunately often mixed up different concepts, indiscriminately employing very different wordings, such as restoration of undistorted competitive conditions and repayment of the financial advantage enjoyed.[37] Repayment of the undue benefit (*i.e.*, of the direct or indirect financial benefit) obtained is ontologically different from restoration of a given market situation (*i.e.*, that existing before the aid was granted).

To begin with, one must choose from at least three alternative concepts of recovery before raising the further question as to whether other restorative or re-dressive measures are appropriate and, if so, in which cases: (i) repayment of the undue benefit (financial concept); (ii) repayment of the economic advantage that the aid immediately and directly produces in the beneficiary's sphere (economic concept); and (iii) the overall advantage caused by the aid, including indirectly or together with other factors and over time (functional concept). However, only the second concept is consistent with the theoretical framework based on primary law.

The first concept, on which case law seems to have settled uncritically since the *Aer Lingus* case,[38] is very unsatisfactory both conceptually and in practice: conceptually because, as explained above, it is very far from the substantialist approach of EU law as reinforced by modernisation; and in practice because there are numerous cases in which reference to restoration of the pre-existing situation is a mere formalism, a *fictio iuris*.[39] What is more, the inadequacy of a concept of recovery equated to the repayment of undue payments (*i.e.*, the simple withdrawal from the beneficiary's finances of the financial burden borne by the State) is not evident only in extreme circumstances, such as the lapse of a long period before recovery is implemented, changes in the beneficiary's corporate structure, or the beneficiary's overcoming of insolvency and subsequent economic revival. Upon reflection, in all cases of investment aid in which the incentive effect has been real, recovery could turn out to be a punitive tool or, at the opposite, not restorative enough depending on the factual circumstances.

Moreover, taking the purely financial concept as the benchmark would suggest that a different concept should be used for indirect aid, as witnessed in the Commission's practice, or otherwise that the possibility of recovery in such cases be completely excluded. It is in fact impossible in many cases to precisely calculate the share of the

37. To cite but one example, *see* Judgment of the Court of 12 December 2002, Case C-209/00, *Commission of the European Communities v. Federal Republic of Germany*, EU:C:2002:747, paras 34-41, where the two concepts coexist in the same judgment. *See also* Part One, section I.A.2.4 and footnote 43.
38. *See* Part One, section II.A.3 and footnote 150.
39. Among many possible examples, consider a case in which the aid saved the beneficiary company from bankruptcy at the time it was paid out, and the company subsequently recovered profitability and even strengthened its market position by launching new products or services.

financial advantage transferred to each category of indirect beneficiaries - nor is it acceptable for the Commission, as it has sometimes done, to place the burden of repayment of the full nominal amount on one of the categories, chosen based on considerations related to mere administrative simplification, thereby leaving those affected by recovery to bring claims against the other beneficiaries.[40]

The third concept - which consists of setting the repayment amount in correspondence to the amount that would be necessary to restore, as closely as possible, the counterfactual scenario that would have occurred in the aid's absence - is theoretically unsatisfactory and practically inapplicable: unsatisfactory because it would require the Commission to make a prognostic judgment on hypothetical scenarios that are no longer relevant; and inapplicable because it is in fact impossible to isolate the effects of a given aid measure from those of all the possible concomitant causes of the market situation that has arisen. It would also be inapplicable because it would be impossible to achieve the desired result by merely modulating the amount to be recovered; instead, the Commission would probably need to adopt regulatory measures that would be difficult to reconcile with the system of aid control designed by the Treaty's authors.

Ultimately, the only concept of recovery that is consistent with the State aid system is the second one outlined above. It would therefore be desirable to refer to the economic concept of recovery for both direct and indirect aid. This should be understood as the advantage that the aid directly and immediately (without taking into account other concurrent circumstances or subsequent events) produces in the recipient's sphere of assets, on condition that the advantage persists at the time of recovery.

Admittedly, this is not fully in line with the currently prevailing case law. However, it is not entirely without grip in part of the case law[41] and plainly addresses the broad criticism against the current system of remedies, echoed in legal scholarship.[42] What then can justify the Court's choice? It must be recognised that the concept of recovery of the economic advantage as set out above, while certainly the most logically suitable, has its own drawbacks.

40. *See* Judgment of the Court of First Instance (Fifth Chamber) of 4 March 2009, cited in footnote 199 of Part One, paras 199-204. For a more recent example, *see* Judgment of the General Court of 8 May 2024, Joint Cases T-700/13 and others, *Caixabank SA and other v. European Commission*, which rejected the ground of lack of reasoning on the identification of the (partial) beneficiaries. To be noted that in the latter case the Court of Justice eventually overturned the General Court's assessment as explained in section III.A.2 of Part One.

41. As mentioned above, case law has often used the concept of elimination of the economic advantage, though it ended up confusing it with that of repayment of the nominal amount of the aid plus interest; case law has also clarified that there is no need for an exact correspondence between the burden on the State (public resources) and the economic advantage for the recipient (though the former must give rise to the latter through a causal link in order for the conditions for the existence of State aid to be fulfilled). *See* Judgment of the Court of 12 December 2002, cited in footnote 37 of this Part Four. It is therefore reasonable to assume that, similarly, it is not necessary to establish a correspondence between the burden borne by the State and the repayment amount.

42. *See*, among others, D. Borde, P. Kirch, *La restitution des aides d'Etat*, RTD eur., 29(3), 1993, p. 498, and M. Karpenschif, *La récupération des aides nationales versées en violation du droit communautaire à l'aune du règlement n. 659/1999: du mythe à la réalité?* RTD eur., 37(3), 2001, p. 551 (and more specifically, pp. 573-577).

First, the selected approach might give rise to perplexity from a purely restorative standpoint, as recovery of the economic advantage could in certain (far from exceptional) circumstances cause the State responsible for breach of the Treaty to be enriched in relation to the financial burden incurred. In other cases, when the economic advantage has vanished due to the aid measure's ineffectiveness or unforeseen market changes, application of the concept of recovery explained above would lead to recognition of the futility of recovery (because there would be no point in harassing the recipient, which has not gained any long-term benefit if it was only to the advantage of the State responsible for breach of the Treaty)[43] – despite recovery being mandatory under currently applicable positive law.

Furthermore, application of this approach would require complex investigations in the case of disposal of the beneficiary company's assets or shares. Indeed, one would have to verify not only whether the economic advantage has been transferred to the buyer, as is already the verification to be carried out based on the concept of economic continuity/discontinuity but also – if the advantage has not been transferred – whether it persists at the level of the initial recipient (the target in the corporate transaction), the seller or the seller's shareholders. Consideration of these difficulties, together with the fear of undermining the deterrent effect,[44] may have conditioned the Court's choice to apply a purely financial concept of recovery.[45]

Yet, the drawbacks listed above are all inherent not in the concept of recovery itself – whichever it may be – but in the impossibility of achieving all the desired goals with a single remedy. Put simply, recovery is not fit for all purposes under all circumstances; indeed, there is no such thing as a catch-all remedy. This reflection leads to the conclusion that a greater focus on the limits of recovery and the need of a *variety of remedies* could produce very positive effects on the coherence and credibility of the system of remedies, even though it would remain incomplete. This initial objective can be achieved through soft law instruments and a jurisprudential overhaul – so that case law realigns with the theoretical basis of recovery.

The necessary prerequisite, however, is to acknowledge that the two jurisprudential formulas of 're-establishment of the *status quo ante*' and 'recovery as a natural consequence of the finding of unlawfulness' are not closely related (despite often being linked in the case law) and perhaps even irreconcilable. Re-establishment of the *status quo ante* is obviously the indispensable reference because it derives from primary law,

43. From the beneficiary undertaking's standpoint, this would amount to a sort of penalty more than to a mere re-establishment of the situation existing before the aid was granted, despite all the statements to the contrary in the case law.
44. In the end, unlike a competitive advantage, a financial benefit is almost always recoverable (except in the event of insolvency).
45. Even so, if one wants to concede that considerations of this kind were the basis for the Court's choice to depart from its own repeated statements about the need to eliminate the 'distortion of effective competition' or 'the actual advantage on the market' and to 'restore the competitive situation' in favour of a nominal concept of the aid to be recovered, the choice remains unconvincing. It would have been more logical to admit – as Advocate General Van Gerven did as far back as in the *Alfa Romeo* case (Opinion of 10 January 1991, Case C-305/89, *Italian Republic v. Commission of the European Communities*, EU:C:1991:4, para. 22) – that although it might be impossible to remedy the distortion of competition, recovery is still necessary to counteract the infringement.

from the landmark *Kohlegesetz* case and from the preamble to the Procedural Regulation. The concept of recovery advocated for in this book totally disregards the infringement's characteristics. It is one thing to speak of the infringement, which can take various forms; it is another thing to speak of the resulting competitive advantage, which is a possible consequence and totally detached from the infringement's characteristics.

Moreover, the wrongful act (*i.e.*, the infringement of procedural obligations) is always attributable to the State and at most could involve the complicity of the measure's addressee (*i.e.*, the aid recipient); whereas the competitive advantage could extend to one or more categories of direct and/or indirect beneficiaries. Likewise, the wrongful act could have numerous natural consequences that affect various parties, *i.e.*, not just the undertaking that obtains the competitive advantage; conversely, re-establishment of the previous situation could also entail a recovery or compensation obligation that goes beyond the wrongful act's natural consequences. The first step towards setting out a path of reform without unjustified constraints is to stop considering different concepts to be similar and to use exclusively the elimination of competitive advantage as a benchmark.

Finally, the notion of 'recovery as a natural consequence of the infringement' was initially developed by the case law to reject claims based on the principle of proportionality,[46] which was often invoked as a general principle of law that could stand in the way of recovery under Article 16(1) of the Procedural Regulation. Now, if, as suggested above, the strict approach whereby the notion of 'absolute impossibility of enforcement' is considered an inherent limitation on recovery is softened so that recovery is assessed against the benchmark of the properly defined restorative goal of removing the distortion of competition, the principle of proportionality will remain invocable in exceptional circumstances only. If recovery – or an alternative remedy – serves the pre-defined goal, it cannot be considered disproportionate; but if the goal is unattainable, proportionality need not be invoked. Its scope of application would thus remain limited to cases in which a remedy additional to, or different from, mere recovery of the undue payment has been applied and is alleged to be unfair.

It goes without saying that, however relevant and fruitful it might be to reform the system of remedies only through soft law instruments and less formalist case law, with a focus on the real needs of an effective functioning of the internal market, much more could be done by reforming secondary legislation. In fact, soft law instruments are limited from several perspectives – even more so in a period of erratic case law, which hardly provides a stable, coherent and convincing framework.[47] It would suffice to get to grips with a few provisions of the Procedural Regulation to shape, at least in the area of public enforcement, a system fully in line with the times and the spirit of modernisation. This would inevitably spread to private enforcement, as explained below.

46. *See* Part One, section I.A.2.6.
47. For a detailed examination of the characteristics and limits of the soft law instrument in State aid law, *see* Merola, *Rimedi per violazione delle norme sugli aiuti di Stato: misure repressive o di ripristino*, cited in footnote 3 of Part One, pp. 359-366.

It seems suitable to distinguish between three essential components in a reform of the procedural rules of secondary legislation: (i) the essential principles that should underlie the reform; (ii) the changes concerning the remedies imposed by the Commission (public enforcement); and (iii) the regulatory developments concerning the powers of national courts (private enforcement). These three components are examined one by one in the next three chapters, before drawing some conclusions.

II ESSENTIAL PRINCIPLES THAT SHOULD UNDERLIE A REFORM OF SECONDARY LAW

This chapter identifies the essential principles which should guide a reform of secondary law that overcomes the rigidity of the current system of remedies. It proposes the introduction of restorative and redressive measures to improve the effectiveness of remedies and singles out the case of remedies in insolvency proceedings as a prime example of the beneficial changes that a modernised view of remedies would entail.

II.A Overcoming the Rigidity of the Current System of Remedies

As mentioned above, the main problem with the current system stems from its excessive rigidity, caused by a total lack of adaptation to the evolution of public competition law over several decades. Practice and case law have aggravated this situation because, instead of attempting to innovate, they have developed imprecise definitions and unnecessary constraints mainly as a result of a lack of a holistic view of the State aid *corpus juris* when dealing with specific topics.[48] Moreover, the legal framework in secondary law is now too simplified and out of step with the times – all the more reason to consider some developments appropriate and necessary.

Against this background, it is essential to rediscover the full value of the Treaty's wording and return to the origin of the concept of restoring the competitive situation altered by unlawful aid. To achieve this, the objective of re-establishing undistorted competitive conditions must be kept distinct from and uncontaminated by other purposes, such as avoiding situations of unjust enrichment, punishing elusive behaviour, or deterring violations of procedural obligations. This, however, necessarily implies that alternative or complementary measures must be found that fulfil these collateral objectives, all of which are in themselves worthy.

Hence, first the notion of recovery, the goal pursued, and the alternative restorative measures that the Commission may adopt should be clarified in the Procedural Regulation; then, other measures of a redressive nature should likewise be identified, along with ancillary remedies. The shift from a rigid system of recovery (or put more correctly, of recovery of the nominal amount of aid) to a system of case-by-case assessment of the most appropriate restorative and, if necessary, redressive measures would help address both the main objective of re-establishing undistorted competition and the collateral objectives.

There is a reason for distinguishing between restorative measures and redressive measures. The typical restorative measures remain total or partial recovery and some

48. This is a general remark, of course, which obviously does not apply to case law in its entirety. Some judgments of great value in the field under discussion have been issued even in recent years (in the modernisation era), especially (but not only) from the Court of Justice's Grand Chamber. Still, in several cases both the General Court and the Court of Justice have failed, in this author's opinion, to deliver the clear, wise and systematic guidance that stakeholders would expect from them.

limited alternative measures with the same or similar effect. The concept of redressive measures should be introduced in the Procedural Regulation as an *alternative* or *complement* to restorative measures whenever the latter are impossible (in the meaning already explained) or ineffective (*i.e.*, insufficient). In those cases, the Commission should be given the power to restore, to the extent possible, a situation of undistorted competition through other means, despite those means not being capable of genuinely reproducing the pre-existing situation in the true sense of the expression.

Redressive measures are essentially similar to the alternative restorative measures that the Commission may take under Article 8(4) of the Merger Regulation in circumstances where restoration of the situation prevailing before the implementation of the concentration is not possible through dissolution of the transaction.[49] Redressive measures are also similar, content-wise, to: (i) prospective measures (*i.e.*, 'conditions' according to the wording of the Merger Regulation) that the Commission may impose within the framework of conditional positive decisions in accordance with Article 9(4) of the Merger Regulation; and (ii) behavioural or structural commitments that the Commission may accept when reviewing a notified concentration in accordance with the second sentence of Article 8(2) of the Merger Regulation.[50]

The difference is that, when referring to unlawful aid, the remedies would be directly *imposed* by the Commission and could differ from any proposals or commitments made by the State concerned or the beneficiary.[51] The closest benchmark for this reform is the FSR, which, as mentioned, does not differentiate between the content of redressive measures based on whether the Commission is reviewing notified or unnotified (including unlawful) subsidies. A definition of all these notions should be included in Article 1 of the Procedural Regulation,[52] and a clear explanation of the goal (or goals) pursued should be added in the Procedural Regulation's recitals.

If one accepts the idea that the Commission may impose restorative and/or redressive measures in the sense explained above, the obvious consequence is that the Commission would have to regain a margin of discretion that the Procedural Regulation currently denies it. This is not a major problem, as it can be achieved simply through a new interpretation of the existing intrinsic and extrinsic limitations to recovery and by empowering the Commission to order redressive measures to restore

49. *See* Council Regulation (EC) No 139/2004 of 20 January 2004 on the control of concentrations between undertakings, OJ L 24, 29.1.2004, p. 1. Notably, Art. 8(4) states that 'the Commission may take any other measure appropriate to achieve such restoration *as far as possible* [emphasis added]'. This can only mean that the Commission may adopt other measures with the knowledge that the measures will only imperfectly restore the pre-existing situation. In other words, this may be read as giving the Commission the power to adopt measures that restore undistorted competition, even though they cannot genuinely restore the *status quo ante* but a different, albeit comparable, market situation. This is what this book refers to with the wording 'redressive measures'.
50. The Merger Regulation refers to these as 'conditions and obligations'.
51. Under the Merger Regulation, the Commission may only 'attach to its decision conditions and obligations *intended to ensure that the undertakings concerned comply with the commitments they have entered into* [emphasis added] *vis-à-vis* the Commission with a view to rendering the concentration compatible with the common market' (Art. 8(2)).
52. By adding a point k) to Art. 1.

undistorted competition as far as possible only when purely restorative measures are either impossible to implement or ineffective.

An important implication of the reform advocated here is that, in modulating restorative and redressive measures, the Commission would not be required to verify and prove how - step by step, through precise causal links, and hypothetically even years after the payment of unlawful aid - the situation existing before the aid changed to the situation existing at the time of the decision. Such an exercise would indeed be arbitrary and often impossible. Instead, as in other sciences, recourse to an 'effective theory' would be justified: in other words, the remedies would be chosen based on the market change prompted by the aid and the resulting competitive situation (which must be remedied), leaving aside the intermediate series of causal links.

The choice of the legal basis for a reform of the Procedural Regulation is not problematic. Article 109 TFEU - which was the sole legal basis of both Council Regulation (EC) No 659/1999 and Council Regulation (EU) No 2015/1589 - is perfectly fit to encapsulate the content of the proposed reform, which is intended simply to implement Article 108 TFEU and contribute to the effectiveness of State aid rules. Indeed, Article 109 TFEU empowers the Council, upon a proposal from the Commission and after consulting the European Parliament, to adopt 'any appropriate regulations for the application of Articles 107 and 108'. In this connection, it is worth noting that the preamble to the Procedural Regulation emphasises the importance of the regulation in contributing to the achievement of the overarching objectives of a modernised system of State aid rules through legal certainty and transparency.[53] Hence, a modernised system of remedies, which is - as explained - the missing piece of the modernisation process, perfectly fits into this mission.

II.B Clarifying the Consequences of a Modernised Concept of Absolute Impossibility

Another important aspect of the advocated reform is the development of agreed remedies for when aid recovery is an absolute impossibility, in the sense clarified earlier in this chapter. Even now, in the case of absolute impossibility, it is up to the Member State concerned to inform the Commission thereof and to propose appropriate alternative measures.[54] Once the concept of absolute impossibility has been adjusted to the need of a reformed system of remedies, the State - when it considers that recovery would not have the desired restorative effects and would risk being unnecessary or even harmful to competition - could inform the Commission thereof. It could also propose appropriate restorative or redressive measures. The Commission would enjoy wide administrative discretion in assessing the proposed measures, subject to restraint control (limited to manifest error or misuse of powers) by the EU courts.[55] The removal

53. *See* recital 3 of Council Regulation (EC) No 659/1999 and, more explicitly, recital 3 of Council Regulation (EU) No 2015/1589.
54. *See* Part One, section I.A.2.8.
55. The Commission's discretionary assessment would encompass at least the following: (i) examination of the actual uselessness or ineffectiveness of repayment, as argued by the State;

of an automaticity in recovery would also greatly reduce the risk of undesirable economic effects contrary to the general interest, *e.g.*, by discouraging restructuring operations of companies in difficulty.[56]

Recourse to the instrument of negotiated settlement of remedies would, in principle, raise a major problem of potential conflict between the granting Member State and the beneficiary undertaking. In cases in which the State no longer has any interest in defending the beneficiary but rather wishes to recoup the funds, it might not resort to the instrument for its own purposes, regardless of the effectiveness of recovery as a restorative measure. The beneficiary itself should therefore be allowed to notify the Member State and, at the same time, the Commission of the occurrence of circumstances justifying the use of alternative measures, and to submit a proposal.

There does not seem to be any argument against this solution given that, at the implementation stage of a recovery decision, the State is no longer planning to intervene in the economy to replace the ineffective action of the market in order to achieve primary policy objectives. Thus, there is no reason not to involve the beneficiary in the negotiation of an effective solution. Allowing the beneficiary to signal the occurrence of the aforementioned circumstances would therefore help avoid the risk of a conflict of interest, prevent unjust enrichment of the State, and orient remedies towards objectives of common interest.

If the initiative came from the beneficiary undertaking, the latter would be obliged not only to elaborate on the commitments it is willing to undertake – including by illustrating their restorative or, lacking that, redressive effects – but also to specify the internal measures taken. These measures should: (i) be aimed at enforcing directors' liability where possible, to discourage future moral hazard; and (ii) seek to prevent or remedy the unjust enrichment of shareholders. Directors' moral hazard and unjust enrichment of shareholders are objective risks any time that share or asset deals have been executed in the interval between the granting of the aid and the implementation of remedies.

As explained before, one of the milestones of the advocated reform would be to avoid recourse to recovery as a catch-all remedy and instead use different remedies to achieve different objectives: restoring the pre-existing situation whenever possible; redressing the competition distortion to the extent possible; avoiding undue advantages for the Member State liable for infringing State aid provisions; and fostering deterrence, possibly *vis-à-vis* both the State and the beneficiary (if the latter was, or should have been, aware of the infringement of procedural rules and was therefore complicit).

A distinction between different objectives and the consequent provision of separate remedies would also promote greater complementarity between public and private enforcement. Today, in essence, the same remedy is largely pursued in both

(ii) appropriateness of the alternative measures proposed; and (iii) elimination or prevention of any unjust enrichment or advantage for beneficiaries or their shareholders.

56. This risk has been emphasised by legal scholars. *See* O. Billard and S. Martin, *Les mesures de soutien public aux entreprises en difficulté au regard de la prohibition des aides d'Etat*, Revue de la Concurrence Lamy, No. 38, 2014, p. 175.

public and private enforcement. Conversely, after the reform, the role of private enforcement would be strengthened in cases in which recovery or other restorative remedies have to be dropped (because they conflict with general principles of law, or it is impossible to restore the previous competitive situation).

Moreover, having the option of not pursuing recovery could facilitate recognition of the measures needed to repair the damage caused by the aid, at the very least because *the irreversibility of the damage itself would be confirmed and, at the same time, the risk of bis in idem would be eliminated* and defences based on this principle would automatically be ruled out. Moreover, the reform would also make it possible to reintroduce, for measures that are not merely restorative, a balancing test whereby other relevant general interests of the Union are considered. The Commission had in some circumstances taken such general interests into account in the lead-up to codifying the recovery obligation,[57] based on the concept of recovery as a natural consequence of infringement. Once that concept is properly reshaped, nothing would preclude a balancing of different Union interests if the Commission imposed alternative or ancillary remedies.[58]

II.C Progressing Towards a Modernised View of Remedies in Cases of Insolvency

The possibility of balancing several Union interests should also lead to a thorough revision of the relationship between recovery and insolvency proceedings, which constitutes one of the least pragmatically satisfying and least theoretically convincing aspects of the current system of remedies. Underlying all the difficulties encountered in practice are the principles of timeliness and effectiveness set out in Article 16(3) of the Procedural Regulation, which limit Member States' autonomy in the execution of recovery decisions and interfere with insolvency proceedings governed by national law in a way that is not always warranted to guarantee the *effet utile* of Union law.

In summary, these limits make it necessary in practice to liquidate a company that benefitted from aid when the aid cannot be repaid promptly and in full by the company (not by the group to which it belongs, as it is the production unit that benefitted from the aid that logically must repay it). In essence, liquidation is considered the only alternative to recovery because, if the beneficiary cannot timely repay the aid, it can be presumed that it would have already gone bankrupt without the aid. In this sense, liquidation is presumed to restore the *status quo ante* by freeing up market share and thus re-establishing a situation of undistorted competition. Even so,

57. *See* M. Karpenschif, *La récupération des aides nationales versées en violation du droit communautaire à l'aune du règlement n. 659/1999: du mythe à la réalité?*, in RTD eur., v. 37, n. 3, 2001, p. 551.

58. One possible example (among many) is a situation in which unlawful aid has proved to be very beneficial to the attainment of environmental objectives but did not comply with all the requirements of the applicable guidelines at the time it was granted. If the pre-existing competitive situation cannot be restored and the project would be discontinued if the aid was recovered, it would make sense to consider redressive measures that would allow the project to go ahead.

liquidation does not have to be judicial and does not require a declaration of bankruptcy, as a liquidation arrangement whereby the company's assets are sold at market terms is generally permissible. However, the constraints imposed as a matter of practice are so pervasive that the autonomy of national law in designing liquidation procedures is severely impaired.

To cite an example:[59] Although prompt registration of a State's claim for repayment of aid is, in theory, considered a suitable measure to enforce a recovery decision,[60] in practice national insolvency proceedings are required to guarantee the desired result of effective and timely recovery within the meaning of Article 16(3) of the Procedural Regulation.[61] Given that the State remains liable even if its national proceedings are unable to guarantee the aforementioned result, this translates *de facto* into a situation of paralysis of insolvency proceedings under national law. The State can in fact never participate in debt restructuring agreements or accept a partial write-off of its claim in an arrangement with creditors.

As to the possibility of selling the beneficiary's shares or business as a going concern, one must consider the requirements, set out in the case law and in the Commission's practice, relating to economic discontinuity between the purchaser and the beneficiary company.[62] The rigidity of these requirements is such that, in essence, a sale is possible only by creating a bad company that is put into compulsory liquidation or by hiving off profitable assets. This approach solves the problem of restoring undistorted competitive conditions only if the sale takes place through a competitive procedure - which the Commission, however, has failed to constantly require.[63] This practice also leaves unchanged the unnecessary formalism of (fictitious) recovery from the company in liquidation. Instead, it would be much more logical to allow the Commission to carry out an overall assessment of the effects of pre-bankruptcy proceedings by favouring instruments that can most concretely and effectively restore undistorted competitive conditions and safeguarding the proper functioning of national bankruptcy law as far as possible.

As a result, the very choice of the type of insolvency proceedings to which an unlawful aid beneficiary is admitted is not left to the normal dynamic between creditor, debtor, and authorities (once the claim is registered as a liability), because State aid law extends its influence to this realm, too. This invasion of the remit of national insolvency law would be justified if it could achieve the objective of restoring the pre-existing

59. Further and more detailed examples from Italian bankruptcy law can be found in Merola, *Rimedi per violazione delle norme sugli aiuti di Stato: misure repressive o di ripristino: Modernizzazione e scenari di riforma*, cited in footnote 3 of Part One, especially pp. 406-414.
60. *See*, among others, Judgment of the Court of 21 March 2003, Case C-613/11, *Commission v. Italian Republic*, EU:C:2013:192, para. 43.
61. *See* New Recovery Notice, cited in footnote 125 of Part One, para. 66.
62. *See* Part One, section I.A.2.8 and the case law referred to therein.
63. There are several examples of the Commission waiving the competitive tender requirement or waiving the requirement that the beneficiary's assets must be sold to a purchaser totally unrelated to the beneficiary's shareholder(s). *See* the case concerning the sale of SEA Handling, to mention but one example (Commission Decision of 5 July 2016, C(2016) 4103 final, OJ L 317, 1.12.2017). Even in the *ITA* case (*see* footnote 14 of this Part Four), only some of the assets were sold through a competitive procedure.

competitive situation effectively (or at least more effectively than other measures); however, determining whether it would indeed achieve that objective would require a case-by-case analysis by the Commission (or by national authorities and courts, under the Commission's supervision).

Instead, this invasion stems from a mechanistic application of general criteria, without even an assessment of the Union's concrete interest in favouring a certain type of proceedings over another based on its effects on the market. Yet, it makes no sense to oblige the State to hinder the reaching of any agreement between creditors involving even the slightest mitigation of the debt to be repaid, just as it makes no sense to challenge any creditors' arrangement allowing even the partial continuation of business without considering whether such an inflexible position is useful for removing the distortion caused by the aid. Indeed, one must ultimately aim at this essential objective and, if possible, consider also certain ancillary goals, such as preventing a bankrupt entrepreneur from continuing to run a business or preventing forms of unjust enrichment of a beneficiary's shareholders.

II.D Considering State Aid Law's Internal Market Goal When Reforming the System of Remedies

Before concluding this section and examining in detail the main secondary law amendments required for the reform advocated for in this book, a final principle needs to be recalled, which, just as the others discussed in this section, should underlie the reform. As is well known, State aid rules have two aims: protect competition and ensure compliance with internal market objectives. An organic regulation of recovery must consider both.

Three macro situations must be considered: (i) one in which the aid's effects have not yet materialised, so it is possible to intervene urgently to prevent them from materialising; (ii) one in which the (unlawful and incompatible) aid has caused a real and lasting distortion of competition; and (iii) one in which the aid has failed, *i.e.*, it has proved to be of no use to the beneficiary and has made no real contribution to strengthening its position on the market. The latter scenario is in fact twofold, as the aid may have produced, at least in part, the effect desired by the State, but failed to durably strengthen the beneficiary's position, or it may have been totally useless even from the standpoint of the public objective pursued.

In all these situations, the State has infringed the Treaty by adopting a unilateral measure in conflict with the rules of the internal market; yet only in some of them has this infringement been accompanied by a distortive effect from a competition and market standpoint. These are clearly different situations – and it would be pointless to treat them the same way by applying the same remedies, which is what happens today.

The first scenario (the aid's effects have not yet materialised) is sufficiently well addressed by the rules in force. Both the Commission and national courts have the means to require recovery in due time or to stop disbursement of the aid if it has not been entirely disbursed. The Private Enforcement Notice is well developed in this respect. Clearly, though, a harmonisation initiative would help achieve greater convergence and level up the enforcement of State aid rules in this scenario.[64]

In the second scenario (the aid resulted in a distortion of competition that is still affecting market dynamics), the adoption of the most effective restorative measures is warranted. The adoption of suitably devised measures would neutralise the distortion of competition while at the same time frustrate the achievement of the unilateral goals that led the Member State to infringe the Treaty. Therefore, it would inherently have a deterrent effect.

In the third scenario, either the aid has been totally ineffective,[65] or the State has partially or entirely achieved its objectives but the distortion of competition did not materialise or was quickly reabsorbed by market developments.[66] If the aid has been totally ineffective, there is no need to restore undistorted competition; therefore, a mere acknowledgment of the infringement in a negative decision seems to be an appropriate remedy,[67] as an equivalent to the infringement procedure for other breaches of Treaty obligations. The State would, however, remain liable to private operators that claim they suffered damage during a certain, albeit limited, period as a result of the aid.

As to the beneficiary, if harmonisation was achieved,[68] private enforcement could develop in a way that would allow the State to hold beneficiaries jointly liable if it can prove that the beneficiaries knew or should have known that the aid infringed the Treaty. If, by contrast, the State achieved its objectives but the related distortion of competition quickly vanished, recovery would not only be useless but it would also be biased and counterproductive. Indeed, it would entail giving the State an unfair benefit at the beneficiary's expense. If the latter was complicit in the infringement, it would make sense to recover the aid, but the amount should be allocated to purposes in conformity with the common interest; whereas if the beneficiary has no liability, the situation is once again that in which only the State's infringement of the Treaty needs remedying – and the only sensible remedy in that case is a formal negative decision as an equivalent to the ordinary infringement procedure.[69]

64. The challenges inherent in the adoption of a private enforcement harmonisation directive are discussed in Chapter IV below.
65. To give but a few examples, consider research aid that did not lead to any concrete results, aid for the implementation of a project that was later abandoned because of unexpected market developments or because it was not selected in a competitive procedure, or aid for the development of a product that did not obtain the necessary authorisations.
66. Consider, for instance: (i) social aid or training/education aid that the beneficiary was eventually unable to exploit because it went bankrupt or for other reasons, with the workforce relocating to other companies; (ii) rescue/restructuring aid that permitted the State to sell a company in difficulty through a competitive procedure without, however, preventing the company's liquidation and exit from the market, or even merely delaying bankruptcy and thus alleviating the associated social problems; or (iii) State equity intervention in a company in difficulty, with the shareholding being resold to private companies after restructuring through a competitive procedure.
67. To increase public reprobation as a means of deterrence, yearly statistics could be published concerning State aid negative decisions declaring aid unlawful.
68. *See* Chapter IV below for a comprehensive analysis of this scenario.
69. *See also* Art. 28 of the Procedural Regulation for infringements of previous Commission decisions or abusive aid.

III MODIFICATION OF THE PROCEDURAL REGULATION'S PROVISIONS ON REMEDIES

This chapter analyses the main amendments to the Procedural Regulation's provisions on remedies advocated for in the book, including as concerns ancillary remedies. It suggests amendments that allow for greater flexibility and adaptability of the system of remedies and discusses the implications of such amendments on decision-making procedures and third parties' rights.

If, in light of the abovementioned guidelines - which in turn are based on the in-depth analysis carried out in the first two parts of this book regarding the current system's shortcomings - one asks what concrete changes in positive law would be necessary to remedy these shortcomings, it immediately appears that a few changes might suffice to entirely rebuild the system of remedies. Those few changes, however, must be incisive, audacious and far-reaching.

III.A Amendment of Article 16(1) of the Procedural Regulation

The first suggested amendment concerns Article 16(1) of the Procedural Regulation, which currently reads as follows:

> Where negative decisions are taken in cases of unlawful aid, the Commission shall decide that the Member State concerned shall take all necessary measures to recover the aid from the beneficiary ('recovery decision'). The Commission shall not require recovery of the aid if this would be contrary to a general principle of Union law.

To start with, it would be worth deleting the word 'negative' in the opening parenthetical clause. This would empower the Commission to order restorative remedies also within the framework of conditional[70] or even positive decisions if warranted in light of the effects the aid has already caused.[71] Second, it is recommended to amend the main provision by replacing the subordinate clause 'to recover the aid from the beneficiary ('recovery decision')' with the following (or similar) wording: 'to restore undistorted competition to the extent possible'.

This simple change would have the twofold effect (illustrated above) of ensuring a more flexible definition of restorative remedies, adaptable to the specific circumstances of any given case while giving the Commission some discretionary power (concerning not the imposition of remedies[72] but rather the choice of remedies), which

70. If the Commission imposed restorative remedies within the framework of conditional decisions, they would be in addition to the prospective remedies that accompany the compatibility assessment and that are based on proposals by the Member State concerned.
71. It would make sense to at least neutralise the financial advantage gained by the beneficiary during the period of unlawfulness (*i.e.*, between the granting of the aid and the Commission decision). This would be coherent with Art. 16(2) of the Procedural Regulation and with the *CELF II* case law (*see* Part Two, footnote 146).
72. Unless the aid has proved to be totally ineffective (as explained in section III.D) and the recipient was not complicit in the infringement of the Treaty, as in such circumstances a formal reprimand

will ultimately improve the system's effectiveness. The following (*i.e.*, last) sentence should likewise be rephrased as follows:

> The Commission shall not impose restorative measures if this would be contrary to a general principle of Union law.

The fully amended provision would thus read as follows:

> Where final decisions are taken in cases of unlawful aid, the Commission shall decide that the Member State concerned shall take all necessary measures to restore undistorted competition to the extent possible. The Commission shall not impose restorative measures if this would be contrary to a general principle of Union law.

Once this amendment is in place, it would be possible to complement the abovementioned provision with an explicit reference to a subordinate category of remedies (*i.e.*, redressive measures) that would be available to the Commission whenever restorative measures are considered ineffective (for the market situation that existed before the aid was granted cannot be restored).[73] The EU legislator could also consider extending this provision to situations in which the aid cannot be recovered because recovery would be contrary to general principles of Union law (*i.e.*, extrinsic limits to recovery).[74] If restorative measures are not possible because they would conflict with the principles of legal certainty or protection of legitimate expectations, that does not necessarily mean the same conclusion would apply to redressive measures, which might be less invasive for the beneficiary and enable a balancing of the need to respect general principles with the need to safeguard competition and the market. When considering redressive measures, the principle of proportionality - which, as a rule, is considered irrelevant in relation to recovery - would also be fully applicable.

As to the content of redressive measures, inspiration can be drawn from the FSR for the reasons set out in Part Three of this book and in Chapter 1 of Part Four. To take just one example, if unlawful aid was used to develop infrastructure, including

---

of the State through a negative decision without recovery would be the most appropriate course of action, with no further remedy needed.

73. In this respect, the rules governing remedies would be similar, but not identical, to those in the FSR. Indeed, as explained in Part Three, the FSR envisages a limited priority for repayment of the subsidy on condition that the beneficiary requests it. In this case, the Commission is obliged to prefer it to other remedies if it considers recovery to be at least as effective in removing the distortion. In the case of aid, alternative (*i.e.*, redressive) measures would clearly be subordinate to restorative measures, in the sense that the Commission could impose them only in the case of absolute impossibility to restore the *status quo ante*, defined in the manner explained above (with a relaxation of the current rigidity). The partial difference that would persist between remedies for foreign subsidies and for State aid would be fully justified by the fact that in the State aid system, the remedy is imposed on Member States. Nonetheless, a broad convergence between the two systems would be achieved.
74. As opposed to the internal or intrinsic limit, which is absolute impossibility. As explained in Part One, the Commission is under a duty to consider the extrinsic limits before adopting a restorative measure in its final decision, whereas the intrinsic limit should be invoked by the State (or the beneficiary undertaking - *see* below) in the decision's execution phase.

essential facilities or production capabilities of essential input that cannot be replicated, at least in the short term, the company in question could be obliged to offer fair, reasonable and non-discriminatory conditions for third-party access to the infrastructure, facility or input concerned unless such access is already provided for by sectoral legislation. It should be borne in mind, however, that the list in Article 7(4) FSR is not exhaustive. The legislator could therefore decide to reproduce roughly the same list, to add other measures, or to avoid providing any list at all, which would increase flexibility even more. If no list were provided, it would be important to set some criteria which any redressive measure should meet. In this regard, the criteria of *transparency, verifiability, effectiveness and proportionality* (*i.e.*, not putting undue constraints on the undertaking concerned to implement its market strategy) seem entirely appropriate.

Likewise, if the aid helped develop significant production capacity, the beneficiary could be obliged to reduce capacity or market presence, including by means of a temporary restriction on commercial activity, by complying with an output growth rate below the growth rate of the relevant market, or by refraining from promotional initiatives or from certain investments. If these remedies were ineffective, the redressive measure could go as far as obliging the beneficiary to divest certain assets or business operations, or even to dissolve a concentration if it was subject to a notification requirement that was not complied with.

As usual in merger control and State aid practice, for a remedy to be effective, it should not lead to a deterioration in the market's structure. This means that a divested ongoing business should be viable on a standalone basis and competitive in the long term if operated by a suitable purchaser. Alternatively, the aid beneficiary should carve out adequate activities and assets to create a new entity that should be able to compete. Similarly, if the aid that comes under the Commission's scrutiny was used to support R&D&I activities whose results are likely to enhance the beneficiary's competitive capacity, publication of those results could be an effective way to remove the competitive advantage, enabling other market players to exploit or replicate them.

The only remedies among those mentioned in Article 7(4) FSR that would clearly be unsuitable as redressive measures in the field of State aid are requiring the undertakings concerned to adapt their governance structure[75] and ordering repayment of the aid (as this would fall under the category of restorative measures as explained above).

To make the system of remedies even more effective, the Commission could be given the power, under exceptional circumstances, to order that aid be repaid not to the State budget in general (or to the local authorities or intermediary public body which administered the funds used to grant the unlawful and incompatible aid), but *to a specific chapter of the State budget to be indicated by the State itself.* The objective would be to increase the financial envelope available to fund IPCEIs, previously authorised aid schemes, or aid under national recovery and resilience plans (NRRPs). In this manner, recovery would maintain its non-punitive nature, and the funds would

75. This remedy is controversial even in the field of foreign subsidies – *see* Part Three, section III.B.4.

be given back to the State but would be earmarked for an objective of common interest so as to ensure deterrence and avoid the State's unjust enrichment.

The exceptional circumstances referred to here could be those indicated in section II.D above (cases in which the State did in fact achieve its objective but competition was eventually not distorted, for example, when restructuring aid permitted the State to sell a company in difficulty through a competitive procedure and recover the funds invested but without preventing the company from being liquidated and exiting the market) if two conditions are met: (i) the State's objectives have been at least partially attained; and (ii) it has been ascertained that the recipient undertaking was complicit in the infringement because it was - or should have been - aware of the infringement of the procedural obligations.

III.B Amendment of Article 16(2) and (3) of the Procedural Regulation

Moving forward, Article 16(2) of the Procedural Regulation - which refers to the interest to be added to recovered amounts - would not need to be changed. After the reform, however, it would refer to only one remedy among others; the legislator might therefore prefer, for systematic reasons, to move it to the implementing regulation.

As to Article 16(3), it currently reads as follows:

> Without prejudice to any order of the Court of Justice of the European Union pursuant to Article 278 TFEU, recovery shall be effected without delay and in accordance with the procedures under the national law of the Member State concerned, provided that they allow the immediate and effective execution of the Commission's decision. To this effect and in the event of a procedure before national courts, the Member States concerned shall take all necessary steps which are available in their respective legal systems, including provisional measures, without prejudice to Union law.

This wording is quite convoluted and certainly not an example of clarity. In essence, apart from unnecessary repetition and a reference to the possibility for the Court of Justice to suspend the effects of a recovery decision through interim measures, it establishes the rule of procedural autonomy of Member States in executing such decisions and establishes the limits of that autonomy, *i.e.*, promptness and effectiveness of recovery.

Basically, this provision, too, would not need to be changed from a reform perspective, as long as it was made clear that it refers to the whole range of restorative and redressive measures that the Commission can take. The concepts of procedural autonomy, promptness and effectiveness would remain appropriate. The time limit within which the decision must be enforced would obviously be set by the Commission *according to the type of remedy* and would not necessarily be the same for all remedies. More details on this could be established in soft law or through the implementing regulation. The reform would also be an opportunity to simplify the wording. One proposal could be the following:

> Without prejudice to any order of the Court of Justice of the European Union pursuant to Article 278 TFEU, the Member State concerned shall implement

> restorative or redressive measures ordered by the Commission in accordance with the procedures in force under national law, provided that those procedures allow the timely and effective execution of the Commission's decision, including through provisional measures if appropriate. If necessary, Member States shall adapt their national law to ensure the timely and effective execution of the Commission's decisions.

With this amendment, the principle that Member States are subject to an obligation of result in this respect, in accordance with *Scott* case law,[76] would be fully justified because the consequences, difficulties and implications of the various measures would already be considered *ex ante*.[77] Finally, it should be borne in mind that Article 16(3) concerns the prolongation of public enforcement by national authorities and courts, not private enforcement. Obviously, however, the concepts of promptness and effectiveness are based on those of effectiveness and equivalence that jurisprudence has extensively developed in relation to the national enforcement of directly applicable EU rules.[78] In this context, equivalence is the fundamental rule, to which effectiveness is added - however, the latter must be read not in relation to specific, pre-defined measures but rather in relation to the measures the national court considers necessary for the full and correct application of EU law.

III.C Clarifying the Interest Pursued in Ordering Remedies

An additional change would be required to clarify the precise interest pursued in ordering remedies, as this would also help better shape the role of national courts (as explained below).[79] As things stand today, great uncertainty and controversy surround this issue based on the current status of case law. There is no need to reiterate here the contradictory indications arising from case law and soft law, nor the difficulty to reconcile them with the Procedural Regulation's preamble.[80] It can be argued that the ambiguity stems directly from the Treaty, as the reference to abolition of aid in Article 108(2) can be read as referring both to the measure instituting the aid and to its effects. However, as explained above, the second reading of the provision appears to be more in line with the substantialist approach of EU law, especially its internal market and competition provisions.

If one accepts this position, the question arises as to whether the objective of eliminating the aid's effects (or, to put it another way, of restoring the competitive situation that existed before the aid was granted) is to be pursued through public enforcement alone or through a combination of private and public enforcement. If the first option is preferred, the reform should clearly introduce the concept of elimination of the distortion of competition and restoration of the competitive situation that existed before the aid was granted, thus departing from the formalistic approach (*i.e.*,

76. *See* Part One, section I.A.2.4 and footnote 39.
77. The (not insignificant) changes that this amendment would imply in terms of procedure are analysed below in this section.
78. *See* Part One, section II.B.2 and footnotes 187 and 188.
79. *See* Chapter IV.
80. *See* Part One, section I.A.2.3.

elimination of the mere financial benefit by ordering repayment of the aid's nominal amount) that recent case law has leaned toward. Conversely, if the second option is preferred, the approach could be confirmed in the reform, but it would become necessary to establish an express obligation on national courts to adopt complementary remedies in follow on cases when necessary to achieve the stated objective. A harmonisation directive would thus become ineluctable from this perspective - and not only the best possible solution for fostering the convergence and effectiveness of national laws.

The preference advocated for in this book is clearly for a system of public enforcement remedies that, by itself, is coherent with the rationale of State aid control and capable of achieving its objectives and that does not have to rely on the potential for private enforcement, which is not under the Commission's control. This does not mean that private enforcement (and the related paths for reform) loses its significance but simply that the two tools remain separate and that each of them has its own scope and mission - as explained in the case law[81] - rather than being intertwined. In any case, it is imperative that this issue be clarified, as the coherence and credibility - not to mention the effectiveness - of the overall system of remedies depends on it.

Finally, a further change would be useful to restore credibility to the system of remedies - credibility that has been weakened in recent times by a formalistic approach that ignores the effects of the aid subject to recovery. Presently, as is well known, in the event of non-implementation of a recovery obligation, the Commission assesses whether - and, if so, when and how - to take legal action against the Member State responsible for the breach, as in any other infringement procedure. In fact, although Article 16(1) of the Procedural Regulation provides for the Commission's obligation to order recovery, it says nothing about the consequences of incorrect recovery or failure to order recovery altogether. This is due to the approach taken in primary law, as Article 108(2) TFEU gives the Commission and the Member States (other than the one granting the aid) the choice to start an infringement procedure before the Court of Justice. In the framework of the proposed reform, it would be appropriate for the Commission - in continuity with the Commission's obligation to take the necessary restorative or redressive measures with reference to a given case - to self-limit its discretion by committing, through a reference in the revised Recovery Notice, to pursue legal action against any Member State that fails to enforce remedies imposed by the Commission or that enforces them partially or incorrectly.

The opportunity to harmonise national rules established to implement restorative or redressive measures adopted by the Commission could also be reconsidered[82] - and it would help win over resistant German courts and scholars,[83] although this is not an absolute must for the proposed reform to be successful and attain its objectives.

81. *See* Judgment of the Court of Justice of 14 February 1990, *Boussac*, cited in footnote 13 of Part One.
82. As is well known, at the time the first Recovery Notice was enacted back in 2009, the EU legislator discarded the Commission's initial proposal to harmonise national procedures for the recovery of unlawful aid following a Commission decision. *See* Part One, section II.A.2.
83. *See* Part One, section I.A.2.4 and footnote 47.

III.D Amendments Related to Ancillary Remedies

Another issue to be carefully considered in the context of the reform concerns ancillary remedies, in particular the remedy arising from the *Deggendorf* doctrine.[84] This remedy, of jurisprudential origin, has been consolidated and clarified through case law and concrete application, in addition to references in various soft law acts.[85] With the reform, the remedy should be adapted to refer to the non-execution of measures imposed by the Commission in a final decision, regardless of their nature. The necessity to clarify this could lead the EU legislator to include a specific provision on ancillary remedies in the reformed Procedural Regulation.

This development would be desirable in terms of legal certainty, as it would codify at least the fundamental principles of this remedy and help correct some deviations from the original approach.[86] Furthermore, anchoring the *Deggendorf* doctrine in positive law would be an opportunity to introduce the concept of beneficiary company liability in the event of complicity with the State in the infringement of procedural rules in this respect, too.[87] If this kind of liability cannot be proven, only the original meaning of the *Deggendorf* doctrine would remain, *i.e.*, a cumulation factor that, when considering the aid's effects as part of the compatibility assessment's balancing test, could push the test towards a negative assessment. Conversely, if the beneficiary company shared liability, nothing in the Treaty would prevent this factor from being taken into account, as the Union may certainly equip itself with the appropriate means to facilitate compliance with Treaty rules through the legal basis of Article 109 TFEU. This would result in an absolute ban on granting new aid to a complicit undertaking that has not yet complied with restorative or redressive measures ordered by the Commission to neutralise previous unlawful and incompatible aid.[88]

If the *Deggendorf* remedy were endowed with a prescriptive source in positive law and the related wording were clear and unambiguous, it would also become available to national courts in private enforcement contexts. Indeed, because national courts would have to draw all consequences from a given breach of the procedural rules without being concerned about compatibility, they could more easily take precautionary measures to block the disbursement of new aid. They would also have

84. The second ancillary remedy – *i.e.*, application of the procedure under Art. 260(2) TFEU – would not require specific attention in the proposed reform, although the critical remarks illustrated in Part One (section I.B.2) remain relevant and will hopefully be considered in the Commission practice and in future case law.
85. *See* Part One, section I.B.1.
86. *Ibid.*, where the risk of a punitive drift of the *Deggendorf* doctrine is flagged.
87. As suggested below (*see* section IV.E.3), the subjective factor of whether beneficiary undertakings were, or should have been, aware of the infringement could be considered when determining remedies.
88. Moreover, this change would yield a second improvement of the system of remedies. Indeed, the analysis of the beneficiary's complicity with the State would allow to establish the concept of co-liability of the beneficiary with the State, with the consequences explained above in section I.D of this Part Four.

the tools to weigh all available evidence and circumstantial elements in order to assess whether the beneficiary company is liable.

Other ancillary remedies could also be included in the scope of a reform. Indeed, with the amendment of the Procedural Regulation, the system of remedies could be completed with the provision of safeguards and penalties modelled on the FSR to ensure the proper enforcement of all remedies, whether restorative or redressive. Not only should the Commission be empowered to impose reporting and transparency requirements to facilitate the monitoring of compliance with remedies and the detection of infringements; but Member States should also be required to adopt a law establishing appropriate penalties for non-compliance with remedies or with reporting and transparency requirements. The Commission could establish the level of such penalties (fines or penalty payments) and link them with the aggregate turnover generated by the liable undertaking in the year preceding the infringement, as is customary in competition law.

In terms of enforcement, it would also be useful to insert a provision in the reformed Procedural Regulation empowering the Commission to take a decision based on the facts available not only when the Member State concerned does not cooperate with the Commission in the investigation but also when the beneficiary undertaking provides incomplete, incorrect or misleading information to the Member State during a State aid investigation or directly to the Commission if the latter uses the investigative tools available to it under Article 27 of the Procedural Regulation to monitor compliance with a previous decision.

Conversely, it would not be advisable to rely on the foreign subsidy model with respect to Article 18 FSR, which empowers the Commission to revoke a decision containing redressive measures or making commitments binding on the undertaking concerned and replace it with a new decision – not only when the revoked decision was based on incomplete, incorrect or misleading information or when the undertaking acts contrary to its commitments or fails to comply with redressive measures but also *when the commitments or redressive measures turn out to be ineffective*.[89] Indeed, this would be at odds with the cornerstone of legal certainty that a reform would aim to lay.

Rather, giving the Commission the possibility to revoke a decision whenever the Member State or undertakings concerned fail to cooperate would be appropriate and would be consistent with a substantive approach to the re-establishment of competitive conditions before the aid was granted by eliminating the competitive advantage gained by the beneficiary.

III.E Amendments Related to the Decision-Making Procedure

The third suggested amendment – *i.e.*, in addition to that of Article 16 of the Procedural Regulation and that concerning ancillary remedies (with the latter being not indispensable but certainly desirable) – should concern procedures. If the system of remedies

89. As explained in Part Three, section III.B.4, this provision is very intrusive and could be challenged before the EU courts through an objection of illegality.

were given greater flexibility, with the possibility of multiple remedies and a distinction between restorative and redressive measures, it would immediately follow that absolute impossibility (within the meaning explained above)[90] would have to be invoked either during the compatibility assessment – so that the Commission can examine it and take it into account when determining the most appropriate remedies – or within a mandatory time limit after the final decision. This leads to the question of how to shape procedures for establishing and monitoring remedies.

First, the Commission should be given the choice of either establishing remedies in a final negative decision or reserving the right to do so at a later stage, albeit within a short time limit. Establishment of the remedies in the operative part of a final decision would remain the rule when no reason exists to do otherwise. In such cases, as mentioned, the priority remedy would remain recovery of the principal plus interest – unless the information provided by the Member State or gathered from other sources makes it possible to determine that repayment of the aid would be ineffective, in which case the Commission would be entitled to order, from the outset, the restorative or redressive measures it considers most appropriate among those envisaged in the reformed Procedural Regulation.[91] The Commission would be given ample discretion in determining the most appropriate remedy based on the information in its files. Challenges before the EU courts would be limited to manifest errors in the assessment of facts, violation of general principles, such as proportionality, abuse of power or failure to state reasons.

If the Commission considered that a risk of recovery being ineffective exists, but that the information at its disposal does not enable it to identify the most appropriate alternative measures, it should be given the power to split the decision on compatibility from that on remedies, with the latter to be notified not only to the Member State concerned but also to the beneficiary.[92] Two options could be envisaged in this respect, *i.e.*, the Commission could either: (i) notify the Member State and beneficiary concerned of a draft measure on remedies, with a short period (not exceeding thirty days) to provide any observations, failing which the incompatibility decision would be deemed to be supplemented by the measure on remedies; or (ii) insert an obligation in the operative part of its decision for the Member State to submit a proposal for remedies within a given period (again, not exceeding thirty days) and to transmit any proposals from the beneficiary within that same period.

Second, a precise procedure should be drawn up and put into practice to regulate cases in which, following the issuance of a final decision containing a recovery order,

90. *See* sections I.C and II.B of this Part Four.
91. Unless, of course, the legislator prefers to refrain from drawing up any list of redressive measures and leaves their content entirely open.
92. As a matter of fact, compatibility assessments and recovery orders can already be understood as two different – albeit related – decisions, as becomes apparent when considering judicial control. For instance, a compatibility decision concerning an aid scheme can be challenged by the beneficiaries only if they are exposed to recovery (*see*, among others, Judgment of the Court of Justice (Grand Chamber) of 19 December 2013, Case C-274/12 P, *Telefónica SA v. European Commission*, EU:C:2013:204); if the decision does not contain a recovery order, the beneficiaries lack standing. Moreover, the EU courts can uphold an assessment of incompatibility and still annul the related recovery order.

the Commission is informed that it is absolutely impossible to execute the order. The notion of absolute impossibility should of course, here too, be understood in the broader sense explained above,[93] based on the substantive concept of effectiveness of the remedy. Moreover, again as explained above, the possibility of reporting absolute impossibility should be granted not only to the Member State (which would be obliged to do so under Article 4(3) TEU) but also to the aid recipient (through the Member State, which would be obliged to transmit the undertaking's request, possibly accompanied by its own observations).[94]

A peremptory deadline should be set for reporting absolute impossibility, which could be thirty days from the decision. At the same time or, at the latest, within a further thirty days (*i.e.*, within a total of two months from the decision), the Member State concerned, or the beneficiary undertaking (through the Member State), would have the possibility of submitting a request to replace recovery with appropriate restorative or redressive measures, which would have to meet the requirements of *transparency*, *verifiability* and *effectiveness* laid down in the reformed Procedural Regulation.

Third, the Commission should have the power (but not the obligation) to conduct a market test to explore the views of other interested parties on the effectiveness of proposed remedies before adopting a final decision on remedies to supplement an incompatibility decision. If the Commission chooses to exercise this power, the test should be conducted within two months from the request to replace recovery with alternative measures (*i.e.*, within a total of four months from the substantive decision in the worst-case scenario, or three months if the request was filed at the same time as the notification of the absolute impossibility).

At that point, it would not be necessary to set a new deadline for enforcement by the Member State and the company concerned because the remedies would be based on their proposal or would in any case have already been discussed with them. In the event of non-compliance, the Commission would have recourse to the procedure under Article 28 of the Procedural Regulation against the Member State (and subsequent recourse, if necessary, to the procedure under Article 260(2) TFEU) and/or have the power to penalise the company by imposing fines or penalty payments just as in cases of non-cooperation (provision of incomplete, inaccurate or misleading information).

If this decision-making procedure were put in place, it would lead to several further benefits for the coherence and modernisation of State aid procedures and the system of State aid control altogether. Indeed, this very procedure could be applied in two situations that are currently unregulated, *i.e.*: (i) when the Commission has ordered recovery in its final decision but has left it to the national authorities, under the supervision of national courts, to calculate the amount to be repaid by the various beneficiaries (which in most cases are identified by the national authorities themselves), which is a very frequent situation that arises in the context of decisions

93. *See* above, sections I.C and II.B of this Part Four.

94. Member States should be under an obligation to inform the Commission of proposals received from beneficiaries because a conflict of interest between the State and beneficiaries cannot be excluded.

concerning aid schemes with multiple beneficiaries;[95] and (ii) when aid cannot be recovered because the company that must repay it is insolvent, the alternative restorative remedy of the cessation of business operations and sale of assets is ordered, and the purchaser (or potential purchaser) wishes to obtain legal certainty through a Commission decision that no element of aid will (or would) be transferred to it.

In the first case, the Member State would be obliged to inform the Commission of the results of its verifications and calculations within two months from the decision, after which the procedure would proceed as outlined above, with the Commission being allowed to carry out its own verifications and to adopt a final decision on remedies within the following two months – a decision to be executed without delay. In the second case, instead of Member States submitting a notification for the sake of legal certainty, as is current practice,[96] and requesting the Commission for a decision under Article 4(2) of the Procedural Regulation, the procedure described above could be used just as for all other cases in which recovery cannot be applied: *i.e.*, a request would be submitted to the Commission with the proposed methods of sale,[97] and the Commission would issue a decision on the remedies, after possible market testing, within two months from the request (or, in the worst-case scenario, within four months from the negative decision).

III.F Possible Amendments Relating to Third Parties' Rights

An important aspect of the reform envisaged here is determining what rights third parties would have under the new procedure. Aid recipients exposed to remedies should logically be granted the right to be closely associated with the procedure for determining remedies. This approach is in accordance with the prevailing view in case law as to the rights of interested parties during the investigation procedure,[98] although

95. The Commission almost invariably relies on Member States' cooperation when an investigation concerns an aid scheme with multiple beneficiaries, limiting its assessment to the general features of the scheme without delving into the specificities of each beneficiary's position.
96. *See*, for example, the Commission Decision of 4 April 2012, C(2012) 2401 final, OJ C 305, 10.10.2012. In this case, the French authorities notified the Commission about the asset deal in order to obtain confirmation that the obligation to recover the aid was not transferred to the acquirers, as there was no economic continuity with the former entity.
97. More precisely, the request should include at least the following: (i) indications on the envisaged procedure (if any) for selecting the purchaser; (ii) the selection requirements relating to the purchaser's identity and its shareholding structure, up to the ultimate beneficiary/beneficial owner; (iii) the conditions imposed on, or commitments required of, the purchaser; (iv) the method for calculating the sale price; and (v) the warranties offered by the seller and any spin-offs, debt restructuring or similar transactions preceding the sale.
98. *See*, among others, Judgment of the Court of Justice of 29 July 2024, Case C-697/22 P, *Koiviston Auto Helsinki Oy (formerly Helsingin Bussillikenne Oy) v. European Commission*, EU:C:2024:641, where the Court held that where new issues arising after the decision to initiate the formal investigation procedure are 'relevant issues of fact and law' within the meaning of Art. 6(1) of the Procedural Regulation, the Commission's obligation to inform all interested parties thereof so that they are able to submit their comments can only be complied with by means of the publication of a supplementary opening decision (para. 53). The Court also held that there may be circumstances in which the establishment of facts that are new or different from those referred to in the decision initiating the formal investigation procedure or the adoption of

thus far has not translated into any concrete progress when it comes to procedural guarantees for aid recipients in relation to the imposition of remedies. In the context of the reform advocated for in this book, this approach must be fully implemented at least within the framework of procedures specifically intended to set remedies ('*remedy procedures*').

Once a remedy procedure is underway, it is no longer a matter of discussing whether and, if so, how a Member State's aid measure is compatible or can be made compatible with the internal market, but rather only a matter of determining how the aid's distortive effects can be neutralised by constraining the beneficiary's operations. Consequently, interested parties and specifically aid beneficiaries must be given appropriate procedural guarantees to make their views known and to be involved in the discussions between the Member State and the Commission. This can also help streamline the investigation procedure and avoid delays when complex issues arise in relation to the identification of beneficiaries and/or the remedies to be imposed (*e.g.*, the possibility or quantification of recovery), while building on the principles already established in the case law.[99]

This is even more crucial considering that the risk of conflicts of interest between the granting Member State and the beneficiary is significant in a negative decision's execution phase.[100] Therefore, either the beneficiary must be given the right to address the Commission directly - by submitting its considerations on the impossibility of restoring the *status quo ante* through recovery and the identification of suitable redressive measures - or a provision must be included in the reformed Procedural Regulation to oblige Member States to liaise with beneficiaries and to bring beneficiaries' views to the Commission's attention. The Commission should then have the possibility of hearing the beneficiary directly.

The position of third parties that qualify as interested parties under the Procedural Regulation - especially if they are competitors of beneficiaries - also deserves careful consideration. Their guarantees of defence in remedy procedures must at least correspond to those they have in formal investigation procedures. Consequently, it is only reasonable that interested third parties that have made submissions in a formal investigation procedure be allowed to do the same in the related remedy procedure. Third parties that have not made themselves known during the formal investigation procedure should be allowed to make submissions only if they can substantiate their

substantial amendments to the relevant legal framework may require greater involvement of the interested parties, or even require that a supplementary or corrected opening decision be published (para. 52). *See also* Judgment of the Court of 11 November 2021, Case C-933/19, *Autostrada Wielkopolska v. European Commission*, EU:C:2021:905, para. 71. Finally, the Court clarified in para. 51 that relevant issue of fact and law are, among others, those concerning the remedies (*i.e.*, the obligation to recover the aid).

99. *See* Judgment of the Court of Justice of 29 July 2024, Case C-697/22 P, *Koiviston Auto Helsinki Oy*, cited above in footnote 98. Although the Court takes the view that the recipient of the aid does not have more extensive rights than other interested parties (*see also* Judgment of the Court of 11 March 2020, C-56/18 P, *European Commission v. Gmina Miasto Gdynia and Port Lotniczy Gdynia Kosakowo*, EU:C:2020:192, para. 75), the situation could be different, if the proposal advocated for here is implemented, in the framework of a remedy procedure (*e.g.*, when the aid recipient submits a proposal for alternative remedies).

100. *See* Part One, section III.C.2., and Part Four, section I.D.

own, specific interest in relation to the determination of redressive measures, which must be different from, and additional to, the interest they might have had when the merits of the case were being examined. Furthermore, the Commission, irrespective of any third-party safeguards, should be empowered to use its investigative tools to consult potential interested parties if it deems it useful, either by way of a market test or on an individual basis.

The procedure would be streamlined because – differently from the case of formal investigation procedures under Article 108(2) TFEU – there would be no need to publish the opening of a remedy procedure in the Official Journal, as in the case of the formal investigation procedure under Article 180(2), given that the procedure would automatically start with the publication of the final decision. Indeed, as explained above, the final decision would contain either a request for the Member State to propose possible alternative remedies (or to transmit to the Commission the beneficiary's proposal for alternative remedies) within two months from notification of the decision, or a request for the Member State (possibly also on the beneficiary's behalf) to submit observations on the alternative remedies outlined in the decision within the same time limit.

Interested third parties (within the meaning outlined above) could submit their comments within one month from publication of the decision.[101] If in a given case the Commission limited itself to ordering recovery, the Member State concerned could, on its own initiative, submit its own (or the beneficiary's) proposal for alternative remedies within the same two-month time limit, with sufficient reasoning as to why alternatives to recovery are necessary to effectively pursue the objective of re-establishing the situation existing before the aid was granted or of removing the distortions caused by the aid.

III.G Clarification Concerning Judicial Control

All decisions on remedies would obviously be challengeable: both the remedies provision of final decisions on incompatibility, as is the case even today, and decisions taken at the end of the remedy procedure, as defined above. However, proper account would have to be taken of the various procedural steps and the wide discretion granted

101. The final decision would have to be published expeditiously so as not to delay the conduct of the remedy procedure, given that its publication would also serve *to open the remedies phase* and determine the *dies a quo* to set the deadlines for the proposal of alternative remedies (or any counterproposals to the alternative remedies outlined by the Commission) and for the submission of third parties' observations. If the time limit for third parties to submit comments was one month, as is the case for comments under a formal investigation procedure, publication should ideally take place within one month from adoption. This would maintain the current two-month timeframe for Member States to inform the Commission of measures taken to implement a recovery decision and would avoid delays in the execution of the decision. Within the same two-month timeframe, the Member State would have to propose and justify alternative remedies if the Commission ordered recovery of the aid. Any information in the decision that could give rise to confidentiality problems and thus delay publication would have to be appropriately redacted, taking care to provide the essential information for third parties to express their views.

to the Commission, to ensure that the system of judicial protection would be balanced and would not favour delay tactics. Thus, it could be useful to clarify within the framework of the reform that, if the Commission, in its decision, requests the Member State to submit its own or the beneficiary's proposal for alternative remedies because it finds that recovery is impossible (including in the sense of ineffective, as explained above), that part of the decision would not be challengeable *per se* by the Member State or beneficiary. It could instead be challenged by a third party that participated in the formal investigation procedure and that meets the other *locus standi* requirements, but judicial review would be limited to manifest error, misuse of power or failure to state reasons.

The same situation would arise in the case of decisions that outline alternative remedies and give the Member State and beneficiary (or beneficiaries) concerned time to submit observations and counterproposals: that part of the operative part would not be open to challenge on a standalone basis by Member States or beneficiaries, whereas it would be open to challenge by interested third parties under the same conditions indicated above.[102] Final decisions on remedy packages would, of course, also be appealable by the Member State that granted the aid and the actual beneficiary, as defined by case law,[103] whose interest and standing would be apparent from the nature of the case itself.

As to the standard of judicial review, it would be reasonable for it to be modulated according to the type of challenge brought against a decision on remedies. If the appellant challenged the assessment of the category of remedy – *i.e.*, the choice of an alternative restorative remedy instead of recovery or of a redressive remedy instead of a restorative one – the standard of review should be pervasive, as this kind of assessment entails determining which category of remedy is 'superior', so to speak, *i.e.*, closer to the goal of restoring the *status quo ante*. However, as these are still complex economic assessments, the EU courts would not be able to substitute their own opinion for that of the Commission – instead, they would have to verify that the Commission did not misrepresent the facts and that it drew logical and plausible inferences from them (in other words, that the established facts were sufficient to support the decision taken). Conversely, the standard of review should be narrower if the appellant challenged the choice of remedy package within the same category (restorative or redressive remedies), as the Commission's discretion would be greater there.

To conclude on this point, endorsing the reform approach advocated for in this book would also have the positive side effect of making it possible to solve the serious and longstanding problem of procedural and defence guarantees, as follows: (i) absolute impossibility could be assessed *ex ante* – as is already the case for extrinsic

102. Of course, if a third party challenged the Commission's assessment that recovery is impossible, this would not prevent the Commission – except in the case of interim measures under Art. 278 TFEU – from continuing the procedure and adopting a final decision on remedies. The third party could then also challenge the latter, in which case the cases would presumably be joined by the Court of Justice.
103. Beneficiaries of individual aid or beneficiaries of aid schemes within the limits indicated in the *Telefónica* case law (*see* footnote 92 of this Part Four).

limits to recovery – if the information available to the Commission allowed it; (ii) the compatibility assessment – which is already conceptually separated from the determination of remedies – would be separated from the latter also in practice; (iii) the beneficiary would finally be able to participate in the determination of remedies in accordance with a natural and all-too-often sacrificed right of defence, and the rights of interested third parties would also be more precisely delineated; and (iv) the need – repeatedly pointed out by scholars – to regulate the procedure for the execution of recovery would disappear, as the remedy procedure would be applicable also to cases in which the Commission delegates the identification of beneficiaries and the calculation of the amount to be reimbursed to national authorities, in addition to cases involving investigations into economic continuity or discontinuity in the event of the sale of the beneficiary company's assets.

Lastly, there would be no need for the legislator to detail the rules and steps of this procedure in the reformed Procedural Regulation. It would be enough to establish a principle whereby the impossibility of recovery must be assessed against the ultimate goal of restoring the *status quo ante*, and that alternative remedies aimed at neutralising distortions of competition caused by aid are possible as a secondary, alternative option. For the remainder of the reform, the legislator could delegate the Commission to adopt the rules of procedure applicable to the remedy procedure.

IV HARMONISATION OF NATIONAL LAWS GOVERNING THE PRIVATE ENFORCEMENT OF STATE AID RULES

This chapter explores the possibility of harmonising national laws governing the private enforcement of State aid rules. It identifies key areas where harmonisation could improve the effectiveness of remedies and facilitate the enforcement of State aid rules. It also thoroughly reviews the issue of the most appropriate legal basis for holding aid recipients liable for damages.

When it comes to the potential development of private enforcement within the framework of a reform of the system of remedies, the first question to address is whether a harmonisation directive would be necessary to achieve a minimum degree of uniformity of national laws – at least on key aspects for the mechanism's effectiveness.

The 2009 Study on the enforcement of State aid law at national level already emphasised the necessity of reasonably uniform rules across the Member States to promote the use of private actions but did not delve into the reasons supporting this conclusion. To answer the question above, the starting point is to focus on the role of private enforcement as a complementary remedy to public enforcement. The procedures used in national law to ensure the proper enforcement of Commission-imposed remedies (*i.e.*, the procedures referred to in Article 16(3) of the Procedural Regulation), and the related principles of effectiveness and equivalence, are of no relevance in this context because those procedures are used simply for the execution of public enforcement remedies. Rather, what is at stake here are the procedural rules applicable to actions brought by private parties seeking to enforce, directly before national courts, a breach of the notification and/or standstill obligations for new aid under Article 108(3) TFEU and Article 2(1) of the Procedural Regulation.[104]

Therefore, what essential role would national courts have to play in view of the proposed reform? In a nutshell:

(i) a preventive role: *i.e.*, they would have to ensure, through appropriate interim measures, that unauthorised aid is not disbursed, irrespective of any assessment of its effects on the market; they would have to immediately suspend disbursement if aid is to be paid in several instalments or phases, *e.g.*, because it is linked to the progress of an investment project or to the fulfilment of certain conditions; and they would have to freeze (*e.g.*, through seizure) funds already received by a beneficiary but not yet spent;

(ii) a complementary or integrative role: *i.e.*, they would have to ensure effective compliance with aid rules through appropriate remedies in all cases that might escape public enforcement, including cases of non-compliance with block exemptions of various kinds, non-compliance with conditions/obligations imposed in conditional approval decisions, and even cases of

104. *See also* recital 5 and Art. 1(c) of the Procedural Regulation.

incorrect or abusive application of aid schemes and cases of minor importance that would likely not be brought to the Commission's attention; and

(iii) a supplementary remedies role: *i.e.*, they would have to supplement public enforcement remedies, especially through damages actions, in cases in which the Commission's remedies are insufficient to eliminate all distortive effects. Indeed, Honoré and Jensen observed as follows concerning damages actions:

> [T]his remedy is crucial to the private enforcement of State aid law, because it is one of the strongest incentives that third parties have to litigate in this area – for ... the benefit that they derive from securing recovery is more remote, since the financial advantage initially bestowed upon State aid beneficiaries simply goes back to the State.[105]

These three roles of private enforcement are analysed in as many sections below. The reason for this is that, if political consensus is coagulated around the need of a harmonisation directive to foster State aid private enforcement, it would be preferable to opt for a comprehensive legislative proposal – a proposal encompassing all the various actions that can be brought before national courts based on the infringement of the notification or standstill obligations and not limited to damages claims (as is the case with Directive 2014/104 in the field of antitrust).

IV.A The Preventive Role

As to the preventive role, the situation in relation to State aid is not very different from that in other areas of EU law where interim relief is invoked at national level to prevent the effects of non-compliance with directly applicable EU rules. The Court of Justice's case law has precisely delineated national courts' role in this respect and the requirements which national law must comply with, illustrating how the principles of effectiveness and equivalence must apply in the context of precautionary protection. Soft law is also sufficiently detailed on this point: the Private Enforcement Notice devotes several pages to it,[106] which are among the clearest sections of the existing rules and the subject of extensive commentary by scholars.[107]

In this context, a harmonisation directive could be useful in giving greater legal certainty to economic operators and would obviously increase national courts' attention to, and awareness of, the need to adopt preventive measures whenever possible (the circumstances in which this might be the case are indeed manifold, as explained above); however, it would not entail any radical changes to the current system. Indeed, similar results could be achieved – albeit over a reasonable period – through moral

105. M. Honoré and N.E. Jensen, *Damages in State Aid Cases*, European State Aid Law Quarterly (ESTaL), 2011, Issue 2, pp. 265 ff. https://doi.org/10.21552/estal/2011/2/227. *See also* A.U. Almeida, *Private Enforcement of EU State Aid Law Through Damages Claims*, European State Aid Law Quarterly, 2019, Issue 2, pp. 169-179 https://doi.org/10.21552/estal/2019/2/6.

106. *See* Part Two, section IV.

107. *See* Part Two, section IV and footnotes 174, 178, 191 and 195.

suasion and training work, which the Commission has already engaged in for quite some time.

IV.B The Complementary or Integrative Role

As to the role of private enforcement in completing/integrating the system of remedies, the objective of a harmonisation directive would be to facilitate standalone actions[108] in cases which, as explained above, the Commission is unlikely to prioritise or the national court is in a better position – given its proximity to the facts and knowledge of the relevant legal or regulatory framework – to effectively remedy the breach of aid rules. There are two situations in which standalone actions could be useful.

The first is when the Commission has already exercised its exclusive competence to assess the effects of aid through implementing measures, such as decisions authorising an aid scheme, block exemptions or the like. Errors of this kind are increasingly common, given the huge recourse to block exemptions, as also highlighted by the Court of Auditors.[109] Under these circumstances, the action – which would remain standalone because it generally establishes a remedy as opposed to executing or supplementing a remedy already ordered by the Commission – would originate from the Member State's and/or beneficiary's failure to comply with conditions or obligations imposed in a previous authorisation decision or from the erroneous or abusive application of an exemption regulation. In these cases, national courts would have full freedom, within the limits set by the applicable national law, to modulate the remedy according to their assessment of the seriousness of the distortion caused by the aid and of the best means at their disposal to re-establish the previous situation (if possible) or to neutralise or compensate for the distortion.

It is debatable whether room for manoeuvre would exist in all the above-mentioned cases or whether it would depend on the circumstances of each case: not complying with the conditions of an exemption, whether block or individual, does not necessarily mean that the aid that is non-compliant is also incompatible, but only that it has not been authorised and is therefore unlawful. In fact, authorisation decisions and exemption regulations do not produce automatic negative effects.

In many cases, however, the reasoning of an authorisation decision or the recitals to a regulation – which form an integral part of the act and in light of which the operative part must be read – are so detailed and precise that it is possible to understand the importance of one condition/obligation or another and draw conclusions as to whether aid which does not comply with them could still be authorised or is to be deemed outright incompatible. National courts may also informally consult the Commission through a request for information or for an opinion, as explained in the

108. Standalone actions are actions brought by interested parties based on alleged infringements of the procedural obligations embodied in Art. 108(3) TFEU that neither are nor have been the subject of public enforcement proceedings.
109. *See* section III.C.5 and footnote 276 of Part One.

Private Enforcement Notice, and then ask for any necessary clarification on the scope of the Commission's decision.[110]

It can be inferred from these considerations that, regarding this first situation in which private enforcement can play a complementary role and complete the system of remedies, a harmonisation directive would be useful to: (i) drive an upwards convergence of the remedies available to national courts; (ii) determine a common standard of proof, in particular by codifying the principle laid down in the Private Enforcement Notice that the first two requirements for establishing Member State liability in accordance with the *Brasserie du Pêcheur* case law can be presumed;[111] (iii) establish uniform admissibility and standing requirements; (iv) regulate the summoning of beneficiaries by the State against which an action is brought; and even possibly (v) make it possible in all legal systems for interested third parties to bring an action directly against a beneficiary (which EU law currently does not support, as explained above)[112] when the unlawfulness arises from the breach of conditions imposed in a previous decision or from the misuse of an authorised or block-exempted aid scheme due to non-compliance with the conditions laid down therein after the aid has been granted; or when it can be proved that the beneficiary colluded with the State in breaching the State's procedural obligations under the Treaty. A similar solution would be to consider the aid recipient and the granting Member State jointly and severally liable in such circumstances.[113]

The level of harmonisation to be achieved would, of course, depend on the degree of consensus that can be built between the Member States; whereas the ultimate usefulness of harmonisation compared with the improvements achievable through mere soft law instruments would greatly depend on how much consensus coalesces around the level of harmonisation.[114]

The second situation in which standalone actions can be useful is when no act implementing aid rules has been adopted by the Commission, but the parties interested in contesting an aid measure nevertheless prefer to go to national courts rather than file a complaint with the Commission (which is the only authority with competence to assess not only the existence of aid but also its compatibility with the internal market). This could happen because interested parties consider a standalone action preferable for practical reasons (speed, costs, *etc.*) or because they believe that the factual elements or the legal framework can be more easily understood and examined by a national court.

110. *See* Part Two, sections II.D and III.C.
111. According to these two requirements, the EU provision breached by the Member State must confer rights on individuals, and the breach must be sufficiently serious. *See* Part Two, section V.E.4.1.b).
112. *See* Part Two, section V.E.4.2.
113. Joint and several liability is also one of the steps that Almeida suggests taking to enhance the private enforcement of State aid provisions. However, the author does not explain the conditions under which the aid recipient's liability can be established alongside that of the State. His broader suggestion of extending the scope of the Damages Directive is critically discussed below. *See* Almeida, *Private Enforcement of EU State Aid Law Through Damages Claims*, cited in footnote 105 of this Part Four.
114. On the usefulness and limits of soft law instruments, *see* Part Two, especially Final Remarks.

In this case, however, they must be aware that the national court would have less room for manoeuvre. In fact, because national courts lack the competence to assess an aid measure's negative effects on competition - let alone to balance those effects with any positive effects for the sector concerned or the economy as a whole - they would not have the elements, if recovery is determined to be impossible or ineffective, to modulate remedies according to the real possibility of re-establishing the *status quo ante* or to the distortion produced (assuming that this possibility is envisaged post-reform). Therefore, an action for the annulment or declaration of invalidity of the aid measure, whenever applicable, could lead only to a recovery order if this remedy is considered at least partially effective to restore the situation that existed before the aid was granted. National courts would instead be unable - given their limited competence - to effectively modulate any redressive measures as an alternative to recovery.

Of course, a standalone damages action against the State would be possible also in the second situation just described, in addition to an action for the annulment or declaration of invalidity of the aid measure. However, it would present all the difficulties of this type of standalone actions - difficulties that would have to be addressed mainly through general provisions on the gathering of evidence under a harmonisation directive.[115] As regards a direct horizontal action against an aid beneficiary by a third party, even if it were envisaged in a harmonisation directive, it would encounter serious difficulties because national courts would have to assess the aid's effects on competition from scratch and would thus have difficulties in quantifying the harm that the beneficiary should compensate the third party for. Finally, as to the classification of the measure as State aid, the possibility of requesting the Commission's assistance as *amicus curiae* would be more problematic in this scenario because Commission intervention in national proceedings would be time-consuming in this situation and would, in practice, oblige the Commission to conduct its own investigation as if it had received a complaint.

These considerations explain why a harmonisation directive in this scenario would have a more limited scope than in the previous scenario. Consequently, if a Treaty infringement were established, national courts would necessarily limit themselves to: (i) ordering the State to recover the aid if they considered that this could serve the objective of restoring the competitive conditions that existed before the aid was granted; or (ii) establishing alternative measures of a restorative nature, if available and useful; and (iii) adjudicating on damages claims against the State and/or the beneficiaries although with the difficulties explained above. The objective of a harmonisation directive in this scenario would thus be limited to determining common standards of proof, establishing uniform admissibility and standing requirements, and possibly regulating the summoning of a complicit beneficiary by the State.

115. *See* section IV.D of this Part Four.

IV.C The Supplementary Role

Lastly, as to the role of private enforcement in supplementing the remedies imposed through public enforcement - *i.e.*, through follow-on actions[116] - private enforcement's usefulness would remain substantially unchanged after a reform of the public enforcement system of remedies. However, it could build upon the possible finding of complicity of aid recipients.

Currently, if the Commission orders recovery of aid - thus re-establishing the *status quo ante* - a national court can in theory order the Member State to pay damages to an interested third party if the latter proves that it suffered an injury as a result of the aid and that the injury cannot be remedied by repayment. The aid may in fact result in competitive damage which goes beyond the nominal amount, or damage which, irrespective of its magnitude in relation to the repayment amount, cannot be remedied by the latter because of the time which has elapsed and the circumstances which have arisen in the meantime. Conversely, a third party may not base a damages action brought directly against a beneficiary on a breach of the Treaty - unless the breach constitutes a tort under national law.

In a post-reform scenario, the possibility of an ineffective remedy would be reduced, given the wider range of measures available and the greater discretion granted to the Commission; consequently, there would be a less obvious need for additional intervention by national courts. In any event, national courts would still have to comply with the *ne bis in idem* principle, based on the criteria set out in EU case law, which basically refers to the legal interest protected in adopting a given remedy.[117] This shows just how important it is to precisely identify the interest protected by the remedies that the Commission is empowered to impose. This is not the case as State aid law currently stands, considering the unclear and even contradictory interpretations

116. Follow-on actions for damages are actions that follow up on public enforcement proceedings concerning the same alleged State aid. Actions that run parallel with public enforcement proceedings concerning the same alleged State aid are a different type of follow-on action (*i.e.*, those which are brought while the Commission is investigating an alleged aid measure, and the applicant requests interim relief from national courts pending the outcome of the public enforcement proceedings).
117. *See*, among others, Judgment of the Court of Justice (Grand Chamber) of 22 March 2022, *Bundeswettbewerbsbhörde v. Nordzucker AG and Others*, C-151/20, EU:C:2022:203. The Court of Justice ruled that it is not an infringement of the *ne bis in idem* principle to initiate several proceedings concerning the same unlawful conduct, and as a result of which several national competition authorities have imposed a penalty on the same undertakings, if those proceedings are aimed at pursuing *different legal interests*. Two or more national authorities are considered to pursue different legal interests in relation to the same unlawful conduct when they investigate the anticompetitive effects of the same conduct on their respective national markets. Conversely, the *ne bis in idem* principle prevents two or more national competition authorities from penalising, in application of Art. 101(1) TFEU, the same undertaking to protect competition not in separate national markets but within the single market, as in that case both proceedings would be aimed at protecting the same legal interest. The same problem does not arise in the case of a normal recovery order issued by the Commission, as in this scenario national courts would obviously not be allowed to order a second repayment of the aid, and they would be allowed only to award damages to the affected parties to be paid by the Member State if it is proved that the actual damage went beyond the aid's nominal value.

given to the notion of restoring the *status quo ante*.[118] As stated above, the proposed reform should definitely clarify this crucial aspect of the system of remedies, for this would not only bring consistency to public enforcement practice but also indirectly define the role of national courts in follow-on cases.[119]

The usefulness of a harmonisation directive in this area would be largely independent of the proposed reform of the system of remedies in public enforcement, except for the potential co-liability of aid recipients. A harmonisation directive would increase legal certainty and awareness among national courts and economic operators. In this respect, Almeida emphasises that the main difficulty in the development of State aid private enforcement stems from the difference between substantive and procedural rules, *i.e.*, substantive rules ensue from EU law whereas procedural rules are only those set out in national legal systems. Based on this consideration, the author argues that there is a need to establish uniform conditions for the application of Article 108(3) TFEU at national level. Almeida also submits that competitors and third parties should be entitled to bring damages actions against both the aid-granting authority and the aid recipient.[120] However, as there is no EU legal basis to sue aid recipients, legal bases will vary significantly among Member States. The author does not develop this idea further.

Nevertheless, given the absence of a direct legal basis in EU primary law for establishing an aid beneficiary's liability for lack of notification, the EU legislator could consider including a provision in a harmonisation directive whereby Member States would be required to construe a beneficiary's complicity with the State in infringing Article 108(3) – if proved in the public enforcement investigation – as unlawful conduct giving rise to liability under national tort law, or adopting a specific provision for this purpose if the aforementioned interpretative solution is not possible under national law. This would be a very significant development, complementary to the already discussed obligation that the revised procedural regulation would place on the Commission to ascertain the possible complicity of the beneficiary company, and

118. *See* Part One, section I.A.2.3, and the Introduction to this Part Four.
119. The same criterion – *i.e.*, the need for a precise definition of the legal interests protected by remedies – developed by the Court of Justice in relation to antitrust matters (*see* footnote 115 of this Part Four) could apply in the case of parallel public and private enforcement of State aid provisions. If the remedy ordered by the Commission addressed the competition distortion in full, there would be no room left for national courts to impose further remedies in follow-on actions. Conversely, if the remedy ordered by the Commission fell short of restoring the competitive situation existing before the aid was granted – either because it was limited to a repayment of the nominal amount when the actual advantage is higher, or because it neutralised the advantage but did not by itself compensate interested third parties for damage – national courts could fill the gap and impose supplementary measures.
120. Almeida, *Private Enforcement of EU State Aid Law Through Damages Claims*, cited in footnote 105 of this Part Four. Establishing joint and several liability between Member States and aid recipients is one of the five steps suggested by Almeida to foster private enforcement of State aid rules. The others (discussed below when appropriate) are: (i) amplifying the scope of the Damages Directive to State aid infringements; (ii) introducing a presumption of harm to reduce causal uncertainty; (iii) using counterfactuals for quantifying damages; and (iv) giving the aid recipient the possibility of bringing a contractual claim against the Member State to obtain compensation if the aid element is embodied in a concession agreement or a similar legal framework that can be construed as a contract.

capable of generating a real qualitative leap in private enforcement and the system of remedies as a whole.

IV.D General Issues to Be Addressed Through a Harmonisation Directive

IV.D.1 Preliminary Remarks

Given the previous considerations related to the different roles that private enforcement can play in the field of State aid and the importance that a harmonisation directive could have in relation to each, also in connection with the proposed reform of the public enforcement system of remedies, it is now time to identify the main areas where harmonisation or approximation of laws could positively affect the implementation of remedies. These areas concern: (i) the rules on legal standing; (ii) competence of the judiciary at national level (*i.e.*, the identification of a court with jurisdiction to review damages cases concerning State aid matters, thus building up specific competences); (iii) the rules on limitation periods; (iv) the definition of criteria for ascertaining the right to damages and for determining their amount; and (v) the problem of the appropriate standard of proof.[121] Points (i)-(iii) do not need to be addressed here, as they do not raise major problems and are unrelated to the variety and classification of remedies. Conversely, points (iv)-(v) can be relevant.

As to the right to damages, it could be clarified that it depends on proof of damage beyond that inherent in the availability of funds that the aid generates for the beneficiary, as the latter is neutralised by recovery (or, if recovery is impossible because the beneficiary is bankrupt, the damage is neutralised by market developments). The right to damages could also be properly regulated in cases in which recovery is not ordered or executed because it would conflict with general principles of law (exogenous causes) or because it would be absolutely impossible to implement it for reasons unrelated to the undertaking's insolvency. In such cases, it is possible that damages would fill an objective regulatory gap – although, as before, it is less likely that such a gap would materialise post-reform, given the breadth of instruments that the Commission would have at its disposal. In any case, a harmonisation directive could clarify these assumptions.

Beyond this, a harmonisation directive as proposed in this book would simply codify the existing case law, which has clearly set the scene for the recognition by national courts of the right to damages of injured parties. Other ideas put forward in legal scholarship, such as the establishment of specialised national authorities could be a nice addition to the proposed reform but not an absolute must from the standpoint of

121. An accurate summary of the main shortcomings of the current private enforcement framework in State aid law can be found in C. Jadot, *Damages Actions and State aid: Time for Action at EU Level?*, Market and Competition Law Review, April 2022, Volume VI, Issue 1. After identifying three main obstacles to an effective use of the instrument of actions for damages in State aid (*i.e.*, the burden of proof as to the existence of State aid, the causal link, and the quantification of harm), the author puts forward several interesting proposals and ideas, to which reference is made when necessary in the present and in the next sections.

the reform advocated for in this book.[122] The aim here is not to pave the way to successful damages actions and even less to put forward an all-encompassing analysis of the effectiveness of State aid rules and related proposals for amending the State aid framework. The purpose of this book is instead exclusively to develop a proposal for modernising and rationalising the system of remedies, in the assumption that an effective, coherent and credible system of remedies is a fundamental element for the effectiveness of the entire aid control system.

As to the amount of damages, it should first be made clear that it is completely independent of the aid's nominal value and that indeed, if a claimant were to ask the State to pay the same amount in damages, such a claim would conflict with the Union's interest in not extending the scope of unlawful and incompatible aid. However, this is already clear from case law[123] and is recalled in the Recovery Notice;[124] therefore, a harmonisation directive would merely codify the principle. Rather, the issue should be raised of whether, in cases in which the aid can be construed as contractual consideration for an aided investment, the aid recipient can claim an amount corresponding to the aid amount not as damages but rather within the framework of a contractual claim.[125] Although the answer is necessarily negative - as a conflict with the Union's interest would exist regardless of the aid's form, and the contract would be unenforceable if it conflicts with State aid rules - this situation should nonetheless be duly considered by the Commission when evaluating the existence of legitimate expectations and, if remedies are eventually imposed, in shaping the remedies so as to avoid the State's unjust enrichment.

Legal scholarship points to the quantification of harm as one of the elements of a damages action that could benefit from a harmonisation initiative. Armati and Macchi explain that the quantification of harm is problematic in State aid private enforcement because the harm arises in the form of profit loss over a certain period. By referring to

---

122. *Ibid.*

C. Jadot refers to the establishment of specialised national authorities as part of several proposals for the development of the private enforcement of State aid rules. She emphasises the contribution that such authorities could give not only in relation to the proof of the right to damages (*i.e.*, the classification of national measure as State aid) but also to the proof of the causal link and to the quantification of damages. Referring to the suggestion contained in the 2019 Enforcement Study to establish a 'screening mechanism' as a best practice as already done in some Member States, Jadot elaborates on the functions that such mechanism managed by a State aid coordination body might be entrusted with. She also recalls the proposal made by Buts, Joris and Jegers as early as in 2013 to require that all aid plans be notified to the National Competition Authorities' State aid departments to determine whether the measure must be notified to the Commission. A disagreement between the administration granting the aid and the NCA would trigger a notification obligation. The topic is certainly interesting but not directly relevant to the subject of this book. It can therefore certainly be left open, taking note of the various interesting ideas presented by scholars, but also of the difficulty of determining from Brussels even the internal administrative organisation of the Member States in such a sensitive matter as public spending and related competences.

123. *See* Part Two, section V.D and footnote 158.

124. New Recovery Notice, cited in Part One, section II.B and footnote 125 of Part One, §96.

125. In this regard, Almeida refers to situations such as investments agreed within the framework of a concession agreement or forms of selective taxation agreed in the context of an investment agreement between the State and the aid recipient. *See* Almeida, *Private Enforcement of EU State Aid Law Through Damages Claims*, cited in footnote 105 of this Part Four.

Article 17(1) of the Damages Directive, they argue that Member States should ensure that neither the burden nor the standard of proof required for the quantification of harm be such that the right to claim damages becomes practically impossible or excessively difficult to exercise. This principle should apply in the field of State aid, too, which would require national courts to be empowered to estimate harm equitably in accordance with national laws if it appears practically impossible or excessively difficult to precisely quantify the harm based on the evidence available.

A potential harmonisation directive should therefore formally incorporate the principle of effective restoration of damage as a pre-condition for national courts to engage in the judiciary estimation of harm if the available evidence does not enable the damage to be quantified more precisely. Similarly, Almeida argues that the harm resulting from State aid infringements is not significantly different from antitrust harm. Hence, in his opinion, 'the quantification of antitrust damages by counterfactuals, although not an obvious transposition to State aid', should apply also to this field.[126] Building on these considerations, he suggests that a harmonisation initiative would 'benefit from the evolution of the antitrust framework in relation to facilitating damages claims in order to foster effective redress for State aid harm'. Specifically, he argues that the adoption of a counterfactual mechanism consisting of a but-for assumption based on an *ex-ante* but realistic scenario established on business practices could be applied also to the quantification of harm in State aid cases.

However, the fact remains that, as already explained when examining the potential models for a reform of private enforcement,[127] State aid law has its own peculiarities, and State aid measures - unlike business decisions - can aim at generating long-term benefits for society at large. This could have an impact on the quantification of harm. For the rest, national courts would be free to employ the methods that they deem most appropriate for the quantification of harm, including expert witnesses for the assessment of counterfactual scenarios once the possible causal links against which the analysis should be carried out have been clearly defined.[128]

Turning now to the standard of proof, studies have pointed out that proving a causal link in State aid matters can often be fairly more complex than identifying a causal link in antitrust matters, as the claimant must demonstrate the existence of a direct link between the granting of aid and the damage it suffered. More precisely, as discussed elsewhere in this book,[129] a twofold test to determine a causal link is required in the case of State aid, as first it must be examined whether a causal link exists between the granting of the aid and the damaging behaviour (whatever it is, be it a new investment, the submission of a winning bid in a tender procedure, or the avoidance of insolvency, just to cite a few examples), and second whether a causal link exists

126. *Ibid.*
127. *See* Part Three, Chapter IV.
128. For this reason, it is hard to see a need to dictate any specific method to be followed by national courts in a harmonisation directive.
129. *See* Part Two, section V.E.4 on actions for damages and Part Three, section IV.C.2.2, where this difference surfaces when considering the possibility of mirroring the Damages Directive in a reform of private enforcement in the field of State aid.

between the damaging behaviour and the damage suffered by one or more competitors of the aid beneficiary.

As explained, the first analysis is also called 'upstream causation' and in part overlaps with the 'intent' requirement known in several national legal systems. It would help if a harmonisation directive clarified that this requirement must be considered met any time it is established that the aid measure concerned is selective and produces an incentive effect.[130] The second aspect, which is also called 'downstream causation', corresponds to the 'avoidability' requirement in some legal systems – it is considered met when a clear link can be established between the aided project or behaviour and the damage caused to competitors, in the sense that the damage would not have materialised without the aid (and was therefore avoidable). This is the most problematic kind of proof because it requires discarding other possible causal links.[131] Hence, the standard of proof and the burden thereof are particularly relevant in this regard.

IV.D.2 Main Areas to Be Addressed in Relation to the Burden of Proof

Against this background, a harmonisation directive could be useful in several ways. First, it could establish rules on the level of proof required of a causal link by setting out rebuttable presumptions in well-defined situations. To give just one example, a harmonisation directive could stipulate an obligation for national legislations to introduce a presumption as to the incompatibility of aid – thus facilitating proof that the avoidability requirement was met, *i.e.*, that the damage would not have occurred had the procedural rules not been infringed[132] – unless the court seized decides to stay the proceedings and make a preliminary reference to the Court of Justice or to use the cooperation tools provided by the Private Enforcement Notice by asking the Commission for an opinion.

Although rebuttable presumptions are also used in the field of antitrust law by the Damages Directive,[133] the most obvious model to draw inspiration from is the FSR. The

130. *See* Part Two, section V.E.4.
131. In this respect, Armati and Macchi recall that the establishment of a causal link is often problematic because many factors can influence the economic and market position of an undertaking affected by the unlawful granting of aid to a third party. The authors argue that determining a causal link in State aid matters is more complex than in antitrust matters because of the need to prove both upstream and downstream causation. Although the authors' contribution is extremely helpful overall, it is unclear how they propose to overcome these obstacles. It is unconvincing that the little the Commission attempted to do in the New Private Enforcement Notice can be sufficient. *See* L. Armati and F. Macchi, *The Commission Adopts the New Notice on the Enforcement of State Aid Rules Before National Courts*, European State Aid Law Quarterly (EStaL), 2022, Issue 1, pp. 3-19 https://doi.org/10.21552/estal/2022/1/3.
132. *See* Part Two, section V.E.4.2.
133. *See* Part Three, section IV.C. In this respect, Almeida suggests that a parallel approach to antitrust could be adopted and refers to Art. 17 of the Damages Directive. However, he does not elaborate further on this and seems to imply that the scope of the Damages Directive could simply be broadened to include State aid – an approach that is not entirely convincing and that is discussed further below. Almeida also proposes, among the various measures to make the private enforcement system more efficient, to establish presumptions for proof of causation.

circumstances that determine a presumption of competition distortion under Article 5 FSR[134] could also be used to help define the scope of rebuttable presumptions of damage that national courts would be required to apply based on a harmonisation directive.[135] As a result, uniform (or at least similar) conditions for presumptive causation standards would be applied across the EU and the entire field of public competition law.

The FSR could therefore be used as a benchmark in defining cases in which a distortion caused by aid is presumed (*i.e.*, the mere fact of receiving the aid would constitute a harmful conduct). This would apply both to actions against Member States based directly on EU law and to actions against aid recipients based on national legislations adopted to implement the directive. The provision of presumptions for the most distortive forms of aid would at least ease the burden of proving upstream causation, enabling claimants to focus their efforts on providing evidence of the damage suffered (downstream causation). To ease the burden of proving downstream causation, the directive could require that the use of a counterfactual test be accepted in national legislations and could enumerate the most commonly accepted counterfactual test methods.

Beyond the recourse to presumptions, another theoretical possibility would of course be to establish a standard of causation that Member States would be required to apply in their national legal systems. Advocate General Kokott, in her opinion on the *Kone* case in the field of antitrust,[136] suggested the use of the 'sufficiently direct causal nexus' standard to determine causation between the harmful conduct and the loss suffered by the claimant and went as far as proposing the use of the same standard across all the fields of EU law whenever claims for damages based on the breach of EU law provisions are brought against Member States or private parties. The application of

---

However, here too, as already seen in connection with his proposal to consider the granting Member State and the aid recipient jointly and severally liable, the author relies on either broadening the scope of the Damages Directive or reproducing similar provisions in a directive on the private enforcement of State aid, without clearly or thoroughly explaining either solution. On the general topic of broadening the scope of the Damages Directive, *see* the critical remarks in the conclusion of this section.

134. Article 5 FSR lists five categories of foreign subsidies that are deemed most likely to distort the internal market: (a) a foreign subsidy granted to ailing undertakings in the absence of an adequate restructuring plan meeting certain specific conditions; (b) a foreign subsidy in the form of unlimited guarantees; (c) an export financing measure that is not in line with the OECD Arrangement on officially supported export credits; (d) a foreign subsidy directly facilitating a concentration; and (e) a foreign subsidy enabling an undertaking to submit an unduly advantageous tender.

135. Similar categories could be used to identify State aid that can be presumed to have damaged competitors – this applies at least to points (a), (b), (d) and (e) of Art. 5. Point (c) would also be relevant if the measure is classified as State aid. Other categories could be added, too. If the legislator opted for the use of presumptions for the most distortive forms of aid, it would shift the burden of proof relating to the existence of downstream causation from the claimant to the respondent. The subsequent step would of course be to quantify the damage.

136. Opinion of Advocate General Kokott of 30 January 2014 in Case C-557/12, *Kone AD and Others v. ÖBB-Infrastruktur AG*, EU:C:2014:45, paras 23-28. The Court did not follow the Advocated General's opinion on this issue and, although limiting the procedural autonomy of Member States in the name of the principle of effectiveness, did not provide any concrete guidelines.

this standard could of course be 'valuable for claimants in the State aid field, since it would be established that the existence of exogenous factors cannot in itself remove the causal link'.[137] If consensus is reached among Member States, a common standard of causation would be a useful addition to the private enforcement system but is in no way a pre-condition for the usefulness of a harmonisation directive and the contribution it could give to a modernised State aid system of remedies, which is the focus of this book.

Moreover, if consensus is reached among Member States, the most innovative contribution of a harmonisation directive is that it would pave the way for direct actions by affected third parties against aid beneficiaries (*i.e.*, not only against Member States) if those parties submit that repayment of the nominal aid amount ordered by the Commission is insufficient to remove the full competitive advantage gained by the beneficiary and that putting the burden of damage compensation on the beneficiary as opposed to the State would be more appropriate and effective given the circumstances of the case.

Today, claimants can sue beneficiaries only if a cause for action exists under national law, and they are usually required to demonstrate that the beneficiary misused the aid to engage in anticompetitive behaviour (*e.g.*, exclusionary practices) or that it leveraged bids in tender procedures thanks to the aid. If a directive required Member States to legislate a course of action for claimants to sue aid recipients, this hurdle would be removed. Establishing common principles on limitation periods and the standard of proof could complete the picture and make damages claims against aid recipients more manageable.

This is a point on which the reform of private enforcement and that of public enforcement can most effectively complement each other. Indeed, if the reform of the remedy procedure postulated in this book were implemented and resulted in the possibility of ascertaining co-responsibility of the beneficiaries (or of their complicity with the State) in the violation of the notification and standstill obligations, this would facilitate the recognition, by means of a harmonisation directive, of co-liability of the beneficiaries to the injured parties.

The new course of action could be independent of any actions for damages against a Member State or could be based on a principle – set out in the directive – of joint and several liability between the granting Member State and the aid beneficiary when the latter was, or should have been, aware of the infringement of notification or standstill obligations.[138] Alternatively, the Member State could be given the right to summon the beneficiary in the course of proceedings initiated by parties seeking damages, so that it could claim that at least the amount corresponding to the competitive advantage obtained in excess of the nominal aid amount be covered by the beneficiary (or a higher amount if the State can prove that the beneficiary was complicit in the breach of a standstill obligation).

137. *See* Jadot, *Damages Actions and State Aid: Time for Action at EU Level?*, cited in footnote 121 of this Part Four.
138. As suggested by Almeida. *See* footnote 105 of this Part Four.

Last but not least, a harmonisation directive could also regulate access to relevant documentation for evidentiary purposes. Although the Court held in the *Boiron* case,[139] back in 2006, that national courts should order the defendants to make documents that can help prove the link between the aid and the harmful conduct available to the claimant, this holding is based on the principle of equivalence and is therefore left to existing provisions of national law. Therefore, the usefulness of this principle from the practical point of view should not be overestimated, and similar considerations apply to the indication in the New Enforcement Notice that national courts can rely on reasonable estimates to determine the actual damage the injured parties are to be compensated for or to the possibility of seeking the Commission's assistance.[140]

On this specific point, the Damages Directive may offer a good model to replicate, of course with some adjustments to take account of the specificity of State aid cases, in particular when an action is directed against a State or the production of evidence is requested from a State. Certain necessary safeguards will have to be foreseen for this purpose, especially to protect exchanges within the administration, without which it would be difficult to gain the necessary consensus for the approval of this provision. Beyond this difficulty, however, it is hard to see why the concept of access to documents for evidentiary purposes should not also apply in the area under consideration, given that it is a principle common to the other instances of private enforcement harmonisation rules in EU law (the public procurement Remedies Directive and the antitrust Damages Directive). Indeed, this would also ensure a desirable convergence within the various areas of competition law and the internal market.

Finally, if the recommendation for specifically tailored procedural rules based on the principle of investigation put forward in the 2019 Enforcement Study were retained, private parties would be able to bring legal actions before national courts under the assumption that they can rely on the courts' investigative powers - at least if they are able to show a solid *prima facie* case.

IV.E The Conundrum of the Appropriate Legal Basis, Demystified

The previous subsections of this chapter examined the impulse that a directive harmonising national regulations could give to the private enforcement of State aid rules, albeit on the assumption - illustrated at the beginning of this Part Four - that a reform of remedies itself would already be useful and potentially innovative and decisive from a modernisation perspective, even in the absence of such a directive.

139. Judgment of the Court of 7 September 2006, Case C-526/04, *Laboratoires Boiron SA*, cited in footnote 292 of Part Two.

140. C. Jadot seems to exaggerate the practical importance of these principles and tools, although she eventually acknowledges, with reason, that 'the damage quantification remains a major obstacle for third parties'. Likewise, she expresses criticism on the New Enforcement Notice for not providing sufficient guidance. *See* Jadot, *Damages Actions and State Aid: Time for Action at EU Level?*, cited in footnote 121 of this Part Four. On the various factor that can explain the low number of successful actions, *see also* A. Scott, *Co-operation and Good Faith: State Aid Rules and National Courts: Procedural and Interpretative Consequences*, European State Aid Law Quarterly (EStAL), 2017, Issue 3, p. 359.

Attention must now go to the form in which harmonisation could be achieved. To do so, it is appropriate to start with the proposal put forward by scholars for a broadening of the Damages Directive (section IV.E.1 below), briefly illustrate the issue of the legal basis for an ad hoc directive, which does not seem particularly problematic (section IV.E.2 below), and finally add some more specific considerations on the thornier (at least in appearance) issue of the legal basis for possibly holding recipient companies liable for damages, if the legislator decides to pursue this path (section IV.E.3 below). A relatively reassuring picture emerges, which should therefore not deter the Commission from pursuing the initiative.

IV.E.1 The Proposal to Broaden the Scope of the Damages Directive

Legal scholars have imagined and discussed the possibility of broadening the Damages Directive, the main features of which are presented earlier in this book.[141] Specifically, Almeida argues that the Damages Directive, despite being devoted to antitrust redress, has been implemented in such a broad manner in some Member States that it potentially encompasses all categories of competition law infringements. He reports the example of the UK Damages Implementation Act,[142] which applies not only to infringements of Articles 101 and 102 TFEU but also to all competition damages actions brought in the UK.[143] He further suggests that a correspondence can be found with the subject matter and scope of that directive, specifically, Article 1 thereof, which states that the directive 'sets out rules fostering undistorted competition in the internal market and removing obstacles to its proper functioning, by ensuring equivalent protection throughout the Union for anyone who has suffered harm'. Jadot also argues that the Damages Directive can serve 'as a partial model for a more streamlined State aid damages regime' and use it 'as a starting point to establish building blocks that could potentially improve the ability for third parties to obtain compensation', but she concedes that 'a literal transposition is not the solution, due to both shortcomings of the Directive and the peculiarities of State aid law'.[144]

In this respect, it must first be considered that the right that third parties derive from Article 108(3) TFEU is not a right of a substantive nature not to suffer harm as a result of aid, but a right to see the proper procedures for examining aid duly implemented before the aid can be paid. Accordingly, the right to damages cannot be based solely on EU law, even if a breach of Article 108(3) TFEU necessarily entails a tort under the non-contractual liability provisions of national law. This aspect, discussed in detail in Part Two,[145] must be taken into account in a possible harmonisation directive

141. *See* Part Three, section IV.C.
142. In this respect, *see* T. Bolster and J. Groves, *The UK Implements the EU Damages Directive,* May 2017 (| Global Litigation Solutions | Hausfeld (iadclaw.org)).
143. Almeida, *Private Enforcement of EU State Aid Law Through Damages Claims,* cited in footnote 105 of this Part Four. Almeida should be praised for having raised the idea of a harmonisation directive for the first time and having launched the debate on this thorny issue.
144. *See* Jadot, *Damages Actions and State Aid: Time for Action at EU Level?,* cited in footnote 121 of this Part Four.
145. *See* Part Two, section V.E.4.

concerning damages actions for breach of State aid rules. It follows that the issues that compensation for damage raises in the field of State aid are ontologically different from those that characterise antitrust torts. Therefore, extending the scope of a directive designed for different reasons is short-sighted.

For example, in the case of aid, the problem of proving that the conduct (in this case, that of the Member State) is contrary to the Treaty (and therefore incompatible) does not arise because, whenever procedural obligations have been infringed, the claimant need not establish that the aid is incompatible. Hence, there is no need to set out the principle that the Commission's findings have a binding effect on national courts (as in Article 16(1) of Regulation (EC) No 1/2003). Likewise, there is no room for a provision equivalent to Article 9(1) of the Damages Directive, as the Commission has exclusive competence to assess State aid compatibility. Hence, these principles would not help spread the use of private enforcement as they historically did in the antitrust field.[146] For State aid, the main obstacles hindering the development of private enforcement are the cause of action and the proof of the causal link (especially downstream causation), as explained above.

Furthermore, a specific situation occurs when a damages claim arises from the granting of unlawful aid as defined in Articles 1(g) and 20 of the Procedural Regulation,[147] because in such cases the aid can be regarded not only as unlawful but also as incompatible, and thus the right to damages may derive directly from the finding of an infringement. A State aid harmonisation directive should therefore deal separately with this scenario, which cannot be confused with the situation of unnotified aid - something that again would clearly differentiate it from the Damages Directive.

For these reasons alone, proposals to extend the scope *ratione materiae* of the Damages Directive do not seem to be able to flourish, though there is obviously no shortage of similarities on technical aspects - such as the quantification of harm, the standard of proof, standing, and others - which explain Almeida's proposal. It follows that an ad hoc directive seems to be the best option if the Commission decides to take up the idea of harmonisation. Of course, a hypothetical harmonisation directive should be substantive - not merely procedural - in content, committing the Member States to adapting their national systems concerning non-contractual liability. Drawing up the proposal would of course be a daunting task for the Commission. And above all, strong resistance is to be expected from some Member States, which are reluctant to welcome such intrusive changes to national law.

---

146. *See* Wils, *Private Enforcement of EU Antitrust Law and Its Relationship with Public Enforcement: Past, Present and Future*, in World Competition, March 2017, Volume 40, Issue 1, pp. 3-46 https://doi.org/10.54648/woco2017002, already cited in footnote 141 of Part Three. This excellent paper - which provides an illuminating history of private enforcement of EU antitrust law from the 1957 EEC Treaty and Regulation 17/62/EEC to Regulation (EC) No 1/2003 and finally Directive 2014/104/EU - was presented at the Mannheim Centre for Competition and Innovation Law and Economics Conference on Cartel Damages in Europe in November 2016.

147. These articles refer to abusive aid, *i.e.*, aid granted in infringement of an authorised aid scheme or infringing one of the conditions imposed in a conditional decision adopted in accordance with Art. 9(4) of the Procedural Regulation.

However, only a State-aid-specific damages directive could adapt precisely and adequately to the peculiarities of State aid law, by: (i) basing liability on the infringement of a procedural provision, not a substantive one, as in antitrust law; (ii) combining States' and aid recipients' liability in the most appropriate way; and (iii) accounting for the different solutions tailored to the various kinds of infringements (notably, unlawful aid versus abusive aid, and unnotified aid versus infringements of block exemption regulations). Therefore, if the idea of a harmonisation tool were to gain momentum, the obvious preference would be for an entirely new piece of legislation, not for a broadening or amendment of the Damages Directive.

IV.E.2 The Choice of the Appropriate Legal Basis

In connection with the issue just mentioned, another complexity would arise from the choice of the appropriate legal basis. The question of the legal basis for an act of the EU institutions is always a sensitive one, not only because it determines the legislative process but also because it affects the very existence of the Union's competence.[148] Moreover, according to the case law, the choice of legal basis is not a choice in the proper sense of the word, because the criteria determining it are binding in nature.[149]

To approach this issue, one should first turn to the Damages Directive, to check whether the same legal basis could be reproduced in a brand-new State aid harmonisation directive. As clearly emerges from its recital 8, the Damages Directive has dual legal bases:[150] Articles 103 and 114 TFEU. This choice is precisely explained by the Commission in the impact assessment of its proposal, where it clarified as follows:

> The ... proposal is based on both Articles 103 and 114 of the Treaty, because it pursues two equally important goals which are inextricably linked, namely (a) to give effect to the principles set out in Articles 101 and 102 of the Treaty and (b) to ensure a more level playing field for undertakings operating in the internal market,

148. *See* G.M. Roberti, *La giurisprudenza della Corte di Giustizia sulla 'base giuridica' degli atti comunitari*, in A. Tizzano, ed., 'Problematica del Diritto delle Comunità Europee, Edizione de "Il Foro Italiano"', Roma, 1992. As the competences of the Union are attributive competences, the assessment of the appropriate legal basis has the dual purpose of verifying whether the subject matter of the envisaged act relates to an express or tacit competence of the Union and of establishing, within the internal framework of the EU legal system, whether the competence is attributable to this or that institution.
149. *See* Judgment of the Court of Justice of 26 March 1987, C-45/86, *Commission of the European Communities v. Council of the European Communities*, EU:C:1987:53. The Court held that:

> the choice of the legal basis for a measure may not depend simply on an institution' s conviction as to the objective pursued but must be based on objective factors which are amenable to judicial review (para. 11).

This judgment inaugurated a jurisprudential trend that confirmed and strengthened the binding nature of the criteria applicable to the choice of the appropriate legal basis.
150. Recital 8 includes the following statement: 'As the differences in the liability regimes applicable in the Member States may negatively affect both competition and the proper functioning of the internal market, it is appropriate to base this Directive on the dual legal bases of Articles 103 and 114 TFEU'.

> and to make it easier for citizens and businesses to make use of the rights they derive from the internal market.[151]

Legal scholarship has endorsed these dual legal bases, without raising any doubts in this respect,[152] though some authors have underlined that Article 103 TFEU would have been sufficient alone.[153]

When it comes to a hypothetical State aid damages directive, Article 103 TFEU would obviously have to be replaced by the corresponding provision for State aid, which is Article 109 TFEU. However, the latter refers merely to regulations, whereas Article 103 TFEU empowers the Council, upon proposal from the Commission, to adopt regulations or directives. Consequently, the only possible legal basis for a State aid damages directive would be Article 114 TFEU. The alternative would be to adopt a regulation, not a directive, but this would raise other and more serious problems: First, setting up a common legal framework for the private enforcement of State aid provisions would be unnecessary and therefore disproportionate to achieving the desired objectives (*i.e.*, it could be seen as a breach of the subsidiarity principle); second, Article 109 TFEU might be considered unsuited for that purpose, as it is clearly orientated to develop the substantive provisions on State aid of Article 107 and the rules governing the procedures before the Commission contained in Article 108.[154]

---

151. Proposal for a directive of the European Parliament and of the Council on certain rules governing actions for damages under national law for infringements of the competition law provisions of the Member States and of the European Union, COM/2013/0404 final - 2013/0185 (COD).
152. *See, ex multis*, G. Muscolo, *Towards More Effective Antitrust Damages Actions in Europe: The Commission Proposal for a Directive*, in Italian Antitrust Review, 2013, Issue 0.
153. *See, ex multis*, A. Howard, '*Too Little, Too Late? The European Commission's Legislative Proposals on Anti-Trust Damages Actions*', in Journal of European Competition Law & Practice, 2013, Volume 6, pp. 455-464.
154. An analysis of the 1956 Messina Conference Intergovernmental Committee's Report to the Foreign Ministers (better known as 'Spaak Report') – available here: https://www.cvce.eu/obj/rapport_des_chefs_de_delegation_aux_ministres_des_affaires_etrangeres_bruxelles_21_avril_1956-fr-4dd69921-433b-4bc0-acec-808f72fec9ae.html.
confirms that the attention of the Heads of Delegation was focussed on the appropriate balance between Commission's powers and Council's prerogatives in deciding: (i) upon the compatibility of particular forms or categories of public assistance with the common market; and (ii) upon the conditions and time-limits of procedures before the Institutions. Therefore, nothing justifies the assumption that the Treaty authors' will was to oblige the Commission to follow the procedure under Art. 109 TFEU (Art. 94 CEE) to enact harmonisation rules intended to foster the effectiveness of State as remedies through private enforcement. In addition, legal scholarship has emphasised that:

> acts adopted on the basis of Art. 109 TFEU are not legislative acts, because the procedure is not qualified as a legislative procedure in the Treaty. Rather, it is one of the rare examples where the Council exercises executive powers. Furthermore, acts adopted on the basis of Art. 109 TFEU are not implementing regulations in the sense of Art. 292 TFEU, because they do not serve the implementation of an act of Union law.

This is confirmed by the fact that Art. 109 TFEU does not foresee any role for the European Parliament. Moreover:

> All these characteristics have the consequence that it is not possible to combine Art. 109 TFEU with legislative legal bases. They are not compatible.

It is therefore necessary to investigate whether the proposal for a directive harmonising national rules governing State aid private enforcement can be exclusively framed under Article 114 TFEU – in other words, whether it meets the requirements for having recourse to this legal basis. Two essential principles stemming from case law, in addition to those mentioned at the beginning of this section, are relevant here. First, the Court held as follows:

> 'If examination of a Community measure reveals that it pursues a twofold purpose or that it has a twofold component and if one of these is identifiable as the main or predominant purpose or component, whereas the other is merely incidental, the act must be based on a single legal basis, namely that required by the main or predominant purpose or component'.[155] However, 'Exceptionally, if it is established that the act simultaneously pursues a number of objectives, indissociably linked, without one being secondary and indirect in relation to the other, such an act may be founded on the various corresponding legal bases.'[156]

Second, specifically on compliance with the requirements of Article 114 TFEU, the Court stated:

> 'The measures referred to in Article 100a(1) of the Treaty [now Art. 114 TFEU] are intended to improve the conditions for the establishment and functioning of the internal market. To construe that article as meaning that it vests in the Community legislature a general power to regulate the internal market would not only be contrary to the express wording of the provisions cited above but would also be incompatible with the principle embodied in Article 3b of the EC Treaty (now Article 5 EC) that the powers of the Community are limited to those specifically conferred on it.'
>
> 'If a mere finding of disparities between national rules and of the abstract risk of obstacles to the exercise of fundamental freedoms or of distortions of competition liable to result therefrom were sufficient to justify the choice of Article 100a as a legal basis, judicial review of compliance with the proper legal basis might be rendered nugatory.'
>
> 'So, in considering whether Article 100a was the proper legal basis, the Court must verify whether the measure whose validity is at issue in fact pursues the objectives stated by the Community legislature.'
>
> 'It is therefore necessary to verify whether the Directive actually contributes to eliminating obstacles to the free movement of goods and to the freedom to provide services, and to removing distortions of competition'.

See T.M. Rusche, *Article 109 TFEU*, in *The EU Treaties and Charter of Fundamental Rights: A Commentary*, New York 2019, Oxford Academic. Rusche concedes that the legislator has taken a different view in the Damages Directive, but it must be recalled that some scholars disapproved this choice.

155. Judgment of the Court of Justice of 30 January 2001, Case C-36/98, *Kingdom of Spain v. Council of the European Union*, EU:C:2001:64. *See also* Judgment of the Court of Justice (Grand Chamber) of 3 December 2019, Case C-482/17, *Czech Republic v. European Parliament and Council of the European Union*, EU:C:2019:1035, para. 31.
156. Judgment of the Court of Justice of 19 September 2002, Case C-336/00, *Republilk Österreich v. Martin Huber*, EU:C:2002:509, para 31.

> 'In examining the lawfulness of a directive adopted on the basis of Article 100a of the Treaty, the Court is required to verify whether the distortion of competition which the measure purports to eliminate is appreciable.'[157]

Based on these principles, Article 114 TFEU seems to be an appropriate legal basis, at least theoretically. First, it is included in the same Title VII of the TFEU as the competition provisions, which can only mean that for the authors of the Treaty there is a possible link between approximation of laws and competition rules - and the adoption of the Damages Directive relied on this link. In other words, approximation of national laws can very well be one of the means at the disposal of the European Institutions to promote undistorted competition in the internal market. Second, it is certainly true that Article 114 refers to the achievement of the objectives set out in Article 26 TFEU (*i.e.*, the functioning of the internal market), but no one can question the very close link between State aid rules and internal market objectives. Aid rules are traditionally defined as a bridge between the internal market and competition, and legal scholarship has emphasised their dual significance as rules to protect competition and the internal market, so much so as to say that they are not aimed only at ensuring consumers' welfare - through protection of a level-playing field - but more broadly at the general welfare of the EU citizens.[158]

As to the necessity of an approximation of laws in this sector, it is widely recognised, also in the 2019 Enforcement Study, that both Member States and undertakings established and operating in their territories are subject to significantly heterogeneous tort laws and procedural rules, which greatly affect the extent to which they can be held liable for infringements of State aid provisions. This heterogeneity would likely result in uneven enforcement of the right to damages in Union law and translate not only into a competitive advantage for some undertakings which might have been complicit in the Member State's infringement of Article 108(3) TFEU but also into a disincentive for undertakings seeking State aid in support of new investment plans to the exercise of the rights of establishment and provision of goods or services in Member States where the right to damages is enforced more effectively.

This idea is certainly not isolated in legal scholarship. Jadot and others have, for example, pointed out that infringements of the rules set out in Article 108(3) TFEU are frequent, as Member States still make many mistakes in the design and implementation of aid schemes and that this can lead to significant distortions of competition.[159] Jadot

157. Judgment of the Court of Justice of 5 October 2000, Case C-376/98, *Federal Republic of Germany v. European Parliament and Council of the European Union*, EU:C:2000:544, paras 83-85, 95 and 106. *See also* Judgment of the Court of Justice of 11 June 1991, Case C-300/89, *Commission of the European Communities v. Council of the European Communities*, EU:C:199:244, para. 23.

158. *See* T. Kleiner and A. Alexis, *Politique des aides d'État: Une analyse économique plus fine au service de l'intérêt commun*, Concurrences, 2005, Volume 2, pp. 45-52. *See also* J.L. Buendía,*EU State Aid Control: Competition Between Undertakings or Between Member States?*, and M. Merola, *The Forces Shaping State Aid Control in the EU*, both in L. Rubini editor, 'What Shapes the Law? Reflections on the History, Law, Politics and Economics of International and European Subsidy Disciplines', pp. 121 ff.

159. *See* Jadot, *Damages Actions and State Aid: Time for Action at EU Level?*, cited in footnote 121 of this Part Four. *See also* Almeida, *Private Enforcement of EU State Aid Law Through Damages Claims*, cited in footnote 105 of this Part Four.

goes on to say that 'increasing the attractivity of damages claims would act as a strong deterrent to the misapplication of State aid rules' and 'would help to detect cases that have not been noticed'. It is thus not debatable that a harmonisation directive would make a real contribution to reducing distortions of competition within the internal market and that these distortions are certainly material - and increasingly so considering the huge recourse to pre-exempted (under the GBER) aid schemes.

It remains to be examined whether the existence of a more specific provision in the Treaty, which could only be Article 109 TFEU, as argued - without ample argumentation, however - by Jadot,[160] might obstruct the use of Article 114 as a legal basis for a harmonisation directive. It can be argued that Article 109 is not a more appropriate legal basis for the objective pursued because, quite simply and as already emphasised, it does not concern the harmonisation of national provisions but the application/implementation of Articles 107 and 108 by the EU Institutions. It is very clear from the wording of Article 109 that the authors had in mind the adoption of secondary law rules that would both facilitate the application of the substantive criteria of Article 107 and regulate the procedures of Article 108 more precisely, with particular reference to the cases in which the obligation to notify may be waived. The *consequences to be drawn from a breach of the procedural rules* were not the object of the provision, still less the national procedures to be followed to that end.

It cannot therefore be inferred that the authors of the Treaty intended any measure concerning the application of Article 108(3) by national courts to be taken by way of regulation - in other words, having recourse to a harmonisation directive is not a way to circumvent the will of the Treaty's authors in terms of the law-making procedure to be followed but the normal consequence of the link between effective enforcement of State aid rules, which requires a certain approximation of national laws, and internal market objectives. The *dual conditionality requirement* is also necessarily met, as the proposed directive would make a significant contribution to the elimination of competition distortions and of obstacles to the free movement of goods and the freedom to provide services.

Conversely, the use of the internal market legal basis alone would clearly not limit the directive's possible operative content. In fact, the provision for the financial liability of beneficiaries and the conditions thereof, in addition to the harmonisation of rules for asserting the State's liability (standing, means of proof, standard of proof of the causal link, grounds for exonerating liability, *etc.*), are also instrumental to protecting the internal market for the reasons already indicated, which are the same as those evoked in the preamble to the Damages Directive.

As clearly expressed by G.M. Roberti back in 1992, if a basic orientation can be deduced from the case law concerning the problem of the legal basis for acts of EU institutions, it is the following:

> [I]t consists in the tendency to construct the competences of the Union *in functional terms*, thus including all the measures that are indispensable to ensure

160. *See* Jadot, *Damages Actions and State Aid: Time for Action at EU Level?*, cited in footnote 121 of this Part Four.

> their effective exercise; this translates into an interpretation that is both evolutionary and extensive at the same time and that entails a tendency to adapt and broaden both the objectives and the means of the various common policies.[161] [translated by this author, emphasis added].

Considering the above, Article 114 TFEU should be seen as a fully appropriate and suitable legal basis to achieve harmonisation of national laws capable of eventually fostering the private enforcement of State aid rules, which is something that – as experience shows – has thus far proved impossible to achieve through other means. Hence, it would not seem necessary to have recourse to Article 352(1) TFEU.[162]

IV.E.3 The Legal Basis for a Potential Liability of Aid Recipients

The last issue to be examined in connection with the legal basis is whether Article 114 TFEU could also be appropriate if the Commission's envisaged proposal were to hold the beneficiary undertaking (or the group to which it belongs) liable, in parallel with the State, if it is proved that it was (or should have been) aware of the infringement of procedural rules and can therefore be considered complicit with the State.[163] It is to be noted that, if the principle of the liability of the beneficiary were accepted, it could be left to the national legislator to choose between the possibility of a direct action by the injured party and the possibility of the State summoning the beneficiary in the event of an action for damages brought against the State, or both.

The problem of an alleged lack of legal basis in primary law on which to establish aid beneficiary liability would not arise, at least for what concerns compensation amounts corresponding to the competitive advantage obtained in excess of the nominal

---

161. *See* Roberti, *La giurisprudenza della Corte di Giustizia sulla 'base giuridica' degli atti comunitari*, cited in footnote 148 of this Part Four.
162. The first sentence of Art. 352(1) TFEU stipulates as follows:

> If action by the Union should prove necessary, within the framework of the policies defined in the Treaties, to attain one of the objectives set out in the Treaties, and the Treaties have not provided the necessary powers, the Council, acting unanimously on a proposal from the Commission and after obtaining the consent of the European Parliament, shall adopt the appropriate measures.

Not only does it not seem necessary to use this exceptional legal basis, but it would also be inappropriate, as the adoption of a harmonisation directive in the field of State aid cannot be considered absolutely necessary to attain the objectives set out in the Treaties for the reasons already explained. Furthermore, it would be difficult to argue that the Treaties have not provided the necessary powers for a reform of the system of remedies in State aid law. As illustrated above, such a reform can be anchored perfectly well in Art. 109 for the public enforcement part and Art. 114 for the private enforcement part, provided that an amendment of secondary law is considered necessary, given that a sufficient result cannot be achieved through soft law.

163. According to Almeida, liability for damage caused by State aid infringements could extend to the beneficiary undertaking based on the Damages Directive. Other aspects of the Damages Directive that could be relevant for the private enforcement of State aid rules are the provision of rebuttable presumptions to ease the causation hurdle and quantification techniques based on counterfactuals for evaluating damage. *See* Almeida, *Private Enforcement of EU State Aid Law Through Damages Claims*, cited in footnote 105 of this Part Four.

aid amount. A harmonisation of national laws to introduce and regulate this form of liability would serve the objective of complementing the public enforcement system and ensure a true re-establishment of a level playing field, especially if recent case law on recovery amounts (according to which recovery is limited to the aid's nominal amount) were to be confirmed and codified for all kinds of aid. In such a scenario, the complementarity that private enforcement can offer in terms of remedies – typically in the form of follow-on actions – would become even more crucial. In addition, it would ensure a uniform application of the system of remedies across the Union and avoid leaving the possibility of the aid recipient's liability to the peculiarities of each national legal system.

A potentially more controversial issue would be to provide for additional liability (beyond the neutralisation of the entire competitive advantage obtained) – although, in principle, this would not be precluded if considered necessary to attain effective deterrence within the framework of a reform. A development of this kind would be relevant both for standalone actions and for follow-on actions. In a nutshell, the provision of co-liability between the granting Member State and the aid recipients, just like the other provisions of the would-be harmonisation directive, would not be aimed merely at eliminating disparities between national rules but would actually (and not in abstract terms) contribute to eliminating obstacles to the free movement of goods and to the freedom to provide services, and to removing distortions of competition.

IV.F Conclusions on the Scope of a Reform of Private Enforcement of State Aid Rules

To sum up, as things currently stand, private enforcement will not be able to fill the gaps that have been identified by an aggregate analysis of public and private enforcement without a reform of public enforcement remedies; but in a reformed public enforcement system,[164] private enforcement would partly evolve of its own accord, even without the need for harmonisation, and could partly be used in a more targeted manner to fill the gaps of, or supplement, public enforcement.

From this standpoint, a new soft law intervention – adapted to the changed regulatory framework – would already be useful, as it could illustrate *how the role of national courts should evolve to reflect the changes in public enforcement*; but a targeted legislative proposal for a directive of partial harmonisation or approximation of national laws would ensure a definitive, qualitative leap forward in terms of *minimum requirements of national regulations, legal certainty and awareness of economic operators*.[165] It could also be used to push through some innovative developments, such as the provision of presumptions that would help: (i) reduce the main obstacle to both standalone actions and follow-on actions (*i.e.*, the provision of evidence of downstream causation); (ii) introduce the concept of joint and severable liability of

164. *See* section III.B of this Part Four.
165. The need to increase awareness is even more important in the field of State aid because there is no explicit reference in the Procedural Regulation to the possibility of national courts granting damages for a breach of the notification or standstill obligations.

granting Member States and recipient undertakings, at least under some circumstances; and (iii) link the amount of compensation at least to the overall competitive damage caused, while not embracing the concept of punitive damages.

The legal basis for the adoption of a harmonisation directive in the field of State aid exists in the Treaty, namely in Article 114 TFEU. As to possible doubts regarding the lack of legal basis for the liability of aid recipients, it must be emphasised that nothing in the Treaty (certainly not the fact that State aid provisions are addressed to Member States) prevents the recognition of this form of liability, at least for damages exceeding the nominal aid amount and for cases of complicity of aid recipients in the infringement of procedural obligations. Moreover, it is worth recalling that the liability of aid recipients is only one of the issues that a State aid damages directive could address – and this new piece of legislation would make perfect sense even without the provision of such liability.

A would-be harmonisation directive in the field of State aid private enforcement would embrace not only actions for damages but more broadly also any sort of action that can be based on the breach of the procedural rules of Article 108(3), such as actions for the annulment of an award in the framework of a public bid if impacted by the granting of unlawful aid or actions meant to obtain a cease and desist order in case of unlawful aid schemes or individual aid not already entirely disbursed, to mention but a few. Another aspect that would profoundly differentiate the hypothetical State Aid Directive from the model of the Antitrust Damages Directive would be the specific regulation of several cases of unlawfulness that pose different problems, especially from the point of view of proof of damage: unlawfulness for failure to notify new aid or violation of the standstill obligation; violation of the compatibility conditions of authorised or block-exempted aid; incomplete or incorrect application of a previous negative decision. On the contrary, the directive advocated for here could usefully be modelled on the Antitrust Damages Directive for other aspects, such as the rules on access to evidence and in part those on joint and several liability and legal standing.

Conversely, there is no need for a more radical reform that would entail a change in primary law, namely the amendment of Article 108 TFEU. Likewise, there is no need to have recourse to Article 352(1) TFEU.

Final Remarks on Part Four

The final remarks summarise the reform proposals advocated for in the book, emphasising the importance of a comprehensive review of the system of remedies that is fully consistent with modernisation objectives.

The wealth of findings, open issues and suggestions for their solution offered by the first three parts of this book certainly put Part Four – which identifies the content and processes of the desired reform – on a good track; but at the same time, they make it a complex exercise because of the difficulty in selecting, prioritising and giving coherence and unity to the proposal.

The first milestone is simple: the proposed reform, to achieve its objectives, must necessarily entail the revision of public enforcement remedies as a first step. It would be illusory and vain to think of bringing the system of State aid remedies up to the level it should be at – if it wants to keep up with the demands of the times and the modernisation of aid policy and substantive State aid rules – by working only on the powers of national courts, despite the importance of their role. The second milestone follows straight from the first: the reform must embrace an amendment of secondary law – which certainly must include a reform of the Procedural Regulation, accompanied by a new implementing regulation or a new soft law/best practice instrument to regulate, in detail, the procedures for defining remedies, which could under certain circumstances be different from the procedures for assessing aid compatibility (so-called, remedies procedures).

In this context, a reform of the procedures must be seized as an opportunity to at last recognise rights of participation in State aid proceedings and rights of defence worthy of Europe's tradition of guaranteeing fundamental rights and worthy of modern competition law. The distinction between recovery (or remedies) procedures and assessment procedures should facilitate this essential step forward. It should also facilitate the involvement of national authorities in the implementation of remedies. Conversely, a modification of the TFEU, as advocated by some legal scholars,[166] is not

166. In particular, *see* T. Jaeger, *The Future of State Aid*, European State Aid Law Quarterly (EStAL), 2022, Issue 2, pp. 117-119 https://doi.org/10.21552/estal/2022/2/2. Jaeger's acute remarks

necessary, nor need it acknowledge a gap in the instruments the TFEU provides so as to necessitate recourse to Article 352 thereof.

As mentioned above, the proposed reform should entail an amendment - though not a drastic one - of the Procedural Regulation, in particular Article 16 thereof. In this context, one of the most salient and innovative aspects of the reform - if not the most salient and innovative, including for the developments it might trigger - would be the modulation of remedies (restorative or redressive measures), which should take inspiration from the modern framework for foreign subsidies.

As illustrated above, simply adding a margin of flexibility in the modulation of remedies and combining restorative remedies, primarily recovery, with a broad panoply of redressive measures would enable a real qualitative leap forward in the system of remedies and bring it in line with the objectives of modernisation. It would also make it possible to combine various remedies to meet the multiple objectives pursued: restoration of conditions of full competition, elimination of the effects of aid to the extent possible, strong deterrence, and substantive justice (*i.e.*, prevention of situations of undue enrichment).

Another aspect that the reform could touch on is the regulation of ancillary remedies, with the aim of making them more effective and complementary - especially with respect to recovery, when this is the selected remedy - and without expecting that one remedy can serve as a catch-all, *i.e.*, satisfy all needs. Examples of new/revisited ancillary remedies include clarification and development of the *Deggendorf* doctrine in order to increase deterrence, the FSR model for the verification and penalisation of non-compliance with remedies, and some changes in the criteria employed to quantify penalties under Article 260(2) TFEU.

The contribution that less formalistic jurisprudence and more boldness from the Commission in its communications - in particular the Recovery Notice - could make to a reform should also be emphasised (as this book has done). Pending a legislative reform, a jurisprudential rethinking - with particular reference to the concept of absolute impossibility, the conditions for the exclusion of recovery and, possibly, the nominal concept of the amount to be repaid[167] - together with a new version of the

on, and criticism of, the bilateral procedural approach (between Member States and the Commission only) are convincing. Indeed, this bilateralism seems entirely outdated and neither reflects economic reality nor provides sufficient incentives for involving private operators in State aid enforcement, as the author underlines. However, overcoming or significantly downgrading procedural bilateralism does not necessarily require an amendment of Art. 108 TFEU, at least when it comes to the application of remedies in cases of unlawful aid. A change in the Treaty would perhaps be needed to shift from bilateralism to a procedure that is open to the contribution of third parties insofar as existing aid is concerned, because Art. 108(1), unlike Art. 108(2), explicitly refers to a review to be carried out 'in cooperation with Member States'. But even this opinion could be questioned. As Jaeger himself puts it, amending Art. 108 would require strong advocacy and a change in mentality that can only be achieved over the long term. A much faster - yet significant, and even revolutionary - change in the system of remedies is possible. It can be achieved through a relatively simple modernisation of a few provisions of the Procedural Regulation and completed with case law and soft law developments.

167. The need for a reversal of the case law on the nominal aid amount to be recovered depends on whether private enforcement is also reformed, as explained above. If the reform of public enforcement is accompanied by a reform of private enforcement, hopefully culminating in the

Recovery Notice and the Private Enforcement Notice that is braver and more in line with the objectives of modernisation, would indeed already constitute a crucial improvement and pave the way for legislative reform.

Turning to private enforcement, the usefulness of a harmonisation directive has been carefully considered in this Part Four, which discusses its real added value in relation to the various functions of private enforcement and examines the legal basis issue. Lessons should be drawn to the greatest extent possible from other neighbouring areas such as public procurement (with the Remedies Directive) and antitrust law (with the Damages Directive). The two aforementioned directives are indeed examined (for the aspects that are relevant to this book) in Part Three, together with the FSR.

A harmonisation directive, while not strictly necessary for the purposes of reform, would represent a decisive step forward in terms of quality and would finally put an end to the longstanding problem of the dearth of private enforcement cases in the field of State aid. In connection with the nature of remedies, a harmonisation directive could contribute to identifying and testing innovative remedies even beyond those listed in the FSR, which could then serve as inspiration also in the field of public enforcement if the new Procedural Regulation leaves sufficient discretionary power to the Commission. The essential aspects that a directive should cover are: (i) the facilitation of proof of a causal link through the use of certain presumptions (especially for upstream causation); (ii) the recourse to provisions on evidence disclosure inspired by those in the Damages Directive (especially to prove downstream causation); (iii) the harmonisation of a common legal basis to be integrated into national non-contractual liability regimes to ensure a certain uniformity of remedies across the Union; and (iv) the provision of joint and several liability between the State and the aid recipient under specific circumstances based on the 'intent' requirement. The possibility for competitors to sue beneficiaries directly – *i.e.*, horizontal direct effect – should also be considered and would be a plus, although it is not strictly necessary to achieve the reform's objectives and would require coordination with other areas of EU law.

All in all, a reform of the State aid system of remedies that combines an amendment of the Procedural Regulation with a harmonisation directive aimed at stimulating private enforcement would be ideal for achieving all the objectives that it would set out to achieve. Indeed, it would complete the process of modernising State aid control, thus successfully addressing the shortcomings indicated by many scholars; it would provide the system of remedies the flexibility needed to adapt to the aims and mission that the EU legislator and policymakers have envisaged for State aid control in

adoption of a State aid damages directive, the need for such a reversal would be less obvious, and the calculation of the nominal aid amount could continue to be the point of reference in public enforcement. However, the best option would still be to reconsider the nominal concept of the amount to be recovered, thereby eliminating the discrepancy between direct aid and indirect aid (without prejudice to the need to verify whether the repayment of indirect aid amounts should be apportioned between different categories of beneficiaries). National courts would still be entrusted with the task of compensating, if the applicable conditions are met, the greater harm caused by the aid to competitors or other interested parties. Conversely, without a reform of private enforcement, the reform of public enforcement would necessarily have to include the choice for an economic concept of the advantage to be repaid, as explained above.

the last twenty years;[168] it would make the system of remedies more effective, including as a means of restoring credibility to State aid policy altogether; it would bring about the desirable convergence of systems of remedies within the framework of public competition law; and, last but not least, it would initiate a rethinking of control procedures, starting with a separation of remedies procedures from compatibility assessment procedures. And within this framework, it would resolve the longstanding problem of the role of third parties in State aid procedures (the missing piece of the modernisation process), thereby responding to the unanimous request of legal scholars and stakeholders.

The following table summarises some of the main proposals for reform put forward throughout this book – especially in this Part Four – and briefly reiterates their rationale. Though it is certainly not exhaustive, it could be of help for future scholarship contributions that seek to fine-tune these proposals, or even for the Commission if it decides to take them up in its internal work and assess possible initiatives:

Reform Proposal	*Relevance and Rationale*
Better coordination between private enforcement and public enforcement	Private enforcement and public enforcement should not be seen in isolation, despite their different roles as clarified in the case law. Complementarities need to be exploited to serve the multiple objectives of the system of remedies.
Clarification of the interpretation of Article 108(2) TFEU when it comes to the alternative of abolishment or alteration of unlawful aid	There is a need to fill a gap in case law and to rediscover the richness of primary law as a precondition for the advocated reform.
Amendment of Article 16(1) of the Procedural Regulation	The provision's wording should be amended so as to grant the Commission broader discretion in assessing the most appropriate remedies to restore the situation existing before the unlawful aid was granted (*i.e.*, restorative remedies) or in imposing adequate remedial measures, whether retrospective or prospective, if the restorative goal cannot be attained (*i.e.*, redressive measures). This is the essential first step for both a modernisation of the State aid system of remedies and for a convergence of remedies in public competition law.

168. As explained in Part One, section III.C.5 of this book, it is crucial to complete the modernisation toolkit with a reform of the system of remedies that internalises the post-SAM paradigm by: (i) adapting remedies to the new objectives of State aid control; and (ii) taking due account of the enforcement shift towards *ex-post* enforcement and the related increased responsibility placed on national courts. Moving away from the dogma of recovery as the sole catch-all remedy and progressing towards an increasingly flexible remedies' toolkit can be the solution. Obviously, it would imply giving the Commission more discretionary power and would therefore need to be balanced by increasing rights of defence granted to the parties concerned in recovery procedures.

Reform Proposal	*Relevance and Rationale*
Revision of traditional case law on the concept of absolute impossibility	A revision – or at least a softening – of the traditional case law on the concept of absolute impossibility would already make a decisive contribution to the development of a more flexible and effective system of remedies.
Full exploitation of the potential of soft law	Further significant progress towards a more flexible and effective system of remedies could be achieved through simple soft law interventions that would build on a less entrenched, more creative jurisprudence, in line with present times. This especially applies to the interplay between remedies and insolvency proceedings, which is one of the most controversial fields in State aid law.
Clarification of the concept of recovery	Although the approach of the reform suggested and advocated for in this book would lead to moving past recovery as essentially the sole remedy against unlawful aid, recovery would nonetheless remain a central element of the system of remedies. Thus, the concept of recovery should be clarified and unified, overcoming the divergent approach currently followed in relation to direct aid and indirect aid.
Downplay of the rigidity of the current system of remedies	The shift from a rigid system of recovery (or, put more correctly, of recovery of the nominal amount of aid) to a system of case-by-case assessment of the most appropriate restorative and, if necessary, redressive measures would help address both the main objective of re-establishing undistorted competition and the collateral objectives.
A modernised view of remedies in cases of insolvency	The possibility of balancing several Union interests should also lead to a thorough revision of the relationship between recovery and insolvency proceedings, which constitutes one of the least pragmatically satisfying and least theoretically convincing aspects of the current system of remedies.
Consideration of State aid law's internal market goal when reforming the system of remedies	An organic regulation of recovery must consider three different scenarios: (i) one in which the aid's effects have not yet materialised, so it is possible to intervene urgently to prevent them from materialising; (ii) one in which the (unlawful and incompatible) aid has caused a real and lasting distortion of competition; and (iii) one in which the aid has failed, *i.e.*, it has proved to be of no use to the beneficiary and has made no real contribution to strengthening its position on the market.

Reform Proposal	*Relevance and Rationale*
Amendment of Article 16(2) and (3) of the Procedural Regulation	The wording of Article 16(2) of the Procedural Regulation – which refers to the interest to be added to recovered amounts – would not need to be amended. After the reform, however, it would refer to only one remedy among others; the legislator might therefore prefer, for systematic reasons, to move it to the implementing regulation. Article 16(3) should be amended in accordance with the amendment of Article 16(1) to better clarify the scope of procedural autonomy and the meaning of effective/timely remedial action.
Clarification of the interest pursued in ordering remedies	An additional change would be required in the recitals of the Procedural Regulation to clarify the precise interest pursued in ordering remedies, as this would also help better shape the role of national courts (as explained below).
Amendments related to ancillary remedies	Another issue to be carefully considered in the context of the reform concerns ancillary remedies, in particular the remedy arising from the *Deggendorf* doctrine and, to a lesser extent, the system of penalties for incorrect, incomplete or misleading information or for non-execution of Court of Justice judgments.
Amendments related to the decision-making procedure	Splitting the assessment procedure and the remedies procedure would help: (i) involve national authorities in the implementation of remedies; (ii) modulate remedies according to the circumstances of the case, especially in terms of the gravity of the harm done to competition; (iii) promote negotiated remedies (*i.e.*, *sui generis* settlements); and (iv) pave the way to the (long-overdue) recognition of rights of participation and defence in State aid proceedings.
Clarification concerning judicial control	All decisions on remedies would obviously be challengeable: both the remedies provision of final decisions on incompatibility, as is the case even today, and decisions taken at the end of the newly established remedies procedure.
Development of private enforcement's integrative role	As to the role of private enforcement in completing/integrating the system of remedies, the objective of a harmonisation directive would be to facilitate standalone actions in cases which the Commission is unlikely to prioritise or in which the national court is in a better position – given its proximity to the facts and knowledge of the relevant legal or regulatory framework – to effectively remedy the breach of aid rules.

Reform Proposal	*Relevance and Rationale*
Facilitation of private enforcement's supplementary role	The role of private enforcement in supplementing the remedies imposed through public enforcement – *i.e.*, through follow-on actions – would remain substantially unchanged after a reform of the public enforcement system of remedies but would be facilitated by quantification of the harm (non-existent in current practice) and analysis of the beneficiary's complicity with the State.
General issues to be addressed through a harmonisation directive	A State aid harmonisation directive should ideally cover the various forms of private enforcement actions and, in relation to actions for damages, would address crucial issues such as: (i) the provision of a legal basis in national tort law to claim damages based on the infringement of the notification and standstill obligations; (ii) the use of presumptions for the avoidability and foreseeability requirements (mainly in connection with upstream causation); (iii) the rules on evidence disclosure (mainly in connection with downstream causation); and (iv) the application and limits of joint and several liability of the State and the beneficiary.

Adoption of these reform proposals would serve the twofold objective of achieving greater flexibility and greater accountability in the system of remedies in State aid law. It would also lead to a more efficient sharing of responsibilities between the Commission and the Member States and leverage on modernised procedures, which are an essential component of whatever reform can be envisaged.

Conclusions

The book concludes with a reflection on the importance of reforming the system of remedies in State aid law. These concluding remarks highlight that the proposed reform has a solid theoretical basis and could be achieved in a reasonable timeframe, thus completing the modernisation of the corpus juris in the field of State aid. Lastly, the need for a system of remedies that can adapt to modern needs and ensure the effectiveness and credibility of State aid control is emphasised.

This book has analysed remedies in State aid law with a view to promoting their reform as well as their convergence with the remedies in the field of foreign subsidies, so as to set up a common system of remedies in public competition law altogether.

The system of remedies in State aid law is the result of an evolutionary process that spans over half a century but that has failed to see progress precisely when progress is most imperative given the breathtaking development of substantive law, fuelled by both modernisation and the use of State aid control as a crisis management tool. The result is before all stakeholders' eyes and has been clearly flagged by legal scholarship: a system that not only seems entirely outdated but that is also ineffective, does not reflect the economic reality, does not provide sufficient incentives for involving private operators in State aid enforcement, does not serve the objectives pursued, and ultimately weakens the credibility of State aid control.

Overcoming the many weaknesses of the present system and significantly upgrading it does not necessarily require an amendment of primary law, notably Article 108(2) TFEU. Amending Article 108 would require strong advocacy and a change in mentality that can be achieved only over the long term. Therefore, this book advocates for a much faster - yet significant, and even revolutionary - change in the system of remedies: a change that the new Von der Leyen Commission could easily take on and deliver within its mandate. Although this book thus endeavours to propose a pragmatic and feasible reform - one that can be achieved in the short term to complete the modernisation of the *corpus juris* in the field of State aid - it also has the more general ambition to provide a solid theoretical background for the future of the policy on remedies, so as to serve as a useful reference in the field also in the medium-to-long term.

Indeed, to avoid losing its way, the reform proposal must rest on solid theoretical foundations. The maturity of a system of remedies is a critical indicator of the maturity of the related legal system as a whole: the latter is mature (*i.e.*, it can be considered solid and resilient) if it minimises the social cost of control and maximises the social function of the remedies. In other words, the remedies applied in any given case must impose themselves as an absolute necessity for lack of better alternatives and must optimise the contribution to achieving the system's objectives. As Norberto Bobbio[169] once observed, a legal system could forego reacting to an infringement only if it had the *a priori* guarantee of absolute compliance by all legal subjects; but such absolute compliance is conceivable only in two abstract cases: (i) a perfectly rational regulatory system for perfectly rational beings; or (ii) an even non-rational system for completely automated beings. Therefore, no legal system is conceivable that does not react in some way to a breach of mandatory rules, just as no social system is conceivable that does not react, in principle, to a violation of the principle of coexistence. Reaction, however, is a broad concept – it is submitted that the perfect legal system is that which can achieve its objectives with *the most lenient reaction that can be envisaged.*

On this basis, the crucial question for this book's purposes was: what is the most appropriate (lenient, yet efficient) reaction to a violation of State aid rules? A legal system has three different degrees of possible reaction when faced with an infringement of mandatory rules (*i.e.*, unlawful conduct), based on the infringement's gravity and/or on other factors (including political and social factors): a punishment, a pecuniary sanction/penalty, and a remedy. The etymology of the word 'remedy' (from the Latin *remedium,* which in turn derives from *mederi* – to heal) indicates that this is the softest reaction a legal system can envisage and consists essentially of either restoring the situation that existed before the unlawful conduct was committed (a concept similar to that of *restitutio in integrum*) or erasing the infringement's harmful consequences.

When compared with the concepts of 'punishment' or 'sanction/penalty', the concept of 'remedy' displays some common elements but also some significant differences. Punishment is of course the strongest reaction a legal system can envisage and is associated with a crime. If a crime is committed, a punishment must necessarily be imposed. Punishment is indeed the consequence of the principle of the offensiveness of a crime, which legal scholarship almost unanimously considers to be an indispensable element of an offence, even for crimes of mere endangerment.[170] In other words, the ineluctable nature (or infallibility) of punishment in criminal law is the

169. Norberto Bobbio was a great Italian philosopher of law and a historian of political thought (18 October 1909-9 January 2004). Bobbio was a social liberal in the tradition of, among others, Piero Gobetti, and as a philosopher of law was mainly influenced by Hans Kelsen. Appointed senator-for-life by Italian President Sandro Pertini in 1984, he received honours and awards at a global level, including election into the American Academy of Arts and Sciences in 1994 and the Hegel Prize for his contribution to the development of the humanities in 2000.

170. For a fascinating illustration of this and other general features of criminal law, *see* F. Ramacci, *Corso di diritto penale,* Roberto Guerrini ed., ottava edizione, Giappichelli, Torino 2023.

consequence of the ontological offensiveness of a crime. Furthermore, for punishment to exist, the afflictive nature of the legal system's reaction to the unlawful conduct must exceed the gain or advantage generated by that very conduct.[171] Other quintessential characteristics of a punishment are that it must be certain in its form and in its quantification criteria, and it must be established beforehand.

When it comes to the second degree of possible reaction to unlawful conduct (*i.e.*, administrative sanctions/penalties), the elements indicated above remain basically unchanged. A sanction or penalty is a similar but broader concept when compared to punishment. Legal systems indeed often decriminalise offences which do not severely impair peaceful coexistence (*i.e.*, the 'social contract') and envisage a pecuniary sanction in the form of a fine or penalty. In EU law, as well as in Member States' individual legal systems, competition law infringements are typically downgraded from the criminal to the administrative sphere. With administrative sanctions, the legal system foregoes only the *reprehensibility (i.e., moral signalling) function* typically associated with punishment or pursues a reprehensibility objective through other means - not through the reaction itself but through transparency (publication of the decision or judgment ascertaining the infringement). The ineluctability requirement, however, remains intact (unless the act-of-State defence can be successfully invoked), as well as the certainty of its form and quantification. When a legal system envisages a remedy (*e.g.*, *restitutio in integrum*, the third and softest reaction that can be envisaged), as in State aid law, the ineluctability and certainty requirements remain equally intact, but they must be correctly understood: in that context, they mean that the watchdog or regulator must ensure that at least all harmful consequences of the infringement are erased.

Moreover, violations of EU rules are not all and under all circumstances necessarily 'offensive', *i.e.*, harmful. This consideration provides a theoretical basis for the essentially political choice of the EU legal system not to envisage penalties for violations of certain treaty rules by Member States (including State aid rules). As the legal system's reaction to unlawful conduct in the field of State aid is the typical *restitutio in integrum* remedy, this implies that the reaction must not exceed the gain or advantage obtained and that it can and should be logically modelled on the characteristics and potential offensiveness of the unlawful conduct (rule of reason). If a remedy were applied despite it being unnecessary to erase the consequences of an infringement, that would imply shifting to the idea of sanction or punishment, whereas the EU system has clearly chosen mere 'remedies' as the appropriate reaction to a breach of the rules.

It follows that the choice to bind the body exercising centralised control (the Commission) to order a specific remedy (recovery of the aid) is not an obligatory choice of the legal system but a political choice - as is also shown by the fact that such an obligation was not initially envisaged - and a choice which is at odds with the concept

171. This statement is attributed to Cesare Bonesana di Beccaria (better known as Cesare Beccaria, 15 March 1738-28 November 1794), an Italian criminologist, jurist, politician and philosopher. Author of the famous treatise 'On Crimes and Punishments', Beccaria is widely considered one of the greatest thinkers of the Age of Enlightenment.

of 'remedy'. It also follows that it is not contrary to the Union's 'constitutional' principles or to general principles of law to envisage a broad range of remedies and to grant the Commission, under the control of the EU courts, a degree of discretion as to the choice of remedy depending on the factual circumstances, with recovery remaining a minimum requirement when the harmful consequences cannot be duly measured or neutralised (*e.g.*, in the case of some tax benefits).

Another perspective from which a comparison of different legal system responses/reactions to unlawful conduct can be of help for this book's purposes concerns the functions they pursue. Various functions have been attributed to criminal sanctions throughout the history of law: a retributive function, a preventive function, a social promotion function, a making-amends function, and so on. Of these, only a preventive function can be found in remedies in general, and for what is relevant here, in remedies for violations of the competition rules addressed to Member States. However, the preventive function is always considered an ancillary function in the general theory of law. What, then, is the main or essential function of State aid remedies? To identify it, one must reflect on the protected legal good (not to be confused with the pursued objective – *e.g.*, consumer welfare or general welfare – because the relationship between protected good and pursued objective depends on the economic theory that pervades the system concerned). In the case of State aid, the protected legal good is twofold: equal opportunity (which means full/undistorted competition) and protection of the internal market. It follows that the main or essential function of State aid remedies is to restore equal opportunity and safeguard the internal market. The choice of the remedy must therefore serve this function through its quintessential nature, which, as mentioned above, is either to restore the situation that existed before the unlawful conduct or to erase the harmful consequences of the infringement, if not both. The preventive function cannot become predominant and, above all, cannot be exclusive: the main function defined above must be present in every form of remedy.

With these general concepts in mind, the conclusions drawn from the research underlying this book acquire more value, as they fit perfectly into the theoretical framework outlined above. Indeed, these conclusions – which are summarised in the final remarks on Part Four of this book (and need not be repeated here) – call for the introduction of a flexible and modern system of remedies that is: (i) characterised by a broad possibility of calibrating remedies according to the substantive characteristics of the aid concerned and the effects that aid produced; and (ii) administered through procedures that allow the participation of interested parties, in particular undertakings exposed to the recovery order or other remedies. The current system's rigidities – which make it ineffective and lacking in credibility (because in the end, it is too often circumvented for political reasons) – are unnecessary given the theoretical foundations mentioned above and would therefore be removed, both in public enforcement and private enforcement. In the case of private enforcement, application of the principle of procedural autonomy would finally be clarified and correctly framed, favouring uniform application across the whole Union regardless of which national courts are entrusted with the task.

From a conceptual perspective, which can be of value in concluding the analysis carried out in this book, the following key takeaways bear summarising:

(i) The effectiveness and efficacy of the overall State aid enforcement system under the SAM paradigm has been questioned in legal scholarship and remains to be proved.
(ii) An effective and modernised system of remedies for breaches of the notification and standstill obligations is an essential component of the proposed solution to restore the control system's credibility, along with efficient *ex-post* monitoring and cooperation with Member States' authorities in a way that is consistent with the modernisation paradigm.
(iii) The long-awaited modernisation of the system of remedies together with the enhancement of *ex-post* monitoring and the strengthening of cooperation with Member States' authorities must become true political priorities for the Commission.
(iv) The comprehensive reform of the system of remedies advocated for in this book would by no means entail weakening the remedies; rather, it would entail strengthening the system's deterrent effect and reinforcing the objective of forfeiting market distortions by establishing a correspondence between the substantive assessment of the effects of aid and the calibration of remedies.
(v) The framework of the advocated reform would have to include the reinstatement of a certain degree of discretion in the Commission's choice of suitable restorative measures and/or redressive measures (including to take into account the nature of *ex-post* control).
(vi) The Commission should consider redressive measures when suitable and effective restorative remedies are unavailable or insufficient to serve the multiple objectives of the system of remedies, as explained in the final remarks on Part Four.
(vii) The FSR's system of remedies, which is based on the multidisciplinary approach that characterises this new instrument, can serve as a model for the reform of the system of remedies in the field of State aid.
(viii) Reconsideration of fundamental concepts such as reestablishment of the *status quo ante*, absolute impossibility and legitimate expectations should also find a place in the reform to ensure internal coherence.
(ix) Clarification of the abovementioned concepts would also help develop national public enforcement along with centralised public enforcement, in accordance with the *Eesti Pagar* and *Provinz Bozen* case law.
(x) The reform should encompass all remedies, including the *Deggendorf* doctrine and, to a lesser extent, the penalty system under Article 260(2) TFEU.
(xi) An extension of the Commission's sanctioning power should be possible and would even be warranted when sanctions (as opposed to remedies) are necessary (for incorrect, incomplete or misleading information or for

the non-execution of judgments), but it should be unrelated to the assessment of the effects of the aid concerned.

(xii) Recovery procedures should be laid down and considered separately from compatibility procedures so that aid beneficiaries (and other interested parties, to the extent possible) can be closely associated with them.

(xiii) The determination of whether the amount recovered should accrue to the State budget or to an earmarked State fund to be managed in compliance with specific rules and in pursuit of horizontal objectives of common interest should depend on the economic consequences of the aid concerned.

(xiv) Private enforcement as it presently stands, even after the enactment of the New Private Enforcement Notice, is unsuitable to complement public enforcement to the degree necessary to overcome the latter's weaknesses and can have only little overall impact on the effectiveness of the system of remedies.

(xv) A part of private enforcement would automatically evolve of its own accord in a reformed public enforcement system, even without harmonisation – especially in follow-on actions if, as suggested, beneficiaries' complicity in an infringement becomes part of the typical assessment in remedy procedures.

(xvi) The recent shift from *ex-ante* to *ex-post* control means that a high rate of flawed application of the GBER is to be expected, which will translate into an increased need for private enforcement and a heavier burden for national courts, especially in light of the Commission's weak enforcement.

(xvii) The degree of independence granted to national courts by the principle of procedural autonomy extends to the choice of the most appropriate and effective remedies to achieve the system's declared objectives/substantial function (as determined by EU law), although different views have been expressed on this issue in legal scholarship, and the lack of ad hoc provisions in most national laws limits the efficacy of this independence.

(xviii) The complexity of this issue and the increasing importance of private enforcement in the current post-modernisation paradigm of *ex-post* control both underline the need for the EU legislator to take up the challenge of reshaping the system of remedies also in the field of private enforcement.

(xix) The comparative analysis carried out in Part Three has shown that, although the Remedies Directive (in the field of public procurement) and the Damages Directive (in the field of antitrust) can offer some useful indications for the reform of private enforcement in State aid law, only a specific State aid directive can ensure the definitive qualitative leap that the proposed reform would set out to achieve.

(xx) A State aid harmonisation directive should ideally cover the various forms of private enforcement actions and, in relation to actions for damages, would address crucial issues such as the use of presumptions for the avoidability and foreseeability requirements (mainly in connection with upstream causation) and the rules on evidence disclosure (manly in connection with downstream causation).

(xxi) Secondary law, soft law and case law developments should ideally be combined to streamline the reform and ensure that it is not unduly delayed.

In this context, a reform of the decision-making procedure - by introducing a specific remedy procedure - must be seized as an opportunity to at last grant rights of participation in State aid proceedings and rights of defence worthy of Europe's tradition of guaranteeing fundamental rights and worthy of modern competition law. The distinction between recovery (or remedies) procedures and assessment procedures should facilitate this essential step forward and would help involve national authorities in the implementation of remedies. Conversely, a modification of the TFEU - as advocated by some legal scholars - is not strictly necessary, nor need the reform acknowledge a gap in the instruments the TFEU provides so as to necessitate recourse to Article 352 thereof.

A mature system of remedies (one that is modern, ductile, efficient and uniform) is an achievable goal and one within reach in a reasonably short term. Such an achievement would help restore credibility and realistic efficiency for the entire control system and halt the current drift towards increasingly politicised enforcement. As explained above, the maturity of a given system of remedies (or of a given administrative or criminal penalty, for that matter) is measured by its ability to protect the protected legal good in the best possible way and at the least possible cost for society. It is submitted that the system of remedies advocated for in this book - which is based on convergence within the field of public competition law - meets this requirement, whereas the current system of remedies clearly does not.

Bibliography

Monographs and Contributions in Collective Works[1]

P. Adriaanse, *Public and Private Enforcement of EU State Aid Law*, in H.J. Blankel, S. Mangiameli (eds), 'The European Union after Lisbon: Constitutional Basis, Economic Order and External Action', Springer, 2012, pp. 456-470

H. Andersson, *The Quest for Evidence: Still an Uphill Battle for Cartel Victims!*, in M. Strand, V. Bastidas, M.C. Iacovides (eds), 'EU Competition Litigation, Transposition and First Experiences of the New Regime', Hart Publishing, 2019, pp. 107-120

J.B. Auby, D. Dero-Brugny, *Les Principes de Sécurité Juridique et de Confiance Légitime*, in J.B. Auby, J. Dutheil de la Rochére (eds), 'Droit Administratif Européen', Bruylant, 2007, pp. 473-491

K. Bacon, *European Union Law of State Aid*, Oxford University Press, 2017

S. Bastianon, *La tutela del legittimo affidamento nel diritto dell'Unione europea*, Giuffrè, 2012

G. Biagioni, *Le modalità di calcolo dell'aiuto di Stato da recuperare e del risarcimento danni per violazione degli artt. 107 e 108 § 3 TFUE*, in L. Pace, 'Dizionario sistematico del diritto della concorrenza', Jovene, 2013, pp. 662-671

A. Biondi, E. Righini, *An Evolutionary Theory of State Aid Control*, in D. Chalmers and A. Arnull (eds), 'The Oxford Handbook of European Union Law', Oxford Handbooks; online edn, Oxford Academic, 2015, pp. 670-690

A. Biondi, *State Aid Control, Government Spending and the Virtue of Loyalty*, in A. Biondi, P. Birkinshaw (eds), 'Britain Alone! The Implications and Consequences of United Kingdom Exit from the EU', Kluwer Law International, 2016, pp. 291-309

J.L. Buendia Sierra, *EU State Aid Control: Competition Between Undertakings or Between Member States?*, in L. Rubini, J. Hawkins (eds), 'What Shapes the Law?

1. This and the following sections of the bibliography include all the legal scholarship's contributions and official sources (i.e., legislation and cases) that have been examined in drafting this book. It is to be noted than not all of them are mentioned in the footnotes but only those explicitly referred to and discussed in the text of the book.

Reflections on the History, Law, Politics and Economics of International and European Subsidy Disciplines', European University Institute, 2016, pp. 121-128

V. Butorak Malnar, *The Kone Case: A Missed Opportunity to Put the Standard of Causation under the Umbrella of the EU*, in V. Tomljenović, N. Bodiroga - Vukobrat, V. Butorak Malnar, I. Kunda (eds), 'EU Competition and State Aid Rules: Public and Private Enforcement', Springer - Verlag, 2017, pp. 175-196

S. Calmes, *Du Principe de Protection de la Confiance Légitime en Droits Allemand, Communautaire et Français*, Dalloz, 2001

U. Classen, M. Seegers, *The State of Private Enforcement of Competition Law: A Practitioner's Perspective*, in M. Strand, V. Bastidas, M.C. Iacovides (eds), 'EU Competition Litigation, Transposition and First Experiences of the New Regime', Hart Publishing, 2019, pp. 19-40

P. Craig, C. Harlow, *Lawmaking in the European Union*, Kluwer Law International, 1998

N. Cunha Rodrigues, *Filling the Regulatory Gap to Address Foreign Subsidies: The EC's Search for a Level Playing Field within the Internal Market*, in N. Cunha Rodrigues (ed.), 'Extraterritoriality of EU Economic Law', Book series 'European Union and its Neighbours in a Globalized World', Springer, 2021, pp. 197-227

L. Daniele, *Private enforcement in materia di aiuti di Stato e ruolo dei giudici nazionali, la nuova Comunicazione della Commissione europea*, in C. Schepisi (ed.), 'La 'modernizzazione' della disciplina sugli aiuti di Stato: il nuovo approccio della Commissione europea e i recenti sviluppi in materia di *public* e *private enforcement*', Giappichelli, 2011, pp. 159-174

W. De Cock, T. Joris, *COVID-19 and EU State Aid Law: An Impression*, in S. Van Puyvelde & C. Buts (eds), 'Critical Contributions to Economics and Beyond', Lexxion, 2021, pp. 577-602

R. Dehousse, J. Weiler, *EPC and the Single Act: From Soft Law to Hard Law?*, in M. Holland (ed.), 'The Future of European Political Cooperation', Macmillan, 1991, pp. 121-142

V. di Bucci, *The Modernisation of State Aid Control and Its Objectives: Clarity, Relevance, Effectiveness*, in E.A. Raffaelli (ed.), 'Antitrust fra diritto Nazionale e diritto dell'Unione Europea', Bruylant, 2015, pp. 419-436

M. Dony, *Le contrôle des aides d'Etat*, Editions de l'Université de Bruxelles, 3ème édition, 2007

M. Dony, *Aides d'Etat*, Bruylant, 2019

H.W. Friederiszick, L. Röller, V. Verouden, *European State Aid Control: An Economic Framework*, in P. Buccirossi (ed.), 'Handbook of Antitrust Economics', Massachussetts Institute of Technology, 2008, pp. 625-669

D. Grespan, *Recovery of Unlawful and Incompatible Aid*, in W. Mederer, N. Pesaresi e M. Van Hoof (eds), 'EU Competition Law Volume IV: State Aid', Claeys & Casteels, 2008, pp. 647-684

L. Hancher, F. Salerno, M. Schutte, *The Different Stages in the State Aid Procedure*, in H. Hofmann, C. Micheau (eds), 'State aid law of the European Union', Oxford University Press, 2016, pp. 348-380

K. Havu, *Causation and Damage: What the Directive Does Not Solve and Remarks on Relevant EU Law*, in C. Strand, V. Bastidas, M.C. Iacovides (eds), 'EU Competition Litigation, Transposition and First Experiences of the New Regime', Hart Publishing, 2019, pp. 19-40

A. Heimler, *State Aid Control: Recent Developments and Some Remaining Challenges*, in P.L. Parcu, G. Monti, M. Botta (eds), 'EU State Aid Law: Emerging Trends at the National and Eu Level', Edward Elgar, 2020, pp. 54-69

H. Hofmann, C. Micheau, *State Aid Law of the European Union*, Oxford University Press, 2016

M.C. Iacovides, *Article 17(3) of the Damages Directive and the Interaction Between the Swedish Competition Authority and Swedish Courts*, in M. Strand, V. Bastidas, M.C. Iacovides (eds), 'EU Competition Litigation, Transposition and First Experiences of the New Regime', Hart Publishing, 2019, pp. 215-233

P. Iannuccelli, *La Responsabilità Civile Antitrust delle Imprese e la Direttiva 104/2014*, Giuffrè, 2017

M. Jimeno-Bulnes, *The CJEU Case Law after Preliminary Ruling on Behalf of Private Enforcement of EU Competition Law*, in S. Marino, L. Biel, M. Bačić, V. Sosoni (eds), 'Language and Law', Springer, 2018, pp. 39-67

T. Joris, W. De Cock, *Belgium and Forum 187 v. Commission Once Again Revisited*, in C. Buts & J.L. Buendía Sierra (eds), 'Milestones in State Aid Case Law EStAL's First 20 Years in Perspective', Lexxion, 2022, pp. 121-137

A.P. Komninos, *Damages Actions in Article 102 TFEU Case: The New Frontier for Private Enforcement*, in Strand, V. Bastidas, M.C. Iacovides (eds), 'EU Competition Litigation, Transposition and First Experiences of the New Regime', Hart Publishing, 2019, pp. 155-171

V. Kreuschitz, H.P. Nehl, *Decentralized Judicial Review and Enforcement of EU State Aid Rules*, in H.C.H. Hofmann, C. Micheau, 'State Aid Law of the European Union', Oxford University Press, 2016, pp. 450-466

V. Kreuschitz, N. Bermejo, *The Role of National Courts in the Enforcement of the European State Aid Rules*, in V. Tomljenović, N. Bodiroga-Vukobrat, V. Butoran Malnar, I. Kunda (eds), 'EU Competition and State Aid Rules, Europeanization and Globalization', Springer, 3/2017, pp. 221-222

K. Lenaerts, *L'articulation entre ordres juridiques à l'œuvre: le régime de récupération des aides d'Etat versées en violation du droit communautaire*, in C.N. Kakouris (ed.), 'Problèmes d'interprétation: à la mémoire de Constantinos N. Kakouris', Bruylant, 2004, pp. 259-283

J. Lever, *The EC State Aid Regime: The Need for Reform*, in A. Biondi, P. Eeckhout, J. Flynn (eds), 'The Law of State Aid in the European Union', Oxford University Press, 2004, pp. 303-322

F. Mariatte, *Développements récents sur les questions de recevabilité des recours dans le contentieux des aides d'Etat*, in S. Mahieu (ed.), 'Contentieux de l'Union européenne. Questions choisies', Larcier, 2014, pp. 259-286

A. Matthias-Werner, *The Procedural Regulation: Is the time Ripe for a Revision?*, in M. Sanchez-Rydelsky (ed.), 'The EC State Aid Regime: Distortive Effects of State Aid on Competition and Trade', Cambridge University Press, 2006, pp. 631-652

M. Merola, A. Cogoni, *Chronique of the 2022 Main Developments in State Aid*, in C. Blumann, F. Picod (eds), 'Annuaire de Droit Européen 2022', Editions Panthéon-Assas, 2023, pp. 1201-1218

M. Merola, G. Theodorakopoulous, *Brève chronique des developpements en matière d'aides d'Etat en 2023*, in C. Blumann, F. Picod (eds), 'Annuaire de Droit de l'Union européenne 2023', Editions Panthéon-Assas, 2024, undergoing publication

M. Merola, L. Armati, *Complainants' Rights in State Aid Matters: Lost in Modernisation?*, in I. Govaere, D. Hanf (eds), 'Scrutinizing Internal and External Dimensions of European Law: Liber amicorum Paul Demaret', College of Europe and P.*i.e.* Peter Lang, 2013, pp. 569-592

M. Merola, T. Ubaldi, *Il recupero degli aiuti di Stato illegali e incompatibili e le relative controversie dinanzi ai giudici nazionali*, in L. Pace (ed.), 'Dizionario sistematico del diritto della concorrenza', Jovene, 2013, pp. 623-637

M. Merola, *Mediaset III: The Recovery Revolution Deactivated*, in C. Buts, J.L. Buendía Sierra (eds), 'Milestones in State Aid Case Law', Lexxion, 2017, pp. 703-717

M. Merola, *Rimedi per violazione delle norme sugli aiuti di Stato: misure repressive o di ripristino*, Giappichelli, 2018

U. Mörth, *Soft Law and Governance and Regulation: An Interdisciplinary Perspective*, Edwar Elgar, 2004

F. Pastor-Merchante, *The EU Perspective on the Private Enforcement of State Aid Law*, in W. Wurmnest, F. Wollenschläger, T. Möllers (eds), 'Private Enforcement of European Competition and State Aid Law: Current Challenges and the Way Forward', Kluwer International, 2019, pp. 197-214

F. Pastor-Merchante, G. Monti, *The Functions of National Courts in the Private Enforcements of State Aid Law*, in P.L. Parcu, G. Monti, M. Botta (eds), 'EU State Aid Law', Edward Elgar, 2020, p. 121-140

F. Picod, *L'Office des juridictions nationales en l'absence de notification d'un projet d'aide d'État à la Commission européenne*, in 'Mélanges offerts à Louis Vogel', LGDJ, 2024, pp. 553-561

J.J. Piernas López, *Enforcement of State Aid Law at the National Level: Recent Trends in Spain*, in P.L. Parcu, G. Monti, M. Botta (eds), 'EU State Aid Law: Emerging trends at the national and EU level', Edward Elgar, 2020, pp. 218-239

C. Quigley, *European State Aid Law and Policy*, Hart Publishing, 2009

F. Ramacci, *Corso di diritto penale*, R. Guerrini (ed.), Giappichelli, 2023

G.M. Roberti, *La giurisprudenza della Corte di Giustizia sulla 'base giuridica' degli atti comunitari*, in A. Tizzano (ed.) 'Problematica del Diritto delle Comunità Europee, Edizione de 'Il Foro Italiano'', 1992, pp. 99-121

B.J. Rodger, M. Sousa Ferro, F. Marcos, *The EU Antitrust Damages Directive: Transposition in the Member States*, Oxford University Press, 2018

V. Rose, D. Bailey, *17 State Aids, Judicial Remedies*, in V. Rose, D. Bailey (eds), 'Bellamy & Child: European Union Law of Competition', Oxford University Press, 2013, pp. 1269-1376

F-J. Säcker, F. Montag, *European State Aid Law: A Commentary*, C.H. Beck - Hart Publishing - Nomos, 2016

M. Sánchez Rydelski, *The EC State Aid Regime: Distortive Effects of State Aid on Competition and Trade*, Cameron May, 2006

C. Schepisi, *Il private enforcement dell'art. 108 § 3 TFUE e i rimedi in capo al giudice nazionale*, in L. Pace (ed.), 'Dizionario sistematico del diritto della concorrenza', Jovene, 2013, pp. 599-614

S. Schonberg, *Legitimate Expectations in Administrative Law*, Oxford University Press, 2000

M. Schütte, *Procedural Aspects of EU State Aid Law and Practice*, in E. Szyszczak (ed.), 'Research Handbook on European State Aid Law', Edward Elgar, 2011, pp. 336-353

J. Schwarze, *European Administrative Law*, Sweet & Maxwell, 2006

O. Ştefan, *Soft Law in EU Competition and State aid: an Imperfect Solution to Grand Regulatory Challenges*, in C.M. Colombo, K. Wright, & M. Eliantonio (eds), 'The Evolving Governance of EU Competition Law in a Time of Disruptions: A Constitutional Perspective', Hart Publishing, 2022, pp. 213-231

M. Strand, V. Bastidas, M.C. Iacovides, *EU Competition Litigation, Transposition and First Experiences of the New Regime*, Hart Publishing, 2019

L. Strisower, *L'extraterritorialité et ses principales applications*, in Académie de droit international de La Haye (ed.), 'Recueil des Cours. Académie de droit international de La Haye', Hachette-Sirey, 1923, pp. 227-287

J. Temple Lang, *Legal Certainty and legitimate expectations as general principles of law*, in U. Bernitz, J. Nergelius (eds), 'General Principles of European Community Law', The Hague, 2000, pp. 163-184

J. Temple Lang, *The Charter and EU State Aid Procedure*, in S. de Vries, U. Bernitz, S. Weatherill (eds), 'The EU Charter of Fundamental Rights as a Binding Instrument: Five Years Old and growing', Bloomsbury Publishing, 2014, pp. 343-364

A.H. Türk, *Judicial Review in EU Law*, Edward Elgar, 2009

A. Van Waeyenberge, *Nouveaux instruments juridiques de l'Union européenne: Évolution de la méthode communautaire*, Larcier, 2015

A. Van Waeyenberge, L. Fromont, *Actualités de la protection juridictionnelle dans et par l'Union européenne*, Larcier, 2016

J. Weinzierl, *Recent Developments in German State Aid Jurisprudence: A Scrutiny from the Perspective of the Preliminary Reference Procedure (Art. 267 TFEU)*, in P.L. Parcu, G. Monti, M. Botta (eds), 'EU State Aid Law: Emerging Trends at the National and EU Level', Edward Elgar, 2020, pp. 194-217

F.G. Wilman, *Private Enforcement of EU Law Before National Courts: The EU Legislative Framework*, Edward Elgar Publishing, 2015

F. Wollenschläger, W. Wurmnest, T.M.J. Möllers, *Private Enforcement of European Competition and State Aid Law: Current Challenges and the Way Forward*, Kluwer Law International, 2020

Contributions in Journals

A. Alexis, *Foreign Subsidies Control: The New European Commission Proposal*, Concurrences, 4/2021, Art. N° 102822

A. Alexis, *Control of Foreign Subsidies Distorting the Internal Market: Main Amendments Introduced by the Co-legislators*, February 2023, Concurrences, 1/2023, Art. N° 111241

A.U. Almeda, *Private Enforcement of EU State Aid Law Through Damages Claims*, EStAL, 2019, pp. 169-179

M. Angeli, *The European Commission's 'New Policy' on State Aid Control: Some Reflections on Public and Private Enforcement of Recovery of Illegal Aid*, European Competition Law Review, 11/2009, pp. 533-541

C. Arhold, *Recovery of Unlawful State Aid by the Member States: The New German Approach*, EStAL, 2006, pp. 6-11

L. Armati, F. Macchi, *The Commission Adopts the New Notice on the Enforcement of State Aid Rules Before National Courts*, EStAL, 2022, pp. 3-19

R. Baratta, *La cosa giudicata non limita il principio della primauté..., peraltro espunto dal progetto di riforma dell'Unione europea*, Giustizia civile, 12/2007, pp. 2657-2736

J.A. Barciela Pérez, *El principio de protección de la confianza legitima en el ámbito tributario: jurisprudencia del TJUE*, Quincena Fiscal, 22/2010, pp. 79-92

W-J. Barends, *Judicial Protection in the Field of Public Procurement: The Transposition into Dutch Law of Directive 2077/66/EC, Amending the Remedies Directive*, Utrecht Journal of International and European Law, 71/2010, pp. 17-25

C. Beccaria, *Dei delitti e delle pene*, in G. Francioni Mediobanca (ed.), 'Edizione nazionale delle opere di Cesare Beccaria: Volume I', Milano, 1984, available at https://archiviostorico.mediobanca.com/pubblicazione/edizione-nazionale-delle-opere-di-cesare-beccaria/

L. Biegurński, *Forms of State Aid Authorities in Associated Countries of Central and Eastern Europe*, EStAL, 2012, pp. 567-572

O. Billard, S. Martin, *Les mesures de soutien public aux entreprises en difficulté au regard de la prohibition des aides d'Etat*, Revue Lamy de la Concurrence: droit, économie, régulation, 38/2014, pp. 151-180

S. Blazek, R. Van der Hout, *The Court's Judgments in the Ryanair and Aer Lingus Cases: Adding Another Layer of Complexity in Fiscal State aid – Case T-500/12 (Ryanair) and Case T-473/12 (Aer Lingus)*, EStAL, 2015, pp. 340-344

J. Blockx, *New State Aid Recovery Notice: Obtaining a Pound of Flesh (Without a Jot of Blood?)*, EStAL, 2019, pp. 540-544

D. Borde, P. Kirch, *La restitution des aides d'Etat: Le point de vue français*, Revue trimestrielle de droit europeen (RTD Eur.), 3/1993, pp. 477-502

B. Brandtner, T. Beranger, C. Lessenich, *Private State Aid Enforcement*, EStAL, 2010, pp. 23-33

H.J. Brinkhorst, *Note on Cases 77/72 (Capolongo) and 70/72 (Kohlegesetz)*, Common Market Law Review, 1974, pp. 199-210

J.L. Buendía Sierra, M.Á. Bolsa Ferruz, *State Aid Assessment: What National Courts Can Do and What They Must Do,* EStAL, 2017, pp. 406-415

C. Buts, T. Joris, M. Jegers, *Determinants of the European Commission's State Aid Decisions,* Journal of Industry, Competition and Trade, 4/2011, pp. 399-426

C. Buts, T. Joris, M. Jegers, *State Aid Policy in the EU Member States. It's a Different Game They Play,* EStAL, 2013, pp. 330-340

D. Calciu, L. Armati, A.B. Alcaraz Riaño, *Cooperation Tools Between National Courts and the European Commission,* EsTAL, 1/2025

A. Carnelutti, *L'arrêt 'Francovich Bonifaci'. L'obligation des états membres de réparer les dommages causés par les violations du droit communautaire,* Revue du marché unique européen, 1/1992, pp. 187-192

J.Y. Chérot, *Le droit communautaire s'oppose à l'application d'une disposition de droit national visant à consacrer le principe de l'autorité de la chose jugée, en tant que son application fait obstacle à la récupération d'une aide d'Etat octroyée en violation du droit communautaire, et dont l'incompatibilité avec le marché commun a été constatée par une décision de la Commission devenue définitive,* Concurrences, 4/2007, pp. 108-110

J.Y. Chérot, *Le plan d'action de la Commission dans le domaine des aides d'Etat: Progrès et limites de l'analyse économique dans me contrôle communautaire des aides d'Etat,* Actualité juridique Droit administratif (AJDA), 44/2007, pp. 2412-2419

M. Cini, *The Soft Law Approach: Commission Rule-Making in the EU's State Aid Regime,* Journal of European Public Policy, 2/2001, pp. 192-207

C.M. Colombo, *State Aid Control in the Modernisation Era: Moving Towards a Differentiated Administrative Integration?,* European Law Journal, 3/2019, pp. 292-316

C. Dackö, C. Brodin, A. Arlebo, *The FDI Screening Mechanisms and the Draft EU Foreign Subsidy Regulation: Potential Conflicts of Interests and in Application,* Zeitschrift für europarechtliche Studien (ZEuS), 2022, pp. 505-518

W. Den Ouden, *Enforcement of State Aid Law in the Netherlands. Legislative Initiative for Effective Recovery Procedures in Dutch Law,* EStAL, 2009, pp. 15-26

J. Derenne, C. Barbu-O'Connor, *State Aid and Private Enforcement: An Overview of EU and National Case Law,* 7 May 2020, e-Competition State Aid Private Enforcement, Art. N. 92521

J. Derenne, C. Chilaru, *Renvoi préjudiciel en appréciation de validité et recours en annulation: quelle protection juridictionnelle effective en particulier en matière d'aides d'Etat?,* Revue des Affaires Européennes, 2/2019, pp. 267-275

J. Derenne, D. Jouve, *State aid & National Enforcement: An Overview of EU and National Case Law,* 2 March 2023, e-Competitions State aid & National enforcement, Art. N° 110999

T. Doleys, *Managing the Dilemma of Discretion: The European Commission and the Development of EU State Aid Policy,* Journal of Industry, Competition and Trade, 13/2013, pp. 23-38

M. Dony, *Aides d'Etat, concurrence et libre circulation,* Revue des Affaires Européennes, 3/2005, pp. 371-462

S. Donzelli, *The Commission's New Recovery Notice: A Handbook for the Recovery of Unlawful and Incompatible Aid*, EStAL, 2019, p. 528-539

N. Dunne, *Courage and Compromise: The Directive on Antitrust Damages*, European Law Review, 4/2015, pp. 581-597

A. Estoa Pérez, *La jurisprudencia Deggendorf como medio de forzar la recuperación de las ayudas ilegales*, Revista de Derecho Comunitario Europeo, 29/2008, pp. 193-211

U. Galetta, *Riflessioni sulla più recente giurisprudenza comunitaria in materia di giudicato nazionale (ovvero sull'autonomia procedurale come competenza procedurale funzionalizzata)*, Il Diritto dell'Unione europea, 4/2009, pp. 961-984

G. Gattinara, A. Di Mario, *The Mediaset Judgment of the Court of Justice: Remarks on Its Consequences on Damages for Breach of the Standstill Obligation*, Revue des affaires européennes, 1/2014, pp. 201-210

L. Ghazarian, *Binding Effect of Opening Decisions: Lufthansa AG v. FFH*, EStAL, 2014, pp. 108-114

L. Ghazarian, *Recovery of State Aid: The Obligations of Member States, National Courts, and National Authorities in State Aid Recovery and Recent Developments in the Case-Law of the Court of Justice of the European Union*, EStAL, 2016, pp. 228-234

A. Gjievori, *Modernisation of EU State Aid Procedures: Are the Rights of Third Parties More Protected?*, Juridical Tribune, 5/2015, pp. 45-59

J. Goodliffe, *State Aids and Recalcitrant Members*, New Law Journal, 1990, pp. 1238-1239

J. Goyder, M. Dons, *Damages Claims Based on State Aid Law Infringements*, EStAL, 2017, pp. 416-428

G. Greco, *Sovvenzioni e tutela dell'affidamento*, Rivista trimestrale di diritto pubblico, 2/2000, pp. 375-388

M.A. Hermitte, *Chronique de jurisprudence de la Cour de justice des Communautés européennes*. Concurrence, Journal du droit international, 1991, pp. 483-494

M. Honoré, N.E. Jensen, *Damages in State Aid Cases*, EStAL, 2011, pp. 265-286

M. Hoskins, *Case C-188/92, TWD Textilwerke Deggendorf GmbH v. Bundesrepublik Deutschland, Judgment of 9 March 1994, [1994] ECR I-833*, Common Market Law Review, 1994, pp. 1399-1408

A. Howard, *Too Little, Too Late? The European Commission's Legislative Proposals on Anti-Trust Damages Actions*, Journal of European Competition Law & Practice, 6/2013, pp. 455-464

K. Jacobsson, *Soft Regulation and Subtle Transformation of States: The Case of EU Employment Policy*, Journal of European Social Policy, 4/2004, pp. 359-370

C. Jadot, *Damages Actions and State Aid: Time for Action at EU Level?*, Market and Competition Law Review, 1/ 2022, pp. 89-122

T. Jaeger, *The CELF Judgment: A Precarious Conception of the Standstill Obligation*, EStAL, 2008, pp. 279-289

T. Jaeger, *The Future of State Aid*, EStAL, 2022, pp. 117-119

K. Jaros, N. Ritter, *Pleading Legitimate Expectations in the Procedure for the Recovery of State Aid*, EStAL, 2004, pp. 11-21

T. Joris, *The Concept of an 'Economic Unit' in State Aid Matters and the Deggendorf Principle*, EStAL, 2012, pp. 149-162

M. Karpenschif, *La récupération des aides nationales versées en violation du droit communautaire à l'aune du règlement n. 659/1999: du mythe à la réalité?*, Revue trimestrielle de droit européen (RTD Eur.), 3/2001, pp. 551-596

M. Kekelekis, *DEI v. European Commission, C-590/14 P, Annotation*, EStAL, 2017, pp. 291-294

A. Knade-Plaskacz, *Enforcement of State Aid Law at National Level. The Relationship Between National Courts and the European Commission*, Juridical Tribune, 2/2013, pp. 116-125

A. Knaul, *The SMI-Judgment: A New Course for Recovery of Illegal State Aid?*, EStAL, 2004, pp. 427-430

C. Koenig, J. Lindner, *Criminal Liability: An Efficient Tool of EU State Aid Law Enforcement?*, EStAL, 2015, pp. 19-24

M. Köhler, *Private Enforcement of State Aid Law: Problems of Guaranteeing EU Rights by Means of National (Procedural) Law*, EStAL, 2012, pp. 369-387

K.P.E. Lasok, *The Commission's Powers over Illegal State Aids*, European Competition Law Review, 1990, pp. 125-127

J. Lever, *EU State Aid Law: Not a Pretty Sight*, EStAL, 2013, pp. 5-10

R.G. Lipsey, K. Lancaster, *The General Theory of Second Best*, in Review of Economic Studies, 1/1956, pp. 11-32

T. Lock, *Is Private Enforcement of EU Law Through State Liability a Myth? An Assessment 20 Years after Francovich*, Common Market Law Review, 2012, pp. 1675-1702

T. Lübbig, T. Morgan, *State Aid, National Courts and the Separation of Powers: Should Judges Be Bound to the European Commission's Unfinished State Aid Businesses?*, Journal of European Competition law & Practice, 5/2014, pp. 256-260

R. Luja, *The Foreign Subsidies Regulation*, EStAL, 2021, pp. 187-199

S. Maes, C. Buts, W. De Cock, *National Courts and the Enforcement of EU State Aid Law: Survey Results*, EsTAL, 1/2025.

R.S. Mehta, *The Court of Justice of the EU Rules That under article 4(3) TFEU a National Court Must Take Into Account the Commission's Statement of Position on the Meaning and Consequences of a Commission Decision (Mediaset)*, 13 February 2014, Concurrences, e-Competitions February 2014, Art. N°64362

M. Merola, *Recouvrement des aides: recherche d'une solution uniforme pour le calcul des montants à récupérer*, L'Observateur de Bruxelles, 108/2017, pp. 40-44

A. Metaxas, S. Spyrou S., *Alteration of Existing State Aid and New Aid: On the Criteria of this Legal Categorisation*, EStAL, 2017, pp. 73-76

M. Muñoz de Juan, J.M. Panero Rivas, *Locus Standi and the Private Creditor Test after the Judgment of the General Court on Buczek Automotive v. Commission*, EStAL, 2012, pp. 273-274

M. Muñoz de Juan, *National Courts and Interim Measures*, EStAL, 2013, pp. 421-423

M. Muñoz de Juan, *Monitoring of State Aid: From Ex Ante to Ex Post Control,* EStAL, 2018, pp. 483-493

G. Muscolo, *Towards More Effective Antitrust Damages Actions in Europe: The Commission Proposal for a Directive,* Italian Antitrust Review, 0/2013, pp. 60-70

M. Negenman, *A State Aid Network?*, EStAL, 2011, pp. 621-627

P. Nicolaides, *Decentralised State Aid Control in An Enlarged European Union: Feasible, Necessary, or Both?*, World Competition: Law & Economics Review, 2/2003, pp. 263-277

P. Nicolaides, *Are National Courts Becoming and Extension of the Commission?*, EStAL, 2014, pp. 409-413

P. Nicolaides, *The EU Court of Justice Rules That the National Courts Dealing with a Case of Recovery of Illegal State Aid May Not Disregard the Statement of Position Made by the Commission in the Relevant Decision (Mediaset)*, 13 February 2014, e-Competitions, 2014, Art. N° 64075

N. Niejahr, *It May Be Zero! CJEU Highlights National Courts' Authority to Review and Determine Amounts of Aid to Be Recovered,* EStAL, 2014, pp. 707-711

V. Noël, S. Thomas, *Locus Standi in State Aid Litigation after Montessori,* EStAL, 2021 pp. 512-528

M. O'Regan, *Private Enforcement of EU Competition Law: The Impact of the Damages Directive,* Volume 18, 1/2019, Competition Law Journal, 2019, pp. 51-53

A. Pappas, *Aides d'Etat et le principe de continuité économique: la cohérence de la notion et la protection effective des concurrents et des repreneurs*, September 2017, Concurrences, 3/2017, Art. N° 84413

O. Peiffert, *Le juge national des référés octroyant une nouvelle aide d'État: syllogisme ou sophisme dans la jurisprudence de la Cour de justice?*, Revue Lamy de la Concurrence: droit, économie, regulation, 2016, pp. 38-42

N. Petit, *Traité de Lisbonne et politique de concurrence – Rupture?*, Revue de la Faculté de Droit de l'Université de Liège, De Boeck & Larcier, 1/2008, pp. 265-279

S. Peyer, *Compensation and the Damages Directive,* European Competition Journal, 8/2016, pp. 87-112

G. Pitruzzella, *Foreign Direct Investment Screening in the EU,* in G. Napolitano (ed.), 'Foreign Direct Investment Screening. Il controllo sugli investimenti esteri diretti', Il Mulino, 2020, pp. 63-70

H. Priess, *Recovery of Illegal State Aid: An Overview of Recent Developments in the Case Law,* Common Market Law Review, 1996, pp. 69-91

N. Ritter, *The CDA Case: New Answers to the Issue of How to Determine the Addressee of a Decision Ordering Recovery?*, EStAL, 2006, pp. 183-186

N. Robins, Z. Xiong, *The Effectiveness of Compensatory Measures in Maintaining the Level-Playing Field,* EStAL, 2024, pp. 268-281

W. Rodriguez Curiel, *Procedimientos sobre ayudas de Estado,* Gaceta Jurídica de la CEE, Boletín, 78/1990, pp. 17-18

A. Ronzano, *Recovery of aid: The EU Court of Justice Urges National Judges to Render Decisions on Illegal State Aid Recovery Requests Even When the State Aid Compatibility Is Still Being Debated (CELF),* 11 March 2010, Concurrences, 2/2010, Art. N° 65434

F. Rossi Dal Pozzo, *Il private enforcement delle regole sugli aiuti di Stato nella giurisprudenza italiana,* Eurojus, 4/2019, pp. 116-131

A. Sánchez-Graells, *Digging Itself Out of the Hole? A Critical Assessment of the European Commission's Attempt to Revitalise State Aid Enforcement after the Crisis*, Journal of antitrust enforcement, 1/2016, pp. 157-187

G. Schohe, *May the Commission Select the Debtor of State Aid Repayment? Where the Commission's Power over State Aid Ends*, EStAL, 2004, pp. 423-426

M. Schonberg, *The EU Foreign Subsidies Regulation: Substantive Assessment Issues and Open Questions*, EStAL, 2022, pp. 143-152

J. Scott, *In Legal Limbo: Post-Legislative Guidance as a Challenge for European Administrative Law*, Common Market Law Review, 2011, pp. 339-343

A. Scott, *Co-operation and Good Faith: State Aid Rules and National Courts: Procedural and Interpretative Consequences*, EStAL, 2017, pp. 354-366

P.J. Slot, *Procedural and Substantive Compliance Required*, European Law Review, 1991, pp. 38-49

J. Smela Wolski, *Legal Basis of the Proposal for a Regulation on Foreign Subsidies Distorting the Internal Market*, EStAL, 2022, pp. 153-172

U. Solstész, *Effet Utile Taken to Extremes*, EStAL, 2013, pp. 635-645

U. Solstész, *Foreign Subsidies Control: A Bureaucratic Monster?*, EStAL, 2023, pp. 175-180

V. Squaratti, *Gli aiuti pubblici alle imprese: la giurisprudenza Deggendorf e l'applicazione del criterio del creditore privato in una economia di mercato a una misura fiscale nell'ambito di una procedura concordataria*, Diritto pubblico comparato ed europeo, 1/2012, pp. 207-215

P. Staviczky, *Analysis of the State Aid-Related Proposals in the Letta Report*, EStAL, 2024, pp. 258-267

O. Ştefan, *Hybridity Before the Court, a Hard Look at Soft Law in State Aid Regulation*, European Law Review, 1/2012, pp. 49-69

O. Ştefan, *Helping Loose Ends Meet? The Judicial Acknowledgement of Soft Law as a Tool of Multi-Level Governance*, Maastricht Journal of European and Comparative Law, 2014, pp. 359-379

J. Temple Lang, *EU State Aid Rules: The Need for Substantive Reform*, EStAL, 2014, pp. 440-453

P. Trapp, C. Montgomery Vollert, *The Foreign Subsidies Regulation and European Top-Class Football: Finally a financial fair play?*, EStAL, 2024, pp. 56-61

E. Truli, *Will Its Provisions Serve Its Goals? Directive 2014/104/EU on Certain Rules Governing Actions for Damages for Competition Law Infringements*, Journal of European Competition Law & Practice, 5/2016, pp. 299-312

A. Vallery, H. Wiame, *The Private Creditor Test: Anything New under the Sun?*, EStAL, 2014, pp. 528-537

F. Viala, S. Petit, *The EU Court of Justice Clarifies the Concept of 'Existing Aid' in a Private Enforcement Case and Holds That Unlawful Aid Cannot Be Retroactively Legalized under a Limitation Period That Has Lapsed (Fallimento Traghetti del Mediterraneo)*, 23 January 2019, e-Competition, 2019, Art. No. 90591

M. Weaver, *Convergence Through the Crisis: State Aid Modernisation & West European Capitalism*, Columbia Journal of European Law, 2015, pp. 587-614

W. Weiß, *Ex Officio Third Country Subsidies' Review*, EStAL, 2022, pp. 132-142

F.G. Wilman, *The End of the Absence? The Growing Body of EU Legislation on Private Enforcement and the Main Remedies It Provides for*, Common Market Law Review, 2016, pp. 887-935

W.P.J. Wils, *Ten Years of Regulation 1/2003: A Retrospective*, Journal of European Competition Law e-Practice, 2013, pp. 293-301

Other Sources

M. Bacci, *L'evoluzione del principio del legittimo affidamento nel diritto dell'Unione europea e degli Stati membri*, Collana di diritto privato europeo, 2015, available at https://masterdirittoprivatoeuropeo.it/

A. Becquet, *Analyse du Règlement subventions étrangères à la lumière du droit des aides d'Etat: Contexte, Objectifs, Contenu et Mise en Œuvre*, thesis presented for a master's degree in European Legal Studies from the College of Europe, 2023-2024 academic year, under the supervision of Prof. Massimo Merola, available at the College library

M. Blauberger, *From Negative to Positive Integration? European State Aid Control Through Soft and Hard Law*, MPIfG Discussion Paper 08/4, 2008

T. Bolster, J. Groves, *The UK Implements the EU Damages Directive,* May 2017. Available at https://www.iadclaw.org/assets/1/7/8.1-_Hausfeld_The_UK_Implements_the_EU_Damag.pdf

A. Carpi, *Charting the Path: Administrative and Judicial Remedies Available to Third Parties under the Foreign Subsidies Regulation*, in Rivista del Contenzioso Europeo, 3/2024, available at https://europeanlitigation.eu/2024/10/02/charting-the-path-administrative-and-judicial-remedies-available-to-third-parties-under-the-foreign-subsidies-regulation/

Y. Chevalier, *L'article 14 du règlement (CE) n. 659/1999, la réforme oubliée du droit des aides d'Etat,* thesis presented for a master's degree from the College of Europe, 2012-2013, under the supervision of Prof. Massimo Merola, available at the College library

J. Derenne, C. Kaczmarek, *La recuperation des aides illegals: le role du juge national dans le* 'private enforcement' *du droit des aides d'Etat*, ERA Forum 10/2009, pp. 251-268

European Commission, L. Armati, F. Macchi, State Aid Brief, 2/2022, Publications Office of the European Union, 2022

European Commission, State Aid Brief – S. Donzelli, The 2019 Commission notice on the recovery of unlawful and incompatible state aid, Publications Office of the European Union, 2019

European Commission, State Aid Brief – L. Armati, F. Macchi, The review of the notice on the enforcement of state aid rules before national courts, Publications Office of the European Union, 2022

European Commission, Green Paper on Damages actions for breach of the EC antitrust rules, COM(2005) 672 final, 19.12.2005

European Commission, White paper on European Economic and Social Committee, Opinion of the on the 'Proposal for a Council Regulation (EC) laying down detailed rules for the application of Article 93 of the EC Treaty', OJ C 284/41, 24.9.1998

damages actions for breach of the EC antitrust rules, COM(2008) 165 final, 2.4.2008

European Economic and Social Committee, Opinion on the 'European State Aid Modernisation (SAM)', OJ C 11/49, 15.1.2013

European Commission, White paper on levelling the playing field as regards foreign subsidies, COM(2020)253 final, 17.06.2020

F. Genoni, *The Interplay Between the Foreign Subsidies Regulation and FDI Screening: Synergies, Convergences and Contradiction*, thesis presented for a master's degree in European Legal Studies from the College of Europe, 2023-2024 academic year, under the supervision of Prof. Massimo Merola, available at the College library

W. Hu, D. Gros, *Policy Brief: The BEV Anti-Subsidy Investigation of the Commission: Industrial Policy and Geopolitics in Disguise?*, in IEP@BU Institute for Policymaking, Università Bocconi, 2024, available at https://iep.unibocconi.eu/policy-brief-bev-anti-subsidy-investigation-commission-industrial-policy-and-geopolitics-disguise

L. Idot, *De la mise en oeuvre de l'obligation de restitution en cas de faillite d'une entreprise*, Europe 6/2004, pp. 27-28

L. Idot, *La suspension, par un juge des référés, de la résiliation d'un contrat, qui était le support juridique d'une aide existante, conduit à une modification de cette dernière et peut être qualifiée d'aide nouvelle*, Europe 12/2016, pp. 36-37

L. Iera, *Il quadro regolatorio italiano sul recupero degli aiuti di Stato nell'ambito delle regole di public enforcement*, Training course 'Il regime degli aiuti di Stato', 2023, available at 2459bada-2125-5869-decf-cd035048e6ba

H. Jennings, *State Aid Modernisation: Trying To Do More With Less*, Competition Policy International Chronicle, 2/2014

M. Kaeding, F. Voskamp, *Better Implementation of EU Legislation Is Not Just a Question of Taking Member State to Court*, European Institute of Public Administration, Working Paper 1/2011

P. Nicolaides, *Enforcement of State Aid Rules by National Courts*, Lexxion, 2019, available at https://www.lexxion.eu/en/stateaidpost/enforcement-of-state-aid-rules-by-national-courts/

P. Nicolaides, *Existing v. New Aid and Role of National Courts*, Lexxion, 2016, available at https://www.lexxion.eu/stateaidpost/existing-v-new-aid-and-role-of-national-courts/

P. Nicolaides, *The EU's State Aid Modernisation: Taking Stock of Its Initial Results*, College of Europe Policy Brief #12.16, July 2016, available at https://aei.pitt.edu/93091/

R. Musone, *La 'repetitio indebiti' della pubblica amministrazione nell'evoluzione giurisprudenziale: l'ordinamento vincolista*, Filodiritto, 2013, available at https://www.filodiritto.com/la-repetitio-indebiti-della-pubblica-amministrazione-nellevoluzione-giurisprudenziale-la-fase-vincolista

F. Pastor-Merchante, *The Role of Competitors in the Enforcement of State Aid* Law, Doctoral dissertation, European University Institute, 2014

S. Thomas, *The Spanish Tax Lease Case: Identifying the Beneficiary under the Selectivity Test in Fiscal Aid Schemes*, European Law Blog, 2016, available at https://www.europeanlawblog.eu/pub/the-spanish-tax-lease-case-identifying-the-beneficiary-under-the-selectivity-test-in-fiscal-aid-schemes/release/1

B. Van Rompuy, *The Impact of the Lisbon Treaty on EU competition Law: A Review of Recent Case Law of the EU Courts*, in Competition Policy International Antitrust

Chronicle, 1/2011, available at https://papers.ssrn.com/sol3/papers.cfm?abstract_id=1970081

A. Weitbrecht, *Book Review: Private Enforcement of European Competition and State Aid Law: Current Challenges and the Way Forward*, in F. Wollenschläger, W. Wurmnest, T.M.J. Möllers (eds), Common Market Law Review, 2022, pp. 283-284

Table of Legislation

EU Primary Law

Treaty on European Union (Consolidated Version), OJ C 202/13, 7.6.2016
Treaty on the Functioning of the European Union (Consolidated Version), OJ C 202/47, 7.6.2016

EU Secondary Law

Regulations

Council Regulation (EC) No 659/1999 of 22 March 1999 laying down detailed rules for the application of Article 93 of the EC Treaty, OJ L 83/1, 27.3.1999, no longer in force
Regulation (EC) No 1049/2001 of the European Parliament and of the Council of 30 May 2001 regarding public access to European Parliament, Council and Commission documents, OJ L 145/43, 31.5.2001
Commission Regulation (EC) No 794/2004 of 21 April 2004 implementing Council Regulation (EU) 2015/1589 laying down detailed rules for the application of Article 108 of the Treaty on the Functioning of the European Union, OJ L 140/1, 30.04.2004
Commission Regulation (EC) No 1628/2006 of 24 October 2006 on the application of Articles 87 and 88 of the Treaty to national regional investment aid, OJ L 302/29, 1.11.2006, no longer in force
Commission Regulation (EU) No 651/2014 of 17 June 2014 declaring certain categories of aid compatible with the internal market in application of Articles 107 and 108 of the Treaty, OJ L 187/1, 26.6.2014
Council Regulation (EU) 2015/1589 of 13 July 2015 laying down detailed rules for the application of Article 108 of the Treaty on the Functioning of the European Union (codification), OJ L 248/9, 24.9.2015
Regulation (EU) 2019/452 of the European Parliament and of the Council of 19 March 2019 establishing a framework for the screening of foreign direct investments into the Union, OJ L 79/1, 21.3.2019

Regulation (EU) 2019/712 of the European Parliament and of the Council of 17 April 2019 on safeguarding competition in air transport, and repealing Regulation (EC) No 868/2004, OJ L 123/4, 10.5.2019

Regulation (EU) 2021/241 of the European Parliament and of the Council of 12 February 2021 establishing the Recovery and Resilience Facility, OJ L 57/17, 18.2.2021

Regulation (EU) 2022/2560 of the European Parliament and of the Council of 14 December 2022 on foreign subsidies distorting the internal market, OJ L 330/1, 23.12.2022

Commission Regulation (EU) 2023/1315 amending Regulation (EU) No 651/2014 declaring certain categories of aid compatible with the internal market in application of Articles 107 and 108 of the Treaty and Regulation (EU) 2022/2473 declaring certain categories of aid to undertakings active in the production, processing and marketing of fishery and aquaculture products compatible with the internal market in application of Articles 107 and 108 of the Treaty, OJ L 167/1, 30.6.2023

Commission Implementing Regulation (EU) 2023/1441 of 10 July 2023 on detailed arrangements for the conduct of proceedings by the Commission pursuant to Regulation (EU) 2022/2560 of the European Parliament and of the Council on foreign subsidies distorting the internal market, OJ L 177/1, 12.7.2023

Regulation (EU) 2024/795 of the European Parliament and of the Council of 29 February 2024 establishing the Strategic Technologies for Europe Platform (STEP), and amending Directive 2003/87/EC and Regulations (EU) 2021/1058, (EU) 2021/1056, (EU) 2021/1057, (EU) No 1303/2013, (EU) No 223/2014, (EU) 2021/1060, (EU) 2021/523, (EU) 2021/695, (EU) 2021/697 and (EU) 2021/241, OJ L 2024/795, 29.2.2024

Directives

Directive 2007/66/EC of the European Parliament and of the Council of 11 December 2007 amending Council Directives 89/665/EEC and 92/13/EEC with regard to improving the effectiveness of review procedures concerning the award of public contracts, OJ L 335/31, 20.12.2007

Directive 2009/81/EC of the European Parliament and of the Council of 13 July 2009 on the coordination of procedures for the award of certain works contracts, supply contracts and service contracts by contracting authorities or entities in the fields of defence and security, and amending Directives 2004/17/EC and 2004/18/EC, OJ L 216/76, 20.8.2009

Directive 2014/104/EU of the European Parliament and of the Council of 26 November 2014 on certain rules governing actions for damages under national law for infringements of the competition law provisions of the Member States and of the European Union, OJ L 349/1, 5.12.2014

Directive (EU) 2019/1023 of the European Parliament and of the Council of 20 June 2019 on preventive restructuring frameworks, on discharge of debt and disqualifications, and on measures to increase the efficiency of procedures concerning restructuring, insolvency and discharge of debt, and amending Directive (EU) 2017/1132 (Directive on restructuring and insolvency), OJ L 172/18, 26.6.2019

Decisions of the European Commission

Commission Decision of 24 January 2007 on State aid C 52/2005 (ex NN 88/2005, ex CP 101/2004) implemented by the Italian Republic for the subsidised purchase of digital decoders, OJ L 147/1, 8.6.2007

Commission Decision of 17 July 2013 on the aid scheme SA.21233 C/11 (ex NN/11, ex CP 137/06) implemented by Spain - Tax scheme applicable to certain finance lease agreements also known as the Spanish Tax Lease System, OJ L 114/1, 16.4.2014

Commission Decision of 30 March 2015 on State aid SA.38517 (2014/C) (ex 2014/NN) implemented by Romania - Arbitral award Micula v Romania of 11 December 2013, OJ L 232/43, 4.9.2015

Commission Decision of 1 October 2014 on State aid SA 27339 (12/C) (ex 11/NN) implemented by Germany for Zweibrücken airport and airlines using the airport, OJ L 34/68, 10.02.2016

Commission Decision of 15 October 2014, on State aid SA.26500 C/12 (ex 2011/NN, ex CP 227/2008) implemented by Germany for Flugplatz Altenburg-Nobitz GmbH and Ryanair Ltd, OJ L 59/22, 04.03.2016

Commission Decision of 12 September 2019 on state aid SA.55121 (2019/N), implemented by Italy for Banca Monte dei Paschi di Siena - Amendments to the list of commitments of the Republic of Italy to the European Commission, OJ C 7/1, 10.1.2020

Commission Decision of 10 September 2023 on state aid SA.58173 (2021 N) (ex 2020 PN) implemented by Italy for Newco ITA, OJ C 177/1, 29.4.2022

Commission Decision of 10 September 2021 on State aid SA.48171 (2018/C) (ex 2018/NN, ex 2017/FC) implemented by Italy for Alitalia, OJ L 141/53, 20.5.2022

Commission Decision of 2 August 2022 on State Aid SA.103450 (2022/N) implemented by Italy for Banca Monte dei Paschi di Siena - Second amendment to the list of commitments related to the aid granted to Banca Monte dei Paschi di Siena in 2017, OJ C 387/1, 7.10.2022

Commission Decision of 27 March 2023 on State aid SA.55678 (2019/NN), implemented by Italy for Alitalia, OJ L 2023/2160, 20.10.2023

Soft Law and Other Official Documents

European Commission, Fifteenth Report on Competition Policy, Publications Office of the European Communities, 1986

European Commission, Notice on cooperation between national courts and the Commission in the State aid field (1995), OJ C 312/8, 23.11.1995

European Commission, Report on the application of EC State aid law by the Member State courts, Publications Office of the European Union, 1999

European Commission, Communication on the application of Article 228 of the EC Treaty, OJ C 126/15, 7.6.2007

European Commission, Community guidelines on State aid for rescuing and restructuring firms in difficulty, OJ C 244/2, 1.10.2004, no longer in force
European Commission, State Aid Action Plan – Less and better targeted state aid: a roadmap for state aid reform 2005-2009, COM(2005) 107 final, 7.6.2005, Publications Office of the European Union, 2005
European Commission, Study on the enforcement of State aid law at national level. Part I, Application of EC State aid rules by national courts. Part II, Recovery of unlawful State aid: enforcement of negative Commission decisions by the Member States, coordinated by T. Derenne, J. Jestaedt, T. Ottervanger, Publications Office of the European Union, 2006
European Commission, Towards an effective implementation of Commission decisions ordering Member States to recover unlawful and incompatible State aid, OJ C 272/4, 15.11.2007
European Commission, Notice on the enforcement of State aid law by national courts, OJ C 85/1, 9.4.2009
European Commission, 2009 update of the 2006 Study on the enforcement of State aid rules at national level. Final report, directed by J. Derenne, Publications Office of the European Union, 2009
European Communication, EU State Aid Modernisation (SAM), COM(2012) 209 final, 8.5.2012
European Commission, Guidelines on State aid for environmental protection and energy 2014–2020, OJ C 200/1, 28.6.2014
European Commission, Study on the enforcement of state aid rules and decisions by national courts: Final study, Monti, G., Bas, P., Meindert, L., et al., Caselex, Ecorys, European University Institute, Sparks, Publications Office of the European Union, 2019
EFTA Surveillance Authority, Study on the private enforcement of State aid rules by national courts in the EEA EFTA States, Publications Office of the European Union, 2019
European Commission, Commission Notice on the recovery of unlawful and incompatible State aid, OJ C 247/1, 23.7.2019
European Commission, Final Study on the enforcement of State aid rules and decisions by national courts, Publications Office of the European Union, 2019
European Commission, Commission Notice on the enforcement of State aid rules by national courts, OJ C 305/1, 30.7.2021
European Commission, Communication on criteria for the analysis of the compatibility with the internal market of State aid to promote the execution of important projects of common European interest, OJ C 528/10, 30.12.2021
European Commission, Guidelines on State aid for climate, environmental protection and energy, OJ C 80/1, 18.2.2022

Table of Cases

European Union

Court of Justice

Judgement of the Court of Justice of 16 January 2025, Case C-588/23, *Scai Srl v. Regione Campania*, EU:C:2025:23

Judgment of the Court of Justice of 5 February 1963, Case 26/62, *NV Algemene Transport – en Expeditie Onderneming van Gend & Loos v. Nethderlands Inland Revenue Administration*, EU:C:1963:1

Judgment of the Court of Justice of 15 July 1963, Case 25/62, *Plaumann & co v. Commission of the European Community*, EU:C:1963:17

Judgment of the Court of Justice of 19 June 1973, Case 77/72, *Carmine Capolongo v. Azienda Agricole Maya*, EU:C:1973:65

Judgment of the Court of Justice of 12 July 1973, Case 70/72, *Commission of the EC v. The Federal Republic of Germany*, EU:C:1973:87

Judgment of the Court of Justice of 11 December 1973, Case 120/73, *Gebrüder Lorenz GmbH v. Federal Republic of Germany and Land Rheinland-Pfalz*, EU:C:1973:152

Judgment of the Court of Justice of 22 March 1977, Case 78/76, *Steinike & Weinlig v. Federal Republic of Germany*, EU:C:1977:52

Judgment of the Court of Justice of 9 March 1978, Case 106/77, *Amministrazione delle finanze dello Stato v. Simmenthal SpA (known as Simmenthal)* EU:C:1978:49

Judgment of the Court of Justice of 29 October 1980, Case 22/80, *Boussac Saint-Frères SA/Brigitte Gerstenmeier*, EU:C:1980:251

Judgment of the Court of Justice of 12 July 1984, Case 170/83, *Hydrotherm Gerätebau GmbH v. Compact del Dott. Ing. Mario Andreoli & C. Sas.*, EU:C:1984:271

Judgment of the Court of Justice of 15 January 1986, Case 52/84, *EC Commission v. Kingdom of Belgium*, EU:C:1986:3

Judgment of the Court of 28 January 1986, Case 169/84, *Compagnie française de l'azote (Cofaz) SA and Others v. Commission of the EC*, EU:C:1986:42

Judgment of the Court of Justice of 24 February 1987, Case 310/85, *Deufil GmbH & Co. KG v. Commission of the EC*, EU:C:1987:96

Judgment of the Court of Justice of 26 March 1987, Case 45/86, *Commission of the European Communities v. Council of the European Communities*, EU:C:1987:53

Judgment of the Court of Justice of 9 April 1987, Case 5/86, *Commission of the European Communities v. Kingdom of Belgium*, EU:C:1987:198

Judgment of the Court of Justice of 22 October 1987, Case 314/85, *Foto-Frost v. Hauptzollamt Lübeck-Ost*, EU:C:1987:452

Judgment of the Court of Justice of 24 November 1987, Case 223/85, *Rijn-Schelde-Verolme (RSV) Machinefabrieken en Scheepswerven NV v. Commission of the EC*, EU:C:1987:502

Judgment of the Court of Justice of 2 February 1988, Joined Cases 67/85, 68/85 and 70/85, *Kwekerij van der Kooy BV and others v. Commission*, EU:C:1988:38

Judgment of the Court of Justice of 13 July 1988, Case 102/87, *French Republic v. Commission of the European Communities*, EU:C:1988:391

Judgment of the Court of Justice of 27 September 1988, Joined Cases 106 to 120/87, *Asteris and others v. Greece and EEC*, EU:C:1988:457

Judgment of the Court of Justice of 2 February 1989, Case C-94/87, *Commission of the EC v. Federal Republic of Germany*, EU:C:1989:46

Judgment of the Court of Justice of 14 February 1990, Case C-301/87, *French Republic v. Commission of the EU*, EU:C:1990:67

Judgment of the Court of Justice of 19 June 1990, Case C-213/89, *Factortame Ltd and others v. Commission of the EC*, EU:C:1990:257

Judgment of the Court of Justice of 20 September 1990, Case C-5/89, *Commission of the EC v. Federal Republic of Germany*, EU:C:1990:320

Judgment of the Court of Justice of 21 February 1991, Joined Cases C-143/88 and C-92/89, *Zuckerfabrik Süderdithmarschen AG v. Hauptzollamt Itzehoe and Zuckerfabrik Soest GmbH v. Hauptzollamt Paderborn (Zuckerfabrik)*, EU:C:1991:65

Judgment of the Court of Justice of 21 March 1991, Case C-305/89, *Italy v. Commission of the European Communities*, EU:C:1991:142

Judgment of the Court of Justice of 19 November 1991, Joined Cases C-6/90 and C-9/90, *Andrea Francovich and Danila Bonifaci and others v. Italian Republic*, EU:C:1991:428

Judgment of the Court of Justice of 21 November 1991, Case C-354/90, *Fédération Nationale du Commerce Extérieur des Produits Alimentaires and Syndicat National des Négociants et Transformateurs de Saumon v. French Republic*, EU:C:1991:440

Judgment of the Court of Justice of 9 March 1994, Case C-188/92, *Textilwerke Deggendorf GmbH v. Federal Republic of Germany*, EU:C:1994:90

Judgment of the Court of Justice of 9 March 1994, Case C-188/92, *TWD Textilwerke Deggendorf GmbH v. Federal Republic of Germany*, EU:C:1994:90

Judgment of the Court of Justice of 9 August 1994, Case C-44/93, *Namur-Les Assurances du Crédit SA v. Office National du Ducroire and the Belgian State*, EU:C:1994:311

Judgment of the Court of Justice of 14 September 1994, Case C-42/93, *Kingdom of Spain v. Commission of the EC*, EU:C:1994:326

Judgment of the Court of Justice of 4 April 1995, Case C-350/93, *Commission of the European Communities v. Italian Republic (ENI-Lanerossi)*, EU:C:1995:96

Judgment of the Court of Justice of 9 November 1995, Case C-465/93, *Atlanta Fruchthandelsgesellschaft mbH and others v. Bundesamt für Ernährung und Forstwirtschaft (Atlanta)*, EU:C:1995:369

Judgment of the Court of Justice 14 December 1995, Case C-312/93, *Peterbroeck, Van Campenhout & Cie SCS v. Kingdom of Belgium*, EU:C:1995:437

Judgment of the Court of Justice of 5 March 1996, Joined Cases C-46/93 and C-48/93, *Brasserie du Pêcheur SA v. Bundesrepublik Deutschland and The Queen v. Secretary of State for Transport, ex parte: Factortame Ltd and others*, EU:C:1996:79

Judgment of the Court of Justice of 11 July 1996, Case C-39/94, *Syndicat Français de l'Express International (SFEI) and Others v. La Poste and Others*, EU.C:1996:285

Judgment of the Court of Justice of 20 March 1997, Case C-24/95, *Land Renania Palatinato v. Alcan Deutschland GmbH*, EU:C:C:1997:163

Judgment of the Court of Justice of 15 May 1997, Case C-355/95 P, *Textilwerke Deggendorf GmbH (TWD) v. Commission of the European Communities and Federal Republic of Germany (Deggendorf II)*, EU:C:1997:241

Judgment of the Court of Justice of 29 January 1998, Case C-280/95, *Commission of the EC v. Republic of Italy*, EU:C:1998:28

Judgment of the Court of Justice of 27 June 2000, Case C-404/97, *Commission of the European Communities v. Portuguese Republic*, EU:C:2000:345

Judgment of the Court of Justice of 19 September 2000, C-156/98, *Germany v. Commission*, EU:C:2000:467

Judgment of the Court of Justice of 12 October 2000, Case C-480/98, *Kingdom of Spain v. Commission of the EC (Magefesa)*, EU:C:2000:559

Judgment of the Court of Justice of 19 October 2000, Joined Cases C-15/98 and C-105/99, *Italy and Sardegna Lines v. Commission*, EU:C:2000:570

Judgment of the Court of Justice of 3 July 2001, Case C-378/98, *Commission of the European Communities v. Kingdom of Belgium*, EU:C:2001:370

Judgment of the Court of Justice of 20 September 2001, Case C-390/98, *H.J. Banks & Co. Ltd v. The Coal Authority et Secretary of State for Trade and Industry*, EU:C:2001:456

Judgment of the Court of Justice of 20 September 2001, Case C-453/99, *Courage Ltd v. Bernard Crehan and Bernard Crehan v. Courage Ltd and others*, EU:C:2001:465

Judgment of the Court of Justice of 8 November 2001, Case C-143/99, *Adria-Wien Pipeline GmbH and Others v. Finanzlandesdirektion fur Karnten*, EU:C:2001:598

Judgment of the Court of Justice of 7 March 2002, Case C-310/99, *Italian Republic v. Commission of the European Communities*, EU:C:2002:143

Judgment of the Court of Justice of 2 July 2002, Case C-499/99, *Commission of the European Communities v. Kingdom of Spain*, EU:C:2002:408

Judgment of the Court of Justice of 12 December 2002, Case C-209/00, *Commission of the European Communities v. Federal Republic of Germany*, EU:C:2002:747

Judgment of the Court of Justice of 21 March 2003, Case C-613/11, *Commission v. Italian Republic*, EU:C:2013:192

Judgment of the Court of Justice of 24 July 2003, Case C-280/00, *Altmark Trans GmbH*, EU:C:2003:415

Judgment of the Court of Justice of 30 September 2003, Case-224/01, *Köbler*, EU:C:2003:513

Judgment of the Court of Justice of 29 April 2004, Case C-277/00, *Federal Republic of Germany v. Commission of the European Communities*, EU:C:2004:238

Judgment of the Court of Justice of 29 April 2004, Case C-298/00 P, *Italian Republic v. Commission*, EU:C:2004:240

Judgment of the Court of Justice of 29 June 2004, Case C-110/02, *Commission v. Council*, EU:C:2004:395

Judgment of the Court of Justice of 13 January 2005, Case C-174/02, *Streekgewest Westelijk Noord-Brabant v. Staatssecretaris van Financiën*, EU:C:2005:10

Judgment of the Court of Justice of 12 May 2005, Case C-415/03, *Commission of the EC v. Hellenic Republic (Olympic Airways)*, EU:C:2005:287

Judgment of the Court of Justice of 12 July 2005, Case C-304/02, *Commission of the European Communities v. French Republic*, EU:C:2005:444

Judgment of the Court of Justice of 15 December 2005, Case C-148/04, *Unicredito Italiano SpA v. Agenzia delle Entrate, Ufficio Genova 1*, EU:C:2005:774

Judgment of the Court of Justice of 23 February 2006, Joined Cases C-346/03 and C-529/03, *Giuseppe Atzeni and Others, Marco Scalas and Renato Lilliu v. Regione autonoma della Sardegna*, EU:C:2006:130

Judgment of the Court of Justice of 13 June 2006, Case C-173/03, *Traghetti del Mediterraneo*, EU:C:2019:51

Judgment of the Court of Justice of 15 June 2006, Joined Cases C-393/04 and C-41/05, *Air Liquide Industries Belgium SA v. Ville de Seraing et Province de Liège*, EU:C:2015:403

Judgment of the Court of Justice of 13 July 2006, Joined Cases C-295/04 to C-298/04, *Vincenzo Manfredi v. Lloyd Adriatico Assicurazioni SpA*, EU:C:2006:461

Judgment of the Court of Justice of 7 September 2006, Case C-526/04, *Laboratoires Boiron*, EU:C:2006:528

Judgment of the Court of Justice of 12 September 2006, Case C-300/04, *M.G. Eman and O.B. Sevinger v. College van burgemeester en wethouders van Den Haag*, EU:C:2006:545

Judgment of the Court of Justice of 19 September 2006, Joined Cases C-392/04 and C-422/04, *i-21 Germany GmbH and Arcor AG & Co. KG v. Bundesrepublik Deutschland*, EU:C:2006:586

Judgment of the Court of Justice of 5 October 2006, Case C-368/04, *Transalpine Ölleitung in Österreich GmbH and Ohers v. Finanzlandesdirektion für Tirol and Others (Transalpine Ölleitung)*, EU:C:2006:644

Judgment of the Court of Justice of 5 October 2006, Case C-232/05, *Commission of the EU v. French Republic (Scott)*, EU:C:2006:651

Judgment of the Court of Justice of 18 July 2007, Case C-119/05, *Ministero dell'Industria, del Commercio e dell'Artigianato v. Lucchini SpA (Lucchini)*, EU:C:2007:434

Judgment of the Court of Justice of 12 February 2008, Case C-199/06, *Centre d'exportation du livre français (CELF) et Ministre de la Culture et de la Communication v. Société internationale de diffusion et d'édition (SIDE)*, EU:C:2008:79

Judgment of the Court of Justice of 21 February 2008, Case C-426/05, *Tele2 Telecommunication GmbH v. Telekom-Control-Kommission*, EU:C:2008:103

Judgment of the Court of Justice of 13 November 2008, Case C-214/07, *EC Commission v. French Republic*, EU:C:2008:619

Judgment of the Court of Justice of 18 December 2008, Case C-384/07, *Wienstrom GmbH/Bundesminister fuur Wirtschaft und Arbeit*, EU:C:2008:747

Judgment of the Court of Justice of 7 July 2009, Case C-369/07, *Commission of the European Communities v. Hellenic Republic*, EU:C:2009:428

Judgment of the Court of Justice of 3 September 2009, Case C-2/08, *Amministrazione dell'Economia e delle Finanze e Agenzia delle entrate v. Fallimento Olimpiclub Srl ('Olimpiclub')*, EU:C:2009:506

Judgment of the Court of Justice of 11 March 2010, Case C-1/09, *Centre d'Exportation du livre français (CELF) and Ministre de la Culture et de la Communication v. Société internationale de diffusion et d'édition (SIDE)*, EU:C:2010:136

Judgment of the Court of Justice of 20 May 2010, Case C-210/09, *Scott SA and Kimberly Clark SAS v. Ville d'Orléans*, EU:C:2010:294

Judgment of the Court of Justice of 18 November 2010, Case C-322/09 P, *NDSHT Nya Destination Stockholm Hotell & Teaterpaket AB v. European Commission*, EU:C:2010:701

Judgment of the Court of Justice of 16 December 2010, Case C-362/09 P, *Athinaïki Techniki AE v. European Commission*, EU:C:2010:783

Judgment of the Court of Justice of 22 December 2010, Case C-507/08, *European Commission v. Slovak Republic*, EU:C:2010:802

Judgment of the Court of Justice of 9 June 2011, Joined Cases C-71/09 P, C-73/09 P and C-76/09 P, *Comitato «Venezia vuole vivere», Hotel Cipriani Srl and Società Italiana per il gas SpA (Italgas) v. European Commission*, EU:C:2011:368

Judgment of the Court of Justice of 14 July 2011, Case C-303/09, *European Commission v. Italian Republic ('Tremonti bis')*, EU:C:2011:483

Judgment of the Court of Justice of 28 July 2011, Case C-403/10 P, *Mediaset SpA v. European Commission*, EU:C:2011:533

Judgment of the Court of Justice of 17 November 2011, Case C-496/09, *European Commission v. Italian Republic*, EU:C:2011:740

Judgment of the Court of Justice of 8 December 2011, Case C-81/10 P, *France Télécom SA v. European Commission*, EU:C:2011:811

Judgment of the Court of Justice of 8 December 2011, Case C-275/10, *Residex Capital IV CV v. Gemeente Rotterdam*, EC:C:2011:814

Judgment of the Court of Justice of 29 March 2012, Case C-243/10, *Commission v. Italy*, EU:C:2012:182

Judgment of the Court of Justice of 11 December 2012, Case C-610/10, *European Commission v. Kingdom of Spain ('Magefesa II')*, EU:C:2012:781

Judgment of the Court of Justice of 21 November 2013, Case C-284/12, *Deutsche Lufthansa v. Flughafen Frankfurt-Hahn GmbH*, EU:C:2013:755

Judgment of the Court of Justice of 10 December 2013, Case C-272/12 P, *European Commission v. Republic of Ireland and Others*, EU:C:2013:812

Judgment of the Court of Justice of 19 December 2013, Case C-274/12 P, *Telefónica SA v. European Commission*, EU:C:2013:204

Judgment of the Court of Justice of 13 February 2014, Case C-69/13, *Mediaset SpA v. Ministero dello Sviluppo economico*, EU:C:2014:71

Judgment of the Court of Justice of 4 December 2014, Case C-243/13, *European Commission v. Kingdom of Sweden*, EU:C:2014:2413

Judgment of the Court of Justice of 19 March 2015, Case C-672/13, *OTP Bank Nyrt. v. Magyar Állam and Magyar Államkincstár*, EU:C:2015:185

Judgment of the Court of Justice of 6 May 2015, Case C-674/13, *European Commission v. Federal Republic of Germany*, EU:C:2015:302

Judgment of the Court of Justice of 17 September 2015, Case C-367/14, *European Commission v. Italian Republic*, EU:C:2015:611

Judgment of the Court of Justice of 1 October 2015, Case C-357/14 P, *Electrabel SA and Dunamenti Erőmű Zrt v. European Commission*, EU:C:2015:642

Judgment of the Court of Justice of 11 November 2015, Case C-505/14, *Klausner Holz Niedersachsen*, EU:C:2015:742

Judgment of the Court of Justice of 21 July 2016, Case C-493/14, *Dilly's Wellnesshotel GmbH/Finanzamt Linz*, EU:C:2016:577

Judgment of the Court of Justice of 26 October 2016, Case C-590/14 P, *Dimosia Epicheirisi Ilektrismou AE (DEI)*, EU:C:2016:797

Judgment of the Court of Justice of 21 December 2016, Case C-524/14 P, *European Commission v. Hansestadt Lübeck*, EU:C:2016:971

Judgment of the Court of Justice of 21 December 2016, Joined Cases C-164/15 P and C-165/15 P, *European Commission v. Aer Lingus Ltd and Ryanair Designated Activity Company*, EU:C:2016:990

Judgment of the Court of Justice of 9 November 2017, Case C-481/16, *European Commission v. Hellenic Republic ('Larco')*, EU:C:2017:845

Judgment of the Court of Justice of 17 January 2018, Case C-363/16, *European Commission v. Hellenic Republic ('United Textiles')*, EU:C:2018:12

Judgment of the Court of Justice of 6 March 2018, Case C-284/16, *Slowakische Republik v. Achmea BV*, EU:C:2018:158

Judgment of the Court of Justice of 26 April 2018, Case C-233/16, *Asociación Nacional de Grandes Empresas de Distribución (ANGED) v. Generalitat de Catalunya*, EU:C:2018:280

Judgment of the Court of Justice of 25 July 2018, Case C-135/16, *Georgsmarienhütte GmbH and Others v. Bundesrepublik Deutschland*, EU:C:2018:582

Judgment of the Court of Justice of 6 November 2018, Joined Cases C-622/16 P to C-624/16 P, *Scuola Elementare Maria Montessori Srl v. European Commission, European Commission v. Scuola Elementare Maria Montessori Srl and European Commission v. Pietro Ferracci*, EU:C:2018:873

Judgment of the Court of Justice of 5 March 2019, Case C-349/17, *Eesti Pagar AS v. Ettevõtluse Arendamise Sihtasutus and Majandus- ja Kommunikatsiooniministee-rium, EG*, EU:C:2019:172

Judgment of the Court of Justice of 13 June 2019, Case C-505/18, *Copebi SCA v. Etablissement national des produits de l'agriculture et de la mer (FranceAgriMer)*, EU:C:2019:500

Judgment of the Court of Justice of 11 December 2019, Case C-332/18 P, *Mytilinaios Anonymos Etairia – Omilos Epicheiriseon v. European Commission*, EU:C:2019:106

Judgment of the Court of Justice of 3 March 2020, Case C-75/18, *Vodafone Magyarország Mobil Távközlési Zrt. v. Nemzeti Adó- és Vámhivatal Fellebbviteli Igazgatósága*, EU:C:2020:139

Judgment of the Court of Justice of 30 April 2020, Case C-627/18, *Nelson Antunes da Cunha*, EU:C:2020:321

Judgment of the Court of Justice of 29 April 2021, Case C-277/00, *Federal Republic of Germany v. Commission of the European Communities ('SMI')*, EU:C:2004:238

Judgment of the Court of Justice of 29 April 2021, Case C-890/19 P, *Fortischem a.s. v. European Commission*, EU:C:2021:345

Judgment of the Court of Justice of 20 January 2022, Case C-51/20, *European Commission v. Hellenic Republic*, EU:C:2022:36

Judgment of the Court of Justice of 25 January 2022, Case C-638/19 P, *European Commission v. European Food and others*, EU:C:2022:50

Judgment of the Court of Justice of 7 March 2022, Case C-310/99, *Italy v. Commission*, EU:C:2002:143

Judgment of the Court of Justice of 22 March 2022, Case C-151/20, *Bundeswettbewerbsbhörde v. Nordzucker AG and Others*, EU:C:2022:203

Judgment of the Court of Justice of 12 January 2023, Joined Cases C-702/20 and C-17/21, *SIA 'DOBELES HES' and Sabiedrisko pakalpojumu regulēšanas komisija*, EU:C:2023:1

Judgment of the Court of Justice of 31 January 2023, Case C-284/21 P, *Commission v. Braesch and Others*, EU:C:2023:58

Judgment of the Court of Justice of 7 December 2023, Case C-700/22, *Regiolet a.s. and Student Agency k.s./České dráhy a.s. and others*, EU:C:2023:960

Judgment of the Court of Justice of 29 July 2024, Case C-697/22 P, *Koiviston Auto Helsinki v. Commission*, EU:C:2024:641

Order of the Court of Justice of 4 April 2014, Case C-27/13, *Flughafen Lübeck GmbH v. Air Berlin plc & Co. Luftverkehrs KG*, EU:C:2014:240

Order of the Court of Justice of 21 September 2022, Case C-333/19, *Romatsa and Others*, EU:C:2022:749

Court of First Instance and General Court

Judgment of the Court of First Instance of 27 April 1995, Case T-435/93, *ASPEC and Others v. Commission*, EU:T:1995:79

Judgment of the Court of First Instance of 13 September 1995, Joined Cases T-244/93 and T-486/93, *TWD Textilwerke Deggendorf GmbH v. Commission of the European Communities*, EU:T:1995:160

Judgment of the Court of First Instance of 28 September 1995, Case T-95/94, *Sytraval v. Commission*, ECLI:EU:T:1995:172

Judgment of the Court of First Instance of 25 June 1998, Joined Cases T-371/94 and T-394/94, *British Airways and Others v. Commission*, EU:T:1998:140

Judgment of the Court of First Instance of 15 June 2000, Joined Cases T-298/97, T-312/97, T-313/97, T-315/97, T-600/97 to T-607/97, T-1/98, T-3/98 to T-6/98 and T-23/98, *Alzetta and Others v. Commission*, EU:T:2000:151

Judgment of the Court of First Instance of 29 June 2000, Case T-234/95, *DSG Dradenauer Stahlgesellschaft mbH v. Commission of the European Communities*, EU:T:2000:174

Judgment of the Court of First Instance of 8 July 2004, Case T-198/01, *Technische Glaswerke Ilmenau GmbH v. Commission of the EC*, EU:T:2004:222

Judgment of the Court of First Instance of 21 October 2004, Case T-36/99, *Lenzing AG v. Commission*, EU:T:2004:312

Judgment of the Court of First Instance of 6 September 2006, Joined Cases T-304/04 and T-316/04, *Italian Republic and Wam SpA v. Commission of the European Communities*, EU:T:2006:239

Judgment of the Court of First Instance of 15 April 2008, Case T-348/04, *Société internationale de diffusion et d'édition (SIDE) v. Commission CE*, EU:T:2008:109

Judgment of the Court of First Instance of 4 March 2009, Case T-445/05, *Associazione italiana del risparmio gestito and Fineco Asset Management v. EC Commission*, EU:T:2009:50

Judgment of the Court of First Instance of 8 September 2009, Case T-303/05, *AceaElectrabel Produzione SpA v. Commission of the European Communities*, EU:T:2009:312

Judgment of the Court of First Instance of 25 November 2009, Case T-376/07, *Federal Republic of Germany v. European Commission*, EU:T:2009:467

Judgment of the General Court of 15 June 2010, Case T-177/07, *Mediaset SpA v. European Commission*, EU:T:2010:233

Judgment of the General Court of 7 October 2010, Case T-452/08, *DHL Aviation SA/NV and DHL Hub Leipzig GmbH v. European Commission*, EU:T:2010:427

Judgment of the General Court 27 September 2012, Case T-303/10, *Wam Industriale SpA v. European Commission*, EU:T:2012:505

Judgment of the General Court of 22 January 2013, Case T-308/00, *Salzgitter AG v. European Commission*, EU:T:2013:30

Judgment of the General Court of 16 July 2014, Case T-52/12, *Hellenic Republic v. European Commission*, EU:T:2014:677

Judgment of the General Court of 8 October 2014, Case T-542/11, *Alouminion v. European Commission*, EU:T:2014:859

Judgment of the General Court of 21 October 2014, Case T-268/13, *Italian Republic v. European Commission*, EU:T:2014:900

Judgment of the General Court of 5 February 2015, Case T-473/12, *Aer Lingus Ltd v. European Commission*, EU:T:2015:78

Judgment of the General Court of 5 February 2015, Case T-500/12, *Ryanair Ltd v. European Commission*, EU:T:2015:73

Judgment of the General Court of 20 March 2015, Case T-456/13, *Sea Handling*, OJ C 155, 11.5.2015

Judgment of the General Court of 17 December 2015, Joined Cases T-515/13 and T-719/13, *Kingdom of Spain and Others v. European Commission,* EU:T:2015:1004

Judgment of the General Court of 3 March 2016, Case T-15/14, *Simet SpA v. European Commission,* EU:T:2016:124

Judgment of the General Court of 22 April 2016, Joined Cases RENV II and T-69/06 RENV II, *Ireland and Aughinish Alumina Ltd v. European Commission,* EU:T:2016:227

Judgment of the General Court of 13 March 2018, Case T-542/11 RENV, *Alouminion tis Ellados VEAE v. European Commission,* EU:T:2018

Judgment of the General Court of 14 February 2019, Joined Cases T-131/16 and T-263/16, *Royaume de Belgique et Magnetrol International v. European Commission,* EU:T:2019:91

Judgment of the General Court of 18 June 2019, Case T-624/15, *European Food and others v. European Commission,* EU:T:2019:423

Judgment of the General Court of 13 May 2020, Case T-607/17, *Volotea SA v. European Commission,* EU:T:2020:180

Judgment of the General Court of 10 November 2021, Case T-678/20, *Solar Electric Holding and Others v. European Commission,* EU:T:2021:780

Judgment of the General Court of 21 September 2022, Case T-95/21, *Portuguese Republic v. European Commission,* EU:T:2022:567

Judgment of the General Court of 20 September 2023, Joined Cases T-278/16 and T-370/16, *Atlas Copco Airpower and Atlas Copco v. Commission* EU:T:2023:568

Judgment of the General Court of 2 October 2024, Cases T-624/15 RENV, T-694/15 RENV and T-704/15 RENV, *European Food SA and others v. European Commission,* EU:T:2024:659

Order of the President of the General Court of 19 September 2012, Case T-52/12 R, *Hellenic Republic v. European Commission,* EU:T:2012:447

Order of the General Court of 3 March 2015, Case T-251/13, *Gemeente Nijmegen v. European Commission,* EU:T:2015:142

Order of the General Court of 2 September 2015, Case T-688/14, *Airport Handling SpA v. European Commission,* EU:T:2015:588

Order of the President of the General Court of 13 March 2020, Case T-603/19 R, *Helsingin Bussiliikenne Oy v. European Commission,* EU:T:2020:110

Opinions of Advocates General

Opinion of Advocate General Tesauro of 19 September 1989, Case C-142/87, *Kingdom of Belgium v. Commission (Tubemeuse)* of the CE, EU:C:1989:335

Opinion of Advocate General Jacobs of 4 October 1989, Case C-301/87, *French Republic v. Commission of the EU (Boussac),* EU:C:1990:357

Opinion of Advocate General Cosmas of 15 February 1996, Case C-63/93, *Fintan Duff and others v. Minister for Agriculture and Food and Attorney General,* EU:C:1995:170

Opinion of Advocate General Tesauro of 10 December 1996, Case C-355/95 P, *Textilwerke Deggendorf GmbH (TWD) v. Commission of the European Communities and Federal Republic of Germany (Deggendorf II and III)*, EU:C:1996:483

Opinion of Advocate General Ruiz-Jarabo Colomer of 28 April 2005, Joined Cases C-346/03 and C-529/03, *Atzeni and Others v. Regione autonoma della Sardegna*, EU:C:2005:256

Opinion of Advocate General Bot of 3 April 2008, Case C-521/06 P, *Athinaïki Techniki AE v. EC Commission*, EU:C:2010:492

Opinion of Advocate General Kokott of 26 May 2011, Case C-275/10, *Residex Capital IV CV v. Gemeente Rotterdam*, EU:C:2011:354

Opinion of Advocate General Wathelet of 19 September 2017, Case C-284/16, *Slowakische Republik v. Achmea BV* EU:C:2017:699

Opinion of Advocate General Sharpston of 10 October 2017, Case C-363/16, *European Commission v. Hellenic Republic*, EU:C:2017:746

Opinion of Advocate General Wathelet of 11 April 2018, Joined Cases C-622/16 P and C-624/16 P, *Scuola elementare Maria Montessori v. European Commission*, EU:C:2018:229

Opinion of Advocate General Szpunar of 1 July 2021, Case C-638/19 P, *European Commission v. European Food and others*, EU:C:2021:529

Member States

France

Conseil d'Etat, Judgment No. 450892 of 29 September 2021, *Collectivité de Corse v. Sté Corsica Ferries*, FR:CECHS:2021:450892.20210929

Administrative Court of Appeal of Marseille, Judgment No. 17MA31582 of 22 February 2021, *Collectivité de Corse*

Italy

Administrative Court of Lombardy (*TAR Lombardia*), Milan, Division III, Order of 22 May 2013, *Comune di Milano v. Presidenza del Consiglio dei Ministri*, Reg. Ric. No. 1084/2013

Index

A

B

C

G

H

I

J

L

M

N

T

U

W

www.ingramcontent.com/pod-product-compliance
Lightning Source LLC
Chambersburg PA
CBHW071236230926
51849CB00001B/123
* 9 7 8 9 4 0 3 5 3 2 5 7 8 *